Biology
for the IB Diploma

Brenda Walpole
Ashby Merson-Davies
Leighton Dann

Course consultant:
Peter Hoeben

Cambridge University Press's mission is to advance learning, knowledge and research worldwide.

Our IB Diploma resources aim to:

- encourage learners to explore concepts, ideas and topics that have local and global significance
- help students develop a positive attitude to learning in preparation for higher education
- assist students in approaching complex questions, applying critical-thinking skills and forming reasoned answers.

CAMBRIDGE
UNIVERSITY PRESS

CAMBRIDGE UNIVERSITY PRESS
Cambridge, New York, Melbourne, Madrid, Cape Town,
Singapore, São Paulo, Delhi, Mexico City

Cambridge University Press
The Edinburgh Building, Cambridge CB2 8RU, UK

www.cambridge.org
Information on this title: www.cambridge.org/9780521171786

First published 2011
3rd printing 2013

Printed in India by Replika Press Pvt. Ltd

A catalogue record for this publication is available from the British Library

ISBN 978-0-521-17178-6 Paperback

The publisher would like to thank the following teachers for reviewing the content:
Jennifer Clarke
Impington Village College, Impington
Sarah Jinks
St. Clare's, Oxford

Contents

Introduction

The International Baccalaureate Diploma course is designed to provide a broad education for students who will become our future citizens. Unlike other courses, the programme of study requires the study of six academic subjects, one of which must be an experimental science.

Biology has advanced at a rapid rate over recent decades and is truly the science of the 21st century. Advances in genetics, biochemistry, medicine and cell biology have kept the subject in the forefront of international news. To keep pace with new developments, the IB Biology course is regularly updated so that IB students can understand not only the principles of modern science but also the processes and the ethical implications that go with them. Theory of Knowledge (TOK) provides a cross-curricular link between different subjects and stimulates thought and consideration of these issues.

Biology may be studied at Standard Level (SL) or Higher Level (HL) and both share a common core of six compulsory topics, which are covered in Chapters 1–6. At HL the core is extended to include a further five topics, covered in Chapters 7–11. In addition, at both levels, students then chose two Options to complete their studies. Options A – C are additional topics for SL only, Options D – G can be studied at either level with extra material covered at HL, and Option H is for HL only.

All the topics required for the core at both SL and HL, as well as all eight Options, are included in this book. Throughout, the colour of the page border indicates the level of the material on the page. Standard Level material has a mid-green page border all the way round, while Higher Level has a darker green at the top of the page and red at the bottom.

Each chapter is divided into sections which include the syllabus assessment statements as starting and reference points. Short-answer questions appear throughout the text so students can check their progress and become familiar with the style and command terms used, and examination style questions appear at the end of each chapter. Answers to all questions are given at the back of the book.

The study of Biology has a vital part to play in the future of the world. It is crucial to understanding our planet, the effect human activities have on it and how the organisms which live on it will survive in the future. The IB Biology course provides opportunities for scientific study in this global context that will both challenge and stimulate students.

How to use this book

As you read this book you will see that certain features are shown in different coloured boxes.

At the start of each section you will find a list of Assessment statements, which form the syllabus for the IB Biology course. They are the objectives for the section and give you the command terms such as 'State', 'Describe' and 'Explain' which will appear in the IB Biology examination papers. Command terms give an idea of the depth of knowledge that is required for a given Assessment statement.

Assessment statements

- Define 'polygenic inheritance'.
- Explain that polygenic inheritance can contribute to continuous variation, using two examples, one of which must be human skin colour.

Photosynthesis means 'making things with light'. Glucose is the molecule most commonly made.

Evolution cumulative change in the heritable characteristics of a population

Throughout the text, side boxes and definition boxes give additional information on various subjects related to the text. The content of the boxes is included to broaden your background knowledge of a topic and to help you remember key information.

Theory of Knowledge (TOK) boxes are also found throughout the text. These will provide food for thought and support the TOK you will be studying in your IB Diploma programme. You will be able to consider important questions about scientific knowledge, including ethical considerations and the development of new theories.

Questions to consider

1 Consider the shape of mitochondria in Figure **2.9**. Why do some mitochondria appear cylindrical and others circular?
2 Plant cells have a single central vacuole. Examine the plant cell in Figure **2.11**. How many vacuoles can you see? How can you explain this?

Can we believe our eyes?

Our own perception is a crucial source of knowledge. The way we see things depends on the interaction between our sense organs and our mind, and what we perceive is a selective interpretation.

When studying material that has been prepared for microscopic examination, we must always bear in mind that staining and cutting cells will alter their appearance. Interpreting images requires care, and what we perceive in a particular image is likely to be influenced by these techniques as well as our own expectations.

1 Look carefully at the eight gametes in Figure **10.2**. How many different gametes are there?

As you read, you will also see short-answer questions at various points in the text, usually at the end of a section. These will allow you to keep a check on your progress as you work through each chapter.

At the end of each chapter, examination style questions will give you the chance to check that you have understood each topic and help you prepare for your final examinations.

Statistical analysis 1

Introduction

Scientists use statistics to help them analyse and understand the evidence they collect during experiments. Statistics is an area of mathematics that measures variation in data, and the differences and relationships between sets of data. By using statistics, we can examine samples of populations or experimental results and decide how certain we can be about the conclusions we draw from them.

1.1 Mean and distribution

Assessment statements

- State that error bars are a graphical representation of the variability of data.
- Calculate the mean and standard deviation of a set of values.
- State that the term 'standard deviation' is used to summarise the spread of values around the mean, and that 68% of all values fall within plus or minus one standard deviation of the mean.
- Explain how the standard deviation is useful for comparing the means and the spread of data between two or more samples.
- Deduce the significance of the difference between two sets of data using calculated values for t and the appropriate tables.
- Explain that the existence of a correlation does not establish that there is a causal relationship between two variables.

Calculating the mean

The **mean** is an average of all the data that has been collected. For example, if you measure the height of all the students in your class, you could find the mean value by first calculating the sum of all the values and then dividing by the number of values.

$$\overline{x} = \frac{\Sigma x}{n}$$

A normal distribution

If you measured the height of ten students and plotted the values on a graph, with the height on the x-axis and the number in each height group on the y-axis, you would get a result that did not show an obvious trend. If you measured the height of 100 students, your graph would begin to look bell shaped, with most values in the middle and fewer on either side. As you measured more and more students' heights, your graph would eventually become a smooth curve as in Figure **1.1** (overleaf). This bell-shaped graph of values is called a **normal distribution**.

Normal distribution curves may be tall and narrow, if all the values are close together, or flatter and wider when the data are more spread out. The mean value is at the peak of the curve.

Mathematical vocabulary

You will find it helpful to understand some mathematical vocabulary first.

- x represents a single value – for example, a person's height $x = 1.7\,\text{m}$
- n represents the total number of values in a set
- $\overline{x}$, called 'x bar', represents the mean of a set of values
- Σ represents the sum of the values
- s represents the standard deviation of the sample
- $\pm$ represents 'plus-or-minus'
- t is a value calculated using a formula called the 't-test'

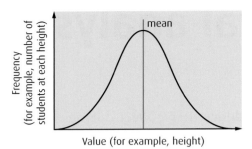

Figure 1.1 A normal distribution.

Statistical analysis using standard deviation or the *t*-test requires a spread of data that is close to a normal distribution. This is why when measuring samples from a population it is best to get as many samples as possible.

Standard deviation

The **standard deviation** shows the spread of all the values around the mean, and therefore it has the same units as the values.

In a normal distribution, 68% of all the values in a sample fall within ±1 standard deviation of the mean, and this increases to 95% within ±2 standard deviations of the mean (Figure **1.2**).

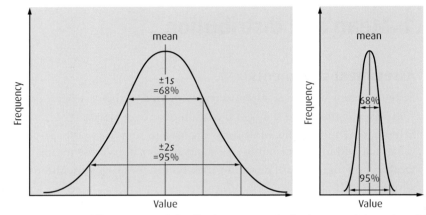

Figure 1.2 Two different normal distribution curves – for both, 68% of the values fall within 1 standard deviation of the mean, and 95% fall within 2 standard deviations.

These percentages are the same for all shapes of normal distribution curves. The standard deviation tells us how much the data spreads out each side of the mean – that is, whether the distribution is tall and narrow or wide and flat – and this allows us to compare sets of data.

Any observable difference between a characteristic in a species is called **variation**.

1   In Figure **1.2**, which sample shows the greatest variation?

Calculating the standard deviation

Check that you know how to calculate standard deviation on your calculator.

The symbol for standard deviation is *s*. Remember that *s* is normally calculated for a sample from the population. Standard deviation is calculated by entering the data into a scientific or graphical calculator, or a spreadsheet.

2   The length of the index finger of five students was measured. Calculate the standard deviation.

Finger length /mm
12
18
15
16
14

Using the standard deviation

The standard deviation can be used to give more information about differences between two sample areas or sets of data that are being studied. We use standard deviation to compare the means and the spread of data in two sets of samples.

For example, if a biologist compared the height of pine trees growing on a west–facing mountain slope with that of trees on an east-facing slope, data might be recorded as in Table **1.1**.

	Height of west-facing trees / m ± 0.5	Height of east-facing trees / m ± 0.5
Measurements	16	18
	12	20
	14	19
	13	10
	18	12
	16	9
	16	11
	15	21
Total	120	120
Mean	15	15

Table 1.1 Data recorded for the heights of pine trees on west- and east-facing mountain slopes.

Looking at the mean values, it seems that the heights of the trees in the two areas are similar. By calculating the standard deviations of the data we can examine the results more closely and see whether this is correct. We can work out the standard deviation of each set of data (using the standard deviation function in a spreadsheet or on a graphical computer) and compare the spread of the data in each case.

The mean values do not show any difference between the two sets of data, but the standard deviation for the west–facing trees is 1.9 m and that for the east-facing trees is 5.0 m. This information tells us that there is much wider variation in the heights of the trees on the east-facing slope. A biologist presented with this information would need to consider other factors besides the direction of the slope that may have affected the height of the trees. Calculation of the standard deviation has given additional information which allows us to think about whether the differences between two samples are likely to be significant.

Error bars on graphs

Error bars are a way of showing either the range or the standard deviation of data on a graph. When data are collected there is usually some variability in the values and the error bars extend above and below the points plotted on a graph to show this variability.

For example, Table **1.2** shows data collected on heart rate during exercise. A different value is recorded in each trial. For a small number of values (three or four), the mean is plotted and the error bar added to show the highest and lowest values, as in Figure **1.3**. This shows the **range** of the values. For a larger number of values (five or more), the standard deviation is calculated and this is shown in the same way (Figure **1.4**).

Trial number	Heart rate/ beats min^{-1}
1	135
2	142
3	139
mean	139

Table 1.2 For a small number of values, only the mean is calculated.

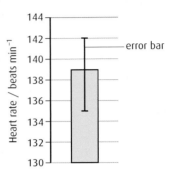

Figure 1.3 Here, the error bar shows the range of the data. The mean value of 139 is plotted with the error bar ranging from the highest value, 142, to the lowest value, 135.

Trial number	Heart rate/ beats min^{-1}
1	137
2	141
3	134
4	136
5	140
6	139
mean	138
standard deviation	2.6

Table 1.3 For five or more values, the standard deviation is also calculated.

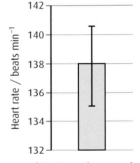

Figure 1.4 This time, the error bar shows the standard deviation from the mean. The mean value of 138 is plotted with the error bar showing ±1s.

In Table **1.3**, where the mean is 138 and s is 2.6, this means that 68% of the values fall within 138 ± 2.6, that is between 135.4 and 140.6, and 95% of the values fall within 138 ± 5.2, that is between 132.8 and 143.2.

Significance

5% significance means that if an investigation was carried out 100 times and each time there was a difference, then 95 of those differences are probably due to the factor being investigated and only 5 are probably due to chance.

1.2 The *t*-test

In order to decide whether the difference between two sets of data is important, or **significant**, we use the **t-test**. It compares the mean and standard deviation of the two sets of samples to see if they are the same or different.

A value for *t* is calculated using a statistical formula. We then look up this value in a standard table of *t*-values, like the one in Table **1.4**. Note that *t*, unlike standard deviation, does not have units. You do not need to know the formula for calculating t, but if you are interested you can find it in the glossary.

There are two important column headings in a table of t-values: '**degrees of freedom**' and '**significance level or probability**'.

'Probability' shows whether chance alone could make a difference between two sets of data that have been collected. There are four different levels of probability shown in Table **1.4**. The most important column to biologists is the one headed '5% or 0.05'. If values fall into this category, it means that 95% of the time the differences between the two sets of values are due to significant differences between them and not due to chance. These are called the '**critical values**'. Biologists use the '5% or 0.05' value because living things have natural, inbuilt variation that must be taken into account.

Degrees of freedom	Significance level or probability			
	10% or 0.1	5% or 0.05	1% or 0.01	0.1% or 0.001
18	1.73	2.10	2.88	3.92
19	1.73	2.09	2.86	3.88
20	1.72	2.09	2.85	3.85
21	1.72	2.08	2.83	3.82
22	1.72	2.07	2.82	3.79
23	1.71	2.07	2.81	3.77
24	1.71	2.06	2.80	3.75
25	1.71	2.06	2.79	3.73
26	1.71	2.06	2.78	3.71
27	1.70	2.05	2.77	3.69
28	1.70	2.05	2.76	3.67
29	1.70	2.05	2.76	3.66
30	1.70	2.04	2.75	3.65
40	1.68	2.02	2.70	3.55
60	1.67	2.00	2.66	3.46
120	1.65	1.98	2.62	3.37
	← decreasing significance increasing →			

Table 1.4 Table of t-values.

'Degrees of freedom' is calculated from the sum of the sample sizes of the two groups of data, minus 2:

$$\text{degrees of freedom} = (n_1 + n_2) - 2$$

where n_1 is the number of values in sample 1 and n_2 is the number of values in sample 2.

Remember, to use the t-test, there must be a minimum of 10 to 15 values for each sample and they must form a normal, or near-normal, distribution.

Worked example 1

Two sets of soybean plants were grown, with and without the addition of fertiliser. The heights of the plants were measured after 30 days. Both sets of data formed near-normal distributions so a t-test was carried out.

Is there a significant difference in growth between the two sets of plants?

Sample number	Increase in height of plants after 30 days/cm ±0.5	
	Group 1 – no fertiliser	Group 2 – 0.1% fertiliser
1	10.0	12.5
2	7.0	13.0
3	9.5	13.0
4	8.5	12.5
5	7.5	15.5
6	10.0	12.5
7	9.5	10.5
8	9.5	14.0
9	8.5	10.0
10	8.5	10.5
mean	8.9	12.4
calculated value for t	5.96	

Step 1 Determine the number of degrees of freedom for the data:

$$\text{degrees of freedom} = (10 + 10) - 2$$
$$= 18$$

Step 2 Go down the degrees of freedom column on the t-table in Table **1.4** to the 18 value.

Step 3 Go across the table and find the critical value of t – that is, the number in the '5% or 0.05' column. In this example, it is 2.10.

Step 4 Calculate a value for t, using the appropriate statistical formula in your calculator or spreadsheet. In this case, the calculated value for t is 5.96.

Step 5 Compare the calculated value for t with the critical value from the table. If the calculated value of t is greater than this critical value, then there is a significant difference between the sets of data. If the calculated value of t is lower than the critical value, then the difference is due to chance.

In this case, 5.96 is greater than 2.10, so we conclude that there is a significant difference between the means. This indicates that the fertiliser may have caused the increase in growth.

Use Table **1.4** to help you answer these questions.

3 In an investigation to compare two groups of plants grown with different levels of minerals, the degrees of freedom (df) was 20 and the calculated value for t was 4.02. Was there a significant difference between the two sets of data?

4 In another investigation the body mass of crabs living on a west-facing shore was compared with that of crabs from an east-facing shore. The degrees of freedom was 37 and the calculated value for t was 1.82. Was there a significant difference between the two sets of data?

If the calculated value of t is close to the critical value, the conclusion is less certain than if there is a greater difference between the values.

Worked example 2

An investigation was carried out to see if light intensity affected the surface area of ivy leaves. A random sample of 10 leaves was collected from each side of a wall, one sunny and the other shaded. The surface area for each leaf was found and t was calculated as 2.19.

The t-value of 2.19 is greater than the critical value of 2.10 for 18df shown in Table **1.4**. This indicates that light intensity does affect the surface area of these ivy leaves.

The value 2.19 is very close to the critical value of 2.10, and so this conclusion is quite weak. If the calculated value for t were much higher, say 2.88, we could feel much safer with the conclusion, and if it were as high as 3.92, for example, we could feel very certain.

5 An investigation was carried out on the effect of pollution on the density of branching coral off the Indonesian island of Hoga. The number of corals found in $9\,m^2$ was counted in a clean area and in a polluted area. Both sets of data formed near-normal distributions so a t-test was carried out.

Sample number	Branching corals / number per $9\,m^2$	
	Clean area	**Polluted area**
1	7	6
2	8	6
3	5	5
4	9	4
5	8	6
6	7	5
7	10	7
8	8	4
9	8	7
10	9	5
11	6	6
12	7	6
13	6	8
14	9	4
15	11	—
16	8	—
mean	7.9	5.6
calculated value of t	4.50	

Determine if the pollution has an effect on the density of branching coral.

How certain is your conclusion?

Why are statistics important?

In science, statistics are often used to add credibility to an argument or support a conclusion. International organisations such as the United Nations collect data on health to ensure aid programmes are properly directed.

Being able to use and interpret statistics is an important skill.

Questions to consider

1 Do you believe the following statements? If not why not?
   - There is a 75% chance that in a group of 30 people, two will have the same birthday.
   - 8 out of 10 dentists recommend Zappo toothpaste.
   - 85% of lung cancers are related to smoking.

2 Can statistics be manipulated to produce misleading claims?

1.3 Correlation and cause

Correlation is one of the most common and useful statistics. It describes the degree of relationship between two variables.

In the last 30 years, the number of people taking a holiday each year has increased. In the last 30 years, there has also been an increase in the number of hotels at holiday resorts. Plotting this data on a graph and adding a trend line as shown in Figure **1.5** shows a **positive correlation**.

Similarly, a graph can be plotted to show annual deaths from influenza and the number of influenza vaccines given. In this case, there is a **negative correlation**, as shown in Figure **1.6**.

With these examples, we might feel safe to say that one set of data is linked to the other and that there is a **causal relationship** – because there are more tourists, more hotels have been built; greater use of the influenza vaccine has resulted in fewer deaths from influenza.

However, it is important to realise that just because the graph shows a **trend** it does not necessarily mean that there is a causal relationship. For example, plotting the number of people using mobile phones in the last

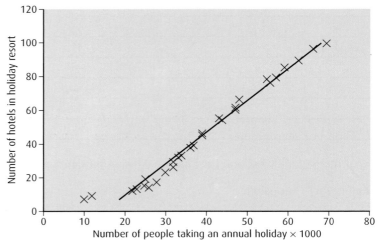

Figure 1.5 A positive correlation.

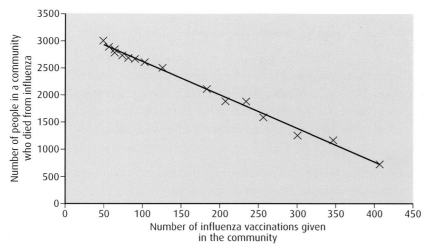

Figure 1.6 A negative correlation.

10 years against the area of Amazon rainforest cut down would show a positive correlation. But this does not mean that the use of mobile phones has caused rainforest to be cut down – nor does it mean that a reduction in rainforest area results in more mobile phone use.

Observations without experiments can show a correlation but usually experiments must be used to provide evidence to show the cause of the correlation.

End-of-chapter questions

1 An error bar drawn on a graph or chart must always be a representation of:

        A   the mean
        B   the standard deviation
        C   the variation shown by the data
        D   the t-value   (1)

2 The width of 10 leaves was measured and the values in mm were 12, 13, 13, 14, 14, 14, 14, 15, 15, 16. The mean is 14.0 mm. What is the best estimate of the standard deviation?

        A   1 mm
        B   2 mm
        C   7 mm
        D   14 mm   (1)

3 Measurements of trunk diameter were taken for 23 trees in one wood, and the trunk diameters of 19 trees were measured in a second wood. If a t-test were carried out, the degrees of freedom used would be:

        A   23
        B   19
        C   42
        D   40   (1)

4   A student examined two walls, one facing east and the other facing west. He measured the percentage of each wall that was covered with lichens. Sixteen samples from each wall were recorded. The calculated value of t was 1.84. Using the t-table (Table **1.4**), the conclusion is:

    A   degrees of freedom are 16 and there is a significant difference between the walls
    B   degrees of freedom are 14 and there is no significant difference between the walls
    C   degrees of freedom are 30 and there is a significant difference between the walls
    D   degrees of freedom are 30 and there is no significant difference between the walls   (1)

5   1000 bananas were collected from a single plantation and weighed. Their masses formed a normal distribution. How many bananas would be expected to be within 2 standard deviations of the mean?

    A   680
    B   950
    C   68
    D   95   (1)

6   In a normal distribution, what percentage of values fall within ±1 standard deviation of the mean and ±2 standard deviations of the mean?   (2)

7   The lengths of the leaves of dandelion plants growing on a lawn were measured. The mean length was 35 mm and the standard deviation was 4 mm. A second set of data on dandelion leaf length was collected from a wasteland area some distance away. The mean was 97 mm and the standard deviation 20 mm. What can you say about the differences in the lengths of the dandelion leaves from the two different habitats?   (2)

8   Salmon live and reproduce in two rivers in Norway – the Namsen and Gaula rivers. Data were collected on the number of eggs laid by the salmon in these two rivers. In the River Namsen, the mean number laid was 1200 eggs per salmon and the standard deviation was 45. For the River Gaula, the mean was 770 eggs per salmon and the standard deviation was 48. Is there a difference between the number of eggs laid by the fish in the two different rivers?   (2)

9   Over a period of 20 years, the number of elephants in the Moremi game reserve in Botswana was recorded each year. Data were also collected on the number of fallen and broken trees. The data are shown on the graph on the right.

    a   State the trend shown by the graph.

    b   What can you say about the relationship between the two sets of data?

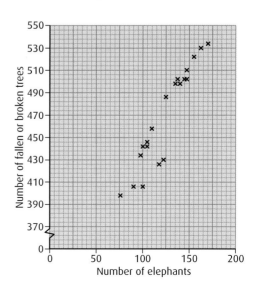

   (3)

10 Dung beetles collect fresh dung in which to lay their eggs. There are two groups – those that bury dung ('buriers'), and those that roll away balls of dung ('rollers'). An investigation was carried out to see if there was any difference in the quantity of dung removed from a field by these two groups. Both sets of data formed near-normal distributions so a *t*-test was carried out.

Sample number	Mass of dung buried/g ±1	Mass of dung rolled away/g ±1
1	56	54
2	58	52
3	56	53
4	55	51
5	53	55
6	60	54
7	58	54
8	56	55
9	51	53
10	55	52
11	57	53
12	52	56
13	54	51
14	57	52
15	59	53
mean	55.8	53.2
calculated value of *t*	3.55	

Using Table **1.4** on page **5**, what conclusion can you draw concerning any difference in the mass of dung removed by the two groups of beetles?

(3)

2 Cells

Introduction

In the middle of the 17th century, one of the pioneers of microscopy, Robert Hooke (1635–1703), decided to examine a piece of cork tissue with his home-built microscope. He saw numerous box-shaped structures that he thought resembled 'monks' cells' or rooms, so he called them 'cells'. As microscopes became more sophisticated, other scientists observed cells and found that they occurred in every organism. No organism has yet been discovered that does not have at least one cell. Living things may vary in shape and size but scientists agree that they are all composed of cells. The study of cells has enabled us to learn more about how whole organisms function.

2.1 Cell theory

Assessment statements

- Outline the cell theory.
- Discuss the evidence for the cell theory.
- State that unicellular organisms carry out all the functions of life.
- Compare the relative sizes of molecules, cell membrane thickness, viruses, bacteria, organelles and cells, using the appropriate SI unit.
- Calculate the linear magnification of drawings and the actual size of specimens in images of known magnification.
- Explain the importance of the surface area to volume ratio as a factor limiting cell size.
- State that multicellular organisms show emergent characteristics.
- Explain that cells in multicellular organisms differentiate to carry out specialised functions by expressing some of their genes but not others.
- State that stem cells retain the capacity to divide and have the ability to differentiate along different pathways.
- Outline one therapeutic use of stem cells.

The cell theory

Today, scientists agree that the cell is the fundamental unit of all life forms. **Cell theory** proposes that all organisms are composed of one or more cells and, furthermore, that cells are the smallest units of life. That is, an individual cell can perform all the functions of life. Conversely, anything that is not made of cells, such as the viruses, cannot be considered living.

One of the functions carried out by all living organisms is reproduction. Therefore, the first principle of the cell theory is that cells can only come from pre-existing cells. They cannot be created from non-living material. Louis Pasteur (1822–1895) provided evidence for this. He showed that bacteria could not grow in a sealed, sterilised container of chicken soup. Only when living bacteria were introduced would more cells appear in the soup.

Extensive examination of many organisms has supported the cell theory, although one or two examples have been found that do not fit the theory perfectly. Fungi consist of long threads called hyphae (Figure **2.1**), which have many nuclei but are not divided into separate cells by cell walls, and skeletal muscle is composed of muscle fibres that are much larger than a single cell and contain several hundred nuclei. Bone cells are also somewhat anomalous because they have a matrix of extracellular material around them, which seems to be greater than the cells themselves, and mammalian erythrocytes (red blood cells) do not contain nuclei once they have matured and been released into the bloodstream.

Figure 2.1 Fungal hyphae grow through material that nourishes the fungus.

Unicellular organisms

By definition, a living organism comprising just one cell has to perform all the necessary functions for survival.

The functions of life are:

- metabolism
- growth
- response (or sensitivity)
- homeostasis
- nutrition
- reproduction

A unicellular organism such as *Amoeba* (Figure **2.2**) needs to **metabolise** organic materials in order to make the chemicals needed to sustain life. It must be able to detect changes in its environment, so it can **respond** to more favourable or less favourable conditions. Some unicellular organisms photosynthesise and they have a light spot that enables them to move to a brighter environment to maximise photosynthesis. A unicellular organism must also be able to control its internal environment (**homeostasis**), as large changes in water or salt concentrations may have a detrimental

> **Key principles of the cell theory:**
>
> - living organisms are composed of cells
> - cells are the smallest units of life
> - all cells come from pre-existing cells

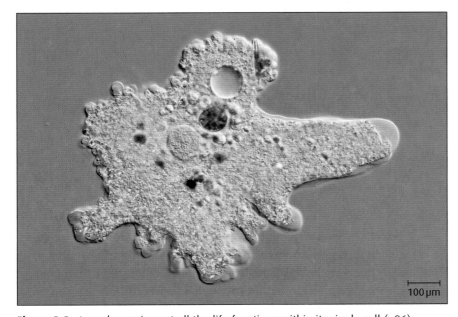

100 μm

Figure 2.2 *Amoeba* carries out all the life functions within its single cell (×86).

Questions to consider

1 How can evidence be obtained for the principles of the cell theory? Can we prove that cells always arise from pre-existing cells?

2 Do the examples of fungal hyphae and muscle cells disprove the cell theory?

3 What should happen if evidence is collected that cannot be explained by a theory?

4 What happens if evidence is collected that disproves a hypothesis?

Hypotheses and theories

A **theory** is a well-established principle that has been developed to explain some aspect of the natural word. A theory arises from repeated observation and testing and incorporates facts, laws, predictions and tested hypotheses that are widely accepted.

A **hypothesis** is a specific, testable prediction about what is expected to happen in an investigation or research project.

Note these important distinctions between the two concepts:

- A theory predicts events in general terms, while a hypothesis makes a specific prediction about a specified set of circumstances.
- A theory has been extensively tested and is generally accepted, while a hypothesis is a speculative guess that has yet to be tested.

effect on metabolism and other cellular functions. It must also obtain food, whether produced by itself through photosynthesis or ingested from outside, as a source of organic and inorganic material (**nutrition**). If the species is to survive, then **reproduction** needs to take place. This could be either asexual or sexual reproduction.

Cell size

One of the few cells large enough to be visible to the unaided eye is the mature human ovum, which has a diameter of approximately $150\,\mu m$. However, most cells are much smaller than this, and can only be seen using a microscope. Light microscopes, which can magnify up to 1000 times, reveal some internal structures such as the nucleus, but greater detail requires the use of more powerful microscopes such as the electron microscope, which magnifies up to 500 000 times. Viruses can only be seen in the electron microscope, so the structure of viruses was unknown until the invention of electron microscopes in the 20th century. Even the electron microscope cannot distinguish individual molecules. Other techniques such as X-ray crystallography are needed to do this. Figure **2.3** indicates the relative sizes of some biological structures.

Surface area to volume ratio

Cells are very small, no matter what the size of the organism that they are part of. Cells do not and cannot grow to be very large and this is important in the way living organisms are built and function. The volume of a cell determines the level of metabolic activity that takes place within it. The surface area of a cell determines the rate of exchange of materials with the outside environment. As the volume of a cell increases, so does its surface area, but not in the same proportion, as Table **2.1** (page 16) shows for a theoretical cube-shaped cell.

SI units – International System

1 metre (m) = $1\,m$

1 millimetre (mm) = $10^{-3}\,m$

1 micrometre (μm) = $10^{-6}\,m$

1 nanometre (nm) = $10^{-9}\,m$

1 centimetre cubed = $1\,cm^3$

1 decimetre cubed = $1\,dm^3$

1 second = $1\,s$

1 minute = $1\,min$

1 hour = $1\,h$

concentration is measured in $mol\,dm^{-3}$

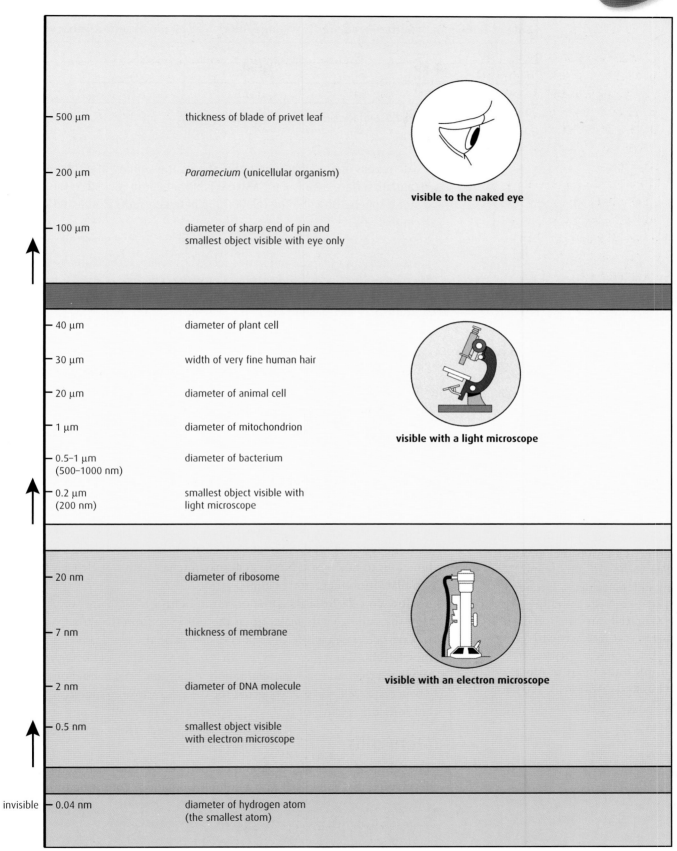

500 µm — thickness of blade of privet leaf

200 µm — *Paramecium* (unicellular organism)

visible to the naked eye

100 µm — diameter of sharp end of pin and
smallest object visible with eye only

40 µm — diameter of plant cell

30 µm — width of very fine human hair

20 µm — diameter of animal cell

1 µm — diameter of mitochondrion

0.5–1 µm — diameter of bacterium
(500–1000 nm)

0.2 µm — smallest object visible with
(200 nm) light microscope

visible with a light microscope

20 nm — diameter of ribosome

7 nm — thickness of membrane

2 nm — diameter of DNA molecule

0.5 nm — smallest object visible
with electron microscope

visible with an electron microscope

invisible — 0.04 nm — diameter of hydrogen atom
(the smallest atom)

Figure 2.3 The sizes of some biological structures.

Side of cube/mm	Surface area/mm²	Volume/mm³	Ratio of surface area : volume
1	6	1	6 : 1
2	24	8	3 : 1
3	54	27	2 : 1

Table 2.1 Surface area to volume ratios for a cube.

1 Many cells are roughly spherical in shape. The volume of a sphere is $\frac{4}{3}\pi r^3$ and its surface area is $4\pi r^2$. Make a table similar to Table **2.1**, this time for a sphere. Describe the relationship between surface area and volume in this case.

As a cell grows larger, in relative terms it has less surface area to obtain the materials it needs and to dispose of waste. The rate of exchange of materials across the outer membrane becomes limiting and cannot keep up with the cell's requirements. Some cells in multicellular organisms have specialised structures, such as folds and microvilli, which increase the surface area so that the rate of diffusion and absorption increases. Other cells are elongated or flattened, which also means they have a larger surface area relative to their volume. But there is a limit to the size of a single cell. Beyond this, a cell must divide and an organism must become multicellular.

Becoming multicellular has enormous advantages. An organism can grow in size and its cells can differentiate – that is, they can take on specific functions, so the organism can grow in complexity as well as size. Examples are nerve cells for communication and interaction with the outside, and muscle cells for movement. Differentiation is said to allow for **emergent properties** in a multicellular organism. This means that different cell types interact with each other to allow more complex functions to take place. Nerve cells may interact with muscle cells to stimulate movement, for example.

How do cells from the same organism behave in different ways? They have the same genetic make-up, as they all arose from the same parent cell. In a particular organism, all the nerve cells have the same genes as all the muscle cells. The logical answer is that in some cells particular genes are expressed that are not expressed in other cells, and vice versa. For example, a pancreatic cell will express genes for the production of digestive enzymes or insulin, but this will not occur in a skin cell.

Stem cells

The fertilised egg of any organism contains all the information needed for developing that single cell into a complex organism consisting of many different types of cell. This information is all within the genes, inherited from the maternal and paternal DNA as fine threads called chromosomes. A fertilised egg divides rapidly and produces a ball of cells called a blastocyst in which all the cells are alike. Gradually, after this stage, the cells

Take a 2 cm cube of modelling clay. Change its shape so that it becomes a cuboid, a thin cylinder or a sphere. Calculate its surface area each time. Try creating folds in the surface. Which shape produces the greatest surface area?

Emergent properties

One person playing the piano can produce a simple, recognisable tune. If several musicians with other instruments join in and play together as a group, they produce a wide variety of sounds and many different effects. Emergent properties in cells are rather like this. One cell can function on its own, but if it interacts with other cells in a group, the organism can carry out a range of more complicated functions.

become specialised, destined to become particular cells such as muscle or liver. This process of specialisation is called **differentiation** and produces cells for specific purposes – muscle cells for contraction, liver cells for metabolism of toxins, and so on. Once differentiation has happened, it cannot be reversed. This shows us that the cells in the blastocyst have the potential to turn into a great many different cell types: they are said to be **pluripotent** and are known as **embryonic stem cells**.

Embryonic stem cells are unique in their potential versatility to differentiate into all the body's cell types. However, some adult tissues contain a different form of stem cell – one that can only differentiate into cells associated with that tissue. For example, bone marrow contains stem cells that can form all the different types of blood cell, but not muscle cells or liver cells (Figure **2.4**).

Stem cells differ from most other cells in the following ways.

- They are unspecialised.
- They can divide repeatedly to make large numbers of new cells.
- They can differentiate into several types of cell.
- They have a large nucleus relative to the volume of the cytoplasm.

Scientists began to investigate and culture stem cells in the 1980s and it soon became apparent that there was enormous potential in using these cells therapeutically. Some of the most recent research aims to grow stem cells to replace damaged or diseased tissue in patients suffering from degenerative conditions such as multiple sclerosis or Alzheimer's disease. Early work concentrated on using embryonic stem cells, but these can only be obtained from discarded embryos from IVF clinics. There is much debate about the ethics of doing this kind of work, and many people feel that the destruction of an embryo to obtain stem cells is morally unacceptable. Others argue that this type of research will contribute significantly to the treatment of disease and can therefore be fully justified.

A less controversial area of research has been in the area of growing and using adult stem cells. In this case, cells are obtained from bone marrow or other tissue from a donor who has given consent. Bone marrow transplants already help many leukaemia patients to a full recovery.

Therapeutic use of stem cells

One important source of stem cells, which has been successfully used in medical treatments, is the blood in the umbilical cord of a newborn baby. These stem cells can divide and become any type of blood cell. Cord blood can be used to treat certain types of leukemia, a cancer which causes overproduction of white blood cells in the bone marrow. Cells from the cord blood are collected and their tissue type is determined. After chemotherapy to destroy the patient's own bone marrow cells, stem cells which are the correct match to the patient's tissue are given by transfusion. They become established in the person's bone marrow and start producing blood cells as normal.

This treatment can work well in young children, but there are not enough cells in a single cord to meet the needs of an adult patient.

Plants also contain stem cells. These are found in the meristems just behind the tips of growing stems and roots. These cells can differentiate to become various tissues of the stem and roots.

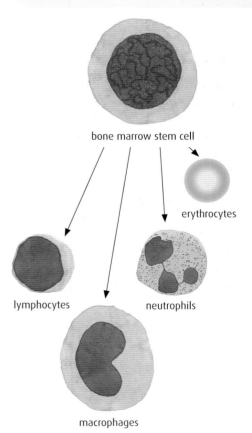

Figure 2.4 Bone marrow cells differentiate into the different types of blood cell.

Scientists have been looking for ways to either combine the cells from more than one baby, or to increase the number of cells in the laboratory. Allowing the stem cells to divide in the laboratory produces many blood cells, but not more stem cells. In 2010, scientists at the Fred Hutchinson Cancer Research Center in Seattle, USA, managed to alter a signalling pathway in the stem cells so they could increase in number without losing stem cell properties. As a result, cord blood may prove to be an even more valuable source of stem cells in the future.

Stem cell therapy has also been successfully used in the treatment of type 1 diabetes. Research is also continuing into therapies to treat a range of conditions involving neurological damage, such as multiple sclerosis and Alzheimer's disease.

Magnification and scale

Cells are extremely small but knowing the sizes of objects viewed under the microscope can be very useful. For example, a plant scientist might want to compare the relative sizes of pollen grains from plants in the same genus to help identify different species.

Magnification is defined as the ratio of the size of the image to the size of the object:

$$\text{magnification} = \frac{\text{size of image}}{\text{size of object}}$$

With a compound microscope, the magnification is the product of both lenses, so if a microscope has a ×10 eyepiece and ×40 objective, the total magnification is ×400.

Printed images of structures seen with a microscope usually show a scale bar or give the magnification, so that the size of an object can be calculated. For example, the magnification of the micrograph in Figure **2.5** is given as ×165.

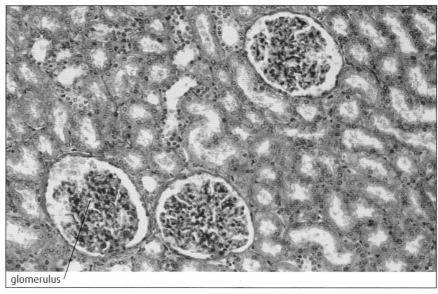

glomerulus

Figure 2.5 Light micrograph of a section through the cortex of a kidney (×165).

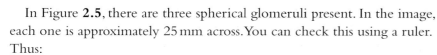

In Figure **2.5**, there are three spherical glomeruli present. In the image, each one is approximately 25 mm across. You can check this using a ruler. Thus:

$$\text{actual size of glomerulus} = \frac{\text{size of image}}{\text{magnification}}$$

$$= \frac{25\,\text{mm}}{165}$$

$$= 0.15\,\text{mm}$$

In micrographs, most measurements are expressed in micrometres.
A micrometre (μm) is 10^{-3} mm, so 1 mm is 1000 μm.
    So the diameter of the glomerulus = $0.15 \times 1000 = 150$ μm.

Worked example 1

Because cells are small, they are viewed through lenses and microscopes. Photographs and diagrams often have scale bars to show the degree of magnification of the image.

    This image shows a red blood cell. The scale bar shows 2 μm. From this, you can calculate both the size of the cell and the magnification of the image.

Size of the cell

Step 1   Use a ruler to measure the diameter of the cell. This is 30 mm.

Step 2   Use a ruler to measure the length of the scale bar. This is 9 mm.

Step 3   Use the ratio of these two values to work out the actual length of the cell.

$$\frac{2\,\mu\text{m}}{9000\,\mu\text{m}} = \frac{\text{actual length of cell}}{30\,000\,\mu\text{m}}$$

(Remember to convert all the units to μm. 1 mm = 1000 μm.)
Rearranging the equation:

$$\text{actual length of the cell} = 2\,\mu\text{m} \times \frac{30\,000\,\mu\text{m}}{9000\,\mu\text{m}}$$

$$= 6.7\,\mu\text{m}$$

Magnification of the image

Use the formula:

$$\text{magnification} = \frac{\text{measured length of the cell}}{\text{actual length of the cell}}$$

So in this case

$$\text{magnification} = \frac{30\,000\,\mu\text{m}}{6.7\,\mu\text{m}}$$

$$= \times 4500$$

    If you are given a value for the magnification you can measure the length of the object in the image and then rearrange the equation to work out the actual length of the object.

2 Calculate how many cells of 100 μm diameter will fit along a 1 mm line.

3 List examples of where the concept of emergent properties can be found in a multicellular animal, such as a bird or a flowering plant.

4 Suggest **one** therapeutic use of stem cells.

5 Explain how cells in multicellular organisms are able to carry out specialised functions.

6 Use the scale bar on Figure **2.2** to calculate the width of the *Amoeba* in the photograph.

2.2 Prokaryotic cells

Assessment statements

- Draw and label a diagram of the ultrastructure of *Escherichia coli* as an example of a prokaryote.
- Annotate the diagram with the functions of each named structure.
- Identify named structures in an electron micrograph of *E. coli*.
- State that prokaryotic cells divide by binary fission.

Cells are divided into two types according to their structure. Cells in the first group, the prokaryotic cells, are usually much smaller than those in the second group, the eukaryotic cells. They have a much simpler structure and are thought to be the first cells to have evolved. Bacteria are all prokaryotic cells.

Prokaryotic cells are so called because they have no nucleus ('prokaryote' comes from the Greek, meaning 'before the nucleus'). They also have no organelles (internal structures), so there is little compartmentalisation of function within them. From the mid–20th century, when the electron microscope was developed, it became possible to study the internal detail of cells. Figures **2.6** and **2.7** show the main features of a typical prokaryotic cell.

- The **cell wall** surrounds the cell. It protects the cell from bursting and is composed of peptidoglycan, which is a mixture of carbohydrate and amino acids.
- The **plasma membrane** controls the movement of materials into and out of the cell. Some substances are pumped in and out using active transport.
- **Cytoplasm** inside the membrane contains all the enzymes for the chemical reactions of the cell. It also contains the genetic material.
- The **chromosome** is found in a region of the cytoplasm called the nucleoid. The DNA is not contained in a nuclear envelope and also it is 'naked' – that is, not associated with any proteins. Bacteria also contain

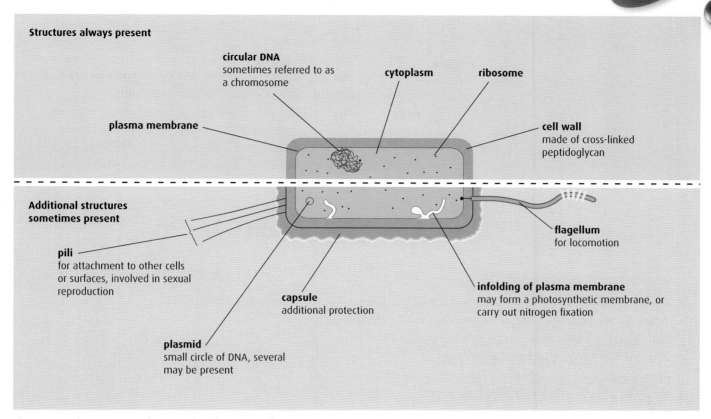

Structures always present

circular DNA
sometimes referred to as
a chromosome

cytoplasm

ribosome

plasma membrane

cell wall
made of cross-linked
peptidoglycan

**Additional structures
sometimes present**

pili
for attachment to other cells
or surfaces, involved in sexual
reproduction

capsule
additional protection

flagellum
for locomotion

infolding of plasma membrane
may form a photosynthetic membrane, or
carry out nitrogen fixation

plasmid
small circle of DNA, several
may be present

Figure 2.6 The structure of a typical prokaryotic cell.

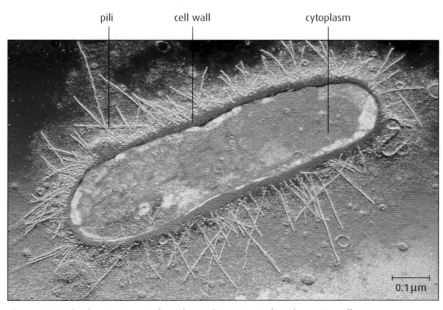

pili   cell wall   cytoplasm

0.1 μm

Figure 2.7 The bacterium *Escherichia coli* is a typical prokaryotic cell.

additional small circles of DNA called **plasmids**. Plasmids replicate
independently and may be passed from one cell to another.

- **Ribosomes** are found in all prokaryotic cells, where they synthesise
proteins. They can be seen in very large numbers in cells that are
actively producing protein.

- A **flagellum** is present in some prokaryotic cells. A flagellum, which projects from the cell wall, enables a cell to move.
- Some bacteria have **pili** (singular **pilus**). These structures, found on the cell wall, can connect to other bacterial cells, drawing them together so that genetic material can be exchanged between them.

Prokaryotic cells are usually much smaller in volume than more complex cells because they have no nucleus. Their means of division is also simple. As they grow, their DNA replicates and separates into two different areas of the cytoplasm, which then divides into two. This is called **binary fission**. It differs slightly from mitosis in eukaryotic cells (see page **34**).

2.3 Eukaryotic cells

Assessment statements

- Draw and label a diagram of the ultrastructure of a liver cell as an example of an animal cell.
- Annotate the diagram with the functions of each named structure.
- Identify named structures in an electron micrograph of liver cells.
- Compare prokaryotic and eukaryotic cells.
- State three differences between plant and animal cells.
- Outline two roles of extracellular components.

Eukaryotic organisms have cells that contain a nucleus. Animals, plants, fungi and protoctista all have eukaryotic cells.

The complexity of a eukaryotic cell cannot be fully appreciated using a compound light microscope. In images made using an electron microscope, however, the fine details of many different organelles are visible. Figure **2.8** shows what can be seen of animal and plant cells using a light microscope – compare these images with the electron micrographs and interpretive drawings in Figures **2.9** to **2.12** (pages **24–25**).

Eukaryotic cells contain structures called **organelles**, each of which has its own specific function. Organelles enable a cell to carry out various chemical reactions or processes in separate parts of the cell. Different types of cell have different organelles in different proportions, depending on the role of the cell.

The largest and most obvious structure in a eukaryotic cell is the **nucleus**, which contains the cell's chromosomes. **Chromosomes** are composed of DNA combined with protein, to form a material known as chromatin. The nucleus is surrounded by a double-layered membrane, the **nuclear envelope**. Small gaps in the envelope, called nuclear pores, are visible and it is through these that material passes between the nucleus and the rest of the cell. A distinctive feature of the nucleus is the darkly staining **nucleolus**. This is the site of production of ribosomes.

Continuous with the nuclear envelope is a series of membranes known as the **endoplasmic reticulum** (ER). Ribosomes attach to this network to form **rough endoplasmic reticulum** (rER), the site of protein

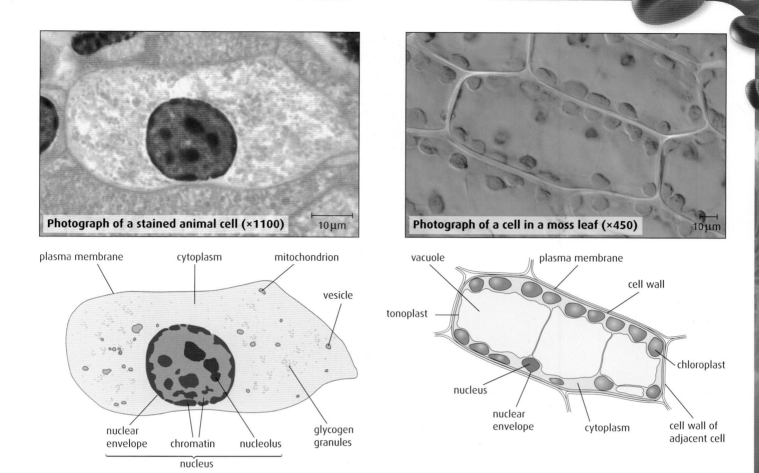

Photograph of a stained animal cell (×1100)   10 μm

Photograph of a cell in a moss leaf (×450)   10 μm

plasma membrane   cytoplasm   mitochondrion

vesicle

nuclear envelope   chromatin   nucleolus   glycogen granules

nucleus

vacuole   plasma membrane

cell wall

tonoplast

chloroplast

nucleus

nuclear envelope   cytoplasm   cell wall of adjacent cell

Figure 2.8 Photographs and diagrams to show typical animal and plant cells as they appear using a light microscope.

synthesis. As proteins are produced, they collect in the space between the membranes, known as the **cisternae**. From here they can be transported in **vesicles** to other parts of the cell such as the Golgi apparatus. ER that has no ribosomes attached is known as **smooth endoplasmic reticulum** (sER). The membranes of smooth ER have many enzymes on their surfaces. Smooth ER has different roles in different types of cell – in liver cells, it is where toxins are broken down; in the ovaries, it is the site of oestrogen production. Smooth ER also produces phospholipids for the construction of membranes and lipids for use in the cell.

The **Golgi apparatus** is similar in appearance to the sER, composed of stacks of flattened, folded membranes. It processes proteins made in the rER, collecting, packaging and modifying them, and then releasing them in vesicles for transport to various parts of the cell or for secretion from the cell. The pancreas contains many secretory cells, which have large areas of Golgi apparatus.

Eukaryotic cells also contain **mitochondria** (singular **mitochondrion**). These are elongated structures surrounded by a double membrane that are found throughout the cytoplasm. Mitochondria are known as the cell's 'powerhouses' because they are the site of aerobic respiration. The inner membrane is folded to form **cristae**, which greatly

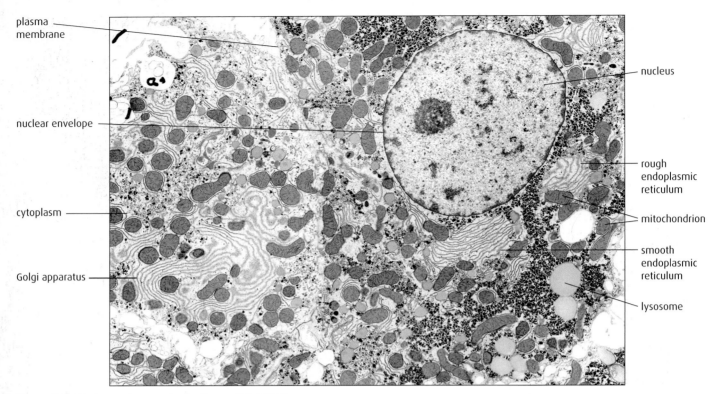

plasma membrane

nuclear envelope

cytoplasm

Golgi apparatus

nucleus

rough endoplasmic reticulum

mitochondrion

smooth endoplasmic reticulum

lysosome

Figure 2.9 Electron micrograph of a liver cell (×9000).

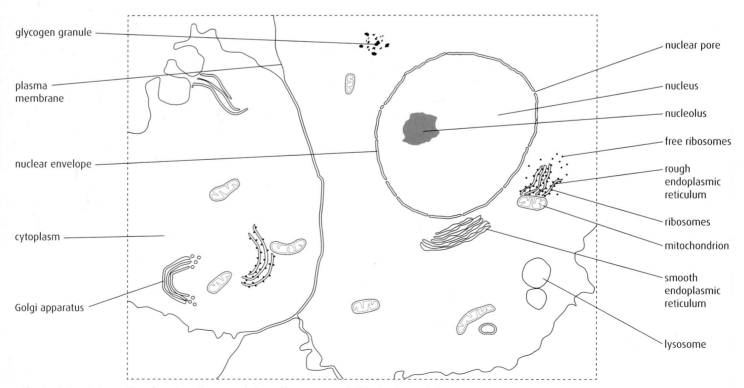

glycogen granule

plasma membrane

nuclear envelope

cytoplasm

Golgi apparatus

nuclear pore

nucleus

nucleolus

free ribosomes

rough endoplasmic reticulum

ribosomes

mitochondrion

smooth endoplasmic reticulum

lysosome

Figure 2.10 Interpretive drawing of some of the cell structures visible in Figure **2.9**.

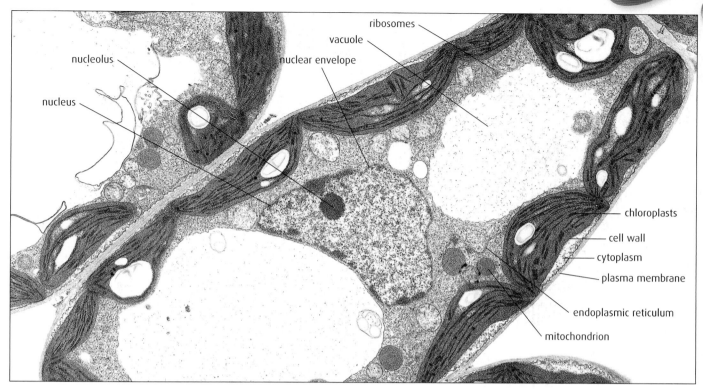

Figure 2.11 Electron micrograph of a plant cell (×5600).

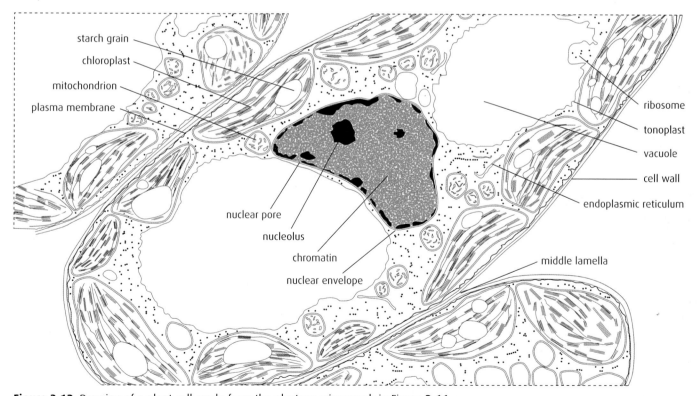

Figure 2.12 Drawing of a plant cell made from the electron micrograph in Figure **2.11**.

increase the surface area for the production of ATP in the cell. Cells that respire rapidly, such as muscle cells, have numerous mitochondria.

Lysosomes are spherical organelles with little internal structure which are made by the Golgi apparatus. They contain hydrolytic enzymes for breaking down components of cells. They are important in cell death, in breaking down old organelles and, in white blood cells, digesting bacteria that have been engulfed by phagocytosis. Plant cells do not normally contain lysosomes.

Ribosomes are the site of protein synthesis in cells. They may be free in the cytoplasm or attached to the rER. They are made of RNA and protein but they do not have a membrane around them.

Plant cells have three additional structures. All plant cells have an outer cellulose cell wall and most have a large central vacuole. Some plant cells contain chloroplasts.

The **chloroplasts** are found in cells exposed to the light, as they are the sites of photosynthesis. Chloroplasts have a double membrane and are about the same size as bacteria. Both chloroplasts and mitochondria have their own DNA and ribosomes and are able to reproduce independently of the cell.

The large central **vacuole** contains water and salts. The membrane that surrounds it is under pressure from within and exerts a force on the cytoplasm, which in turn exerts a force on the cell wall, making the cell turgid and firm. The outer **cell wall** is composed of cellulose and other carbohydrates such as lignin and pectin, giving plant cells further support and a more rigid structure than animal cells. The cell walls and turgidity of plant cells give strength and support to tissues like leaves, holding them in the optimum position to catch the energy from sunlight for photosynthesis.

As in prokaryotic cells, the **plasma membrane** controls the movement of materials into and out of the cell, and the gel-like **cytoplasm**, which fills much of the volume of the cell, provides a medium for many metabolic reactions. However, comparison of Figure **2.6** with Figures **2.10** and **2.12** shows numerous differences between prokaryotic and eukaryotic cells. These are summarised in Table **2.2**. Note, for example, the

Structure	Eukaryotic cell	Prokaryotic cell
nucleus	usually present, surrounded by a nuclear envelope and containing chromosomes and a nucleolus	no nucleus, and therefore no nuclear envelope or nucleolus
mitochondria	usually present	never present
chloroplasts	present in some plant cells	never present
endoplasmic reticulum	usually present	never present
ribosomes	relatively large, about 30 nm in diameter, or 80S	relatively small, about 20 nm in diameter, or 70S
chromosomes	DNA arranged in long strands, associated with proteins	DNA present, not associated with proteins, circular plasmids may also be present
cell wall	always present in plant cells, made of cellulose, never present in animal cells	always present, made of peptidoglycan
cilia and flagella	sometimes present	some have flagella, but these have a different structure from those in eukaryotic cells

Table 2.2 Differences between prokaryotic and eukaryotic cells.

difference in size of ribosomes between prokaryotic and eukaryotic cells. The unit 'S' is a Svedberg unit, used to compare sizes of cell organelles.

Similarly, although they are both eukaryotic cells, there are several key differences between animal and plant cells. These are summarised in Table **2.3**.

Animal cells	Plant cells
cell wall absent	cell wall present
small vacuoles sometimes present	large central vacuole present in mature cells
no chloroplasts	chloroplasts often present
cholesterol in plasma membrane	no cholesterol in plasma membrane
centrioles present (see page **36**)	centrioles absent
stores glycogen	stores starch

Table 2.3 Differences between animal and plant cells.

Can we believe our eyes?

Our own perception is a crucial source of knowledge. The way we see things depends on the interaction between our sense organs and our mind, and what we perceive is a selective interpretation.

When studying material that has been prepared for microscopic examination, we must always bear in mind that staining and cutting cells will alter their appearance. Interpreting images requires care, and what we perceive in a particular image is likely to be influenced by these techniques as well as our own expectations.

Questions to consider

1 Consider the shape of mitochondria in Figure **2.9**. Why do some mitochondria appear cylindrical and others circular?

2 Plant cells have a single central vacuole. Examine the plant cell in Figure **2.11**. How many vacuoles can you see? How can you explain this?

Role of the extracellular components of cells

The **extracellular matrix** (ECM) of animal cells forms a supporting network for the cell membrane and allows adjacent cells to attach to one another and communicate. Most of the matrix is made of collagen fibres and 'sticky' glycoproteins, which are made in the Golgi apparatus from sugars and proteins.

Cell walls form the extracellular component of all plant cells. They are made of cellulose fibres embedded in a glycoprotein matrix which helps maintain the shape of each cell, resists osmotic pressure and allows cells to communicate. Plant cells fit closely together to form tissues and their walls help to bind them to one another.

Recent research suggests that the ECM may be important in interactions between cells that cause them to differentiate and move. Stem cells may be encouraged to become new cell types as a result of interaction with the ECM.

7 List **three** differences between prokaryotic and eukaryotic cells.

8 Distinguish between these pairs of terms:
  a 'cell wall' and 'plasma membrane'
  b 'flagella' and 'pili'

9 Outline **two** roles of extracellular components.

10 State what is meant by the term 'binary fission'.

2.4 Membranes

Assessment statements

- Draw and label a diagram to show the structure of a membrane.
- Explain how the hydrophobic and hydrophilic properties of phospholipids help to maintain the structure of cell membranes.
- List the functions of membrane proteins.
- Define 'diffusion' and 'osmosis'.
- Explain passive transport across membranes by simple diffusion and facilitated diffusion.
- Explain the role of protein pumps and ATP in active transport across membranes.
- Explain how vesicles are used to transport materials within a cell between the rough endoplasmic reticulum, Golgi apparatus and plasma membrane.
- Describe how the fluidity of the membrane allows it to change shape, break and re-form during endocytosis and exocytosis.

It might be thought that membranes are present primarily to provide shape for a cell. Whilst this is certainly important, there is also considerable activity at membrane surfaces, especially at the plasma membrane in contact with the extracellular space. The current model for membrane structure was proposed by Singer and Nicolson in 1972. Their **fluid mosaic model**, illustrated in Figure **2.13**, was based on the knowledge available at the time but has been supported by more recent research, with only minor modifications.

The structure of membranes

All membranes, wherever they occur in cells, have the same basic structure. Membranes are usually between 7 and 10 nm thick, and are composed of two layers of phospholipid, which form a bilayer. **Phospholipids** are made up of a polar, hydrophilic area containing a phosphate group bonded to glycerol, and a non-polar, hydrophobic area containing fatty acids. In the bilayer, the **hydrophobic** (water-hating) parts all point towards each other, and the **hydrophilic** (water-loving) areas point outwards, as Figure **2.14** shows.

It is the different properties of each end of the molecule that cause the phospholipids to arrange themselves in this way. The hydrophilic 'heads' of the molecules always appear on the outside of the membrane where water is present, while the hydrophobic 'tails' orientate inside the double layer, away from water. The whole structure is flexible or 'fluid' because the phospholipids can float into a position anywhere in the membrane. There is much evidence to support the plasma membrane as a 'fluid

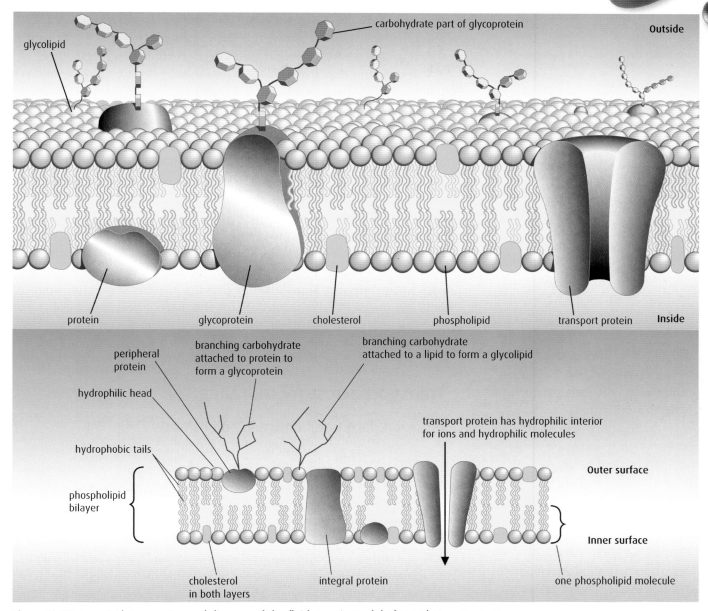

Figure 2.13 An artist's impression and diagram of the fluid mosaic model of membrane structure.

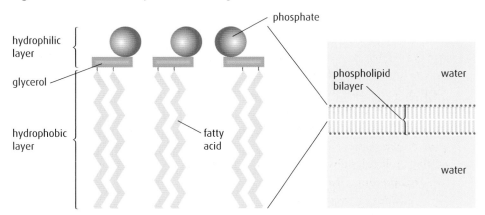

Figure 2.14 In a watery environment, the phospholipids become arranged in a bilayer, because of the hydrophilic and hydrophobic properties of the 'heads' and 'tails' of the molecules.

'mosaic'. Further evidence has come from using radioactively labelled phospholipids. Research shows that these molecules move not only within their own layer, but also between the two layers of the membrane.

Embedded in the bilayer are different molecules that contribute to the functions of membranes. Cholesterol is often present in animal cells and is most commonly found in the plasma membrane. Cholesterol molecules align themselves with the phospholipids making the membrane more rigid, and less permeable to water-soluble molecules.

There are also different types of protein in the bilayer. **Integral proteins** are embedded in the bilayer, whereas **peripheral proteins** are attached to the surface. Many of the proteins on the outer surface are glycoproteins – that is, they have carbohydrate groups attached to them. Some of these serve as hormone binding sites and have special shapes to recognise the specific hormones to which the cell will respond. Others are important in cell-to-cell communication and adhesion. Some integral proteins are enzymes immobilised within the membrane structure and perfectly placed to carry out sequences of metabolic reactions. Finally, there are proteins that span the bilayer acting as channels for ions and molecules to pass by passive transport, or forming pumps that use active transport to move molecules into or out of the cell.

Transport across membranes

Diffusion, facilitated diffusion and osmosis

Many molecules pass across the plasma membrane. Water, oxygen, carbon dioxide, excretory products, nutrients and ions are continuously exchanged and many cells also secrete products such as hormones and enzymes through the membrane.

The simplest way in which a molecule could move into or out of a cell is by **diffusion**. No energy is required, and movement occurs by way of a simple concentration gradient. For example, as carbon dioxide concentration builds up in cells because of respiratory activity, it begins to diffuse through the plasma membrane to an area where the concentration is lower. Diffusion occurs where the membrane is fully permeable to the substance or where protein channels in the membrane are large enough for it to pass through.

In cases where molecules are large, or where charged particles such as chloride ions (Cl^-) must pass, simple diffusion is impossible. These substances are often transported across membranes by **facilitated diffusion**. Here an integral protein in the membrane forms a channel so that the substance particles can pass through them into or out of the cell (Figure **2.15**). Some of these channels are permanently open whereas others can open and close to control the movement of the substance. Furthermore, they are specific – that is, they only allow a particular substance to pass through. As in simple diffusion, no energy is used by the cell. In both cases, the transport relies on the kinetic energy of the particles moving down their concentration gradient.

Passive transport the movement of substances down a concentration gradient from an area of high concentration to an area of lower concentration without the need for energy to be used

Diffusion one example of passive transport; many molecules pass into and out of cells by diffusion e.g. oxygen, carbon dioxide and glucose

Osmosis another example of passive transport but the term is only used in the context of water molecules; osmosis is the movement of water molecules across a partially permeable membrane from a region of lower solute concentration, where there is a high concentration of water molecules, to a region of higher solute concentration, where the concentration of water molecules is lower

Active transport the movement of substances against the concentration gradient, which always involves the expenditure of energy in the form of ATP

A special case of diffusion is **osmosis** (Figure **2.16**). This is the passive movement of water across a partially permeable membrane from an area of lower solute concentration to an area of higher solute concentration.

Active transport

Many of the substances a cell needs occur in low concentrations in the surroundings outside the plasma membrane. Plants must take in nitrate ions from very dilute solutions in the soil to build their proteins, and muscle cells actively take in calcium ions to enable them to contract. To move these substances into the cell against a concentration gradient, the cell must use metabolic energy released from the breakdown of ATP. This is called **active transport** (Figure **2.17**). Specific proteins in the plasma membrane act as transporters or 'carriers' to move substances through. Many of the carrier proteins are specific to particular molecules or ions so that these can be selected for transport into the cell.

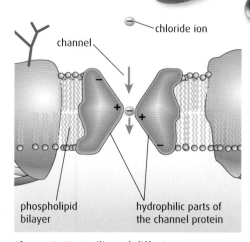

Figure 2.15 Facilitated diffusion.

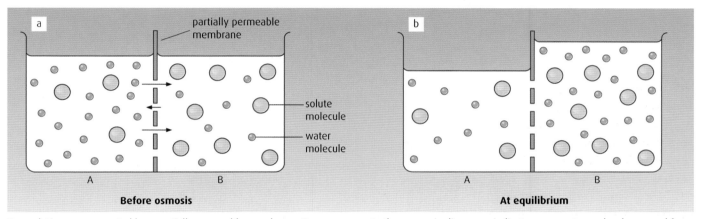

Before osmosis

At equilibrium

Two solutions are separated by a partially permeable membrane. B has a higher solute concentration than A. The soluble molecules are too large to pass through the pores in the membrane but the water molecules are small enough.

As the arrows in diagram **a** indicate, more water molecules moved from A to B than from B to A, so the net movement has been from A to B, raising the level of the solution in B and lowering it in A. The solute concentrations in A and B are now equal.

Figure 2.16 Osmosis.

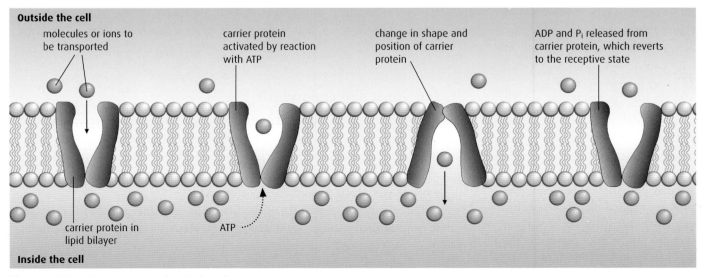

Figure 2.17 Active transport of a single substance.

Figure **2.18** illustrates a very important example of active transport. The sodium–potassium pump maintains the concentration of sodium and potassium ions in the cells and extracellular fluid. Cells are able to exchange sodium ions for potassium ions against concentration gradients using energy provided by ATP. Sodium ions are pumped out of the cell and potassium ions are pumped into the cell.

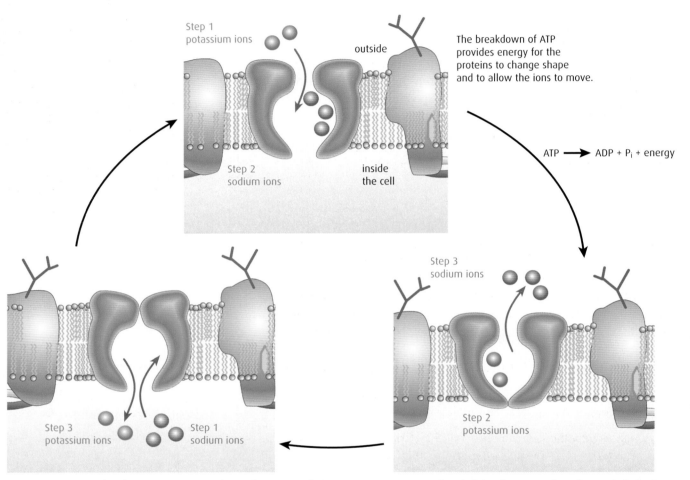

Step 1
potassium ions

outside

The breakdown of ATP provides energy for the proteins to change shape and to allow the ions to move.

Step 2
sodium ions

inside
the cell

ATP → ADP + P$_i$ + energy

Step 3
sodium ions

Step 2
potassium ions

Step 3
potassium ions

Step 1
sodium ions

Figure 2.18 An example of active transport – the sodium–potassium pump. Start at step 1 for each ion in turn and work round clockwise.

Exocytosis and endocytosis

Cells often have to transport large chemical molecules or material in bulk across the plasma membrane. Neither diffusion nor active transport will work here. Instead, cells can release or take in such materials in vesicles, as shown in Figure **2.19**. Uptake is called **endocytosis** and export is **exocytosis**. Both require energy from ATP.

During endocytosis, part of the plasma membrane is pulled inward and surrounds the liquid or solid that is to be moved from the extracellular space into the cell. The material becomes enclosed in a vesicle, which pinches off from the plasma membrane and is drawn into the cell. This is how white blood cells take in bacteria (Figure **2.19**).

There are two types of endocytosis. If the substances being taken in are particles, such as bacteria, the process is called phagocytosis. If the substances are in solution, such as the end products of digestion, then it is called pinocytosis.

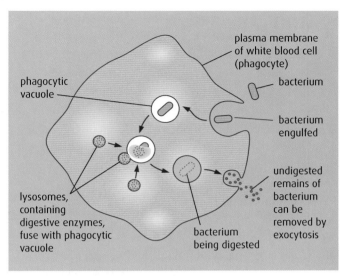

Phagocytosis of a bacterium by a white blood cell – an example of endocytosis.

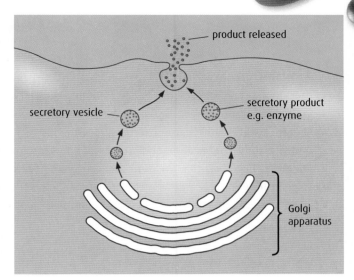

Exocytosis in a secretory cell. If the product is a protein, the Golgi apparatus is often involved in chemically modifying the protein before it is secreted, as in the secretion of digestive enzymes by the pancreas.

Figure 2.19 Examples of endocytosis and exocytosis.

Materials for export, such as digestive enzymes, are made in the rER and then transported to the Golgi apparatus to be processed. From here they are enclosed within a membrane-bound package known as a vesicle, and moved to the plasma membrane along microtubules. The vesicles fuse with the plasma membrane and in doing so release their contents to the outside. The flexibility and fluidity of the plasma membrane allow this to happen.

11 Outline the difference between simple diffusion and facilitated diffusion.

12 Suggest why the term 'fluid mosaic' is used to describe membrane structure.

13 Suggest why the fatty acid 'tails' of the phospholipid molecules always align themselves in the middle of the membrane.

14 Outline the difference between integral membrane proteins and peripheral membrane proteins.

15 List the **six** ways that substances move from one side of a membrane to the other.

16 State which of these transport mechanisms require energy from ATP.

17 List the functions of proteins that are found in a membrane.

2.5 Cell division

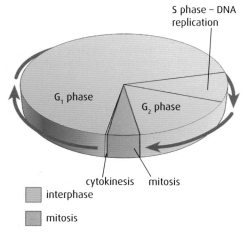

Figure 2.20 The cell cycle.

Summary of the cell cycle
G_1 phase
- cell grows
- DNA is transcribed
- protein is synthesised

S phase
- DNA is replicated

G_2 phase
- cell prepares for division

mitosis
- cell nucleus divides

cytokinesis
- cytoplasm divides

New cells are needed to replace cells which have died or to allow an organism to grow. Cells divide by a process known as **mitosis**, which is one phase of a series of events known as the **cell cycle**.

The cell cycle

The cycle of a cell's life can be divided into three stages, as shown in Figure **2.20**:
1 interphase
2 mitosis (division of the nucleus)
3 cytokinesis (division of the cytoplasm).

Interphase

During most of the life of a cell, it performs the task for which it has been pre-programmed during differentiation. This period is called **interphase**. Part of interphase is spent in preparation for cell division (the **G_2 phase**) and part of it is the period immediately after division (the **G_1 phase**). The two stages of cell division are the separation and division of the chromosomes (mitosis), and the division of the cell into two daughter cells (**cytokinesis**).

If a cell is examined during interphase using a light microscope, very little activity is visible. The cell carries out its normal activities, but also prepares itself for mitosis. The DNA in the chromosomes is replicated (**S phase**) so that after cell division there will be exactly the same number of chromosomes in the two daughter cells. Many proteins necessary for the division need to be synthesised. The number of mitochondria increases so that the respiratory rate can be rapid to provide energy for cell division. In the case of plant cells with chloroplasts, the number of chloroplasts increases so there are sufficient for each daughter cell.

Mitosis

There are four distinct stages in mitosis, though the process is continuous, with each stage running into the next. There are no intervals in between stages. Figures **2.21** and **2.22** show in detail the stages of mitosis.

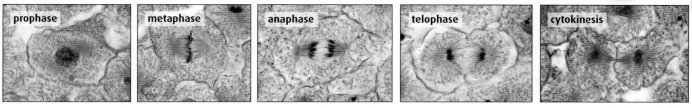

Figure 2.21 Stages of mitosis in an onion cell.

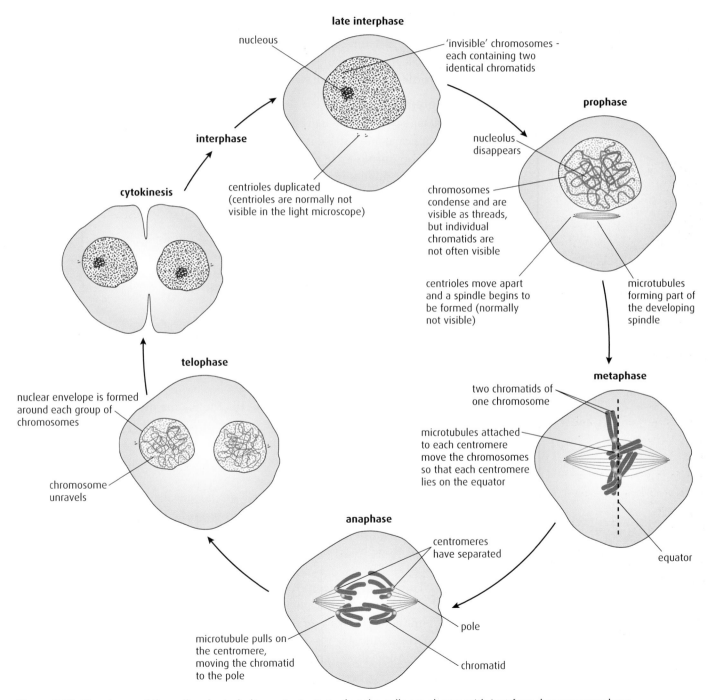

Figure 2.22 The stages of the cell cycle, including mitosis. Note that the cells are shown with just four chromosomes here, to make it easier to understand the process.

Prophase

During prophase, the chromosomes become visible. During interphase they have been drawn out into long threads, allowing the cellular machinery access to the genes. Now, the chromosomes coil several times to produce a supercoil. The chromosomes appear shorter and thicker, and can now be seen using a microscope. Each chromosome is composed of two threads of DNA, the two identical copies that were made during interphase. These two copies are called the **sister chromatids** and are attached to each other at a place called the **centromere**. Also visible at this time are structures known as **centrioles**, which move to opposite sides of the cell as microtubules form between them. This structure is called the **spindle**. As prophase draws to a close, the nuclear envelope breaks down.

Metaphase

Metaphase begins when the nuclear envelope has broken down. As it disappears, more space is created so that the chromosomes can move into position during their division. The sister chromatids align themselves on the microtubules in the middle, or equator, of the spindle and are attached by their centromeres.

Anaphase

During anaphase, the centromeres split and the sister chromatids pull apart and move towards the centrioles at opposite sides, or poles, of the cell as the spindle fibres shorten. Each sister chromatid is now called a chromosome again.

Telophase

Once the two sets of chromosomes reach their opposite poles, the spindle fibres break down and a nuclear envelope forms around each set of chromosomes. At the same time, the chromosomes uncoil and become invisible through a light microscope.

Following telophase, in animal cells, the plasma membrane pinches in and the two new nuclei become separated. Eventually, during cytokinesis, the two sides of the plasma membrane meet and two completely new cells are formed. Each has a complete set of chromosomes, cytoplasm, organelles and a centriole.

It is vital that these two new cells are genetically identical. Mitosis allows an organism to grow more cells from the original fertilised egg during development of an embryo. It also means an organism casn repair injured tissue by replacing damaged cells, and make new cells to replace old ones.

Many organisms reproduce themselves using mitosis. One example is binary fission in unicellular *Amoeba*, and budding in yeast is another. Reproducing in this way is known as **asexual reproduction** as no gametes are involved and the offspring are genetically identical to the parent. Asexual reproduction is very common in the plant kingdom. For example, strawberry plants produce runners that develop into genetically identical new plants, and bulbs like lilies produce miniature bulbils that grow into mature plants genetically the same as the parent.

Mitosis and tumours

In most cases, mitosis continues until a tissue has grown sufficiently or repairs have been made to damaged areas. But sometimes mitosis does not proceed normally. Cell division may continue unchecked and produce an excess of cells, which clump together. This growth is called a **tumour**. Tumours can be either benign, which means they are restricted to that tissue or organ, or malignant, where some of the abnormal cells migrate to other tissues or organs and continue to grow further tumours there. In animals, these abnormal growths are known as cancers and can take many different forms in different tissues. If they are allowed to grow without treatment they can cause obstructions in organs or tissues and interfere with their functions. Cancer is caused by damage to genes, but it cannot be thought of as a single disease because the gene damage can be caused by different factors. Mistakes in copying DNA, environmental factors that cause damage or genetic predisposition as a result of inheritance can all be important factors in causing cancer.

18 List the main stages of the cell cycle in order.

19 Name the stage of the cell cycle that:
    a precedes mitosis
    b follows mitosis

20 State the result of uncontrolled cell divisions.

21 Describe what happens in a cell during interphase.

22 List in order the **four** stages of mitosis.

23 State **three** uses of mitosis in plants and animals.

End-of-chapter questions

1 Prokaryotic cells differ from eukaryotic cells because prokaryotic cells:

      A   have larger ribosomes
      B   have smaller ribosomes
      C   contain mitochondria
      D   have more than one nucleus   (1)

2 The correct order of the stages in the cell cycle is:

      A   cytokinesis $\rightarrow$ mitosis $\rightarrow$ G$_1$ $\rightarrow$ G$_2$ $\rightarrow$ S
      B   mitosis $\rightarrow$ S $\rightarrow$ G$_2$ $\rightarrow$ G$_1$ $\rightarrow$ cytokinesis
      C   mitosis $\rightarrow$ G$_1$ $\rightarrow$ G$_2$ $\rightarrow$ S $\rightarrow$ cytokinesis
      D   cytokinesis $\rightarrow$ G$_1$ $\rightarrow$ S $\rightarrow$ G$_2$ $\rightarrow$ mitosis   (1)

3 Explain how the properties of phospholipids help to maintain the structure of the plasma membrane. (2)

4 Explain how the surface area to volume ratio influences cell size. (3)

5 a Some ions can move across the membrane by passive or active transport. Distinguish between active transport and facilitated diffusion of ions. (2)

b Digestive enzymes leave the cell by exocytosis. Describe the process of exocytosis. (2)

6 A study was carried out to determine the relationship between the diameter of a molecule and its movement through a membrane. The graph below shows the results of the study.

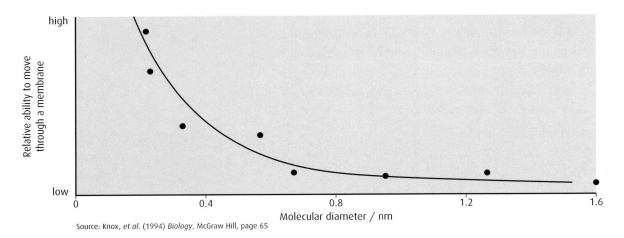

Source: Knox, *et al.* (1994) *Biology*, McGraw Hill, page 65

a From the information in the graph alone, describe the relationship between the diameter of a molecule and its movement through a membrane. (2)

A second study was carried out to investigate the effect of passive protein channels on the movement of glucose into cells. The graph below shows the rate of uptake of glucose into erythrocytes by simple diffusion and facilitated diffusion.

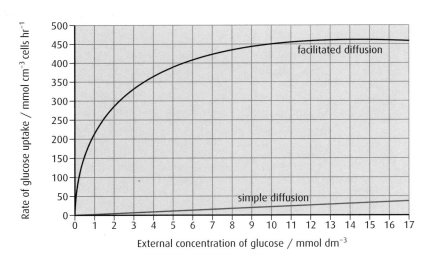

b Identify the rate of glucose uptake at an external glucose concentration of $4\,\mathrm{mmol\,dm^{-3}}$ by:

   i simple diffusion (1)

   ii facilitated diffusion (1)

c **i** Compare the effect of increasing the external glucose concentration on glucose uptake by facilitated diffusion and by simple diffusion. (3)

   ii Predict, with a reason, the effect on glucose uptake by facilitated diffusion of increasing the external concentration of glucose to $30\,\mathrm{mmol\,dm^{-3}}$. (2)

(total 9 marks)

7 **a** Identify the cell organelle shown in the micrograph below. (1)

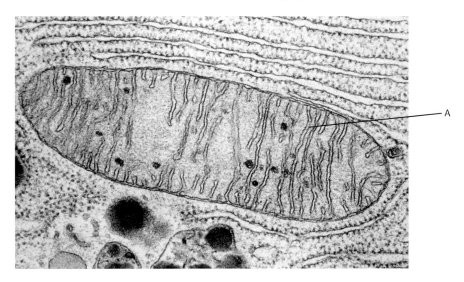

b Identify the structure labelled A above and explain how it is adapted for the organelle to function efficiently. (4)

(total 5 marks)

3 The chemistry of life

Introduction

Living things are built up of many chemical elements, the majority of which are bonded together in organic, carbon-containing compounds. Most organic compounds in living things are carbohydrates, proteins, nucleic acids or lipids. Other inorganic, non-carbon-containing substances are also important but are present in much smaller quantities.

3.1 Chemical elements and water

Assessment statements

- State that the most frequently occurring chemical elements in living things are carbon, hydrogen, oxygen and nitrogen.
- State that a variety of other elements are needed by living organisms, including sulfur, calcium, phosphorus, iron and sodium.
- State one role for each of the above elements.
- Draw and label a diagram showing the structure of water molecules to show their polarity and hydrogen bond formation.
- Outline the thermal, cohesive and solvent properties of water.
- Explain the relationship between the properties of water and its uses in living organisms as a coolant, medium for metabolic reactions and transport medium.

Elements in living things

Carbon, hydrogen, oxygen and nitrogen are the four most common elements found in living organisms.

Carbon, hydrogen and oxygen are found in all the key **organic** molecules – proteins, carbohydrates, nucleic acids and lipids. Proteins and nucleic acids also contain nitrogen.

Any compound that does not contain carbon is said to be **inorganic**. A variety of inorganic substances are found in living things and are vital to both the structure and functioning of different organisms. Some important roles of inorganic elements are shown in Table **3.1**.

Structure and properties of water

Water is the main component of living things. Most human cells are approximately 80% water. Water provides the environment in which the biochemical reactions of life can occur. It also takes part in and is produced by many reactions. Two of its most important properties (its solvent properties and its heat capacity) are due to its molecular structure, which consists of two hydrogen atoms each bonded to an oxygen atom by a covalent bond (Figure **3.1**).

The water molecule is unusual because it has a small positive charge on the two hydrogen atoms and a small negative charge on the oxygen atom.

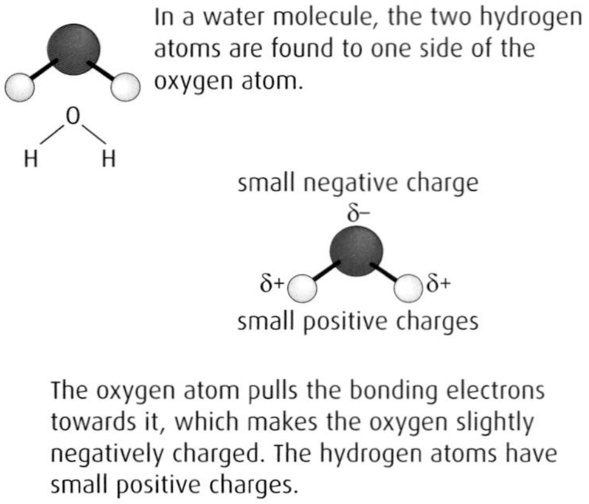

In a water molecule, the two hydrogen atoms are found to one side of the oxygen atom.

small negative charge

small positive charges

The oxygen atom pulls the bonding electrons towards it, which makes the oxygen slightly negatively charged. The hydrogen atoms have small positive charges.

Figure 3.1 The structure of a water molecule.

Element	Example of role in prokaryotes	Example of role in plants	Example of role in animals
sulfur (S)	a component of two amino acids	a component of two amino acids	a component of two amino acids, needed to make some antibodies
calcium (Ca)	co-factor in some enzyme reactions	co-factor in some enzyme reactions	important constituent of bones, needed for muscle contraction
phosphorus (P)	a component of ATP and DNA	a component of ATP and DNA	a component of ATP and DNA
iron (Fe)	a component of cytochrome pigments	a component of cytochrome pigments	a component of hemoglobin and cytochrome pigments
sodium (Na)	important in membranes, changes solute concentration and affects osmosis	important in membranes, changes solute concentration and affects osmosis	important in membranes, changes solute concentration and affects osmosis; also important in transmission of nerve impulses

Table 3.1 Roles of inorganic elements in living things.

Because of this arrangement, water is said to be a **polar** molecule. Polar molecules are those that have an unevenly distributed electrical charge so that there is a positive region and a negative region. Sugars and amino acids are also polar molecules.

A weak bond can form between the negative charge of one water molecule and the positive charge of another, as shown in Figure **3.2**. This type of bond, known as a **hydrogen bond**, is responsible for many of the properties of water.

Hydrogen bonds between water molecules hold them together in a network, resulting in a phenomenon known as **cohesion**. Cohesive forces give water many of its biologically important properties. For example, they enable water to be drawn up inside the xylem of a plant stem in a continuous column. Strong pulling forces, produced as water evaporates from the leaves at the top of tall trees, draw water and dissolved minerals up great distances to the tips of branches high above the ground. Cohesion is also responsible for surface tension, which enables some small organisms to 'walk on water', and contributes to the thermal properties of water too.

Water has unusual **thermal properties**. A large amount of energy is needed to break the many weak hydrogen bonds between the water molecules. This gives water a high specific heat capacity – it can absorb or give off a great deal of heat energy without its temperature changing very much. A stable temperature is important to living things because the range of temperatures in which biological reactions can occur is quite narrow. The thermal properties of water allow it to keep an organism's temperature fairly constant. Within the body, water can act as a temperature regulator – for example, blood carries heat from warmer parts of the body, such as the liver, to cooler parts such as the feet.

When liquid water evaporates and becomes vapour, many hydrogen bonds between the molecules must be broken, so evaporation requires a lot of energy. As a result, water is a liquid at most temperatures found on Earth, and it has a high boiling point. When it evaporates – for example, when an animal sweats – it carries a great deal of heat with it and thus acts as a coolant for the body.

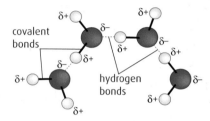

Figure 3.2 Hydrogen bonding in water.

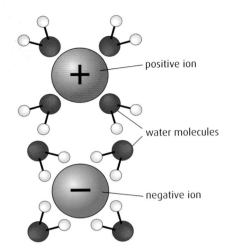

Figure 3.3 The positive and negative charges of water molecules attract ions with negative or positive charges so that they dissolve.

Water is sometimes known as a universal **solvent**. Its polarity makes it an excellent solvent for other polar molecules. Most inorganic ions, such as sodium, potassium and chloride ions, dissolve well as their positive or negative charges are attracted to the charges of water molecules (Figure **3.3**). Polar organic molecules, such as amino acids and sugars, are also soluble in water. Water is the medium in which most biochemical reactions take place since almost all the substances involved dissolve well in it. Protein synthesis and most of the reactions of photosynthesis and respiration take place in an aqueous (water) solution.

The solvent properties of water also make it an excellent medium for transporting substances around the bodies of all organisms. In plants, the xylem carries dissolved minerals from the roots to the leaves, while the phloem transports soluble sugars up and down the plant. Many animals have blood as their transport medium. Blood is predominantly water, and the blood plasma carries dissolved sugars, amino acids and carbon dioxide as well as many other solutes.

The properties of water are summarised in Table **3.2**.

Property	Reason	Consequence
cohesion	Hydrogen bonds hold water molecules together.	Water can travel in continuous columns, for example in the stems of plants, and act as a transport medium.
solvent	The polar molecules of water can interact with other polar molecules.	Ions dissolve easily. Large molecules with polar side groups, such as carbohydrates and proteins, can also dissolve. So water acts as an excellent transport medium and as a medium for metabolic reactions.
thermal	Water has a high heat capacity. Large amounts of energy are needed to break hydrogen bonds and change its temperature.	The temperature of organisms tends to change slowly. Fluids such as blood can transport heat round their bodies.
	Water has a high boiling point compared with other solvents because hydrogen bonds need large amounts of energy to break them.	Water is liquid at most temperatures at which life exists, so is a useful medium for metabolic reactions.
	Water evaporates as hydrogen bonds are broken and heat from water is used.	Sweating and transpiration enable animals and plants to lose heat. Water acts as a coolant.

Table 3.2 Summary of the properties of water.

3.2 Carbohydrates, lipids and proteins

Assessment statements

- Distinguish between 'organic' and 'inorganic' compounds.
- Identify amino acids, glucose, ribose and fatty acids from diagrams showing their structure.
- List three examples each of monosaccharides, disaccharides and polysaccharides.
- State one function of glucose, lactose and glycogen in animals and of fructose, sucrose and cellulose in plants.
- Outline the role of condensation and hydrolysis in the relationships between monosaccharides, disaccharides and polysaccharides; between fatty acids, glycerol and triglycerides; and between amino acids and polypeptides.
- State three functions of lipids.
- Compare the use of carbohydrates and lipids in energy storage.

Organic and inorganic compounds

Chemical compounds are divided into two groups: organic and inorganic. Organic compounds include all the complex compounds of carbon found in living organisms, but not simple carbon-containing compounds such as carbon dioxide, carbonates and hydrogencarbonates. These and all other compounds are inorganic. Both groups are found in living organisms.

Building blocks of organic molecules

Many organic molecules are very large and complex but they are built up of small subunits, which can be relatively simple. Figure **3.4** shows some of these building blocks. Subunits called monomers are built into complex polymers.

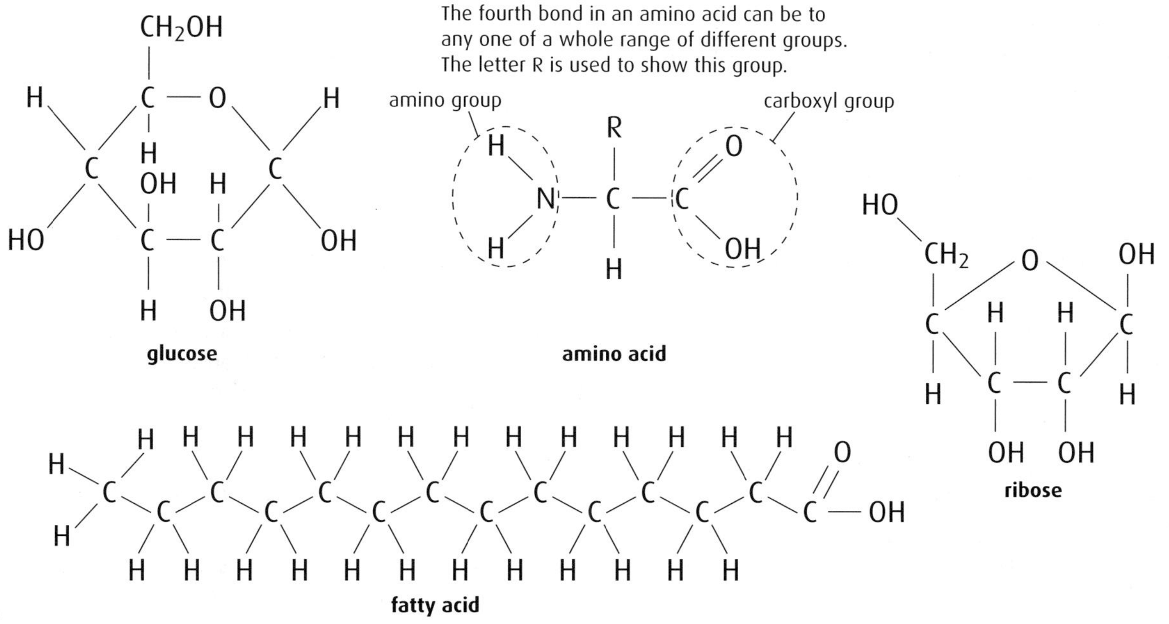

Figure 3.4 The basic structures of glucose, amino acids, fatty acids and ribose – the building blocks of organic molecules.

Carbohydrates

Carbohydrates contain only carbon, hydrogen and oxygen and they are the most abundant category of molecule in living things. In both plants and animals they have an important role as a source of energy, and in plants they also have a structural function. Carbohydrates occur in different forms: **monosaccharides**, which contain only one subunit; **disaccharides**, which have two; and **polysaccharides**, which are formed from long chains of monosaccharides. Table **3.3** (overleaf) shows examples of carbohydrates and their uses.

Condensation and hydrolysis

In a **condensation reaction**, two molecules can be joined to form a larger molecule, held together by strong **covalent bonds**. Each condensation reaction requires an enzyme to catalyse the process

Form of carbohydrate	Examples	Example of use in plants	Example of use in animals
monosaccharide	glucose, galactose, fructose	fructose is a component of fruits, making them taste sweet and attracting animals to eat them, thereby dispersing the seeds inside	glucose is the source of energy for cell respiration – it is obtained from the digestion of carbohydrate foods
disaccharide	maltose, lactose, sucrose	sucrose is transported from leaves to storage tissues and other parts of the plant to provide an energy source	lactose is found in milk and provides energy for young mammals
polysaccharide	starch, glycogen, cellulose	cellulose is a structural component of plant cell walls starch is used as a food store	glycogen is the storage carbohydrate of animals, found in the liver and muscles

Table 3.3 Examples and roles of carbohydrates.

and it produces one molecule of water. The condensation of two monosaccharides produces a disaccharide. For example:

$$\text{glucose} \quad + \quad \text{galactose} \quad \rightarrow \quad \text{lactose} \quad + \quad \text{water}$$
$$\text{(monosaccharide)} \quad \text{(monosaccharide)} \quad \text{(disaccharide)}$$

If further monosaccharides are added to a disaccharide, a polysaccharide is formed, as you can see in Figure **3.5**.

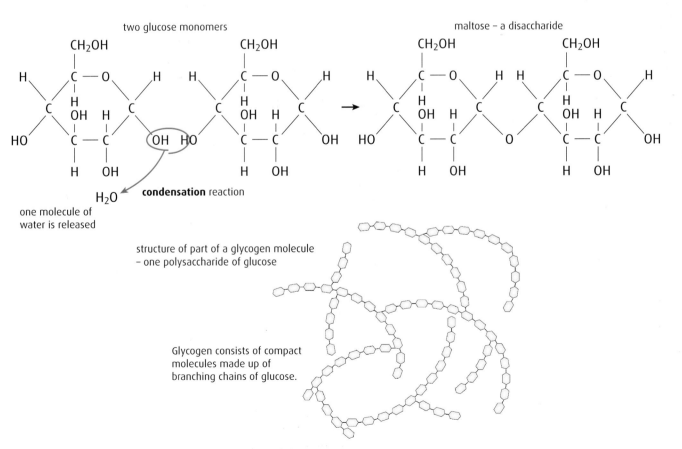

Figure 3.5 Monosaccharide subunits (glucose in this case) are joined in a condensation reaction, forming a disaccharide (maltose) and water. Glycogen is a polysaccharide, formed from long chains of glucose subunits.

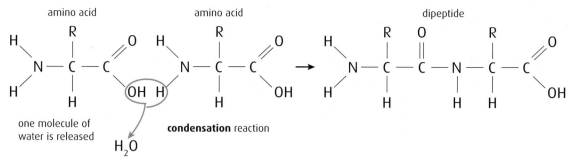

Figure 3.6 Two amino acids combine to form a dipeptide.

In a similar way, two amino acids can be linked to form a **dipeptide** (Figure **3.6**):

amino acid + amino acid → dipeptide + water

When more than two amino acids are joined in this way, a **polypeptide** is formed. Polypeptide chains form protein molecules.

In another condensation reaction, glycerol links to fatty acids to produce triglyceride **lipid** molecules (Figure **3.7**):

glycerol + 3 fatty acids → triglyceride lipid + water

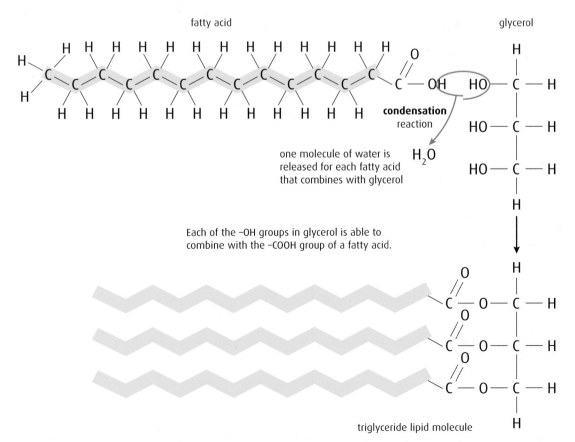

Figure 3.7 How a triglyceride lipid is formed from glycerol and three fatty acids in a condensation reaction.

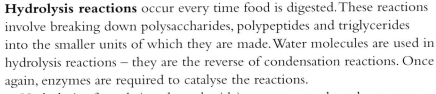

Hydrolysis reactions occur every time food is digested. These reactions involve breaking down polysaccharides, polypeptides and triglycerides into the smaller units of which they are made. Water molecules are used in hydrolysis reactions – they are the reverse of condensation reactions. Once again, enzymes are required to catalyse the reactions.

- Hydrolysis of starch (a polysaccharide) uses water and produces many molecules of glucose.
- Hydrolysis of protein (made of polypeptide chains) uses water and produces many amino acids.
- Hydrolysis of a triglyceride (a lipid) uses water and produces fatty acids and glycerol molecules.

Lipids

Lipids are used as energy storage molecules in plants and animals. Triglyceride lipids that are solid are generally referred to as fats, while in liquid form triglycerides are known as oils. Animals store energy as fat whereas plants store oils – for example, linseed oil and olive oil. Lipid contains about twice as much energy per gram as carbohydrate but each type of storage molecule has its own advantages.

- Lipids contain more energy per gram than carbohydrates, so lipid stores are lighter than carbohydrates storing an equivalent amount of energy.
- Lipids are also less dense than water, so fat stores help large aquatic animals to float.
- Lipids are non-polar, insoluble molecules so they do not affect the movement of water in and out of cells by osmosis.
- Lipids are also important in providing heat insulation. Fat stored under the skin reduces heat loss and is vital for animals, such as seals, polar bears and whales, which live in cold conditions.
- However, carbohydrates can be digested more easily than lipids, making carbohydrate stores more readily available sources of energy.

Molecule	Approximate energy content per gram / kJ
carbohydrate	17
lipid	39
protein	18

1 Explain why water makes a good coolant for animals.

2 State why glucose is not used as an energy storage molecule.

3 Distinguish between hydrolysis and condensation reactions.

3.3 DNA structure

Assessment statements

- Outline DNA nucleotide structure in terms of sugar (deoxyribose), base and phosphate.
- State the names of the four bases in DNA.
- Outline how DNA nucleotides are linked together by covalent bonds into a single strand.
- Explain how a DNA double helix is formed using complementary base pairing and hydrogen bonds.
- Draw and label a simple diagram of the molecular structure of DNA.

DNA (deoxyribonucleic acid) molecules make up the genetic material of living organisms. DNA is an extremely long molecule but, like proteins and carbohydrates, it is built up of many subunits. The subunits of DNA are called **nucleotides**.

Each nucleotide consists of three parts – a sugar (deoxyribose), a phosphate group and a nitrogenous base (Figure **3.8**). DNA contains four different bases: adenine, guanine, cytosine and thymine. These are usually known by their letters: A, G, C and T (Figure **3.9**).

To form a DNA molecule, nucleotides are linked together. The phosphate group of one nucleotide links to the deoxyribose of the next molecule to form a chain of nucleotides, as shown in Figure **3.10** (overleaf). The sugar and phosphate groups are identical all the way along the chain and form the backbone of the DNA molecule. The sequence of bases in the chain will vary and it is this sequence that forms the genetic code determining the characteristics of an organism.

Two strands of nucleotides are linked by hydrogen bonds that form between the bases and this double strand makes up the double helix of a complete DNA molecule (Figure **3.10**). Adenine always pairs with thymine and is bonded with two hydrogen bonds, while cytosine is paired with guanine by three hydrogen bonds. The arrangement is known as **complementary base pairing**. Notice that the two DNA chains run in opposite directions and are said to be **antiparallel**.

You can imagine the molecule rather like a rope ladder with the sugar–phosphate backbone being the sides of the ladder and the rungs being formed by the hydrogen-bonded base pairs. To form the characteristic double helix of a DNA molecule, the ladder must be twisted to resemble a spiral staircase.

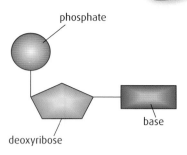

Figure 3.8 The general structure of a DNA nucleotide.

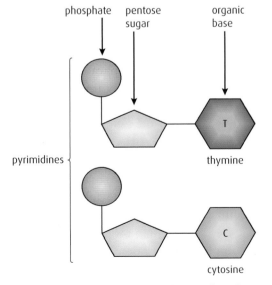
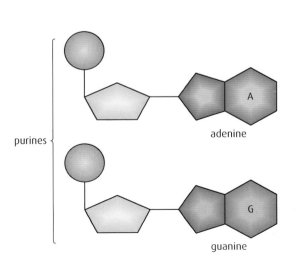

Figure 3.9 The structure of the four nucleotides in DNA.

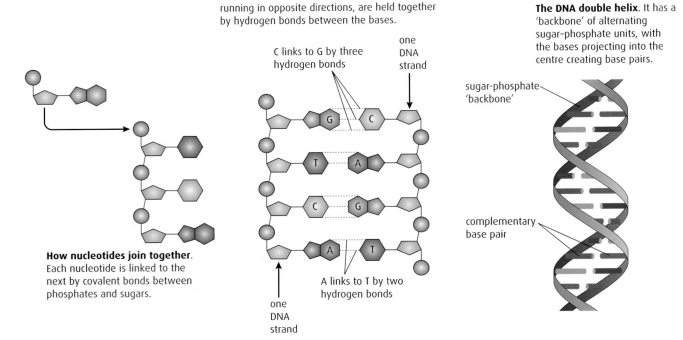

Part of a DNA molecule. Two DNA strands, running in opposite directions, are held together by hydrogen bonds between the bases.

C links to G by three hydrogen bonds

one DNA strand

The DNA double helix. It has a 'backbone' of alternating sugar–phosphate units, with the bases projecting into the centre creating base pairs.

sugar-phosphate 'backbone'

complementary base pair

How nucleotides join together. Each nucleotide is linked to the next by covalent bonds between phosphates and sugars.

A links to T by two hydrogen bonds

one DNA strand

Figure 3.10 The structure of DNA.

3.4 DNA replication

Assessment statements

- Explain DNA replication in terms of unwinding the double helix and separation of the strands by helicase, followed by formation of the new complementary strands by DNA polymerase.
- Explain the significance of complementary base pairing in the conservation of the base sequence of DNA.
- State that DNA replication is semi-conservative.

An essential feature of DNA is that it must be able to replicate itself accurately, so that when a cell divides the genetic code it carries can be passed on to the daughter cells. **DNA replication** copies DNA precisely so that new molecules are produced with exactly the same sequence of bases as the original strands. DNA replication takes place in the nucleus during the S phase of the interphase of the cell cycle when DNA is not tightly coiled.

As Figure **3.11** shows, this process does not occur in a haphazard manner. An enzyme called helicase unzips one region of the DNA molecule and nucleotides are added in a step-by-step process that links them to one another and to their complementary bases in an area known as the replication fork.

1 The first step in the process is the 'unzipping' of the two strands. Helicase moves along the double helix, unwinding the two strands, which separate from one another as the relatively weak hydrogen bonds between the bases are broken.

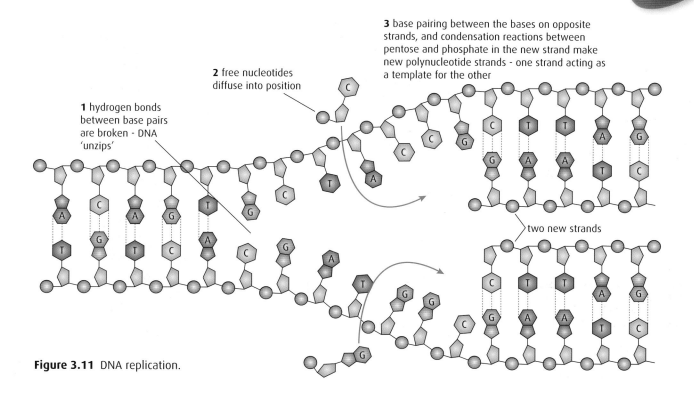

1 hydrogen bonds between base pairs are broken - DNA 'unzips'

2 free nucleotides diffuse into position

3 base pairing between the bases on opposite strands, and condensation reactions between pentose and phosphate in the new strand make new polynucleotide strands - one strand acting as a template for the other

two new strands

Figure 3.11 DNA replication.

2 The unpaired nucleotides are exposed and each single strand now acts as a template for the formation of a new complementary strand. Free nucleotides move into place: C pairs with G and A pairs with T.

3 The free nucleotide bases form complementary pairs with the bases on the single DNA strands. DNA polymerase is the enzyme involved in linking the new nucleotides into place. Finally, the two new DNA molecules are rewound, each one forming a new double helix.

The two new DNA strands that are produced are absolutely identical to the original strands. Complementary base pairing between the template strand and the new strand ensures that an accurate copy of the original DNA is made every time replication occurs. DNA replication is said to be **semi-conservative** because no DNA molecule is ever completely new. Every double helix contains one 'original' and one 'new' strand.

3.5 Transcription and translation

Assessment statements

- Compare the structure of RNA and DNA.
- Outline DNA transcription in terms of the formation of an RNA strand complementary to the DNA strand by RNA polymerase.
- Describe the genetic code in terms of codons composed of triplets of bases.
- Explain the process of translation leading to polypeptide formation.
- Discuss the relationship between one gene and one polypeptide.

The main role of DNA is to direct the activities of the cell. It does this by controlling the proteins that the cell produces. Enzymes, hormones and many other important biochemical molecules are proteins, which control what the cell becomes, what it synthesises and how it functions. Protein synthesis can be divided into two sets of reactions: the first is **transcription** and the second, **translation**. In eukaryotes, transcription occurs in the nucleus and translation in the cytoplasm.

The sections of DNA that code for particular proteins are known as **genes**. Genes contain specific sequences of bases in sets of three, called **triplets**. Some triplets control where transcription begins and ends.

Transcription

The first stage in the synthesis of a protein is the production of an intermediate molecule that carries the coded message of DNA into the cytoplasm where the protein can be produced. This intermediate molecule is called **messenger RNA** or **mRNA**. RNA (ribonucleic acid) has similarities and differences with DNA and these are shown in Table **3.4**.

DNA	RNA
contains the 5-carbon sugar deoxyribose	contains the 5-carbon sugar ribose
contains the bases adenine, guanine, cytosine and thymine	contains the bases adenine, guanine, cytosine and uracil (instead of thymine)
a double-stranded molecule	a single-stranded molecule

Table 3.4 Comparing DNA and RNA.

The building blocks for RNA are the RNA nucleotides that are found in the nucleus. Complementary base pairing of RNA to DNA occurs in exactly the same way as in the replication process but this time uracil (U) pairs with adenine since there is no thymine (T) found in RNA. Transcription results in the copying of one section of the DNA molecule, not its entire length. Figure **3.12** describes the process.

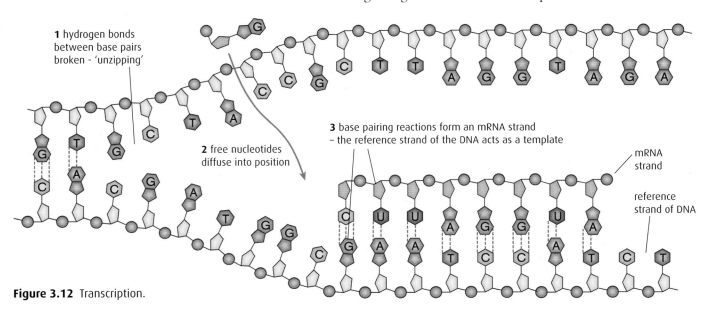

1 hydrogen bonds between base pairs broken - 'unzipping'

2 free nucleotides diffuse into position

3 base pairing reactions form an mRNA strand – the reference strand of the DNA acts as a template

mRNA strand

reference strand of DNA

Figure 3.12 Transcription.

1 DNA is unzipped by the enzyme RNA polymerase, and the two strands uncoil and separate.
2 Free nucleotides move into place along one of the two strands.
3 The same enzyme, RNA polymerase, assembles the free nucleotides in the correct places using complementary base pairing. As the RNA nucleotides are linked together, a single strand of mRNA is formed. This molecule is much shorter than the DNA molecule because it is a copy of just one section – a gene. The mRNA separates from the DNA and the DNA double helix is zipped up again by RNA polymerase.

Once an mRNA molecule has been transcribed, it moves via the pores in the nuclear envelope to the cytoplasm where the process of translation can take place.

Translation

Due to complementary base pairing, the sequence of bases along the mRNA molecule corresponds to the sequence on the original DNA molecule. Each sequence of three bases, called a triplet, corresponds to a specific amino acid, so the order of these triplets determines how amino acids will be assembled into polypeptide chains in the cytoplasm.

Translation is the process by which the coded information in mRNA strands is used to construct polypeptide chains, which in turn make functioning proteins. Each triplet of mRNA bases is called a **codon** and codes for one amino acid. Translation is carried out in the cytoplasm by structures called **ribosomes** (Figure **3.13**, overleaf) and molecules of another type of RNA known as **transfer RNA** or **tRNA** (Figure **3.14**, page **53**).

Ribosomes have binding sites for both the mRNA molecule and tRNA molecules. The ribosome binds to the mRNA and then draws in specific tRNA molecules with **anticodons** that match the mRNA codons.

Only two tRNA molecules bind to the ribosome at once. Each one carries with it the amino acid specified by its anticodon. The anticodon of the tRNA binds to the complementary codon of the mRNA molecule with hydrogen bonds.

When two tRNA molecules are in place on the ribosome, a **peptide bond** forms between the two amino acids they carry to form a dipeptide. Once a dipeptide has been formed, the first tRNA molecule detaches from both the amino acid and the ribosome. The ribosome moves along the mRNA one triplet to the next codon.

These processes, shown in Figure **3.13** (overleaf) are repeated over and over again until the complete polypeptide is formed. The final codon that is reached is a 'stop' codon, which does not code for an amino acid but tells the ribosome to detach from the mRNA. As it does so, the polypeptide floats free in the cytoplasm.

'One gene, one polypeptide' hypothesis

In the 1940s, scientists proposed that each gene was responsible for the production of one protein. Later, the hypothesis was modified to state that

The mRNA codons that code for each amino acid are shown in Table **4.1** on page **68**.

Transfer RNA (tRNA) is a single strand of RNA that is folded into a 'clover leaf' shape (Figure **3.14**, page **53**). Within the molecule, sections are bonded together by complementary base pairing but one particular area is exposed to reveal a triplet of bases called an **anticodon**. This triplet corresponds to one of the codons found in mRNA. At the opposite end of the tRNA molecule is a binding site for one amino acid, which corresponds to the codon on mRNA that matches the anticodon of the tRNA.

the genetic code in part of an mRNA molecule

the mRNA molecule is read in this direction ⟶

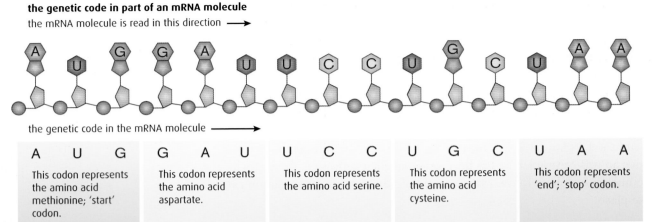

the genetic code in the mRNA molecule ⟶

A U G	G A U	U C C	U G C	U A A
This codon represents the amino acid methionine; 'start' codon.	This codon represents the amino acid aspartate.	This codon represents the amino acid serine.	This codon represents the amino acid cysteine.	This codon represents 'end'; 'stop' codon.

Translation on a ribosome

1 Complementary base pairing between codon and anticodon.

2 Another amino acid is brought in attached to its tRNA.

3 A condensation reaction forms a peptide bond.

4 The ribosome moves along the mRNA by one triplet and a tRNA is released.

5 Another amino acid is brought in.

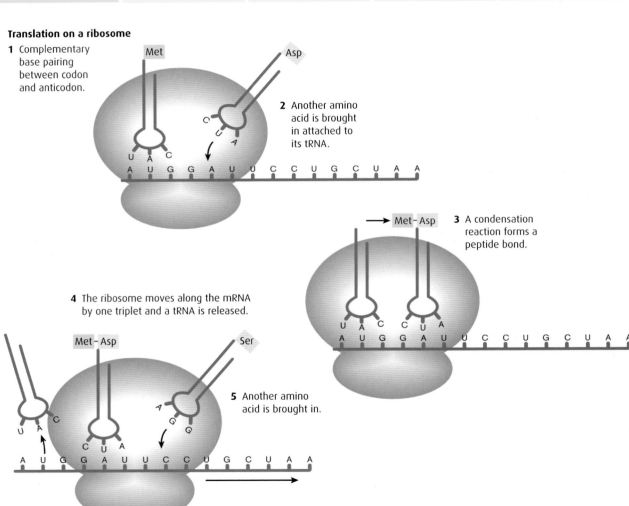

Figure 3.13 Translation.

one gene produces one polypeptide, when it was discovered that some proteins are composed of more than one polypeptide subunit and that each subunit is coded for by its own specific gene. An example of this is hemoglobin, which is composed of two pairs of subunits and is coded for by two genes.

Today, it is generally agreed that each gene does code for a single polypeptide, but that there are some exceptions to the rule. For example, some DNA sequences act as regulators for the expression of other genes and are not transcribed or translated themselves. Others code for mRNA or tRNA but not for proteins. Most recently, researchers have found that some genes code for single mRNA strands which are then modified in the cytoplasm. Variations in the modifications can lead to the production of different polypeptides when the mRNA is translated. For example, when antibodies are produced, lymphocytes splice together sections of RNA in different ways to make a range of antibody proteins. In a few cells, there is differential expression of certain genes, influenced by the type of tissue in which the cells are found. One example of this is the expression of genes that produce the insulin-like growth factors (IGF–1 and IGF–2) in the liver.

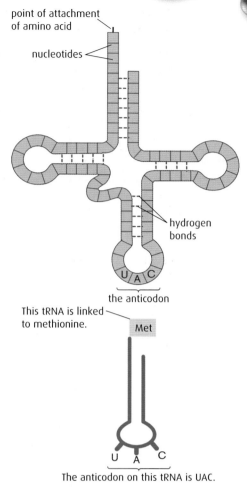

Figure 3.14 The structure of a tRNA molecule.

4 Draw and label a nucleotide.

5 Where in a cell does translation take place?

6 List the differences between DNA and RNA.

7 What is complementary base pairing?

3.6 Enzymes

Assessment statements
- Define 'enzyme' and 'active site'.
- Explain enzyme–substrate specificity.
- Explain the effects of temperature, pH and substrate concentration on enzyme activity.
- Define 'denaturation'.
- Explain the use of lactase in the production of lactose-free milk.

Enzymes and active sites

An **enzyme** is a biological **catalyst**. Catalysts speed up biochemical reactions, such as digestion and respiration, but they remain unchanged at the end of the process. All enzymes are proteins with long polypeptide chains that are folded into three-dimensional shapes. The arrangement of these shapes is very precise and gives each enzyme the ability to catalyse one specific reaction. If the three-dimensional shape of an enzyme is destroyed or damaged, it can no longer carry out its job and is said to be

denatured. Extremes of temperature, heavy metals and, in some cases, pH can cause permanent changes in an enzyme.

The three-dimensional shape of an enzyme is crucial to the way it works. In the structure of every enzyme is a specially shaped region known as an **active site** (Figure **3.15**). It is here that the substrates are brought together. The substrates are the chemicals involved in the reaction catalysed by the enzyme. The shapes of the enzyme and substrates are complementary, so that they fit together perfectly like a key fits into a lock. The 'lock-and-key hypothesis' is a way of explaining how each enzyme can be so specific. To unlock a door requires just one special key. To catalyse a reaction requires one special enzyme. Just as only one key fits perfectly into the lock, only one substrate fits perfectly into the active site of an enzyme.

Once in place in an active site, substrates may be bonded together to form a new substance or they may be broken apart in processes such as digestion and respiration. For example, one type of enzyme bonds amino acids together to form a polypeptide, while very different enzymes are involved in digesting them.

Factors affecting enzyme action

Enzymes work in many different places in living organisms and they require special conditions to work at their greatest, or optimum, efficiency. Temperature, pH and the concentration of the substrates involved all affect the rate at which enzymes operate and produce their products.

Enzyme a globular protein that functions as a biological catalyst of chemical reactions
Denaturation irreversible changes to the structure of an enzyme or other protein so that it can no longer function
Active site region on the surface of an enzyme molecule where a substrate molecule binds and which catalyses a reaction involving the substrates

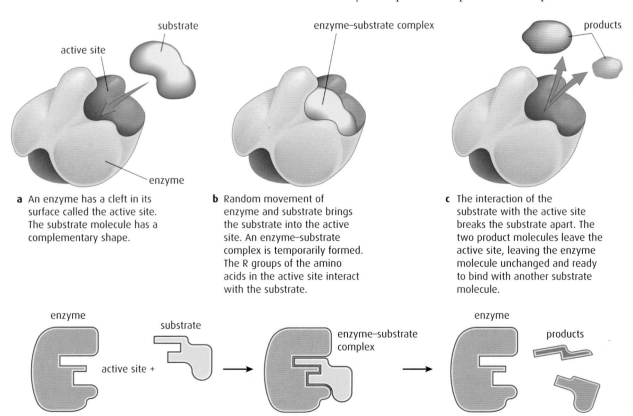

a An enzyme has a cleft in its surface called the active site. The substrate molecule has a complementary shape.

b Random movement of enzyme and substrate brings the substrate into the active site. An enzyme–substrate complex is temporarily formed. The R groups of the amino acids in the active site interact with the substrate.

c The interaction of the substrate with the active site breaks the substrate apart. The two product molecules leave the active site, leaving the enzyme molecule unchanged and ready to bind with another substrate molecule.

Figure 3.15 How an enzyme catalyses the breakdown of a substrate molecule into two product molecules.

Temperature

Enzymes and their substrates usually meet as a result of random collisions between their molecules, which float free in body fluids or cytoplasm. In the human body, most reactions proceed at their greatest rate at a temperature of about 37 °C and deviations from this **optimum temperature** affect the reaction rate, as the graph in Figure **3.16** shows.

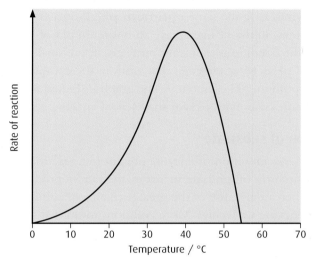

Figure 3.16 The effect of temperature on the rate of an enzyme-controlled reaction. An enzyme works most efficiently at its optimum temperature.

Below 37 °C, molecules in solution move more slowly so the likelihood of collision between them is reduced. This slows down the production of products. At very low temperatures, enzymes hardly work at all and the rate of reaction is very low. As the temperature rises, molecular collisions are more frequent and energetic, and therefore the rate of the enzyme-controlled reaction increases.

As the temperature rises above the optimum, the enzyme and substrate molecules move faster – but atoms within the enzyme molecule itself also move faster, straining the bonds holding it together. Eventually, these bonds may be stressed or broken to such an extent that the enzyme loses its three-dimensional shape and the active site can no longer receive substrate molecules. At these high temperatures, the structure is permanently destroyed and the enzyme is denatured and can no longer catalyse the reaction.

pH

pH is a measure of the relative numbers of H^+ and OH^- ions in a solution. A solution with a low pH value has many free H^+ ions and is acidic, whereas a high pH value indicates more OH^- ions and a basic solution. Pure water is neutral and has a pH value of 7 indicating that the number of OH^- and H^+ ions is equal.

Enzyme action is influenced by pH because the amino acids that make up an enzyme molecule contain many positive and negative regions, some of which are around the active site. An excess of H^+ ions in an acidic solution can lead to bonding between the H^+ ions and negative charges in the active site or other parts of the enzyme. These interactions can inhibit the matching process between the enzyme and its substrate, and slow down or even prevent enzyme activity. A similar effect occurs if a solution becomes too basic – the excess of negative ions upsets the enzyme in the same way. At extremes of pH, the enzyme may even lose its shape and be denatured.

Not all enzymes have the same **optimum pH**. Proteases (protein-digesting enzymes) in the stomach have an optimum pH of 2 and work well in the acidic conditions there, but proteases in the small intestine have an optimum of pH 8. Most enzymes that work in the cytoplasm of body cells have an optimum pH of about 7. The graph in Figure **3.17** shows how reaction rate varies with pH for this type of enzyme.

Concentration of substrate

If there is a set concentration of enzyme present in a reaction mixture, and the concentration of substrate increases, the rate of production of the products will increase because of the greater chance of collisions between substrate and enzyme molecules. More collisions mean that the enzyme is able to process or 'turn over' more substrate molecules. But there is a limit to this increase in reaction rate. If the concentration of substrate increases too much, it will exceed the maximum rate at which the enzyme can work. When this happens, at any one moment all the active sites are occupied by substrate or product molecules, and so adding further substrate has no effect. The rate reaches its limit; you can see this as the plateau in the graph in Figure **3.18**.

Lactose intolerance and the enzyme lactase

All young mammals are fed on milk for the early part of their lives. Milk contains the sugar lactose, which is digested in the intestine by an enzyme

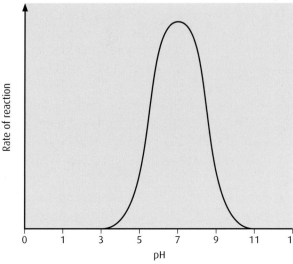

Figure 3.17 The effect of pH on the rate of an enzyme-controlled reaction.

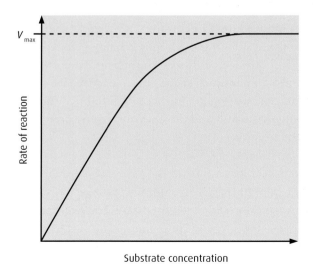

Figure 3.18 The effect of substrate concentration on the rate of an enzyme-catalysed reaction.

called lactase. This produces two simple sugars (glucose and galactose) that can be absorbed into the body. Lactase can be obtained commercially from a yeast that grows in milk and this enzyme is used to produce lactose-free milk.

Lactose-free milk is useful because some people are lactose intolerant and cannot digest lactose properly. If they take more than a small amount of milk, they suffer symptoms such as cramps or diarrhoea. Milk that contains glucose and galactose rather than lactose tastes sweeter and so manufacturers need to add less sweetener to milk products such as yoghurt made with lactose-free milk. Glucose and galactose are also more soluble than lactose, so they produce smoother textures in dairy products such as ice cream. In fermented dairy products such as yoghurt, the fermentation of the simple sugars present in lactose-free milk is much quicker so production rates of these foods can be increased by using lactose-free milk.

8   What is an enzyme?

9   'Enzymes are proteins but not all proteins are enzymes.' Explain this statement.

10 Describe what is meant by the optimum temperature for enzyme activity.

11 Why does increasing the amount of substrate in an enzyme-controlled reaction not always increase the rate of the reaction?

The distribution of lactose intolerance around the globe shows considerable variation. Only 4% of the Scandinavian population is affected, while countries around the Mediterranean have incidences of the order of 50–75% and in Africa the figure reaches 80%. Asia is affected even more with about 90% of the population suffering from lactose intolerance.

The control of lactase production was disputed by scientists for many years. Some researchers in the 1960s argued that lactase production was stimulated in the presence of its substrate, lactose from milk. They proposed that populations that did not use milk as adults lost the ability to produce lactase, whereas groups that did consume milk continued to make the enzyme. More recent studies have cast doubt on this theory and shown that lactase production is controlled by a gene that is located on chromosome 2.

Milk and milk products are valuable sources of protein, calcium, carbohydrates and other nutrients, so the consequences of lactose intolerance in babies and young children can be serious. Other sources of the nutrients must be given: artificial milk for babies can be produced using soybeans, and adults can get protein from meat and vegetables. Yoghurt with live bacterial cultures are usually tolerated well and dark green vegetables are a good source of calcium. Lactose-free dairy products are also readily available in many countries.

3.7 Cell respiration

Assessment statements

- Define 'cell respiration'.
- State that in cell respiration, glucose in the cytoplasm is broken down by glycolysis into pyruvate, with a small yield of ATP.
- Explain that during anaerobic cell respiration, pyruvate can be converted in the cytoplasm into lactate, or ethanol and carbon dioxide with no further yield of ATP.
- Explain that during aerobic respiration, pyruvate can be broken down in the mitochondrion into carbon dioxide and water with a large yield of ATP.

Cell respiration the controlled release of energy in the form of ATP from organic compounds in a cell

ATP (adenosine triphosphate) is the energy currency of a cell. It is needed for every activity that requires energy. Cells make their own ATP in mitochondria. When energy is used, ATP is broken down to ADP (adenosine diphosphate) and inorganic phosphate. This conversion releases energy for use and a cyclic process will reform the ATP during respiration.

$$\text{ADP} + \text{P}_i \underset{\text{during metabolic activity}}{\overset{\text{during respiration}}{\rightleftharpoons}} \text{ATP} + \text{H}_2\text{O}$$

Cell respiration and ATP

All living cells need energy to stay alive. The energy is used to power all the activities of life including digestion, protein synthesis and active transport. A cell's energy sources are the sugars and other substances derived from nutrients, which can be broken down to release the energy that holds their molecules together.

Cell respiration is the gradual breakdown of nutrient molecules such as glucose and fatty acids in a series of reactions that ultimately release energy in the form of **ATP**.

Glucose is probably the most commonly used source of energy. Each glucose molecule is broken down by enzymes in a number of stages, which release energy in small amounts as each covalent bond is broken. If there is insufficient glucose available, fatty acids or amino acids can be used instead.

Glycolysis

The first stage in cell respiration is **glycolysis**. Glucose that is present in the cytoplasm of a cell is broken down by a series of enzymes, to produce two molecules of a simpler compound called pyruvate. As this occurs, there is a net production of two molecules of ATP (Figure **3.19**).

$$\underset{\text{6-carbon sugar}}{\text{glucose}} \quad \rightarrow \quad \underset{2 \times \text{3-carbon sugar}}{2 \text{ pyruvate}} \quad + \quad 2\,\text{ATP}$$

Aerobic and anaerobic respiration

The next stage of cell respiration depends on whether or not oxygen is available. In the presence of oxygen, aerobic respiration can take place; without it, respiration must be anaerobic.

Aerobic respiration is the most efficient way of producing ATP. Aerobic respiration is carried out by cells that have mitochondria and it produces a great deal of ATP. Pyruvate molecules produced by glycolysis enter the mitochondria and are broken down, or oxidised, in a series of reactions that release carbon dioxide and water and produce ATP.

The two pyruvate molecules from glycolysis first lose carbon dioxide and become two molecules of acetyl CoA in the **link reaction**, as shown in Figure **3.19**. Acetyl CoA then enters a stage called the **Krebs cycle** and is modified still further, releasing more carbon dioxide. Finally, products of the cycle react directly with oxygen and the result is the release of large amounts of ATP. The original glucose molecule is completely broken down to carbon dioxide and water so the equation for aerobic respiration is often shown as:

glucose + oxygen → carbon dioxide + water + 38 ATP

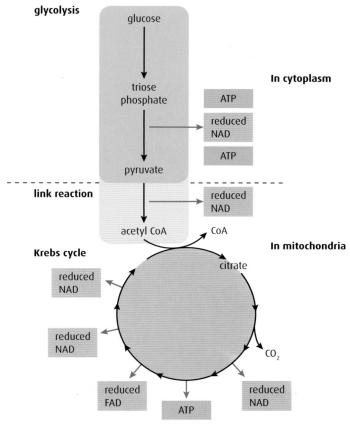

Glycolysis actually uses 2 molecules of ATP to get the process underway, but produces 4 molecules of ATP in total. Thus, we say there is a net production of 2 ATPs.

Figure 3.19 Summary of glycolysis, the link reaction and the Krebs cycle.

Anaerobic respiration occurs in the cytoplasm of cells. In animal cells, the pyruvate produced by glycolysis is converted to lactate (Figure **3.20**, overleaf), which is a waste product and is taken out of the cells. Anaerobic respiration occurs in cases where, for example, a person is doing vigorous exercise and their cardiovascular system is unable to supply sufficient oxygen for aerobic respiration. One consequence of anaerobic respiration and a build–up of lactate in the muscles is the sensation of cramp.

Lactate is taken by the blood to the liver, where it is converted back to pyruvate. This may either be used as a fuel, producing carbon dioxide and water, or be converted back to glucose using energy.

pyruvate → lactate

In other organisms, such as yeast, anaerobic respiration is also known as fermentation, and produces a different outcome. The pyruvate molecules from glycolysis are converted to ethanol (alcohol) and carbon dioxide (Figure **3.21**, overleaf).

pyruvate → ethanol + carbon dioxide

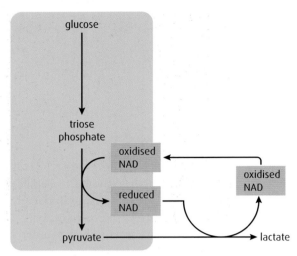

Figure 3.20 Anaerobic respiration in animal cells.

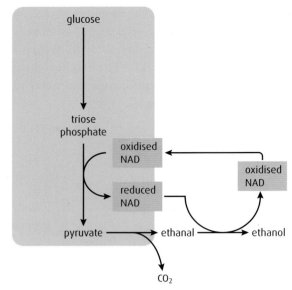

Figure 3.21 Anaerobic respiration in yeast cells.

No further ATP is produced by the anaerobic respiration of pyruvate. Respiration is described in greater detail in Chapter **8**.

12 What are the **two** products of anaerobic respiration in muscles?

13 Where does aerobic respiration take place in a eukaryotic cell?

14 Where in a cell does glycolysis occur?

3.8 Photosynthesis

Assessment statements

- State that photosynthesis involves the conversion of light energy into chemical energy.
- State the light from the Sun is composed of a range of wavelengths (colours).
- State that chlorophyll is the main photosynthetic pigment.
- Outline the differences in absorption of red, blue and green light by chlorophyll.
- State that light energy is used to produce ATP, and to split water molecules (photolysis) to form oxygen and hydrogen.
- State that ATP and hydrogen (derived from the photolysis of water) are used to fix carbon dioxide to make organic molecules.
- Explain that the rate of photosynthesis can be measured directly by the production of oxygen or the uptake of carbon dioxide, or indirectly by an increase in biomass.
- Outline the effects of temperature, light intensity and carbon dioxide concentration on the rate of photosynthesis.

Photosynthesis means 'making things with light'. Glucose is the molecule most commonly made.

Photosynthesis and light

The Sun is the source of energy for almost all life on Earth. Light energy from the Sun is captured by plants and other photosynthetic organisms, and converted into stored chemical energy. The energy is stored in molecules such as glucose, which provide a source of food for organisms that cannot use light energy directly.

Visible light is composed of a spectrum of colours, which can be separated using a prism (Figure **3.22**). A prism bends rays of light and separates the colours because each one has a slightly different wavelength and is refracted (bent) to a slightly different degree. Visible light has a range of wavelengths but the most important regions of the spectrum for photosynthesis are red and blue.

The colour of any object is determined by the wavelength of the light that it reflects back into our eyes. A blue shirt appears blue because it reflects blue light, which our eyes can perceive, but the shirt absorbs other wavelengths that fall on it and we do not see those colours. A black object absorbs all wavelengths of light, while something white reflects them all.

Most plants have green leaves. This tells us that they do not absorb the green part of the spectrum – green light is reflected and makes the leaf appear green. Looking closely at the structure of plant cells such as those shown in Figure **2.8** (page **23**) we can see that the green colour is due to the chloroplasts, which contain a green pigment called **chlorophyll**. Chlorophyll is unable to absorb green light, which it reflects, but it does absorb other wavelengths well. Red and blue light are absorbed particularly well and provide the energy needed for photosynthesis. The top graph in Figure **3.23** (overleaf) shows that the red and blue ends of the visible spectrum are the wavelengths that the photosynthetic pigments in plants absorb most efficiently. The bottom graph shows that the rate of photosynthesis is highest when plants absorb these wavelengths.

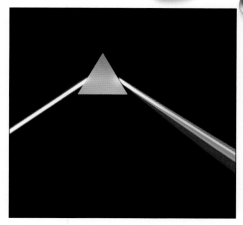

Figure 3.22 'White light', such as sunlight, is composed of a range of wavelengths, which become separated as they pass through a glass prism.

15 If you wanted to make plants grow as well as possible, what colour of light should you shine on them?

16 What would happen to a plant's growth if it were kept in green light?

The chemistry of photosynthesis

Photosynthesis is a complex series of reactions catalysed by a number of different enzymes. To aid understanding, we can consider photosynthesis in two stages.

Light-dependent reactions

The first stage is known as the 'light-dependent reactions' because light is essential for them to occur.

Chlorophyll absorbs light energy and this energy is used to produce ATP. The energy is also used to split water molecules into hydrogen and oxygen in a process called **photolysis**. Hydrogen ions and electrons (from the hydrogen part of water) and oxygen are released. Oxygen is a waste product of photosynthesis but is vital to sustain the lives of aerobic organisms once it has been released into the atmosphere. The ATP, hydrogen ions and electrons are used in the light-independent reactions.

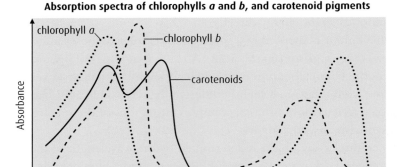

Figure 3.23 These graphs show the wavelengths (colours) of light absorbed by plants and the rate of photosynthesis that occurs at each wavelength.

Light-independent reactions

ATP and hydrogen ions and electrons are used in the second stage of photosynthesis, the 'light–independent reactions'.

During the 'light–independent reactions', carbon dioxide, taken in from the air, is combined with hydrogen and ATP to form a range of organic molecules for the plant. The conversion of inorganic carbon dioxide to organic molecules such as glucose is known as **carbon fixation**. ATP provides the energy for the process.

The series of reactions that occurs during photosynthesis is summarised as:

$$\text{carbon dioxide} + \text{water} \rightarrow \text{glucose} + \text{oxygen}$$
$$6CO_2 + 6H_2O \rightarrow C_6H_{12}O_6 + 6O_2$$

Measuring the rate of photosynthesis

The equation above shows that when photosynthesis occurs, carbon dioxide is used and oxygen is released. The mass of the plant (its **biomass**) will also increase as glucose is used to produce other plant materials. Any of these three factors can be used to measure how quickly the reactions of photosynthesis are occurring.

Aquatic plants release bubbles of oxygen as they photosynthesise and if the volume of these bubbles is measured for a period of time, the rate of photosynthesis can be determined directly (Figure **3.24**).

Aquatic plants also remove carbon dioxide from their environment, causing the pH of the water to rise. Carbon dioxide dissolves in water to form a weak acid so as it is removed, the pH will go up. Therefore, another way of determining the rate of photosynthesis experimentally is to monitor the change in pH of the water surrounding an aquatic plant over a period of time.

Terrestrial plants also remove carbon dioxide from their surroundings but this is difficult to measure. It can be done experimentally by supplying a confined plant with radioactive carbon dioxide, which can be measured as it is taken up and released from the plant.

A third method of measuring the rate of photosynthesis in plants is to determine their biomass at different times. This is an indirect method. Samples of the plants can be collected and measured at different times and the rate of increase in their biomass calculated to determine their rate of photosynthesis.

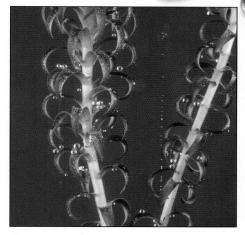

Figure 3.24 The rate of oxygen production can be used as a direct measure of the rate of photosynthesis.

Limits to photosynthesis

The rate at which a plant can photosynthesise depends on factors in the environment that surrounds it. On a warm, sunny afternoon, photosynthesis will be more rapid than on a cool, shady morning. More oxygen will be produced and more carbon dioxide used. But photosynthesis cannot increase beyond certain limits. The effect of light, temperature and carbon dioxide in the air can be measured experimentally, varying one factor while keeping the others the same, and graphs such as those in Figure **3.25** (overleaf) can be drawn.

An increase in light intensity, when all other variables are unchanging, will produce an increase in the rate of photosynthesis that is directly proportional to the increase in light intensity. However, at a certain light intensity, enzymes will be working at their maximum rate, limited by temperature and the availability of carbon dioxide. At very high light intensities, light absorption (and therefore the rate of photosynthesis) reaches its maximum and cannot increase further. At this point, the graph reaches a plateau (Figure **3.25a**).

Increasing temperature also increases the rate of photosynthesis as the frequency and energy of molecular collision increases (Figure **3.25b**). Photosynthesis has an optimum temperature above which the rate will decrease sharply as enzymes are denatured, or the plant wilts and is unable to take in carbon dioxide.

An increase in the concentration of carbon dioxide causes the rate of photosynthesis to increase, as carbon dioxide is a vital raw material for the process. At very high concentrations, the rate will plateau as other factors such as light and temperature limit the rate of reaction (Figure **3.25c**).

a The rate of photosynthesis at different light intensities and constant temperature

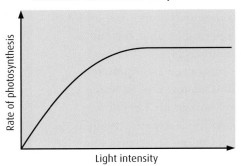

b The rate of photosynthesis at different temperatures and constant light intensities

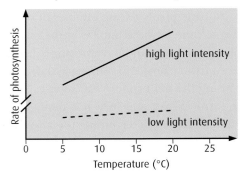

c The rate of photosynthesis at different temperatures, carbon dioxide concentrations and light intensities

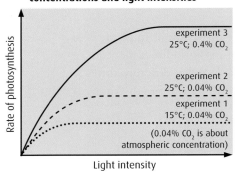

Figure 3.25 These graphs show the effects on photosynthesis of varying light intensity, carbon dioxide concentration and temperature.

The effects of temperature, light and carbon dioxide concentration are well known to horticulturalists who grow crops in glasshouses. Commercial producers of cucumbers and tomatoes keep their glasshouses warm and well lit. They may also introduce carbon dioxide to boost photosynthesis to its maximum rate, thereby increasing crop production and profits.

Photosynthesis is described in more detail in Chapter **8**.

17 What is photolysis?

18 Which colours of the spectrum are used in photosynthesis?

19 Describe **two** ways in which the rate of photosynthesis can be measured.

End-of-chapter questions

1 Which of the following statements is correct?

    A   The most frequently occurring chemical elements in living organisms are carbon, hydrogen, oxygen and calcium.

    B   A water molecule can form hydrogen bonds with other water molecules due to its polarity.

    C   Sweating cools an animal because body heat is required to break the covalent bonds in the water in the sweat, allowing it to evaporate.

    D   Increasing substrate concentration causes enzymes to denature.   (1)

2 Which of the following statements is correct?

    A   The components of a nucleotide are a sugar molecule attached to two phosphate groups and a base.

    B   In a molecule of DNA, the bases thymine and uracil are held together by hydrogen bonds.

    C   During the process of transcription, tRNA molecules bond to mRNA using complementary base pairing.

    D   During DNA replication, new nucleotides are added using the enzyme DNA polymerase.   (1)

3 Outline how monosaccharides are converted into polysaccharides.   (2)

4 State why each step in a biochemical pathway often requires a separate enzyme.   (2)

5 The unicellular green alga *Phaeodactylum tricornutum* is photosynthetic. Cell biologists genetically modified this organism by adding a glucose transporter gene. The modified and unmodified algae were grown in a nutrient medium under a series of different conditions and the growth rate of the cells was measured.

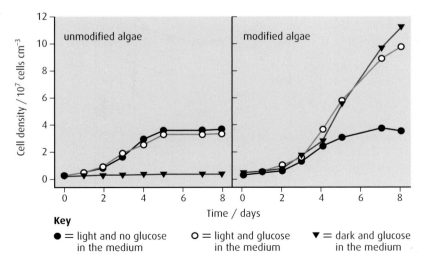

source: L A Zaslavskaia, et al., adapted (2001) *Science*, **292**, pages 2073–2075

a State the role of glucose in the metabolism of cells. (1)

b Deduce where you would expect to find the glucose transporter protein in the modified algae cells. (2)

c Compare the effect of light on the modified and the unmodified cells. (2)

Commercially, unmodified algae are grown in shallow sunlit ponds or illuminated containers. The cells only grow in the top few centimetres. However, the modified algae can grow at any depth.

d Explain why the modified algae can grow at any depth whereas the unmodified algae can only grow at the surface. (3)

(total 8 marks)

© IB Organization 2009

6 The rate of carbon dioxide uptake by the green succulent shrub *Aeonium goochiae* can indicate the amount of photosynthesis taking place in the plant. This rate was measured at 15 °C and 30 °C over a 24–hour period. The units of carbon dioxide absorption are $mg\,CO_2\,h^{-1}$.

The results are shown below. The centre of the graph corresponds to $-2\,mg\,CO_2\,h^{-1}$ and the outer ring is $+2.5\,mg\,CO_2\,h^{-1}$.

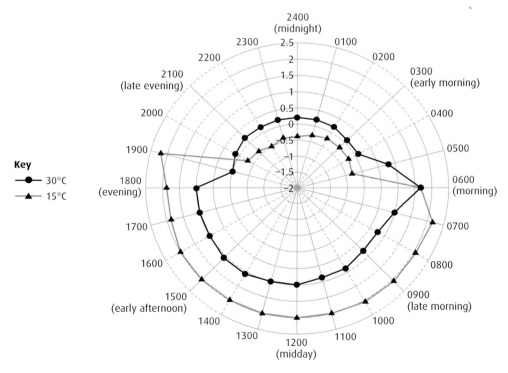

source: adapted from www.biologie.uni-hamburg.de/d-online/e24/9.htm

a Identify a time that carbon dioxide uptake was the same at both temperatures. (1)

b State the maximum rate of carbon dioxide uptake at 15 °C. (1)

c Compare the rate of carbon dioxide uptake at each temperature in daylight and darkness. (3)

d Suggest why the carbon dioxide uptake may at times be negative. (1)

(total 6 marks)

© IB Organization 2009

Genetics I 4

Introduction

Chimpanzees are set apart from all other organisms because their parents were chimpanzees and their offspring will also be chimpanzees. The study of genetics attempts to explain this process of heredity and it also plays a very significant role in the modern world, from plant and animal breeding to human health and disease.

4.1 Chromosomes, genes, alleles and mutation

Assessment statements

- State that eukaryotic chromosomes are made of DNA and proteins.
- Define 'gene', 'allele' and 'genome'.
- Define 'gene mutation'.
- Explain the consequence of a base substitution mutation in relation to the processes of transcription and translation, using the example of sickle–cell anemia.

Chromosome structure

During the phase of the cell cycle known as **interphase**, **chromosomes** are in the form of long, very thin threads, which cannot be seen with a simple microscope. As the nucleus prepares to divide, these threads undergo repeated coiling and become much shorter and thicker (Figure **4.1**). When stained, they are clearly visible even at low microscope magnifications.

Eukaryotic cells contain chromosomes surrounded by a nuclear envelope. The chromosomes of eukaryotic cells are associated with proteins. Each chromosome contains a single molecule of DNA along with these associated proteins. Some of these proteins are structural and others regulate the activities of the DNA.

Chromosome structure is described in greater detail in Chapter **7**.

Chromosomes, genes and mutations

A DNA molecule comprises a pair of strands, each strand consisting of a linear sequence of nucleotides, held together by weak bonds between the bases. This linear sequence of bases contains the genetic code in the form of triplets of bases. A **gene** is a particular section of a DNA strand that, when transcribed and translated, forms a specific polypeptide. (Transcription and translation are described in Chapter **3** and in more detail in Chapter **7**.)

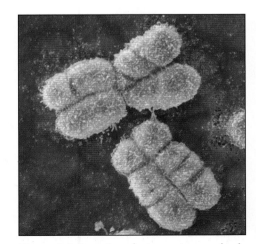

Figure 4.1 Scanning electron micrograph of human chromosomes. They have replicated prior to cell division and so consist of two identical strands (chromatids) linked at the centromere (×7080).

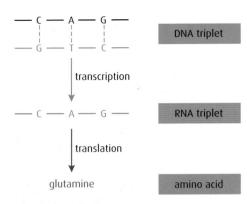

| — C — A — G — |
| — G — T — C — |

DNA triplet

↓ transcription

| — C — A — G — |

RNA triplet

↓ translation

glutamine

amino acid

Figure 4.2 The base sequence in DNA is decoded via transcription and translation.

A triplet of bases in the DNA molecule is transcribed into a triplet of bases in the mRNA molecule, which is then translated into a specific amino acid, as shown in Figure **4.2**.

The process of DNA replication is complex and mistakes sometimes occur – a nucleotide may be left out, an extra one may be added, or the wrong one inserted. These mistakes are known as **gene mutations**. The insertion of an incorrect nucleotide is called a **base substitution mutation.** When the DNA containing an incorrect nucleotide is transcribed and translated, errors may occur in the polypeptide produced.

Table **4.1** shows the amino acids that are specified by different mRNA codons. Most amino acids are coded for by more than one codon and so many substitution mutations have no effect on the final polypeptide that is produced. For example, a mutation in the DNA triplet CCA into CCG would change the codon in the mRNA from GGU to GGC but it would still result in the amino acid glycine being placed in a polypeptide. Some substitution mutations, however, do have serious effects and an important human condition that results from a single base substitution is sickle-cell anemia.

Gene a heritable factor that controls a specific characteristic, or a section of DNA that codes for the formation of a polypeptide
Allele a specific form of a gene occupying the same gene locus or position (page **77**) as other alleles of that gene, but differing from other alleles by small differences in its base sequence
Genome the whole of the genetic information of an organism
Gene mutation a change in the sequence of bases in a gene

There are several thousand human disorders that are caused by mutations in single genes and about 100 'syndromes' associated with chromosome abnormalities.

First base		Second base								Third base
		U		C		A		G		
U		UUU	phenylalanine	UCU	serine	UAU	tyrosine	UGU	cysteine	U
		UUC		UCC		UAC		UGC		C
		UUA	leucine	UCA		UAA	'stop'	UGA	'stop'	A
		UUG		UCG		UAG		UGG	tryptophan	G
C		CUU	leucine	CCU	proline	CAU	histidine	CGU	arginine	U
		CUC		CCC		CAC		CGC		C
		CUA		CCA		CAA	glutamine	CGA		A
		CUG		CCG		CAG		CGG		G
A		AUU	isoleucine	ACU	threonine	AAU	asparagine	AGU	serine	U
		AUC		ACC		AAC		AGC		C
		AUA		ACA		AAA	lysine	AGA	arginine	A
		AUG	methionine or 'start'	ACG		AAG		AGG		G
G		GUU	valine	GCU	alanine	GAU	aspartic acid	GGU	glycine	U
		GUC		GCC		GAC		GGC		C
		GUA		GCA		GAA	glutamic acid	GGA		A
		GUG		GCG		GAG		GGG		G

Table 4.1 To show the amino acids and their associated mRNA codons.

Sickle-cell anemia – the result of a base substitution mutation

Sickle-cell anemia is a blood disorder in which red blood cells become sickle shaped and cannot carry oxygen properly (Figure **4.3**). It occurs most frequently in people with African ancestry – about 1% suffer from the condition and between 10% and 40% are carriers of it. Sickle-cell anemia is due to a single base substitution mutation in one of the genes that make **hemoglobin**, the oxygen-carrying pigment in red blood cells.

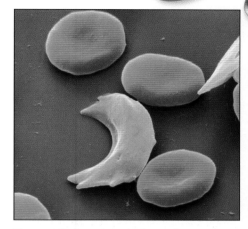

Figure 4.3 Scanning electron micrograph showing a sickle cell and normal red blood cells.

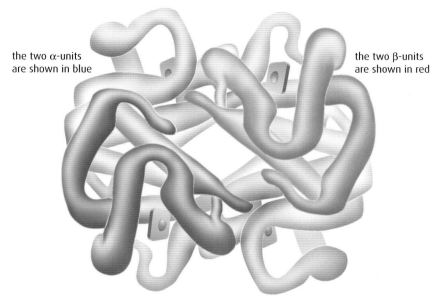

the two α-units are shown in blue

the two β-units are shown in red

Figure 4.4 The structure of a hemoglobin molecule showing the three-dimensional arrangement of the subunits that make it up.

Hemoglobin is made up of four subunits, as shown in Figure **4.4** – two α-chains and two β-chains. The 9 β-chains are affected by the sickle-cell mutation. To form a normal β-chain, the particular triplet base pairing in the DNA is:

```
— G — A — G —
  |   |   |
— C — T — C —
```

The C–T–C on the coding strand of the DNA is transcribed into the mRNA triplet G–A–G, which in turn is translated to give glutamic acid in the polypeptide chain of the β-subunit.

If the sickle-cell mutation occurs, the adenine base A is substituted for thymine T on the coding strand, so the triplet base pairing becomes:

```
— G — T — G —
  |   |   |
— C — A — C —
```

C–A–C on the coding strand of the DNA is now transcribed into the mRNA triplet G–U–G, which in turn is translated to give the amino acid valine. Valine replaces glutamic acid in the β-chain.

Only one strand of DNA is transcribed into mRNA for any gene. The transcribed strand is called the coding strand.

Valine has different properties from glutamic acid and so this single change in the amino acid sequence has very serious effects. The resulting hemoglobin molecule is a different shape, it is less soluble and when in low oxygen concentrations, it deforms the red blood cells to give them a sickle shape. Sickle cells carry less oxygen, which results in anemia. They are also rapidly removed from the circulation, leading to a lack of red blood cells and other symptoms such as jaundice, kidney problems and enlargement of the spleen.

1 The β-chain of the hemoglobin molecule contains 146 amino acids. How many nucleotides are needed to code for this protein?

2 a List the **two** structural components of a eukaryotic chromosome.

   b How does this structure differ from that of a prokaryotic chromosome?

3 Define the following terms.
   a 'gene'
   b 'allele'
   c 'genome'
   d 'gene mutation'

4 What is meant by the term 'base substitution mutation'?

5 a In the normal allele for the β-chain of hemoglobin, there is a triplet on the coding strand of the DNA that is C–T–C. In people suffering from sickle-cell anemia, what has this triplet mutated to?

   b Because of this mutation, one amino acid in the polypeptide chain of the β-subunits in hemoglobin is abnormal. Name the normal amino acid and also the amino acid resulting from the sickle-cell mutation.

   c Explain why this mutation leads to sickle-cell anemia.

6 The following is a sequence of bases in a DNA molecule that has been transcribed into an RNA molecule.

CGGTAAGCCTA

Which is the correct sequence of bases in the RNA molecule?
A CGGTAAGCCTA
B GCCATTGGAT
C CGGUAAGCCUA
D GCCUUTCGGAU

4.2 Meiosis

Assessment statements

- State that meiosis is a reduction division of a diploid nucleus to form haploid nuclei.
- Define 'homologous chromosomes'.
- Outline the process of meiosis, including pairing of homologous chromosomes and crossing over, followed by two divisions, which results in four haploid cells.
- Explain that non-disjunction can lead to changes in chromosome number, illustrated by reference to Down's syndrome (trisomy 21).
- State that, in karyotyping, chromosomes are arranged in pairs according to their size and structure.
- State that karyotyping is performed using cells collected by chorionic villus sampling or amniocentesis, for prenatal diagnosis of chromosome abnormalities.
- Analyse a human karyotype to determine gender and whether non-disjunction has occurred.

Meiosis is a reduction division

Meiosis is a type of cell division that produces **gametes** (sex cells). In any organism, each cell that is produced as a result of meiosis has half the number of chromosomes of other cells in the body.

Eukaryotic body cells have a **diploid** nucleus, which contains two copies of each chromosome, in **homologous** pairs. For example, humans have a diploid number of 46 chromosomes in 23 pairs, mangos and soybean both have 40 chromosomes in 20 pairs, and the camel has 70 chromosomes in 35 pairs.

During sexual reproduction, two gametes fuse together so, in order to keep the chromosome number correct in the offspring that are produced, each gamete must contain only one of each chromosome pair. That is, it must contain half the diploid number of chromosomes, which is called the **haploid** number. During gamete formation, meiosis reduces the diploid number to the haploid number. At the moment of fertilisation, the normal diploid number is restored as the gametes fuse.

So, in the camel, the haploid sperm (35 chromosomes) and haploid egg (35 chromosomes) fuse at fertilisation to form the diploid zygote, with 70 chromosomes.

> **Homologous chromosomes**
> a pair of chromosomes with the same genes but not necessarily the same alleles of those genes

> There are a few organisms that are haploid, for example the male honey bee, *Apis mellifera*. This means it produces gametes through mitosis.

The process of meiosis

Meiosis occurs in a series of stages, as illustrated in Figure **4.5** (overleaf), which result in the production of four cells.

Whereas mitosis, used to replace or repair cells, is achieved with one cell division, meiosis involves two divisions – the first reduces the number of chromosomes by half and the second produces four gametes each containing the haploid number of chromosomes. Exactly the same terms are used for the names of the stages, but since meiosis involves two divisions, the phases are numbered I and II.

The first division is very similar to mitosis and the second division is exactly the same as mitosis.

Meiosis I

1 Prophase I

nuclear envelope breaks up as in mitosis

crossing over of chromatids may occur

homologous chromosomes pair up to form a bivalent

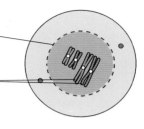

Bivalent showing crossing over that may occur:

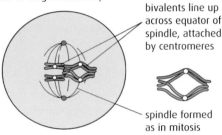

chromatids may break and may reconnect to another chromatid

centromere

chiasma – point where crossing over occurs (plural, chiasmata)

one or more chiasmata may form, anywhere along length

At the end of prophase 1, a spindle is formed.

2 Metaphase I (showing crossing over of long chromatids)

bivalents line up across equator of spindle, attached by centromeres

spindle formed as in mitosis

3 Anaphase I

Centromeres do not divide, unlike mitosis.

Whole chromosomes move towards opposite ends of spindle, centromeres first, pulled by microtubules.

4 Telophase I

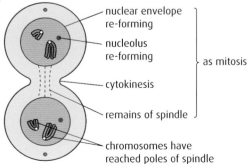

nuclear envelope re-forming

nucleolus re-forming

cytokinesis

remains of spindle

chromosomes have reached poles of spindle

as mitosis

Meiosis II

5 Prophase II

nuclear envelope and nucleolus disperse

centrioles replicate and move to opposite poles of the cell

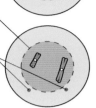

6 Metaphase II

chromosomes line up separately across equator of spindle

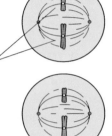

7 Anaphase II

centromeres divide and spindle microtubules pull the chromatids to opposite poles

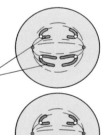

8 Telophase II

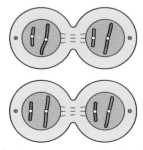

telophase II as mitosis telophase but four haploid daughter cells formed

Figure 4.5 The stages of meiosis in an animal cell. Note that the cells are shown with just two homologous pairs of chromosomes to make it easier to understand the process.

Prophase I

The chromosomes, which have replicated during interphase, now supercoil. Each one consists of two sister chromatids joined by the centromere. The homologous pairs of chromosomes line up side by side.

Although the genes carried by each chromosome pair are identical, the alleles may not be. Exchange of genetic material between the pair can occur at this point. Sister chromatids may become entangled, break and rejoin so that alleles are exchanged between them during a process called **crossing over**. New combinations of alleles are formed and genetic variety in the resulting gametes increases.

The final step in prophase I is the formation of spindle microtubules and the breakdown of the nuclear envelope.

Metaphase I

Chromosomes line up on the equator at the centre of the cell. Each one attaches by a centromere to the spindle microtubules. The alignment of the chromosomes is random so that maternal and paternal chromosomes can appear on either side of one another on the equator. This also increases the genetic variety in the gametes.

Anaphase I

The microtubules now contract towards opposite poles. The pairs of sister chromatids remain together but the homologous pairs are separated. This is the **reduction division** where the chromosome number is halved from diploid to haploid.

Telophase I

Now spindles break down and a new nuclear envelope forms. Cytokinesis follows and the cell splits into two cells, each containing only one chromosome of each homologous pair. Each chromosome, however, still consists of two sister chromatids at this point.

The second division of meiosis now follows to separate the two sister chromatids.

Prophase II

In each of the two cells resulting from meiosis I, new spindle microtubules start to form, the chromosomes recoil and the nuclear envelope begins to break down.

Metaphase II

The nuclear envelope is broken down and individual chromosomes line up on the equator of each cell. Spindle fibres from opposite ends of the cell attach to each chromatid at the centromere.

Anaphase II

Sister chromatids are separated as the centromere splits and spindle fibres pull the chromatids to opposite ends of the cell.

Telophase II

Nuclear envelopes form around the four new haploid nuclei and the chromosomes now uncoil. A second cytokinesis occurs, resulting in four cells.

In each homologous pair, one chromosome is a maternal chromosome and the other a paternal chromosome. After crossing over, the chromatids recombine to produce new and unique combinations of alleles. This is called recombination.

Comparing mitosis and meiosis

Table **4.2** summarises the differences between cell division by mitosis and by meiosis.

Mitosis	Meiosis
occurs to replace and repair cells	occurs in gamete formation
chromosomes line up individually on the spindle microtubules	chromosomes line up in homologous pairs on the spindle microtubules at metaphase I
produces two cells with the same number of chromosomes as the original cell, the diploid number	produces four haploid cells
the two daughter cells are genetically identical	the four daughter cells are usually genetically different

Table 4.2 Some differences between mitosis and meiosis.

7 In which phase or phases of meiosis do the following events occur?
   a homologous chromosomes separate
   b the nuclear envelope breaks down
   c the centromere splits
   d the sister chromatids line up on the equator
   e the chromosomes uncoil
   f reduction division occurs

Non-disjunction

Non-disjunction is a failure of homologous pairs of chromosomes to separate properly during meiosis. It results in gametes that contain either one too few or one too many chromosomes. Those with too few seldom survive, but in some cases a gamete with an extra chromosome does survive and after fertilisation produces a zygote with three chromosomes of one type, as shown in Figure **4.6**. This is called a **trisomy**.

Trisomy in chromosome 21 results in the human condition known as **Down's syndrome** (Figure **4.7**). A gamete, usually the female one, receives 24 chromosomes instead of 23 and a baby with 47 instead of the usual 46 chromosomes in each cell is born.

Karyotyping

Chromosomes have unique banding patterns that are revealed if they are stained with specific dyes during prophase. Each chromosome is a characteristic length and has its centromere at a fixed place, and each one has a homologous partner. In a **karyogram**, chromosomes are stained and photographed. The image is then manipulated to arrange the chromosomes in order of their size, as shown in Figure **4.8**. Karyograms indicate the sex of an individual because they show the sex chromosomes,

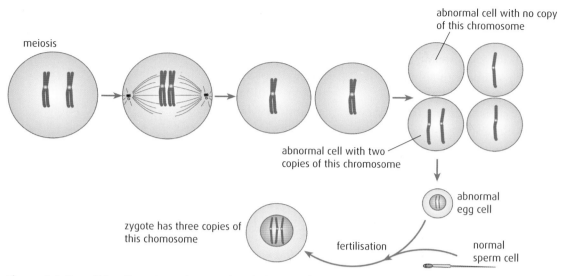

abnormal cell with no copy
of this chromosome

meiosis

abnormal cell with two
copies of this chromosome

abnormal
egg cell

zygote has three copies of
this chomosome

fertilisation

normal
sperm cell

Figure 4.6 Non-disjunction at anaphase II of meiosis. Non-disjunction can also occur at anaphase I.

and they are also used in prenatal diagnosis to check for chromosome abnormalities.

In the procedure called karyotyping, cells from an unborn child are collected in one of two ways – chorionic villus sampling (CVS) or amniocentesis (page **76**). The cells are grown in the laboratory and a karyogram is prepared. This is checked for extra or missing chromosomes. The procedure is normally used when there is concern about potential chromosome abnormalities – for example, if the mother is over the age of 35 years. Down's syndrome, which is more common in babies of older mothers, can be detected using this method.

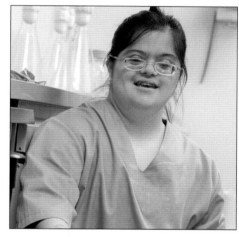

Figure 4.7 People with Down's syndrome have characteristic physical features.

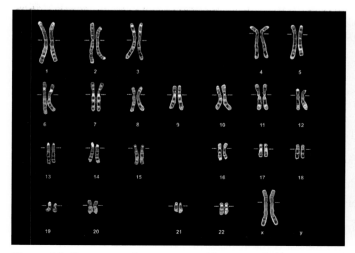

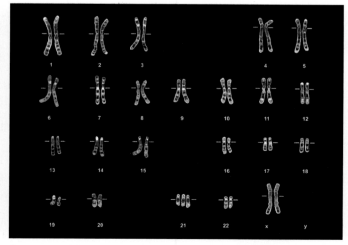

Figure 4.8 Karyograms for a person with a normal chromosome complement, and for a person with trisomy 21 (Down's syndrome).

Prenatal screening

Obtaining fetal cells for karyotyping by amniocentesis involves taking a sample of amniotic fluid from the mother between weeks 14 and 16 of her pregnancy. Chorionic villus sampling (CVS) involves taking a sample of cells from the chorionic villi, which are the fine projections of the placenta embedded in the lining of the uterus. This can be done 8–10 weeks into the pregnancy. Both methods carry a small risk of damaging the fetus or even causing a miscarriage. Once the results of the test are known, the parents may be offered the option to terminate the pregnancy if abnormalities are discovered. The test may reveal an abnormality but it cannot give any indication about the likely severity of the condition.

Questions to consider

1 Karyotyping is a procedure involving medical and ethical decisions. Who should make the decision to carry out the procedure – the parents or health care officials? How important are legal and religious arguments?

2 Both procedures carry the risk of a miscarriage. How can this potential risk to the unborn child be balanced with the parents' desire for information? What safeguards should be in place when the karyotyping procedure is used?

3 Does the information that can be obtained from the karyogram outweigh the risk to the unborn child?

4 If the karyogram indicates a genetic abnormality, should the parents be permitted to consider a termination of the pregnancy?

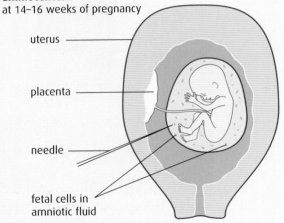

amniocentesis
at 14–16 weeks of pregnancy

uterus

placenta

needle

fetal cells in amniotic fluid

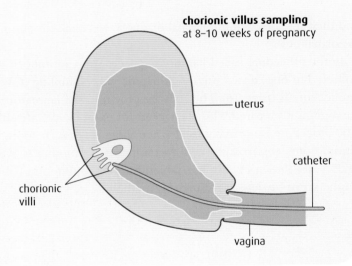

chorionic villus sampling
at 8–10 weeks of pregnancy

uterus

catheter

chorionic villi

vagina

---

8 Define the term 'homologous chromosomes'.

9 Meiosis is a reduction division. What does this mean?

10 How many cells are formed when meiosis in one parent cell is completed?

11 What is a trisomy?

12 State **one** example of non-disjunction in humans.

13 State **two** characteristics of chromosomes that are used to identify them when karyotyping.

14 The soybean has 40 chromosomes in its root cells. What is the name given to this number of chromosomes?

4.3 Theoretical genetics

Assessment statements

- Define 'genotype', 'phenotype', 'dominant allele', 'recessive allele', 'codominant alleles', 'locus', 'homozygous', 'heterozygous', 'carrier' and 'test cross'.
- Determine the genotypes and phenotypes of the offspring of a monohybrid cross using a Punnett grid.
- State that some genes have more than two alleles (multiple alleles).
- Describe ABO blood groups as an example of codominance and multiple alleles.
- Explain how the sex chromosomes control gender by referring to the inheritance of X and Y chromosomes in humans.
- State that some genes are present on the X chromosome and absent from the shorter Y chromosome in humans.
- Define 'sex linkage'.
- Describe the inheritance of colour blindness and hemophilia as examples of sex linkage.
- State that a human female can be homozygous or heterozygous with respect to sex-linked genes.
- Explain that female carriers are heterozygous for X-linked recessive alleles.
- Predict the genotypic and phenotypic ratios of offspring of monohybrid crosses involving any of the above patterns of inheritance.
- Deduce the genotypes and phenotypes of individuals in pedigree charts.

In the study of genetics, there are a number of specialist terms used. It will be helpful to understand and remember these key words.

Genotype the alleles possessed by an organism; each allele is represented by a letter; chromosomes come in pairs and so alleles come in pairs – a genotype is therefore represented by a pair of letters – for example, **TT** or **Tt**

Phenotype the characteristics of an organism; a characteristic may be an external feature, such as the colour of flower petals, or internal, such as sickle-cell anemia

Dominant allele an allele that has the same effect on the phenotype when in either the homozygous or heterozygous state; the dominant allele is always given a capital letter – for example, **T**

Recessive allele an allele that only has an effect on the phenotype when in the homozygous state; a recessive allele is always given the lower case of the same letter given to the dominant allele – for example, **t**

Codominant alleles pairs of alleles that both affect the phenotype when present in the heterozygous state; these alleles are represented in a different way in genetics; a capital letter is chosen to represent the gene and then other (superscript) letters represent the alleles (for example, in human blood grouping, A and B are codominant alleles and are represented as I^A and I^B)

Locus the specific position of a gene on a homologous chromosome; a gene locus is fixed for a species – for example, the insulin gene is always found at the same position on chromosome 11 in humans.

Homozygous having two identical alleles at a gene locus; the alleles may both be dominant or both recessive – for example, **TT** or **tt**

Heterozygous having two different alleles at a gene locus – for example, **Tt**

Test cross testing a dominant phenotype to determine if it is heterozygous or homozygous – for example, crossing either **TT** or **Tt** with **tt**; if there are any offspring with the recessive phenotype, then the parent with the dominant phenotype must be heterozygous (**Tt**)

Carrier an individual with one copy of a recessive allele which causes a genetic disease in individuals that are homozygous for this allele

Determining genotypes and phenotypes in genetics problems

Using a Punnett grid

A genetic diagram called a Punnett grid can be used to work out all the possible combinations of alleles that can be present in the offspring of two parents whose **genotypes** are known. Punnett grids show the combinations and also help to deduce the probabilities of each one occurring.

When working out a problem, it is helpful to follow a few simple steps.

- Choose a letter to represent the gene. Choose one that has a distinctly different upper and lower case for the alleles – so for example O, P and W would not be good choices. It is useful to base the letter on the dominant **phenotype** – so for example R = red could be used for petal colour.
- Represent the genotype of each parent with a pair of letters. Use a single letter surrounded by a circle to represent the genotype of each gamete.
- Combine pairs of the letters representing the gametes to give all the possible genotypes of the offspring. A Punnett grid provides a clear way of doing this.
- From the possible genotypes, work out the possible phenotypes of the offspring.

Worked examples 1 and 2 show how to tackle genetics problems using these steps.

Parental generation the original parent individuals in a series of experimental crosses
F₁ generation the offspring of the parental generation
F₂ generation the offspring of a cross between F₁ individuals

---

Worked example 1

Suppose that fur colour in mice is determined by a single gene. Brown fur is dominant to white. A mouse **homozygous** for brown fur was crossed with a white mouse. Determine the possible genotypes and phenotypes of the offspring.

Step 1 Choose a letter. Brown is dominant so let **B** = brown fur and **b** = white fur.

Step 2 We are told the brown mouse is homozygous so its genotype must be **BB**. Since white is recessive, the genotype of the white mouse can only be **bb**. If a **B** were present, the mouse would have brown fur.

Step 3 Set out the diagram as on the right.

Step 4 The Punnett grid shows that all the offspring will be phenotypically brown and their genotype will be **Bb**.

parental phenotypes:	brown	white
parental genotypes:	**BB**	**bb**
gametes:	Ⓑ Ⓑ	Ⓑ Ⓑ

Punnett grid for F₁:

		gametes from brown parent	
		Ⓑ	Ⓑ
gametes from white parent	Ⓑ	**Bb** brown	**Bb** brown
	Ⓑ	**Bb** brown	**Bb** brown

Worked example 2

Seed shape in the pea plant is controlled by a single gene. Smooth shape is dominant to wrinkled shape. A plant that was **heterozygous** for smooth seeds was crossed with a plant that had wrinkled seeds. Determine the possible genotypes of the offspring and the phenotype ratio.

Step 1 Choose a letter. Smooth is the dominant trait but **S** and **s** are hard to distinguish so use another letter, such as **T**.

Step 2 We are told the smooth plant is heterozygous so its genotype must be **Tt**.
Since 'wrinkled' is a recessive trait, the genotype of the wrinkled seed plant must be **tt**.

Step 3 Set out the diagram as shown opposite, in exactly the same way as before. Notice that, in this case, the smooth–seeded parent produces two different types of gamete because it is heterozygous.

Step 4 Here the Punnett grid shows us that half of the offspring will have smooth seeds with the genotype **Tt** and half will have wrinkled seeds with the genotype **tt**.
The ratio of the phenotypes is 1:1.

parental phenotypes:	smooth	wrinkled
parental genotypes:	Tt	tt
gametes:	(T) (t)	(t) (t)

Punnett grid for F₁:

		gametes from smooth-seed parent	
		(T)	(t)
gametes from wrinkled-seed parent	(t)	Tt smooth	tt wrinkled
	(t)	Tt smooth	tt wrinkled

....

15 Define each of the following terms.
a genotype	**d** recessive allele	**g** heterozygous
b phenotype	**e** locus	**h** carrier
c dominant allele	**f** homozygous	**i** test cross

16 If red **R** is dominant to yellow **r**, what is the phenotype of each of the following genotypes?
  a RR   **b** Rr   **c** rr

17 What would be the gametes produced by a parent with each of the following genotypes?
  a RR   **b** rr   **c** Rr

18 Copy and complete the Punnett grid opposite. Green seed colour **G** is dominant to purple seed colour **g**.

		gametes from green parent	
		(G)	(g)
gametes from green parent	(G)	GG green	
	(g)		

Genotype	Phenotype or blood group
I^AI^A	A
I^Ai	A
I^BI^B	B
I^Bi	B
I^AI^B	AB
ii	O

Table 4.3 Human blood groups and their genotypes.

Codominance and multiple alleles

In the two worked examples above, one of the alleles completely dominates the other, so in a heterozygous genotype the phenotype is determined solely by the dominant allele. In **codominance**, both alleles have an affect on the phenotype.

The examples of the mouse coat colour and the smooth and wrinkled peas are both known as **monohybrid crosses** because they involve just one gene with two alleles: brown **B** and white **b**, or smooth **T** and wrinkled **t**. There are many other cases in which genes have more than two alleles. One example of this is human blood groups.

The ABO human blood grouping is an example of both codominance and multiple alleles. There are three alleles – I^A, I^B and **i**. I^A and I^B are codominant and both are dominant to **i**. This results in four different phenotypes or blood groups.

A person's blood group depends on which combination of alleles he or she receives. Each person has only two of the three alleles and they are inherited just as though they are alternative alleles of a pair. Table **4.3** shows the possible combinations of alleles and the resulting phenotypes.

Worked example 3

Celia is blood group A and her husband Sanjeev is blood group B. Their daughter Sally is blood group O. Determine the genotypes of Celia and Sanjeev.

Step 1 The alleles are represented by I^A, I^B and **i**.

Step 2 To be blood group A, Celia could have genotype I^AI^A or I^Ai.
To be blood group B, Sanjeev could have genotype I^BI^B or I^Bi.
To be blood group O, Sally could **only** have the genotype **ii**.

Step 3 Each of Sally's two alleles have come from her parents, so she must have received one **i** from her mother and one **i** from her father, as shown in the Punnett grid.

		gametes from Sanjeev	
		I^B	i
gametes from Celia	I^A		
	i		ii Sally group O

Step 4 Celia is blood group A so must have the genotype I^Ai and Sanjeev's genotype has to be I^Bi.

Worked example 4

Hair shape in humans is a codominant characteristic. Straight hair and curly hair are codominant alleles and the heterozygote has wavy hair. Daryll and Shaniqua both have wavy hair. Deduce the probabilities that their children will have straight hair, curly hair or wavy hair.

H^S = straight hair and H^C = curly hair.

Since both Daryll and Shaniqua have wavy hair their genotypes must be $H^S H^C$.

The Punnett grid shows that the probabilities of a child inheriting each hair type are:

- straight hair 25%
- curly hair 25%
- wavy hair 50%.

parental phenotypes:	wavy	wavy
parental genotypes:	$H^S H^C$	$H^S H^C$
gametes:	H^S H^C	H^S H^C

Punnett grid:

		gametes from Shaniqua	
		H^S	H^C
gametes from Daryll	H^S	$H^S H^S$ straight hair	$H^S H^C$ wavy hair
	H^C	$H^S H^C$ wavy hair	$H^C H^C$ curly hair

Sex chromosomes and the control of gender

Humans have one pair of chromosomes that determine whether the person is male or female. These chromosomes are called the **sex chromosomes**. Each person has one pair of sex chromosomes, either **XX** or **XY**, along with 22 other pairs known as **autosomes**. The **X** chromosome is longer than the **Y** and carries more genes. Human females have two **X** chromosomes and males have one **X** and one **Y**.

Sex chromosomes are inherited in the same way as other chromosomes.

parental phenotypes:	female	male
parental genotypes:	XX	XY
gametes:	X X	X Y

Punnett grid for F_1:

		gametes from male parent	
		X	Y
gametes from female parent	X	XX female	XY male
	X	XX female	XY male

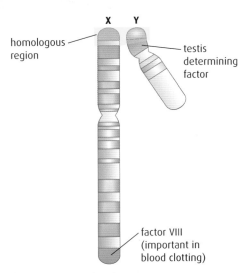

homologous region

testis determining factor

factor VIII (important in blood clotting)

Figure 4.9 X and Y chromosomes.

Sex linkage the pattern of inheritance that is characteristic for genes located on the X chromosome

The ratio of phenotypes female : male is 1 : 1. This means, at fertilisation, there is always a 50% chance that a child will be a boy and 50% that it will be a girl.

Sex chromosomes and genes

The sex chromosomes not only carry the genes that control gender, the X chromosome also carries genes called sex linked or X-linked genes. These genes occur only on the X chromosome and not on the Y chromosome, which is much shorter (Figure **4.9**). The Y chromosome carries alleles that are mainly concerned with male structures and functions.

Sex linkage has a significant effect on genotypes. Females have two X chromosomes, so they have two alleles for each gene and may be homozygous or heterozygous. In a female, a single recessive allele will be masked by a dominant allele on her other X chromosome. Males only have one allele on their X chromosome with no corresponding allele on the Y chromosome, so a recessive allele will always be expressed in a male.

A female who is heterozygous for a sex-linked recessive characteristic that does not affect her phenotype is called a **carrier**.

Examples of sex-linked characteristics

Two examples of sex-linked human characteristics are hemophilia and red–green colour blindness.

Hemophilia is a condition in which the blood of an affected person does not clot normally. It is a sex-linked condition because the genes controlling the production of the blood-clotting protein factor VIII are on the X chromosome. A female who is $X^H X^h$ will be a carrier for hemophilia. A male who has the recessive allele $X^h Y$ will be a hemophiliac. Figure **4.10** is a pedigree chart showing how a sex-linked condition like hemophilia may be inherited. Notice that hemophilia seldom occurs in females, who would have to be homozygous for the recessive allele $X^h X^h$. This condition is usually fatal *in utero*, resulting in a

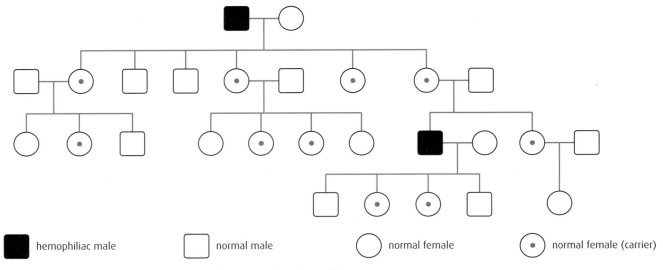

■ hemophiliac male   □ normal male   ○ normal female   ⊙ normal female (carrier)

Figure 4.10 Pedigree for a sex-linked recessive disease, such as hemophilia.

miscarriage. Today, hemophilia is treated by giving the affected person the clotting factor they cannot produce.

A person with red–green colour blindness has difficulty distinguishing between red and green. Red–green colour blindness is inherited in a similar way to hemophilia. A female who is $X^B X^b$ is a carrier for colour blindness and a male with just one copy of the recessive allele will be colour blind. Remember that a man cannot be a carrier for a sex-linked gene.

Worked example 5

A woman who is homozygous for normal vision married a man who is red–green colour blind. Determine the possible types of vision inherited by their two children, one girl and one boy.

Step 1   Standard letters are used for these alleles – normal vision is X^B and colour blind is X^b. The X is always included.

Step 2   The woman is homozygous for normal vision so her genotype must be $X^B X^B$. Since the man is colour blind, his genotype must be $X^b Y$.

Step 3   Set out the diagram as below.

		woman		man	
parental phenotypes:		woman		man	
parental genotypes:		$X^B X^B$		$X^b Y$	
gametes:	X^B		X^B	X^b	Y

Punnett grid for F$_1$:

		gametes from man	
		X^b	Y
gametes from woman	X^B	$X^B X^b$ girl, normal vision, carrier	$X^B Y$ boy, normal vision
	X^B	$X^B X^b$ girl, normal vision, carrier	$X^B Y$ boy, normal vision

Step 4   The Punnett grid shows that a daughter will have normal vision, but be a carrier for red–green colour blindness. A son will have normal vision.

Pedigree charts

Pedigree charts, like the one shown in Figures **4.10** and **4.11** (overleaf), are a way of tracing the pattern of inheritance of a genetic condition through a family. Specific symbols are always used, and the chart is set out in a standard way. The horizontal lines linking the male and female in a generation indicate a marriage (or mating) and the vertical lines indicate their offspring. Offspring are shown in the order of their birth. For example, in the family shown in Figure **4.11**, the oldest individual affected with the genetic condition is II2, who is a male.

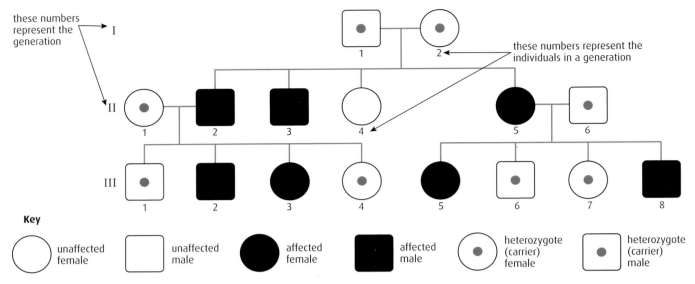

these numbers represent the generation → I

these numbers represent the individuals in a generation

Key

◯	unaffected female
▢	unaffected male
●	affected female
■	affected male
◉	heterozygote (carrier) female
▣	heterozygote (carrier) male

Figure 4.11 This pedigree chart shows the occurrence of a genetic condition known as brachydactyly (short fingers) in a family.

Worked example 6

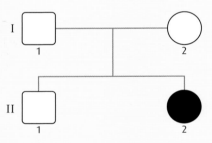

Cystic fibrosis (CF) is a genetic disorder that causes the excessive production of thick sticky mucus. It is due to a recessive allele that is not sex linked. The pedigree chart below shows two generations of a family. A filled-in symbol represents an individual who has cystic fibrosis.
Deduce the genotypes of the parents I1 and I2.
Deduce the probability that II1 is heterozygous.

Step 1 Cystic fibrosis is a recessive disorder so the 'normal' condition, without cystic fibrosis, is dominant. It is useful to choose **N** to represent the normal allele.

Step 2 Neither of the parents, I1 and I2, have cystic fibrosis so both must have at least one normal allele **N**. Since cystic fibrosis is recessive and II2 has the condition, she must have the genotype **nn**.
II2 received one allele from each of her parents so both of them must have passed one **n** allele to her. Both parents must have one **n** but they do not have cystic fibrosis so their genotype must be heterozygous **Nn**.
The pedigree chart could now be redrawn, to show that the parents are heterozygous carriers.

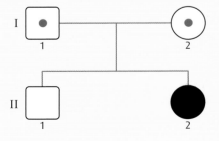

Step 3 Now that both parents are known to be heterozygous, a Punnett grid can be drawn.

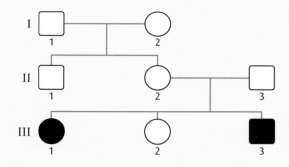

		gametes from I1	
		N	**n**
gametes from I2	**N**	**NN** normal	**Nn** normal
	n	**Nn** normal	**nn** II2 with CF

Step 4 Person II1 does not have cystic fibrosis and so could have the allele combination shown by any of the shaded boxes. The probability of being heterozygous is 2 out of 3, or $\frac{2}{3}$, or 66%.

Worked example 7

The pedigree chart below shows the family history of a recessive human condition called woolly hair. A filled-in symbol indicates that the person has woolly hair. Deduce whether this condition is sex linked or not.

Step 1 Remember that in a sex-linked condition, the allele occurs only on the X chromosome and males only have one X chromosome.
Step 2 Using **N** to represent the condition, we can see that female III1 must be **nn** as she has the condition and thus has inherited one **n** from each parent.
Step 3 If woolly hair is not sex linked, both her parents would be **Nn** as they have normal hair.
Step 4 If it is sex linked, her mother (II2) would be $\mathbf{X^N X^n}$ and her father (II3) would be $\mathbf{X^n Y}$. This would mean he has the recessive allele and no dominant allele. If the condition is sex linked, he would have woolly hair, which he does not. This proves that it is not sex linked.

Worked example 8

The pedigree chart below shows the inheritance of a particular genetic condition in a family. A filled in circle or square means that the individual is affected, that is, shows the genetic condition. The condition is not sex linked. Deduce whether the characteristic is dominant or recessive.

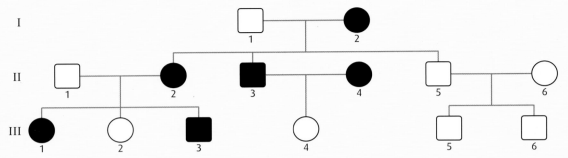

We can see that the genetic condition is dominant because of the following reasons:

- affected individuals occur in every generation
- every affected individual has at least one affected parent
- two affected parents (II3 and II4) can have a non-affected child (III4), so the parents must be heterozygous.

Genetics pioneers rejected and ignored

Gregor Mendel (1822–1884) was an Augustinian monk in the Abbey of St Thomas in Brno, a town in what is now the Czech Republic. Over a period of seven years, he cultivated and tested different pea plants and studied their visible characteristics. In 1866, he published a paper on the inheritance of characteristics in pea plants, which he called 'Experiments on Plant Hybridization', in *The Proceedings of the Natural History Society of Brünn*. In it, he set out his two laws of inheritance. Although Mendel sent copies to well-known biologists, his ideas were rejected. For the next 35 years, his paper was effectively ignored yet, as scientists later discovered, it contained the entire basis of modern genetics.

In 1951, two years before the structure of DNA was determined, Dr Barbara McClintock presented a paper on 'jumping genes' at a symposium at the Cold Spring Harbor research laboratories in North America. She explained how genes could be transferred from one chromosome to another. Her work was rejected by fellow scientists and ignored for 30 years until rediscovered. Now she is recognised as a pioneer in the field and her work is acknowledged as a cornerstone of modern genetics. In 1983, Dr McClintock received a Nobel Prize for her work.

Gregor Mendel, genetics pioneer.

Questions to consider

1 Why is the work of some scientists ignored while that of others becomes readily accepted?

2 How important is it for a new theory to be presented in a famous journal or at a well-attended meeting?

3 Do you think Mendel's work was ignored because it was not widely published, or because he was not a well-known scientist, or for some other reason?

4 Barbara McClintock was a young woman when she presented her work. Her work represented a completely different view of how genes might behave. How significant is this type of paradigm shift in gaining acceptance for a new theory or discovery?

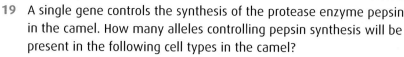

19 A single gene controls the synthesis of the protease enzyme pepsin in the camel. How many alleles controlling pepsin synthesis will be present in the following cell types in the camel?

    a a stomach cell   **b** a brain cell   **c** an egg cell

20 Which phenotype (blood group) in the ABO human blood grouping system always has a homozygous genotype?

21 State **two** sex-linked characteristics in humans.

22 What is the standard symbol in a pedigree chart for a woman who shows a particular genetic condition?

23 What are alleles called if they both have an effect on the phenotype in a heterozygous genotype?

24 State the name given to an individual who has one copy of a recessive allele that would cause a genetic disease when homozygous.

4.4 Genetic engineering and biotechnology

Assessment statements

- Outline the use of the polymerase chain reaction (PCR) to copy and amplify minute quantities of DNA.
- State that, in gel electrophoresis, fragments of DNA move in an electric field and are separated according to their size.
- State that gel electrophoresis of DNA is used in DNA profiling.
- Describe the application of DNA profiling to determine paternity and also in forensic investigations.
- Analyse DNA profiles to draw conclusions about paternity or forensic investigations.
- Outline three outcomes of the sequencing of the complete human genome.
- State that, when genes are transferred between species, the amino acid sequence of polypeptides translated from them is unchanged because the genetic code is universal.
- Outline a basic technique used for gene transfer involving plasmids, a host cell (bacterium, yeast or other cell), restriction enzymes (endonucleases) and DNA ligase.
- State two examples of the current uses of genetically modified crops or animals.
- Discuss the potential benefits and possible harmful effects of one example of genetic modification.
- Define 'clone'.
- Outline a technique for cloning using differentiated animal cells.
- Discuss the ethical issues of therapeutic cloning in humans.

Genetic engineering and **biotechnology** have opened up new opportunities in forensic science, agriculture, medicine and food technology. As knowledge has grown, science has enabled people to manipulate the unique genetic identity of organisms. Gene transfer, cloning and stem cell research have raised questions about the safety and ethics of techniques that have been unknown to previous generations.

DNA profiling

At a crime scene, forensic scientists check for fingerprints because a person's fingerprint is unique and can be used to identify them. Forensic scientists also collect samples of hair, skin, blood and other body fluids left at a crime scene because they all contain a person's DNA and that too is a unique record of their presence.

Matching the DNA from a sample to a known individual is called **DNA profiling**. In forensic science, DNA profiles from crime scenes can be used to establish the possibility of guilt or prove a suspect innocent (Figure **4.13**). DNA profiling can also be used to determine paternity. For example, a woman might claim that a particular man is the father of her child. By comparing DNA samples from all three individuals – the woman, the man and the child – paternity can be established.

The polymerase chain reaction (PCR)

DNA profiles can only be done if there is sufficient DNA to complete the procedure. Sometimes, at a crime scene or when a body is found after a very long time, only a minute amount can be collected. The **polymerase chain reaction** is a simple method that makes millions of copies of tiny amounts of DNA so there is sufficient to produce a profile. This is done at high temperature using a special type of DNA polymerase enzyme. Technicians must take great care when handling the original sample so that it is not contaminated with their own or other DNA.

Questions to consider

1 DNA profiles do not show individual base sequences but only identify repeated sequences. How much confidence should be placed on DNA evidence?
2 How secure is DNA profiling?
3 What are the implications for society if the authorities were to hold a DNA profile for every person?
4 What safeguards should be in place to protect the rights of individuals whose DNA profiles have been placed on a database but who have not been convicted of a crime?
5 Is it right to convict a person on DNA evidence alone?

DNA profile databases

In the USA, the FBI has a national database of DNA profiles from convicted criminals, suspects, missing persons and crime scenes. The data that is held may be used in current investigations and to solve unsolved crimes. There are many commercial laboratories that carry out DNA profiling analysis on behalf of law enforcement agencies. Many of them check 13 key 'short tandem repeat' sequences in DNA samples, which vary considerably between individuals. The FBI has recommended that these should be used because they provide odds of one in a thousand million that two people will have the same results.

CODIS is a computer software program that operates the national database of DNA profiles. Every American State has a statutory right to establish a DNA database that holds DNA profiles from offenders convicted of particular crimes. CODIS software enables laboratories to compare DNA profiles electronically, linking serial crimes to each other and identifying suspects from profiles of convicted offenders. CODIS has contributed to thousands of cases that have been solved by matching crime scene evidence to known convicted offenders.

Gel electrophoresis

Gel electrophoresis is a method used to separate fragments of DNA on the basis of size and the electric charge they carry. It can identify natural variations found in every individual's DNA.

Any DNA sample usually contains long molecules that are too large to be used for profiling. Enzymes, called **restriction enzymes**, are used to cut DNA into fragments at very precise points in the base sequences. Since each individual has a unique DNA sequence, the positions of these cutting sites will vary, giving a mixture of different fragment sizes.

The DNA fragments are placed in a well in a plate of gel (a jelly-like material) and an electric field is applied. Each DNA fragment has a small negative charge and so will move in the electric field, through the gel. The distance a fragment can move depends on its size – smaller fragments move most easily through the gel matrix and travel further, while larger fragments are left behind close to their starting point. After the fragments have been separated in the gel, they are stained and produce a unique pattern of bands called a **DNA profile** (Figures **4.12** and **4.13**).

The Human Genome Project

In 1990, the Human Genome Project was started as an international collaboration to determine the entire base sequence of the human **genome**. The project was publicly funded in a number of countries and the sequencing of three billion base pairs was completed in 2003. Work continues on locating genes and mapping their specific positions on chromosomes. Identifying and studying the proteins produced by these genes may soon give a better understanding of genetic disorders. Since 2003, other genome-sequencing projects have been undertaken to gather data on populations from different parts of the world and analyse genetic

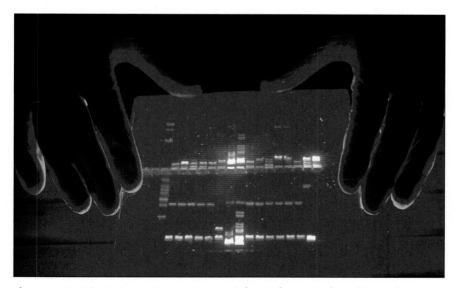

Figure 4.12 Scientist examining an agarose electrophoresis gel used to prepare a DNA profile. The sample of DNA is marked with a radioactive substance, so the DNA banding pattern appears pink under ultraviolet light. The pattern is preserved by applying radiographic film to the gel.

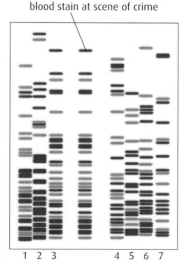

Figure 4.13 DNA profile of a blood stain found at the scene of a crime compared with profiles from seven suspects. Which suspect was at the scene of the crime? What is the evidence to support your answer?

variation. Simply knowing the base sequence of a chromosome does not have much scientific value, but knowing the sequence of the genes on that chromosome will be of great value in molecular medicine, as well as in forensic science and the study of evolution.

Some of the medical benefits that are already being investigated include:

- improved diagnosis of disease – faulty genes can be found during prenatal diagnosis, for example, allowing earlier treatment
- earlier detection of genetic susceptibility to disease so that environmental factors that trigger the disease can be avoided
- better identification of carriers of genetic conditions
- gene therapy, which aims to repair or replace a faulty gene
- drug design to find new classes of drugs that act on specific genes
- pharmacogenomics, where the drug is tailored specifically to an individual.

Gene technology

Gene technology, which is also called **genetic modification** (GM) or **genetic engineering**, involves the transfer of genes from one species to another in order to produce new varieties of organisms with useful or desirable characteristics.

Selective plant and animal breeding has been carried out by humans for thousands of years as people tried to develop cattle that produced high milk yields or crops with better resistance to disease, for example. In these cases, animals or plants of the same species were chosen for breeding because of their particular characteristics. Over many generations of selection, the desired characteristics increase in frequency in the population.

Gene technology gives us the new ability to transfer genes from one species to another completely different species in just one generation. For example, bacterial genes have been transferred to plants, human genes transferred to bacteria and spider genes transferred to a goat.

GM sheep benefit humans

Factor XI was first recognised in 1953. Factor XI is part of the cascade of clotting factors that form the chain leading to a protective clot. The incidence of Factor XI deficiency is estimated at 1 in 100 000. Although, in some people, the symptoms are similar to hemophilia, it is not a sex-linked condition and it affects men and women equally. In many countries, treatment involves obtaining factor XI from fresh-frozen plasma and since factor XI is not concentrated in plasma, considerable amounts of it are needed. It is hoped that the production of clotting factors in GM sheep's milk will lead to new and better treatments.

Ethics and the Human Genome Project

Although the sequencing of the bases of the human genome has been completed, the task of identifying all of the genes is ongoing. As these genes are found, it would be possible for a person to be screened for particular genes that could affect them – for example, by increasing their susceptibility to cancer or the likelihood that they will develop Alzheimer's disease in later life.

Questions to consider

1 Does simply knowing the sequence of the three billion base pairs of the human chromosomes tell us anything about what it means to be human?
2 Should third parties such as health insurance companies have the right to see genetic test results or demand that a person is screened before offering insurance cover or setting the level of premiums?
3 If treatment is unavailable, is it valuable to provide knowledge of a genetic condition that a person may carry?
4 Knowledge of an individual's genome has implications for other members of their families. Should their rights be protected?

Gene transfer is possible because **the genetic code is universal**. No matter what the species, the genetic code spells out the same information and produces an amino acid sequence in one species that is exactly the same in any other species.

Usually, in gene transfer, only single genes are used – for example, the gene for producing human blood-clotting factor XI has been transferred to sheep, which then produce the factor in their milk.

The technique of gene transfer

One of the first important uses of gene transfer was to produce insulin for diabetic patients who do not produce insulin properly. Many years ago, insulin was obtained from cow or pig pancreases but the process was difficult and the insulin was likely to be contaminated. Today, diabetics inject themselves with human insulin that has been made by modified *E. coli* bacteria (Figure **4.14**, overleaf).

There are key three steps in the process:

- obtaining the desired human insulin gene in the form of a piece of DNA
- attaching this DNA to a **vector**, which will carry it into the **host cell** (*E. coli*) – the vector used is the **plasmid** found inside the bacterium
- culturing *E. coli* bacteria so that they translate the DNA and make insulin, which is collected.

Genetically modified organisms (GMOs)

By 2009, almost 100 plant species had been genetically modified and many trials have taken place to assess their usefulness. In comparison, there are very few examples of genetically modified animal species. Most genetic engineering has involved commercial crops such as maize, potatoes, tomatoes and cotton. Plants have been modified to make them resistant to pests and disease and tolerant to herbicides. Genetically engineered animals, on the other hand, have mainly been farmed for the products of the inserted genes – most common are proteins such as factor XI and α1 antitrypsin, which are needed for the treatment of human diseases.

Herbicide tolerance

Herbicides are used to kill weeds in crop fields but they are expensive and can affect local ecosystems as well as cultivated areas. One commonly sprayed and very powerful herbicide is glyphosate, which is rapidly broken down by soil bacteria. For maximum crop protection, farmers needed to spray several times a year. But now, the genes from soil bacteria have been successfully transferred into maize plants making them resistant to the herbicide.

Farmers can plant the modified maize seeds, which germinate along with the competing weeds. Spraying once with glyphosate kills the weeds and leaves the maize unaffected. The maize then grows and out-competes any weeds that grow later when the glyphosate has broken down in the soil. Yields are improved and less herbicide has to be used.

New developments in genetic modification

While strawberries, pineapples, sweet peppers and bananas have all been genetically modified to remain fresh for longer, a new variety of golden-coloured rice has been genetically modified so that it contains high levels of a substance called beta-carotene. Beta-carotene gives carrots their orange colour but, more importantly, the body converts it to vitamin A, which is essential for the development of pigments in the retina of the eye. Three genes had to be introduced into rice so it could produce beta-carotene. Two of these came from daffodils and the third was taken from a bacterium.

Enriched Golden Rice™ is a valuable dietary supplement for people whose diet is low in vitamin A and who might otherwise suffer vision problems or blindness. Since Golden Rice™ was developed in the 1990s, research has continued into its use and help in enriching diets. Some interesting and controversial issues have arisen about the ownership of the rights to the seeds, the flavour of the rice and the publication of research data from experimental studies. You may like to read more about this in *Plant Physiology*, March 2001, vol. 125, pages 1157–1161, www.plantphysiol.org.

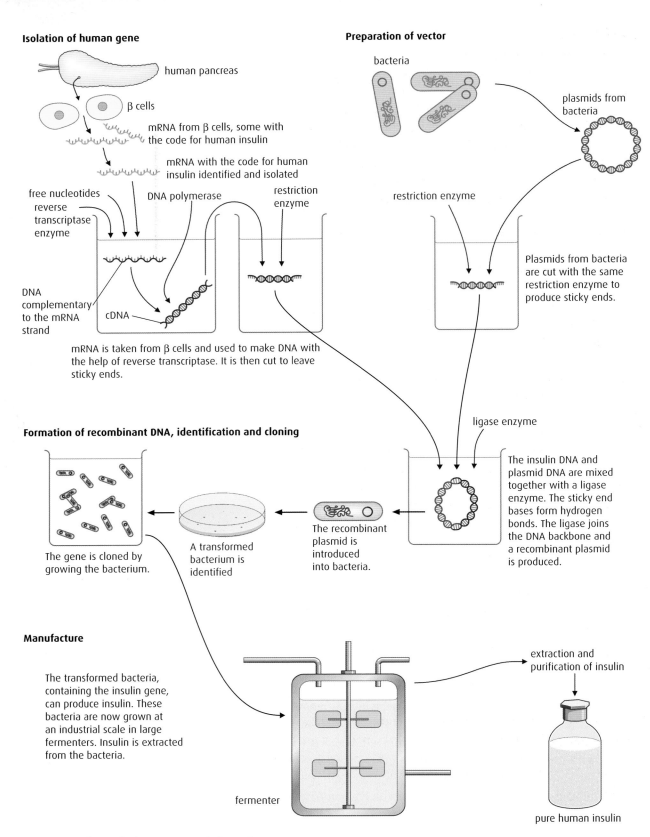

Isolation of human gene

human pancreas

β cells

mRNA from β cells, some with the code for human insulin

mRNA with the code for human insulin identified and isolated

free nucleotides
reverse transcriptase enzyme

DNA polymerase

restriction enzyme

DNA complementary to the mRNA strand

cDNA

mRNA is taken from β cells and used to make DNA with the help of reverse transcriptase. It is then cut to leave sticky ends.

Preparation of vector

bacteria

plasmids from bacteria

restriction enzyme

Plasmids from bacteria are cut with the same restriction enzyme to produce sticky ends.

Formation of recombinant DNA, identification and cloning

The gene is cloned by growing the bacterium.

A transformed bacterium is identified

The recombinant plasmid is introduced into bacteria.

ligase enzyme

The insulin DNA and plasmid DNA are mixed together with a ligase enzyme. The sticky end bases form hydrogen bonds. The ligase joins the DNA backbone and a recombinant plasmid is produced.

Manufacture

The transformed bacteria, containing the insulin gene, can produce insulin. These bacteria are now grown at an industrial scale in large fermenters. Insulin is extracted from the bacteria.

fermenter

extraction and purification of insulin

pure human insulin

Figure 4.14 Stages in producing a transgenic bacterium.

Reducing pollution

Pigs fed on grains and soybean meal produce a lot of phosphate in their manure. Phosphate causes pollution and eutrophication in the environment. Genetically modified pigs have been developed with a gene from the bacterium *E. coli*. The bacteria make an enzyme, phytase, which releases the digestible phosphorus found in grains and soybeans. Genetically modified pigs produce this enzyme in their saliva and so digest their food better. More phosphorus becomes available to them and less goes undigested. The pigs absorb the nutrients into their blood, so they grow better, and much less phosphate is released in their manure.

Potential benefits and possible harm from genetic modification

Genetic modification of plants and animals is potentially enormously helpful to the human race but it raises ethical and social questions, which are the source of heated debate. Some of the possible benefits for the future are listed below.

- As our population increases and more people need feeding, modifying plants and animals to increase yield or to be able to grow in places where they previously could not, will provide more food. Plants can be made tolerant to drought or salt water so that food can be grown in difficult areas.
- Crop plants that are disease resistant not only increase yields but also reduce the need for applying potentially harmful pesticides.
- Many substances, such as human growth hormone, a blood–clotting factor, antibodies, and vitamins, are already being made by genetically modified organisms to improve human health.

On the other hand, there are those who are greatly concerned by the use of genetically modified plants and animals.

- They argue that animals could be harmed by having these genes inserted.
- There is concern that people consuming genetically modified plants and animals could be harmed.
- The long-term effects of genetically modified crops in the environment are not known. Plants or animals could 'escape' into the environment and their genes might become incorporated into wild populations, with unknown effects.
- Human food crops could become controlled by a small number of biotechnology companies.
- GM seeds/plants may be more expensive, preventing poorer farmers from buying them. Wealth might become concentrated in a smaller percentage of the population, which might damage the local economy.
- More genetically modified organisms might lead to a reduction in natural biodiversity.

Ethics and genetic modification

There is much discussion in the media about genetic modification. On the one hand, some see it as 'the next green revolution, capable of saving the world from starvation', while others are extremely concerned about 'unleashed genes having catastrophic effects on the environment'.

Questions to consider

1 Keeping in mind that the genetic code is universal, what do you consider to be the differences between genetic modification and standard plant and animal breeding?
2 Read about the precautionary principle, which is explained on pages **108–109** in Chapter **5**. How should the precautionary principle be applied to genetic modification of farmed plants and animals?
3 At what level should gene technology be controlled – laboratory, government or international?
4 Is gene technology so potentially dangerous that it should be banned completely?

Clone a group of genetically identical organisms or a group of cells derived from a single parent cell

Cloning

Cloning happens naturally – identical twins or triplets are a **clone**. Cloning is also very widespread in agriculture and horticulture and has been used for many years to propagate new plants from cuttings, taken from roots, stems or leaves. Animal clones can be produced after *in vitro* fertilisation. The ball of cells formed as the zygote begins to divide can be separated into several parts in a Petri dish and each part can go on to form a genetically identical embryo. This type of reproductive cloning produces more individual animals with desirable characteristics for farmers and animal breeders.

Cells from a newly fertilised egg are not differentiated and have not specialised into the different cells they will become. Until recently, cloning an animal from another animal was impossible because the cells in an animal's body had already become nerves, skin, muscles and so on. Differentiated cells have many of their genes switched off, so before they can be used for cloning, the genes have to be switched back on.

The first successful clone made from an adult animal was Dolly the sheep (Figure **4.15**). The breakthrough was made in 1997 by Sir Ian Wilmut and his team at a laboratory at the Roslin Institute in Edinburgh, Scotland, where Dolly was created. Unlike previous clones, Dolly was created from the fusion of an ovum with the mammary cell of an adult sheep, creating a genetic replica of the original adult animal.

Therapeutic cloning

Therapeutic cloning is used to produce tissue or even organs that may be needed by a human patient. Human embryos are used as a source of embryonic stem cells, which are undifferentiated and can become any type of human cell. The potential value of stem cells is that they could be used to repair damaged parts of the body, such as liver or kidneys or brain, because they will grow to become those tissues.

There are many ethical issues that arise when human cloning is considered and stem cell research has been banned in some countries. Currently, embryos are not specially created for the purpose of therapeutic

A cell was taken from the udder of a ewe of the Finn Dorset breed.

An egg cell was taken from a Scottish Blackface ewe.

The nucleus was removed.

The two cells were fused together.

The egg grew to become an embryo.

The embryo was put into the uterus of a Scottish Blackface ewe.

Dolly was born – a clone of the Finn Dorset ewe.

Figure 4.15 Stages in the creation of Dolly, the first successful clone.

cloning. Embryos that are used come from the *in vitro* fertilisation (IVF) process and are surplus embryos that were not implanted into the mother.

In the future, embryos could be created using differentiated cells from the patient so that the stem cells they produce are genetically identical to the patient.

25 What is the purpose of the polymerase chain reaction?

26 What is the characteristic of DNA fragments that causes them to separate during electrophoresis?

27 State **two** uses of DNA profiling.

28 What characteristic of the genetic code allows a gene to be transferred between species?

29 Name the rings of DNA found in prokaryotic cells that can act as gene vectors.

30 Name the **two** enzymes used to make a recombinant plasmid.

31 Name the **two** cell types used to make Dolly the sheep.

Ethics and therapeutic cloning

As we have seen, there are two types of cloning – reproductive and therapeutic. Reproductive cloning involves an embryo that has been created and implanted into a surrogate mother, where it is allowed to develop into a new organism. This has now been done for many different species of animals but not, as yet, for humans. In the therapeutic cloning process, no sperm fertilisation is needed nor is it necessary to implant an embryo into the uterus to create a child.

In the future, human therapeutic cloning could begin with the extraction of a nucleus from a donated egg. This nucleus holds the genetic material from the donor. Scientists might then take a body cell from their patient and extract the nucleus from it. The patient might need a stem cell transplant to treat a health condition or disease.

The patient's nucleus would be substituted into the egg cell so that the egg then contains the patient's genetic material. The egg could be stimulated to divide and soon form a cluster of cells rich in stem cells. Stem cells could be isolated and infused into the patient where they are needed to restore structure or function.

One of the major benefits of therapeutic cloning is that the stem cells are **pluripotent**, which means they can give rise to almost any cell type in the body. Another advantage is that there is no risk of immunological rejection because the patient's own genetic material is used. Therapeutic cloning has the potential to dramatically reduce waiting times for organ transplants as well as eliminating the immunological concerns associated with organ transplants.

Questions to consider

1 Therapeutic cloning is still at the research stage, using unused IVF embryos. Is it appropriate to take it to the next stage and create patient-specific embryos for therapeutic use?

2 The creation of an embryo requires a human egg cell. Some women are willing to donate eggs but is it ethical to buy them from willing donors?

3 The embryonic stem cells are genetically identical to the patient's cells and therefore there is no need to use immunosuppressant drugs and no danger of tissue rejection. Is this a useful argument supporting therapeutic cloning?

4 Since embryonic stem cells can develop into any cell type, how can a surgeon be certain that the implanted cells will develop into the desired differentiated cells and not some other cell type such as cancer cells? Are these risks worth taking?

End-of-chapter questions

1 Which of the following statements is correct?

     A   Both men and women can be carriers of a sex-linked allele.

     B   Mitosis reduces the number of chromosomes in a cell from the diploid to the haploid number.

     C   All of the genetic information in an organism is called a genome.

     D   The polymerase chain reaction separates fragments of DNA in a gel.   (1)

2 The fruit fly, *Drosophila*, has sex chromosomes X and Y, the same as humans. 'White eye' is caused by a sex-linked allele, which is recessive. In the pedigree shown opposite, which **two** individuals must be carriers of the white allele?

     A   I4 and II3

     B   I4 and II2

     C   II1 and II2

     D   II2 and III2

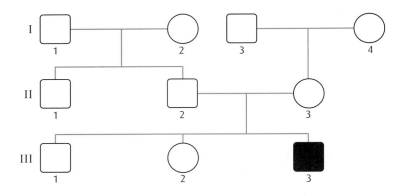

■ this fly has white eye

(1)

3 The karyogram below shows:

     A   Down's syndrome

     B   a sex chromosome trisomy

     C   a normal human female

     D   a normal human male

(1)

4 Which of the following describes the behaviour of chromosomes during prophase I and metaphase II of meiosis?

	Prophase I	Metaphase II
A	Chromosomes undergo supercoiling.	Sister chromatids are separated.
B	Homologous chromosomes pair up together.	Homologous pairs of chromosomes line up on the equator.
C	Homologous chromosomes pair up together.	Chromosomes line up on the equator.
D	The nuclear envelope reforms.	Chromosomes line up on the equator.

(1)

5 A test cross is carried out on a plant of unknown genotype; 50% of the offspring have the same phenotype as the test–cross parent. The conclusion is:

        A   the unknown parent is homozygous recessive
        B   the unknown parent is homozygous dominant
        C   the gene is sex linked
        D   the unknown parent is heterozygous

(1)

6 The diagram shows a DNA electrophoresis gel. The results are from a single probe showing a DNA profile for a man, a woman and their four children.

Which child is least likely to be the biological offspring of the father?

        A   Child 1
        B   Child 2
        C   Child 3
        D   Child 4

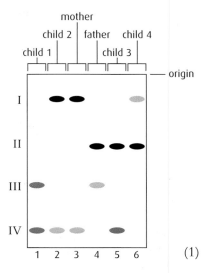

(1)

7 Ludovica is blood group AB and is expecting a baby with her husband Mikhail who is blood group A. Mikhail's mother was group O. Deduce the possible genotypes and phenotypes of their baby using a Punnett grid.

(4)

8 Discuss the ethical arguments for and against the therapeutic cloning of humans.

(4)

9 Genetic modification involves the transfer of DNA from one species to another. Discuss the potential benefits and possible harmful effects of genetic modification. Include a named example.

(8)

10 Outline how a DNA profile is obtained, including one way in which it has been used.

(5)

11 Karyotyping involves arranging the chromosomes of an individual into pairs. Describe one application of this process, including the way in which the chromosomes are obtained.

(5)

12 Outline **two** positive outcomes of the Human Genome Project. Do not include international cooperation. (2)

13 The diagram opposite shows the pedigree of a family with red–green colour-blindness, a sex-linked condition.

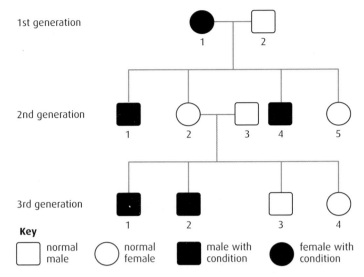

1st generation

2nd generation

3rd generation

Key

| normal male | normal female | male with condition | female with condition |

a Define the term 'sex-linkage'. (1)

b Deduce, with a reason, whether the allele producing the condition is dominant or recessive. (2)

c i Determine all the possible genotypes of the individual (2nd generation 1) using appropriate symbols. (1)
ii Determine all the possible genotypes of the individual (3rd generation 4) using appropriate symbols. (1)

(total 5 marks)

© IB Organization 2009

14 Potatoes with more starch have a lower percentage water content. This has an advantage in the transport, cooking and processing of potatoes.

In a strain of *Escherichia coli*, scientists found an enzyme that increases the production of starch. Using biotechnology, the gene for this enzyme was transferred to potatoes, increasing their starch content (transgenic potatoes). The gene was transferred to three potato varieties to create three transgenic lines. The table shows the mean amount of starch and sugar contained in three lines of transgenic potatoes and normal potatoes (control), after storage for four months at 4 °C.

| Potato | Line | Carbohydrate/% of fresh weight | |
		Sugar	Starch
transgenic	I	0.60	11.07
	II	1.56	11.61
	III	1.46	12.74
	mean	1.21	11.81
control	I	5.14	5.88
	II	5.61	3.70
	III	4.32	6.35
	mean	5.02	5.31

source: Stark et al, (1999), *Annals of the New York Academy of Sciences*, 792, pages 26–36

a State which line of transgenic potato has the greatest amount of starch. (1)

b **i** Compare the levels of carbohydrate between the transgenic lines and the control potatoes. (2)

   ii Suggest reasons for these differences. (2)

Potato tubers were harvested from the field and stored in high humidity at 4 °C for three months. After this period, the tubers were stored at 16 °C, and samples were removed after 0, 3, 6 or 10 days, cut into strips, and fried. The colour of the fried potatoes was then measured and values reported using a 0 to 4 rating (light to dark), where a score of 2 or lower indicates acceptable colour. The results are shown in the table.

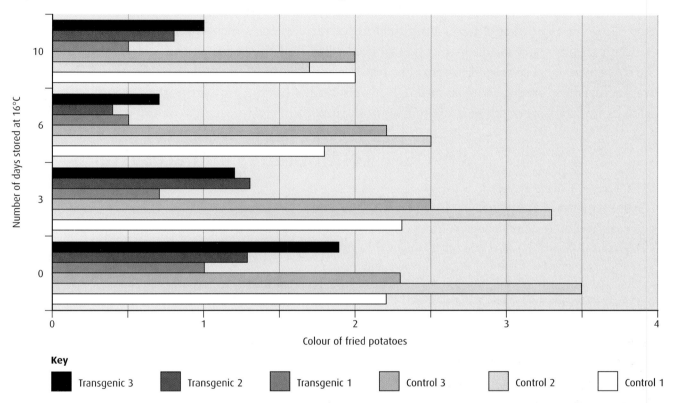

source: Stark *et al*, (1999), *Annals of the New York Academy of Sciences*, **792**, pages 26–36

c Evaluate the effect of transferring the *E. coli* gene on the suitability of the potatoes for frying. (2)

(total 7 marks)

© IB Organization 2009

5 Ecology and evolution

Introduction

Almost the entire surface of the Earth – the land, rivers, lakes, seas and oceans – is home to organisms of one kind or another. It has been estimated that there are as many as 10 million different species on Earth and understanding where and how they live and interact is a branch of biology known as **ecology**. Over long periods of time, species may change their genetic make-up as they adapt to new surroundings or changing conditions. One result of these changes is the evolution of new varieties and species. Humans are not the most numerous species on Earth (there are many more bacteria and insects, for example), but mankind is having a disproportionate effect on the world's ecosystems as damage is caused by pollution, rainforest destruction and global warming.

5.1 Communities and ecosystems

Assessment statements

- Define 'species', 'habitat', 'population', 'community', 'ecosystem' and 'ecology'.
- Distinguish between 'autotroph' and 'heterotroph'.
- Distinguish between 'consumers', 'detritivores' and 'saprotrophs'.
- Describe what is meant by a food chain, giving three examples, each with at least three linkages (four organisms).
- Describe what is meant by a food web.
- Define 'trophic level'.
- Deduce the trophic level of organisms in a food chain and a food web.
- Construct a food web containing up to ten organisms, using appropriate information.
- State that light is the initial energy source for almost all communities.
- Explain the energy flow in a food chain.
- State that energy transformations are never 100% efficient.
- Explain reasons for the shape of pyramids of energy.
- Explain that energy enters and leaves ecosystems, but nutrients must be recycled.
- State that saprotrophic bacteria and fungi (decomposers) recycle nutrients.

'*A true conservationist is a man who knows that the world is not given by his father but borrowed from his children.*'

John James Audubon (1785–1851)

Food chains

Every organism needs food to survive but eventually it too is eaten. In any **ecosystem**, there is a hierarchy of feeding relationships that influences how nutrients and energy pass through it. The sequence of organisms that provide food for one another is known as a **food chain**.

Consider a hyena eating a cheetah. The cheetah could have eaten an antelope, which in turn had eaten leaves from a plant. Thus, the four organisms form a food chain:

plant → antelope → cheetah → hyena

Every organism fits somewhere in a food chain, and although the organisms that make up the food chain will vary from place to place, almost every food chain starts with a green plant. It may be any part of the plant – the leaves, roots, stems, fruits, flowers or nectar. Green plants start food chains because they are able to capture light energy from the Sun and synthesise sugars, amino acids, lipids and vitamins, using simple inorganic substances such as water, carbon dioxide and minerals. Plants are called **autotrophs** (which means 'self feeding') or **producers** because they 'produce' organic compounds by photosynthesis. Every other organism in a food chain gets its organic compounds from its food and so is called a **heterotroph** or **consumer**.

Figure **5.1** shows three examples of food chains from different ecosystems. Notices that the arrows in a food chain always point in the direction in which the energy and nutrients flow.

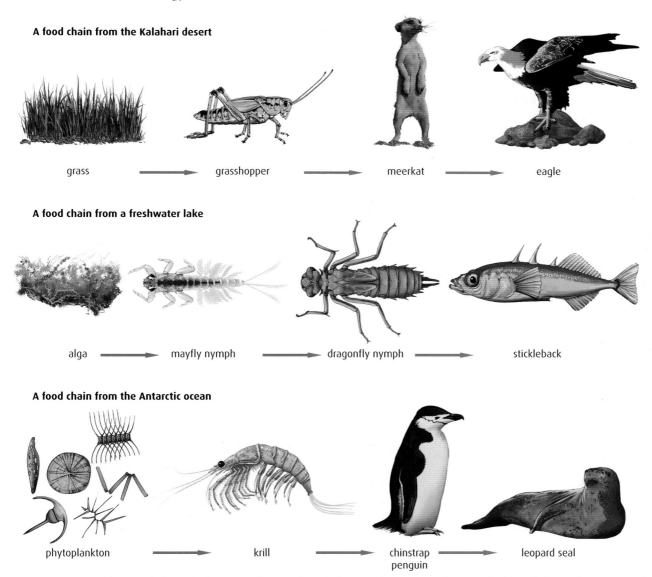

A food chain from the Kalahari desert

grass ⟶ grasshopper ⟶ meerkat ⟶ eagle

A food chain from a freshwater lake

alga ⟶ mayfly nymph ⟶ dragonfly nymph ⟶ stickleback

A food chain from the Antarctic ocean

phytoplankton ⟶ krill ⟶ chinstrap penguin ⟶ leopard seal

Figure 5.1 Grass, algae and phytoplankton are all examples of photosynthesising producers, which use light as their source of energy. Almost all food chains start with light as the initial source of energy.

In order to understand the topics in this chapter, it is important to remember the following terms, which are used in the study of ecology.

Species a group of organisms that can interbreed and produce fertile offspring

Habitat the environment in which a species normally lives or the location of a living organism

Population a group of organisms of the same species who live in the same area at the same time

Community a group of populations living and interacting with each other in an area

Ecosystem a community and its abiotic environment

Ecology the study of relationships between living organisms and between organisms and their environment

Trophic level the position of an organism in a food chain

The end of the chain

When an organism dies, its remains provide nutrients for other groups of organisms called **detritivores** and **saprotrophs**. Detritivores are organisms that ingest dead organic matter, whereas saprotrophs are organisms that secrete digestive enzymes onto the organic matter and then absorb their nutrients in a digested form. Saprotrophs are therefore responsible for the decomposition of organic matter and are often referred to as **decomposers.** Saprotrophic bacteria and fungi are the most important decomposers for most ecosystems and are crucial to the recycling of nutrients such as nitrogen compounds.

Trophic levels

Every ecosystem has a structure that divides organisms into **trophic levels** on the basis of their food sources. Trophic means 'feeding' and every organism in a food chain is on a particular feeding level.

Green plants are producers and are at the lowest trophic level. Above them come all the consumer levels. The first consumers, or **primary consumers**, are always herbivores. Any organism above the herbivores will be a carnivore and these can be listed as **secondary consumer**, **tertiary consumer** and so on. A food chain can therefore be summarised as:

producer → primary consumer → secondary consumer → tertiary consumer

Food webs

Few consumers feed on only one source of food. For example, this food chain describes one set of feeding relationships:

grass → beetle → tree creeper → sparrowhawk

But beetles eat a wide range of plants, tree creepers eat other types of insect and sparrowhawks eat other birds. So this food chain could be interlinked with many others. A **food web** like the one shown in Figure **5.2** shows a much more realistic picture of the feeding relations of the organisms in a habitat. Notice how organisms change trophic levels depending on what they are eating at any particular time. In Figure **5.2**, for example, the fox is a primary consumer when it is eating a crab apple but a secondary consumer when it is eating a woodmouse.

1 In the food web in Figure **5.2**, what is the trophic level of:
   a the tree creeper when eating a caterpillar?
   b the fox when eating a great tit?

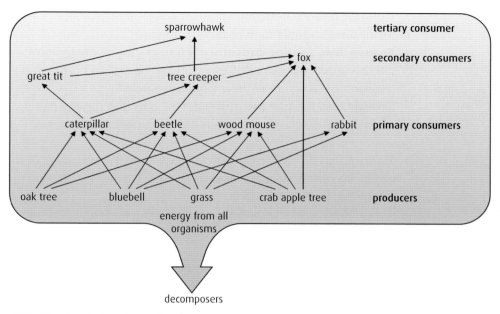

Figure 5.2 A food web in oak woodland.

Energy and food chains

Arrows in a food chain show the direction of flow of both the energy and nutrients that keep organisms alive. Energy flow through an ecosystem can be quantified and analysed. These studies reveal that, at each step in the food chain, energy is lost from the chain in various ways. Some is not consumed, some leaves the food chain as waste or when an animal dies, and some is used by living organisms as they respire (Figure **5.3**). In all three cases, the lost energy cannot be passed to the next trophic level.

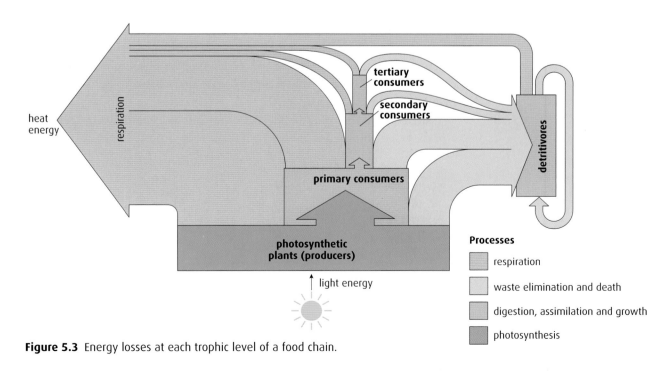

Figure 5.3 Energy losses at each trophic level of a food chain.

Consider an area of African savannah where grass, antelopes and cheetahs form a simple food chain.

- **Energy loss 1 – not consumed.** The grass stores energy from photosynthesis but the antelopes only eat some parts of the grass, so they do not consume all the energy it has stored.
- **Energy loss 2 – not assimilated.** The grass that is eaten passes through the digestive system of the antelope but not all of it is digested and absorbed, so some passes out in the faeces.
- **Energy loss 3 – cell respiration.** The antelope uses energy to move and to keep its body temperature constant. As a result, some energy is lost to the environment as heat.

The assimilated energy remaining after respiration goes into building the antelope's body and this energy becomes available to the cheetah when it eats the antelope.

Ecologists represent the transfer of energy between trophic levels in diagrams called **energy pyramids**. The width of each of the layers in the pyramid is proportional to the amount of energy it represents. So the antelope → cheetah energy transfer would appear as in Figure **5.4**. This section of an energy pyramid shows that only about 10% of energy from the antelope passes to the cheetah and about 90% has been lost.

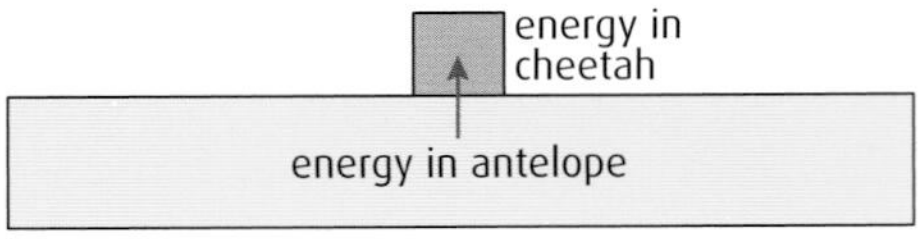

Energy losses occur at every step in a food chain, as the energy pyramid in Figure **5.5** illustrates. Every link in the chain results in losses, so that eventually there will be insufficient energy to support any further trophic levels. Most food chains commonly contain between three and five organisms, and seldom more than six. The energy that enters an ecosystem as light is converted to stored chemical energy and finally lost as heat.

Energy flow and nutrient recycling

All the organic matter from an organism, including everything from living or dead material to waste, is eventually consumed by other organisms. All these organisms respire and release energy as heat. All the energy that enters ecosystems as light energy, and is trapped by photosynthesis, will eventually be converted to heat and become unavailable to be used again by living things.

Nutrients, on the other hand, are continually **recycled**. A nitrogen atom may be absorbed as nitrate by a plant root and used to make an

Figure 5.4 A simple energy pyramid for a single energy transfer.

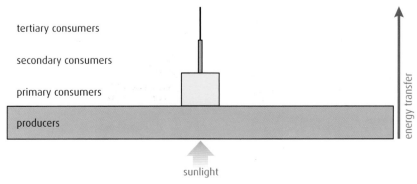

Figure 5.5 A generalised energy pyramid.

amino acid. The amino acid may pass into an animal when the plant material is eaten, and then pass out of the animal's body during excretion. Soil bacteria may convert urea in the excreted material back into nitrate and the cycle begins again.

Decomposers in the soil, the saprotrophic bacteria and fungi, are essential for the recycling of nutrients. You can find out more about nutrient cycles on pages **106** and **443**.

2 Define the following terms.
  a 'species'   **d** 'community'
  b 'habitat'   **e** 'ecosystem'
  c 'population'   **f** 'ecology'

3 Distinguish between an autotroph and a heterotroph.

4 Distinguish between consumers, detritivores and saprotrophs.

5 Give an example of a food chain containing four named organisms.

6 What do the arrows represent in a food chain?

7 Describe what is meant by a food web.

8 What is the initial energy source for most food chains?

9 Define 'trophic level'.

10 List the **three** ways energy is lost when moving from one trophic level to the next.

11 The leaves of a tree store $20\,000\,\mathrm{J\,m^{-2}\,y^{-1}}$ of energy. What is the approximate amount of energy stored by the caterpillars that feed on the leaves?

12 Name the **two** types of decomposer.

13 State the difference between energy movement and nutrient movement in an ecosystem.

5.2 The greenhouse effect

Assessment statements

- Draw and label a diagram of the carbon cycle to show the processes involved.
- Analyse the changes in concentration of atmospheric carbon dioxide using historical records.
- Explain the relationship between rises in concentrations of atmospheric carbon dioxide, methane and oxides of nitrogen and the enhanced greenhouse effect.
- Outline the precautionary principle.
- Evaluate the precautionary principle as a justification for strong action in response to the threats posed by the enhanced greenhouse effect.
- Outline the consequences of a global temperature rise on arctic ecosystems.

The carbon cycle

Carbon is one of the most important elements that are recycled in an ecosystem (Figure **5.6**). Inorganic carbon dioxide in the atmosphere is trapped or 'fixed' as organic carbon compounds during photosynthesis. Some of this carbon is soon returned to the atmosphere as the plants respire. The other steps in the cycle follow the same path as food chains. As herbivores eat plants, and carnivores eat herbivores, the carbon compounds move from plants to animals. Respiration by any organism in this sequence returns carbon to the atmosphere as carbon dioxide and when a plant or animal dies, carbon compounds that move to detritivores and saprotrophs may also be respired.

In some conditions, plants and animals do not decay when they die. They become compressed and fossilised in a process that takes millions of years and forms **fossil fuels**. Vast coal, oil and natural gas deposits have been formed and the carbon trapped in these fuels cannot return to the atmosphere unless the fuels are burned. Over a very long period of time, fossil fuel formation has gradually lowered the carbon dioxide level of the Earth's atmosphere, but in more recent times this balance has been upset.

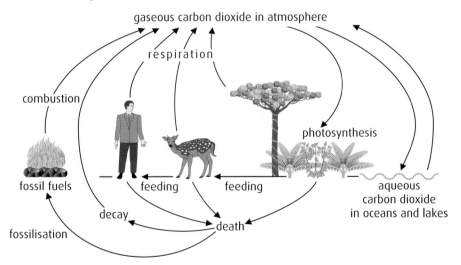

Figure 5.6 The carbon cycle.

How the greenhouse effect works

Certain gases, including carbon dioxide, enable the atmosphere to retain heat. Without these gases in the atmosphere, the Earth's temperature would be too low to support life. The warming effect of these gases is known as the **greenhouse effect** because it is caused in a similar way to the warming of a greenhouse.

A greenhouse is made of glass, which allows shorter-wave radiation from the Sun to pass through it. As the sunlight passes through the glass, the radiation is changed into heat, which has a longer wavelength. Glass is less transparent to these long wavelengths and heat is trapped in the greenhouse, making it warmer inside. So-called 'greenhouse gases' in the Earth's atmosphere (such as carbon dioxide, methane and water vapour) act in a similar way to the greenhouse glass. They trap heat that is radiated from the Earth's surface and keep the Earth at a comfortable temperature for life to exist.

Greenhouse gases, human activity and global warming

Carbon dioxide currently forms only 0.04% of the atmospheric gases but it plays a significant part in the greenhouse effect. Other greenhouse gases include water vapour, methane, oxides of nitrogen and fluorocarbons (FCs). Chlorofluorocarbons (CFCs) were used in aerosols and as refrigerants but were found to damage the ozone layer when released into the atmosphere. They are being replaced by hydrofluorcarbons (HFCs), but this is leading to an additional problem because HFCs are greenhouse gases.

The human population has increased dramatically in recent history, with a consequent increase in demand for energy in industry, transport and homes. Most of this energy demand has been met by burning fossil fuels, mainly oil, coal and gas. Burning fossil fuels releases both carbon dioxide and oxides of nitrogen. This activity has raised the concentration of carbon dioxide in the Earth's atmosphere by more than 20% since 1959 (Figure **5.7** and Table **5.1**, overleaf).

In the tropical regions of the world vast rainforests trap carbon dioxide through photosynthesis and have been important in maintaining the low level of atmospheric carbon dioxide. Humans have upset this balance by deforesting vast areas of forest for agriculture and timber production. Forest destruction has multiple effects, but the most important for the atmosphere are the loss of carbon dioxide uptake by photosynthesis and the increase in carbon dioxide released from the rotting or burnt vegetation.

Another important result of rising CO_2 levels is lowering of the pH of the oceans as CO_2 dissolves in them. Acidic oceans may inhibit the growth of producers and so affect food chains.

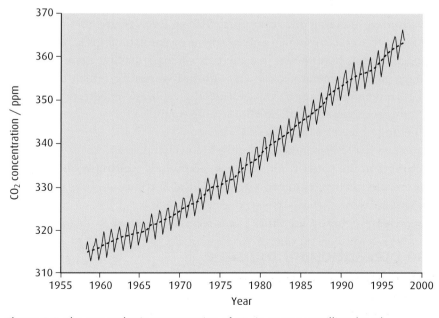

Figure 5.7 The atmospheric concentration of CO_2 in parts per million (ppm) measured at monthly intervals in Hawaii, showing the annual variation and increasing overall trend. The peaks and troughs indicate seasonal variations.

Year	Carbon dioxide concentration/ parts per million (ppm)	% increase from the previous value	% increase from 1959
1959	316		
1965	320	1.3	1.3
1970	326	1.9	3.2
1975	331	1.5	4.7
1980	339	2.4	7.3
1985	346	2.1	9.5
1990	354	2.3	12.0
1995	361	2.0	14.2
2000	369	2.2	16.8
2002	373	1.1	18.0
2004	378	1.3	19.6
2006	382	1.1	20.9
2008	386	1.0	22.2

Table 5.1 The atmospheric carbon dioxide levels monitored at the Mauna Loa laboratory in Hawaii since 1959. Although the percentage increase from the previous year tends to show a downward trend from 2000, the percentage increase from 1959 continues to rise (source: NOAA Earth System Research Laboratory).

The term 'global warming' is somewhat simplistic because some areas of the world will be colder as a result of an increase in greenhouse gases. A better term is 'climate change'. Climatologists try to make predictions about changes in weather patterns using computer-generated climate models.

Methane is another important greenhouse gas. It is produced by human activity when organic waste decomposes in waste tips. It also comes from rice paddies and from cattle farming. More rice is being planted as the human population increases and more cattle are being farmed for meat. Cattle release methane from their digestive systems as they process their food.

Climatologists are concerned that, as a result of all this activity, humans are adversely affecting our atmosphere. Rising levels of greenhouse gases are believed to be causing an enhancement of the natural greenhouse effect. Scientists have shown that the Earth is experiencing a rise in average global temperature, known as **global warming**, which is thought to be happening because of this enhanced greenhouse effect.

Some possible results of global warming might be:
- melting of ice caps and glaciers
- a rise in sea levels, causing flooding to low-lying areas
- changes in the pattern of the climate and winds – **climate change** – leading to changes in ecosystems and the distributions of plants and animals
- increases in photosynthesis as plants receive more carbon dioxide.

The precautionary principle

The **precautionary principle** suggests that if the effect of a change caused by humans is likely to be very harmful to the environment, action should be taken to prevent it, even though there may not be sufficient data to prove that the activity will cause harm. The precautionary principle is most often applied to the impact of human actions on the environment

Ethics and fossil fuels

To run a 100-watt bulb constantly for a year would use 325 kg of coal in a coal-fired power station. The thermal efficiency of such a power plant is about 40%.

One litre of petrol comes from 23.5 tonnes of ancient organic material deposited on the ocean floor.

The total amount of fossil fuels used in 1997 was estimated to have been produced from all plant matter that grew on the surface and in all the oceans of the ancient Earth for a period of more than 400 years.

At current usage, the Earth's coal supply will last for 1500 years. However, at a 5% growth rate, the coal supply will last only 86 years. As the supplies of other fossil fuels diminish, even greater quantities of coal are likely to be used.

Burning fossil fuels is responsible for environmental issues that are high on the political agenda of many countries. Examples include not only global warming, but also acidification, air pollution, water pollution and damage to land surface.

Questions to consider

1 How should an individual react to this information? What can one person do to limit their own impact on the environment?
2 Developing countries need electricity and transport to fuel their industries and to provide for the basic needs of their populations. How should developed nations respond to increasing fossil fuel consumption in these countries?

and human health, as both are complex and the consequences of actions may be unpredictable.

One of the cornerstones of the precautionary principle, and a globally accepted definition, comes from the Earth Summit held in Rio in 1992.

'In order to protect the environment, the precautionary approach shall be widely applied by States according to their capabilities. Where there are threats of serious or irreversible damage, lack of full scientific certainty shall not be used as a reason for postponing cost-effective measures to prevent environmental degradation.'

There are many warning signs to indicate that climate change will have a serious effect on ecosystems across the world. It is clear that global temperatures are increasing and there is a significant probability that this is caused by human activities. It is also likely that weather patterns will alter and cause changes in sea levels and the availability of land for farming. The precautionary principle challenges governments, industries and consumers to take action without waiting for definitive scientific proof to be forthcoming.

 Are there any reasons to doubt that climate change is occurring?

Evaluating the precautionary principle

Should the precautionary principle be used to justify action to reduce the impact of the release of greenhouse gases into the atmosphere before irreparable harm is done? Here are some arguments to discuss:

- Global warming has consequences for the entire human race and an international solution is needed to tackle the problems. It is not always the case that those who produce the most greenhouse gases suffer the greatest harm so it is essential that measures to reduce emissions are taken with full international cooperation.

- If industries and farmers in one area invest money to reduce their greenhouse gases while those in other areas do not, an economic imbalance may be created in favour of the more polluting enterprises, who can offer services more cheaply.
- Consumers can be encouraged to use more environmentally friendly goods and services.
- Scientists can argue that it is better to invest in a sustainable future and prevent further harm.
- It is unethical for one generation to cause harm to future generations by not taking action to address the problem of greenhouse gases.

Global temperature rise and Arctic ecosystems

The ecosystems of the Arctic include the tundra, permafrost and the sea ice, a huge floating ice mass surrounding the North Pole (Figure **5.8**). Scientists studying these regions have recorded considerable changes in recent years. Average annual temperatures in the Arctic have increased by approximately double the increase in global average temperatures and the direct impacts of this include melting of sea ice and glaciers.

Melting sea ice affects many species. Algae, which are important producers in Arctic food chains, are found just beneath the sea ice. As the ice disappears, so do the algae and this affects numerous other organisms

Trouble in Greenland

The snow in Greenland is not all pristine white. There are patches of brown and black dotted all over the landscape. This is cryconite, a mixture of desert sand, volcanic ash and soot from burnt fossil fuels carried by the wind to Greenland from hundreds or thousands of kilometres away. The more soot there is, the blacker the snow becomes. Black objects absorb the Sun's heat more quickly than white ones do, so the sooty covering makes the underlying snow melt faster. As it melts, the previous year's layer of cryconite is exposed, which makes the layer even blacker. This positive feedback is causing rapid melting of the Greenland ice sheets.

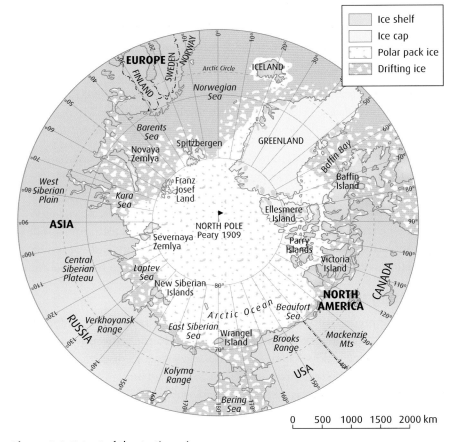

Figure 5.8 Extent of the Arctic region.

that use them as food. Populations of marine mammals, caribou and polar bears are also affected and have already been forced to adapt to changes in their habitats. According to scientists, the retreat of sea ice has reduced the platform that seals and walruses traditionally use to rest between searches for fish and mussels. Caribou are falling through once-solid sea ice and polar bears, which live on sea ice while hunting their prey, now have shorter feeding periods and decreased access to the seals that they hunt. Polar bear numbers are decreasing at an alarming rate.

Forest and tundra ecosystems are important features of the Arctic environment. In Alaska, substantial changes in forest life, including increases in insect pests, have been observed. Rising temperatures have allowed spruce bark beetles to reproduce rapidly and one outbreak of the beetles caused the loss of over 2.3 million acres of trees. Outbreaks of other leaf-eating insects in the boreal forest, such as spruce budworm and larch sawfly, have also increased sharply. In addition, some species from temperate climates are extending their ranges to the north. One insect causing concern is the mosquito, which is responsible for the transmission of malaria.

Detritus trapped in frozen tundra is released as the ground thaws. The detritus decomposes and the carbon dioxide and methane produced are released into the atmosphere, contributing to rising greenhouse gas levels.

14 List **three** groups of organisms in the carbon cycle that transfer carbon dioxide to the atmosphere.

15 State the process in the carbon cycle by which carbon dioxide is fixed as organic carbon-containing compounds.

16 List **three** greenhouse gases.

17 List **five** human activities that are causing an increase in the levels of greenhouse gases in the atmosphere.

18 State briefly what you understand by the precautionary principle.

19 List **three** ways in which a rise in average global temperature is having an effect on Arctic ecosystems.

5.3 Populations

Assessment statements

- Outline how population size is affected by natality, immigration, mortality and emigration.
- Draw and label a graph showing a sigmoid population growth curve.
- Explain the reasons for the exponential growth phase, the plateau phase and the transitional phase between these two phases.
- List three factors that set limits to population increase.

A **population** is a group of individuals of the same species that live in the same area. Population numbers can and do change over time and are affected by a number of factors in the environment.

Population size and growth

Consider what happens if a few individuals of a species enter an unoccupied area. Perhaps a few rabbits arrive on an uninhabited island covered by lush grassland or some fish are washed into a newly established pond. Assuming there is enough food and there are few predators, the newcomers will reproduce and the population will increase rapidly. After a time, when there are large numbers of individuals, the food supply will start to be used up faster than it can be replaced. The population will be unable to increase any further and the population numbers will stabilise.

This typical pattern of population growth can be represented on a graph, shown in Figure **5.9**. As reproduction gets underway, the population shows exponential growth (the steepest part of the curve). At this time, there is abundant food, little competition for space and the effects of predation and disease are minimal.

After a time, the exponential phase ceases and one or more of the resources individuals need become limited. These may be food or water, light (in the case of plants) or shelter. Predation, disease, and in some cases the accumulation of toxic wastes, such as carbon dioxide, can also limit a population. The shape of the curve shows that population growth is decreasing and the population is said to be in the transitional phase.

Eventually population numbers become more or less constant and the curve levels off, in the plateau phase.

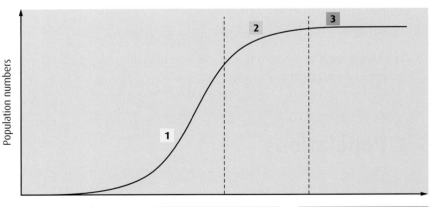

1 Exponential phase

Population increases with no restraint on growth. Nutrents are abundant and there is little accumulation of waste.

2 Transitional phase

One or more factors in the environment are limiting the rate of reproduction. These might be competition for resources such as food, space or mates, increased predation and disease, or an abiotic factor such as oxygen might be in short supply.

3 Plateau phase

In this phase the number of births plus immigration is equal to the number of deaths plus emigration.

Figure 5.9 A sigmoid population growth curve.

Why do population sizes vary?

There are a number of important reasons why a population may change in size:

- **natality** – the birth rate may change (the number of new individuals joining the population due to reproduction)
- **mortality** – the number of deaths may change
- **emigration** – members of the population may move away to new habitats
- **immigration** – new members of the species may arrive from elsewhere.

Factors that limit population increases

There are certain key factors that affect a population, no matter what species is considered. These include:

- availability of key resources such as food, water, oxygen, light, space, mates and shelter
- disease and predation
- levels of waste products, such as carbon dioxide or nitrogenous waste.

....

20 Suggest factors that might lead to an increase in a bird population in a woodland.

21 Complete this equation for the plateau phase of a growth curve:

birth + ... = ... + ...

....

5.4 Evolution

Assessment statements

- Define 'evolution'.
- Outline the evidence for evolution provided by the fossil record, selective breeding of domesticated animals and homologous structures.
- State that populations tend to produce more offspring than the environment can support.
- Explain that the consequence of the potential overproduction of offspring is a struggle for survival.
- State that the members of a species show variation.
- Explain how sexual reproduction promotes variation in a species.
- Explain how natural selection leads to evolution.
- Explain two examples of evolution in response to environmental change; one must be antibiotic resistance in bacteria.

What is evolution?

Life on Earth is always changing. Just by looking at any group of individuals of any species – whether humans, cats or sunflowers, for example – you can see that individuals are not all the same. For example, the people in Figure **5.10** (overleaf) vary in height, hair colour, skin tone and in many other ways. How do these differences arise? Where do different species come from?

Figure 5.10 Most of the variation between humans is continuous variation, and is influenced by the environment as well as genes.

Evolution cumulative change in the heritable characteristics of a population

Variation within a species is a result of both genetic and environmental factors. We say that **selection pressures** act on individuals: because of variation, some may be better suited to their environment than others. These are likely to survive longer and have more offspring.

The characteristics of a species are inherited and passed on to succeeding generations. The cumulative change in these heritable characteristics is called **evolution**. If we go back in time, then existing species must have evolved from pre-existing ones. All life forms can therefore be said to be linked in one vast family tree with a common origin.

What evidence is there for evolution?

The fossil record

Fossils, such as the one shown in Figure **5.11**, are the preserved remains of organisms that lived a long time ago. They are often formed from the hard parts of organisms, such as shell, bone or wood. Minerals seep into these tissues and, over time, deposit and harden. As the living tissue decays, the minerals form a replica that remains behind. Soft tissue can sometimes be preserved in the same way, as can footprints and animal droppings. Most fossils become damaged or are crushed through land or sea movement, but some are remarkably well preserved. The earliest fossils date from over three billion years ago, so the time scale of the fossil record is immense. Most fossils are of species that died out long ago, because they did not adapt to new environmental conditions.

The study of fossils is called palaeontology. Palaeontologists have been collecting and classifying fossils for over two hundred years, but they have only been able to date them since the 1940s. Scientists do this by studying the amount of radioactivity in fossils. Over time, the amount of radioactivity decreases. This is because the reactive elements decay, so there is less radioactive material left. The rate of decay is fixed for each element, so it is possible to date fossils by measuring the amount of radioactivity in each specimen. Carbon-14 is used to study material up to 60 000 years old. For older material, other elements are used.

Although the fossil record is incomplete and fossils are very rare, it is possible to show how modern plants and animals might have evolved from previous species that existed hundreds or thousands of millions of years ago. For example, fossil sequences suggest how modern horses may have evolved from earlier species (Figure **5.12**). It is important to recognise, though, that we can never say that '**this** species evolved into **that** species', based on a fossil sequence – even when we have many fossils. All that we can say is that they appear to be related – that they probably share a common ancestor. Other species could well have existed too, for which no fossils have ever been found.

A few organisms seem to have changed very little. The horseshoe crab we see today is very similar to fossil specimens a million years old. This would seem to suggest that there has been little selection pressure on these crabs.

Observations of fossils provide evidence that life on Earth changes and that many of the changes occur over millions of years.

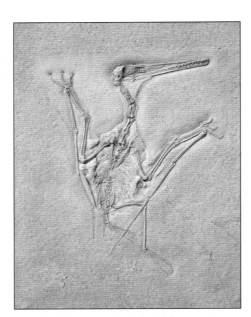

Figure 5.11 A fossil of a Pterosaur.

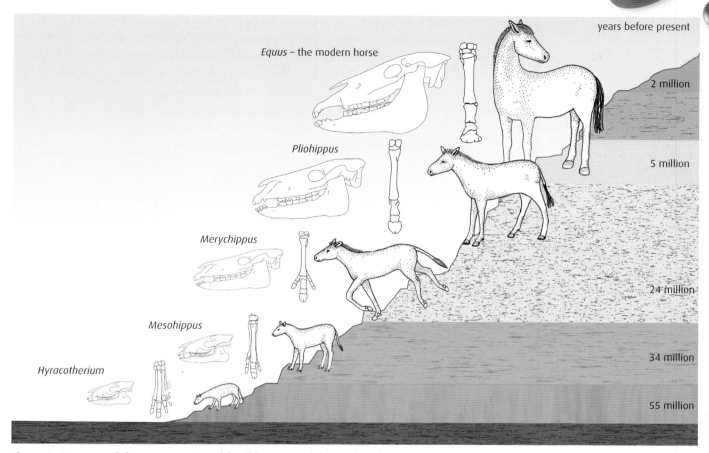

years before present

Equus – the modern horse

2 million

Pliohippus

5 million

Merychippus

24 million

Mesohippus

34 million

Hyracotherium

55 million

Figure 5.12 Some of the many species of fossil horses, and the modern horse, *Equus*. The fossil sequence shows that, over time, horses have developed single-toes hooves, longer legs and longer faces, with larger teeth for grazing.

Selective breeding

Further evidence for the way evolution might have occurred comes from observations of selective breeding. In this process, plants or animals with favourable characteristics are bred to increase their numbers in a population. Humankind has been domesticating and breeding plants and animals for thousands of years. Modern varieties of wheat produce higher yields and are shorter and stronger than varieties of a hundred years ago, and these in turn have many differences from the grasses that wheat was originally bred from 10 000 years ago. Similarly, farmers and animal breeders may look for favourable characteristics in a cow or a sheep, such as milk yield or quality of wool, and then use individuals displaying these characteristics to breed more animals with the same features (Figure **5.13**).

Although the driving force for artificial selection is human intervention, which is quite different from natural evolution, selective or artificial breeding does show that species can change over time.

Homologous structures

Further evidence for evolution is provided by **homologous structures**, which are anatomical features showing similarities in shape or function in different organisms. Their presence suggests that the species possessing

Figure 5.13 Selective breeding of cows over many centuries has produced many breeds including the Guernsey. Guernseys have been bred for the production of large quantities of fat-rich milk.

them are closely related and derived from a common ancestor. A good example is the vertebrate pentadactyl limb. This is found in a large range of animals including bats, whales and humans, as shown in Figure **5.14**. In each group, limbs have the same general structure and arrangement of bones but each one is adapted for different uses.

Bird wings and reptile limbs are also homologous structures. Even though a bird uses its wings for flying and reptiles use their limbs for walking, they share a common arrangement of bones.

A mechanism for evolution

The theory of evolution by means of natural selection was proposed by Charles Darwin and Alfred Wallace. Darwin explained his ideas in a book called *On the Origin of Species by Means of Natural Selection*, published in 1859. The explanation remains a theory because it can

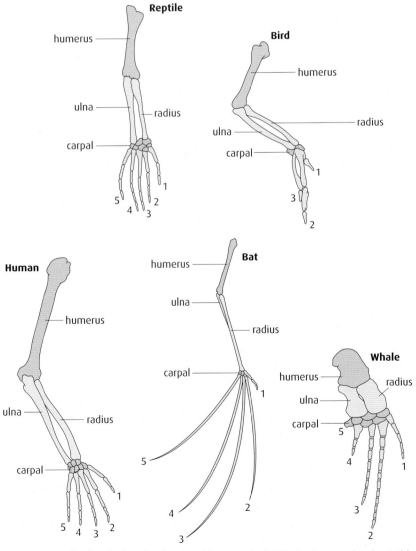

Figure 5.14 The forelimbs of animals with pentadactyl limbs have a clearly visible humerus, radius, ulna and carpals.

never be completely proved but there is an abundance of evidence to support the key ideas, which are based on the following observations and deductions. Some terms we use now were not used by Darwin, who had no knowledge of genes or alleles. However, the fundamental basis of his argument was the same as outlined here.

- All organisms are potentially capable of producing large numbers of offspring and far more than the environment can support. Trees can produce thousands of seeds and fish hundreds of eggs. Yet few of these survive to maturity and we rarely see population explosions in an ecosystem.
- Both plants and animals in a growing population will compete for resources. These may be food, territory or even the opportunity to find a mate. In addition, predators and disease will take their toll. This competition will bring about a struggle for survival between the members of a population. Organisms that are well adapted to the conditions will be good at competing and will tend to survive, while others die.
- Different members of the same species are all slightly different and this variation is due to the mechanism of sexual reproduction. The process of meiosis produces haploid gametes and furthermore the genes in the gametes an individual produces may be present in different forms or alleles. When an egg is fertilised, the zygote contains a unique combination of genetic material from its two parents. Sexual reproduction gives an enormous source of genetic diversity, which gives rise to a wide variation within the individuals of a species.
- As a result of variation, some members of a population may be better suited to their surroundings than others. They may have keener eyesight, or have better camouflage to avoid predators. These individuals will out-compete others; they will survive better, live longer, and pass on their genes to more offspring. Gradually, as the process is repeated generation after generation, the proportion of these genes in the population as a whole increases. This is called **natural selection**, and it occurs as the fittest survive to reproduce.

Natural selection and evolution

Usually natural selection tends to keep things much the same. Species that are living today have evolved to be suited to their environment. However, if the environment changes, a population will need to adapt if it is to survive in the new conditions. Two examples of how this can happen are the response of a moth population to pollution, and the emergence of new strains of bacteria following the introduction of antibiotics.

Industrial melanism

The peppered moth (*Biston betularia*) is a night-flying moth that rests during the day on the bark of trees, particularly on branches that are covered with grey–green lichen. It is a light speckled grey, and relies on camouflage against the tree branches to protect it from predatory birds.

In Britain in the mid-19th century, a black form of the moth was noticed (Figure **5.15**, overleaf). The appearance of this new colour

Sexual reproduction promotes variation

Mutations in genes cause new variations to arise, but sexual reproduction increases variation in a population by forming new combinations of alleles.

- During meiosis, crossing over at prophase I and random assortment in metaphase I produce genetically different gametes (see pages **71–75**).
- Different alleles are also brought together at fertilisation, promoting more variation.

In species that reproduce asexually, variation can arise only by mutation.

Figure 5.15 Light and melanic forms of peppered moths on light and dark tree bark.

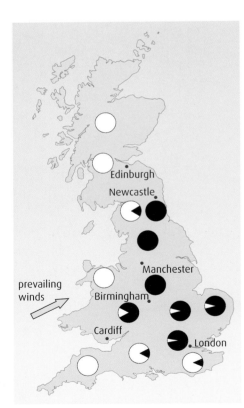

Figure 5.16 The distribution of the light and melanic forms of the peppered moth in Britain in the early 1960s. The ratio of dark to light areas in each circle shows the ratio of dark to light moths in that part of the country.

coincided with the period of the industrial revolution when many factories were built and contributed to growing pollution in the atmosphere. This pollution killed the lichens that grow on the bark of trees, which became blackened with particles of soot.

The colour of the moth is due to a single gene, which can be present in two forms. The common recessive form gives rise to a light speckled colour. The much less common dominant form gives rise to the black, melanic moth.

In the polluted areas, the speckled form was no longer camouflaged on the blackened tree bark, and was easily seen by birds that ate speckled moths. The black moths were better suited to the changed environment as they were camouflaged. Black moths survived and bred and the proportion of black moths with the dominant allele grew in the population.

In 1956, the Clean Air Act became law in Britain and restricted air pollution. Lichen grew back on trees and their bark became lighter. As a consequence, the speckled form of the peppered moth has increased in numbers again in many areas, and the black form has become less frequent (Figure **5.16**).

Antibiotic resistance

Antibiotics are drugs that kill or inhibit bacterial growth. Usually, treating a bacterial infection with an antibiotic kills every invading cell. But, because of variation within the population, there may be a few bacterial cells that can resist the antibiotic. These individuals will survive and reproduce (Figure **5.17**). Because they reproduce asexually, all offspring of a resistant bacterium are also resistant, and will also survive in the presence of the antibiotic. The resistant bacteria have enormous selective advantage over the normal susceptible strain, and quickly out-compete them.

Treating a disease caused by resistant strains of bacteria becomes very difficult. Doctors may have to prescribe stronger doses of antibiotic or try different antibiotics to kill the resistant bacteria.

The problem of antibiotic resistance is made more complex because bacteria frequently contain additional genetic information in the form of plasmids, which they can transfer or exchange with other bacteria, even those from different species. Genes for enzymes that can inactivate antibiotics are often found on plasmids, so potentially dangerous bacteria can become resistant to antibiotics by receiving a plasmid from a relatively harmless species. Many bacteria are now resistant to several antibiotics, so pharmaceutical companies are constantly trying to develop new antibiotics to treat the multiple resistance forms of bacteria.

Antibiotic resistance and so-called 'superbugs', such as MRSA and *Clostridium difficile*, are bacteria resistant to many antibiotics. They have arisen partly as a result of overuse of antibiotics. Antibiotics used incorrectly or too frequently, help to 'select' the resistant individuals, which then increase in numbers. Patients failing to take a complete course of medication can also encourage the survival of slightly resistant bacteria that might have been killed if the antibiotic had been taken properly.

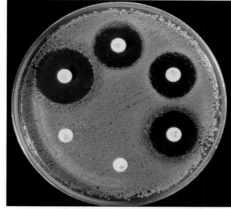

Figure 5.17 The grey areas on the agar jelly in this Petri dish are colonies of the bacterium *Escherichia coli*. The white card discs are impregnated with different antibiotics. This strain of *E. coli* is resistant to the antibiotics at the bottom left and has been able to grow right up to the discs.

22 Define 'evolution'.

23 Why is sexual reproduction important for evolution?

24 Individuals in a population are often said to be 'struggling for survival'. What is the key fact that causes this struggle?

25 If an environment changes, individuals with particular combinations of genes are more likely to survive. What is the name given to this phenomenon?

26 Give **two** examples of evolution in response to environmental change.

5.5 Classification

Assessment statements

- Outline the binomial system of classification.
- List seven levels in the hierarchy of taxa – kingdom, phylum, class, order, family, genus and species – using an example from two different kingdoms for each level.
- Distinguish between the following phyla of plants, using simple external recognition features: bryophyta, filicinophyta, coniferophyta and angiospermophyta.
- Distinguish between the following phyla of animals, using simple external recognition features: porifera, cnidaria, platyhelminthes, annelida, mollusca and arthropoda.
- Apply and design a key for a group of up to eight organisms.

Biological classification attempts to arrange living organisms into groups that enable them to be identified easily and that show evolutionary links between them. The system of classification we use today has its origins in a method devised by the Swedish scientist Carolus Linnaeus (1707–1778).

Figure 5.18 Carolus Linnaeus, also known as Carl Linnaeus, was a Swedish botanist, physician and zoologist, who laid the foundations for the modern scheme of binomial nomenclature.

By convention, the genus name starts with a capital, while the species does not. Both are written in italic or underlined. Once an organism has been referred to by its full Latin name in a piece of text, further references abbreviate the genus to the first letter only – for example, *U. maritimus.*

	Polar bear	Lemon tree
Kingdom	Animalia	Plantae
Phylum	Chordata	Angiospermata
Class	Mammalia	Dicoyledoneae
Order	Carnivora	Geraniales
Family	Ursidae	Rutaceae
Genus	*Ursus*	*Citrus*
Species	*maritimus*	*limonia*

Table 5.2 The taxonomic hierarchy for a plant species and for an animal species.

The binomial system of classification

The **classification** of living organisms is simply a method of organising them into groups to show similarities and differences between them. More than two thousand years ago, the Greek philosopher Aristotle (384–322 BC) classified organisms into two groups – plants and animals. This was useful as a starting point, but as the two main groups were sub-divided, problems started to appear. At that time, organisms were seen to be unchanging, so there was no understanding of evolutionary relationships. Many organisms discovered later did not fit into the scheme very well.

Birds were separated into a group defined as 'Feathered animals that can fly' so no place could be found for the flightless cormorant, a bird that does not fly. Bacteria, which were unknown at the time, were not included at all.

In 1735, Carolus Linnaeus (Figure **5.18**) adapted Aristotle's work, and his system forms the foundation of modern taxonomy. **Taxonomy** is the science of identifying, naming and grouping organisms.

Linnaeus gave each organism two Latin names – the first part of the name is a genus name and the second part a species name. Thus the **binomial**, or two-part, name for the American grizzly bear is *Ursus americanus* whereas a polar bear is *Ursus maritimus*. Linnaeus used Latin for his names. Latin has long been the language of medicine and science, and it is unchanging. If *Ursus maritimus* is mentioned anywhere in the world, scientists will know that polar bears are being discussed.

- The **genus** part of the name indicates a group of species that are very closely related and share a common ancestor.
- The **species** is usually defined as a group of individuals that are capable of interbreeding to produce fertile offspring.

Linnaeus developed structure in his classification system – for example, he grouped birds into birds of prey, wading birds and perching birds. Although it is possible to group living things in many different ways, over the last two hundred years a hierarchical classification system has emerged and it is now used by biologists everywhere.

There are seven levels to the hierarchy:

- kingdom
- phylum (plural: phyla)
- class
- order
- family
- genus
- species

Two examples of how species are classified are shown in Table **5.2**.

Aristotle's original grouping of organisms into just two kingdoms has also been refined. Today the most widely accepted method of classification uses five kingdoms:

- Kingdom Plantae – plants
- Kingdom Animalia – animals
- Kingdom Fungi – fungi
- Kingdom Protoctista – protozoa and algae
- Kingdom Prokaryotae – bacteria.

The main phyla of the plant kingdom

Members of the plant kingdom are eukaryotic, have cellulose cell walls and carry out photosynthesis. The kingdom is divided into several different phyla based on other similarities.

Bryophyta

Plants in this phylum include the mosses (Figure **5.19**) and liverworts. These are the simplest land plants and are probably similar to the first plants to colonise the land some 400 million years ago.

- Bryophytes are usually small and grow in damp places because they have no vascular system to carry water.
- They reproduce by way of spores, and these are contained in capsules on small stalks held above the plants.
- They have no roots, just thin filamentous outgrowths called rhizoids. They have no cuticle and absorb water across their whole surface.
- Liverworts have a flattened structure called a thallus but mosses have small simple leaves.

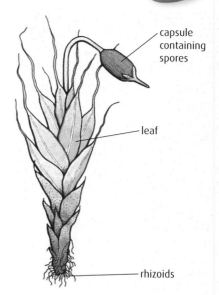

Figure 5.19 A moss, *Grimmia pulvinata*.

Filicinophyta

This group includes the club mosses, horsetails and ferns (Figure **5.20**).

- They have roots, stems and leaves and possess internal structures.
- Because of the support from woody tissue, some tree ferns grow to over 5 m in height.
- Some have fibrous roots, while others produce an underground stem called a rhizome.
- Like the bryophytes, they also reproduce by producing spores. In the ferns, these are found in clusters called sori on the undersides of the leaves.

Coniferophyta

Conifers include shrubs or trees, such as pine trees, fir and cedar, which are often large and evergreen (Figure **5.21**, overleaf). Some of the world's largest forests are comprised of conifers.

- Conifers produce pollen rather than spores, often in huge amounts, as conifers are wind-pollinated plants.
- They produce seeds, which are found in cones on the branches.
- Most have needle-like leaves, to reduce water loss.

Angiospermophyta

This group includes all the flowering plants, which are pollinated by wind or animals (Figure **5.22**, overleaf). They range from small low-lying plants to large trees. Many of them are important crop plants.

- Angiosperms all have flowers, which produce pollen.
- They all produce seeds, which are associated with a fruit or nut.

Figure 5.20 Club moss hanging from a maple tree in Washington, USA.

Figure 5.21 A western white pine tree (*Pinus monticola*) in the Sierra Nevada, USA.

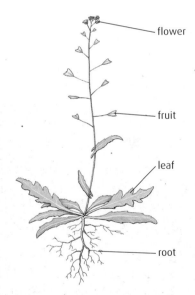

— flower

— fruit

— leaf

— root

Figure 5.22 Shepherd's purse, *Capsella bursa-pastoris* – an example of a flowering plant.

Some phyla of the animal kingdom

Organisms in the animal kingdom are characterised by being able to move and getting their nutrition by eating plants, other animals or both. Animals are divided into two groups – those that have a backbone (vertebrates) and those that do not (invertebrates). The phyla described below are all invertebrates.

Porifera

This group contains the sponges (Figure **5.23**). They have different types of cell, but no real organisation into tissues and no clear symmetry. All sponges are aquatic and many produce a skeleton of calcium carbonate or silicon. They pump water through the numerous pores in the body wall and filter out food. Sponges have no nerves or muscular tissue.

Cnidaria

These are the sea anemones, corals and jellyfish (Figure **5.24**). Almost all are marine, and have cells organised into tissues in two body layers. They feed on other animals by stinging them with special cells called nematocysts and trapping them in their tentacles. They have a mouth to take in food and use the same opening to get rid of waste. The box jellyfish and the Portuguese man-of-war are two of the most venomous animals on Earth.

Platyhelminthes

These have three layers of cells and have a body cavity with a mouth and an anus. Some are free living in water while others are parasites, living inside other organisms. They have a flattened appearance, hence their common name 'flatworms' (Figure **5.25**). Most flatworms are small, but the tapeworm found in the intestines of animals may grow to several metres long.

Figure 5.23 A giant barrel sponge (*Xestospongia testudinaria*) in the Sulawesi Sea of Indonesia is around 10–20 cm in diameter and 10–20 cm tall.

Annelida

This group, known as the 'segmented worms', contains lugworms, earthworms and leeches. Some are aquatic, living in rivers, estuaries and mud, and others inhabit soil. All annelids have bodies that are divided into sections called segments. All of them have a simple gut with a mouth at one end and an anus at the other. Earthworms are important in agriculture, because their burrowing aerates the soil and brings down organic matter from the surface, which helps to fertilise it.

Mollusca

This is the second largest animal phylum, containing over 80 000 species. The group includes small organisms like slugs and snails, as well as large marine creatures like the giant squid and octopuses (Figure **5.26**). Many produce an outer shell of calcium carbonate for protection.

Arthropoda

The arthropods comprise the largest animal phylum, and include aquatic animals such as the crustaceans (the crabs and lobsters), and terrestrial animals such as insects, spiders and scorpions. All have an **exoskeleton** made of chitin. They have segmented bodies and jointed limbs for walking, swimming, feeding or sensing. An exoskeleton places a restriction on their size: arthropods are never very big because they must shed their exoskeleton and produce a new, larger one in order to grow. The largest arthropod is the Japanese spider crab, which can be 4 m long. These crabs are marine so water gives their bodies buoyancy, enabling them to move. Well over one million arthropods are known and it is estimated that there may be at least as many more that have not yet been identified.

27 List in order the levels in the hierarchy of taxa.

28 State the **two** names from the hierarchy of taxa that are used in the binomial system.

29 Identify the group of plants that is characterised by producing pollen and having seeds in cones.

30 State which group of plants is characterised by producing spores, having no root system and no cuticle.

31 State which group of animals is characterised by having jointed limbs and an exoskeleton.

32 State which group of animals is characterised by having segmented bodies with a mouth at one end and an anus at the other.

Figure 5.24 *Dendrophyllia* coral polyps in the Red Sea. These polyps are 2–4 cm in diameter.

The Platyhelminthes, Annelida, Mollusca and Arthropoda are animals that are 'bilaterally symmetrical'. They have a definite front and back end, and a dorsal (back) and ventral (belly) side.

Figure 5.25 The Hawaiian spotted flatworm (*Pseudobiceros* sp.) is about 5 cm long.

Figure 5.26 The giant squid (*Architeuthis* sp.) is one of the largest invertebrates and can be up to 20 m long.

Designing a dichotomous key

A **dichotomous key** is a series of steps, each involving a decision, that can be used to identify unknown organisms. The key prompts us to decide, through careful observation, whether or not a specimen displays particular visible features, and allows us to distinguish between specimens on this basis.

When constructing a key to identify organisms such as those shown in Figure **5.27**, first examine each specimen in the set carefully, and choose a characteristic that is present in about half of the individuals and absent in the others. For example, the presence of wings could be this first distinguishing characteristic, which effectively divides the specimens into two smaller groups.

Now for each group, another diagnostic feature must be chosen whose presence or absence divides the specimens into two further groups. A branching tree diagram can be constructed, as shown in Figure **5.27**, progressively dividing the specimens into smaller and smaller groups, until at the end of each branch a single individual is identified.

Finally, the tree diagram is 'translated' into a written key, in which the branch points are expressed as alternative statements. Each alternative either names the identified specimen or leads the user to a subsequent pair of statements, until an identification is reached. A well-written key is composed of a series of questions or steps, such that an organism that is being studied can only be placed in one of two groups. The style of the questions is therefore very important in the design of a good key.

So, for example, the dichotomous key arising from the tree diagram in Figure **5.27** would be as follows.

1	Wings present	go to **2**
	No wings	go to **5**
2	Two pairs of wings	go to **3**
	One pair of wings	fly
3	Legs all approximately the same length	go to **4**
	Hind pair of legs much longer than front two pairs	locust
4	Wings covered in scales	butterfly
	Wings transparent, not covered in scales	dragonfly
5	Four pairs of legs	go to **6**
	More than four pairs of legs	go to **7**
6	Pair of claws present	crab
	No claws	spider
7	Body clearly divided into equal-sized segments	centipede
	Body in two regions, segments only clear on hind region	prawn

33 If you were making a dichotomous key to identify leaves, explain why the question 'Is the leaf large?' would not be useful.

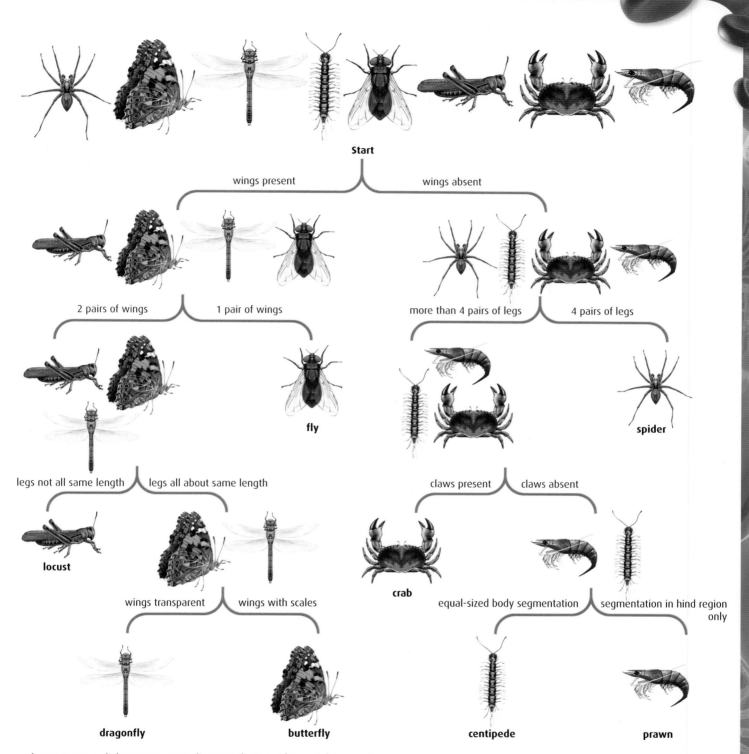

Figure 5.27 A dichotomous tree diagram distinguishing eight organisms.

End-of-chapter questions

1 Which of the following statements is correct?

    A   A community is the place where several different species live.

    B   Heterotrophs are organisms that feed off organic matter.

    C   Decomposer bacteria are detritivores.

    D   A habitat is a community and its abiotic environment.   (1)

2 Which of the following statements is correct?

    A   The precautionary principle states that if the effects of a human-induced change would be very large, those responsible for the change must prove that it will not be harmful before proceeding.

    B   The greenhouse gases methane and oxides of nitrogen have increased global temperatures by converting short-wave radiation to long-wave radiation.

    C   In the carbon cycle, the process of complete decomposition of plant remains stores carbon in the form of fossil fuels.

    D   A dichotomous key can be used for the identification of organisms because all organisms have a binomial classification.   (1)

3 Which of the following is the correct sequence for the hierarchy of taxa?

    A   kingdom, phylum, family, order, species

    B   kingdom, order, class, genus, species

    C   kingdom, class, phylum, order, species

    D   kingdom, phylum, family, genus, species   (1)

4 If two organisms are members of the same order, then they are also members of the same

    A   genus

    B   class

    C   family

    D   species.   (1)

5 The total energy in an area of grassland was analysed and found to be $400\,kJ\,m^{-2}\,y^{-1}$. Construct a labelled pyramid of energy for this grassland for the first three trophic levels, assuming an energy loss of 90% at each level. It is not necessary to draw it to scale.   (3)

6 Outline the role of variation in evolution.   (3)

7 Outline **three** factors that cause the transitional phase in the growth of a population.   (3)

8 Phenologists are biologists who study the timing of seasonal activities in animals and plants, such as the opening of tree leaves and the laying of eggs by birds. Data such as these can provide evidence of climate changes, including global warming.

The date in the spring when new leaves open on horse chestnut trees (*Aesculus hippocastaneum*) has been recorded in Germany every year since 1951. The graph below shows the difference between each year's date of leaf opening and the mean date of leaf opening between 1970 and 2000. Negative values indicate that the date of leaf opening was earlier than the mean. The graph also shows the difference between each year's mean temperature during March and April and the overall mean temperature for these two months. The data for temperature were obtained from the records of thirty-five German climate stations.

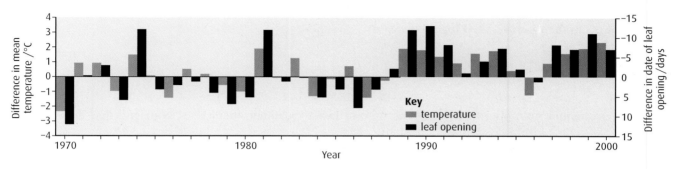

source: Walther *et al.*, *Nature* (2002), **416**, pages 389–395

a Identify the year in which there was the:
  i earliest opening of horse chestnut leaves (1)
  ii lowest mean temperature in March and April (1)

b Use the data in the graph to deduce the following:
  i the relationship between temperatures in March and April and the date of opening of leaves on horse chestnut trees (1)
  ii whether there is evidence of global warming towards the end of the 20th century (2)

From 1973 onwards, phenologists in the Netherlands have been studying a population of great tits (*Parus major*) in a forest on the Hoge Veluwe. Nest boxes are checked every week to find out when the great tits lay their eggs and how many eggs they lay. Young birds are ringed when they are seven days old, to allow the reproductive success of their parents to be monitored. Great tits feed on arthropods, especially caterpillars. The phenologists found that the date of maximum caterpillar biomass each year in the forest could be estimated accurately using temperature records. The graphs below show the mean date of egg laying and the estimated date of maximum caterpillar biomass for each year from 1973 to 1995.

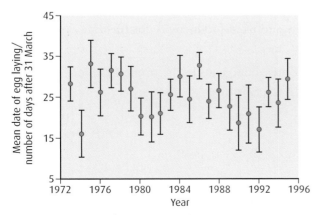
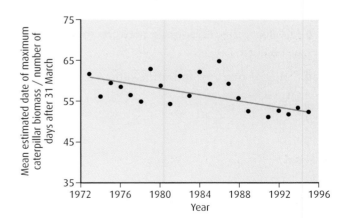

source: Visser, Noordwijk, Tinbergen and Lessells, *Proceedings of the Royal Society of London*, (1998), **265**, pages 1867–1870

c i Compare the date of egg laying with the date of maximum caterpillar biomass. (1)

　　ii Suggest an advantage to great tits of the difference in dates. (1)

d State the trend, shown in the graph, for the date of maximum caterpillar biomass. (1)

There was no statistically significant change in the date of egg laying between 1973 and 1995, but the phenologists found evidence that natural selection will eventually cause a change in the date of egg laying.

e Explain how natural selection could cause a change in the date of egg laying in the population of great tits in the forest on the Hoge Veluwe. (2)

(total 10 marks)

© IB Organization 2009

9 Ecosystems require an input of energy, water and nutrients to maintain themselves. Nutrients may be re-used through recycling within ecosystems.

Nutrient cycling within an ecosystem has been studied in many types of region. One factor studied is the mean residence time (MRT), which is the amount of time needed for one cycle of decomposition (from absorption by organism to release after death). The table below gives the mean residence time for certain nutrients in four different types of region. In addition, the plant productivity is also shown. (Plant productivity gives an indication of the quantity of plant material potentially available to consumers.)

Type of region	Mean residence time / years						Plant productivity/ $g\,cm^{-2}\,y^{-1}$
	Carbon	Nitrogen	Phosphorus	Potassium	Calcium	Magnesium	
sub-arctic forest	353.0	230.0	324.0	94.0	149.0	455.0	360
temperate forest	4.0	5.5	5.8	1.3	3.0	3.4	540
chaparral	3.8	4.2	3.6	1.4	5.0	2.8	270
tropical rainforest	0.4	2.0	1.6	0.7	1.5	1.1	900

source: W H Schlesinger (1991), in M Bush, *Ecology of a Changing Planet* (1997), Prentice Hall, page 67

a i State which nutrient shows the shortest mean residence time in a temperate forest. (1)

　　ii Identify the type of region in which potassium has the longest mean residence time. (1)

b Compare the mean residence time for nutrients in the temperate forest and chaparral. (2)

c Evaluate the relationship between the mean residence time and plant productivity for the different types of habitat. (2)

d Suggest **one** reason for the difference in mean residence time of nutrients in the tropical rainforest and the sub-arctic forest. (1)

(total 7 marks)

© IB Organization 2009

10 The graph below shows the variation in the concentration of atmospheric carbon dioxide since 1970.

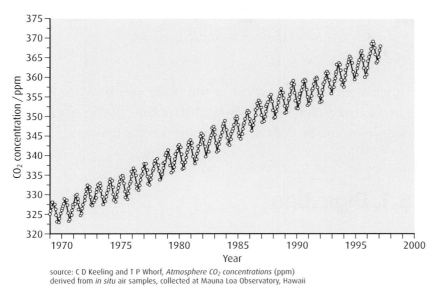

source: C D Keeling and T P Whorf, *Atmosphere CO₂ concentrations* (ppm)
derived from *in situ* air samples, collected at Mauna Loa Observatory, Hawaii

The annual fluctuation is mainly the result of changes in the levels of photosynthesis associated with the seasons in Northern Hemisphere forests.

a **i** Describe the overall trend shown in the graph. (1)

   ii Suggest a cause for the overall trend throughout the period 1970–1999. (1)

b **i** Using a clear label, identify any **one** point on the graph which shows the CO_2 level in mid-summer. (1)

   ii Explain why the concentration of CO_2 varies with the seasons. (2)

c Identify **one** gas, other than CO_2, which is contributing to the enhanced greenhouse effect. (1)

(total 6 marks)
© IB Organization 2009

6 Human health and physiology I

Introduction

Human physiology is the study of the organs and organ systems of the body and how they interact to keep us alive. Physiologists examine anatomy, which is the physical structure of the organs, and investigate the biochemical processes occurring inside cells and tissues to keep our organs working efficiently.

6.1 Digestion

Assessment statements

- Explain why the digestion of large food molecules is essential.
- Explain the need for enzymes in digestion.
- State the source, substrate, products and optimum pH conditions for one amylase, one protease and one lipase.
- Draw and label a diagram of the digestive system.
- Outline the function of the stomach, small intestine and large intestine.
- Distinguish between 'absorption' and 'assimilation'.
- Explain how the structure of the villus is related to its role in absorption and transport of the products of digestion.

Ingestion the act of eating

Digestion a series of biochemical reactions that converts large ingested molecules into small, soluble molecules

Why is digestion necessary?

When we eat, we take in food consisting of large, complex organic molecules, which are not suitable to be used as they are. Large molecules cannot pass through membranes to enter the cells that line the intestine or pass on into the bloodstream. **Digestion** is the biochemical breakdown of large, insoluble food molecules into small, soluble molecules. This process is essential because only small molecules can enter cells and be used in the body. Molecules produced by digestion pass through the wall of the intestine by diffusion, facilitated diffusion or active transport. They enter the bloodstream and travel to the cells, where they are reassembled into new structures.

Three main types of food molecule that must be digested are carbohydrates, proteins and lipids. Table **6.1** shows how these molecules are **ingested** and what is produced when they are digested.

Type of molecule	Form of the molecule in ingested food	Products of digestion
carbohydrates	monosaccharides, disaccharides, polysaccharides	monosaccharides (for example, glucose)
proteins	proteins	amino acids
lipids	triglycerides	fatty acids and glycerol
nucleic acids	DNA, RNA	nucleotides

Table 6.1 Large food molecules are broken down in digestion, into the small molecules of which they are made.

Digestion of large molecules occurs very slowly at body temperature. **Enzymes** are essential to speed up the rate of digestion so that it is fast enough to process nutrients to supply our needs.

There are many different enzymes in the human digestive system. Different enzymes are released in different sections of the digestive system and each one is specific for one food type. Some enzymes are specific to the different carbohydrates that we eat, and others work one after another to digest foods such as proteins in a series of stages. All digestive enzymes help to catalyse hydrolysis reactions (Figure **6.1**) and work most efficiently at about 37 °C. Examples of some important enzymes are shown in Table **6.2**.

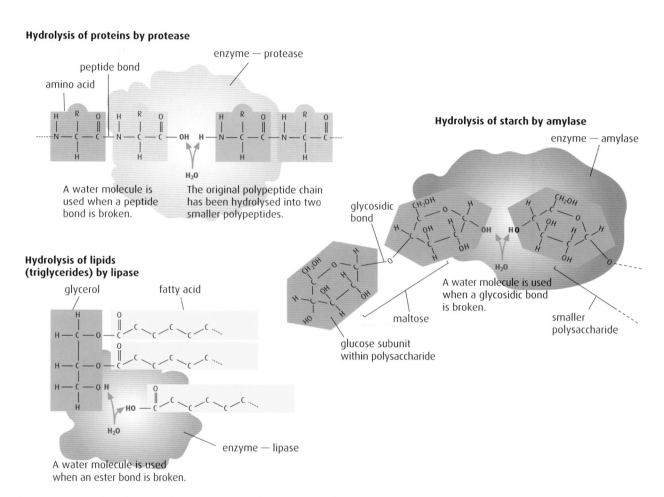

Figure 6.1 Chemical digestion involves hydrolysis to break the links between the subunits of the large molecules. You can refer back to the process of hydrolysis in Chapter **3**.

Enzyme type	Example	Source	Substrate	Products	Optimum pH
amylase	salivary amylase	salivary glands	starch	maltose	7
protease	pepsin	gastric glands in stomach wall	protein	polypeptides	2
lipase	pancreatic lipase	pancreas	triglycerides (fats and oils)	fatty acids and glycerol	7

Table 6.2 Different types of enzyme digest different types of food molecule.

The digestive system

The **digestive system** consists of a long, muscular tube, also called the gut or **alimentary canal** (Figure **6.2**). Associated with it are a number of glands that secrete enzymes and other digestive juices. The gut extends from the mouth to the anus and is specialised for the movement, digestion and absorption of food.

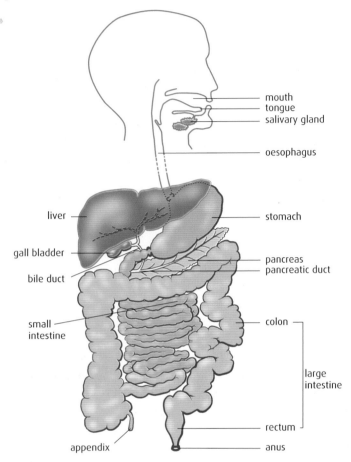

Figure 6.2 The human digestive system.

Mouth, oesophagus and stomach

In the mouth, food is broken into small pieces by the jaws and teeth, and mixed with saliva containing the enzyme salivary amylase, which begins the digestion of any starch the food contains.

The food is then passed down the oesophagus to the stomach by a sequence of muscle contractions known as peristalsis. The stomach is a muscular sac that holds the food for up to four hours while digestion proceeds inside it. As muscles of the stomach contract, food and enzymes are mixed — this gives maximum contact between food and enzyme molecules, and speeds up the digestive process.

Digestion of protein begins here, catalysed by the enzyme pepsin, which is secreted in gastric juice produced by millions of gastric glands in the stomach wall. Gastric juice contains pepsin in an inactive form.

Hydrochloric acid activates the pepsin and maintains a pH of 1.5–2.0 in the stomach. This pH is the optimum for protein digestion and also kills many of the bacteria present in the food we eat. Goblet cells in the stomach lining secrete mucus to protect the interior of the stomach from the acid and enzymes, which might otherwise digest it.

Food is transformed in the stomach to a semi–liquid called chyme and is then ready to move on to the next stage of digestion in the small intestine.

Roles of the small intestine

Little by little, chyme leaves the stomach via a valve at the lower end and moves into the five-metre long small intestine. Digestion is completed in the first section of the small intestine, (Figure **6.2**). Digestive juices are secreted from the liver, gall bladder, pancreas and the intestine walls. Bile is added from the liver and gall bladder, and the pancreas secretes pancreatic juice containing trypsin (a protease), lipase, amylase and bicarbonate ions. The acidity of the chyme is reduced by these ions, allowing the enzymes to work at their optimum pH.

The inner surface of the small intestine is greatly folded to form thousands of tiny **villi** (Figure **6.3**, overleaf). Each **villus** contains a network of capillaries and a lacteal. (A lacteal is a small vessel of the lymphatic system.) Villi greatly increase the surface area of the small intestine and improve its efficiency as an absorbing surface. As small molecules such as glucose, amino acids, fatty acids and glycerol, come into contact with a villus, they are **absorbed**, either passively or by active transport, into the single layer of epithelial cells that cover it. Amino acids and glucose then enter the capillaries and are carried away in the bloodstream. Fatty acids and glycerol are taken into the lacteal and travel in the lymphatic system.

After digested food has been absorbed, it is **assimilated** into the body and enters cells to become part of the body's tissues or reserves. Glucose is transported to the liver, which maintains a constant level of blood sugar. Amino acids form part of the reserve of amino acids used to build new proteins in cells all over the body, and fatty acids and glycerol enter the bloodstream from lymph vessels near the heart to be used as an energy source or to build larger molecules.

Absorption the process by which small molecules are taken through the cells of the intestine and pass into the bloodstream
Assimilation the process by which products of digestion are used or stored by body cells

Role of the large intestine

By the time food reaches the end of the small intestine, most useful substances have been removed from it. Any remaining undigested material passes into the large intestine, which also contains mucus, dead cells from the intestine lining and large numbers of naturally occurring bacteria. Bacteria living here are **mutualistic** organisms, gaining nutrients and a suitable habitat, while synthesising vitamin K for the benefit of their human host.

The main role of the large intestine is reabsorbing water and mineral ions such as sodium (Na^+) and chloride (Cl^-). Water in the gut contents comes not only from our diet, but also from the many additional litres that are added to the intestine in digestive juices. What remains of the original food is now referred to as **faeces** and is **egested**, or eliminated from the body, via the anus.

Egestion the process by which undigested material leaves the body at the end of the gut

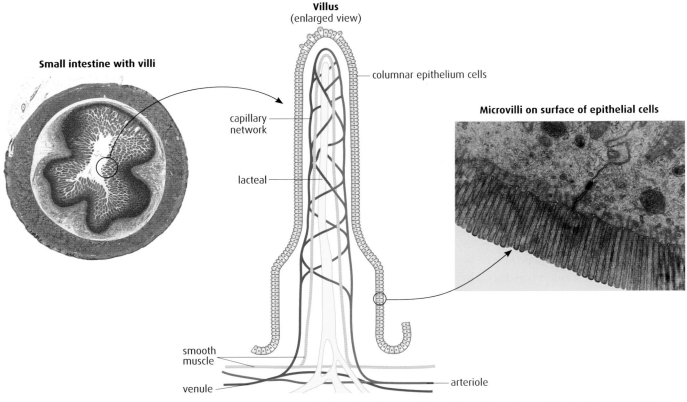

Villus
(enlarged view)

Small intestine with villi

columnar epithelium cells

capillary network

lacteal

Microvilli on surface of epithelial cells

smooth muscle

venule

arteriole

Figure 6.3 The inner surface of the small intestine is highly folded, with millions of finger-like villi. Each epithelial cell is covered in minute microvilli, so the total surface area for absorption is vast.

1 List the reasons why digestion is essential.

2 Distinguish between 'absorption' and 'assimilation'.

3 State why enzymes are needed in digestion.

4 List the ways in which a villus is adapted to increase the efficiency of absorption of nutrients.

6.2 The transport system

Assessment statements

- Draw and label a diagram of the heart showing the four chambers, associated blood vessels, valves and the route of blood through the heart.
- State that coronary arteries supply the heart muscle with oxygen and nutrients.
- Explain the action of the heart in terms of collecting blood, pumping blood and opening and closing of valves.
- Outline the control of the heart beat in terms of myogenic muscle contraction, the role of the pacemaker, nerves, the medulla of the brain and adrenalin (epinephrine).
- Explain the relationship between the structure and function of arteries, capillaries and veins.
- State that blood is composed of plasma, erythrocytes, leucocytes (phagocytes and lymphocytes) and platelets.
- State that the following are transported by the blood: nutrients, oxygen, carbon dioxide, hormones, antibodies, urea and heat.

Our **circulatory system** provides a delivery and collection service for the whole body. The heart, blood and blood vessels make up a most efficient transport system that reaches all cells, bringing the substances they need and taking away their waste. Humans and other mammals have what is known as a closed circulatory system with blood contained inside a network of arteries, veins and capillaries.

The human heart

In the human circulatory system, blood is kept on the move by the pumping action of the powerful heart muscle. It has been estimated that a normal human heart beats more than 2.5×10^9 times in a lifetime, sending a total of more than 1.5 million litres of blood from each ventricle.

A human heart is about the size of a clenched fist. It is double pump with two separate sides (Figure **6.4**). The right-hand side receives deoxygenated blood from all over the body and pumps it to the lungs to pick up more oxygen. The left-hand side receives oxygenated blood from the lungs and pumps it to cells all over the body where the oxygen is unloaded. On any complete journey round the body, blood will pass through the heart twice.

The heart has four chambers – two smaller **atria** (singular **atrium**) at the top and two larger **ventricles** below. The right- and left-hand sides are completely separated from one another. Atria have thin walls as the blood they receive from the veins is under relatively low pressure. Ventricles are stronger and more muscular as their job is to pump blood out of the heart. Both ventricles hold the same volume of blood but the left ventricle wall is thicker than the right as it must generate enough pressure to pump blood all round the body. The right ventricle pumps blood a much shorter distance to the lungs.

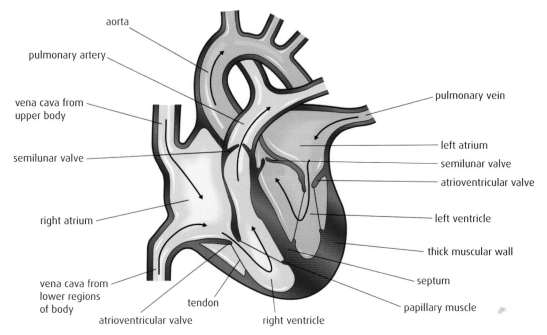

Figure 6.4 Diagram of the human heart, in longitudinal section, showing the direction of blood flow.

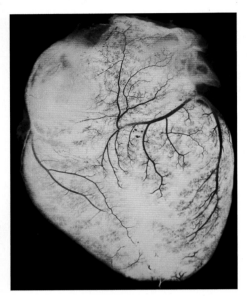

Figure 6.5 A human heart. Clearly visible are the coronary arteries, which supply oxygen to the heart muscle.

Cardiac muscle will contract rhythmically in tissue culture if it is supplied with oxygen and glucose. Its normal resting rate in culture is about 50 beats per minute.

Sympathetic and parasympathetic nerves

Sympathetic and parasympathetic nerves are part of the autonomic nervous system, which controls activities, such as heart rate, that are not under our conscious control.

Atria are separated from ventricles by **atrioventricular valves**, which prevent the blood flowing backwards into the atria. A second set of valves in the aorta and pulmonary arteries – the **semilunar valves** – prevent backflow into the ventricles as they relax after a contraction.

Heart muscle works continuously, beating about 75 times per minute when a person is resting, and so it has a large demand for oxygen. Coronary arteries extend over the surface of the heart and penetrate deep into the muscle fibres to supply oxygen and nutrients for this unremitting activity (Figure **6.5**).

The cardiac cycle

The **cardiac cycle** is the sequence of events that takes place during one heart beat (Figure **6.6** overleaf). As the heart's chambers contract, blood inside them is forced on its way. Valves in the heart and arteries stop the blood flowing backwards.

Control of the heart beat

Heart tissue is made of a special type of muscle that is different from other muscles in our bodies. **Cardiac muscle** is unique because it contracts and relaxes without stimulation from the nervous system. It is said to be **myogenic**. Natural myogenic contractions are initiated at an inbuilt pacemaker, which keeps cardiac muscle working in a coordinated, controlled sequence. The pacemaker, or **sinoatrial node** (SAN), is special region of muscle cells in the right atrium that sets the basic pace of the heart. The rate set by the SAN is also influenced by stimulation from the nervous system and by hormones.

At the start of every heart beat, the SAN produces an impulse that stimulates both atria to contract. A second structure, the **atrioventricular node** (AVN) at the base of the right atrium, is also stimulated. It delays the impulse briefly until the atrial contraction finishes and then transmits it on down a bundle of modified muscle fibres – the bundle of His and Purkinje fibres – to the base of the ventricles. Impulses radiate up through the ventricles, which contract simultaneously about 0.1 seconds after the atria.

The natural rhythm of the pacemaker is modulated by the nervous system so that the heart rate is adjusted to our activity levels. It speeds up when we are exercising and need extra oxygen and nutrients, and slows down as we sleep. Changes to our heart rate are not under our conscious control but result from impulses sent from a control centre in the part of the brain stem known as the medulla. Impulses to speed up the heart pass along the sympathetic nerve, which stimulates the pacemaker to increase its rate. Impulses sent along the parasympathetic (vagus) nerve cause the heart rate to slow down. The medulla monitors blood pressure and carbon dioxide levels using information it receives from receptors in arteries.

Emotions such as stress, as well as increases in activity level, can cause an increase in heart rate. During periods of excitement, fear or stress the adrenal glands release the hormone **adrenalin**, which travels in the blood to the pacemaker and stimulates it to increase the heart rate.

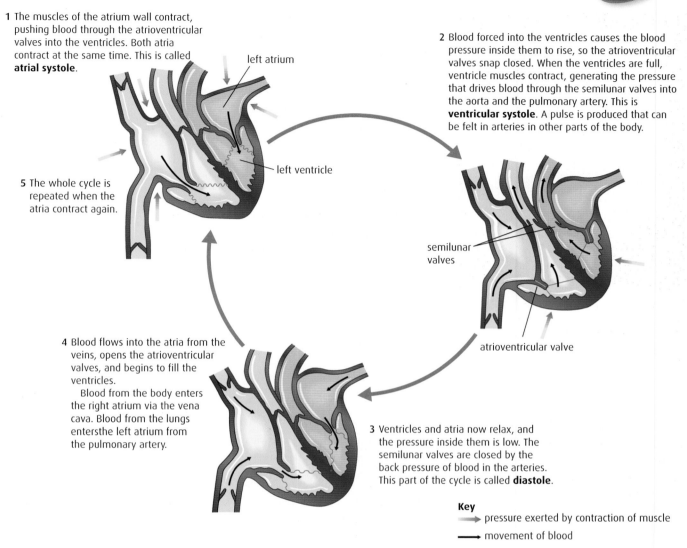

1 The muscles of the atrium wall contract, pushing blood through the atrioventricular valves into the ventricles. Both atria contract at the same time. This is called **atrial systole**.

left atrium

left ventricle

5 The whole cycle is repeated when the atria contract again.

2 Blood forced into the ventricles causes the blood pressure inside them to rise, so the atrioventricular valves snap closed. When the ventricles are full, ventricle muscles contract, generating the pressure that drives blood through the semilunar valves into the aorta and the pulmonary artery. This is **ventricular systole**. A pulse is produced that can be felt in arteries in other parts of the body.

semilunar valves

atrioventricular valve

4 Blood flows into the atria from the veins, opens the atrioventricular valves, and begins to fill the ventricles.
Blood from the body enters the right atrium via the vena cava. Blood from the lungs entersthe left atrium from the pulmonary artery.

3 Ventricles and atria now relax, and the pressure inside them is low. The semilunar valves are closed by the back pressure of blood in the arteries. This part of the cycle is called **diastole**.

Key
→ pressure exerted by contraction of muscle
→ movement of blood

Figure 6.6 The events of a heart beat – the cardiac cycle. The heart normally beats about 75 times per minute, and a complete heart beat takes about 0.8 seconds.

Blood and blood vessels

Arteries are blood vessels that carry blood away from the heart. They branch and divide many times forming **arterioles** and eventually the tiny capillaries that reach all our tissues. Arteries have thick outer walls of collagen and elastic fibres (Figure **6.7**, overleaf), which withstand high blood pressure and prevent vessels becoming overstretched or bursting. Just beneath the outer covering is a ring of circular smooth muscle that contracts with each heart beat to maintain blood pressure and keep blood moving along. Inside an artery, the lumen is narrow to keep blood pressure high. The lumen's lining of smooth epithelial cells reduces friction and keeps blood flowing smoothly.

Capillaries are the smallest vessels – the lumen of a capillary is only about 10 μm in diameter and some are so small that red blood cells must fold up in order to pass along. Networks of these tiny capillaries reach

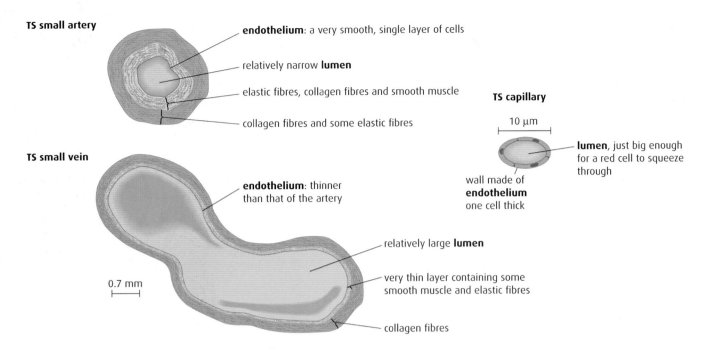

Figure 6.7 The structure of arteries, veins and capillaries.

Plasma that leaks out of tiny capillaries bathes the nearby tissues and supplies oxygen and nutrients to the cells. Once out of the capillary, the fluid is known as **tissue fluid**.

Lymphatic system

The lymphatic system collects tissue fluid that leaks from the capillaries and returns it to the large veins close to the heart.

almost every body cell. Blood flow here is very slow, at less than 1 mm per second, but capillary walls are only one cell thick so the distance for diffusion of materials in and out of them is as small as possible. Some capillaries have spaces between their cells enabling plasma and phagocytes to leak out into the tissues.

Veins carry blood back towards the heart from body tissues. Small veins called venules join up to form large veins, which can be distinguished from arteries by their much thinner walls, which contain few elastic and muscle fibres. Blood inside a vein does not pulse along and the lumen is large to hold the slow-moving flow. The relatively thin walls can be compressed by adjacent muscles and this helps to squeeze blood along and keep it moving. Many veins contain valves to prevent blood flowing backwards, a problem which can arise if flow is sluggish.

Table **6.3** summarises the differences and similarities between the three types of blood vessel.

Artery	Vein	Capillary
thick walls	thin walls	walls one cell thick
no valves	valves present	no valves
blood pressure high	blood pressure low	blood pressure low
carry blood from the heart	carry blood to the heart	link small arteries to small veins

Table 6.3 Comparing arteries, veins and capillaries.

Composition of blood

Blood **plasma** is a pale yellow liquid that makes up 50–60% of our blood volume. Suspended in plasma are three important groups of cells:

- **erythrocytes** (red blood cells), whose job is to carry oxygen
- **leucocytes** (white blood cells), which fight disease
- **platelets** (cell fragments), which are needed for blood clotting

Figure **6.8** shows the appearance of blood when examined under a light microscope.

Functions of blood

Blood has two important roles: it is a vital part of the body's transport network, carrying dissolved materials to all cells, and it helps to fight infectious disease. Table **6.4** (overleaf) summarises the important substances the blood carries. Its role in infection control will be explored in the next section.

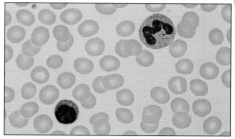

Figure 6.8 Light micrograph of a smear of healthy human blood. Two types of leucocyte can be seen – a lymphocyte (lower left) and a phagocyte (upper right). Lymphocytes produce antibodies, and phagocytes engulf foreign particles, including bacteria, that enter the body. Many erythrocytes can also be seen.

William Harvey (1578–1657)

Harvey, an English physician, is widely acknowledged as being the first man to describe accurately how blood flows in a continuous circulation round the body. Before Harvey, few people questioned the classical writings of authors such as Aristotle (384–322 BC), Hippocrates (460–c.370 BC) and Galen (AD c.130–c.200). Galen believed that two types of blood existed. Darker, venous blood formed in the liver and red, arterial blood flowed from the heart. Blood was thought to be 'consumed' by different organs and converted to 'vital spirits' in the lungs. Harvey was unwilling to believe this doctrine and sought evidence to produce and support his own theories. He carefully recorded all his observations and carried out dissections on which to base his conclusions. He calculated the volume of blood that might pass through the heart in one day to disprove Galen's suppositions. In his famous publication, *Exercitatio Anatomica de Motu Cordis et Sanguinis in Animalibus* ('*An Anatomical Study of the Motion of the Heart and of the Blood in Animals*') in 1628, Harvey proposed that blood circulated in two separate, closed circuits. Illustrations in the book also showed his demonstration of the existence and function of valves in veins.

Sir William Osler (1849–1919), a famous Canadian physician, later wrote of Harvey's book:

> '*It marks the break of the modern spirit with the old traditions … here for the first time a great physiological problem was approached from the experimental side by a man with a modern scientific mind, who could weigh evidence and not go beyond it …*'

Questions to consider

1 Why did people in the 1600s still believe writings of Greek and Roman authors from more than 1400 years earlier?

2 Harvey proposed the existence of capillaries but was never able to prove his theory. Why not?

3 Harvey would not accept doctrines without evidence. Can doctrines ever be accepted if the evidence is provided by authority?

4 21 years after the original publication of his book, Harvey produced a volume of responses to those who had made comments and criticisms of it. Why was this important?

5 What did Osler mean by the phrase 'a modern scientific mind'? How could this be defined today?

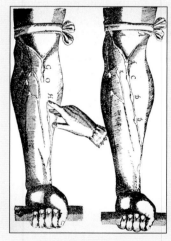

A woodcut from William Harvey's book, showing the veins in the forearm.

Substance transported	Source and destination
nutrients	glucose, amino acids, vitamins and minerals carried in plasma from the small intestine to the cells
oxygen	carried by red blood cells from the lungs to all tissues
carbon dioxide	returned to the lungs in plasma and red blood cells from all respiring tissues
urea	carried in plasma from cells to the kidneys for disposal
hormones	transported in plasma from glands to target cells
antibodies	protein molecules produced by certain lymphocytes to fight infection and distributed in plasma
heat	distributed from warm areas to cooler ones to maintain core temperature

Table 6.4 Some important substances that are transported by the blood.

5 List the structures on the route taken by a red blood cell on a journey from the vena cava to the aorta. Name all the chambers of the heart, valves and blood vessels it passes through.

6 List **five** substances that are carried around the body in blood plasma.

7 Explain why arteries have thicker walls than veins.

8 State **two** reasons why the heart rate increases when we exercise.

9 List the major components of the blood.

6.3 Defence against infectious disease

Assessment statements

- Define 'pathogen'.
- Explain why antibiotics are effective against bacteria but not against viruses.
- Outline the role of the skin and mucous membranes in defence against pathogens.
- Outline how phagocytic leucocytes ingest pathogens in the blood and in body tissues.
- Distinguish between 'antigens' and 'antibodies'.
- Explain antibody production.
- Outline the effects of HIV on the immune system.
- Discuss the cause, transmission and social implications of AIDS.

Pathogens cause disease

A **pathogen** is a living organism or virus that invades the body and causes disease. Most pathogens are bacteria and viruses (Figure **6.9**), but protozoa, parasitic worms and fungi can also be pathogenic.

Relatively few bacteria and fungi are pathogens, but no virus can function outside the cell of its host organism so all viruses have the potential to be pathogenic. A virus takes over the nucleic acid and protein synthesis mechanisms of its host cell and directs them to make more viruses.

Antibiotics

Most bacterial infections can be treated with **antibiotics**. Antibiotics are natural substances that slow the growth of bacteria. Since the discovery of penicillin in 1928, many antibiotics have been isolated and about 50 are now manufactured for medical use. These antibiotics work in different ways but are effective because prokaryotic and eukaryotic cells have different metabolic pathways. Some antibiotics block the protein synthesis mechanism in bacteria while not affecting the process in human cells. Others interfere with the formation of the bacterial cell wall and prevent bacteria growing and dividing.

Viruses are not living and have no metabolic pathways of their own. Since they use their human host's metabolism to build new viruses, antibiotics have no effect against viral infections.

The body's first line of defence

Despite the fact that we come into contact with many pathogens every day, we are seldom ill. This is due to our effective **immune system**, which both prevents pathogens entering the body and also deals with any that do.

The first line of defence against infection is our skin. Unbroken skin is a tough barrier to any potential invaders. It is waterproof and its secretions repel bacteria. Openings in the skin, such as eyes and nose, can provide entry points for pathogens but these are protected by various secretions. Tears, mucus and saliva all contain the enzyme lysozyme, which attacks the cell walls of bacteria. If pathogens are swallowed in food or water, the acidic environment of the stomach helps to kill them.

Pathogens that do enter the body are soon recognised by phagocytic leucocytes, which form a vital part of the body's immune system. These specialised white blood cells circulate in the blood system and, because they are easily able to change their shape, can also squeeze in and out of capillaries. Phagocytic leucocytes respond to invaders by engulfing and destroying them in a process called phagocytosis (Figure **6.10**).

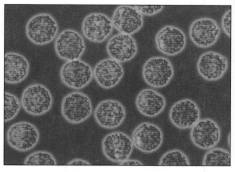

Figure 6.9 Coloured TEM of hepatitis B viruses (×200 000).

Prions

In recent years, new infectious particles called prions have been discovered. Prions do not contain nucleic acid. Prions are proteins that convert normal proteins into infectious prion proteins. They are not destroyed by normal sterilisation techniques and have been spread on surgical instruments and in contaminated meat. Prion diseases include scrapie in sheep, bovine spongiform encephalopathy (BSE) in cattle, variant Creutzfeldt–Jacob disease (discovered in 1996) and kuru in humans. Prions are produced by mutations in genes coding for a cell protein called PrP.

1 Phagocytic leucocyte detects a bacterium and moves towards it. The bacterium attaches to receptors on the cell's plasma membrane.

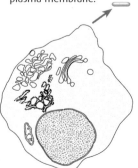

2 Bacterium is engulfed by phagocytosis into a vacuole.

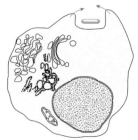

3 Lysosomes inside the cell fuse with the vacuole and release hydrolytic enzymes.

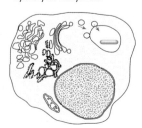

4 Bacterium is destroyed, and any chemicals that are not absorbed into the cell are egested.

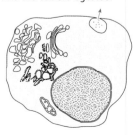

Figure 6.10 Phagocytosis of a pathogen.

Questions to consider

1 **Inductive reasoning** is a method of thinking that involves using a set of specific facts to come to a general conclusion. Was the discovery of penicillin an example of inductive reasoning? If not, why not?

2 Why did the discovery of penicillin have such a profound effect on people at the time?

3 Why was the collaboration of three scientists vital to the discovery of penicillin?

4 What are the ethical issues involved in using a new drug for the first time? Was Fletcher right to use penicillin on his patient?

Alexander Fleming.

Inductive reasoning and collaboration

The discovery of antibiotics began by accident. On 3 September 1928, Professor Alexander Fleming was examining a batch of culture plates on which he had grown *Staphylococcus* bacteria. He noticed that one of the plates had a green mould growing on it. The mould was *Penicillium notatum*. The mould was circular in shape, and the area around it seemed to be free of *Staphylococcus*. On other areas of the plate, the bacteria were continuing to grow well. Fleming deduced that the bacteria around the circular mould had been killed off by a substance produced by the mould.

Fleming discovered that the mould could kill other bacteria and that it could be given to small animals without any harmful effects. However, he moved onto other research and it was not until ten years later that Howard Florey and Ernst Chain, working at Oxford University, isolated the bacteria-killing substance, penicillin, produced by the mould. Chain was a German chemist and Florey an Australian pathologist. It was Chain who isolated and purified penicillin and Florey who tested its safety to use on animals and humans.

One of the first uses of penicillin was in 1941, when Dr Charles Fletcher gave it to patient at a hospital in Oxford who was near to death as a result of bacterial infection in a wound. Fletcher used some penicillin on the patient and the wound made a spectacular recovery. Unfortunately, Fletcher did not have sufficient penicillin to clear the patient's body of bacteria and he died a few weeks later as the pathogen regained a hold.

An American brewing company began mass production of penicillin and soon sufficient was available to treat all the bacterial infections among the troops fighting in World War II. Penicillin was nicknamed 'the wonder drug' and in 1945 Fleming, Chain and Florey shared the Nobel Prize for Medicine.

Antibodies and antigens

Antigens (**anti**body **gen**erating **s**ubstances), are proteins found embedded in the plasma membranes or cell walls of bacteria or in the protein coat of a virus. These antigens enable the body to recognise a pathogen as being 'not self' – that is, not a part of the body – and they give a clear signal to switch on the immune response, with the rapid production of antibodies.

Antibodies are protein molecules that are produced in response to any antigen that enters the body. There are millions of different antibodies and each one is specific to an antigen. For example, the antibodies produced in response to infection by an influenza virus are quite different from those produced in response to a tuberculosis bacterium. Even fragments of pathogens, or their toxins, can stimulate the release of antibodies. Figure **6.11** explains how antibodies are made.

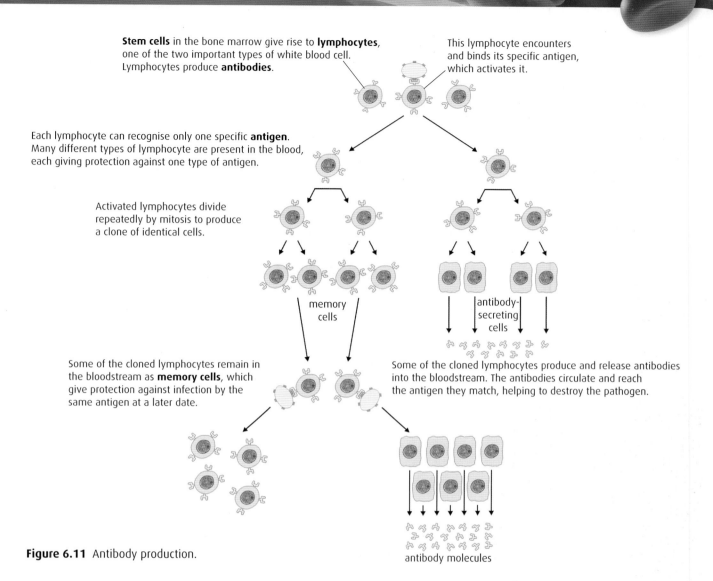

Stem cells in the bone marrow give rise to **lymphocytes**, one of the two important types of white blood cell. Lymphocytes produce **antibodies**.

This lymphocyte encounters and binds its specific antigen, which activates it.

Each lymphocyte can recognise only one specific **antigen**. Many different types of lymphocyte are present in the blood, each giving protection against one type of antigen.

Activated lymphocytes divide repeatedly by mitosis to produce a clone of identical cells.

memory cells

antibody-secreting cells

Some of the cloned lymphocytes remain in the bloodstream as **memory cells**, which give protection against infection by the same antigen at a later date.

Some of the cloned lymphocytes produce and release antibodies into the bloodstream. The antibodies circulate and reach the antigen they match, helping to destroy the pathogen.

antibody molecules

Figure 6.11 Antibody production.

Each antibody molecule has a basic Y shape but at the tops of the Y, specific binding sites give every antibody its unique properties (Figure **6.12**). These specific binding sites attach to the corresponding antigen site on the surface of the pathogen or its toxin. Once an antibody has bound to an antigen, it can destroy it in one of a number of ways. Some cause bacterial cells to clump together, making the job of phagocytes easier. Others cause cell walls to rupture, deactivate toxins, or act as recognition signals for phagocytes, giving a clear indication that action is needed (Figure **6.13**, overleaf).

HIV and AIDS

Human immunodeficiency virus (HIV, Figure **6.14**, overleaf), first identified in the early 1980s, causes the series of symptoms together known as acquired immune deficiency syndrome, or AIDS. HIV infects only the helper T-cells, a type of lymphocyte that is important in maintaining communication between cells of the immune system. After a latent period of months or years, helper T-cells are gradually destroyed and, as their

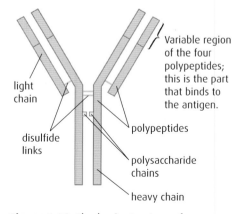

light chain

disulfide links

Variable region of the four polypeptides; this is the part that binds to the antigen.

polypeptides

polysaccharide chains

heavy chain

Figure 6.12 The basic structure of an antibody molecule.

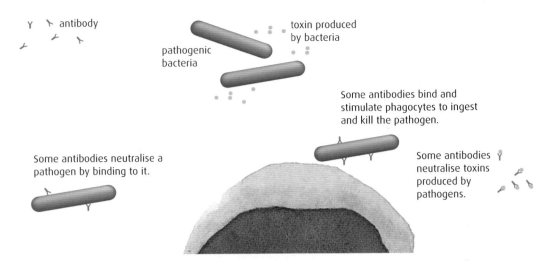

Figure 6.13 The various ways in which different antibodies can destroy bacteria or their toxins.

numbers fall, so does the body's ability to fight infection. Helper T-cells instruct other lymphocytes to clone and generate antibodies, and without them an infected person can no longer fight off pathogens. Secondary infections result and the person is said to be suffering from AIDS.

Cause, transmission and consequences of AIDS

AIDS is the end stage of an HIV infection. It is caused by a severe failure of the immune system as the HIV virus selectively infects helper T-cells. Some infected individuals have no symptoms in the early stages of the disease while others may be slightly unwell when first infected. Symptoms of AIDS develop as the number of active helper T-cells decreases. The symptoms occur as a result of secondary infections caused by bacteria, fungi and viruses that the body is unable to resist due to its compromised immune system (Figure **6.15**, overleaf).

HIV is transmitted in blood, vaginal secretions, semen, breast milk and sometimes across the placenta. In some countries, HIV has been transmitted in blood transfusions but in most places with medical care facilities, blood for

HIV is a retrovirus, which means it can insert its DNA into that of a host cell using a protein called reverse transcriptase. Even if all the viruses in the body could be removed, the T-cells would continue to make new viruses.

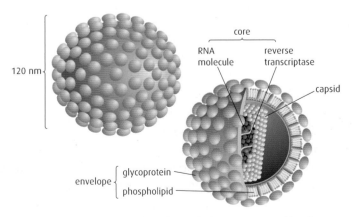

Figure 6.14 HIV viruses consist of a spherical glycoprotein and lipid coat enclosing two strands of RNA. The virus is 60 times smaller than a red blood cell.

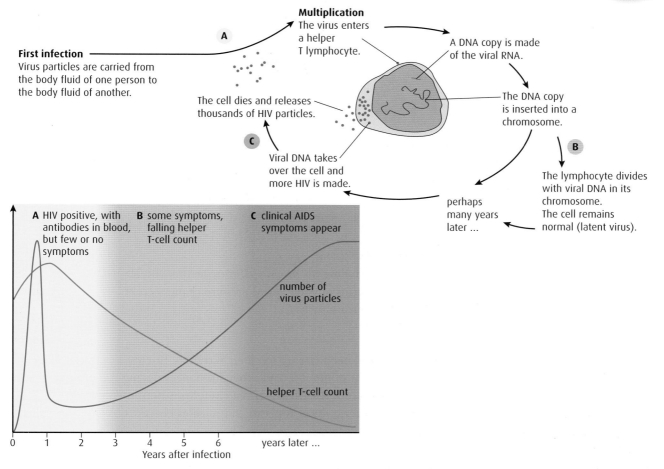

First infection
Virus particles are carried from the body fluid of one person to the body fluid of another.

A

Multiplication
The virus enters a helper T lymphocyte.

A DNA copy is made of the viral RNA.

The DNA copy is inserted into a chromosome.

B

The lymphocyte divides with viral DNA in its chromosome. The cell remains normal (latent virus).

perhaps many years later ...

C

The cell dies and releases thousands of HIV particles.

Viral DNA takes over the cell and more HIV is made.

A HIV positive, with antibodies in blood, but few or no symptoms

B some symptoms, falling helper T-cell count

C clinical AIDS symptoms appear

number of virus particles

helper T-cell count

0 1 2 3 4 5 6 years later ...
Years after infection

Figure 6.15 HIV infection proceeds through three stages – HIV positive with few symptoms, some symptoms and low helper T-cell count, and clinical AIDS with associated symptoms.

transfusion is now screened for the virus. The virus is most frequently passed from person to person in bodily fluids during sex and also when non-sterile syringe needles are used to administer either legal or illegal drugs.

AIDS used to be thought of as a disease that affected only drug abusers and homosexuals but it is now clear that the virus is also transmitted by heterosexual sex. Transmission is most likely among individuals who engage in casual sex with multiple partners.

AIDS is a worldwide pandemic but some regions are more seriously affected than others. In 2008, the number of people living with HIV and AIDS was estimated at 25 million in sub-Sarahan Africa and almost 8 million in South and South East Asia. AIDS is the main cause of death for men and women aged between 16 and 50 years in these countries, Latin America and the Caribbean. Those who die are farmers, workers and parents, so the social and economic consequences are significant – in many communities, the elderly are left caring for children, with little support. Family incomes and national productivity decline as people of working age fall ill. Food production is affected and causes more problems. Caring for the sick and providing medical care form an expensive burden for individual families, companies and governments.

10 Define the term 'pathogen'.

11 Describe what is meant by the term 'antigen'.

12 State why helper T-cells are important in the immune response.

13 Distinguish between a 'phagocyte' and a 'lymphocyte'.

6.4 Gas exchange

Assessment statements

- Distinguish between 'ventilation', 'gas exchange' and 'cell respiration'.
- Explain the need for a ventilation system.
- Describe the features of alveoli that adapt them to gas exchange.
- Draw and label a diagram of the ventilation system, including trachea, lungs, bronchi, bronchioles and alveoli.
- Explain the mechanism of ventilation of the lungs in terms of volume and pressure changes caused by the internal and external intercostal muscles, the diaphragm and abdominal muscles.

All living cells need energy for their activities. Energy is released from the breakdown of glucose and other substances during the process of cell respiration. **Respiration** is a chemical reaction that occurs in mitochondria and the cytoplasm and releases energy as ATP, a form that can be used inside cells.

Our cells use oxygen to carry out aerobic respiration and produce carbon dioxide as a waste product. Oxygen is taken in from the air and carbon dioxide is returned to it in a passive process known as **gas exchange**. Gas exchange occurs in the alveoli of the lungs where oxygen from the air diffuses into blood capillaries, and carbon dioxide passes in the opposite direction. Gases are also exchanged in the tissues where oxygen diffuses into respiring cells and is exchanged for carbon dioxide.

Whenever diffusion occurs, there must always be a concentration gradient with a higher level of the diffusing substance in one area than in another. Air inside the alveoli contains a higher concentration of oxygen than the blood, so oxygen diffuses into the blood. Blood contains a higher level of carbon dioxide than inhaled air, so carbon dioxide diffuses into the alveoli.

For gas exchange to continue, these concentration gradients must be maintained. As oxygen diffuses out of the alveoli, the level of oxygen inside them gradually falls. Stale air must be expelled regularly and replaced with a fresh supply. This is achieved by breathing in and out, a process known as **ventilation**.

The human ventilation system

Our lungs are protected inside the thorax in an air-tight cavity formed by the ribs and diaphragm. The inside of the ribcage is lined with membranes that secrete fluid to lubricate the lungs, making them slippery and

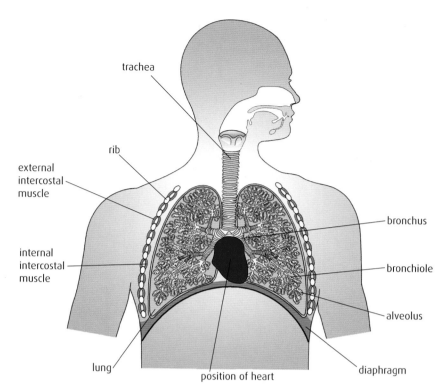

trachea

rib

external
intercostal
muscle

internal
intercostal
muscle

lung

position of heart

bronchus

bronchiole

alveolus

diaphragm

Figure 6.16 The ventilation system.

reducing friction during breathing. Air is drawn in through the nose and passes down the **trachea** to the two **bronchi** (singular **bronchus**), one of which passes to each lung (Figure **6.16**). Bronchi divide into smaller and smaller tubes, called **bronchioles**, which end in tiny air sacs or **alveoli** (singular **alveolus**). The alveoli are covered with a network of capillaries and together provide us with a very large surface area for the exchange of oxygen and carbon dioxide.

Mechanism of ventilation

Lungs have no muscles and cannot move by themselves. Breathing is brought about by two sets of **intercostal muscles** between the ribs, and by the **diaphragm**, the sheet of muscle separating the thorax from the abdomen (Figure **6.17**).

During **inhalation**, contraction of the external intercostal muscles raises the ribs and contraction of the diaphragm lowers the floor of the thorax. These movements increase the volume of the chest cavity and lower the pressure on the lungs to below that of the air outside. As a result, air is drawn down the trachea to fill the lungs.

Gentle **exhalation** occurs as the intercostal and diaphragm muscles relax, reducing the volume of the chest cavity. Elastic fibres around the alveoli return to their original length and pressure forces air out of the lungs.

Long or forced exhalations involve the internal intercostal muscles, which contract to lower the ribs. Muscles in the abdominal wall also

Blowing a trumpet

External and internal intercostal muscles are antagonistic muscles because they have opposite effects when they contract. During relaxed breathing, internal intercostal muscles do not contract, but they are used to force air out of the lungs when we sing or play a wind instrument.

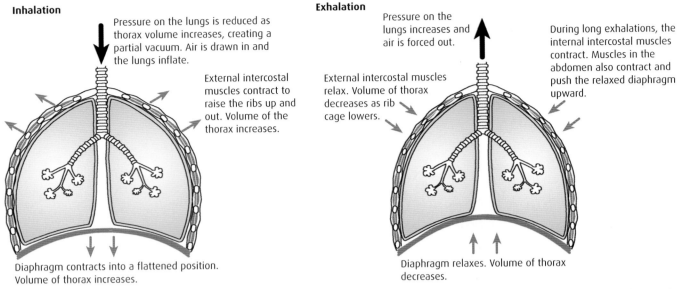

Inhalation

Pressure on the lungs is reduced as thorax volume increases, creating a partial vacuum. Air is drawn in and the lungs inflate.

External intercostal muscles contract to raise the ribs up and out. Volume of the thorax increases.

Diaphragm contracts into a flattened position. Volume of thorax increases.

Exhalation

Pressure on the lungs increases and air is forced out.

During long exhalations, the internal intercostal muscles contract. Muscles in the abdomen also contract and push the relaxed diaphragm upward.

External intercostal muscles relax. Volume of thorax decreases as rib cage lowers.

Diaphragm relaxes. Volume of thorax decreases.

Figure 6.17 The mechanism of ventilation.

contract and push the relaxed diaphragm upward. Pressure inside the chest cavity increases and air is forced out of the lungs.

Importance of alveoli

Alveoli are the body's gas exchanges surfaces. Formed in clusters at the ends of the smallest bronchioles, more than 300 million alveoli in each lung together provide a surface area of about $75\,\text{m}^2$. Alveoli are roughly spherical in shape and made of flat cells less than $5\,\mu\text{m}$ thick (Figure **6.18**). The capillaries that wrap around them also have thin walls of single epithelial cells. These two thin layers make the distance for diffusion of gases as small as possible. Oxygen diffuses through the alveolus and capillary into the blood and carbon dioxide diffuses in the opposite direction (Figure **6.19**). So long as the diffusion gradient is maintained by regular breathing, diffusion continues.

Table **6.5** summarises ways in which the alveoli are well adapted for their role in gas exchange.

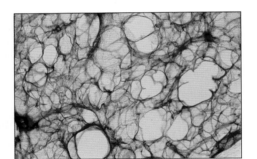

Figure 6.18 Healthy human lung tissue, showing many alveoli (×34).

Feature of alveoli	Importance
many small, spherical alveoli	provide a large area for gas exchange
thin walls of flattened single cells	short diffusion distance
rich blood supply from capillaries	maintains concentration gradient and carries absorbed gases away rapidly

Table 6.5 Adaptations of alveoli for gas exchange.

14 List the structures that a molecule of oxygen would pass on its way into an alveolus from the atmosphere.

15 List the **three** key characteristics of a gas exchange surface.

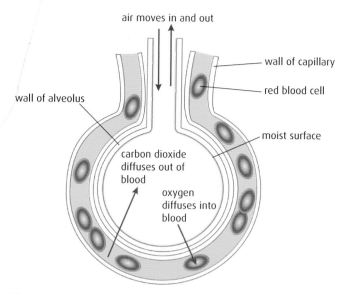

air moves in and out

wall of alveolus

wall of capillary

red blood cell

moist surface

carbon dioxide diffuses out of blood

oxygen diffuses into blood

Figure 6.19 Gas exchange in the alveolus.

16   List the muscles involved in inhalation.

17   Distinguish between 'gas exchange' and 'ventilation'.

6.5 Nerves, hormones and homeostasis

Assessment statements

- State that the nervous system consists of the central nervous system (CNS) and the peripheral nerves, and is composed of cells called neurons that can carry rapid electrical impulses.
- Draw and label the structure of a motor neuron.
- State that nerve impulses are conducted from receptors to the CNS by sensory neurons, within the CNS by relay neurons and from the CNS to effectors by motor neurons.
- Define 'resting potential' and 'action potential' (depolarisation and repolarisation).
- Explain how a nerve impulse passes along a non-myelinated neuron.
- Explain the principles of synaptic transmission.
- State that the endocrine system consists of glands that release hormones that are transported in the blood.
- State that homeostasis involves maintaining the internal environment between limits, including blood pH, carbon dioxide concentration, blood glucose concentration, body temperature and water balance.
- Explain that homeostasis involves monitoring levels of variables and correcting changes in levels by negative feedback mechanisms.
- Explain the control of body temperature, including the transfer of heat in blood and the roles of the hypothalamus, sweat glands, skin, arterioles and shivering.
- Explain the control of blood glucose concentration, including the roles of glucagon, insulin and α and β cells in the pancreatic islets.
- Distinguish between 'type I' and 'type II diabetes'.

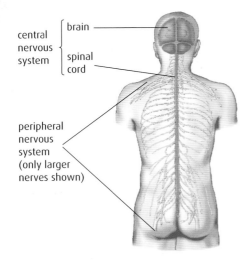

central nervous system { brain
spinal cord

peripheral nervous system (only larger nerves shown)

Figure 6.20 The human nervous system.

The human nervous system

The nervous system consists of **neurons**, or nerve cells, which transmit information in the form of nerve impulses. Figure **6.20** shows the basic layout of the human nervous system.

The **central nervous system**, or CNS, is made up of the neurons of the brain and the spinal cord. The CNS receives information from sensory receptors all over the body. Information is processed and interpreted before the CNS initiates suitable responses.

The **peripheral nerves** are the network of neurons that carry information to and from the CNS. Peripheral nerves include sensory neurons, which carry information to the CNS, and motor neurons, which transmit impulses from the CNS to muscles and glands that then cause a response.

Three types of neuron are found in the nervous system. **Sensory** and **motor neurons** transmit information to and from the CNS, while **relay neurons** within the CNS form connections between them.

The structure of a motor neuron is shown in Figure **6.21**. Many small **dendrites** receive information from relay neurons and transmit the impulses to the cell body. One long **axon** then carries impulses away. The cell body contains the nucleus and most of the cytoplasm of the cell. The axon is covered by a **myelin sheath** formed from Schwann cells, which wrap themselves around it. Myelin has a high lipid content and forms an electrical insulation layer that speeds the transmission of impulses along the axon. Along the length of the axon, junctions where two Schwann cells meet can be seen. These junctions are known as **nodes of Ranvier**.

Transmission of nerve impulses

Neurons transmit information in the form of **impulses**, which are short-lived changes in electrical potential across the membrane of a neuron. All

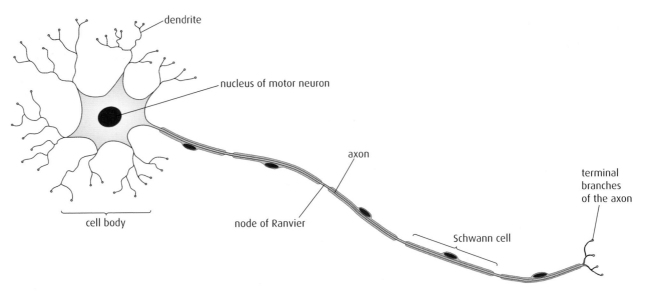

dendrite

nucleus of motor neuron

axon

terminal branches of the axon

cell body

node of Ranvier

Schwann cell

Figure 6.21 A motor neuron.

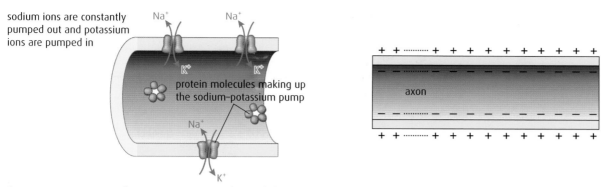

sodium ions are constantly pumped out and potassium ions are pumped in

Na⁺   Na⁺

K⁺   K⁺

protein molecules making up the sodium–potassium pump

Na⁺

K⁺

axon

Figure 6.22 At rest, sodium ions are pumped out of the neuron and potassium ions are pumped in, to establish the resting potential. Inside the neuron is negatively charged because of the presence of chloride and other negative ions.

neurons contain sodium (Na^+) and potassium (K^+) ions. Impulses occur as these important ions move in and out through the plasma membrane.

When a neuron is not transmitting an impulse, it is said to be at its **resting potential**. The resting potential is the potential difference across the plasma membrane when it is not being stimulated – for most neurons, this potential is −70 mV. The inside of the axon is negatively charged with respect to the outside (Figure **6.22**).

As a nerve impulse occurs, the distribution of charge across the membrane is reversed. For a millisecond, the membrane is said to be **depolarised**. As charge is reversed in one area of the axon, local currents depolarise the next region so that the impulse spreads along the axon (Figure **6.23**). An impulse that travels in this way is known as an **action potential**.

Figure **6.24** (overleaf) explains what is happening at the plasma membrane of the neuron as an action potential is generated.

1 When a neuron is stimulated, gated sodium channels in the membrane open and sodium ions (Na^+) from the outside flow in. They follow both the electrical gradient and the concentration gradient, together known as the electrochemical gradient, to move into the cell. The neuron is now said to be depolarised.

2 For a very brief period of time, the inside of the axon becomes positively charged with respect to the outside as sodium ions enter. At this point, the sodium channels close.

3 Now, gated potassium channels open and potassium ions (K^+) begin to leave the axon, moving down their electrochemical gradient to re-establish the resting potential, a process known as **repolarisation**.

4 Because so many potassium ions start to move, the potential difference falls below the resting potential. At this point, both sodium and potassium channels close. The resting potential is re-established by the action of sodium–potassium pumps, which move ions back to restore the resting potential.

An action potential in one part of an axon causes the depolarisation of the adjacent section of the axon. This occurs because local currents are set up between adjacent regions and these cause ion channels to open, allowing sodium ions in and potassium ions out of the axon.

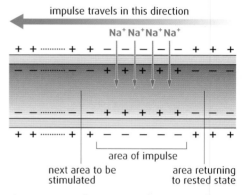

impulse travels in this direction

Na⁺ Na⁺Na⁺ Na⁺

area of impulse

next area to be stimulated

area returning to rested state

Figure 6.23 When an impulse passes along the neuron, sodium ions diffuse via ion channels and the potential is reversed. This process is called an action potential.

Resting potential the electrical potential across the plasma membrane of a neuron that is not conducting an impulse

Action potential the reversal and restoration of the resting potential across the plasma membrane of a neuron as an electrical impulse passes along it

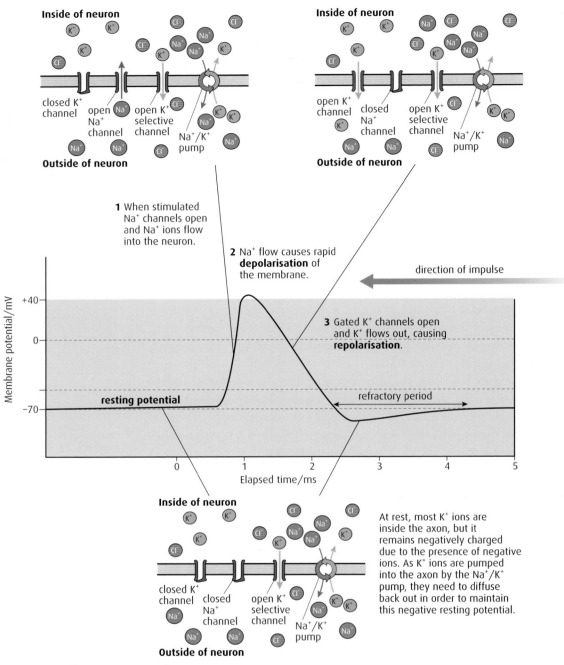

Figure 6.24 The action potential.

The action potential travels along the neuron rather like a 'Mexican wave'. The impulse can only pass in one direction because the region behind it is still in the recovery phase of the action potential and is temporarily unable to generate a new action potential. The recovery phase is known as the **refractory period**.

The synapse

A **synapse** is the place where two neurons meet. Two neurons do not touch one another and the tiny gap of about 20 nm between them is known as the **synaptic cleft**. Action potentials must be transmitted across this gap for the impulse to pass on its way and this is achieved by the presence of chemicals known as **neurotransmitters**. Neurotransmitters are held in vesicles in the pre-synaptic cell until an action potential arrives. They are then released into the synaptic cleft, and diffuse across to the post-synaptic membrane. There they can cause another action potential to be produced.

The synapse shown in Figure **6.25** uses the neurotransmitter acetylcholine (ACh) and is a cholinergic synapse. ACh binds to receptors and causes depolarisation of the post-synaptic membrane and the initiation of an action potential. Once an action potential is generated in the post-synaptic membrane, ACh in the synaptic cleft is deactivated by acetylcholinesterase enzymes and the products are reabsorbed by the pre-synaptic membrane to be remade and repackaged in vesicles.

There are more than 40 different neurotransmitters in the body. Acetylcholine and noradrenalin are found throughout the nervous system, others (e.g. dopamine) are found only in the brain.

Many drugs affect synapses and influence the way nerve impulses are transmitted. Nicotine has a similar molecular shape to acetylcholine and affects the post-synaptic membrane so that it transmits an action potential.

Homeostasis

The internal environment of the body remains constant, within certain limits, despite changes that occur in the external environment. The control process that maintains conditions within these limits is known as **homeostasis**.

The factors that are controlled include water balance, blood glucose concentration, blood pH, carbon dioxide concentration and body temperature.

Each of these has a 'normal' or set point although they may vary slightly above or below it. For example, the normal body temperature for humans is about 37 °C.

Both the nervous system and the endocrine system are involved in homeostasis. The **endocrine system** consists of ductless **endocrine glands**, which release different hormones (Figure **6.26**, overleaf). **Hormones** circulate in the bloodstream but each one is a chemical messenger that only affects the metabolism of specific target cells.

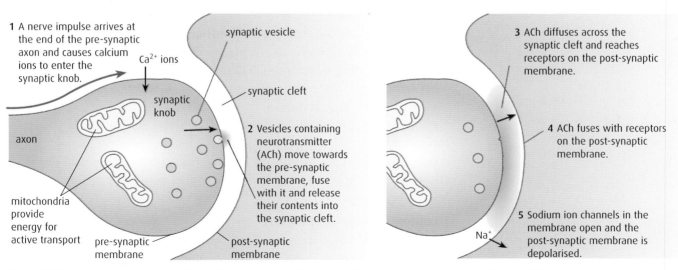

1 A nerve impulse arrives at the end of the pre-synaptic axon and causes calcium ions to enter the synaptic knob.

Ca²⁺ ions

synaptic vesicle

synaptic cleft

synaptic knob

axon

2 Vesicles containing neurotransmitter (ACh) move towards the pre-synaptic membrane, fuse with it and release their contents into the synaptic cleft.

mitochondria provide energy for active transport

pre-synaptic membrane

post-synaptic membrane

3 ACh diffuses across the synaptic cleft and reaches receptors on the post-synaptic membrane.

4 ACh fuses with receptors on the post-synaptic membrane.

Na⁺

5 Sodium ion channels in the membrane open and the post-synaptic membrane is depolarised.

Figure 6.25 A cholinergic synapse. The whole sequence of events of transmission at a synapse takes 5–10 ms.

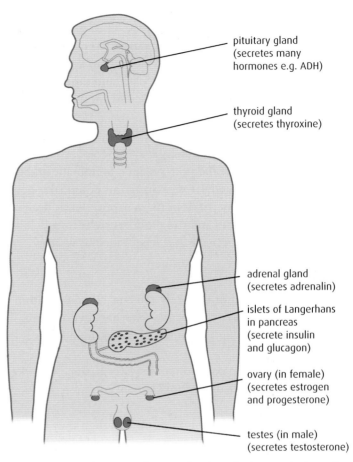

Figure 6.26 The positions of some endocrine glands in the human body. Endocrine glands have no ducts, and secrete directly into the bloodstream, which carries them to target cells.

Monitoring levels and control by negative feedback

Feedback systems work by monitoring the level of a substance, or a product, and feeding this level back to affect the rate of production or use of the substance. **Negative feedback** stabilises the internal environment by reversing the changes within it. For example, if metabolic processes produce heat causing blood temperature to rise, sensors in the hypothalamus in the brain respond and send messages to increase heat loss or slow down heat production.

Negative feedback also controls levels of blood glucose. If a large amount of glucose is absorbed from the intestine, responses are initiated to bring the levels back to normal. The graph shown in Figure **6.27** shows how the level of glucose in the blood changes from its normal level and how the normal level is re-established.

Control of body temperature

Body temperature is monitored and controlled by the hypothalamus in the brain. The 'set point' for body temperature is 36.7 °C. The hypothalamus responds to nerve impulses from receptors in the skin

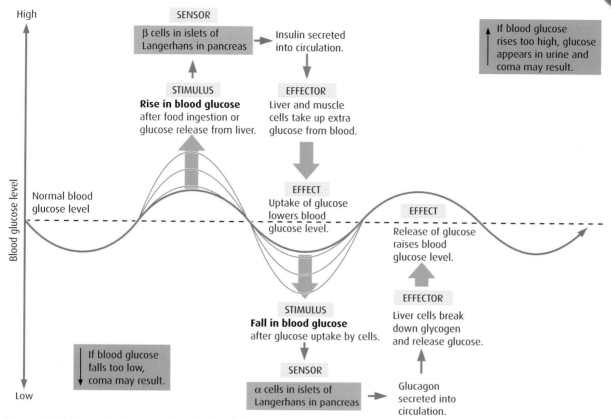

High

SENSOR
β cells in islets of Langerhans in pancreas → Insulin secreted into circulation.

If blood glucose rises too high, glucose appears in urine and coma may result.

STIMULUS
Rise in blood glucose after food ingestion or glucose release from liver.

EFFECTOR
Liver and muscle cells take up extra glucose from blood.

Normal blood glucose level

EFFECT
Uptake of glucose lowers blood glucose level.

EFFECT
Release of glucose raises blood glucose level.

Blood glucose level

If blood glucose falls too low, coma may result.

STIMULUS
Fall in blood glucose after glucose uptake by cells.

EFFECTOR
Liver cells break down glycogen and release glucose.

SENSOR
α cells in islets of Langerhans in pancreas → Glucagon secreted into circulation.

Low

Figure 6.27 The control mechanism for blood glucose.

and also to changes in the body's core temperature. If body temperature fluctuates above or below the set point, the hypothalamus coordinates responses to bring it back to normal. This is another example of negative feedback. Nerve messages are carried from the hypothalamus to organs that bring about warming or cooling of the body. Table **6.6** (overleaf) lists some of the body's responses to changes in temperature.

Control of blood glucose levels

Blood glucose level is the concentration of glucose dissolved in blood plasma. It is expressed as millimoles per decimetre cubed ($mmol\,dm^{-3}$). Normally blood glucose level stays within narrow limits, between $4\,mmol\,dm^{-3}$ and $8\,mmol\,dm^{-3}$, so that the osmotic balance of the blood remains constant and body cells receive sufficient glucose for respiration. Levels are higher after meals as glucose is absorbed into the blood from the intestine and usually lowest in the morning as food has not been consumed overnight.

Glucose levels are monitored by cells in the pancreas. If the level is too high or too low, α and β cells in regions of the pancreas known as the islets of Langerhans produce hormones which turn on control mechanisms to correct it. Table **6.7** (overleaf) summarises these responses.

Diabetes

The most obvious symptom of **diabetes** is the inability of the body to control blood glucose level. A diabetic person will experience wide

Fever is a higher than normal temperature caused as the hypothalamus raises the body's 'set point' to over 37 °C. Fever may be a response to toxins from pathogens or to histamines, released by white blood cells at infection. A high temperature is an important part of the body's defence response to infection.

1 decimetre cubed is the same volume as 1 litre.

	Responses to a rise in body temperature	Responses to a fall in body temperature
Arterioles in the skin	dilate (widen) so that more blood flows to skin capillaries – excess heat from the core of the body is lost from the skin	narrow to restrict flow of warm blood to the skin capillaries – heat is retained in the body
Sweat glands	produce more sweat, which evaporates from the skin surface to cool it	cease production of sweat
Muscles	remain relaxed	muscular activity such as shivering generates heat
Metabolic rate	may decrease to minimise heat production	thyroxine increases metabolic rate

Table 6.6 The body's responses to changes in core temperature.

	Responses to a rise in blood glucose above normal	Responses to a fall in blood glucose below normal
Pancreas	β **cells** in the pancreas produce the hormone **insulin**	α **cells** in the pancreas produce the hormone **glucagon**
Glucose uptake or release	insulin stimulates cells in the liver and muscles to take in glucose and convert it to **glycogen** and fat, which can be stored; inside the cells – blood glucose levels fall	glucagon stimulates the hydrolysis of glycogen to glucose in liver cells – glucose is released into the blood

Table 6.7 The body's responses to changes in blood glucose.

fluctuations in their blood glucose above and below the normal limits (Figure **6.28**).

Type I diabetes is caused when the β cells in the pancreas do not produce insulin. This can be a result of autoimmune disease in which the body's immune system destroys its own β cells. Without insulin, glucose is not taken up by body cells so blood levels remain high, a condition known as **hyperglycaemia**. Excess glucose is excreted in urine and its presence is used to diagnose diabetes. About 10% of diabetics have type I

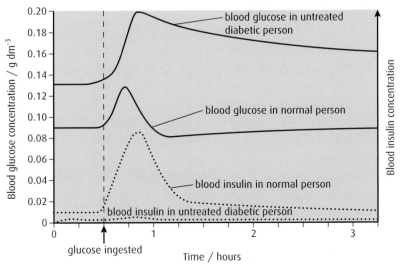

Figure 6.28 Blood glucose and insulin levels following intake of glucose in a normal person and a person with untreated type I diabetes.

diabetes, which must be controlled by insulin injections. Symptoms usually begin in childhood, which is why type I diabetes is sometimes known as 'early onset' diabetes.

Type II diabetes accounts for 90% of all cases. It is caused by body cells failing to respond to the insulin that is produced. Again, the result is that blood glucose level remains too high. This type of diabetes can be controlled by a change to a low carbohydrate diet. It is often associated with obesity, age, lack of exercise and genetic factors. The pancreas does produce insulin although levels may fall as the disease progresses. Type II diabetes is sometimes known as 'late onset' diabetes.

Diabetics must monitor their blood glucose level carefully so that they can control it, since the body's internal control mechanism is not working properly.

18 Draw a labelled diagram of a motor neuron.

19 Define the term 'action potential'.

20 List the key events of synaptic transmission.

21 State the role of negative feedback in homeostasis.

22 Draw a table to compare and distinguish between type I and type II diabetes.

Causes of diabetes

Evidence that type II diabetes is influenced by genes has come from studies of ethnic groups worldwide. Native Americans, Native Australian Aborigines and the Polynesian Maori people all have a higher incidence of diabetes than would occur by chance.

In the last decade, there has been a large increase in the number of people in industrialised countries affected by type II diabetes. Can you suggest a reason for this?

6.6 Reproduction

Assessment statements

- Draw and label diagrams of the adult male and female reproductive systems.
- Outline the role of hormones in the menstrual cycle, including FSH, LH, estrogen and progesterone.
- Annotate a graph showing hormone levels in the menstrual cycle, illustrating the relationship between changes in hormone levels and ovulation, menstruation and thickening of the endometrium.
- List three roles of testosterone in males.
- Outline the process of *in vitro* fertilisation (IVF).
- Discuss the ethical issues associated with IVF.

Reproduction is one of the important characteristics of living things. Human male and female reproductive systems produce the gametes (the sperm cell and egg cell) that must come together to begin a new life. The two reproductive systems enable the gametes to meet and the female reproductive system provides a suitable place for fertilisation to occur and an embryo to develop. The ovaries and testes also produce hormones that regulate sexual development and reproduction.

Male reproductive system

The testes are held just outside the male body in the scrotum (Figure **6.29**, overleaf). Each testis produces both sperm cells and the hormone

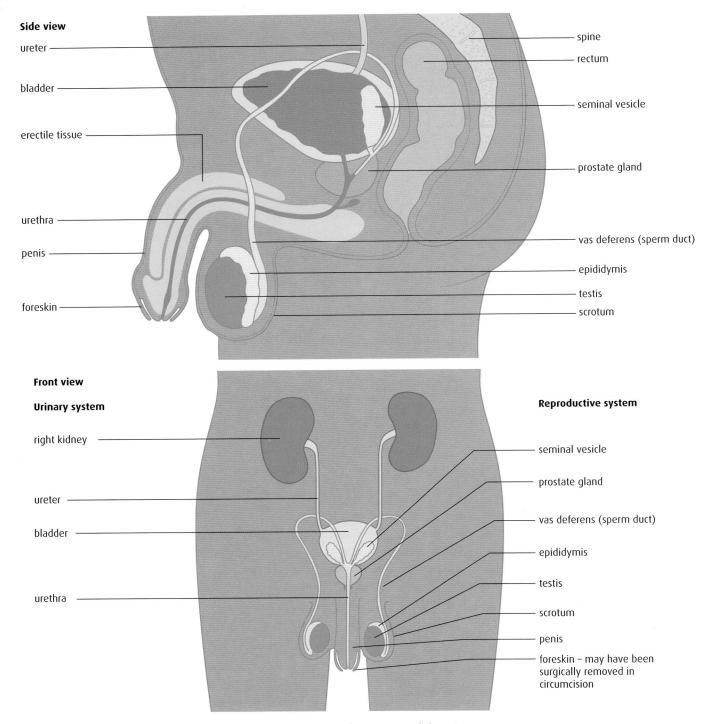

Side view

ureter

bladder

erectile tissue

urethra

penis

foreskin

spine

rectum

seminal vesicle

prostate gland

vas deferens (sperm duct)

epididymis

testis

scrotum

Front view

Urinary system

right kidney

ureter

bladder

urethra

Reproductive system

seminal vesicle

prostate gland

vas deferens (sperm duct)

epididymis

testis

scrotum

penis

foreskin – may have been surgically removed in circumcision

Figure 6.29 The male reproductive system. These diagrams also show organs of the urinary system.

The temperature in the scrotum is about 35 °C, which is ideal for sperm production.

testosterone. Sperm cells are carried from the testes in the sperm ducts, which transport them past the seminal vesicles and prostate glands. These glands together produce the seminal fluid in which the sperm cells travel. Seminal fluid containing sperm cells is known as semen. This fluid travels down the penis in the urethra and is transferred to the vagina during intercourse. The penis contains spongy tissue that can fill with blood during sexual arousal to cause an erection. Sperm production is a continuous process, which begins at puberty and continues throughout a man's life.

Roles of testosterone

The hormone testosterone, which is produced by the testes, has important roles in the sexual development and reproductive behaviour in males.

- During fetal development, testosterone causes the development of the male genitalia.
- At puberty, levels of testosterone rise and cause the development of male secondary sexual characteristics including growth of muscle, deepening of the voice, enlargement of the penis and growth of body hair.
- Testosterone stimulates the continuous production of sperm, and behaviour associated with the sex drive.

Female reproductive system

The female reproductive system includes the ovaries, which produce the female gametes, the oviducts, where fertilisation usually takes place, and the uterus, where the baby grows and develops (Figure **6.30**, overleaf). The vagina is the passageway for sperm cells to enter the body, and the way out for the baby when it is born.

Production of female gametes is a cyclical process, which lasts approximately 28 days. During the first half of this **menstrual cycle** the egg cell is produced, and in the second half the uterus lining thickens to prepare for implantation of a fertilised egg. The cycle involves hormones that are released by the ovaries and the pituitary gland.

Female sex hormones and the menstrual cycle

Ovaries produce two hormones, **estrogen** and **progesterone**. These hormones stimulate the development of female characteristics at puberty and also influence the changes in the uterus lining during the menstrual cycle and pregnancy. The pituitary gland in the brain produces two further hormones, **luteinising hormone** (**LH**) and **follicle–stimulating hormone** (**FSH**). FSH stimulates the development of immature follicles in the ovary, one of which will come to contain a mature egg cell. LH stimulates the follicle to release the egg and subsequently to form the corpus luteum.

The sequence of events begins at the start of **menstruation**, which is often called a period (Figure **6.31**, page **161**). During the first four or five days of the cycle, the endometrium (lining) of the uterus is shed and leaves the body through the vagina. This indicates that fertilisation has not occurred during the previous month.

In this early part of the cycle, the pituitary gland secretes FSH, which stimulates the development of an immature follicle in the ovary. The follicle then secretes estrogen, which enhances the follicle's response to FSH. As the level of estrogen rises, it also stimulates the repair of the uterus lining.

Side view

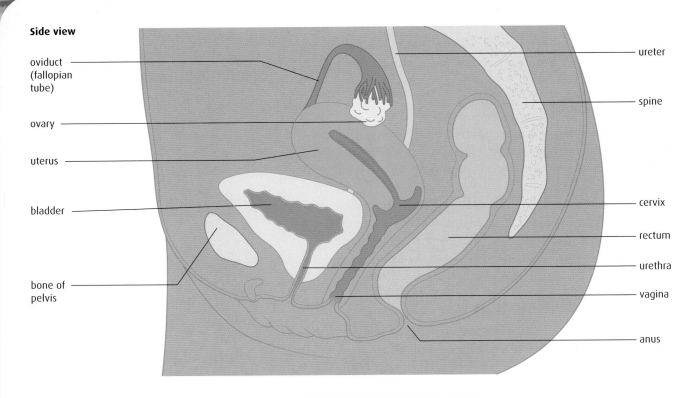

oviduct (fallopian tube)

ovary

uterus

bladder

bone of pelvis

ureter

spine

cervix

rectum

urethra

vagina

anus

Front view

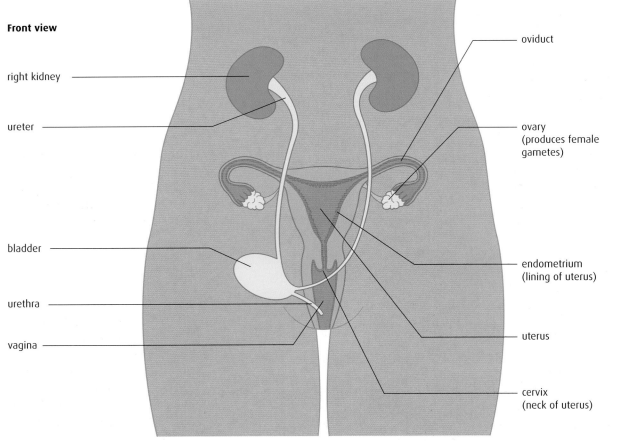

right kidney

ureter

bladder

urethra

vagina

oviduct

ovary (produces female gametes)

endometrium (lining of uterus)

uterus

cervix (neck of uterus)

Figure 6.30 The female reproductive system. The diagrams also show organs of the urinary system – in the front view the bladder has been drawn to one side, to reveal the uterus.

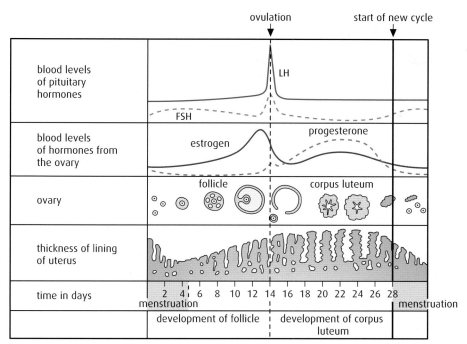

Figure 6.31 The menstrual cycle lasts an average of 28 days and involves changes in hormone levels that influence the follicles and lining of the uterus.

As the follicle grows, estrogen levels rise to a peak at around day 12, when they stimulate the release of LH from the pituitary gland. As LH levels reach their highest point, **ovulation** – the release of the egg cell from the follicle – takes place. Ovulation usually occurs at around the day 14 of the cycle. Immediately afterwards, LH stimulates the empty follicle to form the **corpus luteum**. Levels of estrogen begin to rise and as a result FSH and LH levels fall.

The corpus luteum secretes progesterone, which stimulates the thickening of the endometrium and prepares the uterus to receive an embryo. It also inhibits the production of FSH and LH.

If the egg cell is not fertilised, the LH level falls, the corpus luteum degenerates and progesterone and estrogen levels fall. The fall in progesterone stimulates the breakdown of the uterus lining. FSH is no longer inhibited, so a new follicle is stimulated and the cycle begins again.

In vitro fertilisation

In vitro **fertilisation** (IVF) is a technique used to help couples who have been unable to conceive naturally. There are many reasons for infertility. Males may have a low sperm count, blocked or damaged sperm ducts or be unable to achieve an erection. Females may fail to ovulate or have blocked or damaged oviducts, or produce antibodies in cervical mucus that destroy sperm.

The first step in IVF treatment is an assessment of whether the couple are suitable for treatment. If so, the woman is injected with FSH for about 10 days. This hormone causes a number of egg cells to mature at the same time in her ovaries. Just before the egg cells are released from the

Figure **11.22** on page **276** shows the stages in the development of a follicle in the ovary, right up to ovulation and then the formation of the corpus luteum.

The first successful IVF baby was Louise Brown, born in 1978 following her mother's IVF treatment. Professor Robert Edwards, who pioneered the technique, was awarded the Nobel prize in Physiology or Medicine in 2010.

Questions to consider

1 Are the increased risks of birth defects acceptable? Is it even possible to assess what an acceptable level of risk is?

2 What would you define as a 'birth defect'?

3 The causes of the birth defects are unknown. They could be due to the treatment or to factors associated with the infertility of the parents. Would people's view of the risk be changed if we had enough evidence to identify the causes?

4 Is it important who carries out reviews and studies of these risks? Can scientific evidence be evaluated differently by people who have strong views about the acceptability of assisted reproduction?

Assessing the risks of IVF

When IVF treatment is carried out, a woman is given drug treatments to interrupt her own natural reproductive cycle and induce her body to release more eggs than is normal. Healthy sperm are selected and, in some treatments, injected into the eggs. There is some evidence that babies born after IVF treatment may be at a greater risk of birth defects than children born following natural conception. The largest study into the number of congenital abnormalities in babies born following fertility treatment found that 4.2% were affected by major malformations, compared with a rate of 2–3% for babies not conceived through IVF.

Although this rate is still low, ever more babies are born each year as a result of fertility treatment. In Great Britain, about 200 000 such babies have been born since 1991, suggesting that up to 8000 children may be affected. These figures include not only IVF, but also other treatments such as using drugs to stimulate ovulation.

In France, a survey of 15 000 births in 33 hospitals was carried out between 2003 and 2007. These results also showed increased numbers of malformations. Geraldine Viot from the Maternité Port-Royal hospital in Paris, speaking at an annual meeting of the European Society of Human Genetics, said 'Given that our study is the largest to date, we think that our data are more likely to be statistically representative of the true picture… At a time when infertility is increasing and more couples need to use ART [assisted reproductive technology] to conceive, it is vitally important that we find out as much as we can about what is causing malformations in these children.'

follicles, they are collected using a laparoscope. The egg cells are 'matured' in culture medium for up to 24 hours before sperm cells are added to fertilise them. Fertilised egg cells are incubated for about three days until they have divided to form a ball of cells. These embryos are checked to make sure they are healthy and developing normally. Either two or three will be selected and placed into the woman's uterus for implantation. The pregnancy is then allowed to continue in the normal way. Any remaining embryos can be frozen and stored for use later. Figure **6.32** summarises the stages in IVF treatment.

Ethical issues associated with IVF treatment

IVF has enabled men and women who would naturally be infertile to have children but it has also produced some serious ethical issues. Some of these are outlined in Table **6.8**. Each society needs to think about these issues and decide what should be done about them.

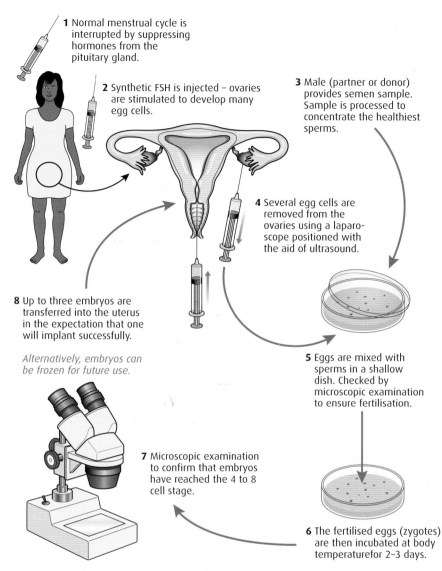

1 Normal menstrual cycle is interrupted by suppressing hormones from the pituitary gland.

2 Synthetic FSH is injected – ovaries are stimulated to develop many egg cells.

3 Male (partner or donor) provides semen sample. Sample is processed to concentrate the healthiest sperms.

4 Several egg cells are removed from the ovaries using a laparoscope positioned with the aid of ultrasound.

8 Up to three embryos are transferred into the uterus in the expectation that one will implant successfully.

Alternatively, embryos can be frozen for future use.

5 Eggs are mixed with sperms in a shallow dish. Checked by microscopic examination to ensure fertilisation.

7 Microscopic examination to confirm that embryos have reached the 4 to 8 cell stage.

6 The fertilised eggs (zygotes) are then incubated at body temperature for 2–3 days.

Figure 6.32 The stages in *in vitro* fertilisation treatment.

Arguments in favour of IVF	Arguments against IVF
• Enables infertile couples to have a family. • Couples willing to undergo IVF treatment must have determination to become parents. • Embryos used in IVF treatment can be screened to ensure they are healthy and do not have certain genetic conditions that would be inherited. • IVF techniques have led to further understanding of human reproductive biology.	• Unused embryos produced by IVF are frozen for a limited period and then destroyed. • Embryos are selected for implantation so humans are choosing which should have the chance of life. • Multiple births often result from IVF and this increases the risks to mother and babies. • Infertility is a natural phenomenon whereas IVF is not and some religions object to it on this basis. • Some causes of infertility are due to genetic conditions, which may be passed on to children born as a result of IVF.

Table 6.8 Arguments for and against IVF treatment.

Questions to consider

1 Should IVF conceptions such as Anna's be permitted?
2 Who should have rights over a child's genetic material in cases like this?
3 Is it right that a child should be created simply to keep another person alive?

Born to give

My Sister's Keeper is a novel by Jodi Picoult, published in 2004. The book, which was made into a film in 2009, follows the life of 13-year-old Anna, who enlists the help of an attorney to sue her parents for rights to her own body. Anna's older sister Kate suffers from leukemia and Anna was conceived through IVF to be a genetic match and donor for her sister. Anna donates bone marrow and blood for her sister throughout her life. As Kate's condition worsens, their parents want Anna to donate a kidney to Kate after she goes into renal failure, but Anna files a lawsuit against her parents for medical emancipation from them despite the consequences for her sister's health.

This novel is a fictional story but already there have been real examples of children being conceived by IVF and born to provide stem cells for siblings who would otherwise die.

End-of-chapter questions

1 Which of the following statements is correct?

    A   Large food molecules need to be digested so that they can be absorbed through the gut wall.

    B   The liver and pancreas both release their digestive enzymes into the small intestine.

    C   The approximate pH of the stomach is 8.

    D   Assimilation is the transfer of the end products of digestion from the gut lumen to the blood. (1)

2 Which of the following statements is correct?

    A   Blood passes from the atria to the ventricles through the semilunar valves.

    B   The coronary and pulmonary arteries supply oxygenated blood to the heart muscle.

    C   The pacemaker, brain and adrenal gland are all involved in the regulation of the heart beat.

    D   A red blood cell travels from the lungs to the stomach via the right atrium, right ventricle and aorta. (1)

3 Which of the following statements is correct?

    A   Antibiotics are effective against viruses but not bacteria.

    B   Antigens are made by lymphocytes.

    C   Phagocytes are white blood cells that can be found in the tissue fluid around cells.

    D   HIV is a bacterium that reduces the number of active lymphocytes in the blood. (1)

4 Which of the following statements is correct?

    A   During breathing in, the rib cage moves up and out and the pressure inside the thorax increases.

    B   Alveoli are small sac-like structures that have walls only two cells thick.

    C   To assist with breathing out, the abdominal and external intercostal muscles contract.

    D   The purpose of ventilation is to increase the rate of gas exchange in the alveoli.   (1)

5 Which of the following statements is correct?

    A   In a motor neuron, the impulse travels from the axon to the cell body.

    B   A nerve impulse travels from a receptor to the CNS via a sensory neuron and from the CNS to an effector via a motor neuron.

    C   The endocrine system produces hormones, which pass from the endocrine glands to the blood through ducts.

    D   The resting potential is divided into two parts, depolarisation and repolarisation.   (1)

6 Which of the following statements is correct?

    A   In the male reproductive system, the sperm ducts are connected to the ureters.

    B   During the process of *in vitro* fertilisation, a woman is injected with FSH to stimulate egg cells to mature.

    C   FSH and oestrogen are hormones released from the ovaries whereas LH and progesterone are hormones released from the pituitary gland.

    D   In the menstrual cycle, the levels of progesterone begin to rise around day 5.   (1)

7 Outline the functions of the stomach, small intestine and large intestine in a table like the one below.   (4)

Stomach	Small intestine	Large intestine
provides acidic environment	provides weakly alkaline environment	

8 Explain the relationship between the structure and function of arteries, veins and capillaries.   (9)

9 Explain antibody production.   (3)

10 Explain how the skin and mucous membranes prevent entry of pathogens into the body.   (3)

11 Explain how blood glucose concentration is controlled in humans.   (8)

12 Discuss the ethical issues of *in vitro* fertilisation (IVF) in humans.   (8)

13 The body mass index (BMI) takes into account the weight and height of a person and can be used to determine if a person is overweight or obese. The nomogram shows the body mass index for a range of weights and heights.

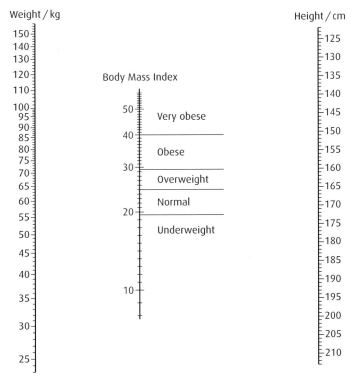

source: adapted with permission from the American College of Neuropsychopharmacology (ACNP), from G Bray, *Obesity, Fat intake and Chronic Disease*, (2000)

a State the weight description of a 75 kg man who is 145 cm tall. (1)

b A woman of height 150 cm has a BMI of 40. Calculate the minimum weight she must lose to be considered 'normal'. (1)

c Outline the relationship between height and BMI for a fixed weight. (1)

(total 3 marks)
© IB Organization 2009

14 Blind mole rats (*Spalax ehrenberghi*) are adapted to live in underground burrows with very low oxygen conditions. Scientists compared blind mole rats and white rats in order to determine whether these adaptations are due to changes in their ventilation system.

Both types of rat were placed on a treadmill and the amount of oxygen consumed was measured at different speeds. This study was done under normal oxygen conditions and under low oxygen conditions. The results are shown in the scatter graphs below.

Blind mole rats

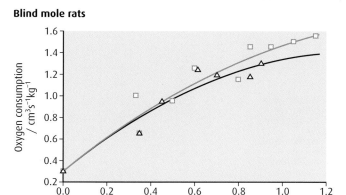

source: Hans R. Widmer *et al.*, 'Working underground: respiratory adaptations in the blind mole rat' *PNAS* (4 March 1997), vol. **94**, issue 4, pp. 2062–2067, Fig 1, © 2003 National Academy of Sciences, USA

White rats

Key
□ normal oxygen   △ low oxygen

a Compare the oxygen consumption of blind mole rats and white rats when the treadmill is not moving. (1)

b Compare the effect of increasing the treadmill speed on the oxygen consumption in both types of rats under normal oxygen conditions. (3)

c Evaluate the effect of reducing the amount of oxygen available on both types of rat. (2)

The lungs of both types of rats were studied and the features important to oxygen uptake were compared. The results are shown in the bar chart below.

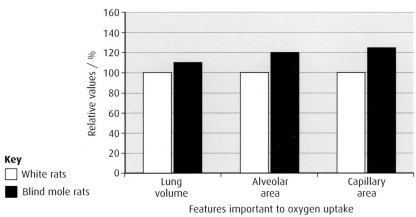

Key
□ White rats
■ Blind mole rats

source: Hans R. Widmer *et al.*, 'Working underground: respiratory adaptations in the blind mole rat' *PNAS* (4 March 1997), vol. **94**, issue 4, pp. 2062–2067, Fig 1, © 2003 National Academy of Sciences, USA

d Using your knowledge of gas exchange in lungs, explain how these adaptations would help the blind mole rats to survive in underground burrows. (3)

(total 9 marks)
© IB Organization 2009

15 Near the middle of pregnancy in humans, the placenta begins to secrete a hormone called corticotrophin-releasing hormone (CRH). CRH influences the production of hormones that stimulate the development of the fetus.

A study was carried out to determine if levels of CRH were correlated with the timing of the baby's delivery. Blood samples were taken from 500 women during their pregnancies and the concentration of CRH was measured. The women were then divided into three groups according to whether their baby was delivered prematurely, at full-term or late.

The graph below shows how the concentration of CRH varied in the mothers' blood (maternal blood) in each of the three groups during pregnancy.

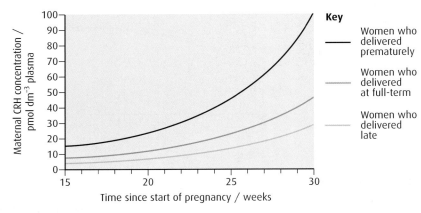

source: R Smith, *Scientific American* (March 1999) pp. 68–75

a Outline how the concentration of CRH in the blood changes during the pregnancies of women who delivered prematurely. (2)

b Compare how the concentration of CRH changes during the pregnancies of women who delivered late with those that delivered at full-term. (2)

c Measure the difference in CRH concentration at 30 weeks between the women who delivered prematurely and those that delivered at full-term. (1)

d Suggest how knowledge of the CRH concentration in maternal blood might be used by doctors monitoring pregnancies. (2)

The Western spadefoot toad (*Scaphiopus hammondii*) lives in desert areas in California and lays its eggs in pools formed by rain. When the egg first hatches, its body form is referred to as the tadpole stage. At some point, it undergoes metamorphosis (a change in body form) to develop into the adult toad.

If the pools where the eggs have been laid shrink due to a lack of rain, the tadpoles quickly develop into small adult toads. If there is sufficient rain and the pools persist, the tadpoles develop more slowly and grow large before developing into adult toads.

e Suggest how undergoing metamorphosis at different times in response to water levels helps the survival of the toad. (3)

It has been suggested that CRH control of development might have evolved in amphibians long before mammals appeared. In toads, increase in CRH concentration leads directly to an increase in the level of the hormone thyroxine and indirectly to an increase in corticosterone levels.

An experiment was carried out to determine what hormones might be involved in triggering development in response to pond drying. Tadpoles were raised in a constant high–water–level environment. They were then divided into two groups. One group was transferred to a tank containing $10\,dm^3$ of water – a high-water environment. The other group was transferred to a tank of the same size containing only $1\,dm^3$ of water – a low-water environment. The concentrations of thyroxine and corticosterone were measured in each group. The results are shown below.

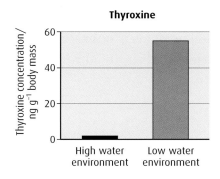

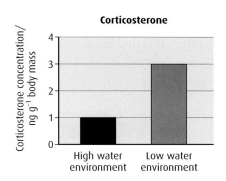

source: R J Denver, *General and Comparative Endocrinology*, (1998), **110**, pp. 326–336

f Compare the concentrations of thyroxine and corticosterone in the two groups. (2)

g Predict how the concentration of CRH would be different in the two groups. (1)

(total 13 marks)
© IB Organization 2009

7 Nucleic acids and proteins

Introduction

Nucleic acids are very large macromolecules composed of a backbone of sugar and phosphate molecules each with a nitrogenous base attached to the sugar. In Chapter **3**, the role of DNA and RNA is outlined. In this chapter, the detailed structure of different nucleic acids is considered, as well as the vital role of nucleic acids in converting the genetic code contained in the chromosomes into the protein molecules that are needed to make all cells function.

7.1 DNA structure

Assessment statements

- Describe the structure of DNA, including the antiparallel strands, 3'–5' linkages and hydrogen bonding between the purines and the pyrimidines.
- Outline the structure of nucleosomes.
- State that nucleosomes help to supercoil chromosomes and help to regulate transcription.
- Distinguish between 'unique or single-copy genes' and 'highly repetitive sequences' in nuclear DNA.
- State that eukaryotic genes can contain exons and introns.

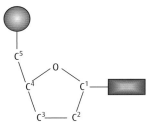

Figure 7.1 The structure of a nucleotide.

The 3'–5' linkage

A nucleotide consists of the sugar deoxyribose to which are attached a phosphate group and a nitrogenous base. The carbons in the sugar are numbered from 1 to 5 in a clockwise direction starting after the oxygen at the apex (Figure **7.1**).

- The base is attached to carbon 1.
- Carbon 2 has just a hydrogen attached instead of an OH group – this is the reason the sugar is called **deoxy**ribose.
- Carbon 3 is where the next nucleotide attaches in one direction.
- Carbon 5 has a phosphate group attached to it, which is where the next nucleotide attaches in the other direction.

This means that each nucleotide is linked to those on either side of it through carbons 3 and 5. The linkages are called **3'–5' linkages**.

Antiparallel strands

Look at Figure **3.10** on page **48**. This shows part of a DNA molecule, in which two polynucleotide strands, running in opposite directions, are held together by hydrogen bonds between the bases. Notice that the deoxyribose molecules are orientated in opposite directions. One strand runs in a 5' → 3' direction whereas the other runs in a 3' → 5' direction. Figure **7.2** also shows this. The strands are described as being **antiparallel**.

The bases and hydrogen bonding

The four DNA bases are cytosine, thymine, adenine and guanine, and they fall into two chemical groups called **pyrimidines** and **purines**. Cytosine and thymine are pyrimidines, and adenine and guanine are purines.

Cytosine pairs with guanine and thymine pairs with adenine – that is, a pyrimidine always pairs with a purine. This is because they are different sizes: pyrimidines are smaller than purines. The pairing of a pyrimidine with a purine ensures that the strands are always the same distance apart.

It is important to notice that cytosine, a pyrimidine, cannot pair with adenine, even though it is a purine. Cytosine and guanine have three hydrogen bonds whereas thymine and adenine only have two hydrogen bonds (Figure **7.2**).

An easy way to remember the two groups of DNA bases is to look at the words. Thymine and cytosine, which both contain a letter y, are in the group pyrimidines, which also contains a letter y.

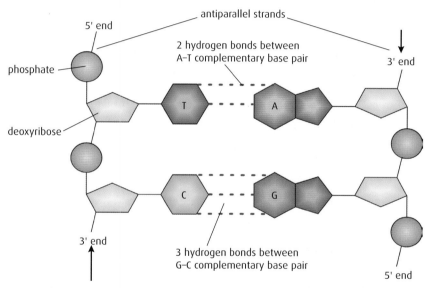

Figure 7.2 Hydrogen bonding between antiparallel strands of DNA.

Nucleosomes

A eukaryotic chromosome is composed of a double strand of DNA combined with proteins. Some of these proteins, called **histones**, combine together in groups of eight to form a bead-like structure (Figure **7.3**). The strand of DNA takes two turns around this bead before continuing on to the next bead. It is held in place on the bead by a ninth histone. The group of nine histones with the DNA is called a **nucleosome**. The function of nucleosomes is to help supercoil the chromosomes during mitosis and meiosis and also to help regulate transcription.

Nuclear DNA

The nucleus of a human cell contains nearly 2 m of DNA, but genes make up only a proportion of this. The DNA in a eukaryotic cell can be divided up into two types:

- **unique** or **single-copy genes**, which make up 55–95% of the total

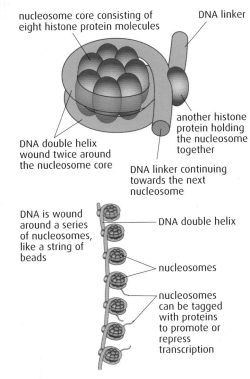

nucleosome core consisting of eight histone protein molecules

DNA linker

DNA double helix wound twice around the nucleosome core

another histone protein holding the nucleosome together

DNA linker continuing towards the next nucleosome

DNA is wound around a series of nucleosomes, like a string of beads

DNA double helix

nucleosomes

nucleosomes can be tagged with proteins to promote or repress transcription

Figure 7.3 The structure of a nucleosome.

- **highly repetitive sequences**, or **satellite DNA**, which account for 5–45%.

The repetitive sequences are typically between 5 and 300 base pairs long and may be duplicated as many as 100 000 times in a genome.

Many genes include sections called **introns** that are transcribed but not translated. Only sections of genes known as **exons** are both transcribed and translated. You will learn more about introns and exons in Section **7.3** (page **175**).

1 Outline what is meant by the term 'antiparallel'.

2 Outline the structure of a nucleosome.

What is junk?

When the highly repetitive sequences of DNA were first discovered, they appeared to have no function. Scientists at the time called them 'junk DNA' and thought they were simply excess baggage. Before scientists began mapping several animal genomes, they had a rather restricted view about which parts of the genome were important. According to the traditional viewpoint, the really crucial things were genes and a few other sections that regulate gene function were also considered useful.

But new findings suggest that this interpretation was not correct. In 2004, David Haussler's team at the University of California, Santa Cruz, USA, compared human, mouse and rat genome sequences. They found – to their astonishment – that several long sequences of repeated DNA were identical across the three species. As David Haussler exclaimed:

'It absolutely knocked me off my chair.'

When the Human Genome Project was planned, there were calls from some people to map only the bits of genome that coded for protein – mapping the rest was thought to be a waste of time. Luckily, entire genomes were mapped and have proved vital to the study of so-called 'junk DNA'. It is now thought that the most likely scenario is that junk DNA controls the activity of vital genes and possibly embryo development.

Questions to consider

1 Do you think it is appropriate to label something as 'junk' simply because it is thought to have no function?

2 Does such labelling hinder scientific progress?

3 Should experiments be carried out to answer fundamental questions even if they have no obvious application?

4 Who should decide which research is most likely to be valuable?

7.2 DNA replication

Assessment statements

- State that DNA replication occurs in a 5' → 3' direction.
- Explain the process of DNA replication in prokaryotes, including the role of enzymes (helicase, DNA polymerase, RNA primase, and DNA ligase), Okazaki fragments and deoxynucleoside triphosphates.
- State that DNA replication is initiated at many points in eukaryotic chromosomes.

DNA **replication** ensures that exact copies of existing molecules are produced before a cell divides. The process is said to be semi-conservative and each strand of an existing DNA molecule acts as a template for the production of a new strand.

The process of DNA replication

As Figure **7.2** shows, at one end of a DNA strand there is a free 3' carbon and at the other there is a free 5' carbon. (Ignore the fact that there is a phosphate group attached to this 5' carbon.) A strand of DNA can therefore be described as running in a 5' → 3' direction or in a 3' → 5' direction.

The process of replication is **semi-conservative** – that is, each original strand acts as a template to build up a new strand (Figure **7.4**). The DNA double helix is unwound to expose the two strands for replication by the enzyme **helicase**, at a region known as a **replication fork**. Eukaryotic chromosomes are very long compared to prokaryotic chromosomes and so, to speed up the process, replication starts at many replication forks along a chromosome at the same time.

Replication must occur in the 5' → 3' direction (just as in transcription and translation, described in Sections **7.3** and **7.4**), because the enzymes involved only work in a 5' → 3' direction. As the two strands are antiparallel, replication therefore has to proceed in opposite directions on the two strands. However, the replication fork where the double helix unwinds moves along in one direction only. This means that on one of the strands replication can proceed in a continuous way, following the replication fork along, but on the other strand the process has to happen in short sections, each moving away from the replication fork (Figure **7.5**, overleaf). The strand undergoing continuous synthesis is called the **leading strand**. The other strand, in which the new DNA is built up in short sections, is known as the **lagging strand**.

Leading strand

Replication to produce the leading strand is straightforward. First **RNA primase** adds a short length of RNA, attached by complementary base pairing, to the template DNA strand. This acts as a primer, allowing the enzyme **DNA polymerase III** to bind. DNA polymerase III then adds free building units called **deoxynucleoside triphosphates** (dNTPs) to

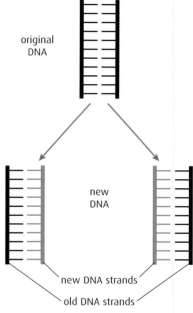

original DNA

new DNA

new DNA strands

old DNA strands

Figure 7.4 DNA replication is semi-conservative. As it is copied one original strand becomes paired with one new strand. One original strand is conserved in each new DNA molecule, hence semi-conservative.

Replication fork the point where the DNA double helix is being separated to expose the two strands as templates for replication
Leading strand the new strand that is synthesised continuously and follows the replication fork
Lagging strand the new strand that is synthesised in short fragments in the opposite direction to the movement of the replication fork
Okazaki fragments short fragments of a DNA strand formed on the lagging strand

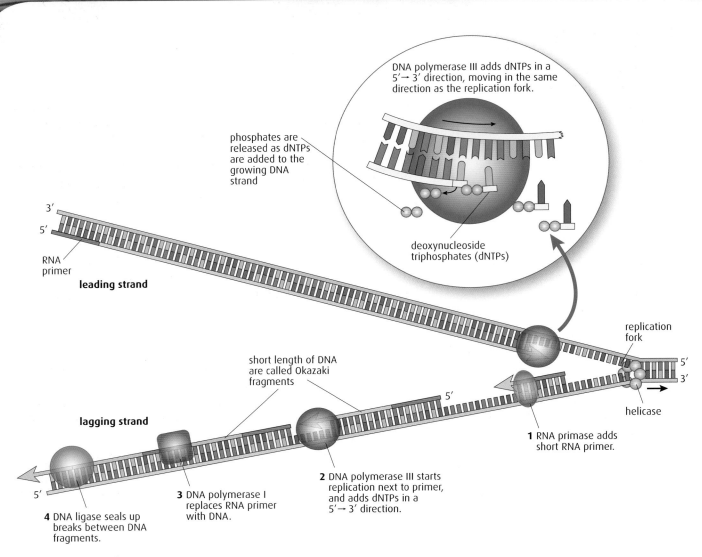

Figure 7.5 DNA replication.

the existing strand of DNA in a 5' → 3' direction, following the progress of helicase as it moves the replication fork along the DNA double helix. The RNA primer will later be removed by DNA polymerase I.

The dNTPs have two extra phosphate groups attached, and are said to be 'activated'. They pair up with their complementary bases on the exposed DNA strand and DNA polymerase III then links together the sugar and the innermost phosphate groups of adjacent nucleotides. The two extra phosphate groups are broken off and released. In this way, a continuous new DNA strand is built up on the leading strand.

Lagging strand

Synthesis of the lagging strand is a little more complicated, as it has to occur in discontinuous sections, which are then joined together.

1 As for the leading strand, **RNA primase** first synthesises a short RNA primer, complementary to the exposed DNA. This happens close to the replication fork.

2 **DNA polymerase III** starts replication by attaching at the 3' end of the RNA primer and adding dNTPs in a 5' → 3' direction. It moves away from the replication fork on this strand.

3 **DNA polymerase I** now removes the RNA primer and replaces it with DNA using dNTPs. Short lengths of new DNA called **Okazaki fragments** are formed from each primer. The new fragment grows away from the replication fork until it reaches the next fragment.

4 Finally, **DNA ligase** seals up each break between the Okazaki fragments by making sugar–phosphate bonds so that a continuous strand of new DNA is created.

3 State the direction in which DNA replication occurs.

4 Explain why Okazaki fragments must be produced on one DNA strand.

There are several chemical names involved in replication, so it is helpful to list them.

Nucleoside triphosphate (NTP) a building unit for RNA – a ribose nucleotide with two additional phosphates, which are chopped off during the synthesis process

Deoxynucleoside triphosphate (dNTP) the same as NTP but with deoxyribose instead of ribose, so it is used to build DNA rather than RNA through base-pairing to the parent DNA strand

Helicase an enzyme found at the replication fork, with two functions – to unwind the two DNA strands, and to separate them by breaking the hydrogen bonds

RNA primase this enzyme adds NTPs to the single-stranded DNA that has been unzipped by helicase, in a 5' → 3' direction, to make a short length of RNA base-paired to the parent DNA strand

DNA polymerase III this enzyme adds dNTPs in a 5' → 3' direction where RNA primase has added a short length of complementary RNA as a primer; it is unable to add dNTPs directly to the single-stranded parent DNA that has been unzipped by helicase

DNA polymerase I this enzyme removes the RNA nucleotides of the primers on the lagging strand in a 5' → 3' direction and replaces them with DNA nucleotides using dNTPs

DNA ligase this enzyme joins adjacent Okazaki fragments by forming a covalent bond between the deoxyribose and the phosphate of adjacent nucleotides

7.3 Transcription

Assessment statements

- State that transcription is carried out in a 5' → 3' direction.
- Distinguish between the 'sense' and 'antisense' strands of DNA.
- Explain the process of transcription in prokaryotes, including the role of the promoter region, RNA polymerase, nucleoside triphosphates and the terminator.
- State that eukaryotic RNA needs the removal of introns to form mature mRNA.

The process by which the DNA code is used to build polypeptides occurs in two stages. The first is transcription, which transfers sections of the genetic code from DNA to an mRNA molecule. Transcription happens in the nucleus. The second stage, known as translation, occurs in the cytoplasm and uses the mRNA, together with ribosomes, to construct the polypeptide. Translation is discussed in the next section.

Transcribing DNA into mRNA in prokaryotes

A single chromosome contains DNA that codes for many proteins. During transcription, genes (short lengths of DNA that code for single polypeptides) are used to produce mRNA. Most genes are about 1000 nucleotides long, a few are longer and a very small number are less than 100 nucleotides. The size of the gene corresponds to the size of the polypeptide it codes for.

Nucleoside triphosphates (NTPs) are the molecules used by RNA polymerase to build mRNA molecules during transcription. As they move into place, two phosphates are removed from them so they become converted into nucleotides.

At the start of **transcription**, the DNA molecule is separated into two strands by the enzyme **RNA polymerase**, which binds to the DNA near the beginning of a gene. Hydrogen bonds between the bases are broken and the double helix unwinds (Figure **7.6**).

Transcription begins at a specific point on the DNA molecule called the **promoter region**. Only one of the two strands is used as a template for transcription and this is called the **antisense strand**. The other DNA strand is called the **sense strand**. RNA polymerase uses free nucleoside triphosphates (NTPs) to build the RNA molecule, using complementary base pairing to the DNA and condensation reactions between the nucleotides. This produces a primary mRNA molecule that is complementary to the antisense strand being transcribed, and has the same base sequence as the sense strand (except that it contains the base U in place of T). RNA polymerase moves along the antisense DNA strand in a 3' → 5' direction. As it does so, the 5' end of a nucleotide is added to the 3' end of the mRNA molecule so that the construction of the mRNA proceeds in a 5' → 3' direction.

RNA polymerase checks the mRNA molecule as it forms to ensure that bases are paired correctly. As the mRNA molecule is extended, the DNA is rewound into a helix once a section has been transcribed. Eventually RNA polymerase reaches another specific sequence on the DNA called the **terminator region**, which indicates the end of the gene. The RNA polymerase releases the completed RNA strand and finishes rewinding the DNA before breaking free.

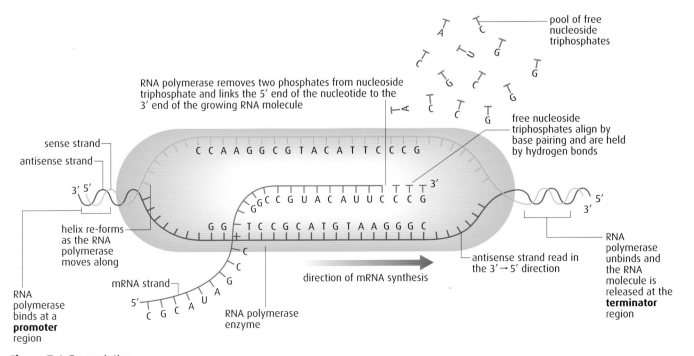

Figure 7.6 Transcription.

Introns and exons

In eukaryotes, many genes contain sequences of DNA that are transcribed but not translated. These sequences, which appear in mRNA, are known as **introns**. After transcription of a gene, the introns are removed in a process known as post-transcriptional modification. The sequences of bases that remain are known as **exons** and these are linked together to form the **mature mRNA** that is translated (Figure **7.7**). Mature mRNA leaves the nucleus via the nuclear pores and moves to the cytoplasm.

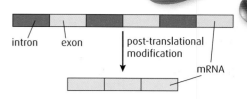

Figure 7.7 Introns and exons in mRNA.

7.4 Translation

Assessment statements

- Explain that each tRNA molecule is recognised by a tRNA-activating enzyme that binds a specific amino acid to the tRNA, using ATP for energy.
- Outline the structure of ribosomes, including protein and RNA composition, large and small subunits, three tRNA binding sites and mRNA binding sites.
- State that translation consists of initiation, elongation, translocation and termination.
- State that translation occurs in a 5' → 3' direction.
- Draw and label a diagram showing the structure of a peptide bond between two amino acids.
- Explain the process of translation, including ribosomes, polysomes, start codons and stop codons.
- State that free ribosomes synthesise proteins for use primarily within the cell, and that bound ribosomes synthesize proteins primarily for secretion or for lysosomes.

Translation is the process by which the information carried by mRNA is decoded and used to build the sequence of amino acids that eventually forms a protein molecule. During translation, amino acids are joined together in the order dictated by the sequence of codons on the mRNA to form a polypeptide. This polypeptide eventually becomes the protein coded for by the original gene.

Transfer RNA (tRNA)

The process of translation requires another type of nucleic acid known as **transfer RNA** or **tRNA**. tRNA is made of a single strand of nucleotides that is folded and held in place by base pairing and hydrogen bonds (Figure **7.8**). There are many different tRNA molecules but they all have a characteristic 'clover leaf' appearance with some small differences between them.

At one position on the molecule is a triplet of bases called the **anticodon**, which pairs by complementary base pairing with a codon on the mRNA strand. At the 3' end of the tRNA molecule is a base sequence CCA which is the attachment site for an amino acid.

An amino acid is attached to the specific tRNA molecule that has its corresponding anticodon, by an **activating enzyme**. As there are 20 different amino acids, so there are also 20 different activating enzymes in

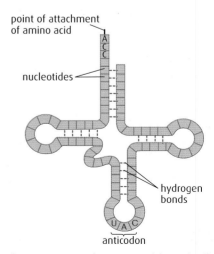

Figure 7.8 Transfer RNA – a 'clover leaf' shape.

the cytoplasm. The tRNA activating enzymes recognise the correct tRNA molecules by their shapes. Energy for the attachment of an amino acid comes from ATP. A tRNA molecule with its attached amino acid is called a **charged tRNA**.

Ribosomes

Ribosomes are the site of protein synthesis. Some ribosomes occur free in the cytoplasm and these synthesise proteins that will be used within the cell. Others are bound to the endoplasmic reticulum, forming rough endoplasmic reticulum, and these synthesise proteins for secretion from the cell or for use within lysosomes.

Ribosomes are composed of two subunits, one large and one small. The subunits are built of protein and ribosomal RNA (rRNA). On the surface of the ribosome are three tRNA binding sites (site 1, site 2 and the exit site), and one mRNA binding site (Figure **7.9**). Two charged tRNA molecules can bind to a ribosome at one time. Polypeptide chains are built up in the groove between the two subunits.

Building a polypeptide

Translation is the process that decodes the information of mRNA into the sequence of amino acids that eventually form a protein. Translation consists of four stages:

1 initiation

2 elongation

3 translocation

4 termination

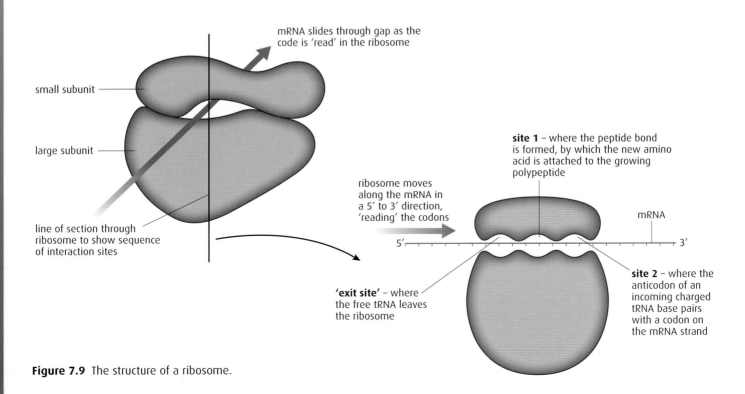

Figure 7.9 The structure of a ribosome.

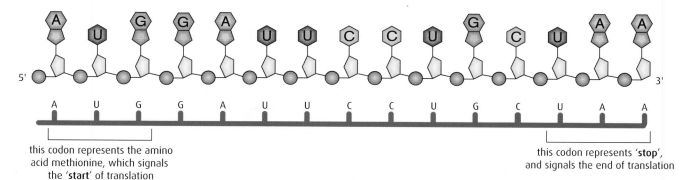

the genetic code in this mRNA is read in this direction →

5'   3'

A   U   G   G   A   U   U   C   C   U   G   C   U   A   A

this codon represents the amino acid methionine, which signals the 'start' of translation

this codon represents 'stop', and signals the end of translation

Figure 7.10 mRNA 'start' and 'stop' codons.

Initiation

Translation begins at a start codon (AUG) near the 5' end of the mRNA strand. This codon codes for the amino acid methionine and is a signal to begin the process of translation (Figure **7.10**). This is called **initiation**. The mRNA binds to the small subunit of a ribosome. Then an activated tRNA molecule, carrying the amino acid methionine, moves into position at site 1 of the ribosome. Its anticodon binds with the AUG codon using complementary base pairing. Hydrogen bonds form between the complementary bases of the mRNA and tRNA and, once this has happened, a large ribosomal subunit moves into place and combines with the small subunit.

Elongation

Initiation is followed by **elongation** and the formation of peptide bonds (Figure **7.11**). tRNA molecules bring amino acids to the mRNA strand in the order specified by the codons. To add the second amino acid, a second

one amino acid   another amino acid

$$H_2N — C — COOH \quad H_2N — C — COOH$$

R   R

| |

H   H

Two atoms of hydrogen and one of oxygen are lost – they form a molecule of water.

H_2O

peptide bond

$$H_2N — C — CO — HN — C — COOH$$

R   R

| |

H   H

The two amino acids are joined at this point by a peptide bond.

Figure 7.11 The formation of a peptide bond by a condensation reaction.

Look back at Table **4.1** on page **68** to see all the mRNA codons and what they represent.

charged tRNA with the anticodon corresponding to the next codon enters site 2 of the ribosome and binds to its codon by complementary base pairing. The ribosome catalyses the formation of a **peptide bond** between the two adjacent amino acids (Figure **7.12**). The ribosome and

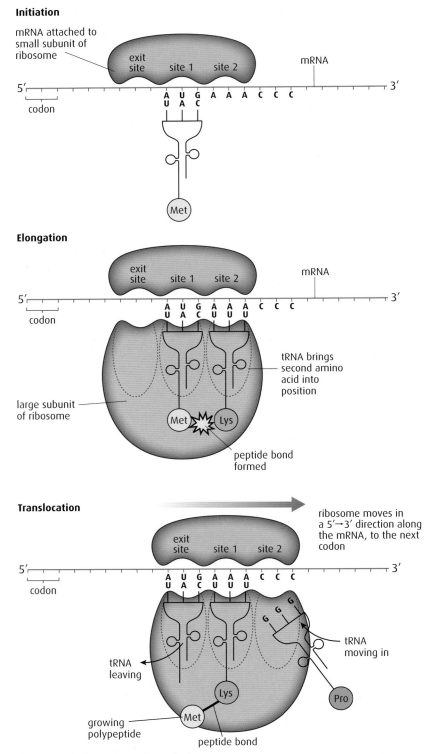

Figure 7.12 The stages of translation.

tRNA molecules now hold two amino acids. The methionine becomes detached from its tRNA. Now the ribosome moves along the mRNA and the first tRNA is released to collect another methionine molecule.

Translocation

Translocation is the movement of the ribosome along the mRNA strand one codon at a time. As the ribosome moves, the unattached tRNA moves into the exit site and is then released into the cytoplasm, where it will pick up another amino acid molecule. The growing peptide chain is now positioned in site 1, leaving site 2 empty and ready to receive another charged tRNA molecule to enter and continue the elongation process. Figure **7.12** shows how initiation, elongation and translocation occur as mRNA is translated.

Termination

Translocation and elongation are repeated until one of the three 'stop' codons aligns with site 2, which acts as a signal to end translocation. There are no tRNA molecules with anticodons corresponding to these stop codons. The polypeptide chain and the mRNA are released from the ribosome and the ribosome separates into its two subunits. This final stage of translation is called **termination**.

Polysomes

Translation occurs at many places along an mRNA molecule at the same time. A **polysome** like that in Figure **7.13** is a group of ribosomes along one mRNA strand.

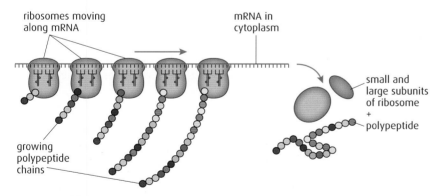

Figure 7.13 A polysome.

---

5 State what is meant by an 'exon'.

6 Distinguish between 'transcription' and 'translation'.

7 Distinguish between the 'sense' and 'antisense' strands of DNA.

8 Outline the role of the promoter region in transcription.

9 Draw a peptide bond between two amino acids.

10 State where the protein that is synthesised by free ribosomes is used.

7.5 Proteins

Assessment statements

- Explain the four levels of protein structure, indicating the significance of each level.
- Outline the difference between fibrous and globular proteins, with reference to two examples of each protein type.
- Explain the significance of polar and non-polar amino acids.
- State four functions of proteins, giving a named example of each.

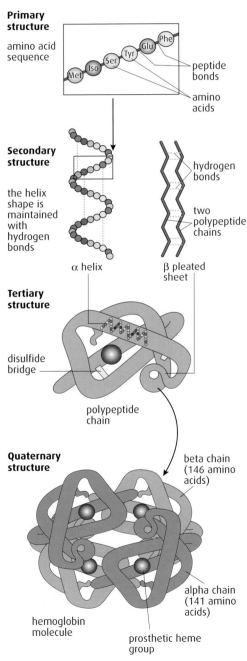

Primary structure

amino acid sequence

peptide bonds

amino acids

Secondary structure

the helix shape is maintained with hydrogen bonds

hydrogen bonds

two polypeptide chains

α helix

β pleated sheet

Tertiary structure

disulfide bridge

polypeptide chain

Quaternary structure

beta chain (146 amino acids)

alpha chain (141 amino acids)

hemoglobin molecule

prosthetic heme group

Figure 7.14 The structure of hemoglobin.

Protein structure

Proteins are large, complex molecules, usually made up of hundreds of amino acid subunits. The way these subunits fit together is highly specific to each type of protein, and is vital to its function. Figure **7.14** illustrates the structure of the protein hemoglobin.

The first stage of protein production is the assembly of a sequence of amino acid molecules that are linked by peptide bonds formed by condensation reactions. This sequence forms the **primary structure** of a protein. There are many different proteins and each one has different numbers and types of amino acids arranged in a different order, coded for by a cell's DNA.

The **secondary structure** of a protein is formed when the polypeptide chain takes up a permanent folded or twisted shape. Some polypeptides coil to produce an α helix, others fold to form β pleated sheets. The shapes are held in place by many weak hydrogen bonds. Depending on the sequence of amino acids, one section of a polypeptide may become an α helix while another takes up a β pleated form. This is the case in hemoglobin.

The **tertiary structure** of a protein forms as the molecule folds still further due to interactions between the R groups of the amino acids (Figure **7.16**, page **184**) and within the polypeptide chain. The protein takes up a three-dimensional shape, which is held together by ionic bonds between particular R groups, disulfide bridges (covalent bonds) between sulfur atoms of some R groups, and by weaker interactions between hydrophilic and hydrophobic side chains. Figure **7.15** shows the different types of bond involved in maintaining the tertiary structure of proteins. Tertiary structure is very important in enzymes because the shape of an enzyme molecule gives it its unique properties and determines which substrates can fit into its active site.

The final level of protein structure is **quaternary structure**, which links two or more polypeptide chains to form a single, large, complex protein. The structure is held together by all the bonds that are important in the previous levels of structure. Examples are collagen (which has three polypeptide chains), hemoglobin (which has four), antibodies (which also have four) and myosin (which has six).

In addition, many proteins contain **prosthetic groups** and are called **conjugated proteins**. Prosthetic groups are not polypeptides but they

Hydrogen bonds form between strongly polar groups. They can be broken by high temperature or by pH changes.

bond to rest of molecule

δ^- δ^+ δ^+
NH   C
O

bond to rest of molecule

shared electrons spend more time around N

shared electrons spend more time around O

hydrogen bond

Disulfide bonds form between cysteine molecules. The bonds can be broken by reducing agents.

cysteine

CH_2 CH_2

SH   S

disulfide bond

SH   S

CH_2 CH_2

cysteine

Ionic bonds form between ionised amine and carboxylic acid groups. They can be broken by pH changes.

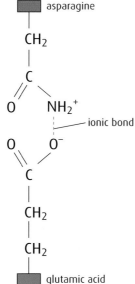

asparagine

CH_2

C

O NH_2^+

ionic bond

O O^-

C

CH_2

CH_2

glutamic acid

Hydrophobic interactions occur between non-polar side chains.

tyrosine

CH_2 — OH

CH_3

HC

CH_3

valine

Figure 7.15 Types of bond that are important in protein structure.

are able to bind to different proteins or parts of them. For example, hemoglobin is a conjugated protein, with four polypeptide chains, each containing a prosthetic heme group.

Fibrous and globular proteins

Protein molecules are categorised into two major types by their shape. **Fibrous proteins** are long and narrow and include collagen, keratin (which is found in hair and nails) and silk. Fibrous proteins are usually insoluble in water and in general have secondary structure. **Globular proteins** have a more rounded, three-dimensional shape and have either tertiary or quaternary structure. Most globular proteins are soluble in water. Globular proteins include enzymes, such as pepsin, and antibodies. Myoglobin and hemoglobin are also globular proteins.

Polar and non-polar amino acids

Amino acids are divided into two groups according to the chemical properties of their side chains or **R groups** (Figure **7.16**, overleaf). Polar

General structure of an amino acid

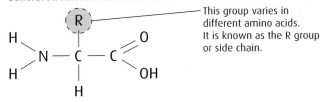

This group varies in different amino acids. It is known as the R group or side chain.

Structure of the simplest amino acid, glycine

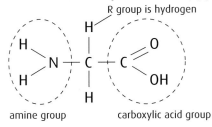

R group is hydrogen

amine group   carboxylic acid group

Figure 7.16 The general structure of an amino acid and the structure of glycine.

serine – a hydrophilic amino acid

alanine – a hydrophobic amino acid

and non-polar amino acids have different properties and their positions in a molecule affect the behaviour and function of the whole protein.

Amino acids with non-polar side chains are **hydrophobic**. Those with polar side chains are **hydrophilic**. Non-polar amino acids are found in parts of proteins that are in hydrophobic areas, while polar amino acids are in areas that are exposed to an aqueous environment such as cytoplasm or blood plasma.

For membrane proteins, the polar hydrophilic amino acids are found on the outer and inner surfaces in contact with the aqueous environment, while the non-polar hydrophobic amino acids are embedded in the core of the membrane in contact with the hydrophobic tails of the phospholipid bilayer (Figure **7.17**). This helps to hold the protein in place in the membrane. Some integral proteins act as channels, and the pore is lined with hydrophilic amino acids to enable polar substances to pass through.

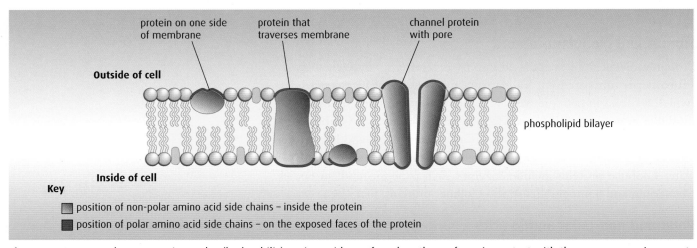

Figure 7.17 In membrane proteins, polar (hydrophilic) amino acids are found on the surfaces in contact with the aqueous environment, while non-polar (hydrophobic) amino acids are embedded inside the phospholipid bilayer.

Polar and non-polar amino acids are also important in enzymes, where they assist in the binding of substrates. An enzyme that acts on a polar substance (for example, amylase) has polar amino acids in its active site, whereas lipases have non-polar amino acids in the active site.

Polar amino acids on the surface of a protein increase its solubility while non-polar amino acids help a protein maintain its structure. Lipases are proteins that have polar groups on the outside so they are soluble in the gut, but non-polar groups in the their active site so that lipids can bind to them.

Protein functions

Some proteins build the structure of an organism's body, some act as chemical receptors and others act as enzymes or hormones. Table **7.1** summarises some important protein functions.

Protein	Function	Comments
hemoglobin	transport	hemoglobin binds oxygen in areas of high concentration and releases it in respiring tissues
actin and myosin	movement	these proteins interact to cause the contraction of muscles
pepsin	digestion	pepsin is an enzyme that digests protein in the stomach
collagen	structural	collagen strengthens bone and is a major component of tendons, ligaments and the skin
immunoglobulin	defence	immunoglobulins act as antibodies

Table 7.1 Some functions of proteins.

7.6 Enzymes

Assessment statements

- State that metabolic pathways consist of chains and cycles of catalysed reactions.
- Describe the induced-fit model.
- Explain that enzymes lower the activation energy of the chemical reactions that they catalyse.
- Explain the difference between competitive and non-competitive inhibition, with reference to one example of each.
- Explain the control of metabolic pathways by end-product inhibition, including the role of allosteric sites.

The basics of enzyme action were introduced in Chapter **3**. It would be useful to re-read that section before beginning this Higher Level topic.

Metabolic pathways

Metabolic pathways consist of chains or cycles of reactions that are catalysed by enzymes. Metabolism includes all the chemical activities that keep organisms alive. Metabolic pathways may be very complex, but most consist of a series of steps, each controlled by an enzyme. Simple pathways involve the conversion of substrates to a final product:

$$\text{substrate X} \xrightarrow{\text{enzyme 1}} \text{substrate Y} \xrightarrow{\text{enzyme 2}} \text{substrate Z} \xrightarrow{\text{enzyme 3}} \text{end product}$$

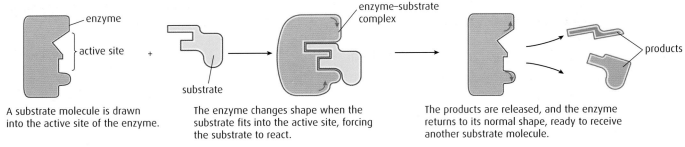

A substrate molecule is drawn into the active site of the enzyme.

The enzyme changes shape when the substrate fits into the active site, forcing the substrate to react.

The products are released, and the enzyme returns to its normal shape, ready to receive another substrate molecule.

Figure 7.18 The induced-fit model of enzyme action.

Each arrow represents the specific enzyme needed to catalyse the conversion of one substrate to the next.

Other metabolic pathways, such as photosynthesis or respiration, involve chains of reactions and cycles of reactions – as you will learn in Chapter **8**.

Induced-fit model of enzyme action

The lock–and–key hypothesis discussed on page **54** explains enzyme action by suggesting that there is a perfect match between the shape of the active site of an enzyme and the shape of its substrate. This theory was proposed in 1890 by Emil Fischer.

In the last century, research published by Daniel Koshland (1958) suggested that the process is not quite this straightforward. The lock–and–key hypothesis cannot account for the binding and simultaneous change that is seen in many enzyme reactions, nor the fact that some enzymes can bind to more than one similarly shaped substrate.

A more likely explanation of enzyme action is that the shape of an enzyme is changed slightly as a substrate binds to its active site (Figure **7.18**). The substrate causes or induces a slight change in the shape of the active site so it can fit perfectly. As the enzyme changes shape, the substrate molecule is activated so that it can react and the resulting product or products are released. The enzyme is left to return to its normal shape, ready to receive another substrate molecule.

This hypothesis is known as the **induced–fit model** of enzyme action.

Activation energy

Enzymes work by lowering the activation energy of the substrate or substrates. In order for a metabolic reaction to occur, the substrate has to reach an unstable, high-energy 'transition state' where the chemical bonds are destabilised, and this requires an input of energy, which is called the **activation energy**. When the substrate reaches this transition stage, it can then immediately form the product. Enzymes can make reactions occur more quickly because they reduce the activation energy of reactions they catalyse to bring about a chemical change (Figure **7.19**).

Metabolic reactions that occur in living organisms have to occur at the body temperature of the organism, which is never high enough to bring substrates to their transition state. The active site of an enzyme is very

Key

1 = activation energy without catalyst

2 = activation energy with catalyst

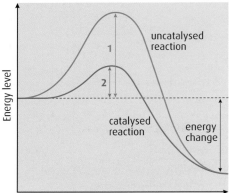

energy change = overall energy change after reaction – most biological reactions release more energy than they take in as activation energy and are said to be exothermic

Figure 7.19 Graph to show activation energy for an exothermic reaction with and without a catalyst.

Enzymes do not change the quantity of product that is formed, only the rate at which the product is formed.

important because it can lower the amount of energy needed to reach a transition state, so the reaction can occur at the temperature of the organism.

Competitive and non-competitive inhibition

Enzyme inhibitors are substances that reduce or prevent an enzyme's activity. Some inhibitors are competitive and others non-competitive.

Competitive inhibitors have molecules whose structure is similar to that of the substrate molecule that normally binds to the active site. They compete with the substrate to occupy the active site of the enzyme, and prevent the substrate molecules from binding (Figure **7.20**). The inhibitors are not affected by the enzyme and do not form products, so they tend to remain in the active site. This means that the rate of reaction is lower because the substrate cannot enter an active site that is blocked by an inhibitor. At low concentrations of substrate, competitive inhibitors have a more significant effect than at higher concentrations, when the substrate can out-compete the inhibitor (Figure **7.21**).

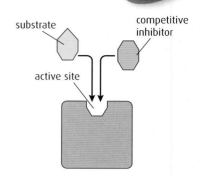

Figure 7.20 Competitive inhibition.

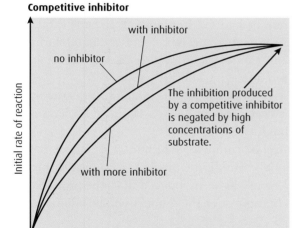

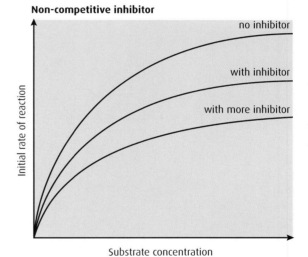

Figure 7.21 Graphs to show the effects of competitive and non-competitive inhibitors on reaction rate, as substrate concentration increases.

Non-competitive inhibitors also combine with enzymes but not at the active site. They bind at another part of the enzyme where they either partly block access of the substrate to the active site or cause a change in the shape of the enzyme so that the substrate cannot enter the active site (Figure **7.22**). Increasing the concentration of substrate in the presence of a non-competitive inhibitor does not overcome inhibition (Figure **7.21**).

Table **7.2** (overleaf) compares the nature and effects of competitive and non-competitive inhibitors.

Controlling metabolic pathways by end-product inhibition

End-product inhibition means that an enzyme in a pathway is inhibited by the product of that pathway. This prevents a cell over-producing a

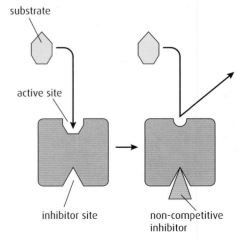

Figure 7.22 Non-competitive inhibition.

Competitive inhibitors	Non-competitive inhibitors

• structurally similar to the substrate molecule
• occupies and blocks the active site
• if concentration of inhibitor is low, increasing the concentration of substrate will reduce the inhibition
• examples include:
  – oxygen, which competes with carbon dioxide for the active site of ribulose bisphosphate carboxylase in photosynthesis
  – disulfiram, which competes with acetaldehyde for the active site of aldehyde dehydrogenase
	• structurally unlike the substrate molecule
	• binds at a site away from the active site, reduces access to it
	• if concentration of substrate is low, increasing the concentration of substrate has no effect on binding of the inhibitor so inhibition stays high
	• examples include:
	  – cyanide and carbon monoxide, which block cytochrome oxidase in aerobic respiration, leading to death

Table 7.2 Comparing competitive and non-competitive inhibitors.

substance it does not need at the time. Many products may be needed by the cell at a specific time or in specific amounts and over-production not only wastes energy but may also become toxic if the product accumulates.

In an assembly-line reaction, such as those described in Figure **7.23**, each step is controlled by a different enzyme. If the end-product begins to accumulate because it is not being used, it inhibits an enzyme earlier in the pathway to switch off the assembly line. In most cases, the inhibiting effect is on the first enzyme in a process, but in other cases it can act at a branch point to divert the reaction along another pathway.

When the end-product starts to be used up, its inhibiting effect reduces, the inhibited enzyme is reactivated and production begins again. This is an example of **negative feedback** (see page **154**).

End-product inhibition may be competitive or non-competitive. Competitive inhibition will only work if the product is a similar shape to the normal substrate and there can be an induced fit of the product or inhibitor onto the enzyme. In most cases, the product will be a different

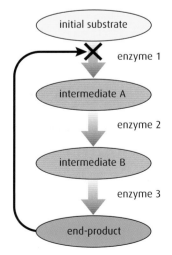

The end-product inhibits the enzyme catalysing the first reaction in the series, so all the subsequent reactions stop.

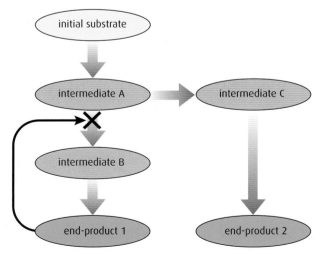

The end-product inhibits an enzyme in the pathway, which causes a different enzyme to come into play and the pathway is diverted down a different route.

Figure 7.23 End-product inhibition.

shape and therefore this has to be non-competitive inhibition. In this case, the enzyme is known as an **allosteric enzyme**, the product is called an **allosteric inhibitor** and the place where it binds to the enzyme is called the **allosteric site** (Figure **7.24**).

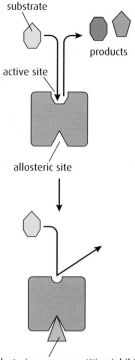

Figure 7.24 Allosteric control. Allosteric inhibitors prevent the active site functioning.

11 Outline the **four** levels of protein structure.

12 List **three** differences between fibrous and globular proteins.

13 List **four** functions of proteins.

14 Outline what is meant by 'activation energy'.

15 Explain how the induced-fit model differs from the lock-and-key hypothesis for enzyme action.

End-of-chapter questions

1 The components of a nucleosome are:

    A   ribosomal RNA and DNA
    B   8 histone proteins and DNA
    C   8 histones proteins in a ball + 1 further histone
    D   9 histone proteins and DNA   (1)

2 Which of the following statements is correct about the structure of DNA?

    A   The purine base cytosine is linked to the pyrimidine base guanine through three hydrogen bonds.
    B   The sugar–phosphate strands are antiparallel and linked by complementary base pairing.
    C   The bases are linked to each other through a 3'–5' linkage.
    D   Complementary base pairing of guanine with cytosine and adenine with uracil means that the two sugar–phosphate strands lie parallel.   (1)

3 Which of the following statements is correct about DNA replication?

A   The enzymes DNA ligase and RNA primase can be found on the lagging strand.

B   Okazaki fragments are produced by DNA polymerase I and DNA polymerase III on the leading strand.

C   On the lagging strand, the RNA primer is synthesised by RNA primase and then converted into a DNA strand with the enzyme DNA polymerase III.

D   The enzyme DNA polymerase III uses deoxynucleoside triphosphates to build a new DNA strand only on the leading strand.　　　　(1)

4 Which of the following statements is correct about transcription?

A   The enzyme RNA polymerase moves along the antisense strand in a $3' \rightarrow 5'$ direction.

B   The sequence of bases in the strand of RNA being synthesised is the same as the sequence of bases in the sense strand of DNA.

C   In eukaryotic cells, exons are removed from the primary RNA in the nucleus to make mature RNA.

D   Messenger RNA is synthesised by RNA polymerase in a $3' \rightarrow 5'$ direction.　　　　(1)

5 Which of the following statements is correct about translation?

A   Ribosomes that are free in the cytoplasm synthesise proteins that are primarily for lysosome manufacture and exocytosis.

B   Ribosomes are made of two subunits and mRNA binds to the larger one.

C   On the larger ribosome subunit there are three binding sites that can be occupied by tRNA molecules.

D   During polypeptide synthesis, the ribosome moves along the mRNA strand in a $3' \rightarrow 5'$ direction until it reaches a stop codon.　　　　(1)

6 Which of the following statements is correct about protein structure?

A   There are four levels of protein structure. The primary level is held together by covalent and hydrogen bonding.

B   Enzymes have an active site that is a three-dimensional structure produced by secondary level folding of the protein.

C   The α helix and β pleated sheet are both types of tertiary level folding.

D   Both tertiary and quaternary level proteins can form conjugated proteins.　　　　(1)

7 Which of the following statements is correct about enzymes?

A   Most enzymes use the lock-and-key model of substrate interaction as it is the most stable.

B   In allosteric control of metabolic pathways, a product within the pathway can act as a non-competitive inhibitor of an enzyme earlier in the pathway.

C   Increasing the concentration of substrate has no effect on the rate of a reaction being inhibited by a competitive inhibitor.

D   Competitive inhibitors bind to an allosteric site and alter the shape of the active site.　　　　(1)

8 Explain the process of translation. (9)

9 Explain how control of metabolic pathways can be brought about by end–product inhibition. (6)

10 It had always been assumed that eukaryotic genes were similar in organisation to prokaryotic genes. However, modern techniques of molecular analysis indicate that there are additional DNA sequences lying within the coding region of genes. Exons are the DNA sequences that code for proteins while introns are the intervening sequences that have to be removed. The graph shows the number of exons found in genes for three different groups of eukaryotes.

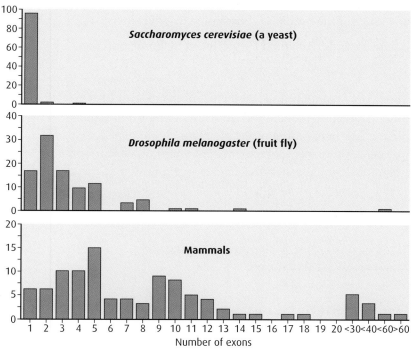

source: Benjamin Lewin (1999) *Genes VII*, OUP, p. 55

a Calculate the percentage of genes that have five or fewer exons in mammals. (1)

b Describe the distribution of the number of exons and the percentage of genes in *D. melanogaster*. (2)

c **i** Compare the distributions of the number of exons found in genes of *S. cerevisiae* and in mammals. (2)

   ii Suggest **one** reason for the differences in the numbers of exons found in genes of *S. cerevisiae* and in mammals. (1)

Human DNA has been analysed and details of certain genes are shown in the table below.

Gene	Gene size / kilobase pairs	mRNA size / kilobase pairs	Number of introns
insulin	1.7	0.4	2
collagen	38.0	5.0	50
albumin	25.0	2.1	14
phenylalanine hydroxylase	90.0	2.4	12
dystrophin	2000.0	17.0	50

source: William S Klug and Michael R Cummings, (2002), *Concepts of Genetics*, 7th edition, Prentice Hall, p. 314

d Calculate the average size of the introns for the albumin gene. (2)

e Analyse the relationship between gene size and the number of introns. (2)

f Determine the maximum number of amino acids that could be produced by translating the phenylalanine hydroxylase mRNA. (1)

Hemoglobin is a protein composed of two pairs of globin molecules. During the process of development from conception to adulthood, human hemoglobin changes in composition. Adult hemoglobin consists of two alpha–globin and two beta–globin molecules. Two globin genes occur on chromosome 16: alpha-globin and zeta-globin. Four other globin genes are found on chromosome 11: beta, delta, epsilon and gamma. The graph below illustrates the changes in expression of the globin genes over time.

g State which globin genes are the first to be expressed after fertilisation. (1)

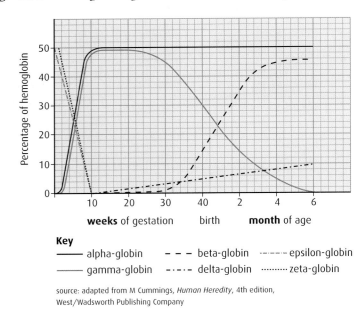

source: adapted from M Cummings, *Human Heredity*, 4th edition,
West/Wadsworth Publishing Company

h Compare the expression of the gamma-globin gene with the beta-globin gene. (3)

i Deduce the composition of the hemoglobin molecules at 10 weeks of gestation and at 2 months after birth. (2)

(total 17 marks)
© IB Organization 2009

11 The enzyme aspartate carbomoyltransferase (ACTase) is a key regulatory enzyme in nucleotide metabolism in bacteria. The activity of this enzyme was studied in the bacterium *Helicobacter pylori*, an important human pathogen. ACTase activity and the growth of *H. pylori* were measured at different concentrations of carbomoyl aspartate (CAA), the end product of the reaction catalysed by ACTase.

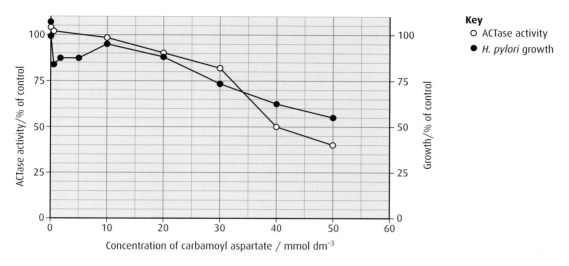

source: Burns, *et al.*, *Biological Procedures Online*, (1998),
htttp://www.biologicalprocedures.com

a **i** State the growth of *H. pylori* at a CAA concentration of 30 mmol dm^{-3}. (1)

    ii Calculate the change in ACTase activity between CAA concentrations of 20 and 40 mmol dm^{-3}. (1)

b Compare the effect of increasing CAA concentration on the growth of *H. pylori* and ACTase activity. (2)

c Explain the effect of CAA on ACTase activity. (2)

d Suggest a direct medical application of this information. (1)

(total 7 marks)

© IB Organization 2009

8 Cell respiration and photosynthesis

Introduction

Respiration and photosynthesis are two key biochemical pathways in ecosystems. Light energy from the Sun is trapped as chemical energy in photosynthesis and then the energy is transferred through food chains and released back to the environment as heat energy from respiration. The two pathways can be simply written as:

$$6CO_2 + 6H_2O + energy \underset{\text{respiration}}{\overset{\text{photosynthesis}}{\rightleftharpoons}} C_6H_{12}O_6 + 6O_2$$

There are a number of similarities between the two pathways, which will be examined in this chapter. The basics of photosynthesis and respiration are covered in Chapter **3**, and it would be useful to review this chapter before proceeding.

8.1 Cell respiration

Assessment statements

- State that oxidation involves the loss of electrons from an element, whereas reduction involves a gain of electrons; and that oxidation frequently involves gaining oxygen or losing hydrogen, whereas reduction frequently involves losing oxygen or gaining hydrogen.
- Outline the process of glycolysis, including phosphorylation, lysis, oxidation and ATP formation.
- Draw and label a diagram showing the structure of a mitochondrion as seen in electron micrographs.
- Explain aerobic respiration, including the link reaction, the Krebs cycle, the role of $NADH + H^+$, the electron transport chain and the role of oxygen.
- Explain oxidative phosphorylation in terms of chemiosmosis.
- Explain the relationship between the structure of the mitochondrion and its function.

Oxidation and reduction

Cell respiration involves several **oxidation** and **reduction** reactions. Such reactions are common in biochemical pathways. When two molecules react, one of them starts in the oxidised state and becomes reduced, and the other starts in the reduced state and becomes oxidised, as shown in Figure **8.1**.

There are three different ways in which a molecule can be oxidised or reduced, as outlined in Table **8.1**. In biological oxidation reactions, addition of oxygen atoms is an alternative to removal of hydrogen atoms. Since a hydrogen atom consists of an electron and a proton, losing hydrogen atoms (oxidation) involves losing one or more electrons.

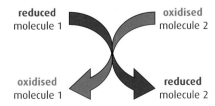

reduced molecule 1   **oxidised** molecule 2

oxidised molecule 1   **reduced** molecule 2

Figure 8.1 Oxidation and reduction are linked processes – as one molecule is reduced another is oxidised in a redox reaction.

Oxidation and reduction occur together in biochemical reactions. As one compound loses electrons, for example, another gains. In the simple equation for respiration, glucose is oxidised as hydrogen atoms, and therefore electrons, are gradually removed from it and added to hydrogen acceptors (the oxygen atoms on the left side of the equation), which become reduced.

$$C_6H_{12}O_6 + 6O_2 \rightarrow 6CO_2 + 6H_2O + energy$$

Chemical reactions like this are referred to as **redox reactions**. In redox reactions, the reduced molecule always has more potential energy than the oxidised form of the molecule. Electrons passing from one molecule to another carry energy with them.

Respiration

Cell respiration is the controlled breakdown of food molecules such as glucose or fat to release energy, which can be stored for later use. The energy is most commonly stored in the molecule adenosine triphosphate, or ATP. The respiration pathway can be divided into four parts:

- glycolysis
- link reaction
- Krebs cycle
- electron transfer chain and chemiosmosis.

Glycolysis

Glycolysis is the first stage in the series of reactions that make up respiration. It literally means 'breaking apart glucose'. The glycolysis pathway occurs in the cytoplasm of the cell. It is anaerobic (that is, it can proceed in the absence of oxygen) and produces pyruvate and a small amount of ATP. One molecule of the hexose sugar glucose is converted to two molecules of the three-carbon molecule called pyruvate with the net gain of two molecules of ATP and two molecules of $NADH + H^+$. The process is shown in detail in Figure **8.2** (overleaf).

1 The first steps are to add two phosphate groups from ATP, in a process called **phosphorylation**. A hexose bisphosphate molecule is produced. (This appears contrary to the purpose of respiration, which is to make ATP, but the two lost ATPs are recovered later.)
2 The hexose bisphosphate is now split into two triose phosphates in a reaction called **lysis**.
3 Now, another phosphorylation takes place but this time an inorganic phosphate ion, P_i, is used and not ATP. Two triose bisphosphates are formed. The energy to add the P_i comes from an **oxidation** reaction. The triose bisphosphate is oxidised and at the same time NAD^+ is reduced to $NADH + H^+$.
4 There now follows a series of reactions in which the two phosphate groups from each triose bisphosphate are transferred onto two molecules of ADP, to form two molecules of ATP – this is **ATP formation**. A pyruvate molecule is also produced.

Oxidation	Reduction
loss of electrons	gain of electrons
loss of hydrogen	gain of hydrogen
gain of oxygen	loss of oxygen

Table 8.1 Changes involved in oxidation and reduction.

An easy way to remember oxidation and reduction is to think of the words OIL RIG:

OIL = **O**xidation **I**s **L**oss (of electrons)

RIG = **R**eduction **I**s **G**ain (of electrons)

Bisphosphate and diphosphate

Although both these molecules contain two phosphate groups, the phosphates are joined in different ways. In a diphosphate molecule such as ADP, the two phosphates are joined to each other; in a bisphosphate molecule such as hexose bisphosphate, each phosphate is joined to a different part of the hexose molecule.

NAD^+ is a hydrogen carrier that accepts hydrogen atoms removed during the reactions of respiration. During glycolysis, two hydrogen atoms are removed and NAD^+ accepts the protons from one of them and the electrons from both of them.

$$NAD^+ + 2H \rightarrow NADH + H^+$$

Note that $NADH + H^+$ must be written in this way and should not be simplified to $NADH_2$.

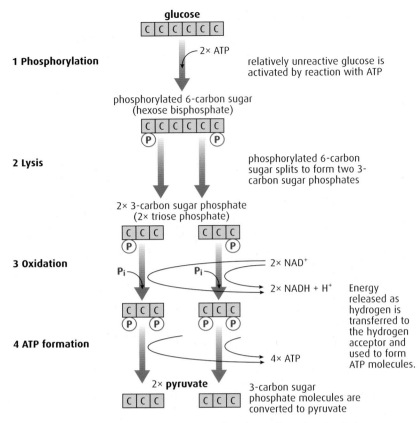

glucose

1 Phosphorylation

2× ATP

relatively unreactive glucose is activated by reaction with ATP

phosphorylated 6-carbon sugar
(hexose bisphosphate)

2 Lysis

phosphorylated 6-carbon sugar splits to form two 3-carbon sugar phosphates

2× 3-carbon sugar phosphate
(2× triose phosphate)

3 Oxidation

P_i P_i

2× NAD⁺

2× NADH + H⁺

Energy released as hydrogen is transferred to the hydrogen acceptor and used to form ATP molecules.

4 ATP formation

4× ATP

2× **pyruvate**

3-carbon sugar phosphate molecules are converted to pyruvate

Figure 8.2 The stages of glycolysis. Note that for each molecule of glucose, two molecules of ATP are used and four are formed, so there is a net gain of two ATPs.

Four molecules of ATP are formed by converting one molecule of glucose to two molecules of pyruvate. However, two molecules of ATP were required to start the pathway and so there is a net gain of two molecules of ATP per glucose. In addition two NADH + H⁺ are formed.

To summarise, the net products of glycolysis per glucose molecule are:

- 2 ATP
- 2 NADH + H⁺
- 2 molecules of pyruvate.

1 List **three** ways in which a substance can be reduced.

2 What molecule is used to phosphorylate glucose at the start of glycolysis?

3 State the name of the process that splits the hexose bisphosphate molecule into two triose phosphate molecules.

4 What is used to phosphorylate each triose phosphate molecule following the above reaction?

5 In the glycolysis pathway, which molecule is oxidised during an oxidation/reduction reaction?

6 What is the net gain of ATP from glycolysis per glucose molecule?

The link reaction and Krebs cycle

If oxygen is present, pyruvate formed during glycolysis moves into the mitochondrial matrix by facilitated diffusion. The structure of a mitochondrion is shown in Figures **8.3** and **8.4**.

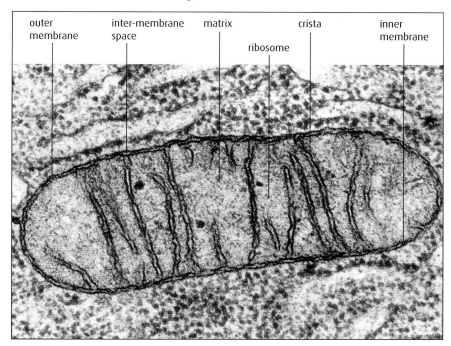

outer membrane   inter-membrane space   matrix   crista   inner membrane

ribosome

Figure 8.3 Electron micrograph of a mitochondrion (×72 000).

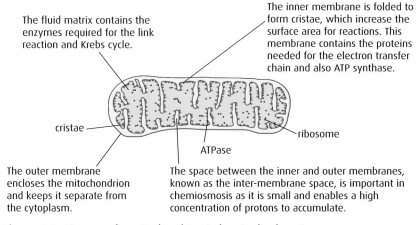

The fluid matrix contains the enzymes required for the link reaction and Krebs cycle.

The inner membrane is folded to form cristae, which increase the surface area for reactions. This membrane contains the proteins needed for the electron transfer chain and also ATP synthase.

cristae

ATPase

ribosome

The outer membrane encloses the mitochondrion and keeps it separate from the cytoplasm.

The space between the inner and outer membranes, known as the inter-membrane space, is important in chemiosmosis as it is small and enables a high concentration of protons to accumulate.

Figure 8.4 Diagram of a mitochondrion in longitudinal section.

Increasing area

Just as the inner lining of the small intestine is folded to increase its surface area to absorb food, so the inner mitochondrial membrane is folded into cristae to increase its surface area. The cristae provide a large area for the enzymes and molecules used in the electron transport chain (see page **199**).

The link reaction and the Krebs cycle pathways occur in the mitochondrial matrix, shown in Figure **8.5** (overleaf).

1 The **link reaction** converts pyruvate to acetyl CoA using coenzyme A, and a carbon atom is removed as carbon dioxide. This is called a **decarboxylation reaction**. At the same time as the carbon dioxide is removed, pyruvate is oxidised by the removal of hydrogen. The hydrogen atoms are removed by NAD^+ to form $NADH + H^+$.

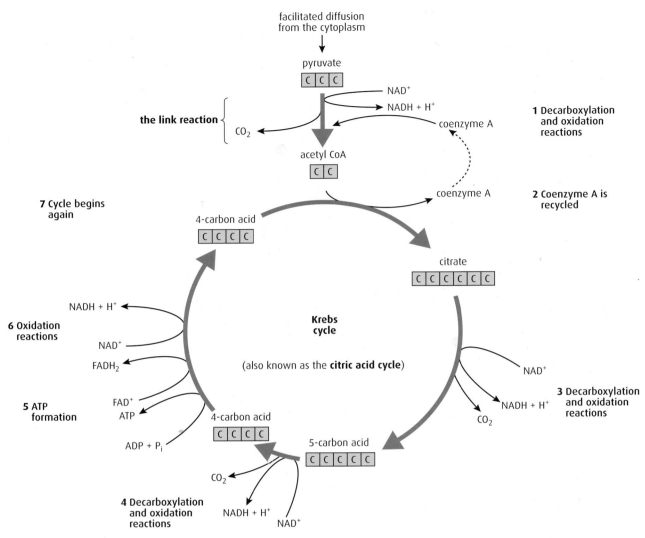

facilitated diffusion
from the cytoplasm

pyruvate
C C C

NAD$^+$

NADH + H$^+$

the link reaction

coenzyme A

CO_2

acetyl CoA
C C

coenzyme A

**1 Decarboxylation
and oxidation
reactions**

**2 Coenzyme A is
recycled**

**7 Cycle begins
again**

4-carbon acid
C C C C

citrate
C C C C C C

NADH + H$^+$

**Krebs
cycle**

NAD$^+$

**6 Oxidation
reactions**

NAD$^+$

(also known as the citric acid cycle)

NAD$^+$

FADH$_2$

NADH + H$^+$

**3 Decarboxylation
and oxidation
reactions**

CO_2

FAD$^+$

ATP

4-carbon acid
C C C C

5-carbon acid
C C C C C

**5 ATP
formation**

ADP + P$_i$

CO_2

**4 Decarboxylation
and oxidation
reactions**

NADH + H$^+$

NAD$^+$

Figure 8.5 The link reaction and Krebs cycle.

2 Acetyl CoA now enters the **Krebs cycle** to continue the processes
   of aerobic respiration. Immediately, the coenzyme A is removed to be
   recycled.

3 The two carbons that enter with acetyl CoA also leave as carbon
   dioxide from two decarboxylation reactions.

4 One molecule of ATP is formed.

5 Hydrogen is removed during oxidation reactions to the two hydrogen
   carriers NAD$^+$ and FAD$^+$.

6 Since the Krebs cycle is a cyclic process, what enters must eventually
   leave so that the cycle begins and ends with the same substances.

Because each molecule of glucose forms two molecules of pyruvate
during glycolysis, each glucose molecule requires two link reactions and
two rotations of the Krebs cycle. Thus, when working out the products

of the cycle we must consider two sets of products. So, to summarise, the products of the link reaction and Krebs cycle, per glucose molecule, are:

- 8 molecules of NADH + H$^+$
- 2 molecules of FADH$_2$
- 2 molecules of ATP
- 6 molecules of CO$_2$.

> Note that the correct method to show reduced FAD is FADH$_2$.

The electron transport chain, oxidative phosphorylation and chemiosmosis

Most of the ATP produced from glucose breakdown occurs in the last phase of respiration at the end of the **electron transport chain**. Reactions take place on the inner mitochondrial membrane of the cristae and in the inter-membrane space between the inner and outer membranes. The inner membrane holds molecules called **electron carriers**, which pick up electrons and pass them from one to another in a series of oxidations and reductions. The pathway is called the electron transport chain (ETC) because electrons from hydrogen are moved along it. Several protein molecules are electron carriers and the three key ones are shown in Figure **8.6**.

Electrons from NADH + H$^+$ are transferred onto the first electron carrier. As they pass through the carrier, they lose energy and this is used to pump a proton (H$^+$) from the matrix to the inter-membrane space, lowering the pH of the space. The electrons are then transferred to two further carriers and the process is repeated. As the electrons from one NADH + H$^+$ pass along the chain, a total of nine protons are pumped

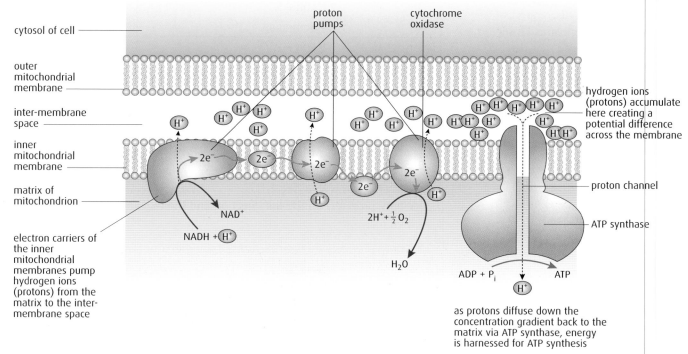

Figure 8.6 The electron transport chain showing oxidative phosphorylation and chemiosmosis.

into the inter-membrane space. At the end of the chain, the electrons are combined with protons and oxygen atoms to make water, in the oxidative part of **oxidative phosphorylation**.

The space between the membranes is very narrow and allows for a rapid increase in the concentration of the protons that are pumped into it during the electron transfer reactions. The protons in the inter-membrane space create a concentration gradient between the space and the matrix. These protons can now flow passively down this concentration gradient back into the matrix, through a very large integral protein. This is called **chemiosmosis**. The large protein contains the enzyme **ATP synthase**, which joins ADP and P_i to form ATP. Three protons flowing through this enzyme results in one ATP being formed. Since the electrons from one NADH + H^+ pump nine protons into the inter-membrane space, each NADH + H^+ results in the formation of three ATP. This is the phosphorylation part of oxidative phosphorylation.

$FADH_2$ also supplies electrons to the electron transport chain but further down the chain than NADH + H^+, missing the first protein pump. $FADH_2$ allows the production of just two ATPs.

Overall ATP production during aerobic respiration

Together, glycolysis, the link reaction and the Krebs cycle yield 36 ATP molecules for each molecule of glucose broken down by aerobic respiration, as summarised in Table **8.2**.

Stage		ATP use	ATP yield
glycolysis	2 ATP used at the start	−2 ATP	
	2 NADH + H^+		+4 ATP
	ATP formation		+4 ATP
link reaction	2 NADH + H^+		+6 ATP
Krebs cycle	ATP formation		+2 ATP
	6 NADH + H^+		+18 ATP
	2 $FADH_2$		+4 ATP
net energy yield			+36 ATP

Table 8.2 Summary of ATP production during aerobic respiration.

7 Where precisely do the link reaction and the reactions of Krebs cycle take place?

8 Where precisely do the reactions of the electron transport chain take place?

9 In the link reaction, is pyruvate oxidised or reduced?

10 Name the molecule that enters the Krebs cycle.

11 During one rotation of the Krebs cycle, how many molecules of carbon dioxide are formed?

Chemiosmosis

Osmosis is the passive flow of water molecules down a concentration gradient through a partially permeable membrane. Chemiosmosis is similar but instead of water moving, it is protons that pass down a concentration gradient.

As Table **8.2** shows, the net production of ATP from one molecule of glucose is, in theory, 36. Biochemists have discovered that the actual production is closer to 30 ATPs and propose that this discrepancy occurs because some protons are used to transfer ATP from the matrix to the cytoplasm. Only about 30% of the energy in a glucose molecule generates ATP.

12 During one rotation of the Krebs cycle, how many molecules of ATP are formed directly by the cycle?

13 What is the purpose of the folding of the inner mitochondrial membrane?

14 What is the function of the electron transport chain (ETC)?

15 What happens to the pH of the inter-membrane space as electrons move along the ETC?

16 How many molecules of ATP are produced from one $NADH + H^+$?

17 Name the molecule that the protons pass through going from the inter-membrane space to the matrix.

8.2 Photosynthesis

Assessment statements

- Draw and label a diagram showing the structure of a chloroplast as seen in electron micrographs.
- State that photosynthesis consists of light-dependent and light-independent reaction.
- Explain the light-dependent reactions.
- Explain photophosphorylation in terms of chemiosmosis.
- Explain the light-independent reactions.
- Explain the relationship between the structure of the chloroplast and its function.
- Explain the relationship between the action spectrum and the absorption spectrum of photosynthetic pigments in green plants.
- Explain the concept of limiting factors in photosynthesis with reference to light intensity, temperature and concentration of carbon dioxide.

The reactions of photosynthesis

Photosynthesis is the process by which light energy is harvested and stored as chemical energy, primarily in sugars but also in other organic molecules such as lipids. It occurs in green plants, algae and some bacteria. All these organisms are known as **autotrophs**, which means they can make their own food.

Photosynthesis can be divided into two parts:
- the light-dependent reaction
- the light-independent reaction.

The light-dependent reaction produces compounds that are used in the light-independent reaction.

Both the light-dependent and the light-independent reactions take place in the **chloroplasts** of plant cells (Figures **8.7** and **8.8**, overleaf). The stroma contains the enzymes required for the light-independent reaction and the stacks of thylakoid membranes increase the surface area for the light-dependent reaction.

The light-dependent and light-independent reactions

Both of these reactions are part of photosynthesis and can only occur when there is sufficient light. The light-independent reactions do not have to take place during darkness.

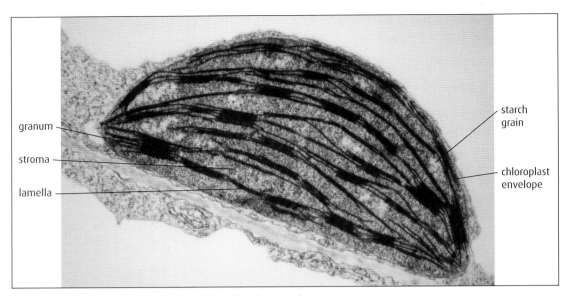

Figure 8.7 Electron micrograph of a chloroplast (×20 000).

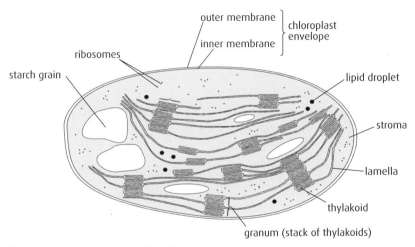

Figure 8.8 Diagram of a chloroplast.

The light-dependent reaction

The **light–dependent reaction** occurs on the **thylakoid membranes** of the chloroplast and is powered by light energy from the Sun. Each thylakoid is a flattened sac so the space in the middle is narrow. The thylakoid membranes form stacks called **grana**, which may be joined together by intergranal membranes. Light is absorbed by photosynthetic pigments such as chlorophyll, which are found on the granal membranes. There are several pigments found in plants and each one absorbs light of a slightly different wavelength. The pigments are associated with proteins that are involved in electron transport, proton pumping and chemiosmosis.

The photosynthetic pigments are combined into two complex groups called **photosystems I and II**, which absorb the light energy and use this to boost electrons to a higher energy level so that they become 'excited', as shown in Figure **8.9**.

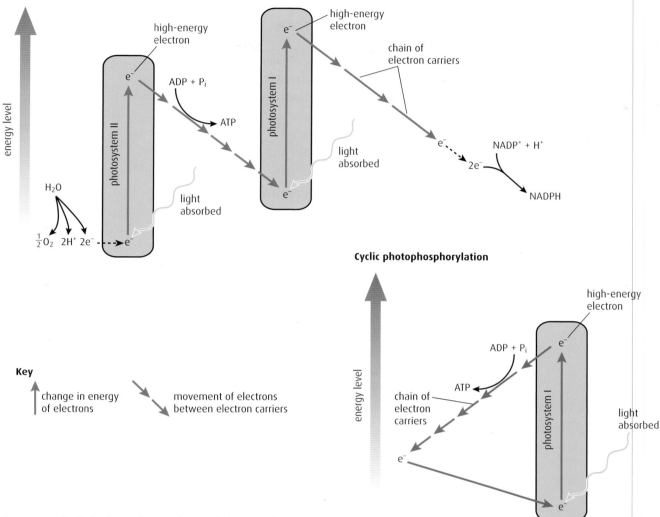

Non-cyclic photophosphorylation

energy level

high-energy electron

ADP + P$_i$

ATP

photosystem II

high-energy electron

photosystem I

chain of electron carriers

light absorbed

NADP$^+$ + H$^+$

2e$^-$

NADPH

H$_2$O

$\frac{1}{2}$O$_2$ 2H$^+$ 2e$^-$

light absorbed

Key

change in energy of electrons

movement of electrons between electron carriers

Cyclic photophosphorylation

energy level

ADP + P$_i$

ATP

chain of electron carriers

photosystem I

high-energy electron

light absorbed

Figure 8.9 The light-dependent pathway of photosynthesis.

1 The first step in the light–dependent reaction is the **photoactivation** of photosystem II. Pigment molecules in the photosystem absorb light energy and boost electrons in a molecule of chlorophyll to a higher energy level. The electrons are accepted by a carrier protein molecule at the start of the electron transport chain.

2 Photosystem II has to replace these lost electrons and it does this by taking them from water. Water is split into electrons, protons (hydrogen ions) and an oxygen atom. Since the splitting is brought about by light energy, it is called **photolysis**. The oxygen is released as an excretory product.

3 Excited electrons travel along the electron transport chain into photosystem I. As they do this, they lose energy but this is used to pump protons into the thylakoid interior (in a similar way as occurs in the electron transport chain in the mitochondrion). The thylakoid interior is small and so a proton concentration gradient builds up quickly. The protons then flow out through a large channel protein,

almost identical to the one in mitochondria, which contains the enzyme ATP synthase. This time though, the formation of ATP is called **photophosphorylation** and it occurs between photosystems II and I (Figure **8.10**).

4 Absorption of light energy causes photoactivation in photosystem I, boosting more electrons to an even higher energy level. The electrons that arrive from photosystem II replace those that are displaced. The electrons at the higher energy level are combined with protons in the hydrogen carrier $NADP^+$ to form $NADPH + H^+$.

The two products of the light-dependent reaction, ATP and $NADPH + H^+$, are used to drive the light-independent reaction.

Cyclic and non-cyclic photophosphorylation

When ATP is produced using energy from excited electrons flowing from photosystem II through photosynthesis I and on to $NADP^+$, the process is called **non-cyclic photophosphorylation**.

When light is not a limiting factor, the light-independent reactions may proceed more slowly than the light-dependent reaction, so that the supply of $NADP^+$ runs out. This means the electrons boosted up from photosystem I have no acceptor available to take them. They rejoin the electron transport chain near the start and generate more ATP for the light-independent reaction. This alternative pathway is called **cyclic photophosphorylation** (Figure **8.9**).

NADP$^+$ is very similar to NAD$^+$ – it simply has a phosphate group attached. An easy way to remember that photosynthesis uses NADP$^+$ is to note that they both have a letter 'P'.

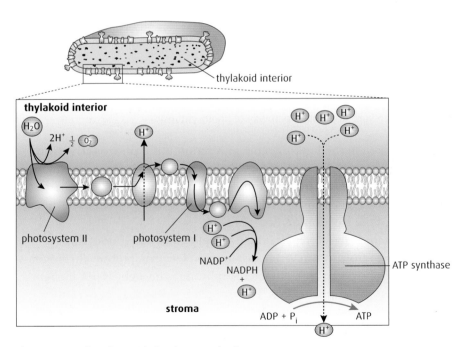

Figure 8.10 Chemiosmosis in photosynthesis.

The light-independent reaction

The **light-independent reaction** occurs in the stroma of the chloroplast and is a cyclic pathway called the **Calvin cycle**. The pathway is shown in Figure **8.11**. (Large organic molecules have been simplified to show just the number of carbon atoms they contain.) ATP and NADPH + H$^+$ formed during the light-dependent stage supply energy and reducing power for the Calvin cycle. The final product of the cycle is carbohydrate.

During each turn of the Calvin cycle one molecule of carbon dioxide is used so Figure **8.11** shows three cycles combined together. As this is a cycle, what goes in must leave, so three carbons enter in three molecules of carbon dioxide and three carbons leave in one molecule of triose phosphate, which can be used to form glucose or other organic compounds.

1 At the start of the cycle, the acceptor molecule ribulose bisphosphate (RuBP) combines with incoming carbon dioxide from the air to form glycerate 3-phosphate (GP). This reaction is called **carbon fixation**. It is catalysed by **RuBP carboxylase**, an enzyme that is sometimes called **rubisco**.

2 The ATP and NADPH + H$^+$ from the light-dependent reaction convert the glycerate 3-phosphate into triose phosphate (TP). Glycerate 3-phosphate therefore becomes reduced to triose phosphate. No more phosphate is added so the only input from ATP is energy.

3 Six molecules of triose phosphate are produced but only five are needed to reform the ribulose bisphosphate to keep the cycle going. The extra triose phosphate leaves the cycle and since it takes a phosphate with it, this is replaced in the cycle from ATP.

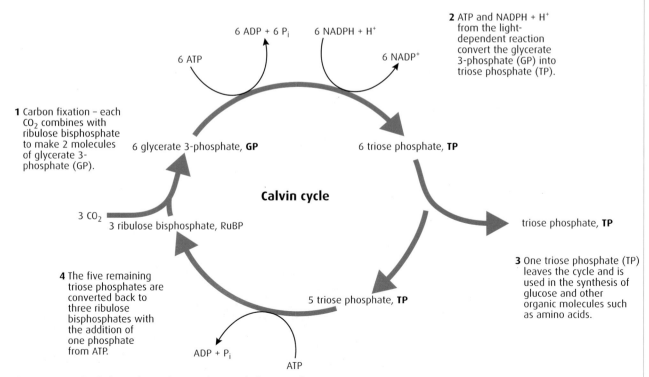

2 ATP and NADPH + H$^+$ from the light-dependent reaction convert the glycerate 3-phosphate (GP) into triose phosphate (TP).

6 ADP + 6 P$_i$ 6 NADPH + H$^+$

6 ATP   6 NADP$^+$

1 Carbon fixation – each CO$_2$ combines with ribulose bisphosphate to make 2 molecules of glycerate 3-phosphate (GP).

6 glycerate 3-phosphate, **GP**   6 triose phosphate, **TP**

Calvin cycle

3 CO$_2$
3 ribulose bisphosphate, RuBP

triose phosphate, **TP**

3 One triose phosphate (TP) leaves the cycle and is used in the synthesis of glucose and other organic molecules such as amino acids.

4 The five remaining triose phosphates are converted back to three ribulose bisphosphates with the addition of one phosphate from ATP.

5 triose phosphate, **TP**

ADP + P$_i$

ATP

Figure 8.11 The light-independent pathway of photosynthesis.

Six 'turns' of the Calvin cycle produces two triose phosphate molecules, which can be combined to form the final product, glucose. Some triose phosphate molecules will follow other pathways to make other organic carbohydrate molecules, such as sucrose or cellulose, or other molecules that the plant needs, such as amino acids, fatty acids or vitamins.

18 Where does the light-independent reaction take place?

19 Where does the light-dependent reaction take place?

20 What is the name given to the absorption of light by the photosystems?

21 Which colour of the light spectrum is not absorbed by plants?

22 What is the light energy used for when it is absorbed by the photosystems?

23 When photosystem II loses electrons, what molecule is used to replace them?

24 What is the name of the process in question **23**?

25 Name the waste product from the light-dependent reaction.

26 Name the **two** products from the light-dependent reaction that are needed for the light-independent reactions.

27 Name the starting acceptor molecule in the Calvin cycle, which reacts with carbon dioxide.

28 Name the product of this reaction.

29 The molecule named in question **28** reacts with the molecules named in question **26**. Name the product of this reaction.

30 What is the name given to the formation of ATP in the light-dependent reaction?

31 Name the pathway where electrons from photosystem I are recycled back into photosystem I.

Creative endeavour

Occasionally, the answer to a question about an unknown biochemical pathway is discovered as a result of designing an investigation that is simple and elegant. To find the steps involved in the light–independent reaction, a team led by Melvin Calvin (1911–1997) designed what he called the 'lollipop' apparatus.

Question to consider

To what extent could an elegant scientific protocol be considered a work of art?

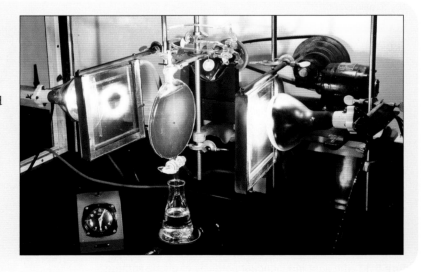

The action spectrum and the absorption spectrum

The spectrum of colours that humans can perceive is just part of the electromagnetic spectrum. The range of wavelengths in visible light is from 400 nm to about 700 nm. Light provides the energy for photosynthesis but not all wavelengths are absorbed equally by the chloroplasts. If white light is shone onto chloroplasts, the wavelengths they absorb depend on the pigments present in them. Figure **8.12** shows an investigation in which the pigments from chloroplasts have been extracted and form a solution. They are illuminated by light that has passed through a prism, so that the whole spectrum is visible. As the spectrum of wavelengths passes through the solution, the red and blue colours are lost, because they have been absorbed by the pigments. The green part of the spectrum is not affected, as chlorophyll does not absorb green light.

The investigation in Figure **8.12** can be made more sophisticated by filtering white light so that only a precise wavelength is shone onto the chlorophyll solution. The proportion of each wavelength that is absorbed by the solution can be measured and an **absorption spectrum,** which shows the relative amounts of each wavelength that is absorbed, can be built up. Each pigment has a characteristic absorption spectrum, as shown in Figure **8.13** (overleaf).

The rate of photosynthesis can be measured in several ways, one of which is to measure the volume of oxygen released. Rapid oxygen production indicates a high rate of photosynthesis. If the rate is measured for a range of wavelengths, a graph known as an **action spectrum** can be built up. Chlorophyll is more sensitive to some wavelengths of light than others and produces excited electrons at the highest rate at these wavelengths. The more excited electrons are produced, the faster the rate of photosynthesis. A typical action spectrum shows that blue and red light are used most efficiently.

Chlorophyll is the most important and abundant plant pigment used to capture light for photosynthesis. There are several forms of chlorophyll and each selectively absorbs certain wavelengths of light at the red and blue ends of the spectrum, while reflecting green light. Terrestrial plants and green algae contain two forms of the pigment, chlorophyll *a* and *b*, but diatoms contain a third type known as chlorophyll *c* instead of chlorophyll *b*.

Plants also contain several other pigments, including carotenoids, which are orange in colour, and anthocyanins, which are red. These pigments also selectively absorb certain wavelengths and reflect others. Absorbed light may be used in chemical reactions, and the reflected light determines the colour of the plant and can be important in attracting pollinators to flowers.

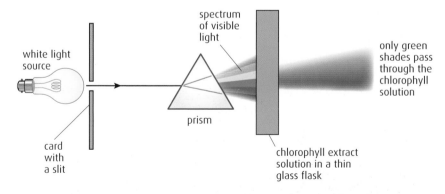

Figure 8.12 Only green light passes through a chloroplast extract solution; red and blue wavelengths are absorbed.

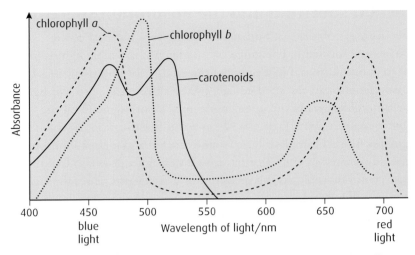

Figure 8.13 Absorption spectra for photosynthetic pigments – chlorophylls *a* and *b,* and carotenoid pigments.

Figure **8.14** shows action and absorption spectra plotted on one graph. The degree of correlation between the light energy absorbed at different wavelengths and the rate of photosynthesis indicates that absorbed light is used in the photosynthetic pathways.

Absorption and action spectra vary for different species of plant. Some plants contain different pigments such as carotene and xanthophylls, which absorb wavelengths that chlorophyll cannot. These pigments, known as accessory pigments, absorb some yellow and green light and account for the photosynthesis that occurs in this range.

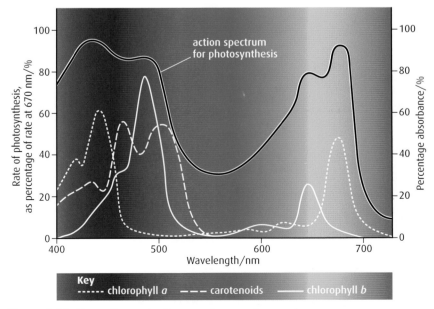

Figure 8.14 Absorption and action spectra superimposed.

Limiting factors

Like all metabolic processes, the photosynthetic pathway requires a number of components to make it work. If any of these components is in short supply, it limits the rate at which photosynthesis works.

Photosynthesis requires a suitable temperature, and sufficient light energy and carbon dioxide – any one of these can become a **limiting factor** and change the rate of photosynthesis.

When one step in photosynthesis is slowed down, the whole process slows down. If light intensity is increased, the rate of photosynthesis increases until a certain point when increasing light has no further effect, as shown in Figure **8.15**.

At low light intensities, there may be a shortage of the products of the light-dependent reaction so photosynthesis is slow. At point A, the plant is saturated with light and cannot photosynthesise at a faster rate even with more light. This indicates that some other factor is limiting the reaction.

Temperature affects enzymes that catalyse the reactions of photosynthesis so that if the temperature is too low the reactions may proceed very slowly and a graph of temperature versus rate of photosynthesis would look similar to Figure **8.16**. At low concentrations of carbon dioxide there may be insufficient carbon dioxide to be fixed in the Calvin cycle. At higher carbon dioxide concentrations, another factor may limit the reaction.

- In Figure **8.16**, experiment 1 shows that as light intensity increases so does the rate of photosynthesis between the points A and B on the graph. At these light intensities, light is the limiting factor. Between points B and C another factor has become limiting.
- In experiment 2, where the temperature has been increased to 20 °C, the line has not changed, showing that it is the carbon dioxide concentration that is the limiting factor – a change in temperature has had no effect.

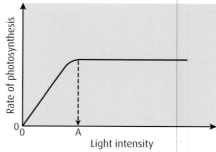

Figure 8.15 Rate of photosynthesis is proportional to light intensity, until point A, when some other factor is limiting.

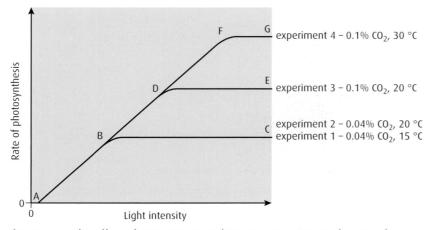

Figure 8.16 The effect of temperature and CO_2 concentration on the rate of photosynthesis.

- In experiment 3, raising the carbon dioxide concentration causes the rate of photosynthesis to increase to point D, but then another limiting factor comes in to play from D to E.
- In experiment 4 we see that, at the higher carbon dioxide concentration, raising the temperature causes the line to rise to F but then again another limiting factor has become limiting from F to G.

The level of carbon dioxide in the atmosphere is relatively low and carbon dioxide is frequently a limiting factor for photosynthesis. Horticulturalists increase the yield of their crops by maximising the rate of photosynthesis in their glasshouses. They do this by keeping the air inside warm with heaters, increasing the intensity of light using lamps and, in some cases, increasing the concentration of carbon dioxide.

Water is also essential for photosynthesis but it is seldom likely to be a limiting factor since all the cells of a plant must contain it to remain alive.

32 If the graphs of the photosynthesis action spectrum and the chloroplast pigment absorption spectrum are superimposed, what can be deduced?

33 What is meant by the term 'limiting factor'?

34 List **three** limiting factors for photosynthesis.

End-of-chapter questions

1 Which of the following statements is correct?

    A   Oxidation can involve the removal of oxygen from a compound.

    B   The solution inside a mitochondrion is called the matrix and the solution inside a chloroplast is called the stroma.

    C   The folds of the inner membrane of a mitochondrion are called grana.

    D   The photosynthetic pigments in a chloroplast are found on the cristae. (1)

2 Which of the following statements about glycolysis is correct?

    A   It is anaerobic, occurs in the cytoplasm, and includes at least one phosphorylation reaction.

    B   It is aerobic and includes a lysis reaction.

    C   In the final stages, two molecules of ATP are used in the formation of pyruvate.

    D   It is aerobic and does not include a lysis reaction. (1)

3 Which of the following statements about the link reaction and Krebs cycle is correct?

    A   Pyruvate in the mitochondrion matrix is oxidised to acetyl CoA.

    B   At the end of the link reaction, coenzyme A is recycled back into the cytoplasm to combine with another pyruvate molecule.

    C   During one rotation of the Krebs cycle there are three decarboxylation reactions.

    D   The link reaction occurs in the mitochondrial matrix and Krebs cycle occurs on the mitochondrial cristae. (1)

4 Which of the following statements about the electron transport chain is correct?

A As electrons flow along the chain, protons are pumped into the mitochondrial matrix.

B ATP is formed as electrons flow through the enzyme ATP synthase.

C The flow of electrons along the chain causes the pH of the inter-membrane space to increase.

D When protons diffuse through ATP synthase into the matrix, ATP is formed. (1)

5 Which of the following statements about the light-dependent reaction is correct?

A Photoactivation of photosystem I causes photolysis.

B Cyclic photophosphorylation involves both photosystems I and II.

C Electrons from the photolysis of water are transferred to $NADP^+$ from photosystem I.

D $NADP^+$ becomes oxidised when it combines with electrons and protons. (1)

6 Which of the following statements about the light-independent reaction is correct?

A The enzyme RuBP carboxylase is used to convert ribulose bisphosphate into triose phosphate.

B The conversion of glycerate 3-phosphate to triose phosphate requires ATP and $NADP^+$ from the light-dependent reaction.

C At the start of the Calvin cycle, carbon dioxide combines with glycerate 3-phosphate to form ribulose bisphosphate.

D The formation of ribulose bisphosphate from triose phosphate requires a phosphorylation reaction. (1)

7 Which of the following statements is correct?

A A limiting factor is one that determines what the end-product of a reaction is.

B A limiting factor is one that determines the rate of a reaction.

C Limiting factors for photosynthesis include light intensity, carbon dioxide concentration and glucose concentration.

D An absorption spectrum can be obtained by measuring the release of oxygen gas from pondweed at different wavelengths of light. (1)

8 Explain the reasons for:

a many grana in the chloroplast (2)

b poor growth of plants growing beneath trees (2)

c large amounts of RuBP carboxylase in the chloroplast (2)

(total 6 marks)

9 Explain the process of aerobic respiration in a cell starting at the end of glycolysis and including oxidative phosphorylation. (8)

10 Explain how the light-independent reaction of photosynthesis relies on the light-dependent reaction. (5)

11   At the start of glycolysis, glucose is phosphorylated to produce glucose 6-phosphate, which is converted into fructose 6-phosphate. A second phosphorylation reaction is then carried out, in which fructose 6-phosphate is converted into fructose 1,6-bisphosphate. This reaction is catalysed by the enzyme phosphofructokinase. Biochemists measured the enzyme activity of phosphofructokinase (the rate at which it catalysed the reaction) at different concentrations of fructose 6-phosphate. The enzyme activity was measured with a low concentration of ATP and a high concentration of ATP in the reaction mixture. The graph below shows the results.

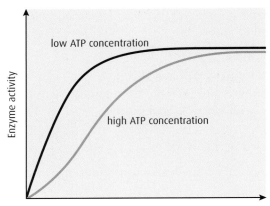

a   **i**   Using **only** the data in the above graph, outline the effect of increasing fructose 6-phosphate concentration on the activity of phosphofructokinase, at a low ATP concentration.   (2)

ii   Explain how increases in fructose 6-phosphate concentration affect the activity of the enzyme.   (2)

b   **i**   Outline the effect of increasing the ATP concentration on the activity of phosphofructokinase.   (2)

ii   Suggest an advantage to living organisms of the effect of ATP on phosphofructokinase.   (1)

(total 7 marks)
© IB Organization 2009

12   There are many abiotic factors that affect the rate of photosynthesis in terrestrial plants. Wheat is an important cereal crop in many parts of the world. Wheat seedlings were grown at three different concentrations of carbon dioxide (in parts per million) and the rate of photosynthesis was measured at various light intensities.

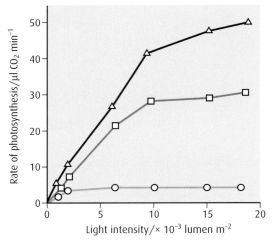

source: adapted from J P Kimmins (1997) *Forest Ecology* (2nd edition) p. 161

a Describe the relationship between the rate of photosynthesis and light intensity for wheat seedlings grown at a CO_2 concentration of 500 ppm. (2)

b Outline the effect of CO_2 concentration on the rate of photosynthesis of the wheat seedlings. (3)

c The normal atmospheric concentration of CO_2 is 370 ppm. Deduce the effect of doubling the CO_2 concentration to 740 ppm on the growth of wheat plants. (2)

Leaf area and chlorophyll levels were measured in sun leaves and shade leaves of *Hedera helix* (English ivy) and *Prunus laurocerasus* (cherry laurel). Sun leaves developed under maximal sunlight conditions while shade leaves developed at reduced sunlight levels in the shadow of other leaves.

Species	Leaf type	Chlorophyll/$\mu g\,ml^{-1}$	Leaf area/cm^2
ivy	shade	4.3	72.6
	sun	3.8	62.9
laurel	shade	4.7	38.7
	sun	4.2	25.7

source: D Curtis, plant ecology independent project (1990)

d Calculate the percentage increase in the amount of chlorophyll in shade leaves of ivy compared to sun leaves of ivy. (1)

e Suggest a reason for the differences in chlorophyll concentration and leaf area in sun and shade leaves in these two species. (2)

(total 10 marks)
© IB Organization 2009

9 Plant science

Introduction

Plants are a vital part of almost every ecosystem. As autotrophs, they start food chains by producing carbohydrates and other organic molecules that are needed by heterotrophs. They also produce oxygen and absorb carbon dioxide from the atmosphere or from water. When they die, their remains contribute to the humus, which is an important part of soil structure.

9.1 Plant structure and growth

Assessment statements

- Draw and label plan diagrams to show the distribution of tissues in the stem and leaf of a dicotyledonous plant.
- Outline three differences between the structures of dicotyledonous and monocotyledonous plants.
- Explain the relationship between the distribution of tissues in the leaf and the functions of these tissues.
- Identify modifications of roots, stems and leaves for different functions: bulbs, stem tubers, storage roots and tendrils.
- State that dicotyledonous plants have apical and lateral meristems.
- Compare growth due to apical and lateral meristems in dicotyledonous plants.
- Explain the role of auxin in phototropism as an example of the control of plant growth.

Tissues in the stem and leaf

A typical land plant is made up of three major organs: the roots, stems and leaves. Roots anchor the plant in the ground and absorb water and minerals for plant growth (Figure **9.1**). Some roots also store reserves of food.

The stem provides support for the leaves. It also contains tissues for the transport of materials from the root to the leaf, and for the distribution of the products of photosynthesis from leaves to the growing parts of the plant, as shown in Figure **9.2**. One of the most distinctive features of a plant stem is the range of different tissues it contains. The outer **cortex** contains cells that contribute strength to the stem maintaining its erect form. Embedded in the cortex are several tissues, particularly the **xylem** and **phloem** vessels, which make up **vascular bundles**. The central part of the stem is called **pith** and is composed of spongy cells that provide an area for storage.

Some plants have just a single large leaf, but most plants have many leaves, distributed on shoots or branches that arise from the main stem. Leaves are often arranged in a mosaic to maximise the efficiency of light capture and so that none of them obscures or shades other leaves. The general structure of plant leaves is shown in Figure **9.3**. Leaves come in a huge range of shapes and sizes, but all share several common features.

The upper **epidermis** is covered by an outer **cuticle** of wax, which lets visible light through, but prevents water loss through the upper

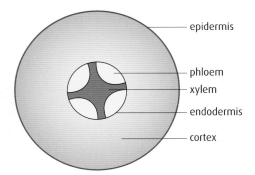

Figure 9.1 A cross-section of a root. The epidermis protects the outer layer of the root. The cortex carries water to the xylem, which transports it to the rest of the plant. The phloem carries nutrients and minerals around the plant.

epidermis —
phloem —
xylem —
endodermis —
cortex —

surface. The epidermis itself contains a layer of flattened, rectangular, transparent cells. These help protect the leaf from invading pathogens such as fungal spores. Below the epidermis is the **palisade layer**, containing elongated cells with numerous chloroplasts. The cells are closely packed together to maximise the amount of photosynthesis that can take place. Chloroplasts often move up towards the upper part of these palisade cells, so they can receive more light. Below the palisade layer, **spongy mesophyll** cells, also containing some chloroplasts, are loosely packed together with large **air spaces** surrounding them. Diffusion of gases to and from the stomata can easily occur through these air spaces.

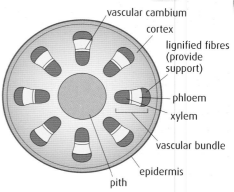

Figure 9.2 Transverse section through a young stem to show the distribution of tissues.

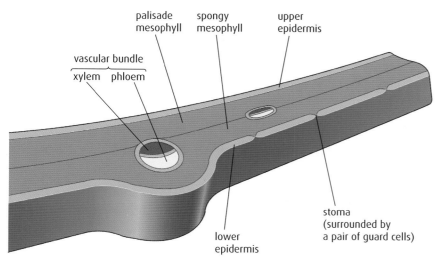

Figure 9.3 The structure of a leaf; water enters the leaf as liquid water in the xylem, and diffuses out as water vapour through the stomata.

The lower epidermis, which covers the lower leaf surface, has **guard cells** embedded in it, in many types of leaf. Guard cells contain chloroplasts and have an uneven thickening of cellulose in their cell walls. As they take in or lose water they change shape, opening or closing the pore or **stoma** (plural **stomata**) between them. This allows carbon dioxide, water vapour and oxygen to pass in and out of the leaf. Stomata on the underside of a leaf are in a shaded position and protected from excess heat, helping to prevent too much water being lost through them.

Leaves also contain vascular bundles, which are continuous with those in the stem. As well as providing support for the leaf, the xylem in the vascular bundles brings water and minerals that are drawn up from the roots directly into the leaves. The water is necessary for photosynthesis, and the minerals are necessary for growth.

Monocotyledons and dicotyledons

Flowering plants, or **angiosperms**, are grouped into two classes: **monocotyledonous** plants (having one seed leaf) and **dicotyledonous** plants (having two seed leaves). Apart from the number of seed leaves, there are several other physical differences between the two groups of plants (Table **9.1**, overleaf).

Advances in plant classification

Recent research into the evolutionary history of angiosperms has revealed new evidence about differences between members of the group. A new classification has been devised by the Angiosperm Phylogeny Group. It divides angiosperms into three groups rather than just two. The three new groups are: monocotyledons, magnoliids and eudicots. Some plant scientists have already started using the new APG system to organise their specimens.

Feature	Monocotyledonous plants	Dicotyledonous plants
seed leaves	one	two
leaf veins	usually parallel	radiating in a net-like pattern
distribution of vascular bundles in the stem	scattered through the stem	arranged in a ring around the outside of the stem
stomata	common in both upper and lower epidermis	mostly found in lower epidermis
flowers	stamens and other structures in the flower occur in multiples of three	stamens and other structures in the flower occur in multiples of four or five
roots	unbranched, fibrous roots usually growing from the stem	main tap root with branches from it

Table 9.1 Monocotyledons and dicotyledons compared.

There are more than 50 000 species of monocotyledons, including orchids, grasses and lilies. Dicotyledons are a much larger group with almost 200 000 known species. They include magnolias, daisies, gentians and proteas.

Adaptations to different environments

If plants from different habitats are compared, they may well look quite different. Their roots, stems and leaves serve the same functions, but their structures may be modified to suit their environments. Such adaptations give the plant the ability to survive in a particular climate or enable it to avoid being eaten by herbivores, for example.

Root modifications

Some plants have large tap roots that act as storage organs for food reserves. Examples of these include carrots, cassava and turnips (Figure **9.4**). Others have swollen roots that can store water. Mangroves produce air roots, which extend above waterlogged soil or water to absorb oxygen (Figure **9.5**). Many cacti have extensive surface roots, which can quickly absorb any rain that falls before it evaporates in hot conditions.

Figure 9.4 The carrot plant has large tap roots where it stores food reserves.

Figure 9.5 The roots of mangrove trees extend above the soil or water so they can absorb oxygen.

Bulbs

Some plants use swollen, underground leaf bases to form food storage organs called **bulbs**. These enable plants to survive over winter when photosynthesis may not be possible. Onions and daffodils are examples of plants that produce bulbs. The leaf bases can be seen arranged over one another around a central shoot in Figure **9.6**.

Leaves

Many plants survive in very arid climates where water loss from leaves would cause problems. They solve this in different ways. Some have very waxy leaves to minimise water loss, while others have reduced leaves or no leaves at all, for the same purpose.

Plants in both temperate and tropical regions have evolved modified leaves called **tendrils** as a mechanism for getting their leaves into sunlight, even when they are shaded by surrounding vegetation. Tendrils enable the plant to cling onto other plants or objects, so that it is supported as it grows and climbs up towards the light (Figure **9.7**).

Stem tubers

Tubers are stems that grow below ground and are used to store food. Potatoes are stem tubers that store carbohydrate in the form of starch (Figure **9.8**).

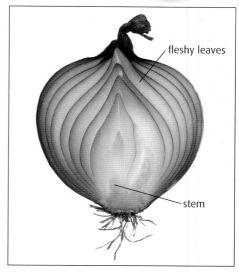

Figure 9.6 An onion bulb is made up of modified leaves.

Figure 9.7 Curly tendrils in the garden pea plant grip on to surrounding objects, allowing the plant to grow up into the light.

Figure 9.8 Potato tubers are modified stems.

Potato production

Most cultivated varieties of potato are descended from a species first grown in Chile about 10 000 years ago. Potatoes are a staple food in many countries, and are the world's largest food crop. Today, a third of all potatoes are grown in China.

Meristems

Meristems are the growing parts of a flowering plant where cells may divide by mitosis throughout the life of the plant. There are two types of meristem in a dicotyledonous plant – the **apical meristems** found at the tip of the root and the shoot, and the **lateral meristems** found in the vascular bundles of the stem. Growth in the main stem occurs at the apical or primary meristem, with fresh tissue forming at the growing tip (Figure **9.9**). This allows a plant to grow upwards from the soil and towards light so that leaves can obtain sufficient light for photosynthesis. In the root, growth of the apical meristem extends the root into the soil.

Many plants also grow at lateral meristems in the vascular **cambium**. This makes stems and roots thicker, and is known as **secondary growth**. Side growth may develop from the main stem as shoots or branches to take advantage of favourable conditions and to avoid competition from other plants.

If plants are damaged at the apical meristems, often the first lateral meristem is induced to grow and take over the role of the apical meristem. If a flower on the apical meristem is cut off, this will induce the lateral meristems to switch to producing flowers.

Auxin and phototropism

Plants produce **growth–regulating substances** that act to control growth and development. These substances are sometimes called plant hormones.

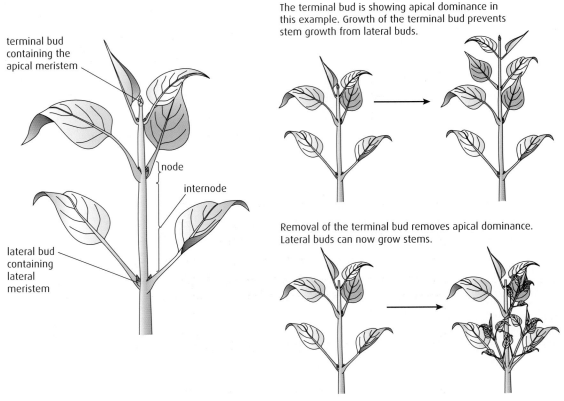

terminal bud containing the apical meristem

node

internode

lateral bud containing lateral meristem

The terminal bud is showing apical dominance in this example. Growth of the terminal bud prevents stem growth from lateral buds.

Removal of the terminal bud removes apical dominance. Lateral buds can now grow stems.

Figure 9.9 Apical meristems exert an inhibitory effect on the lateral meristems, called apical dominance.

Knowledge of these growth substances was noted by Charles Darwin in a report of his experiments that he published in 1880. He observed that oat shoots grew towards light because of some 'influence', which he proposed was transmitted from the shoot tip to the area immediately below. We now know that the substance that causes shoots to bend towards the light is **auxin**, and the response it causes is called **phototropism**. Auxin is found in the embryos of seeds and in apical meristems, where it controls several growth responses.

Auxin seems to act by loosening the bonds between cellulose fibres in plant cell walls and making them more flexible. The exact mechanism of auxin action is not fully understood. It has been suggested that auxin is redistributed to the side of a shoot tip that is away from a light source. The uneven distribution of auxin allows cell elongation on the shaded side of a shoot, which in turn causes bending towards light (Figure **9.10**).

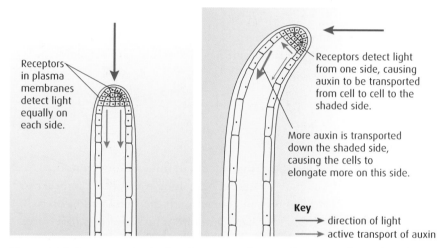

Receptors in plasma membranes detect light equally on each side.

Receptors detect light from one side, causing auxin to be transported from cell to cell to the shaded side.

More auxin is transported down the shaded side, causing the cells to elongate more on this side.

Key

→ direction of light
→ active transport of auxin

Figure 9.10 Some proteins in the plasma membranes of certain cells in plant shoots are sensitive to light. When light falls on them, they cause auxin to be transported to the shaded side of the shoot, which in turn causes the shoot to bend towards the light.

1 Outline the differences between monocotyledons and dicotyledons.

2 Outline the role of auxin in phototropism.

3 Compare the role of apical and lateral meristems in the growth of a plant.

4 Draw a plan of the structure of a typical stem to show the arrangement of tissue inside.

9.2 Transport in angiospermophytes

Assessment statements

- Outline how the root system provides a large surface area for mineral ion and water uptake by means of branching and root hairs.
- List ways in which mineral ions in the soil move to the root.
- Explain the process of mineral ion absorption from the soil into roots by active transport.
- State that terrestrial plants support themselves by means of thickened cellulose, cell turgor and lignified xylem.
- Define 'transpiration'.
- Explain how water is carried by the transpiration stream, including the structure of xylem vessels, transpiration pull, cohesion, adhesion and evaporation.
- State that guard cells can regulate transpiration by opening and closing stomata.
- State that the plant hormone abscisic acid causes the closing of stomata.
- Explain how the abiotic factors light, temperature, wind and humidity affect the rate of transpiration in a typical terrestrial plant.
- Outline four adaptations of xerophytes that help to reduce transpiration.
- Outline the role of phloem in active translocation of sugars (sucrose) and amino acids from source (photosynthetic tissue and storage organs) to sink (fruits, seeds, roots).

Roots

Roots are responsible for absorbing water and mineral ions from the soil. Many plants develop an extensive, branching root system in order to increase the surface area of root in contact with the soil. In addition, as new roots grow, numerous root hairs develop to increase the surface area even more (Figure **9.11**). Root hairs are temporary and die away to be replaced by new ones near the growing tip.

Plants require a number of minerals to make a variety of substances necessary for growth. A few of these are listed in Table **9.2**.

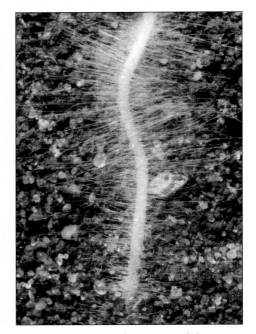

Figure 9.11 A root of a young radish showing the root hairs.

Mineral ion	Importance
calcium	constituent of cell walls
magnesium	needed to make chlorophyll
iron	required as a cofactor for many enzymes

Table 9.2 How plants use some important mineral ions.

Minerals are present in the soil as salts – for example, calcium occurs in the form of carbonates. These dissolve in soil water and the dissolved ions can move into root cells in different ways.

- Dissolved minerals may move into the root by **mass flow** of water carrying the ions, or by **facilitated diffusion** of ions from the soil water into root hairs, down their concentration gradient (Figure **9.12**). Both these processes are passive – that is, they do not require energy in the form of ATP.

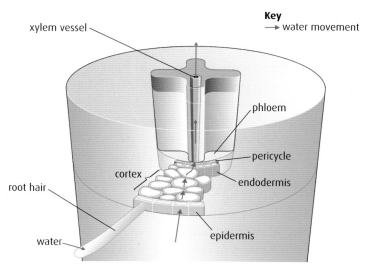

Figure 9.12 The pathway of water movement from root hair to xylem. The water may carry dissolved mineral ions.

- Where the concentration of a mineral is lower in the soil water than in plant cells, **active transport** is needed to take it up. Potassium, nitrate and phosphate are usually absorbed by active transport. Root hair cells contain mitochondria to provide ATP and most roots can only take in minerals if oxygen is available for aerobic respiration, to provide sufficient ATP. Experiments have shown that potassium ions stop moving into root cells from the soil when potassium cyanide is added. Cyanide is a potent blocker of respiration as it inhibits enzyme action, and so it prevents active transport.

- In other cases, there may be a close association, known as a **mutualistic relationship**, between the roots and a fungus (a mycorrhiza) (Figure **9.13**). Roots become covered with an extensive network of hyphae, which increase the surface area for absorption of both water and minerals. Minerals can pass directly from fungal hyphae to root cells.

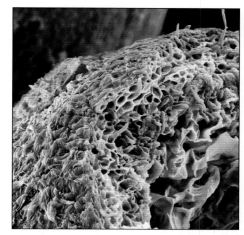

Figure 9.13 Electron micrograph of a fungus and a plant in a mutualistic relationship called a mycorrhiza. The thin, orange threads are fungal hyphae, existing within the cortex of a root (×540).

Support

Plants need to support their leaves and flowers and it is often the stem, which connects the roots to these structures, that supports them. Support is provided by cellulose cell walls, cell turgor and by thickening certain structures with lignin and other materials.

All plant cells are surrounded by a firm **cellulose** cell wall, which also contains hemicelluloses and pectin. Over time, some cells may thicken their cell walls with other carbohydrates such as **lignin**, which provide additional structure around the cell.

Under normal environmental conditions, the large central vacuole in plant cells is filled with fluid containing dissolved minerals. This fluid exerts pressure on the cell wall, so the cell becomes rigid and presses on adjacent cells. Cells in this condition are said to be **turgid**, and each exerts **turgor pressure** on surrounding cells. This is sufficient to support leaves and new, soft tissue. Its effect is most clearly seen in periods of drought when leaves droop and become soft or flaccid.

But turgor pressure is not enough to support the stem, especially if a plant is tall. Here, **xylem tissue** in the vascular bundles not only carries water but also provides support, as shown in Figure **9.14**. The xylem contains elongated cells, which are hollow, and become thickened with lignin forming a 'backbone' to support the stem.

Lignin is a complex substance that is very hard and resistant to decay. Perennial plants like trees lay down more lignin each year, forming wood.

Transpiration

Transpiration is the loss of water vapour from the leaves and stems of plants. Water is absorbed by the roots, travels up the stem in the xylem vessels in the vascular bundles to the leaves, and is lost by evaporation through stomata (Figure **9.15**).

Most plants grow in areas where the amount of water in the air, the **humidity**, is less than in the leaves. During the day when the stomata are open, water vapour leaves the air spaces in the spongy mesophyll through stomata in the lower epidermis and the stem. The evaporating water is drawn from the vascular bundles in the leaf and stem. The vascular bundles are continuous with those in the xylem from the roots so a column of water is formed connecting the roots, stem, leaves and air spaces. This is known as the **transpiration stream**.

Transpiration also carries minerals through the plant, and serves to cool leaves in warm conditions.

Cohesion–tension theory

The movement of water in the xylem can be explained by the cohesion–tension theory.

- Loss of water vapour from the stomata in the leaves results in 'tension' or negative pressure in the xylem vessels.

> **Transpiration** the loss of water vapour from the aerial parts of plants (the leaves and stems)

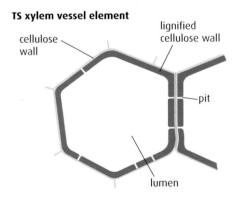

TS xylem vessel element

cellulose wall

lignified cellulose wall

pit

lumen

Types of lignified cell wall thickenings

spiral   annular   reticulate   pitted

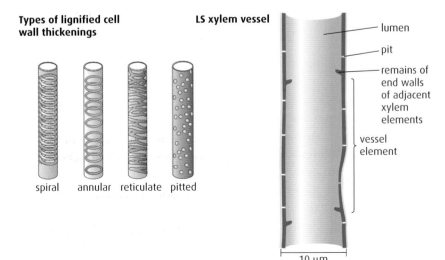

LS xylem vessel

lumen

pit

remains of end walls of adjacent xylem elements

vessel element

10 μm

Figure 9.14 Xylem vessels are not alive and have no plasma membrane, so water can easily move in and out of them.

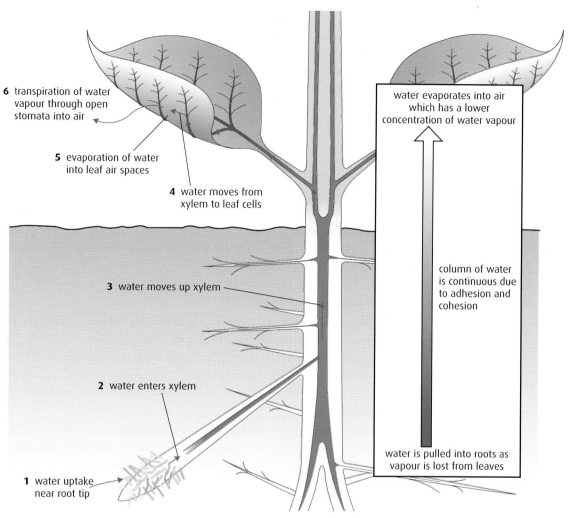

6 transpiration of water vapour through open stomata into air

5 evaporation of water into leaf air spaces

4 water moves from xylem to leaf cells

3 water moves up xylem

2 water enters xylem

1 water uptake near root tip

water evaporates into air which has a lower concentration of water vapour

column of water is continuous due to adhesion and cohesion

water is pulled into roots as vapour is lost from leaves

Figure 9.15 The movements of water through a plant: water moves from the soil to the air (from where there is more water to where there is less water).

- Water vapour re-enters the air spaces in the leaf from the xylem vessels.
- Continuous columns of water are drawn up the xylem due to cohesion between water molecules in the xylem and forces of adhesion between the water molecules and the xylem vessel walls. **Cohesion** is due to hydrogen bonding between water molecules and **adhesion** is caused by the hydrogen bonds between water molecules and molecules in the walls of the xylem vessels.
- The tension in the xylem is strong due to loss of water and there would be a tendency for xylem vessels to collapse inwards. The thickening provided by lignin prevents this happening.
- Water is drawn in from the cortex in the roots to replace water that is lost in transpiration.
- The tension caused by transpiration also causes water to be drawn into the roots from the soil.

Transpiration is largely controlled by the pairs of guard cells that surround the stomata. **Guard cells** have unevenly shaped cell walls with more cellulose on the side adjacent to the stoma. The inner part of the cell wall is less elastic, so that when guard cells take up water and become turgid, they take on a sausage-like shape and an opening – the **stoma** – is formed between them (Figure **9.16**). When the guard cells lose water, the cell walls relax and the stoma closes.

The opening and closing of stomata is controlled by the concentration of potassium ions. In darkness, these ions move out of the guard cells into surrounding cells. In light conditions, potassium ions are actively pumped into the vacuoles of guard cells. This creates an increased solute concentration so that water enters by osmosis, making the cells turgid and opening the stomata. A plant hormone called abscisic acid, produced in the roots during times of drought, affects potassium ion movement in guard cells. When abscisic acid is present, potassium ions leak out and water follows by osmosis. This means that the guard cells lose turgor and stomata close, thus conserving water.

Factors affecting transpiration

Several abiotic environmental factors (notably light, temperature, humidity and wind speed) influence the rate of transpiration in plants.

- Light affects transpiration directly by controlling the opening and closing of stomata. As light intensity increases, stomata open, speeding up the rate of transpiration. In darkness, stomata close, thus restricting transpiration.
- Temperature affects transpiration because heat energy is needed for the evaporation of water. As the temperature rises, the rate of transpiration also rises as water evaporates from the air spaces in the spongy mesophyll and diffuses out of the stomata.

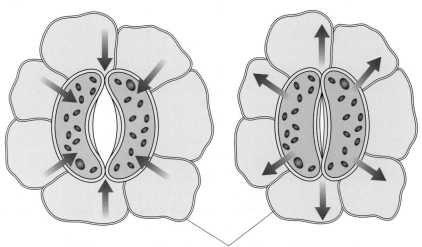

water enters guard cells by osmosis; guard cells become turgid, opening stoma

water leaves guard cells by osmosis; guard cells become flaccid, closing stoma

epidermis cells surrounding guard cells

Figure 9.16 The opening and closing of stomata. Gases can diffuse in and out of open stomata. When stomata are closed, water loss is minimised.

- An increase in atmospheric humidity reduces the rate of transpiration. Air in the mesophyll air spaces tends to be saturated with water vapour so if atmospheric air becomes more humid, the concentration gradient between the air space and the atmosphere is reduced and transpiration is slowed down.
- An increase in wind speed increases the rate of transpiration because it blows away the air just outside the stomata, which is saturated with water vapour. Reduced humidity near the stomata enables water vapour to diffuse more readily from the spongy mesophyll, where the air is very humid, to the air just outside the leaf, which has lower humidity.

Transpiration in xerophytes

Xerophytes are plants that live in arid climates – an example is shown in Figure **9.17**. Some xerophytes grow in areas where there is very little rainfall all the year, while others live in places where rainfall is intense but short lived, with long, dry periods for the rest of the year. In both cases, plants have evolved specialisations that enable them to survive shortages of water by reducing water loss.

Marram grass is well adapted to survive in the dry conditions found in sand dunes. Its leaves are rolled into tube-like shapes, which are protected on the outside by a thick waxy cuticle. Stomata of marram grass are protected deep inside pits (Figure **9.18**, overleaf) which themselves are rolled up inside the leaf. A lining of hairs on the inner side of the leaf keeps humid air trapped inside the rolled-up leaves. Hairs prevent water loss by diffusion. When the humidity of the air rises, marram grass is able to unroll its leaves using specialised hinge cells. When the leaf is unrolled, leaf hairs help conserve a supply of water by trapping moist air. This air remains inside the leaf when it rolls up again.

The Crassulaceae, a group of succulent plants, have evolved a mechanism allowing them to keep their stomata closed during the heat of the day, to reduce water loss. At night, the stomata open and carbon dioxide diffuses into the leaf. It is fixed temporarily in cells, and then is released for photosynthesis during the day when the stomata are closed. This is called crassulacean acid metabolism (CAM).

Translocation in the phloem

Translocation is the movement of organic molecules through the phloem tissue of plants. The phloem consists of two types of living cell: **sieve tube cells**, which are perforated to allow the movement of solutes through them, and **companion cells**, which are connected to the sieve tube cells as shown in Figure **9.19** (page **227**).

Whereas the xylem carries water and mineral salts only in an upward direction, the phloem can transport materials either up or down the plant. Translocation moves materials from a **source**, where they are made or stored, to a **sink**, where they are used, as shown in Figure **9.20** (page **227**).

Figure 9.17 *Opuntia*, or prickly pear, is a cactus with flattened photosynthetic stems that store water. The leaves are modified as spines, and this minimises water loss by reducing the surface area from which transpiration can take place. The spines also protect the plant from being eaten by animals.

Storage structures such as seeds and bulbs are sinks during the growing season but may also act as sources when they begin to sprout.

The leaves can roll up, exposing a tough, waterproof cuticle to the air outside the leaf.

Marram grass is one of the few plants that can thrive in mobile sand dunes, surviving the very dry conditions that are found there.

Specialised cells – hinge cells – cause the opening and closing of the marram grass leaf in response to air humidity. Leaf rolling traps air inside the rolled leaf. This air can remain humid even if the air outside is very dry.

The stomata are found deep in the grooves and open into the enclosed humid space inside a rolled leaf. Water has to diffuse a long way before it reaches moving air outside the leaf, slowing water loss.

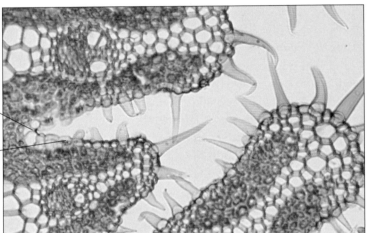

A light micrograph of a transverse section through a marram grass leaf (×137).

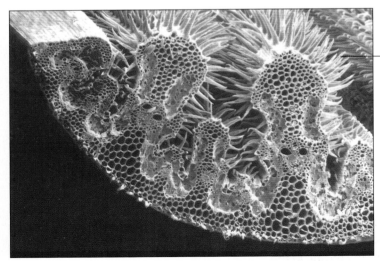

Hairs help to keep the humid air trapped inside a rolled leaf. When the leaf is unrolled, the hairs help to trap a thick layer of moist air close to the leaf surface, reducing air movement. Water vapour has to diffuse through this layer before it can be carried away in air movements. The thicker the layer, the more slowly water is lost by transpiration.

A scanning electron micrograph of a transverse section through part of a rolled leaf of marram grass (×90).

Figure 9.18 Adaptations of the xerophyte marram grass (*Ammophila arenaria*) to dry conditions.

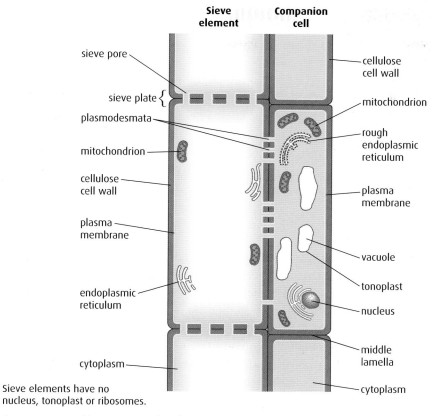

Sieve elements have no nucleus, tonoplast or ribosomes.

Figure 9.19 A phloem sieve tube element and its companion cell.

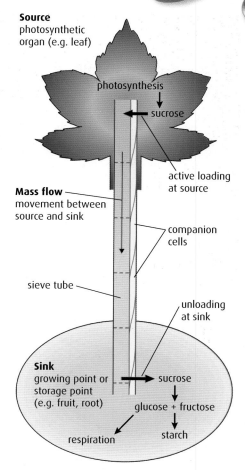

Figure 9.20 Sources, sinks and mass flow in phloem.

The products of photosynthesis, including sugars and amino acids, move from leaf cells, which are a source, into the phloem. Once in the phloem, they are translocated to sink regions, such as growing tissue in the meristems of roots, buds and stems, or storage organs like fruits and seeds.

All the materials that are moved by translocation are dissolved in water to form a solution called 'sap' which also carries plant hormones. Sugar is usually carried as sucrose, which enters and leaves the phloem by active transport using energy provided by the companion cells. Once materials have entered the phloem, they move passively throughout the plant.

5 List ways in which a terrestrial plant is supported.

6 Compare the structure of xylem and phloem.

7 State the substances that are carried in the xylem.

8 Explain how mineral ions enter the root.

9 Explain the importance of root hairs.

10 List the factors that affect the rate of transpiration.

9.3 Reproduction in angiospermophytes

Assessment statements

- Draw and label a diagram showing the structure of a dicotyledonous animal–pollinated flower.
- Distinguish between 'pollination', 'fertilisation' and 'seed dispersal'.
- Draw and label a diagram showing the external and internal structure of a named dicotyledonous seed.
- Explain the conditions needed for the germination of a typical seed.
- Outline the metabolic processes during the germination of a starchy seed.
- Explain how flowering is controlled in long-day and short-day plants, including the role of phytochrome.

Flowers

There is enormous variety in the shapes and structures of flowers. Some are male, some are female, others have both male and female parts. For this reason, there is a huge variety in the appearance of flowers that we see. Flowers also differ in the way they are pollinated. Animal-pollinated flowers need structures to attract a pollinator, whereas flowers that use the wind to carry their pollen do not. An example of an animal-pollinated flower containing both male and female parts is shown in Figure **9.21**.

When the flower is in the bud stage, it is surrounded by **sepals**, which fold around the bud to protect the developing flower. As the flower opens, the sepals become insignificant and resemble small dried petals below the flower.

Petals of animal-pollinated flowers are often brightly coloured to attract

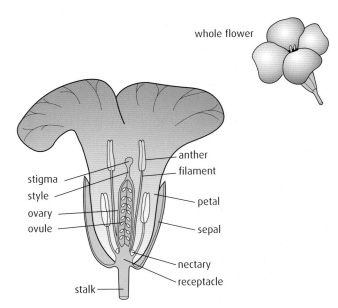

Figure 9.21 Half-flower of wallflower (*Cheiranthus cheiri*). The flower is about 2.5 cm in diameter. It is pollinated by bees and hoverflies. Its petals are usually brightly coloured and fragrant.

insects or other animals that may visit. Many have nectar guides, which are markings on the petals that tempt pollinators deep into the flower.

Pollen, containing the male gametes, is produced in the **anthers**, which are held up on long **filaments** in many flowers, so that as pollinators enter they brush past the anthers and are dusted with pollen.

The female organs are the **stigma**, **style** and **ovary**. The stigma receives pollen grains, which arrive with pollinators as they delve into a flower to obtain nectar. The sticky stigma has sugars present on its surface that cause pollen grains to germinate.

Pollination and fertilisation

Pollination is the transfer of pollen (containing the male gametes) from the anther to the stigma. Pollen may be carried by insects, other animals (such as birds, bats or mice), or by the wind. If pollen travels from the anthers of one plant to the stigma of another plant, the process is known as **cross-pollination**. If pollen is deposited on the stigma of the same plant that produced it, **self-pollination** occurs. Self-pollination produces less genetic variation than cross-pollination.

Fertilisation occurs when male and female gametes fuse to form a **zygote**. This occurs in the ovule of the flower. When pollen grains from a plant of the right species arrive on the stigma, they germinate and produce a **pollen tube**, which grows down the style to the ovary (Figure **9.22**).

The tube enters the ovary and a pollen nucleus passes down the tube to fuse with and fertilise the nucleus of the female gamete in the ovule.

Seeds

Fertilised ovules develop over time into **seeds**, which protect the developing embryo inside. Seeds are held within a seed pod, fruit or nut, which can be dispersed to new locations so that when they germinate, the new plants that develop do not compete with their parents.

Plants have evolved many ingenious means by which to bring about **seed dispersal**. A few are listed below.

- Some seed pods, such as those in the pea family, mature and dry out, so they eventually snap, causing the seed pod to open quite suddenly, ejecting the seeds some distance from the parent plant.
- Fruits containing seeds are frequently eaten by birds or animals. A tasty fruit tempts an animal to eat and digest it, but the tough seeds inside it pass through the digestive tract and emerge in the faeces. These seeds may appear long distances from the parent plant and are contained within a rich fertiliser.
- Nuts are collected by animals like squirrels, which bury them as a reserve of food for the winter. They may bury several groups of nuts and fail to dig them all up during the winter. The nuts remain in the soil ready to germinate when conditions are favourable.

Seeds have all the necessary components to ensure successful germination and the growth of a new plant. Within every seed is an embryo root and shoot, ready to develop when the time is right. Once a seed has been

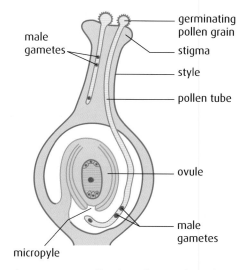

Figure 9.22 Fertilisation of an ovule in the ovary of a plant.

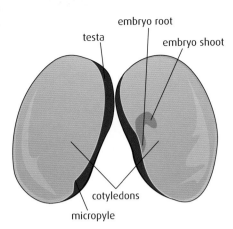

Figure 9.23 The main parts of a dicotyledonous plant seed.

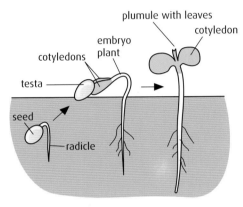

Figure 9.24 Germination and early growth in a dicotyledonous plant.

formed in the ovary, it loses water so that it can enter a dormant phase and not develop further until conditions for growth are favourable.

Inside their seeds, dicotyledonous plants have two seed leaves, or **cotyledons**, which store food reserves needed for germination (Figure **9.23**). The cotyledons are surrounded by a hard protective seed coat called the **testa**.

Many seeds have to endure quite harsh environmental conditions, so the testa protects the delicate tissues inside. In the wall of the testa is a pore called the **micropyle** through which water is absorbed to begin the process of germination.

Germination

Germination is the development of the seed into a new plant (Figure **9.24**). A dormant seed needs three vital factors to be in place for germination to occur.

- **Temperature** – A suitable temperature is essential for the enzymes in a seed to become active. They cannot work in cold conditions, and very high temperatures also inhibit their activity. Many seeds remain dormant until the temperature is at a particular level so that they germinate when the seedling will have the best chance of survival.
- **Water** – Most seeds contain only about 10% water, so water must be taken in to start the germination process. Water rehydrates the seed and the enzymes contained within it. The enzymes break down food stores to provide energy for the emerging root and stem.
- **Oxygen** – This is essential to provide energy for aerobic respiration.

Metabolism and germination

Germination begins as water is absorbed by the seed in a process known as **imbibition**. Water enters through the micropyle of the testa.

Water rehydrates stored food reserves in the seed and, in a starchy seed such as a barley grain, it triggers the embryo plant to release a plant growth hormone called **gibberellin** (Figure **9.25**). The gibberellin in turn stimulates the synthesis of **amylase** by the cells in the outer **aleurone layer** of the seed. The amylase hydrolyses starch molecules in the **endosperm** (food store), converting them to soluble maltose molecules. These are converted to glucose and are transported to the embryo, providing a source of carbohydrate that can be respired to provide energy as the **radicle** (embryo root) and **plumule** (embryo shoot) begin to grow, or used to produce other materials needed for growth, such as cellulose.

Absorption of water by the seed splits the testa, so that the radicle and plumule can emerge and grow. When the leaves of the seedling have grown above ground, they can begin to photosynthesise and take over from the food store in the seed in supplying the needs of the growing plant.

Control of flowering

At certain times of the year, shoot meristems produce flowers. Nearly 100 years ago, plant scientists discovered that light influences the timing of flowering in many plants. In the middle of the 20th century, scientists

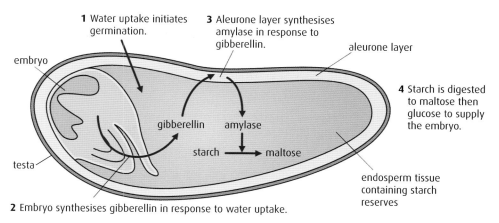

1 Water uptake initiates germination.

3 Aleurone layer synthesises amylase in response to gibberellin.

aleurone layer

embryo

4 Starch is digested to maltose then glucose to supply the embryo.

gibberellin   amylase

starch → maltose

testa

endosperm tissue containing starch reserves

2 Embryo synthesises gibberellin in response to water uptake.

Figure 9.25 Longitudinal section through a barley seed, showing how secretion of gibberellin by the embryo results in the mobilisation of starch reserves during germination.

showed that the period of darkness is the critical factor in controlling flowering. **Photoperiodism** is the term given to plants' responses to the relative periods of darkness and light.

- **Long-day plants** flower when days are longest and the nights are short. A long-day plant requires less than a certain number of hours of darkness in each 24-hour period to induce flowering. In the northern hemisphere, these plants flower during late spring or early summer (April to July) as days become longer and periods of darkness decrease. This situation is reversed in the southern hemisphere, where long-day plants flower between September and December. Examples of long-day plants are carnations, clover and ryegrass.

- **Short-day plants** flower as nights become longer and days are shorter. In the northern hemisphere this is during the late summer or autumn (fall). They require a continuous period of darkness before flowering and the dark period must be longer than a critical length. The length of the dark period differs between species. Examples of short-day plants are chrysanthemum, poinsettia, coffee and tobacco, which require 10–11 hours of darkness in a 24-hour period before they will flower. Short-day plants cannot flower if the period of darkness is interrupted by a pulse of artificial light shone on them even for just a few minutes.

Plants respond to periods of darkness using a leaf pigment called **phytochrome**. This pigment can exist in two inter-convertible forms – inactive P_r and active P_{fr}.

Active P_{fr} is produced from inactive P_r during daylight hours. The conversion occurs rapidly in response to an increase in red light (660 nm), which is absorbed by P_r. In darkness, P_{fr} reverts slowly to the more stable P_r.

red light (660 nm)

$$P_r \rightleftharpoons P_{fr} \rightarrow \text{response}$$

far-red light (730 nm)

darkness

Some short-day plants, such as poinsettias or chrysanthemums, are commercially produced so that they flower at any time of year. Horticulturalists grow them in shaded glasshouses where an extended period of darkness induces them to produce flowers.

During long days, increased amounts of P_{fr} promote flowering in long–

day plants. Flowering in short–day plants is inhibited by P_{fr}, but during long nights, sufficient P_{fr} is removed to allow them to flower.

The exact mechanism of phytochrome action is not fully understood but it is thought that it causes changes in the expression of genes concerned with flowering.

11 Explain why temperature is an important factor in the process of germination.

12 Distinguish between 'pollination' and 'fertilisation'.

13 Name the male parts of an angiosperm flower.

14 Outline why it is important for seeds to be dispersed.

End-of-chapter questions

1 Which of the following statements concerning plant structure and growth is correct?

    A   The veins in a leaf serve both to support the leaf and act as a transport system.

    B   Monocotyledonous plants have apical and lateral meristems.

    C   In an apical meristem, cell division by mitosis results in an increase in the diameter of the stem.

    D   Positive phototropism is due to increased growth as a result of auxin accumulating on the illuminated side of a shoot. (1)

2 Which of the following statements concerning transport in angiospermophytes is correct?

    A   A plant loses support if its cells increase their turgor.

    B   Fungal hyphae can play an important part in the uptake of mineral ions into the root of a plant.

    C   Mineral ions can only move into plant root hairs as a result of active transport.

    D   Transpiration is the flow of water through the phloem tissue of a plant. (1)

3 Which of the following statements concerning transport in angiospermophytes is correct?

    A   Cohesion is important in maintaining a column of water in xylem vessels when transpiration causes a transpiration pull.

    B   The plant hormone abscisic acid causes an increase in transpiration.

    C   An increase in humidity will lead to an increase in transpiration.

    D   Phloem is involved in the transpiration of sugar. (1)

4 Which of the following statements concerning reproduction in angiospermophytes is correct?

    A   Transfer of pollen from the stigma to the anther results in pollination.

    B   In a dicotyledonous seed, the micropyle is part of the embryo root.

    C   During germination, production of gibberellin in the cotyledons opens the micropyle to allow water absorption.

    D   In a long-day plant, flowering is promoted as a result of an increase in the proportion of P_{fr} compared to P_r.

(1)

5 Explain the role of auxin in phototropism. (3)

6 Outline the movement of water in plants from root to leaf, including the effects of environmental abiotic factors on the rate of transport. (6)

7 Explain how manipulating day length is used by commercial flower growers. (6)

8 Describe the metabolic events of germination in a starchy seed. (4)

9 Outline the role of the phloem in the active translocation of food molecules. (6)

10 Seed dispersal is important in the migration of plants from one area to another area. Plants have evolved many methods, both physical and biological, by which to disperse their seeds.

50 maple seeds, which are wind dispersed, were dropped one at a time from two different heights, 0.54 m and 10.8 m respectively. The histograms below show the distribution of the distance the maple seeds travelled.

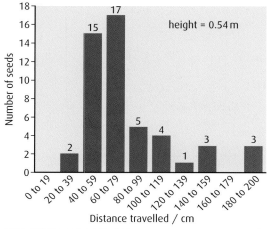
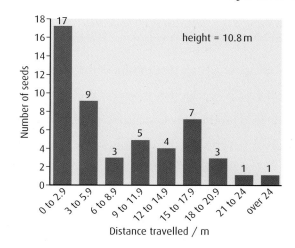

source: student experiment, Guralnick

  a Identify the distance travelled by the greatest number of seeds dropped from:

    i height = 0.54 m

    ii height = 10.8 m (1)

  b State the effect of height on seed dispersal. (1)

  c Suggest **two** reasons for the effect of the drop height on the distance travelled by the seeds. (2)

The following graphs show the rate and timing of seed release from different species of grass in the same area during the summer.

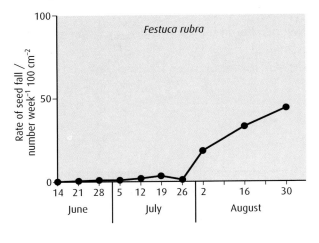

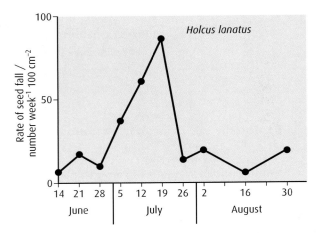

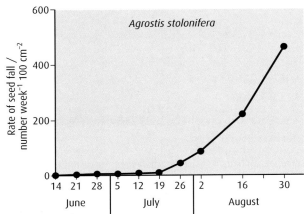

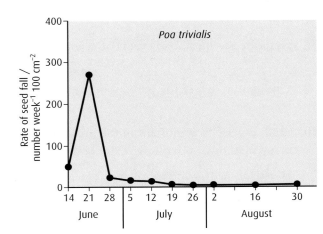

source: J L Harper (1997) *Population Biology of Plants*, Academic Press (Harcourt Brace Jovanovich), p.57

d Identify the grass species that produces the most seeds in this area. (1)

e Identify the grass species that produces the most seeds in June. (1)

f Compare seed production for all species relative to the timing of their release. (3)

g Suggest **two** benefits for these plants in the timing of seed release. (2)

Biological seed dispersal is usually dependent on the nutritional content of the seed or fruit. The following table gives the nutritional content for fruits of different species in temperate and tropical climates.

Common name of plant (*genus*)	Percentage of fruit by dry weight			Dispersal agents
	Protein	Lipid	Carbohydrate	
Temperate				
cranberry (*Vaccinium*)	3	6	89	birds
hawthorn (*Crataegus*)	2	2	73	birds
pin cherry (*Prunus*)	8	3	84	birds
pokeberry (*Phytolacca*)	14	2	68	birds
strawberry (*Fragaria*)	6	4	88	birds
Tropical				
bird palm (*Chamaedorea*)	14	16	55	birds
fig (*Ficus*)	7	4	79	bats
mistletoe (*Viscum*)	6	53	38	birds
monkey fruit (*Tetragastris*)	1	4	94	monkeys
Wild nutmeg (*Virola*)	2	63	9	birds

source: H Howe and L Westley (1988) *Ecological Relationship of Plants and Animals*, Oxford University Press, p. 121

h Compare tropical fruits to temperate fruits in relation to the mean values for lipid, carbohydrate and protein content. (2)

i Explain which fruit would have the highest energy content. (2)

j Suggest **one** advantage and **one** disadvantage of dispersal of seeds by animals. (2)

(total 17 marks)
© IB Organization 2009

10 Genetics II

Introduction

Chapter **4** dealt with meiosis, how gametes are produced and how the genes they carry affect human characteristics. Single genes and monohybrid genetic crosses produce variation, and multiple alleles, such as those that control blood groups, increase the possible variety still further. Here, we consider dihybrid crosses – the simultaneous inheritance of two pairs of characteristics, which involve more than one gene. We see how the processes of random assortment and crossing over of homologous chromosomes result in enormous variety among individuals. Very few characteristics are controlled by single genes and when a number of genes control a characteristic, the phenotype is determined by their combined effect. These groups of genes are known as polygenes, and produce the variety that is essential for evolution.

10.1 Meiosis

Assessment statements

- Describe the behaviour of the chromosomes in the phases of meiosis.
- Outline the formation of chiasmata in the process of crossing over.
- Explain how meiosis results in an effectively infinite genetic variety in gametes through crossing over in prophase I and random orientation in metaphase I.
- State Mendel's law of independent assortment.
- Explain the relationship between Mendel's law of independent assortment and meiosis.

Functions of meiosis

Meiosis is essential in all organisms that reproduce sexually because at fertilisation, when two haploid gametes meet, the chromosome number of the zygote becomes the diploid number for the organism.

Meiosis has two functions:

- **Halving the chromosome number** – Meiosis consists of two nuclear divisions (meiosis I and II) but the chromosomes replicate only once, so the four resulting daughter cells each have half the chromosome number of the parent cell.
- **Producing genetic variety** – This occurs in two ways: through crossing over during prophase I, and through random assortment during metaphase I. In addition, random fertilisation also produces variety since any gamete has an equal chance of combining with any other gamete.

Behaviour of chromosomes during meiosis

Crossing over

During prophase I, chromosomes shorten and coil. Homologous pairs of chromosomes come together to form a bivalent so that maternal and paternal chromosomes are next to one another (Figure **10.1**). Homologous chromosomes contain the same genes, but since they came from different parents, they can have different alleles. As they line up together, the non-sister chromatids may touch and break. The two segments may then rejoin at the corresponding position on the other

Look back at Figure **4.5** on page **72** to remind yourself of the stages of meiosis.

As well as the red hair locus, chromosome 4 also has a locus for a gene coding for dopamine receptors. Imagine that there are two different alleles of this gene.

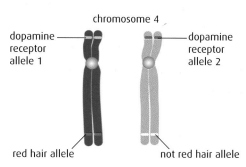

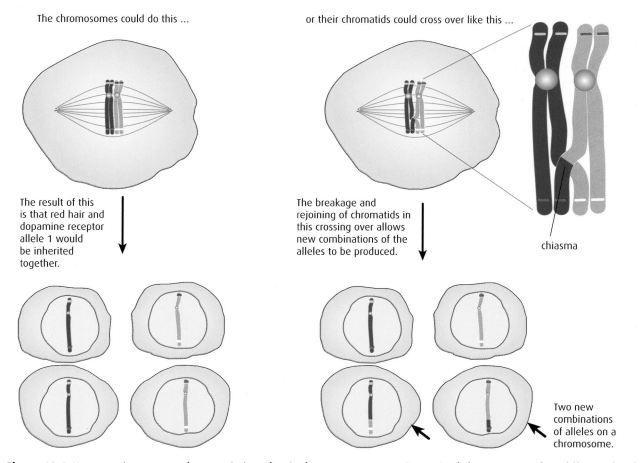

The chromosomes could do this …

or their chromatids could cross over like this …

chiasma

The result of this is that red hair and dopamine receptor allele 1 would be inherited together.

The breakage and rejoining of chromatids in this crossing over allows new combinations of the alleles to be produced.

Two new combinations of alleles on a chromosome.

Figure 10.1 How crossing over produces variation. If a single cross-over occurs in a pair of chromosomes, four different daughter chromatids are produced instead of two.

Crossing over does not occur between the X and Y chromosomes. This is because many of the genes they carry determine gender and so need to remain on their respective chromosomes.

chromatid. In this way, chromatids are formed that are a mixture of paternal and maternal alleles. The region where this happens is called a **chiasma** (plural **chiasmata**).

The point at which a chiasma forms is largely random. However, not all chromatids will form chiasmata and they never occur at all on some chromosomes. In this way, some chromatids will retain their full complement of paternal or maternal alleles. This is shown in Figure **10.1** for two pairs of alleles (for a dopamine receptor gene and a hair colour gene) on human chromosome 4.

Random orientation of chromosomes

During metaphase I, the bivalents line up on the equator and spindle microtubules become attached to their centromeres. However, the way in which they line up is random. This is shown in Figure **10.2**, which illustrates the possibilities for just two chromosomes, 4 and 7.

Imagine body cells containing one pair of alleles for red hair / not red hair and another for blue colour blindness / normal blue vision.

Chromosomes from the father are shown in blue and from the mother in grey.

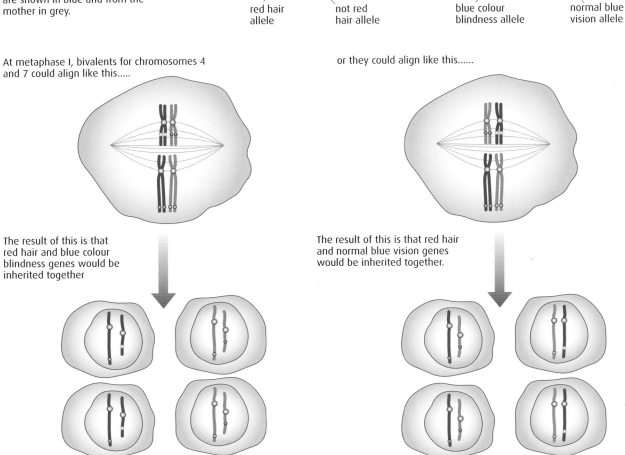

chromosome 4

red hair allele   not red hair allele

chromosome 7

blue colour blindness allele   normal blue vision allele

At metaphase I, bivalents for chromosomes 4 and 7 could align like this.....

or they could align like this......

The result of this is that red hair and blue colour blindness genes would be inherited together

The result of this is that red hair and normal blue vision genes would be inherited together.

Figure 10.2 How independent assortment produces variation.

- The paternal chromosomes could both line up together on one side of the equator with the maternal ones on the other side, as shown on the left in Figure **10.2**. Two of the gametes that are produced then contain just paternal chromosomes while the other two contain just maternal chromosomes.
- Another possibility is that the chromosomes line up as shown on the right in Figure **10.2**, with maternal and paternal chromosomes on both sides of the equator. The end result here is that all four gametes contain a mixture of paternal and maternal chromosomes.

1 Look carefully at the eight gametes in Figure **10.2**. How many different gametes are there?

Your answer should be that there are four different gametes. Now consider what happens if a third pair of chromosomes is added. The number of genetically different gametes will increase to eight.

The number of possible genetic combinations that can occur as a result of random orientation of chromosomes is vast. If only chromosome combinations in a haploid cell are considered, the figure is 2^n where n is the haploid number. For humans, $n = 23$ so the possible combinations are over 8 million for just one gamete. The formula can be used to work out the combinations in Figure **10.2** – for two pairs of chromosomes, $n = 2$, so the number of possible combinations $= 2^2 = 4$. With three pairs of chromosomes, the number of possible combinations $= 2^3 = 8$.

Meiosis and variety

The calculation of the number of genetic possibilities in gametes using the formula 2^n can only be an approximation. It does not account for the fact that there are two types of gametes – male and female. Also it does not include the extra variation that arises from crossing over. If a single cross-over occurs then the number of combinations is doubled, as shown in Figure **10.1**. Since several crossovers normally occur during a meiotic division, it is clear that the amount of genetic variety is almost infinite even in organisms that only have a small haploid number.

Meiosis and Mendel's law of independent assortment

Gregor Mendel's 'law of independent assortment' states that:

When gametes are formed, the separation of one pair of alleles into the new cells is independent of the separation of any other pair of alleles.

Or:

Either of a pair of alleles is equally likely to be inherited with either of another pair.

Random assortment during metaphase I can produce variety in the gametes as shown in Figure **10.2**. How this relates to Mendel's law of

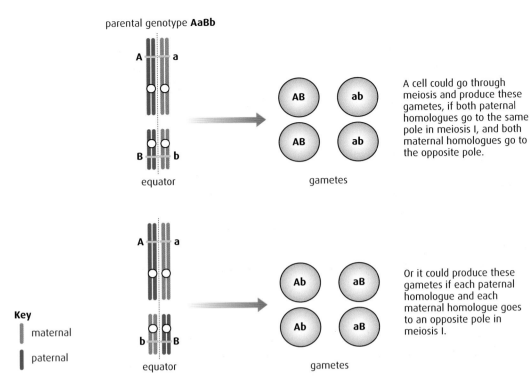

parental genotype **AaBb**

A cell could go through meiosis and produce these gametes, if both paternal homologues go to the same pole in meiosis I, and both maternal homologues go to the opposite pole.

equator   gametes

Or it could produce these gametes if each paternal homologue and each maternal homologue goes to an opposite pole in meiosis I.

Key

  maternal

  paternal

equator   gametes

Figure 10.3 Meiosis and Mendel's law of independent assortment.

independent assortment for two pairs of chromosomes carrying the alleles **Aa** and **Bb** is shown in Figure **10.3**.

As a result of the random alignment, the **A** allele has an equal chance of being in a gamete with either the **B** allele or the **b** allele, and similarly the **a** allele has an equal chance of being in a gamete with either the **B** allele or the **b** allele. Thus, four types of gamete can be produced carrying the alleles **AB**, **Ab**, **aB** or **ab**. They will occur in the ratio 1 : 1 : 1 : 1.

10.2 Dihybrid crosses and gene linkage

Assessment statements

- Calculate and predict the genotype and phenotype ratio of offspring of dihybrid crosses involving unlinked autosomal genes.
- Distinguish between 'autosomes' and 'sex chromosomes'.
- Explain how crossing over between non-sister chromatids of a homologous pair in prophase I can result in an exchange of alleles.
- Define 'linkage group'.
- Explain an example of a cross between two linked genes.
- Identify which of the offspring are recombinants in a dihybrid cross involving linked genes.

Genotypes and gametes

Dihybrid crosses involve characteristics that are controlled by two genes. In a dihybrid genotype, there are two pairs of alleles to consider. Figure **10.3** shows what happens during meiosis in a parent with the genotype **AaBb**. Each pair of alleles can be combined in a mixture of dominant and recessive and some examples of genotypes and gametes are given in Table **10.1**.

Genotype	Gametes
AABB	all **AB**
aaBB	all **aB**
AaBB	**AB** and **aB** in a ratio of 1 : 1
Aabb	**Ab** and **ab** in a ratio of 1 : 1

Table 10.1 Some examples of diploid genotypes and the haploid gametes they produce.

There are more possible genotypes than those shown in Table **10.1**, but each genotype can only produce either one type of gamete, or two, or four. No genotype produces three types of gamete and only the double heterozygous genotype (as in Figure **10.3**, for example) can produce four types of gamete. It is helpful to keep this in mind when working out the possible offspring of dihybrid crosses.

2   What are the gametes produced by the genotypes **Ttrr** and **HhGg**?

3   What is the name of the grid used to determine offspring genotypes and phenotypes?

The dihybrid cross

Although the dihybrid cross involves two pairs of genes instead of just one, the principles of setting out a genetic cross diagram to predict the offspring that will be produced are exactly the same as for the monohybrid crosses you saw in Chapter **4**. The genetic diagrams should include parental phenotypes, parental genotypes, gametes in circles and a Punnett grid for the **F$_1$** or **F$_2$ generation**.

Parental generation the original parent individuals in a series of experimental crosses
F$_1$ generation the offspring of the parental generation
F$_2$ generation the offspring of a cross between F$_1$ individuals

Worked example 1

Fur colour in mice is determined by a single gene. Brown fur is dominant to white. Ear size is also determined by a single gene. Rounded ears are dominant to pointed ears.

A mouse homozygous for brown fur and rounded ears was crossed with a white mouse with pointed ears. Determine the possible phenotypes and genotypes of the offspring.

Step 1 Choose suitable letters to represent the alleles. Brown fur is dominant, so let **B** = brown fur and **b** = white fur. Rounded ears is dominant, so let **R** = rounded and **r** = pointed.

Step 2 The brown mouse with rounded ears is homozygous so its genotype must be **BBRR**.
Since white and pointed are recessive, the genotype of the white mouse with pointed ears must be **bbrr**.

Step 3 Set out the genetic diagram as shown.

Step 4 All the F_1 mice have brown fur and rounded ears

parental phenotypes:	brown fur, rounded ears	white fur, pointed ears
parental genotypes:	**BBRR**	**bbrr**
gametes:	all (BR)	all (br)

Punnett grid for F_1:

		gametes from brown, round-eared parent
gametes from white, pointed-eared parent		(BR)
	(br)	**BbRr** brown, rounded ears

Note that although the gamete **BR** is combined with the gamete **br**, the alleles in the offspring are always paired up, so the genotype of the F_1 is written as **BbRr** (not **BRbr**).

Worked example 2

Mendel carried out genetic studies with the garden pea. Tall plants are dominant to short, and green seeds are dominant to yellow. A homozygous tall plant with yellow seeds was crossed with a short plant homozygous for green seeds. Determine the possible genotypes and phenotypes in the offspring.

Step 1 Tall is dominant to short, so **T** = tall and **t** = short. Green is dominant to yellow so **G** = green and **g** = yellow.

Step 2 Each parent has one dominant and one recessive characteristic but we are told the dominant characteristic is homozygous. The tall, yellow-seeded plant therefore has genotype **TTgg**, and the short, green-seeded plant is **ttGG**.

Step 3 Set out the genetic diagram as shown.

Step 4 All the offspring are tall plants with green seeds.

It was fortunate that Mendel chose these two characteristics for his crosses. Seed colour and height are unlinked genes on different chromosomes. Had they been on the same chromosome and linked, the results would have been different.

parental phenotypes:	tall, yellow seeds	short, green seeds
parental genotypes:	**TTgg**	**ttGG**
gametes:	all (Tg)	(tG)

Punnett grid for F_1:

		gametes from tall, yellow-seeded parent
gametes from short, green-seeded parent		(Tg)
	(tG)	**TtGg** tall, green seeds

Worked example 3

One of the heterozygous F_1 mice with brown fur and rounded ears from the cross in Worked example **1** was crossed with a mouse with white fur and rounded ears. Some of the offspring had pointed ears. Deduce the genotype of the second mouse and state the phenotype ratio of the offspring.

Step 1 Use the same letters as in Worked example **1**: **B** = brown fur and **b** = white fur, **R** = rounded ears and **r** = pointed ears.

Step 2 The first mouse has the genotype **BbRr**.

We are told the second mouse is white, so it must have the alleles **rr**. It has rounded ears but we are not told if this is homozygous or heterozygous, so the alleles could be **RR** or **Rr**.

Reading on, we find that there are some offspring with pointed ears, so they must have the genotype **rr**. This means that the parent genotype must have been heterozygous, **Rr**. If the parent was **RR**, no recessive allele would have been present and none of the offspring would have pointed ears.

Step 3 Having written down your reasoning, as above, now set out the usual genetic diagram.

parental phenotypes: brown, rounded ears | white, rounded ears

parental genotypes: **BbRr** | **bbRr**

gametes: (BR) (Br) (bR) (br) | (bR) (br)

Punnett grid for F_1:

		gametes from brown, rounded-eared parent			
		(BR)	(Br)	(bR)	(br)
gametes from white, rounded-eared parent	(bR)	**BbRR** brown, rounded ears	**BbRr** brown, rounded ears	**bbRR** white, rounded ears	**bbRr** white, rounded ears
	(br)	**BbRr** brown, rounded ears	**Bbrr** brown, pointed ears	**bbRr** white, rounded ears	**bbrr** white, pointed ears

Step 4 The phenotypes produced are:

3 brown fur, rounded ears
3 white fur, rounded ears
1 brown fur, pointed ears
1 white fur, pointed ears.

This produces a ratio of phenotypes of 3 : 3 : 1 : 1, which is an important Mendelian ratio.

Autosomes and sex chromosomes

The pair of sex chromosomes, X and Y, determine the gender of an individual. All the other chromosomes in a nucleus are called **autosomes**. Humans have 22 autosomes and in addition one pair of sex chromosomes – XY for a male and XX for a female.

Chromosomes and genes

The human genome contains between 25 000 and 30 000 genes but there are only 23 pairs of chromosomes. This means that each chromosome must carry very many genes. Chromosome 1 contains over 3000 genes but the much smaller chromosome 21 contains only around 400 genes. Any two genes on the same chromosome are said to be **linked**. Linked genes are usually passed on together. The genes on any chromosome form a **linkage group**, so a human has 23 linkage groups. The difference between unlinked and linked genes is shown in Figure **10.4**.

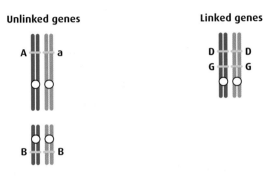

Genes **A** and **B** are on separate chromosomes and so are not linked. They will obey Mendel's law of independent assortment and be inherited independently.

Genes **D** and **G** are on the same chromosomes and so are linked. They will not follow Mendel's law of independent assortment. Genes **D** and **G** form a linkage group.

Figure 10.4 The difference between unlinked and linked genes.

Linkage and genes

If alleles are linked together on a chromosome, then it follows that they will be inherited together because during meiosis they will move together to the same pole as the cell divides. In genetics problems, dihybrid crosses involving linked genes do not produce Mendelian ratios. Linked genes do not follow Mendel's law of independent assortment – they are not inherited independently and can give a variety of different ratios.

Mendelian ratios

In monohybrid crosses, two ratios for the offspring of a genetic cross are possible.

The first is 1:1 if a heterozygous individual (**Aa**) and a homozygous recessive individual (**aa**) are crossed.

The second is 3:1 when two heterozygous individuals are crossed (**Aa × Aa**). These are called Mendelian ratios.

Mendelian ratios also occur in dihybrid crosses, but with more gametes there are more possibilities. A heterozygous individual (**AaBb**) crossed with a homozygous recessive (**aabb**) produces a 1:1:1:1 ratio and the ratio produced by crossing two double heterozygous (**AaBb**) individuals is 9:3:3:1. The 3:3:1:1 ratio in Worked example **3** is another Mendelian ratio. It is helpful to be familiar with these ratios.

Linkage group a linkage group is all the genes that have their loci on a particular chromosome

---

Worked example 4

In the fruit fly, *Drosophila*, red eye colour is dominant to purple eyes and long wings is dominant to dumpy wings. These genes are linked on chromosome 2. A fly that was homozygous for red eyes and long wings was crossed with a fly that had purple eyes and dumpy wings. Determine the genotype and phenotype of the F_2 offspring by using a full genetic diagram.

Step 1 Red eye colour is dominant so **R** = red eye and **r** = purple eye. Long wings is dominant so **N** = long wings and **n** = dumpy wings.

Step 2 The fly with the dominant characteristics is homozygous and the other fly shows both recessive characteristics. The parental genotypes are

$$\frac{R\ N}{R\ N} \text{ and } \frac{r\ n}{r\ n}.$$

Step 3   Set out the genetic diagram as below.

parental phenotypes:
red eyes, long wings   purple eyes, dumpy wings

parental genotypes:
$\dfrac{R\ \ N}{R\ \ N}$ $\dfrac{r\ \ n}{r\ \ n}$

gametes:
all (RN) all (rn)

Punnett grid for F$_1$:

	gametes from red-eyed, long-winged parent
gametes from purple-eyed, dumpy-winged parent (rn)	(RN) $\dfrac{R\ \ N}{r\ \ n}$ red eyes, long wings

All the F$_1$ have red eyes and long wings.

Now, the F$_2$ generation is obtained by crossing two offspring from the F$_1$ generation.

parental phenotypes:
red eyes, long wings   red eyes, long wings

parental genotypes:
$\dfrac{R\ \ N}{r\ \ n}$ $\dfrac{R\ \ N}{r\ \ n}$

gametes:
(RN) (rn) (RN) (rn)

Punnett grid for F$_2$:

		gametes from red-eyed, long-winged parent	
		(RN)	(rn)
gametes from red-eyed, long-winged parent	(RN)	$\dfrac{R\ \ N}{R\ \ N}$ red eyes, long wings	$\dfrac{R\ \ N}{r\ \ n}$ red eyes, long wings
	(rn)	$\dfrac{R\ \ N}{r\ \ n}$ red eyes, long wings	$\dfrac{r\ \ n}{r\ \ n}$ purple eyes, dumpy wings

Step 4   In the F$_2$ generation, the ratio of phenotypes is:
3 red eye, long wing : 1 purple eye, dumpy wing.
Note that this 3:1 ratio is what you would expect in a monohybrid cross. The reason for this is that the two genes are linked and so there is only one pair of chromosomes involved, as in monohybrid crosses.

Writing a linkage genotype

In the dihybrid crosses considered so far, genotypes have been written in the form **AABB**. With linked genes, a different notation has to be used because, although there are still four alleles to be considered, they are found on only one pair of chromosomes. The genotype is therefore always written as shown in Figure **10.5**. The horizontal lines signify that the two genes occur on the same chromosome.

$\dfrac{D\ \ G}{d\ \ g}$ $\dfrac{D\ \ g}{d\ \ G}$

Here, **D** is linked to **G** and **d** is linked to **g**. Therefore **D** and **G** are inherited together and **d** and **g** are inherited together.

Here, **D** is linked to **g** and **d** is linked to **G**. Therefore **D** and **g** are inherited together and **d** and **G** are inherited together.

Figure 10.5 This shows the two possible linkage patterns for these four alleles. The difference between the two linkage patterns makes a very big difference in the ratios of the phenotypes in the offspring of a cross.

Drosophila

Drosophila is a genus of fruit fly that is commonly used in genetic experiments. It breeds quickly, producing large numbers of offspring, and its genetic make-up has been well studied. Various different alleles, controlling characteristics such as eye colour, wing shape and body colour, are used in genetic crosses. These features are easy to see and enable geneticists to deduce the genotypes of the flies from their appearance.

A fruit fly, *Drosophila melanogaster*, of 'wild type' with red eyes and long wings.

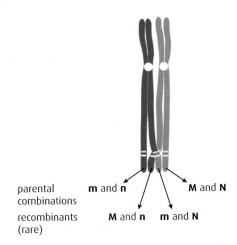

parental combinations   **m** and **n**   **M** and **N**

recombinants (rare)   **M** and **n**   **m** and **N**

Figure 10.6 A single chiasma has formed between two chromatids so crossing over of the alleles will take place to form the recombinant gametes. No crossing over has taken place with the other chromatids and so these will retain the parental combination of alleles.

Recombinant offspring in which the genetic information has been rearranged by crossing over so as to produce phenotypes that are different from those of the parents

Linkage and crossing over

Figure **10.1** showed how crossing over creates genetic variety by exchanging parts of the maternal and paternal chromosomes. Figure **10.6** shows what happens to two closely linked alleles after a cross-over occurs between them.

Look back at the left-hand example in Figure **10.5** (page **245**). Without crossing over, the parental gametes formed will be **DG** and **dg**. If a cross-over does take place (as shown by the blue cross, below) then additional **recombinant** gametes **Dg** and **dG** will be formed.

$$\frac{D \quad G}{d \quad g}$$

Four types of gamete – **DG**, **dg**, **Dg** and **dG** – are possible, but there is a very significant difference in the numbers of each type that are formed. The chance of a chiasma forming between the two loci that are close together is very small. So the chance of forming the gametes **Dg** and **dG** is also very small. The majority of gametes therefore carry the alleles **DG** and **dg** and they will form in equal numbers. If a cross-over does takes place, for every **Dg** gamete there will be a **dG** gamete. The numbers of these two gametes will also be equal but very small.

Now look at the right-hand example in Figure **10.5**. What will be the allele combinations in gametes where crossing over has not taken place? What will be the allele combinations in gametes where crossing over has taken place, and which combinations will be present in greater numbers?

Worked example 5

Grey body and red eyes are dominant to stripe body and cardinal eye in *Drosophila*. They are autosomal, linked genes on chromosome 3. Homozygous grey flies with red eyes were crossed with stripe flies with cardinal eyes. No crossing over occurred.

Then the F$_1$ flies were crossed with stripe, cardinal flies.

- If no crossing over occurs between the two loci, what phenotypes would be expected in the offspring of this second cross?
- If crossing over did occur between the loci, what phenotypes would be expected this time?

First cross, with no crossing over:

Step 1   Grey body is dominant, so **G** = grey body and **g** = stripe body. Red eye is dominant so **R** = red eye and **r** = cardinal eye.

Step 2   The fly with the dominant characteristics is homozygous and the other fly shows both recessive characteristics. The parental genotypes are $\dfrac{G \ R}{G \ R}$ and $\dfrac{g \ r}{g \ r}$.

Step 3   Set out the diagram as on the right.

parental phenotypes:	grey body, red eyes	stripe body, cardinal eyes

parental genotypes:

$$\frac{G}{G}\frac{R}{R} \qquad\qquad \frac{g}{g}\frac{r}{r}$$

gametes: all (GR)   all (gr)

Punnett grid for F$_1$:

		gametes from grey-bodied, red-eyed parent
gametes from stripe-bodied, cardinal-eyed parent		(GR)
	(gr)	$\frac{G}{g}\frac{R}{r}$ grey body, red eyes

Step 4   All the F$_1$ flies have a grey body and red eyes.

Second cross, with no crossing over:

parental phenotypes:	grey body, red eyes	stripe body, cardinal eyes

parental genotypes:

$$\frac{G}{g}\frac{R}{r} \qquad\qquad \frac{g}{g}\frac{r}{r}$$

gametes: (GR)   (gr)   all (gr)

Punnett grid for F$_1$:

		gametes from grey-bodied, red-eyed parent	
gametes from stripe-bodied, cardinal-eyed parent		(GR)	(gr)
	(gr)	$\frac{G}{g}\frac{R}{r}$ grey body, red eyes	$\frac{g}{g}\frac{r}{r}$ stripe body, cardinal eyes

Second cross, with crossing over:

parental phenotypes:	grey body, red eyes	stripe body, cardinal eyes

parental genotypes:

$$\frac{G}{g}\frac{R}{r} \qquad\qquad \frac{g}{g}\frac{r}{r}$$

gametes: (GR)   (gr)   (Gr)*   (gR)*   all (gr)

Punnett grid for F$_1$:

		gametes from grey-bodied, red-eyed parent			
gametes from stripe-bodied cardinal-eyed parent		(GR)	(gr)	(Gr)	(gR)
	(gr)	$\frac{G}{g}\frac{R}{r}$ grey body, red eyes	$\frac{g}{g}\frac{r}{r}$ stripe body, cardinal eyes	$\frac{G}{g}\frac{r}{r}$ grey body, cardinal eyes	$\frac{g}{g}\frac{R}{r}$ stripe body, red eyes

* gametes formed as a result of crossing over

Step 4 The four F₁ phenotypes are:

- grey body and red eyes
- stripe body and cardinal eyes
- grey body and cardinal eyes
- stripe body and red eyes

The 'grey, cardinal' and 'stripe, red' (shown in red type) flies are **recombinants** as they have a phenotype that is different from the parental phenotypes. These recombinant phenotypes will occur in approximately equal numbers. The parental phenotypes (shown in black type) will also be in approximately equal numbers among the offspring, but the recombinant phenotypes will be very few in number compared to the parental phenotypes.

> 4 Individuals from which generation are crossed in order to produce an F₂ generation?

10.3 Polygenic inheritance

Assessment statements

- Define 'polygenic inheritance'.
- Explain that polygenic inheritance can contribute to continuous variation, using two examples, one of which must be human skin colour.

Polygenic inheritance the inheritance of a characteristic that is controlled by two or more genes; polygenic inheritance accounts for the continuous variation that occurs in characteristics such as human height, body mass and skin colour

Continuous variation (for example, human height) can be shown on a graph, which produces an even distribution of frequencies of the characteristic. The bell-shaped curves in Figure **1.1** (page **2**) represent continuous variaton. Discontinuous variation, such as that observed in human blood groups, produces a bar graph, with each distinct category represented separately.

Polygenes

In the genetic examples considered so far, a particular characteristic is controlled by one gene, which can have different alleles at a specific pair of loci. There is a clear difference between organisms with different alleles. An organism either has the characteristic or it does not – there are no intermediate forms. This is called **discontinuous variation.**

Very few characteristics are controlled by single genes. Most are controlled by groups of genes, which together are known as **polygenes**. The genes that form polygenes are often unlinked – that is, they are located on different chromosomes. When two or more genes, each with multiple alleles, are responsible for a characteristic the number of possible phenotypes is greatly increased. Each gene separately may have little impact but their combined effect produces a whole variety of phenotypes. Unlinked polygenes result in a range of degrees of the characteristic from one extreme to another – that is, **continuous variation**.

Human skin colour

Human skin colour depends on the amount of the pigment melanin that is produced in the skin. Melanin synthesis is controlled by genes. The degree of pigmentation can range from the very dark skin of people originating from regions such as Namibia in southern Africa, through to the very pale skin of native Scandinavian people.

Melanin protects the skin from the harmful UV rays from the Sun. In parts of the world close to the equator, the Sun's rays are very intense so people need protection from sunburn, which can lead to a type of skin cancer called melanoma. Dark–skinned people have a high concentration of melanin, which protects them, while fair–skinned people have much less. Although skin colour is genetically determined, environmental factors also influence it. Fair–skinned people who are exposed to sunlight produce extra melanin and develop a protective suntan. They are also able to produce more vitamin D in their skin (see Option **A**).

Several genes are involved in determining skin colour and they produce the almost continuous variation that can be seen in the global human population. In the example, below only three genes are shown. Each gene has two alleles. One allele, **M**, contributes to melanin production and the other, **m**, does not. These three genes, each with two alleles, give rise to seven possible skin tones – numbered 0 to 6 below. The number refers to the number of **M** alleles, which determine the level of skin pigmentation. A person with the genotype **MMMMMM** will have very dark skin (6),

parental phenotypes: light brown skin   light brown skin
| 3 | | 3 |

parental genotypes: $M^1m^1M^2m^2M^3m^3$ $M^1m^1M^2m^2M^3m^3$

gametes:

$(M^1M^2M^3)$ $(M^1M^2m^3)$ $(m^1m^2M^3)$ $(M^1m^2M^3)$ $(M^1M^2M^3)$ $(M^1M^2m^3)$ $(m^1m^2M^3)$ $(M^1m^2M^3)$

$(m^1M^2m^3)$ $(M^1m^2m^3)$ $(m^1M^2M^3)$ $(m^1m^2m^3)$ $(m^1M^2m^3)$ $(M^1m^2m^3)$ $(m^1M^2M^3)$ $(m^1m^2m^3)$

Punnett grid for F_1:

	gametes from light-brown-skinned parent							
	$(M^1M^2M^3)$	$(M^1M^2m^3)$	$(m^1m^2M^3)$	$(M^1m^2M^3)$	$(m^1m^2m^3)$	$(M^1m^2m^3)$	$(m^1M^2M^3)$	$(m^1m^2m^3)$
$(M^1M^2M^3)$	6	5	4	5	4	4	5	3
$(M^1M^2m^3)$	5	4	3	4	3	3	4	2
$(m^1m^2M^3)$	4	3	2	3	2	2	3	1
$(M^1m^2M^3)$	5	4	3	4	3	3	4	2
$(m^1M^2m^3)$	4	3	2	3	2	2	3	1
$(M^1m^2m^3)$	4	3	2	3	2	2	3	1
$(m^1M^2M^3)$	5	4	3	4	3	3	4	2
$(m^1m^2m^3)$	3	2	1	2	1	1	2	0

(left axis label) gametes from light-brown-skinned parent

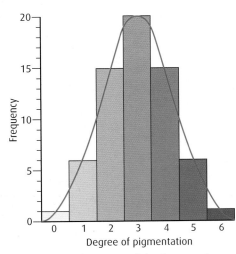

Figure 10.7 Histogram of the frequencies of skin pigmentation from the Punnett grid above. This shows continuous variation.

while a person with **mmmmmm** will have very pale skin (0). The Punnett grid shows the possible combinations of skin colour in children from two parents, both heterozygous for all three genes. The parents' phenotype is light brown skin (3).

Although in this simplified example there are only seven categories of pigmentation, nevertheless you can see that if the frequencies of the skin colour varieties in the Punnett grid are plotted on a histogram, as in Figure **10.7**, it produces a normal distribution. In the case of human skin colour, it is known that more than three genes are involved and the number of categories exceeds seven. The result is a wider distribution curve and more 'continuous' variation.

Beak depth in finches

Finches are birds that eat seeds and have a strong beak to break open the seeds. Three unlinked genes are involved in controlling the depth of the beak, each with two alleles. The **D** allele contributes to beak depth and the **d** allele does not, so the pattern of inheritance is exactly the same as in the example shown above for human skin pigmentation.

Many other examples of **polygenic inheritance** are known. In plants, three genes interact to control the colour of seeds of wheat. Human height and body mass are also controlled in this way, as well as some conditions such as diabetes and autism.

Questions to consider

1 Why do some of these alterations seem more acceptable than others?

2 If the child was genetically altered to make them more competitive and this led to them being aggressive or violent, would the child be responsible? Or would the parent be responsible?

3 Can an individual ever be held responsible for their actions if they are genetically determined?

Scientific advances and ethics

It may one day be possible to isolate and alter certain genes in a fetus. This will raise serious ethical questions. Consider the hypothetical situations that are listed here. Would you have your child's genetic makeup altered in the following circumstances?

• To remove the tendency to develop breast cancer?
• To remove a tendency for short-sightedness?
• To make them taller or shorter?
• To make them better looking?
• To make them more athletic?
• To make them more competitive?
• To give them a better sense of humour?
• To make them more intelligent?
• To make them more musical?
• To change their hair colour?
• To alter their sexual orientation?
• To change their skin colour?

End-of-chapter questions

1 The genotypes **AABb** and **AaBb** were crossed. What would be the ratio of genotypes in the offspring?

    A   1 **AABB** : 1 **AaBB** : 1 **AAbb** : 1 **Aabb** : 2 **AABb** : 2 **AaBb**

    B   1 **AABB** : 1 **AaBb** : 1 **Aabb** : 1 **aaBb**

    C   2 **AABB** : 2 **aaBB** : 2 **AAbb** : 2 **Aabb**

    D   1 **AABb** : 1 **AaBb** : 1 **AABB** : 1 **AaBB** : 2 **AAbb** : 2 **Aabb**   (1)

2 A maize plant homozygous for the genes for green leaves and round stem was crossed with a plant with yellow leaves and square stem. All the offspring had green leaves and round stem. The F_1 plants were crossed among themselves and the 480 F_2 generation individuals were of four different phenotypes.

How many of the F_2 would be expected to have yellow leaves and round stem?

    A   60

    B   30

    C   120

    D   90   (1)

3 A fruit fly of genotype **GgTt** was test crossed. The offspring genotype ratio was 1 : 1. The reason for this was:

    A   The genes assorted independently.

    B   The genes were linked and crossing over occurred.

    C   The genes were linked and no crossing over occurred.

    D   Non-disjunction had taken place.   (1)

4 A fruit fly of the genotype **RrBb** was crossed with another of the same genotype. The genes are linked. The offspring genotype ratio could be:

    A   1 : 1

    B   9 : 3 : 3 : 1

    C   1 : 1 : 1 : 1

    D   7 : 7 : 1 : 1   (1)

5 Outline how meiotic division results in almost infinite genetic variation in the gametes produced.   (2)

6 Using a specific example, explain a cross between two autosomal linked genes, including the way in which recombinants are produced. You are advised to use a test cross.   (9)

7 In the fruit fly, *Drosophila melanogaster*, the allele for dark body (**D**) is dominant over the allele for ebony body (**d**). The allele for straight bristles (**T**) is dominant over the allele for dichaete bristles (**t**). Pure-breeding flies with dark body and straight bristles were crossed with pure-breeding flies with ebony body and dichaete bristles.

a State the genotype and the phenotype of the F_1 individuals produced as a result of this cross. (2)

b The F_1 flies were crossed with flies that had the genotype **ddtt**. Determine the expected ratio of phenotypes in the F_2 generation, assuming that there is independent assortment. (3)
The observed percentages of phenotypes in the F_2 generation are shown below.

dark body, straight bristles	37%
ebony body, straight bristles	14%
dark body, dichaete bristles	16%
ebony body, dichaete bristles	33%

The observed results differ significantly from the results expected on the basis of independent assortment.

c Explain the reasons for the observed results of the cross differing significantly from the expected results. (2)

Human health and physiology II 11

Introduction

This chapter extends ideas introduced in Chapter **6**, and deals in more detail with the processes of reproduction, movement and defence of the body against infection.

11.1 Defence against infectious disease

Assessment statements

- Describe the process of blood clotting.
- Outline the principle of challenge and response, clonal selection and memory cells as the basis of immunity.
- Define 'active' and 'passive immunity'.
- Explain antibody production.
- Describe the production of monoclonal antibodies and their use in diagnosis and in treatment.
- Explain the principle of vaccination.
- Discuss the benefits and dangers of vaccination.

Blood clotting

Arteries, veins and capillaries form a closed system of blood vessels. If skin and blood vessels are broken when tissue is damaged, pathogens have a route into the bloodstream. To prevent blood loss and the entry of pathogens, any blood that escapes from a damaged vessel quickly forms a **clot**, which plugs the gap.

Platelets, erythrocytes (red blood cells) and **leucocytes** (a type of white blood cell) are all important in the clotting process. Platelets are small cell fragments, which form in the bone marrow and circulate in the bloodstream. Also important are two plasma proteins, which are present in the blood in their inactive forms until they are activated

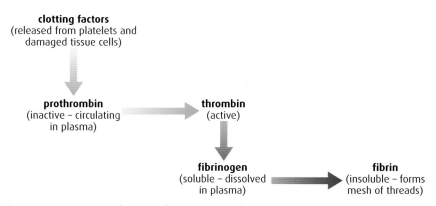

Figure 11.1 Diagram showing the sequence of reactions in the blood-clotting cascade.

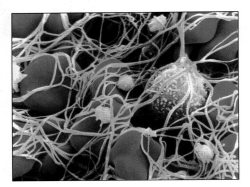

Figure 11.2 False-colour TEM showing red blood cells and threads of fibrin forming a clot (×3600).

when needed (Figure **11.1**). These two inactive proteins are **prothrombin** and **fibrinogen**.

If a small blood vessel is damaged, injured cells or platelets release **clotting factors**, which cause platelets to stick to the area. These factors activate prothrombin, which is converted to its active form, **thrombin**. Thrombin, in turn activates the soluble protein fibrinogen, converting it to active **fibrin**, which is insoluble and forms long threads. This cascade of reactions ensures a speedy response to any damage. Fibrin forms a mesh of fibres that covers the damaged area and traps passing blood cells, forming a soft clot (Figure **11.2**). If a clot is exposed to air, it dries and forms a scab, which will protect the area until the tissue beneath has been repaired.

Immunity: challenge and response

Resistance to an infection is known as **immunity**. Immunity is acquired from childhood onwards as the body is exposed to, and learns to recognise, many different types of pathogen that have the potential to cause disease. We become able to distinguish between cells that are our own 'self' and those that are 'non-self' and are therefore likely to be pathogens or cause harm. Cells are recognised by the proteins on their plasma membranes.

Certain leucocytes are able to recognise 'non-self' proteins, or **antigens**. Antigens may be on the surface of a pathogen, or may have been secreted by a pathogen in a toxin. Antigens are also likely to be present on the cell surfaces of transplanted tissues or organs.

If a pathogen enters the body, the immune system is stimulated to respond. As it is 'challenged' by the pathogen, it 'responds' by setting in motion processes that will destroy it. The first line of defence is phagocytic leucocytes. These are non-specific and will consume bacteria, viruses and other pathogens, as well as dead cells and cell fragments that might accumulate, for example, in a wound. The second line of defence is a specific response to antigens, with **antibodies**. These proteins are the key to the body's immune response, and producing them effectively requires interaction between three types of cell: macrophages and two types of lymphocyte, called B-cells and helper T-cells.

The **immune response** takes several days to become fully active and in the meantime we become ill. Sometimes symptoms are mild, such as with the common cold, but sometimes they are severe, leading to permanent disability or even death.

Clonal selection

B-cells are antibody-producing lymphocytes, but each B-cell can only produce one particular type of antibody. Since the antibody–antigen response is highly specific, there must be a great many types of B-cell in order to be able to respond to all the possible types of antigen. At any time, there can only be a very few of each type of B-cell in the bloodstream because most of the blood volume is taken up with red cells. Look back at the micrograph of a stained blood smear in Figure **6.8** (page **139**) – this shows clearly how red cells heavily outnumber white cells in the blood.

When a pathogen enters the bloodstream, its surface antigen molecules are exposed to the antibodies attached to different B-cells in the blood. If there is a match between an antigen and an antibody, the B-cell with the matching antibody becomes 'selected' while all the other B-cells are rejected. The selected B-cell is stimulated to divide and produces a **clone** of antibody-secreting cells, in a process known as **clonal selection**.

It is likely that any pathogen will have many different antigenic molecules on its surface so several different types of B-cell will probably be selected. Each of these will result in clone of antibody-secreting B-cells. This is therefore called a **polyclonal response** and it will result in a more efficient destruction of the pathogen.

Antibody production

In reality, the response to pathogens is more complex than simple clonal selection and it involves two types of lymphocyte: B-cells and T-cells.

1 When a pathogen enters the bloodstream it is consumed by a macrophage, partly digested and antigen proteins from it are placed on the outer surface of the macrophage. This is called **antigen presentation** because the proteins are being 'presented' to other cells.
2 **Helper T-cells** with matching receptors bind to the macrophages and are activated.
3 Activated helper T-cells then start dividing into two clones of cells. One clone is of active helper T-cells, which are required for the next step in the process, and the other clone is of **memory cells**, which will be used if the same pathogen ever invades the body again.
4 **B-cells** with the matching antibody also take in and process antigen proteins from the pathogen and place them on their outer surface.
5 Active helper T-cells bind to these B-cells and, in turn, activate them.
6 Just like the T-cells, the B-cells now divide into two clones of cells. One is made up of active B-cells, or **plasma cells**, which secrete huge quantities of antibodies into the bloodstream. Antibodies destroy pathogens and also help the macrophages to detect and consume more pathogens. The second clone is made up of **memory cells**, which allow the body to make a large and rapid response should the same pathogen invade again.

Figure **11.3** (overleaf) summarises the process of antibody production.

Active and passive immunity

As we have seen, immunity develops as a result of exposure to a pathogen. This in turn causes the production of antibodies, but developing immunity to a disease can occur either actively or passively.

* **Active immunity** develops when an individual is exposed to an antigen and produces antibodies after their immune system has been stimulated. The antigens may be present in the body as a result of infection or be intentionally introduced during vaccinations. In both cases, the body produces antibodies and specialised lymphocytes.

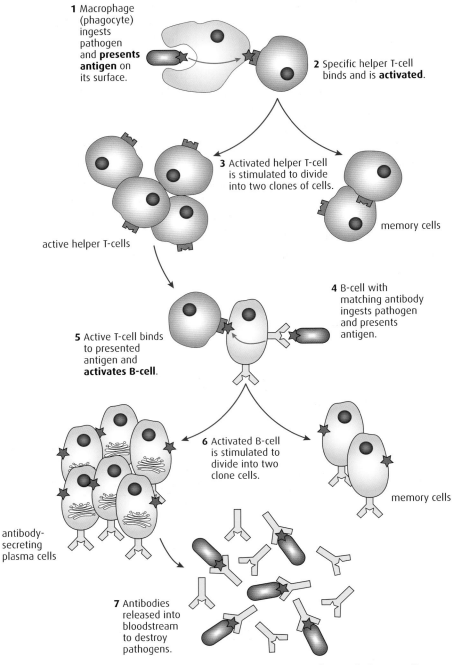

1 Macrophage (phagocyte) ingests pathogen and **presents antigen** on its surface.

2 Specific helper T-cell binds and is **activated**.

3 Activated helper T-cell is stimulated to divide into two clones of cells.

memory cells

active helper T-cells

4 B-cell with matching antibody ingests pathogen and presents antigen.

5 Active T-cell binds to presented antigen and **activates B-cell**.

6 Activated B-cell is stimulated to divide into two clone cells.

memory cells

antibody-secreting plasma cells

7 Antibodies released into bloodstream to destroy pathogens.

Figure 11.3 The production of antibodies involving macrophages, helper T-cells and B-cells. The plasma cells contain large amounts of rER to synthesise the protein antibodies.

- **Passive immunity** is acquired when antibodies are transferred from one person (or other organism) to another. The antibodies will have been produced as a result of active immunity. Antibodies pass from mother to baby across the placenta and are also transferred in colostrum (a special form of milk) in the first few days of suckling after birth. Preformed antibodies can be injected into a person in the form of a serum – for example, to treat a snake bite. Passive immunity is relatively short-lived. It lasts as long as the antibodies are present in the blood and the recipient does not produce any antibodies of their own.

Monoclonal antibodies

The body normally produces a polyclonal response to an invasion by a pathogen. A **monoclonal antibody** is artificially produced to target one specific antigen. These are used both in commercial applications and for laboratory research. Figure **11.4** shows how monoclonal antibodies are obtained.

B-cells are short lived and therefore of little value for commercial antibody production. The **hybridoma cells**, however, have characteristics of both B-cells and cancer cells: they produce antibodies *and* they are almost immortal if they are kept in culture medium. Monoclonal antibodies are produced by clones so they are all identical, they are highly specific, and they can be produced in very large quantities.

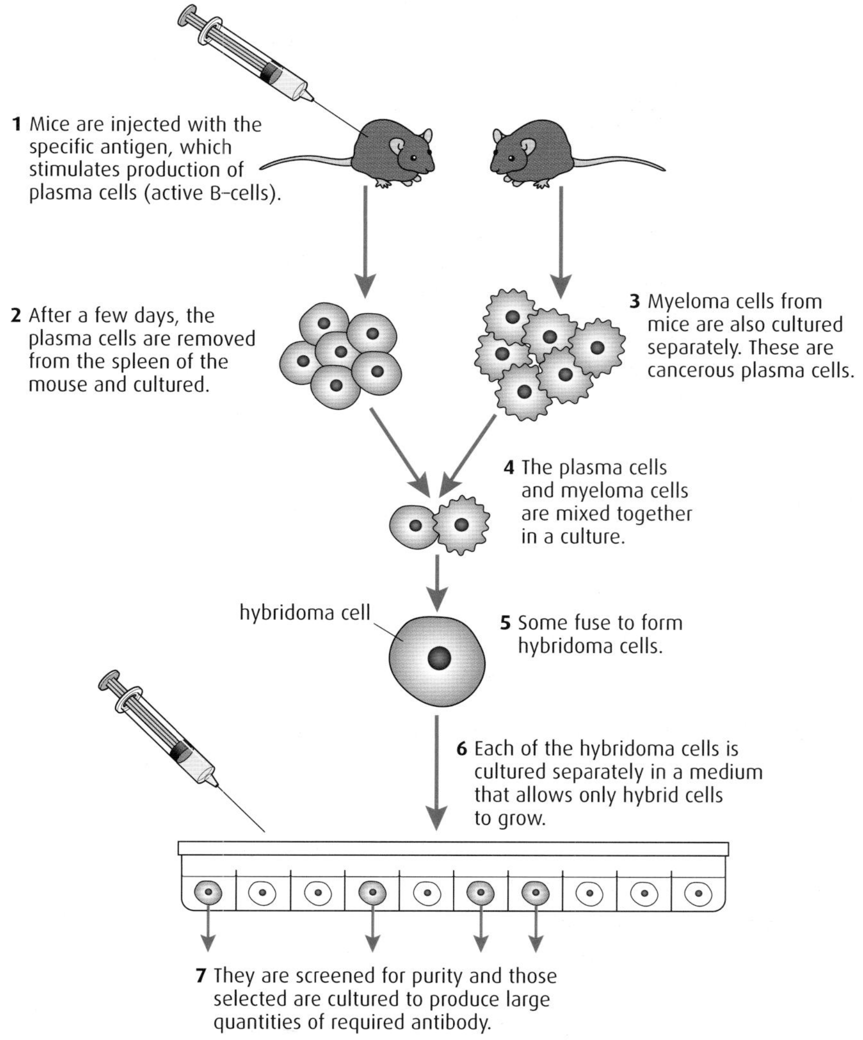

Active immunity resistance to the onset of a disease due to the production of antibodies in the body after stimulation of the immune system by disease antigens; active immunity may occur as a result either of exposure to a disease or vaccination

Passive immunity resistance to the onset of a disease due to antibodies acquired from another organism in which active immunity has been stimulated

1 Mice are injected with the specific antigen, which stimulates production of plasma cells (active B-cells).

2 After a few days, the plasma cells are removed from the spleen of the mouse and cultured.

3 Myeloma cells from mice are also cultured separately. These are cancerous plasma cells.

4 The plasma cells and myeloma cells are mixed together in a culture.

hybridoma cell

5 Some fuse to form hybridoma cells.

6 Each of the hybridoma cells is cultured separately in a medium that allows only hybrid cells to grow.

7 They are screened for purity and those selected are cultured to produce large quantities of required antibody.

Figure 11.4 Formation of monoclonal antibodies.

Monoclonal antibodies are used in diagnosis to detect the presence of pathogens such as streptococcal bacteria and herpes virus. They are also used in pregnancy testing. Monoclonal antibodies can recognise HCG (human chorionic gonadotrophin), which is present in the urine of a pregnant woman (see page **279**).

Monoclonal antibodies may also prove to be invaluable in the treatment of cancer. Cancer cells carry specific antigens on their cell surfaces and if monoclonal antibodies can recognise these, they can be used to target these cancer cells and carry cytotoxic drugs to them. It is hoped that these treatments, which have been called 'magic bullets', could reduce the amount of drugs that need to be taken during chemotherapy treatment. One disease, called mantle cell lymphoma, has already been treated in this way. Mantel cell lymphoma is a cancer of the B-cells (B-lymphocytes) and accounts for about 1 in 20 of all cases of the group of cancers known as non-Hodgkin lymphomas. This disease has been treated with manufactured monoclonal antibodies, with the generic name of rituximab. The antibodies are used in conjunction with chemotherapy and stick to particular surface proteins on the cancer cells, which they stimulate the body's immune system to destroy.

Vaccination

Immunity develops when a person has been exposed to a pathogen. For most mild illnesses, such as the common cold or tonsillitis, this happens naturally as a person comes into contact with the viruses or bacteria that cause them. But some pathogens cause diseases that have dangerous or life-threatening symptoms. For these diseases, which include tetanus, tuberculosis, cholera, poliomyelitis and measles, **vaccines** have been developed to provide a safe first exposure so that a vaccinated person will develop immunity but not the disease.

Vaccines are modified forms of the disease-causing pathogens. A vaccine may contain either weakened (attenuated) or dead pathogens, or their toxins. Vaccines are often produced by treating pathogens with heat or chemicals.

Most vaccines are injected into a person's body, although some, such as polio vaccine, can be taken orally. Antigens in the vaccine stimulate the immune response and the formation of sufficient memory cells to produce antibodies very quickly if the person is infected with the real pathogen later on.

A first **vaccination** produces a primary response but many vaccinations are followed up with another some time later. The second or 'booster' dose of vaccine causes a greater and faster production of antibodies and memory cells, known as a **secondary response** (Figure **11.5**), and provides long-term protection. The time that antibodies and memory cells persist depends on the disease. Rubella vaccination can provide protection for up to 20 years, while vaccinations for tetanus should be repeated every 10 years. Vaccines do not prevent infection by pathogens but they do enable the body to respond quickly to them and prevent serious illness.

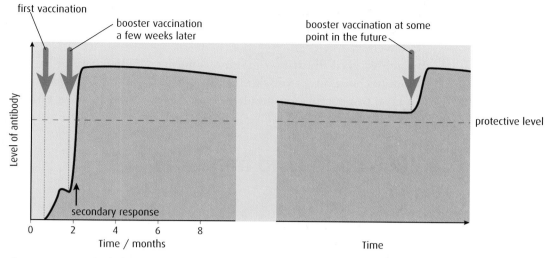

Figure 11.5 Antibody levels after vaccination. The persistance of antibodies varies and depends on the vaccine used.

Benefits and dangers of vaccination

The first vaccine against smallpox was developed by Edward Jenner in 1796. Since then, vaccination programmes in many countries have saved countless lives. Smallpox was eradicated in 1977 as a direct result of a World Health Organization vaccination programme. Since that time, there have been no cases of this once-fatal disease.

The advantages of vaccination include:

- **prevention of epidemics and decrease in the spread of disease** – as people travel more widely and more rapidly all over the world, this has become increasingly important
- **economic benefits** – it is much cheaper to vaccinate large numbers of people and prevent illness rather than bear the healthcare costs of treating the sick
- **complete eradication of some diseases** – this has already occurred for smallpox and the World Health Organization also aims to eliminate measles and polio
- **prevention of disability by vaccination** – before vaccinations were available, polio left many people paralysed after they had been infected, while rubella virus caused blindness and deafness in the babies of mothers who had the disease during their pregnancy.

Although the case for vaccination is a powerful one, some people are concerned that vaccinations may have disadvantages, which include:

- **rare cases of allergic reaction** – although vaccines are thoroughly tested before use and usually cause only minor reactions, such as fever or swelling, a small number of individuals do react badly to them
- **perceived risk of 'overloading' of immune system** – vaccinations for some childhood illnesses, such as measles, mumps and rubella (MMR), are given together in a multiple-vaccine, and some parents fear that such multiple-vaccinations may cause the immune system to overreact, thereby posing a possible danger to their child

- **difficulty of ensuring safe use** – in some countries, it is difficult to keep the vaccines in cool, sterile conditions and administer them effectively
- **breach of civil liberties** – in some countries, children have to have certain vaccinations before they can start school, and there are parents who feel that vaccination should be a matter of personal choice, rather than compulsory.

11.2 Muscles and movement

Assessment statements

- State the roles of bones, ligaments, muscles, tendons and nerves in human movement.
- Label a diagram of the human elbow joint, including cartilage, synovial fluid, joint capsule, named bones and antagonistic muscles (biceps and triceps).
- Outline the functions of the structures in the human elbow joint.
- Compare the movements of the hip joint and the knee joint.
- Describe the structure of striated muscle fibres, including the myofibrils with light and dark bands, mitochondria, the sarcoplasmic reticulum, nuclei and the sarcolemma.
- Draw and label a diagram to show the structure of a sarcomere, including Z lines, actin filaments, myosin filaments with heads and the resultant light and dark bands.
- Explain how skeletal muscle contracts, including the release of calcium ions from the sarcoplasmic reticulum, the formation of cross-bridges, the sliding of actin and myosin filaments and the use of ATP to break cross-bridges and re-set myosin heads.
- Analyse electron micrographs to find the state of contraction of muscle fibres.

Joints

A **joint** is a place where two or more bones meet. Joints between bones in the human body, together with the muscles that are attached to them, enable us to move and also support the body. Most joints involve bones, muscles, cartilage, tendons, ligaments and nerves.

- **Bones** provide a framework that supports the body. They protect vital organs such as the brain and the lungs. Blood cells are formed within bones, which contain bone marrow. Bones also act as a site for the storage of calcium and phosphate.
- **Ligaments** attach bones to one another at a joint. Some strap joints together while others form a protective capsule around a joint. They are tough and fibrous and provide strength and support so that joints are not dislocated.
- **Tendons** attach muscles to bones. They are formed of tough bands of connective tissue made of collagen fibres and are capable of withstanding tension as muscles contract.
- **Muscles** provide the force needed for movement. They are able to contract in length and as they do so they move the joint into new positions. Muscles only cause movement by contraction, so they occur

in **antagonistic pairs** – one muscle of the pair causes a movement in one direction while the other returns it to its original position.
- **Motor neurons** stimulate muscle contraction. Sensory neurons transmit information from proprioceptors (position sensors) in the muscles so that movements can be coordinated and monitored.

The elbow joint

The elbow is a **hinge joint**, so-called because it moves in a manner resembling the opening and closing of a door hinge (Figure **11.6**). It is an example of a **synovial joint**. The capsule that seals the joint is lined by a membrane that secretes lubricating **synovial fluid** so that the bones move smoothly against one another and friction is reduced. Smooth cartilage covers the ends of the bones at the joint and also helps to reduce friction and absorbs pressure as the joint moves.

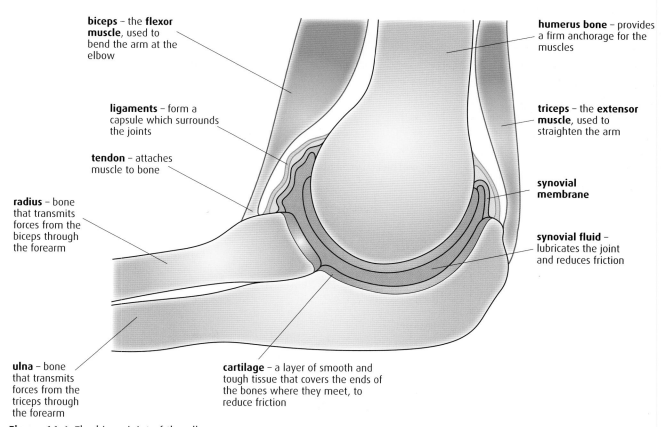

biceps – the **flexor muscle**, used to bend the arm at the elbow

ligaments – form a capsule which surrounds the joints

tendon – attaches muscle to bone

radius – bone that transmits forces from the biceps through the forearm

ulna – bone that transmits forces from the triceps through the forearm

cartilage – a layer of smooth and tough tissue that covers the ends of the bones where they meet, to reduce friction

humerus bone – provides a firm anchorage for the muscles

triceps – the **extensor muscle**, used to straighten the arm

synovial membrane

synovial fluid – lubricates the joint and reduces friction

Figure 11.6 The hinge joint of the elbow.

The elbow joint is formed of three bones – the radius and ulna in the lower arm and the humerus in the upper arm. Tendons attach the biceps and triceps muscles to these bones. The biceps is attached to the radius and the shoulder blade. When it contracts the arm bends. The triceps is attached to the ulna, humerus and shoulder blade and it contracts to straighten the arm. The biceps and triceps are an example of an antagonistic pair of muscles.

The knee and hip joints

The knee joint is another example of a hinge joint and it moves in a similar way to the elbow, allowing movement in only one direction. The hip joint is a **ball-and-socket joint** with the ball-shaped head of the thigh bone (the femur) fitting into a socket in the hip. Ball-and-socket joints allow movement in more than one direction and also permit rotational movements (Figure **11.7**).

Knee joint and movement at the knee

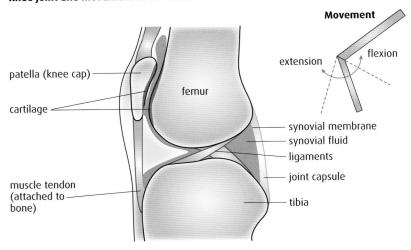

Hip joint and movement at the hip

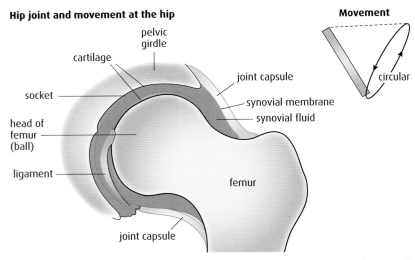

Figure 11.7 Longitudinal sections of the knee and hip joints, and the degree of movement they allow.

Muscles

Skeletal or **striated muscle** is the muscle that causes the movement of our joints. Viewed under the light microscope (Figure **11.8**) it has a striped appearance made up of multinucleate cells known as **muscle fibres**. Surrounding the muscle fibre is a plasma membrane called the **sarcolemma**. Each fibre is made up of many **myofibrils** running parallel to one another (Figure **11.9**).

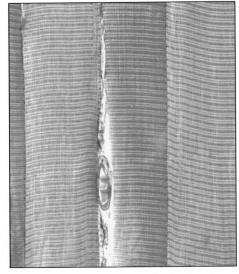

Figure 11.8 Light micrograph of striated muscle, stained to show the banding in muscle fibres.

The body contains three types of muscle – **skeletal** or **striated muscle** attached to the skeleton, **cardiac muscle** found only in the heart, and **smooth** or **non-striated muscle**, which is found in the walls of hollow organs such as the intestines and bladder. Striated muscle can be controlled voluntarily and enables us to move.

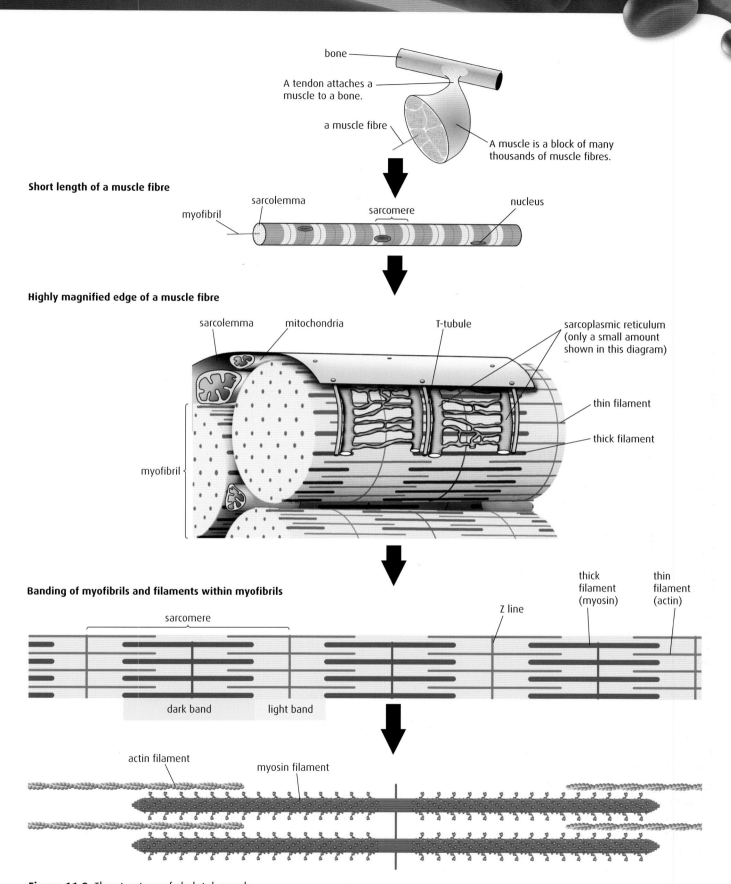

bone

A tendon attaches a muscle to a bone.

a muscle fibre

A muscle is a block of many thousands of muscle fibres.

Short length of a muscle fibre

myofibril

sarcolemma

sarcomere

nucleus

Highly magnified edge of a muscle fibre

sarcolemma

mitochondria

T-tubule

sarcoplasmic reticulum (only a small amount shown in this diagram)

thin filament

thick filament

myofibril

Banding of myofibrils and filaments within myofibrils

sarcomere

Z line

thick filament (myosin)

thin filament (actin)

dark band

light band

actin filament

myosin filament

Figure 11.9 The structure of skeletal muscle.

If skeletal muscle is examined with an electron microscope, it is possible to see that surrounding each myofibril is a system of membranes called the **sarcoplasmic reticulum** (which resembles smooth endoplasmic reticulum) and between the closely packed myofibrils are many mitochondria (Figure **11.9**).

Myofibrils are made up of repeating subunits called **sarcomeres**, which produce the striped appearance of a muscle fibre and are responsible for muscle contraction. The ends of a sarcomere are called the **Z lines**.

There are two types of filament that form the striped pattern of a muscle. These filaments are formed from the contractile proteins **actin** and **myosin**. The narrow filaments of actin are attached to the Z lines and extend into the sarcomere. Thicker filaments of myosin run between them. Where myosin is present, the myofibril has a dark appearance and a light band is seen where only actin is present. Myosin filaments have 'heads' which protrude from their molecules and are able to bind to special sites on the actin filaments.

Muscle contraction

Muscle contraction is explained by the 'sliding filament theory', which describes how actin and myosin filaments slide over one another to shorten the muscle. Contraction is initiated by the arrival of a nerve impulse from a motor neuron which stimulates the sarcolemma of the muscle fibre. This, in turn, causes the release of calcium ions (Ca^{2+}) from the sarcoplasmic reticulum and begins the process that causes actin filaments to slide inward towards the centre of the sarcomere. The series of events is shown in Figure **11.10**.

1 Nerve impulses (action potentials) travel along the muscle fibre membrane, or sarcolemma, and are carried down into the fibre through infoldings called T-tubules. The impulses then spread along the membrane of the sarcoplasmic reticulum, causing Ca^{2+} ions to be released.

2 Before contraction, binding sites for myosin heads on the actin filaments are covered by two molecules, **troponin** and **tropomyosin**. The myosin heads are prepared in an erect position as ATP binds to them.

3 Now Ca^{2+} ions bind to the actin filaments, causing the troponin and tropomyosin to change shape and expose the myosin binding sites. The myosin heads bind to the actin filaments at the exposed binding sites, forming cross-bridges.

4 This causes inorganic phosphate (P_i) to be released and, as each cross-bridge forms, ADP is also released. The myosin heads bend towards the centre of the sarcomere, pulling the actin filaments inward past the myosin filaments, by about 10 nm. This produces a 'power stroke'.

5 New ATP molecules bind to the myosin heads, breaking the cross-bridges and detaching them from the actin filaments. ATP is used and the myosin heads return to the start position. If the muscle receives further stimulation, the process is repeated and the myosin heads attach further along the actin filaments.

Muscle tone

Contraction of a muscle causes shortening, and this in turn moves bones into a new position. If only a few fibres in a muscle contract, the muscle tightens but does not cause movement. Partial contraction produces muscle tone, which is important in maintaining posture and body shape.

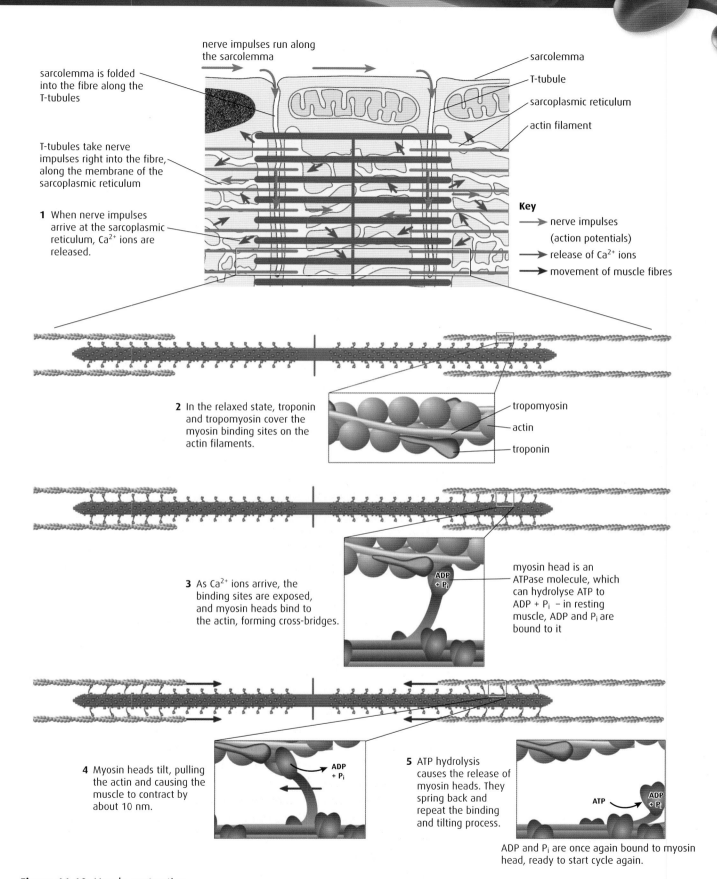

nerve impulses run along the sarcolemma

sarcolemma is folded into the fibre along the T-tubules

sarcolemma

T-tubule

sarcoplasmic reticulum

actin filament

T-tubules take nerve impulses right into the fibre, along the membrane of the sarcoplasmic reticulum

1 When nerve impulses arrive at the sarcoplasmic reticulum, Ca^{2+} ions are released.

Key

→ nerve impulses (action potentials)

→ release of Ca^{2+} ions

→ movement of muscle fibres

2 In the relaxed state, troponin and tropomyosin cover the myosin binding sites on the actin filaments.

tropomyosin

actin

troponin

3 As Ca^{2+} ions arrive, the binding sites are exposed, and myosin heads bind to the actin, forming cross-bridges.

ADP + P$_i$

myosin head is an ATPase molecule, which can hydrolyse ATP to ADP + P$_i$ – in resting muscle, ADP and P$_i$ are bound to it

4 Myosin heads tilt, pulling the actin and causing the muscle to contract by about 10 nm.

ADP + P$_i$

5 ATP hydrolysis causes the release of myosin heads. They spring back and repeat the binding and tilting process.

ATP

ADP + P$_i$

ADP and P$_i$ are once again bound to myosin head, ready to start cycle again.

Figure 11.10 Muscle contraction.

Although the actin and myosin filaments do not change in length when a muscle contracts, the appearance of the banding patterns in the sarcomere is changed. The light bands become reduced, and as the overall length of the sarcomere decreases the dark bands take up a greater proportion of the length (Figure **11.11**).

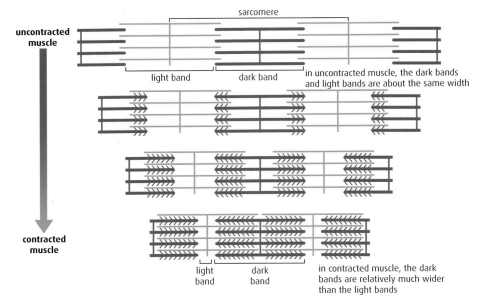

in uncontracted muscle, the dark bands and light bands are about the same width

in contracted muscle, the dark bands are relatively much wider than the light bands

TEM showing myofibrils in an uncontracted skeletal muscle fibre

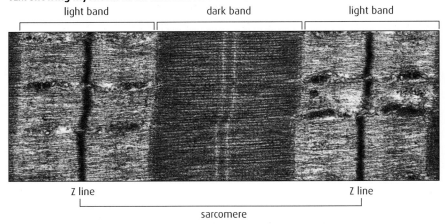

Figure 11.11 When muscle contracts, the interleaved fibres slide inward, past each other. This makes the light bands appear narrower, but the dark bands remain the same width.

1 Explain why muscles occur in antagonistic pairs.

2 Outline the functions of cartilage and synovial fluid in the elbow joint.

3 Compare the movement of a hinge joint and a ball-and-socket joint.

4 Explain how actin and myosin filaments produce the striped appearance of skeletal muscle.

5 Describe the role of ATP in muscle contraction.

Rigor mortis is a partial contraction of muscles that occurs after a person has died. The muscles become stiff and locked in position. It is caused because ATP production stops and myosin heads are unable to detach from actin filaments. It lasts for about 24 hours, at which time decomposition begins to break down the muscle tissues.

11.3 The kidney

Assessment statements

- Define 'excretion'.
- Draw and label a diagram of the kidney.
- Annotate a diagram of a glomerulus and associated nephron to show the function of each part.
- Explain the process of ultrafiltration, including blood pressure, fenestrated blood capillaries and basement membrane.
- Define 'osmoregulation'.
- Explain the reabsorption of glucose, water and salts in the proximal convoluted tubule, including the roles of microvilli, osmosis and active transport.
- Explain the roles of the loop of Henle, medulla, collecting duct and ADH (vasopressin) in maintaining the water balance of the blood.
- Explain the differences in the concentration of proteins, glucose and urea between blood plasma, glomerular filtrate and urine.
- Explain the presence of glucose in the urine of untreated diabetic patients.

Functions of the kidney

The many metabolic processes occurring in cells result in waste substances that must be removed. For example, **urea** is produced as a waste product from the metabolism of amino acids. Waste products such as this are carried away from cells by the bloodstream, but they must be continuously removed from the blood so that they do not reach toxic levels. One of the main functions of the kidneys is to act as filters, removing waste molecules from the blood passing through them. This process is called **excretion**.

The kidneys are also vital in **osmoregulation**. This is the control of the water and salt balance of the body, to maintain a constant internal environment in the blood, tissue fluid and cytoplasm, which is essential to ensure that all cell processes occur effectively. Osmoregulation is achieved mainly by regulating the composition and volume of urine produced by the kidneys.

Excretion the removal from the body of the waste products of metabolic pathways

Osmoregulation control of the water potential of body fluids by the regulation of water and salt content

Structure of the kidney

The kidneys are situated in the lower back, one on either side of the spine, as shown in Figure **11.12** (overleaf). Each receives a blood supply from a renal artery, which is a branch of the main aorta. After filtration, blood leaves the kidney via a renal vein that joins the vena cava.

Figure **11.13** (overleaf) shows a kidney in vertical section. Three regions are visible – the outer cortex, the central medulla and the inner renal pelvis. Urine produced by the kidney collects in the renal pelvis and is carried down to the bladder in the ureter.

Each kidney is made up of more than one million tiny structures called **nephrons**. These are the functional units of the kidney, selectively filtering and reabsorbing substances from the blood. Figure **11.14** (page **269**) shows the structure of a nephron, which consists of a filtering unit (a complex of capillaries called a **glomerulus** surrounded by a **Bowman's capsule**)

Kidney functions at a glance

- excretion of waste products, water-soluble toxic substances and drugs
- regulation of the water and salt content of the body
- retention of substances vital to the body such as protein and glucose
- maintenance of pH balance
- endocrine functions

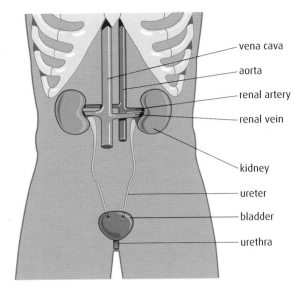

Figure 11.12 Location of the kidneys.

together with a tube that extends from the filtering unit to the renal pelvis. This tube is divided into four regions – the proximal convoluted tubule, the loop of Henle, the distal convoluted tubule and finally a collecting duct. Each of these regions has a specific role to play in urine formation.

How the kidney works

The kidney's complex structure allows it to carry out its functions amazingly efficiently. The process begins as blood from the renal artery reaches each glomerulus.

Blood supply to the kidney is normally about 20% of the heart's output. Approximately 99% of this blood flow goes to the cortex.

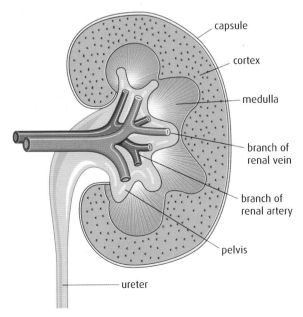

Figure 11.13 Longitudinal section of a kidney.

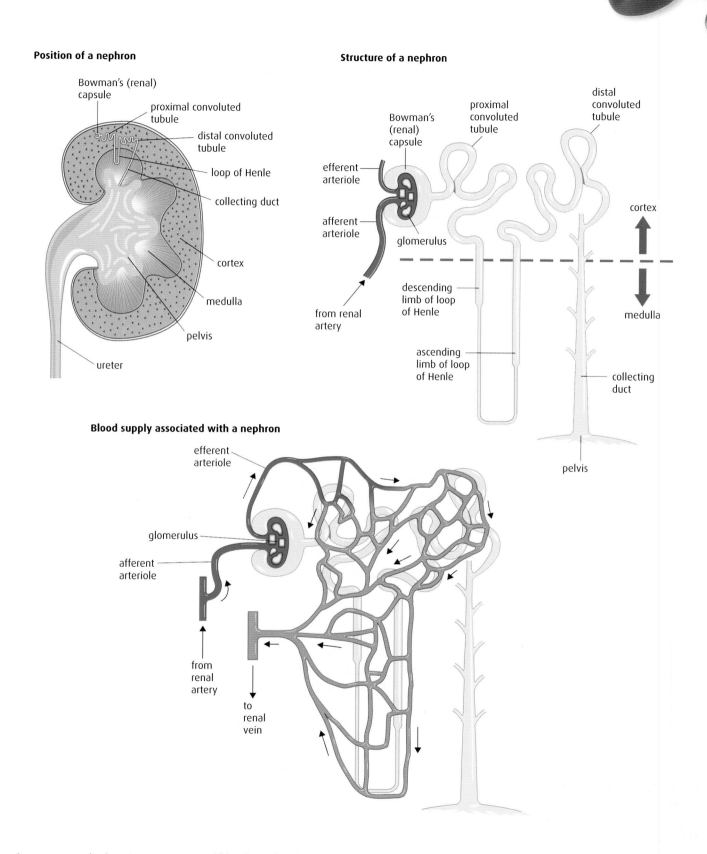

Position of a nephron

- Bowman's (renal) capsule
- proximal convoluted tubule
- distal convoluted tubule
- loop of Henle
- collecting duct
- cortex
- medulla
- pelvis
- ureter

Structure of a nephron

- Bowman's (renal) capsule
- proximal convoluted tubule
- distal convoluted tubule
- efferent arteriole
- afferent arteriole
- glomerulus
- from renal artery
- descending limb of loop of Henle
- ascending limb of loop of Henle
- cortex
- medulla
- collecting duct
- pelvis

Blood supply associated with a nephron

- efferent arteriole
- glomerulus
- afferent arteriole
- from renal artery
- to renal vein

Figure 11.14 The location, structure and blood supply of a nephron.

Ultrafiltration and the glomerulus

Ultrafiltration occurs in the glomerulus, as various small molecules leave the blood.

Because the incoming **afferent** arteriole (a branch of the renal artery) has a wider diameter than the outgoing **efferent** arteriole, blood pressure in the glomerulus capillaries is very high – so high, in fact, that about 20% of the blood plasma leaves the capillaries in the glomerulus and passes into the Bowman's capsule.

The blood plasma passes through three layers – the wall of the capillary in the glomerulus, the **basement membrane** (which acts as a molecular filter) and finally the epithelium of the Bowman's capsule. It leaves the capillaries through small pores or **fenestrations**, which the high blood pressure causes to open in the capillary walls. The fenestrations allow all molecules to pass through easily, but filtration occurs at the basement membrane, which is made of a glycoprotein. Only molecules with a molecular mass smaller than 68 000 are able to pass through. So water, salts, glucose, amino acids and small proteins can all pass through the basement membrane, but it effectively prevents blood cells and large molecules such as plasma proteins from leaving the blood (Figure **11.15**).

The blood plasma that has passed through the basement membrane is now known as **filtrate**. It now passes through the epithelium of the Bowman's capsule into the nephron, and enters the proximal convoluted tubule. Blood cells and large molecules remain in the blood in the glomerulus capillaries and flow on into the efferent arteriole.

The arrows show how the net effect of higher pressure in the capillary and lower solute concentration in the renal capsule is that fluid moves out of the capillary and into the lumen of the capsule.

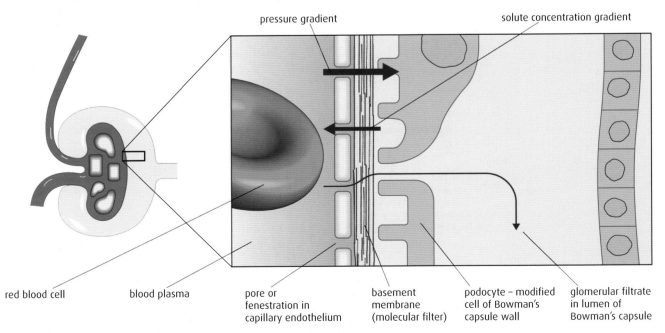

Figure 11.15 Detail of the Bowman's capsule showing the basement membrane, fenestrated capillary and podocytes. Podocytes are supportive, foot-shaped cells of the capsule wall that form a network of slits. Filtrate passes through these slits, and into the capsule.

Reabsorption in the proximal convoluted tubule

Along with the unwanted molecules, many useful substances (water, glucose and ions that the body needs) enter the Bowman's capsule during ultrafiltration. These must be **reabsorbed** into the bloodstream. Between 80% and 90% of the filtrate is reabsorbed in the proximal convoluted tubule of the nephron (Figure **11.16**). The wall of the tubule is a single layer of cells and each one has a border of microvilli to increase its surface area. The cells have many mitochondria fuelling active transport through membrane pumps that selectively reabsorb ions and glucose from the tubular fluid. All the glucose in the filtrate is actively reabsorbed together with almost 80% of sodium (Na^+), potassium (K^+), magnesium (Mg^{2+}) and calcium (Ca^{2+}) ions. Chloride ions (Cl^-) are absorbed passively and water follows by osmosis as the solute concentration of the cells rises due to the active uptake of ions and glucose.

The remaining filtrate now moves into the loop of Henle.

The loop of Henle

The filtrate that enters the **loop of Henle** still contains a good deal of the water that was filtered from the blood. The wall of the descending limb of the loop is permeable to water but relatively impermeable to salts, whereas the ascending limb is impermeable to water, but allows salt to be passed through its walls. The loop passes down into the medulla of the kidney, which has a very high salt concentration, produced by the loop of Henle. A high salt concentration in this area of the kidney is essential for

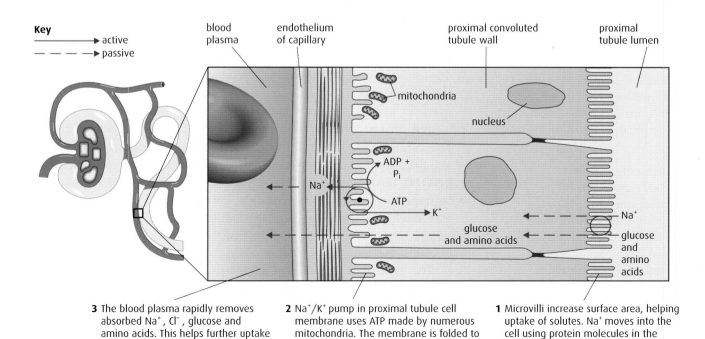

Key
⟶ active
⤍ passive

blood plasma

endothelium of capillary

proximal convoluted tubule wall

proximal tubule lumen

mitochondria

nucleus

ADP + P$_i$

Na$^+$

ATP

K$^+$

glucose and amino acids

Na$^+$

glucose and amino acids

3 The blood plasma rapidly removes absorbed Na$^+$, Cl$^-$, glucose and amino acids. This helps further uptake from the lumen of the tubule.

2 Na$^+$/K$^+$ pump in proximal tubule cell membrane uses ATP made by numerous mitochondria. The membrane is folded to increase surface area. The pump lowers the concentration of Na$^+$ in the cell.

1 Microvilli increase surface area, helping uptake of solutes. Na$^+$ moves into the cell using protein molecules in the membrane, which bring in glucose and amino acids at the same time.

Figure 11.16 Reabsorption in the proximal convoluted tubule.

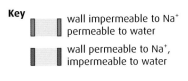

descending limb **ascending limb**

1 Na⁺ and Cl⁻ are actively transported out of the ascending limb.

2 This raises the concentration of Na⁺ and Cl⁻ in the tissue fluid.

3 This in turn causes the loss of water from the descending limb.

4 The loss of water concentrates Na⁺ and Cl⁻ in the descending limb.

5 Na⁺ and Cl⁻ ions diffuse out of this concentrated solution in the lower part of the ascending limb.

Key

▮▮ wall impermeable to Na⁺ permeable to water

▮▮ wall permeable to Na⁺, impermeable to water

Figure 11.17 The counter-current mechanism in the loop of Henle builds up a high Na⁺ ion and Cl⁻ ion concentration in the tissue fluid of the medulla.

the fine-tuning of the water content of the blood by the collecting duct at a slightly later stage.

Water leaves the descending limb passively by osmosis, which is made possible by the active transport of Na⁺ and Cl⁻ ions out of the ascending limb into the tissue fluid of the medulla. The water enters blood capillaries that surround the loop of Henle. The process is summarised in Figure **11.17**.

Despite the loss of water from the loop of Henle, the filtrate that enters the next section of the tubule still has relatively high water content.

The distal convoluted tubule and the collecting duct

Ions are exchanged between the filtrate and the blood in the distal convoluted tubule. Na⁺, Cl⁻ and Ca²⁺ ions are reabsorbed into the blood while H⁺ and K⁺ ions may be actively pumped into the tubule.

The final portion of the nephron is the collecting duct where the final adjustment of water is made (Figure **11.18**). The permeability of the duct depends on the presence or absence of **antidiuretic hormone (ADH)**. If ADH is present, the duct develops membrane channels called **aquaporins** so that it becomes more permeable and water is taken back into the blood. If the water content of the blood is high, ADH is not produced so the duct becomes impermeable and water remains inside the nephron, producing more dilute urine.

The urine now flows from the collecting ducts, into the renal pelvis and down the ureter to the bladder.

A summary of kidney function

Table **11.1** compares the concentration of glucose, urea and protein in the blood plasma that enters the glomerulus, inside the glomerular filtrate and in urine.

ADH and control of water loss

ADH is secreted by the posterior lobe of the pituitary gland, in the brain. If blood volume is low and more water is needed in the body, ADH causes the production of more concentrated urine. Osmoreceptors in the hypothalamus monitor water levels in the blood and control the release of ADH.

Caffeine, alcohol and cold conditions suppress ADH production and can lead to dehydration if too much water is lost in urine. Stress and nicotine increase ADH production producing the opposite effect.

Although the kidney can conserve water already present in the body, only intake of water by drinking or in foods can replace water that has already been lost.

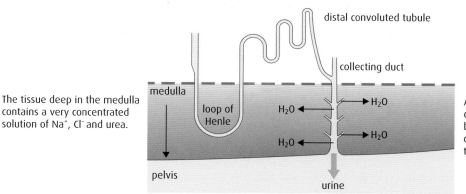

distal convoluted tubule

collecting duct

medulla

The tissue deep in the medulla contains a very concentrated solution of Na⁺, Cl⁻ and urea.

loop of Henle

H_2O

H_2O

H_2O

H_2O

As urine passes down the collecting ducts, water can be reabsorbed. The permeability of the duct is controlled by the hormone ADH.

pelvis

urine

Figure 11.18 Water can be drawn out of the collecting duct by the high salt concentration in the surrounding tissue fluid of the medulla.

Substance	Content in blood plasma/ mg 100 ml⁻¹	Content in glomerular filtrate/ mg 100 ml⁻¹	Content in urine/mg 100 ml⁻¹
urea	30	30	2000
glucose	90	90	0
proteins	750	0	0

Table 11.1 The concentrations of some key substances in blood plasma, glomerular filtrate and urine.

Protein should not be present in the urine of a healthy person whose kidneys are working properly because protein molecules are too large to fit through the membrane filters in the glomerulus.

Urea is toxic in high concentrations and its content increases in urine as water is absorbed from the filtrate.

Glucose, filtered from the blood, forms part of the glomerular filtrate but is reabsorbed by active transport and should not be present in the urine of a healthy person. Glucose in urine is frequently a sign of untreated diabetes. Glucose concentration in a diabetic person's blood rises to a high level because their blood sugar level is not regulated properly by insulin. High blood glucose levels mean the pumps in the proximal convoluted tubule cannot remove it all form the filtrate and return it to the bloodstream. As a result, some glucose remains in the nephron and is lost in the urine because it cannot be reabsorbed in any other regions of the tubule.

6 Define the terms 'excretion' and 'osmoregulation'.

7 Draw and label the functional sections that make up the nephron.

8 Outline the role of the loop of Henle in regulating the content of urine.

9 Outline the role of the efferent and afferent arterioles in ultrafiltration.

10 Explain the role of microvilli in the cells of the proximal convoluted tubule.

11 List the layers through which a glucose molecule passes during ultrafiltration.

12 Outline the role of ADH in controlling the water content of urine.

13 Suggest why a diabetic person may produce urine containing glucose.

11.4 Reproduction

Assessment statements

- Annotate a light micrograph of testis tissue to show the location and function of interstitial cells (Leydig cells), germinal epithelium cells, developing spermatozoa and Sertoli cells.
- Outline the processes involved in spermatogenesis within the testis, including mitosis, cell growth, the two divisions of meiosis and cell differentiation.
- State the role of LH, testosterone and FSH in spermatogenesis.
- Annotate a diagram of the ovary to show the location and function of germinal epithelium, primary follicles, mature follicle and secondary oocyte.
- Outline the processes involved in oogenesis within the ovary, including mitosis, cell growth, the two division of meiosis, the unequal division of cytoplasm and the degeneration of the polar body.
- Draw and label a diagram of a mature sperm and egg.
- Outline the role of the epididymis, seminal vesicle and prostate gland in the production of semen.
- Compare the processes of spermatogenesis and oogenesis, including the number of gametes and timing of the formation and release of gametes.
- Describe the process of fertilisation, including the acrosome reaction, penetration of the egg membrane by a sperm and the cortical reaction.
- Outline the role of HCG in early pregnancy.
- Outline early embryo development up to the implantation of the blastocyst.
- Explain the structure and functions of the placenta, including its hormonal role in secretion of oestrogen and progesterone to maintain pregnancy.
- State that the fetus is supported and protected by the amniotic sac and amniotic fluid.
- State that materials are exchanged between the maternal and fetal blood in the placenta.
- Outline the process of birth and its hormonal control including the changes in progesterone and oxytocin levels and positive feedback.

Spermatogenesis

Spermatogenesis is the production of mature sperm cells (spermatozoa) in the testis. More than 100 million sperm cells are produced each day in a process that takes place in the narrow seminiferous tubules making up each testis (Figures **11.19** and **11.20**).

Sperm production and development takes place from the outer part of the **seminiferous tubules** towards the central lumen, where sperm cells are eventually released. Each tubule is enclosed in a basement membrane beneath which is an outer layer of germinal epithelium cells. These diploid cells (2n) divide regularly by mitosis to produce more diploid cells, which enlarge and are known as **primary spermatocytes**.

Primary spermatocytes divide by meiosis and their first division produces two haploid (n) cells. The second division of these two cells results in four spermatids (n).

Developing sperm are attached to **Sertoli cells** (Figure **11.20**), which are also called nurse cells. These large cells assist the differentiation of immature spermatids into spermatozoa and provide nourishment for them.

Spermatozoa that have developed their tails (Figure **11.21**, overleaf) detach from the Sertoli cells and are carried down the lumen of the tubule to the epididymis of the testis.

Hormones and sperm production

Sperm production is controlled by three hormones – follicle-stimulating hormone (FSH) and luteinising hormone (LH) from the pituitary gland, and testosterone produced by the testes.

- **FSH** stimulates meiosis in spermatocytes, to produce haploid cells.
- **Testosterone** stimulates the maturation of secondary spermatocytes into mature sperm cells.
- **LH** stimulates the secretion of testosterone by the testis.

Epididymis, seminal vesicles and semen production

Sperm cells are stored and mature in the **epididymis** (see Figure **6.29** on page **158**), where they also develop the ability to swim. Sperm cells are released at ejaculation in a nutrient-rich fluid known as **semen**. Semen is produced by two **seminal vesicles** and the **prostate gland**. It is mixed with the sperm cells as they leave the epididymis and move along the

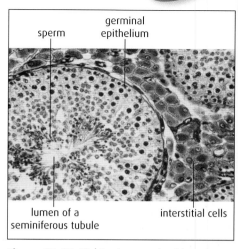

Figure 11.19 Light micrograph of transverse section of a testis showing seminiferous tubules with interstitial cells between them (×170).

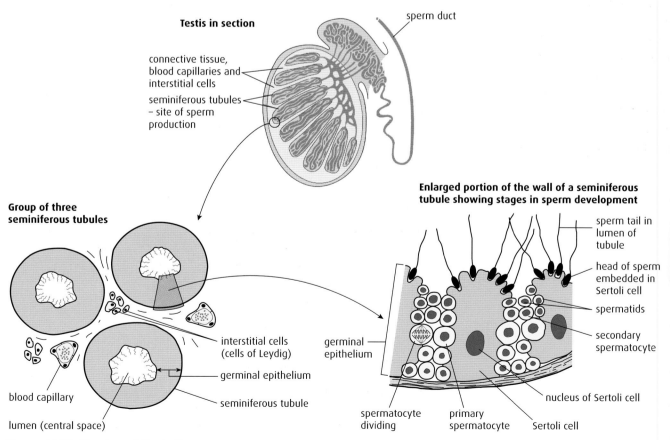

Figure 11.20 Structure of the testis.

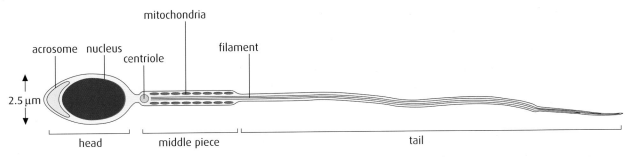

Figure 11.21 Structure of a human sperm cell. Total length is 60 μm.

To remind yourself of the structure of the male reproductive system, look back at Figure **6.29** on page **158**.

vas deferens (sperm duct). Fluid from the seminal vesicles makes up about 70% of semen. It is rich in fructose, which provides energy for the sperm cells to swim, and it also contains protective mucus. The prostate gland produces an alkaline fluid that helps the sperm cells to survive in the acidic conditions of the vagina.

Oogenesis

Oogenesis produces female gametes, the **ova**. Unlike spermatogenesis, which takes place in an adult male, oogenesis begins in the ovaries of a female when she is still a fetus. **Oogonia**, the germinal epithelial cells within the ovaries of the female fetus, divide by mitosis to produce more diploid (2*n*) cells. These enlarge to form **primary oocytes**, which are also diploid. Primary oocytes undergo the first stages of meiosis but this stops during prophase 1 leaving the primary oocyte surrounded by a layer of follicle cells in a structure known as the **primary follicle** (Figure **11.22**).

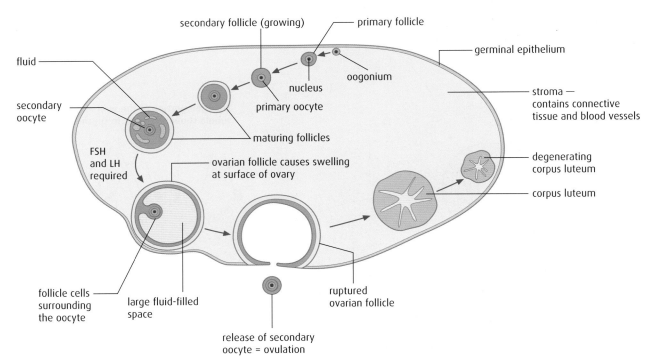

Figure 11.22 Stages in the development of one follicle in a human ovary. The arrows show the sequence of events.

Development now ceases but the ovaries of a baby girl contain around 300 000 primary follicles at birth. The remaining stages of oogenesis are shown in Figure **11.22**.

At puberty, development of the primary follicles continues. During each menstrual cycle, a few follicles proceed to complete the first division of meiosis. Two haploid cells (*n*) are produced but the cytoplasm divides unequally so that one cell is much larger than the other. The larger cell is known as the **secondary oocyte** (*n*) and the smaller cell is the **polar body** (*n*). The polar body degenerates and does not develop further.

The secondary oocyte, protected within its follicle, begins meiosis II but stops in prophase II. At the same time, the follicle cells divide and produce a fluid that causes the follicle to swell. At the point of **ovulation**, the follicle bursts, releasing the secondary oocyte, which floats towards the **oviduct** (fallopian tube). Although ovulation is often described as the release of the ovum, the cell that is released is in fact still a secondary oocyte. The detailed structure of a secondary oocyte is shown in Figure **11.23**, and Figure **11.24** (overleaf) shows secondary oocytes in a rabbit ovary in section.

After fertilisation, the secondary oocyte completes meiosis II, becoming a mature ovum, and expels a second polar body, which degenerates. The empty follicle in the ovary develops to become the **corpus luteum** or yellow body, which produces the hormone progesterone.

To remind yourself about the production of progesterone by the corpus luteum, look back at Chapter **6**, page **161**.

Comparing spermatogenesis and oogenesis

There are a number of similarities and also several differences between the processes of spermatogenesis and oogenesis. Both involve the division of cells in the germinal epithelium by mitosis, and the growth of cells before they undergo meiosis. In both cases, meiosis produces haploid gametes, as shown in Figure **11.25** (overleaf). Table **11.2** (page **279**) summarises the differences and similarities in the two processes.

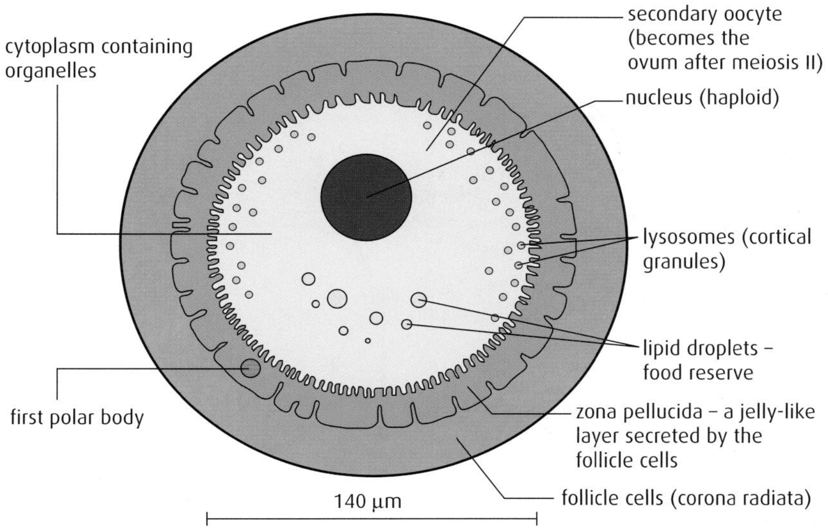

Labels: cytoplasm containing organelles; secondary oocyte (becomes the ovum after meiosis II); nucleus (haploid); lysosomes (cortical granules); lipid droplets – food reserve; first polar body; zona pellucida – a jelly-like layer secreted by the follicle cells; follicle cells (corona radiata); 140 μm

Figure 11.23 Structure of the secondary oocyte and surrounding structures at ovulation.

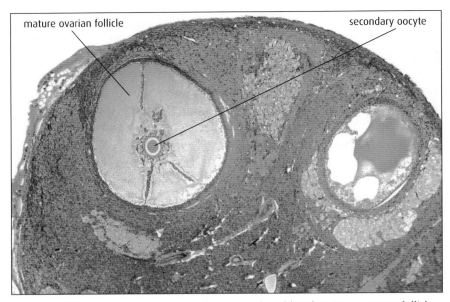

Figure 11.24 Longitudinal section of the ovary of a rabbit showing a mature follicle (×22.5).

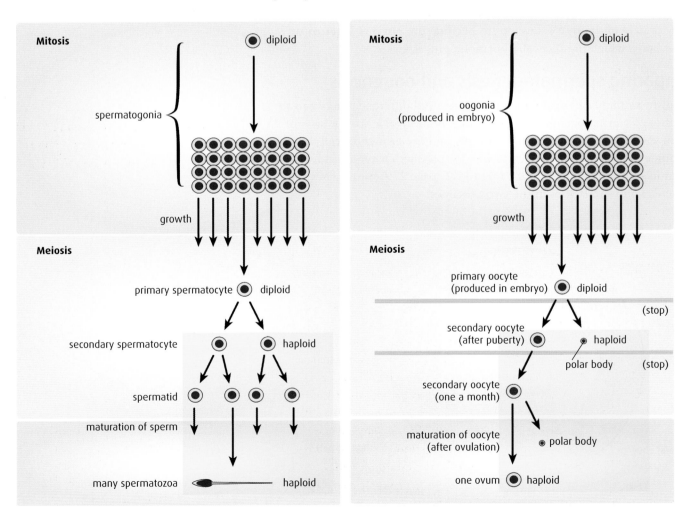

Figure 11.25 A comparison of spermatogenesis and oogenesis.

	Oogenesis	Spermatogenesis
Similarities	both begin with production of cells by mitosis	
	in both, cells grow before meiosis	
	in both, two divisions of meiosis produce the haploid gamete	
Differences	one secondary oocyte is produced per menstrual cycle	millions of sperm cells are produced continuously
	only one large gamete is produced per meiosis	four small gametes are produced per meiosis
	occurs in ovaries, which tend to alternate oocyte production	occurs in testes, which both produce sperm cells
	early stages occur during fetal development	process begins at puberty
	released at ovulation during the menstrual cycle	released at ejaculation
	ovulation ceases at menopause	sperm production continues throughout an adult male's life

Table 11.2 Oogenesis and spermatogenesis compared.

Fertilisation

During sexual intercourse, millions of sperm cells are ejaculated into the vagina and some of them make their way through the cervix and uterus towards the oviducts. Only a very small number of the ejaculated sperm will complete the journey, which is a considerable distance for the tiny cells. For fertilisation to be successful, many sperm cells must be present to penetrate the outer layers of follicle cells covering the secondary oocyte. Only one sperm cell will break through and reach the plasma membrane and enter it. Fertilisation usually occurs in one of the oviducts and is the moment when one sperm cell fuses with the secondary oocyte to form a **zygote**.

The sequence of events is summarised in Figure **11.26** (overleaf).

To remind yourself of the structure of the female reproductive system, look back at Figure **6.30** on page **160**.

Pregnancy

Approximately 24 hours after fertilisation, the zygote begins to divide by mitosis. Mitosis continues and, after about five days of division, produces ball of around 100 cells known as a **blastocyst**, as shown in Figure **11.27** (overleaf). As these divisions are occurring, the ball of cells is moved down the oviduct towards the uterus. After about seven days, it reaches the uterus and settles in the **endometrium** lining, where it implants itself and continues to divide and develop into an **embryo**.

Once the blastocyst has become established in the endometrium, it begins to secrete the hormone **human chorionic gonadotrophin** (**HCG**). HCG travels in the bloodstream to the ovary, where its role is to maintain the corpus luteum, the mass of cells that developed from the empty follicle. The corpus luteum produces progesterone and oestrogen, which – in a non-pregnant woman – maintain the endometrium until the end of the menstrual cycle, when the corpus luteum degenerates. During pregnancy, it is important that the lining remains in place. HCG stimulates the corpus luteum so that it grows and continues to produce its

HCG is excreted in the urine of a pregnant woman and it is this hormone that is detected in a pregnancy test with the use of monoclonal antibodies.

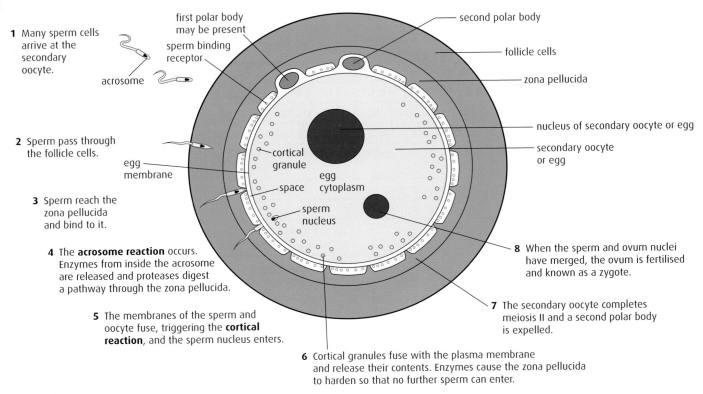

1 Many sperm cells arrive at the secondary oocyte.

2 Sperm pass through the follicle cells.

3 Sperm reach the zona pellucida and bind to it.

4 The **acrosome reaction** occurs. Enzymes from inside the acrosome are released and proteases digest a pathway through the zona pellucida.

5 The membranes of the sperm and oocyte fuse, triggering the **cortical reaction**, and the sperm nucleus enters.

6 Cortical granules fuse with the plasma membrane and release their contents. Enzymes cause the zona pellucida to harden so that no further sperm can enter.

7 The secondary oocyte completes meiosis II and a second polar body is expelled.

8 When the sperm and ovum nuclei have merged, the ovum is fertilised and known as a zygote.

acrosome
sperm binding receptor
first polar body may be present
second polar body
follicle cells
zona pellucida
nucleus of secondary oocyte or egg
secondary oocyte or egg
cortical granule
egg membrane
space
egg cytoplasm
sperm nucleus

Figure 11.26 The stages of fertilisation.

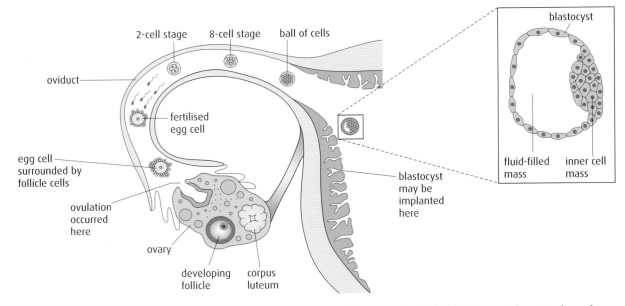

2-cell stage
8-cell stage
ball of cells
blastocyst
oviduct
fertilised egg cell
egg cell surrounded by follicle cells
ovulation occurred here
ovary
developing follicle
corpus luteum
blastocyst may be implanted here
fluid-filled mass
inner cell mass

Figure 11.27 The blastocyst consists of an outer layer of cells enclosing an inner cell mass and a fluid-filled space. The outer layer forms part of the placenta and the inner cell mass develops to become the body of the embryo.

hormones for the first three months (**trimester**) of pregnancy. Thereafter, the placenta is fully formed and produces placental progesterone and oestrogen, so the corpus luteum degenerates.

The embryo grows and develops. After about one month, it is only 5 mm long but has a beating heart and the beginnings of a nervous system.

From two months onwards, it is known as a **fetus**. The fetus at this stage is 30–40 mm long and has recognisable limbs with developing bones. The uterus lining provides nourishment for the early embryo but the placenta soon forms from the endometrium and fetal membranes and by about 12 weeks it is fully functioning. The fetus is connected to the placenta by the **umbilical cord** and is surrounded by a fluid-filled sac called the **amnion**, which contains **amniotic fluid**. The fetus is supported in this fluid throughout its development and is protected by it from bumps and knocks, as the fluid is an effective shock absorber. Amniotic fluid also enables the growing fetus to move and develop its muscles and skeleton.

The placenta

The developing fetus depends on its mother for all its nutrients and oxygen and for the disposal of its waste carbon dioxide and urea. The **placenta** allows these materials to be exchanged between the mother and the fetus and also acts as an endocrine gland, producing estrogen, progesterone and other hormones that maintain the pregnancy.

The placenta is a disc-shaped structure, about 180 mm in diameter and weighing about 1 kg when it is fully developed. It is made up of the maternal endometrium and small projections, or villi, from the outer layers of the **chorion**, which surrounds the embryo. These **chorionic villi**, which are rich in capillaries, grow out into the endometrium to produce a very large surface area for the exchange of gases and other materials. Fetal blood remains inside these capillaries, which penetrate the endometrium tissue until they are surrounded by maternal blood flowing into blood sinuses (spaces) around them. In this way, the mother's blood is brought as close as possible to the fetal blood to allow for efficient diffusion without the two ever mixing. These features are shown in Figure **11.28** (overleaf).

Exchange of materials

Fetal blood is carried to the placenta in two umbilical arteries, which divide to form capillaries in the villi. Nutrients and oxygen from the mother's blood diffuse into the fetal capillaries and are carried back to the fetus in a single umbilical vein. Waste products and carbon dioxide are carried to the placenta in the two umbilical arteries and diffuse into the mother's blood.

Many materials pass to the fetus from its mother. Some of these – such as drugs (both prescription and illegal), nicotine and alcohol – have the potential to seriously harm the fetus, which is why pregnant women are encouraged not to smoke or drink alcohol during pregnancy and to be careful with any medicines they may take.

Substances that pass from mother to fetus include:

- oxygen
- nutrients including glucose, amino acids, vitamins, minerals
- water
- hormones
- alcohol, nicotine and other drugs
- some viruses, including rubella and sometimes HIV.

Prenatal testing – amniocentesis and CVS

Amniocentesis is one of a number of techniques used in prenatal testing to check human fetuses for abnormalities. A fine needle is inserted through the mother's abdomen into the amniotic sac and a small sample of amniotic fluid is taken. The fluid contains fetal cells, which can be cultured for 3–4 weeks until the cells divide and chromosomes become visible. The chromosomes are stained to produce a karyogram, which can be checked for mutations.

An alternative procedure, which can be done earlier in the pregnancy, is chorionic villus sampling (CVS). In this case, a sample of cells is taken for examination from the chorionic villi, via the cervix. More fetal cells are obtained in this way and the results are produced more quickly. However, CVS does have a greater risk of inducing a miscarriage than amniocentesis.

Look back at page **76** in Chapter **4** to see how the techniques of amniocentesis and CVS are carried out.

Substances that pass from fetus to mother include:

- carbon dioxide
- urea
- water
- some hormones, such as HCG.

Fetus in the uterus, showing placenta and umbilical cord

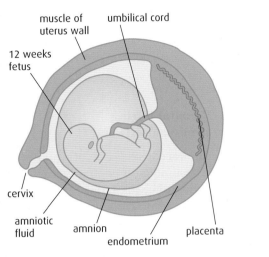

muscle of uterus wall
umbilical cord
12 weeks fetus
cervix
amniotic fluid
amnion
endometrium
placenta

Placenta, showing chorionic villi and fetal and maternal blood supplies

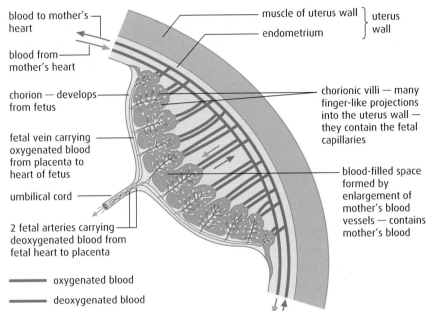

blood to mother's heart
blood from mother's heart
chorion — develops from fetus
fetal vein carrying oxygenated blood from placenta to heart of fetus
umbilical cord
2 fetal arteries carrying deoxygenated blood from fetal heart to placenta

muscle of uterus wall
endometrium
} uterus wall

chorionic villi — many finger-like projections into the uterus wall — they contain the fetal capillaries

blood-filled space formed by enlargement of mother's blood vessels — contains mother's blood

—— oxygenated blood
—— deoxygenated blood

Detail of chorionic villi showing capillaries

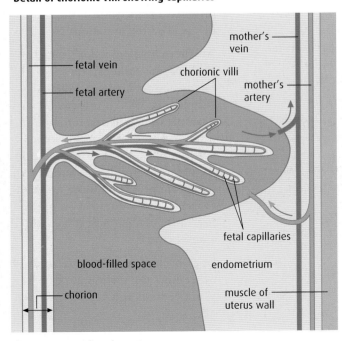

fetal vein
chorionic villi
fetal artery
mother's vein
mother's artery
fetal capillaries
blood-filled space
endometrium
chorion
muscle of uterus wall

Figure 11.28 The placenta.

Hormonal changes and childbirth

For the first 12 weeks of pregnancy, the corpus luteum produces progesterone to maintain the uterus lining (endometrium). After this, the placenta takes over and produces progesterone and estrogen, which suppress the menstrual cycle and promote the growth of breast tissue for **lactation** (milk production).

As the end of pregnancy approaches, the level of progesterone produced by the placenta falls (Figure **11.29**) and this signals the onset of the uterine contractions known as **labour**. At this time, the hormone **oxytocin** is secreted by the posterior lobe of the pituitary gland, in the brain. Oxytocin stimulates the uterus muscles to contract. At first the contractions are mild and infrequent but oxytocin is a hormone that is controlled by **positive feedback**. A small contraction of the uterus muscle stimulates the release of further oxytocin, which in turn stimulates more and stronger contractions. As the uterus contracts, the cervix widens and the amniotic sac breaks, releasing the amniotic fluid. Contractions continue for several hours and the baby is pushed through the cervix and out of the mother's body down the vagina. Gentle contractions continue until the placenta, now known as the afterbirth, is also expelled from the uterus.

After birth, blood levels of the hormone **prolactin**, from the anterior pituitary gland, increase. This hormone stimulates milk production by the mammary glands. As a baby suckles, prolactin secretion is maintained and oxytocin is also released from the posterior pituitary gland. Oxytocin causes milk to be released from milk ducts.

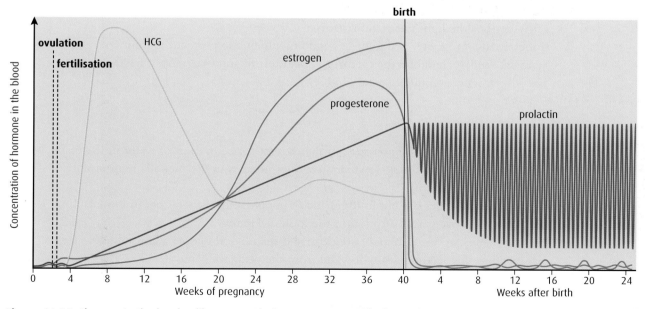

Figure 11.29 Changes in the levels of hormones during pregnancy and birth.

14 Outline the role of the Sertoli cells in spermatogenesis.

15 State the role of testosterone in spermatogenesis.

16 Explain why unequal divisions of cytoplasm are necessary in oogenesis.

17 Outline the role of the prostate gland in semen production.

18 List **three** differences between spermatogenesis and oogenesis.

19 Describe the role of the amnion in the development of the fetus.

20 Describe the role of oxytocin at birth.

End-of-chapter questions

1 Which of the following statements about defence is correct?

    A   During the process of blood clotting, thrombin causes the release of clotting factors
            from the platelets.
    B   Active immunity occurs as a result of the body being challenged by antigens.
    C   Monoclonal antibodies are produced by fusing a hybridoma cell with a myeloma cell.
    D   As a result of vaccination, the primary response of the body will be greater when it
            is invaded by an antigen.   (1)

2 Which of the following statements about muscles and movement is correct?

    A   During muscle contraction, the distance between Z lines decreases, and the dark bands
            get wider but the light bands get narrower.
    B   Bones are held together at a joint by tendons, which also protect the joint.
    C   Synovial fluid, secreted by the cartilage, lubricates the joint to prevent friction.
    D   The elbow is an example of a ball–and–socket joint.   (1)

3 Which of the following statements about the kidney is correct?

    A   Osmoregulation is the maintenance of the correct concentration of water in the urine.
    B   Ultrafiltration occurs in the Bowman's capsules situated in the medulla region of
            the kidney.
    C   Glucose is sometimes present in the urine of people with diabetes because the lack
            of insulin prevents its reabsorption in the loop of Henle.
    D   Human urine can become more concentrated than blood plasma as a result of water
            reabsorption due to the release of ADH from the pituitary gland.   (1)

4 Which of the following statements about reproduction is correct?

    A   The hormones LH and FSH from the pituitary gland and testosterone from the Sertoli cells are involved in spermatogenesis.

    B   During oogenesis polar bodies are formed by meiosis in the follicle cells of the germinal epithelial layer of the ovary.

    C   The role of the hormone HCG early in pregnancy is to prevent further ovulation by blocking the production of oestrogen.

    D   During the process of fertilisation substances released from the cortical granules result in the formation of the fertilisation membrane.   (1)

5 Explain antibody production.   (5)

6 Outline how the fluid in the proximal convoluted tubule is produced by the process of ultrafiltration.   (4)

7 Explain how the cells of the proximal convoluted tubule are adapted to carry out selective reabsorption.   (3)

8 Outline how muscle contraction is brought about, starting with the arrival of a nerve impulse at the muscle.   (5)

9 Outline the process of birth, including hormonal control.   (5)

10 The sense of taste is normally caused by the stimulation of chemoreceptors in the taste buds of the tongue. There are four main 'tastes': sweet, salty, bitter and sour. The tongue also has receptors for temperature. It is known that the taste of food can vary according to whether it is cold, warm or hot. Scientists discovered that just warming or cooling parts of the tongue, even when no food was present, also caused a sensation of taste.

Scientists experimented with a group of people. They gradually cooled the tips of their tongues and measured the intensity of the taste felt by each member of the group. The experiment was repeated, this time warming the tip of the tongue. The graphs show the average values for the group.

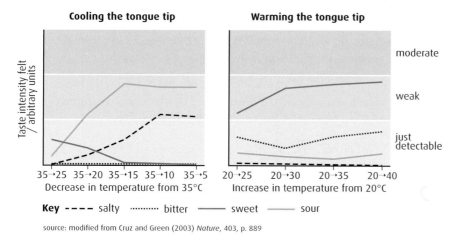

source: modified from Cruz and Green (2003) *Nature*, 403, p. 889

    a   Identify which taste was felt most strongly when the tip of the tongue was:

      i   cooled

      ii warmed   (1)

b Compare the effects on the taste of sweetness, of warming and cooling the tip of the tongue. (2)

c It is important that such experiments use a population sample that is representative. Suggest **two** biological criteria the scientists would have used to select the people to be tested. (1)

d Explain whether cooling or warming the tip of the tongue has the greater effect on the sensation of taste. (2)

The scientists discovered that there were two types of chemoreceptor in the tongue tip. They called these A and B. They tested these chemoreceptors using solutions of sucrose to find out the type of taste and the intensity felt. The results are shown in the bar chart.

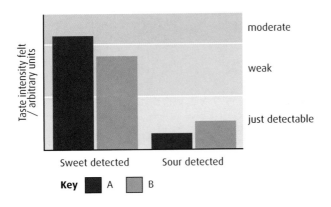

e Compare the effects of sucrose on the A and B chemoreceptors by giving **two** similarities and **two** differences. (4)

(total 10 marks)

© IB Organization 2009

11 Research into how the lungs perform during general anaesthesia has increased because there are so many pulmonary complications during operations. It is believed that many inhaled anaesthetics affect pulmonary epithelial permeability.

Pulmonary clearing is an indication of whether the alveolar–capillary barrier has been damaged. It can be measured as the rate at which radioactivity decreases in lungs after inhalation of a radioactive aerosol. The greater the clearing rate, the greater the damage to the alveolar–capillary barrier. Smoking and lung diseases (such as cancers and asthma) also significantly increase the clearing rate of radioactive aerosols.

In an experiment, doctors wanted to test the effect of inhaled anaesthetics on the permeability between the alveoli and capillaries. Patients were tested by inhaling a radioactive aerosol one day before their operation and one hour after their operation.

Three groups of patients each received a different type of anaesthetic.
Group 1: 1% halotane (inhaled anaesthetic)
Group 2: 1.5% isofluorane (inhaled anaesthetic)
Group 3: phentanyl and propofol (intravenous anaesthetic)

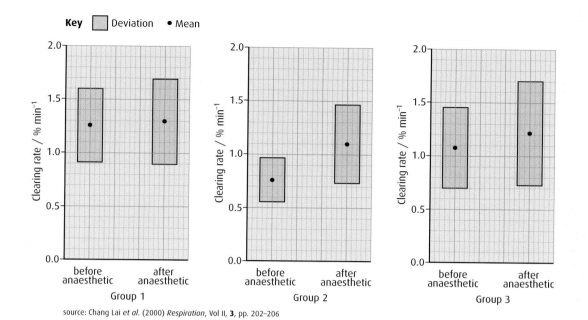

Key ☐ Deviation • Mean

source: Chang Lai *et al.* (2000) *Respiration*, Vol II, **3**, pp. 202–206

a Compare the effect of each inhaled anaesthetic on the permeability of the alveoli. (2)

b Using the data from the graphs, explain whether or not inhaled anaesthetics are more dangerous than intravenous anaesthetics. (3)

(total 5 marks)
© IB Organization 2009

Option A Human nutrition and health

Introduction

The food we eat keeps us alive and provides the nourishment we need to grow, repair our bodies and stay active. A balanced diet gives us all the essential substances that we need in just the right quantities. Our needs differ depending on our age, activities and lifestyles. Some people who do not get the balance right may become overweight, underweight or even seriously ill. Choices people make about what to eat depend on where they live but are also influenced by social issues. Being a vegetarian, whether to breastfeed or bottle-feed infants and taking account of food miles and the environment all have an impact on human nutrition.

A1 Components of the human diet

Assessment statements

- Define 'nutrient'.
- List the types of nutrients that are essential in the human diet, including amino acids, fatty acids, minerals, vitamins and water.
- State that non-essential amino acids can be synthesised in the body from other nutrients.
- Outline the consequences of protein deficiency malnutrition.
- Explain the causes and consequences of phenylketonuria (PKU) and how early diagnosis and a special diet can reduce the consequences.
- Outline the variation in the molecular structure of fatty acids, including saturated fatty acids, *cis* and *trans* unsaturated fatty acids, monounsaturated and polyunsaturated fatty acids.
- Evaluate the health consequences of diets rich in the different types of fatty acid.
- Distinguish between 'minerals' and 'vitamins' in terms of their chemical nature.
- Outline two of the methods that have been used to determine the recommended daily intake of vitamin C.
- Discuss the amount of vitamin C that an adult should consume per day, including the level needed to prevent scurvy, claims that higher intakes give protection against upper respiratory tract infections, and the danger of rebound malnutrition.
- List the sources of vitamin D in human diets.
- Discuss how the risk of vitamin D deficiency from insufficient exposure to sunlight can be balanced against the risk of contracting malignant melanoma.
- Explain the benefits of artificial dietary supplementation as a means of preventing malnutrition, using iodine as an example.
- Outline the importance of fibre as a component of a balanced diet.

Nutrients

Nutrients are chemical substances, found in foods, that are used in the human body. We need a number of nutrients to build our bodies and to stay healthy. We obtain these from the foods we eat. **Essential nutrients** are those that cannot be made in the body and must therefore be included in the diet. Essential nutrients are:

- essential amino acids

Nutrient a chemical substance found in food that is used by the human body for growth or metabolism

- essential fatty acids
- vitamins
- minerals
- water.

Carbohydrates are not included as essential nutrients because they are present in most human diets and there are no specific carbohydrates that are essential. Some diets do not include carbohydrates at all, see page **298**.

Minerals and vitamins are both needed in very small quantities. Their chemical structures are quite different – vitamins are organic compounds, whereas minerals are usually derived from their ions. For example, sodium in the diet is available as Na^+ ions.

Amino acids and protein

To synthesise all the proteins in a human body, 20 different amino acids are needed. We can make some of these in our cells by converting certain nutrients into amino acids, but there are nine that cannot be synthesised and must be taken in as part of a healthy diet. These are known as **essential amino acids**.

Protein deficiency malnutrition can occur if an individual does not have enough of one or more of these essential amino acids. Protein deficiency can lead to poor growth and lack of energy, as well as loss of body mass. One of the most common conditions associated with protein deficiency is swelling of the abdomen (Figure **A.1**). A lack of protein in the diet prevents blood plasma proteins being produced properly. Blood plasma protein assists with the reabsorption of tissue fluid into blood capillaries and without it fluid remains in the tissues causing **oedema** (swelling).

Phenylketonuria

Phenylketonuria (PKU) is a rare genetic metabolic disorder. In the USA, PKU occurs in 1 in 15 000 births. It is caused by a mutation to a gene on chromosome 12. People who suffer from PKU lack an enzyme that is needed to process the amino acid phenylalanine. They are unable to make the liver enzyme tyrosine hydroxylase, which converts phenylalanine into another non-essential amino acid called tyrosine. Phenylalanine is essential for normal growth but if too much builds up in the blood, brain damage can result. The condition is treatable if it is diagnosed soon after birth. Babies and children with untreated PKU develop serious physical and mental health problems as levels of phenylalanine in their blood rise. In many parts of the world, a simple blood test at birth is used to identify babies with PKU. Children who are identified as having PKU must be given a special diet that is low in protein and especially low in the amino acid phenylalanine. They must avoid many common, high protein foods such as milk and dairy products, nuts, fish and meat. PKU only affects children until puberty. After this, they can have a normal diet.

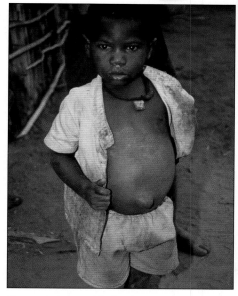

Figure A.1 Kwashiorkor is a protein deficiency disease seen in young children, resulting from a diet low in protein, energy and other nutrients. The children do not grow properly and suffer from oedema, which causes the swollen appearance of their abdomen.

Malnutrition, starvation or deficiency?

Malnutrition occurs when a person does not eat a balanced diet. The diet may mean the person is deficient in one or more nutrients, or suffers an imbalance from eating an excess of a particular nutrient. Malnutrition is defined as the insufficient, excessive or imbalanced consumption of nutrients, which leads to health problems. A person can eat a lot of food but still be malnourished.

Starvation is different from malnutrition – it occurs when an individual simply does not have enough to eat.

A **deficiency** occurs when a person does not have enough of one particular nutrient and suffers health problems as a result.

Fatty acids

All **fatty acids** are composed of a chain of carbon atoms to which hydrogen atoms are bonded, with a carboxyl group (–COOH) at one end and a methyl group (CH$_3$) at the other (Figure **A.2**). The arrangement of carbon and hydrogen atoms in the hydrocarbon chain varies in different types of fatty acids and this gives each type their particular properties.

Saturated fatty acids

Saturated fatty acids get their name from the fact that all the carbon atoms in the hydrocarbon chain are bonded to the maximum number of hydrogen atoms and so are saturated with hydrogen (Figure **A.2**). These fatty acids have straight molecules with up to 20 carbon atoms in the chain. There are no double bonds between any of the carbon atoms. Saturated fatty acids in the human diet come mainly from animal products such as meat, butter, ghee, cream and hard cheese, and a few plant sources such as coconut and palm oils.

Unsaturated fatty acids

Unsaturated fatty acids have one or more double bonds in the hydrocarbon chain, which means they contain less than the maximum number of hydrogen atoms.

   Monounsaturated fatty acids have one double bond and when compared with a saturated fatty acid with the same number of carbon atoms, they have two 'spaces' where hydrogen atoms could bond. These two spaces may be on the same side of the hydrocarbon chain, or on opposite sides (Figure **A.3**). If they are on the same side of the chain, the fatty acid is said to be a *cis* **fatty acid**, and the chain has a kink in it. When the spaces are on opposite sides of the hydrocarbon chain, it is a *trans* **fatty acid** and the chain is straight.

   Polyunsaturated fatty acids have more than one double bond in the hydrocarbon chain. They tend to be liquids at 20 °C and are mainly derived from plant sources. Examples are sunflower oil, corn oil and olive oil.

   One type of *cis* fatty acid is the omega–3 group. These have a double bond at the third bond from the omega end (CH$_3$ end) of the molecule. Omega–3 fatty acids are obtained from eating fish. Omega–6 fatty acids

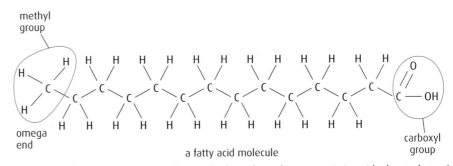

Figure A.2 Fatty acid molecules are hydrocarbon chains. Myristic acid, shown here, is a saturated fatty acid.

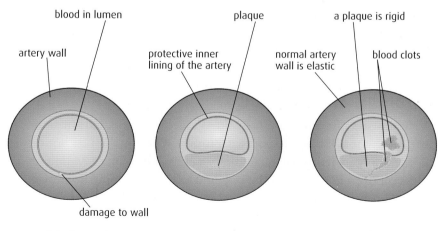

bent *cis* fatty acid – two hydrogen atoms are
absent from the same side of the hydrocarbon chain

straight *trans* fatty acid – one hydrogen atom is
absent from each side of the hydrocarbon chain

Figure A.3 A fatty acid may be in the *cis* or *trans* form, depending on where the 'missing hydrogen spaces' occur.

have a double bond at the sixth position from the omega end. Most
omega-6 fatty acids in the diet come from vegetable oils.

Health and fatty acids

The relative amounts of different types of fatty acid in a person's diet can,
in many cases, be correlated with health issues. Diets in societies around
the world are very different and so is the incidence of coronary heart
disease (CHD) and other diet-related illnesses.

Saturated fatty acids

Eating a diet that is high in saturated fatty acids has been shown to have
a positive correlation with an increased risk of CHD. Saturated fatty acids
can be deposited inside the arteries, and if the deposits combine with
cholesterol they may lead to atherosclerosis, which reduces the diameter of
the lumen and leads to high blood pressure (Figure **A.4**).

Reliable evidence suggests that in countries where the diet is high
in saturated fatty acids and many high-fat foods, animal products and
processed foods are eaten there is likely to be a high incidence of CHD.
Since all fatty acids are high in energy, an excess of these foods in the diet
can also lead to obesity, which places a further strain on the heart.

blood in lumen   plaque   a plaque is rigid

artery wall   protective inner
lining of the artery   normal artery
wall is elastic   blood clots

damage to wall

1 Part of the lining of
the artery is damaged.

2 Gradually, over time,
cells divide in the artery
wall and there is a
build-up of lipids.

3 Exercise or stress can
make the plaque break.
Blood enters the crack.
Platelets in the blood are
activated and a clot forms.
Part of the clot may
break off.

Figure A.4 The development of atherosclerosis in an artery.

Correlation and cause

When studying the occurrence of medical conditions that may be related to diet, it is important to distinguish between **correlation** and **cause**. A correlation between two variables, such as a high incidence of CHD and a high intake of saturated fatty acids, does not mean that the CHD is caused by the fat intake.

Read more about correlation and cause in Chapter **1**, page **8**.

Questions to consider

Think about how the evidence for correlation between diet and health is gathered and what other factors may be important.

1 How can lifestyle indicators be taken into account?
2 What is the importance of genetics and family history?
3 Can it ever be possible to say that one type of diet is good and another is bad for health?

There are some exceptions to this general rule. The Masai people of East Africa have a very low incidence of heart disease despite the fact that most of their traditional diet is derived from milk and meat and the blood of goats and cows. The Masai consume few vegetables so one explanation of their low incidence of CHD could be that they have a low energy intake together with a very active life. Genetic factors may also be important in protecting them from heart disease.

Unsaturated fatty acids

People who eat a Mediterranean-style diet, rich in unsaturated fatty acids from olive oil and fresh vegetables, tend to have a low incidence of CHD. These fats do not combine with cholesterol to form plaques and so arteries tend to remain unblocked and healthy.

Some polyunsaturated fats are modified or 'hydrogenated' so they can be used in processed foods. These hydrogenated fats become *trans* fatty acids. There is a positive link between the intake of these *trans* fatty acids and CHD.

Omega-3 fatty acids found in fish are used to synthesise long-chain fatty acids found in the nervous system. It has been suggested that a lack of omega-3 fatty acids could affect brain and nerve development but no conclusive evidence has yet been found.

Vitamins and minerals

Vitamins and minerals are usually listed together in diet information because, although they are both vital for good health, they are both needed only in very small quantities. Vitamins are chemically quite different from minerals and the two nutrient groups come from many different sources. Some key differences are shown in Table **A.1**.

Vitamins	Minerals
made in plants and animals	substances derived from rocks or found dissolved in water
compounds	elements in ionic form, e.g. phosphate (PO_3^-)
organic e.g. vitamin C ($C_6H_8O_6$)	inorganic, e.g. iron (Fe^{2+}), calcium (Ca^{2+}), iodine (I^-)

Table A.1 Comparing vitamins and minerals.

Vitamin C

Nutritional labels on food products show the quantities of different nutrients that they contain, together with a recommended daily amount (RDA) for each one. The recommended level for vitamin C is about 50 mg per day. Vitamin C helps to protect the body from infection and is important in keeping bones, teeth and gums healthy and for synthesis of the protein collagen. A shortage of the vitamin leads to the deficiency disease called **scurvy**.

Two main techniques have been used to work out how much vitamin C a person needs each day. The first involves the use of animal tests and the second uses human test subjects.

During tests involving animals, small mammals such as guinea pigs are fed diets containing different levels of vitamin C, while all other nutrients are controlled. Levels of vitamin C in the blood can be measured and the health of the animals is monitored. After a time, animals receiving insufficient vitamin C show signs of deficiency, such as poor collagen in bones and increased rates of infection. The data collected can be used to calculate the amount of vitamin C required by a human.

Humans were directly monitored during a number of medical investigations carried out in Sheffield, UK, during the 1939–45 war. The subjects were conscientious objectors – pacifists, who were allowed to volunteer for experiments as an alternative to military service. The young men and women were fed diets lacking in vitamin C for six weeks but were given supplements of 70 mg of L-ascorbic acid each day. (L-ascorbic acid is the chemical term for vitamin C.) The subjects were then divided into three groups. The first group continued to receive 70 mg of L-ascorbic acid per day, the second was given 10 mg per day and the third group received no L-ascorbic acid at all. After 6–8 months on this regime, the volunteers deprived of vitamin C developed signs of scurvy while the other two groups did not.

Vitamin C is found in citrus fruits such as oranges and lemons, but strawberries and kiwi fruit are also rich sources. Fresh vegetables also contain vitamin C but the amount is reduced by cooking.

Recommended daily amounts

Different countries establish different values for RDAs of various nutrients. The RDAs for vitamin C from various authorities are shown in the table below.

World Health Organization	45 mg day^{-1}
Canada	75 mg day^{-1} for women; 90 mg day^{-1} for men
UK	75 mg day^{-1}
USA	60–95 mg day^{-1}

Human experimentation

Between 1942 and 1946, Professor John Pemberton was a Medical Officer to the Research Team that carried out the medical experiments in Sheffield, including those on vitamin C, and he has written about that research. In his paper, published in the *International Journal of Epidemiology* (2006), he says:

'*The Sheffield conscientious objectors demonstrated, once again, how valuable medical knowledge can be obtained by human experimentation, and sometimes in no other way, if volunteers can be found who are willing to undergo considerable discomfort, pain and even serious risks to the health. The contribution of the volunteers to medical knowledge during 1939–45 should not be forgotten.*'

Questions to consider

Today, experiments like these would not be permitted under the Helsinki Agreement of 1975, which promoted human rights.

1 What are the ethical issues involved in such trials?
2 Can experiments in which subjects may be put at risk ever be justified?

The results indicated that 10 mg of vitamin C per day would be sufficient for good health but it is generally agreed that the recommended level should be higher to account for variation between people and provide a suitable level to protect people from scurvy and infection.

1 Why were the human volunteers deprived of vitamin C in their diet for six weeks but given L-ascorbic acid before the experiments?

Excess vitamin C that is eaten or taken as supplements cannot be stored and is excreted in urine. If a person takes in a large excess of vitamin C for a long time, the person's body becomes used to excreting large amounts. It may continue to do so even if the person stops taking the supplement and the level of intake falls. Vitamin C continues to be excreted, so that levels in the body may fall too low, a condition known as **rebound malnutrition**. A diet with regular amounts of fresh fruits and vegetables should always contain sufficient vitamin C for good health, without the need to take vitamin supplements.

Question to consider

How important is reputation in deciding whether or not a new theory or proposal is a good one?

A reputation on the line

Linus Pauling (1901–94) was an American biochemist who won two Nobel Prizes for his work. In 1986, in his book *How to Live Longer and Feel Better*, he suggested that very large doses of vitamin C, as high as 1000 mg per day, would provide protection against colds and other minor respiratory tract infections. There was no conclusive experimental evidence to back up his claims but he was believed by many people because of his reputation and fame.

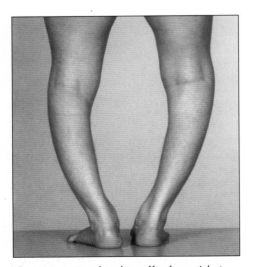

Figure A.5 People who suffer from rickets have bone deformities because vitamin D is vital for the incorporation of calcium and phosphorus into the bone matrix.

Vitamin D

Vitamin D (calciferol) is needed to ensure that sufficient calcium is absorbed in the digestive system to build healthy bones. Vitamin D deficiency can lead to malformation of the bones, a condition known as **rickets** (Figure **A.5**). Rickets can be a problem in growing children and breastfeeding mothers whose vitamin D intake is low.

Vitamin D is obtained from foods such as oily fish, particularly salmon and tuna, egg yolk, liver and dairy products including milk, cheese and butter. In some countries, milk is fortified by adding supplements of vitamin D.

Vitamin D is one of the few vitamins that can be made in the body. It is synthesised in the skin when it is exposed to ultraviolet (UV) rays from the Sun. Only a short exposure is needed but in some countries at extreme latitudes there is insufficient sunlight in winter months for vitamin D to be made. Fortunately, the liver can store vitamin D that is produced during the summer.

For vitamin D to be produced, sufficient light must reach the skin. If an individual stays out of the sunshine, or protects the skin with a sun-blocking cream or clothing, they may not receive enough UV rays. On the other hand, excessive exposure to UV light leads to an increased risk of malignant melanoma, a form of skin cancer. It is important to balance the need for sunlight with the risk of too much exposure. Fair-skinned people should always protect their skin and avoid intense sunlight. To minimise the risk of skin cancer, they should only expose their skin during early morning or late afternoon when the sunlight is less intense.

Individuals with darker skin, which is protected by increased amounts of melanin pigment, require more time in sunlight than fair-skinned people to produce the vitamin D they need. The amount of time depends on the intensity of the sunlight, and therefore varies with distance from the equator and with the seasons of the year.

Both exposure to the Sun and complete protection from it carry some risks. It is important to consider these risks but impossible to avoid them completely.

Dietary supplements

Some diets do not provide all the nutrients needed for perfect health. In these cases, artificial dietary supplements can be added to food. One good example is the mineral iodine, naturally found in foods derived from the sea. People living far from the coast or those who have little seafood in their diet may suffer from a shortage of iodine. Iodine is needed to synthesise the hormone **thyroxine**, which regulates growth and controls metabolism. Without iodine, the thyroid gland can become enlarged, producing a swelling known as **goitre** (Figure **A.6**).

Iodine deficiency disorder (IDD) is a serious problem for babies whose mothers were iodine deficient during pregnancy. Unborn babies with IDD can suffer brain damage and have poor mental development after birth. The most severe cases lead to **cretinism**, which UNICEF estimated affected more than 11 million people in 2000.

Goitre and cretinism are rare in Europe and the Americas because in these regions sodium iodide (NaI) has been added to table salt since the early part of the 20th century. In the mid-western states of the USA, iodine added to salt in the 1920s reduced the incidence of goitre in children from 40% to 10% in just four years.

UNICEF has been involved in efforts to eliminate iodine deficiency since the 1950s. The organisation has persuaded and assisted many governments to iodise salt in an effort to eliminate IDD. It has provided salt iodisation equipment and iodine supplements to many countries. At the time of the World Summit for Children in 1990, only about 20% of households in the world used iodised salt and the campaign was stepped up. By the end of 2000, this figure had risen to around 70%. This global progress has meant that at the start of the 21st century more than 91 million newborn children were protected against significant losses in learning ability caused by IDD.

Vitamin D and evolution

People with dark skin evolved in hot sunny countries where it was more important to be protected against UV damage than vitamin D deficiency. As humans moved across the Earth, some evolved lighter skins in places where it was more of an advantage to produce vitamin D than be protected from UV rays.

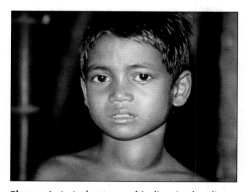

Figure A.6 A shortage of iodine in the diet can lead to enlargement of the thyroid gland in the neck, a condition known as goitre.

Fibre

Dietary fibre consists mainly of cellulose material from plant foods, with additional material from chitin from fungi and crustaceans. It cannot by digested in the human intestine.

The benefits of dietary fibre occur mainly in the stomach and small intestine and include those listed below.

- Fibre tends to slow down the rate of digestion, leading to a more gradual emptying of the food from the stomach into the small intestine. This means that there is less likelihood of large quantities of glucose being absorbed rapidly in the small intestine, which leads to more stable blood glucose levels and a reduced the risk of diabetes. If the digestive process is slower, food spends more time in the small intestine, which may also increase the uptake of minerals and other nutrients.
- Fibre thickens and becomes gel-like when in contact with water in the digestive system. This swelling effect together with slower digestion increases the feeling of being full and so reduces the desire to eat. Fibre is therefore helpful in maintaining a healthy body mass.
- Fibre may help to reduce blood cholesterol levels by binding with it in the intestine and preventing it being absorbed.
- Because it is not digested itself, fibre moves quickly through the large intestine, and promotes healthy egestion of faeces, thus helping to prevent constipation and reducing pressure within the colon.
- Fibre seems to be linked to a reduced likelihood of cancer and other ailments such as haemorrhoids and appendicitis. Although the process is not understood, fibre may interfere with the aggregation of cancer cells to form tumours.

2 Explain the difference between essential and non-essential amino acids.

3 State the cause of phenylketonuria and explain how the consequences of the condition can be reduced.

4 Distinguish between a 'vitamin' and a 'mineral'.

5 Describe what is meant by 'rebound malnutrition', in relation to vitamin C consumption.

6 Explain the benefits of supplementing the diet with iodine.

A2 Energy in human diets

Assessment statements

- Compare the energy content per 100 g of carbohydrate, fat and protein.
- Compare the main dietary sources of energy in different ethnic groups.
- Explain the possible health consequences of diets rich in carbohydrates, fats and proteins.
- Outline the function of the appetite control centre in the brain.
- Calculate the body mass index (BMI) from the body mass and height of a person:
  BMI = (mass in kg)/(height in m)^2
- Distinguish, using the body mass index, between being 'underweight', 'normal weight', 'overweight' and 'obese'.
- Outline the reasons for increasing rates of clinical obesity in some countries, including availability of cheap high-energy foods, large portion sizes, increasing use of vehicles for transport, and a change from active to sedentary occupations.
- Outline the consequences of anorexia nervosa.

Energy content of different nutrients

Carbohydrates and proteins contain a similar amount of energy per gram, but lipids contain more than twice as much, as shown in Table **A.2**.

In these nutrient molecules, the bonds that contain most energy are those between carbon and hydrogen. Bonds between carbon and oxygen also contain energy but in small quantities. Lipids have a higher proportion of C–H bonds than the other nutrients and so they contain more energy per 100 g.

Nutrient	Energy content/ kJ per 100 g
carbohydrate	1760
protein	1720
lipid	4000

Table A.2 Energy content of different nutrients.

Energy sources around the world

Ethnic groups in different parts of the world eat very different diets. In most places, people have one main source of energy, which forms the most important part of their traditional diet.

Rice is widely eaten all over the world and 20% of people rely on it as their main energy source. The vast majority of rice is grown in Asia, but rice is also produced in tropical and temperate areas worldwide. The populations of China, Japan, India, Bangladesh, Thailand and other Asian nations all have rice as a **staple food** and the main source of energy in their diets (Figure **A.7**, overleaf).

Wheat is grown in North America, Russia and Europe. It provides a source of energy in the flour used for making bread, pasta, noodles and couscous in many countries. Top consumers of wheat are Australia, Russia, Turkey and Canada. Wheat was first cultivated about 10 000 years ago and new varieties have been bred from the original wild grasses that grew in the Nile Delta.

Cassava or manioc is a tropical plant, originally found in South America but now grown in many tropical areas that have high rainfall, such as East and West Africa, India and Indonesia. Cassava root is ground to make tapioca flour, called gari in West Africa or farinha in Brazil. Cassava is also eaten as a vegetable in these countries, but careful preparation is needed as the root contains a high level of cyanide, which must be removed by

rice

cassava

maize

wheat

Figure A.7 Different foods, each rich in carbohydrate, form the staple diet for people in different cultures.

grating and drying. It is a very good source of energy and calcium but contains very little protein.

Maize is produced in higher quantities than either rice or wheat. It is described as corn in many foods and corn starch provides energy for the populations of many Central and South American countries. In Mexico, corn provides 50% of the energy intake of most people.

Meat has traditionally provided the main source of energy for nomadic groups such as the Masai people of East Africa. Energy supplied by eating meat is derived from protein and fat.

Fish supplies energy in areas where it is difficult to grow carbohydrate-containing crops. The energy comes from fish protein and fat. The native Inuit people of the Arctic have fish as their staple food and island peoples such as the population of the Maldives also share a fishing tradition.

Health consequences of some different diets

Nutrients taken in excess can lead to health problems. Advertising and social pressures may encourage people to consume an inappropriate diet that damages their health.

Excessive carbohydrate intake

Carbohydrates in the form of sugars and starch are the body's source of energy, but if the energy is not used for day-to-day activities, the excess is stored either as glycogen in the liver and muscles or as fat. The body's capacity to store glycogen is limited so eating an excess of carbohydrate means that fat reserves build up and, over a long period of time, can lead to weight gain and obesity.

An excess of simple sugars found in sweet cakes, biscuits and drinks can also cause tooth decay and type II diabetes. Starchy foods such as pasta and potatoes, which are digested more slowly, are less likely to cause the high blood sugar levels associated with diabetes (see page **303**).

Fibre is indigestible carbohydrate found in fruit and vegetables and has positive effects on health (page **296**). Excessive intake of processed sugary and fatty foods that are low in fibre can mean that individuals eat less high-fibre foods, which are the healthier option.

Excessive fat intake

Fat contains twice as much energy as carbohydrate, so eating an excess of fatty foods is very likely to lead to obesity. There is also a substantial risk of heart disease and other cardiovascular problems associated with an excess of saturated and *trans* fatty acids in the diet (pages **291–292**).

Excessive protein intake

The recommended daily intake of protein for an average adult is 50 g per day but many people in the developed world consume far more than this. Excess protein cannot be stored in the body and is excreted after processing by the liver and kidneys. These organs can be damaged if excess protein is eaten for prolonged periods, as is suggested in some weight-reduction diets. The liver and kidneys may become enlarged and some people develop kidney stones and gout. The kidneys use calcium to excrete amino acids from excess protein and if there is not enough calcium in a person's diet, it may be withdrawn from bones making them weak and even leading to osteoporosis.

Appetite control

The **appetite control centre** is found in the **hypothalamus** at the base of the brain. Its job is to signal to the body when sufficient food has been eaten and the body has reached satiation. The hypothalamus receives information in four important ways:

- When the stomach is full, receptors in the stomach wall send messages to the brain via the vagus nerves.

Diet and the media

Newspapers and magazines are full of advice and information about diet and health issues. Some typical headlines are shown below.

Questions to consider

1 How valid are claims like these, which you can see in the media every day?
2 How much data is needed to provide a statistically valid claim?
3 Will consumers be influenced by big headlines? How do these news stories affect what you do?
4 Does the media provide sufficient information for people to understand scientific research? Will people be put off by too much technical information?
5 How significant do you think studies such as the research on the 'apple diet' really are?

Eating breakfast and fatty diet during early pregnancy increases chances of having a boy
What women eat while they are in the early stages of pregnancy influences the sex and health of their unborn baby, new research suggests.

The truth about the apple diet
Now a small study has shown that the theory that makes eating an apple a better choice than more 'fattening' options, even if your overall calories are under control, may have some validity after all.

Eating at night makes you thin
In a six-week study on 12 mice that were all given the same calories as part of a high-fat diet, those that ate during the day gained twice as much weight as those that fed at night.

Vitamin D 'triggers and arms' the immune system
Vitamin D is crucial to the fending off of infections, claims new research.

Calories on menus: do they work?
Calorie counts on menus and fast food: are they a weapon against obesity, or just more 'nannying' from the Government?

Eggs 'should be considered a superfood' say scientists
The humble egg should be considered a superfood thanks to its ability to boost health and even help tackle obesity, according to researchers behind a new study.

- When food enters it, the small intestine secretes a peptide hormone called PYY 3–36, which suppresses appetite.
- Another hormone, leptin, is released by adipose (fat) tissue and this also suppresses appetite — a person who has more adipose tissue has more leptin-secreting cells.
- Insulin from the pancreas, released as food is absorbed, also suppresses appetite.

Evidence for the importance of the hypothalamus in controlling the feeling of hunger has come from people who have damage in that area of the brain. In many cases, they have severe appetite-control problems being either unable to eat or unable to stop eating. Despite the controls that the hypothalamus provides for us, almost everyone can be encouraged to eat when they are not hungry by the appearance or smells of delicious food, or if we are tempted by enticing advertisements.

Body mass index

Body mass index (BMI) is a scientific, objective measure of whether an individual has an appropriate body mass. It is an internationally used measure for adults over 20 years of age. BMI calculations are based on mass and height and the normal range for a healthy person is between 18.5 and 24.9 (Table **A.3**).

$$BMI = \frac{\text{mass in kg}}{(\text{height in m})^2}$$

BMI was developed in the 19th century by Adolphe Quetelet, a Belgian statistician and scientist. He based the formula on measurements of thousands of soldiers. It provides a useful guide to check on a healthy body mass, but it may not tell the whole story. Fitness training builds up larger muscles, which weigh more than fat and can make the BMI of a very fit athlete with a large frame appear in the 'overweight' category.

Obesity in the modern world

Data collected by the World Health Organization indicates that one billion adults are overweight and more than 300 million are obese worldwide. It is estimated that 2.6 million people each year die as a result of being overweight or obese. Once associated with high-income countries, obesity is now also prevalent in low- and middle-income countries too. Today, 65% of the world's population lives in a country where being overweight or obese kills more people than being underweight. Globally, 44% of cases of diabetes, and 23% of coronary heart disease, are linked to being overweight.

Obesity is caused as a result of an imbalance between the energy a person consumes and the energy he or she uses. So, an increased consumption of high-energy foods, without an equal increase in physical activity, leads to an unhealthy increase in weight (Figure **A.8**).

Decreased levels of physical activity can also result in an energy imbalance and lead to weight gain. In recent times, people have become

BMI	Status
below 18.5	underweight
18.5–24.9	normal weight
25.0–29.9	overweight
30.0 and above	obese

Table A.3 A BMI in a certain range indicates whether a person is underweight, or normal weight, overweight or obese.

Calculate the BMI of a male Olympic weight lifter who has a body mass of 99 kg and is 1.75 m tall. Is he likely to be obese?

less active as machines take over the jobs that used to be done by hand. Young people are more likely to sit and watch TV or play computer games than play active games outside, and we are more likely to travel by car than to walk. In many countries, diet has also changed. Food is plentiful, portions generous and convenience foods that are high in fats and sugars are readily available.

To cure the obesity epidemic, people must take care over what they eat and try to include more physical activity in their daily routine.

Consequences of anorexia nervosa

Anorexia nervosa is an eating disorder. Individuals who suffer from this condition stop eating a balanced diet and become seriously underweight because they have an obsessive fear of gaining body mass. The condition has psychological causes and people with the disorder are unable to appreciate that they have a problem, often perceiving themselves as overweight despite being normal or underweight. The condition affects mostly young women – approximately 90% of cases of anorexia nervosa are in females, with few men or boys being affected.

Among the many consequences of anorexia nervosa are serious disturbances of the endocrine system. Anorexic women and girls stop menstruating and suffer fertility problems. Other physiological problems include anemia, loss of hair and muscle mass and dryness of the skin, with the growth of fine downy hair over the body. The lack of food causes dehydration and low blood pressure, which causes fainting and eventually kidney and liver damage. A shortage of calcium can permanently damage the teeth and weaken bones, while a shortage of other ions can lead to irregular heart beat or even a heart attack. A long period without a balanced diet also weakens the immune system.

Figure A.8 Anyone with a BMI over 30 is classified as obese.

Without medical help, people with anorexia may starve themselves to death. Treatment involves addressing both the physical and psychological aspects of the problem. Medical and nutritional needs are dealt with, as well as promoting a healthy relationship with food, and teaching constructive ways to cope with life and its challenges.

7 State the possible health consequences of a diet rich in fats.

8 Give **three** possible reasons for the increase in obesity in some countries.

9 Outline the consequences of anorexia nervosa.

A3 Special issues in human nutrition

Assessment statements

- Distinguish between the composition of 'human milk' and 'artificial milk' used for bottle-feeding babies.
- Discuss the benefits of breastfeeding.
- Outline the causes and symptoms of type II diabetes.
- Explain the dietary advice that should be given to a patient who has developed type II diabetes.
- Discuss the ethical issues concerning the eating of animal products, including honey, eggs, milk and meat.
- Evaluate the benefits of reducing dietary cholesterol in lowering the risk of coronary heart disease.
- Discuss the concept of food miles and the reasons for consumers choosing foods to minimise food miles.

Human milk and artificial milk

Human mothers, like all mammals, produce milk that perfectly matches their babies' needs. Milk is produced by the mother's breasts after her baby has been born and continues to be produced while the child is suckling. Artificial milk, or formula milk, is often derived from cow's milk, but is manufactured to be as similar as possible to human milk. It is usually supplied as a powder, which is mixed with water when it is needed.

There are a number of key differences between the contents of artificial milk and human milk, which are shown in Table **A.4**.

The benefits of breastfeeding

The composition of breast milk is perfect for the growth and development of a baby and most medical professionals recommend that mothers breastfeed their infants. A small number of women may be unable to produce sufficient milk, or may carry a disease such as HIV or tuberculosis that can be passed to their child in their milk. In these cases, artificial milk is more suitable. In other cases, mothers may prefer bottle-feeding for social or personal reasons.

The advantages of breastfeeding include those listed below.

- Human milk is perfectly matched to a human baby's needs at each stage of its development.
- Human milk is easier for a baby to digest and nutrients are better absorbed.
- Breastfeeding avoids the risk of the baby developing allergies.

Nutrient factor	Human milk	Artificial milk	Comments
Fatty acids	Human butterfat	Oil is added from plant sources – palm, coconut, corn, soy or safflower oils	Babies need lipids to build plasma membranes in cells. The lipid content of human milk changes with the baby's needs whereas that in artificial milk does not.
Proteins	65% whey 35% casein	18% bovine whey 82% bovine casein (or soy proteins for lactose-intolerant babies)	Whey is easier to digest than casein so human milk is more completely absorbed. Heat treatment of animal milk can destroy some proteins and lead to allergies.
Carbohydrates	Lactose	Glucose polymers or lactose	Human milk has nearly 50% more lactose than cow's milk.
Immunity boosters	Macrophages present, and colostrum is rich in antibodies	No human antibodies or white blood cells	Colostrum is produced only for the first few days after birth.
Vitamins and minerals	Many present	Extra iron added	Vitamins and minerals have a higher bioavailability in human milk. A greater percentage is absorbed from milk than from other sources.
Enzymes and hormones	Amylase, lipase and hormones present	No enzymes or hormones	Hormones include prostaglandins, which aid movement of food through the intestine, and cortisol, which helps the growth of the pancreas.

Table A.4 Comparison of the content of human and artificial milk.

- Breastfeeding is safer because it avoids the need to sterilise bottles or make up formula milk, particularly in areas where water may be polluted or contaminated with pathogens.
- Breastfeeding helps the mother and child to bond emotionally.
- Breastfed babies tend to develop fewer infections in childhood than bottle-fed babies.
- Mothers who breastfeed tend to lose the extra weight they have gained during their pregnancy.
- Breast milk is free.

The disadvantages of breastfeeding include the following.

- Some pathogens such as HIV may be passed from mother to baby.
- In some parts of the world, breastfeeding in public is not acceptable.
- Breastfeeding and maintaining a career is difficult for mothers.
- Fathers, and other members of the wider family, cannot contribute to feeding the child, as they can with bottle-feeding.

Type II diabetes

Type II diabetes is the most common form of diabetes, accounting for nine out of ten cases worldwide. It is also known as late-onset diabetes or non–insulin-dependent diabetes mellitus. Individuals who have the condition develop insulin resistance, which means that the receptor cells that normally respond to insulin fail to be stimulated by it, even though the beta cells in the pancreas still produce insulin.

Causes and symptoms

The causes of type II diabetes are not fully understood but there is a strong correlation of risk with weight and diet. High levels of fatty acids in the blood may be a factor causing the condition and people whose diets are high in fat but low in fibre seem to be most at risk. Obesity, associated with a lack of exercise or a genetic makeup that influences fat metabolism, is a key risk factor. The condition is more common in older people but there are an increasing number of cases in overweight children.

Some ethnic groups are more likely to develop type II diabetes and this provides evidence for a genetic link to a predisposition to the condition. Aboriginal Australians, people of Asian and Afro-Caribbean origin, Native Americans and Maori peoples are all at a higher risk.

The symptoms of type II diabetes tend to develop slowly but include:

- high glucose levels in the blood
- glucose in the urine
- frequent need to urinate, which leads to dehydration and increased thirst
- tiredness and fatigue
- some loss of weight.

Glycemic index

Some health professionals recommend that people who have or are at risk from type II diabetes follow a low GI (glycemic index) diet. Low GI foods allow the body to absorb carbohydrates more slowly, which helps to stabilise glucose levels through the day. Low GI foods include apples, oranges, pasta, sweet potato, sweetcorn and noodles.

Dietary advice to treat type II diabetes

Many people who have type II diabetes are advised to control their blood sugar levels by following a healthy diet, taking exercise and losing weight. They are advised to eat foods that are low in saturated fat and salt but high in fibre and complex (slowly absorbed) carbohydrates, such as wholegrain cereals, pulses, beans and lentils. These foods, especially if they are taken at regular intervals during the day, help to keep blood sugar levels steady. Foods that should be avoided include sugary snack foods and drinks, and food with a high level of saturated fat. These foods cause a rapid rise in blood sugar level that the diabetic person is unable to deal with. The fat content of food can be reduced by certain cooking methods. Grilling or steaming is preferable to frying because no fat is used or added to the food.

If left untreated, type II diabetes can lead to long-term health problems such as kidney disease, retinal damage, high blood pressure, stroke and heart attack.

Ethical issues and eating animal products

Some people choose not to eat certain foods because their production involves the killing of an animal. Others choose not to eat meat for religious, cultural or other ethical reasons.

Getting the message across

Many health initiatives and campaigns rely on communicating scientific information to people in the hope that they will change their lifestyle or diet to improve their health. This is true in the cases of type II diabetes, lowering cholesterol levels to prevent CHD and persuading mothers of the benefits of breast feeding.

Truly persuasive health communication messages are difficult to create. For example, fast-paced, flashy messages may grab attention but hinder understanding. In addition, different audiences usually require very different messages, even when the goal is similar.

Many people find statistics hard to understand. Most people overestimate the risk of things like car accidents, but underestimate things like strokes and heart attacks.

Sometimes, even when the message is understood, a change in behaviour is not acceptable to the audience because it takes too much effort or there are cultural issues to overcome. For example, suggesting abstinence has not been a very effective strategy for reducing consumption of alcohol and tobacco. The way the message is presented and by whom is also important. Many health campaigns use celebrities or cartoons to communicate information, rather than scientists or doctors, because the former are more memorable and can be less threatening to the audience.

Questions to consider

1 What important scientific information should be passed to mothers to encourage breast feeding?
2 Who could best communicate this information (**i**) in the developed world and (**ii**) in the developing world?
3 There is an ethical conflict between profit-making companies that advertise artificial milk and health professionals who communicate a different message. Should advertising be restricted in the way that tobacco advertising is limited in some countries?
4 Some populations are more susceptible to type II diabetes than others. Is it possible to communicate messages that include these groups sensitively but effectively?

Vegetarians do not eat meat from any animals but some are willing to eat other animal products such as eggs, milk and honey, which do not involve an animal being slaughtered. **Vegans** are vegetarians who will not eat **any** animal produce but choose to derive all their nutrients from other sources.

Vegetarians might argue that:

- slaughtering animals is unnecessary as humans can survive without meat
- rearing animals specifically for food is wrong and uses more land and resources than arable farming
- intensive farming methods are cruel and cause suffering to animals.

Non-vegetarians would counter the argument as follows:

- animals can be reared in free-range systems that are not cruel and people can choose to eat meat or fish from such producers
- animals reared for food are only bred because they are needed
- some nutrients are simply not present in a vegetarian diet and it is natural for humans to eat meat.

There are other ethical arguments that should be considered in relation to milk, honey and eggs.

- Is it right to breed cows for high milk yields and force them to have calves in order to do so?
- Are the health problems suffered by some cows as a result of breeding and high milk production justifiable?
- Egg-laying hens are often kept in cages in artificial light where they are unable to behave normally. Is this acceptable?
- Only female chickens are kept and these are bred for maximum egg production. Is it right to dispose of male birds and force hens to produce very large numbers of eggs?
- Honey is taken from beehives where it has been stored by bees. Is it right to remove the bees' food source?

Personal choice is important and individuals must consider all the issues before deciding what to eat.

Benefits associated with lowering dietary cholesterol

Cholesterol is a steroid that is synthesised in the liver and found almost exclusively in foods of animal origin. It forms part of the cell membrane and it helps in the transport of substances in and out of cells, communication between cells and the conduction of impulses along nerve cells. Cholesterol is carried around the body in the form of **lipoproteins**. **Low-density lipoproteins** (**LDLs**) are often referred to as 'bad cholesterol'. LDLs don't travel well in the bloodstream and can clog up arteries, causing **atherosclerosis**, CHD or stroke. High LDL levels frequently occur in people with high levels of saturated or *trans* fatty acids in their diet.

HDL stands for **high-density lipoproteins**. These are sometimes known as 'good cholesterol'. HDLs are carried easily around the body

Figure A.9 Foods like cheese and meat, from animal sources, contain high levels of cholesterol. For most people, though, reducing the amount of **saturated fat** they eat has a greater effect in reducing their blood cholesterol than reducing the amount of cholesterol-rich food in their diet.

and don't contribute to blockages in the arteries. Blood vessels carry cholesterol to the liver where it can be broken down or excreted. Evidence suggests that HDL cholesterol can help to remove LDLs from arteries.

A definite link has been found between the intake of saturated fats in the diet and the level of cholesterol in the blood. High levels of saturated fats in food increase both LDL and total blood cholesterol levels. There is also a clear correlation between saturated fats in the diet and CHD. Medical professionals recommend reducing the intake of saturated fats to reduce blood cholesterol and the risk of a heart attack. However, it may be that reducing the levels of cholesterol in the form of LDLs is more important than reducing the total cholesterol level in the blood. It is also important to consider genetic factors and predisposition to high cholesterol levels. Maintaining a low cholesterol level can be achieved by careful dietary choices (Figure **A.9**).

Food miles

Food miles are a measure of how far food has travelled from its place of production to where it is eaten. Transporting food – either from one country to another, or from one part of a country to a warehouse and then to a supermarket – uses fuel, produces greenhouse gases, and causes pollution and traffic congestion. Food may travel hundreds or thousands of miles by air, road and sea. When people drive to shop in large stores, they too contribute to problems of fuel consumption, and therefore to climate change resulting from increased greenhouse gas emissions.

People can choose to eat locally grown food that is in season to reduce their own impact on the environment, but in doing so they may reduce the variety of foods they eat.

From field to plate

Many people argue that it would be more logical to buy food from local suppliers and farmers so that produce has to travel a shorter distance from field to plate and the environmental impact is much smaller. Others suggest that there are many advantages to transporting foods. Some foods are impossible to grow locally and others are only available at certain times of year. Transporting food improves consumer choice and the opportunity to eat a healthy diet. Some crops, such as tomatoes, can be grown with low energy costs in warmer parts of the world where greenhouses and heating are not needed. As a result, even after transportation to cooler countries, the total energy cost is still lower than growing the fruits locally.

Questions to consider

How much do you and your family, as consumers, contribute to climate change as a result of the foods you choose to buy?

1 Think about food items your family have bought in the last week. Are there any you could have sourced closer to your home? Are there any foods you could have substituted with other products in order to reduce your family's 'food miles'?

2 Should all consumers be encouraged to support their local farmers?

10 Give **three** differences between human milk and artificial milk used for babies.

11 Outline the symptoms of type II diabetes.

12 State what is meant by the term 'food miles'.

End-of-chapter questions

1 Outline how absorbed carbohydrates are used by the body. (3)

2 Explain how a healthy diet differs in the amount of saturated and unsaturated lipids it contains, compared to a diet that is less healthy. (4)

3 Compare the energy content of carbohydrate, fat and protein. (3)

4 Outline the causes and symptoms of type II diabetes. (4)

5 Mexico has had an increasing demand for milk and dairy products over the last 30 years. The proportion of the different groups of milk products imported over a 27-year period is shown in the graph below.

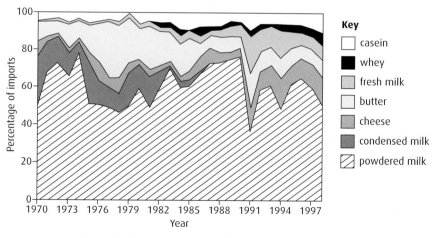

source: Amendola, R D (2002) *A Dairy System Based on Forages and Grazing in Temperate Mexico,* PhD thesis, Wageningen University, p 15

a Identify the year in which the importation of butter was greatest. (1)

b State the relationship between the importation of condensed milk and fresh milk. (1)

c Determine which group of dairy products increased most in percentage of imports from 1973 to 1991. (1)

d Suggest **two** reasons for the increase in importation of fresh products. (2)

e State **two** essential constituents of a balanced diet found in milk products. (1)

(total 6 marks)
© IB Organization 2009

6 Wheat flour in the diet can lower the quantity of lipids in the blood. A study was carried out to determine whether the size of flour particles (coarse or fine) or the amount of the protein gluten in wheat flour (high or normal) contributed more to lowering the lipid level. Volunteers, in addition to their regular diets, were asked to eat bread made from different types of wheat flour over a period of several weeks. Measurements were made of the changes in the amounts of lipids in their blood serum.

The graph below shows the results for each volunteer (indicated by circles) and the mean values for each group (indicated by the squares).

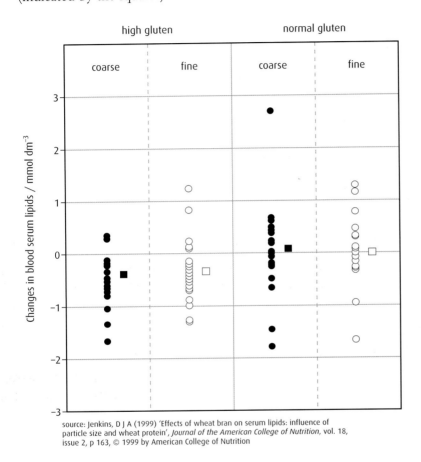

source: Jenkins, D J A (1999) 'Effects of wheat bran on serum lipids: influence of particle size and wheat protein', *Journal of the American College of Nutrition*, vol. 18, issue 2, p 163, © 1999 by American College of Nutrition

a Identify the type of flour in the bread that was least effective in lowering blood serum lipid level. (1)

b Compare the effects of the two types of bread made with fine flour on the lipids in the blood serum. (2)

c Evaluate the hypothesis that the amount of the protein gluten in the flour is more important than the particle size in preventing cardiovascular disease. (3)

d The fibre in the wheat flour may have contributed to lowering the blood serum lipid level. State **one** other function of fibre in the diet. (1)

(total 7 marks)
© IB Organization 2009

7 Cancer of the colon is the fourth most common cancer throughout the world. A number of epidemiological studies have shown that dietary starch and fibre can influence the incidence of colon cancer. The results of two of these studies are shown below. Each point on the graphs represents the human population of one region.

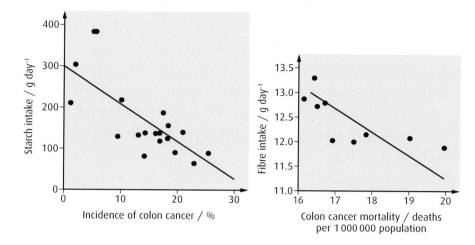

source: adapted from *Food, Nutrition and the Prevention of Cancer: a Global Perspective,*
World Cancer Research Fund, American Institute for Cancer Research (1997) p 380

a Outline the relationship between fibre intake and colon cancer mortality. (1)

b **i** Determine the predicted mortality due to colon cancer at a daily fibre intake of 12.5 g day^{-1}. (1)
   ii Calculate how much more starch a person would have to consume per day to reduce the cancer risk by 10%. (1)

c Compare the effect of fibre intake and the effect of starch intake on cancer of the colon. (2)

d Discuss the effect of daily fibre intake on lowering the mortality rates of cancer of the colon. (2)

(total 7 marks)
© IB Organization 2009

Option B Physiology of exercise

Introduction

Many different muscles, nerves, tendons and joints have to work together when we exercise and whether a person is an elite athlete or simply enjoys a relaxing walk similar mechanisms are involved. Training can improve the cardiovascular and respiratory systems so that athletes can improve their performances but regular exercise has health benefits for almost everyone. Understanding how the body copes with exercise and recovers from it can help us exercise safely, improve our personal fitness and avoid injuries.

B1 Muscles and movement

Assessment statements

- State the roles of bones, ligaments, muscles, tendons and nerves in human movement.
- Label a diagram of the human elbow joint, including cartilage, synovial fluid, joint capsule, named bones and antagonistic muscles (biceps and triceps).
- Outline the functions of the structures in the human elbow joint.
- Compare the movements of the hip joint and the knee joint.
- Describe the structure of striated muscle fibres, including the myofibrils with light and dark bands, mitochondria, the sarcoplasmic reticulum, nuclei and the sarcolemma.
- Draw and label a diagram to show the structure of a sarcomere, including Z lines, actin filaments, myosin filaments with heads and the resultant light and dark bands.
- Explain how skeletal muscle contracts, including the release of calcium ions from the sarcoplasmic reticulum, the formation of cross-bridges, the sliding of actin and myosin filaments and the use of ATP to break cross-bridges and re-set myosin heads.
- Analyse electron micrographs to find the state of contraction of muscle fibres.

Human movement

Movement and exercise are made possible by the interaction of our skeleton and the tendons, ligaments and muscles that move it. Every movement is controlled by nerves, which ensure that all the parts work together as we bend, stretch or run.

Joints

A **joint** is a place where two or more bones meet. Joints between bones in the human body, together with the muscles that are attached to them, enable us to move and also support the body. Most joints involve bones, muscles, cartilage, tendons, ligaments and nerves.

- **Bones** provide a framework that supports the body. They protect vital organs such as the brain, which is surrounded by the skull, and the lungs, which are surrounded by the ribcage. Blood cells are formed within bones such as the femur, breast bone and humerus, which contain bone marrow. Bones also act as a site for the storage of calcium and phosphate.

- **Ligaments** attach bones to one another at a joint. Some strap joints together while others form a protective capsule around a joint. They are tough and fibrous and provide strength and support so that joints are not dislocated.
- **Tendons** attach muscles to bones. They are formed of tough bands of connective tissue made of collagen fibres and are capable of withstanding tension as muscles contract.
- **Muscles** provide the force needed for movement. They are able to contract in length and as they do so they move the joint into new positions. Muscles only cause movement by contraction, so they occur in **antagonistic pairs** – one muscle of the pair causes a movement in one direction while the other returns it to its original position.
- **Motor neurons** stimulate muscle contraction. Sensory neurons transmit information from proprioceptors (position sensors) in the muscles so that movements can be coordinated and monitored.

The elbow joint

The elbow is a **hinge joint**, so-called because it moves in a manner resembling the opening and closing of a door hinge (Figure **B.1**). It is an example of a **synovial joint**. The capsule that seals the joint is lined by a

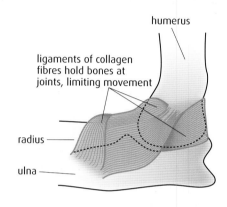

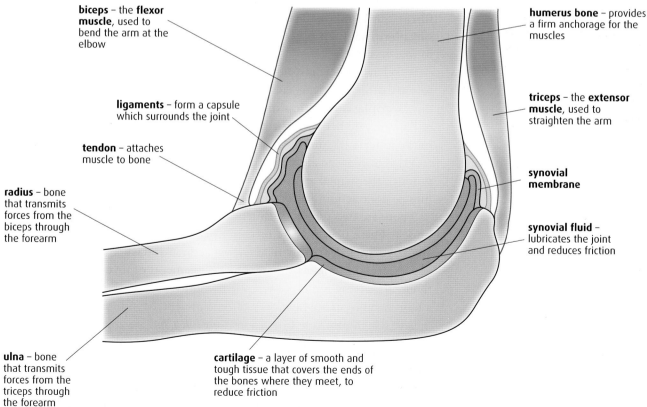

biceps – the **flexor muscle**, used to bend the arm at the elbow

ligaments – form a capsule which surrounds the joint

tendon – attaches muscle to bone

radius – bone that transmits forces from the biceps through the forearm

ulna – bone that transmits forces from the triceps through the forearm

humerus bone – provides a firm anchorage for the muscles

triceps – the **extensor muscle**, used to straighten the arm

synovial membrane

synovial fluid – lubricates the joint and reduces friction

cartilage – a layer of smooth and tough tissue that covers the ends of the bones where they meet, to reduce friction

Figure B.1 The hinge joint of the elbow.

membrane that secretes lubricating **synovial fluid** so that the bones move smoothly against one another and friction is reduced. Smooth cartilage covers the ends of the bones at the joint and also helps to reduce friction and absorbs pressure as the joint moves.

The elbow joint is formed of three bones – the radius and ulna in the lower arm and the humerus in the upper arm. Tendons attach the biceps and triceps muscles to these bones. The biceps is attached to the radius and the shoulder blade. When it contracts the arm bends. The triceps is attached to the ulna, humerus and shoulder blade and it contracts to straighten the arm. The biceps and triceps are an example of an antagonistic pair of muscles.

The knee and hip joints

The knee joint is another example of a hinge joint and it moves in a similar way to the elbow, allowing movement in only one direction. The hip joint is a **ball-and-socket joint** with the ball-shaped head of the thigh bone (the femur) fitting into a socket in the hip. Ball-and-socket joints allow movement in more than one direction and also permit rotational movements (Figure **B.2**).

Muscles

Skeletal or **striated muscle** is the muscle that causes the movement of our joints. If it is viewed under the light microscope, as in Figure **B.3**, it has a striped appearance made up of multinucleate cells known as **muscle fibres**. Surrounding the muscle fibre is a plasma membrane called the **sarcolemma**. Each fibre is made up of many **myofibrils** running parallel to one another.

If skeletal muscle is examined with an electron microscope, it is possible to see that surrounding each myofibril is a system of membranes called the **sarcoplasmic reticulum** (which resembles smooth endoplasmic reticulum) and between the closely packed myofibrils are many mitochondria (Figure **B.4**, page **314**).

Myofibrils are made up of repeating subunits called **sarcomeres**, which produce the striped appearance of a muscle fibre and are responsible for muscle contraction. The ends of a sarcomere are called the **Z lines**.

There are two types of filament that form the striped pattern of a muscle. These filaments are formed from the contractile proteins **actin** and **myosin**. The narrow filaments of actin are attached to the Z lines and extend into the sarcomere. Thicker filaments of myosin run between them. Where myosin is present, the myofibril has a dark appearance and a light band is seen where only actin is present. Myosin filaments have 'heads' which protrude from their molecules and are able to bind to special sites on the actin filaments.

Muscle contraction

Muscle contraction is explained by the 'sliding filament theory', which describes how actin and myosin filaments slide over one another to

The body contains three types of muscle – **skeletal** or **striated muscle** attached to the skeleton, **cardiac muscle** found only in the heart, and **smooth** or **non-striated muscle**, which is found in the walls of hollow organs such as the intestines and bladder. Striated muscle can be controlled voluntarily and enables us to move.

Knee joint and movement at the knee

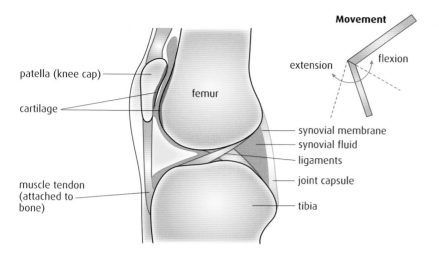

Movement

extension — flexion

patella (knee cap)

femur

cartilage

synovial membrane
synovial fluid
ligaments

joint capsule

muscle tendon (attached to bone)

tibia

Hip joint and movement at the hip

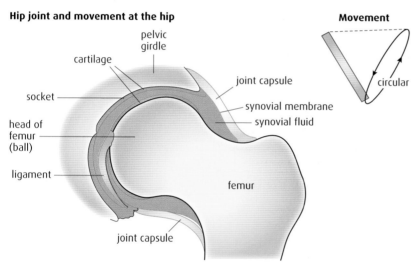

Movement

circular

pelvic girdle

cartilage

joint capsule

socket

synovial membrane
synovial fluid

head of femur (ball)

ligament

femur

joint capsule

Figure B.2 Longitudinal sections of the knee and hip joints, and the degree of movement they allow.

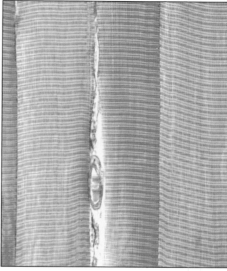

Figure B.3 Light micrograph of striated muscle, stained to show the banding in muscle fibres.

shorten the muscle. Contraction is initiated by the arrival of a nerve impulse from a motor neuron, which stimulates the sarcolemma of the muscle fibre. This, in turn, causes the release of calcium ions (Ca^{2+}) from the sarcoplasmic reticulum and begins the process that causes actin filaments to slide inward towards the centre of the sarcomere. The series of events is shown in Figure **B.5** (page **315**).

1 Nerve impulses (action potentials) travel along the muscle fibre membrane, or sarcolemma, and are carried down into the fibre through infoldings called T-tubules. The impulses then spread along the membrane of the sarcoplasmic reticulum, causing Ca^{2+} ions to be released.

2 Before contraction, binding sites for myosin heads on the actin filaments are covered by two molecules, **troponin** and **tropomyosin**. The myosin heads are prepared in an erect position as ATP binds to them.

Muscle tone

Contraction of a muscle causes shortening, and this in turn moves bones into a new position. If only a few fibres in a muscle contract, the muscle tightens but does not cause movement. Partial contraction produces muscle tone, which is important in maintaining posture and body shape.

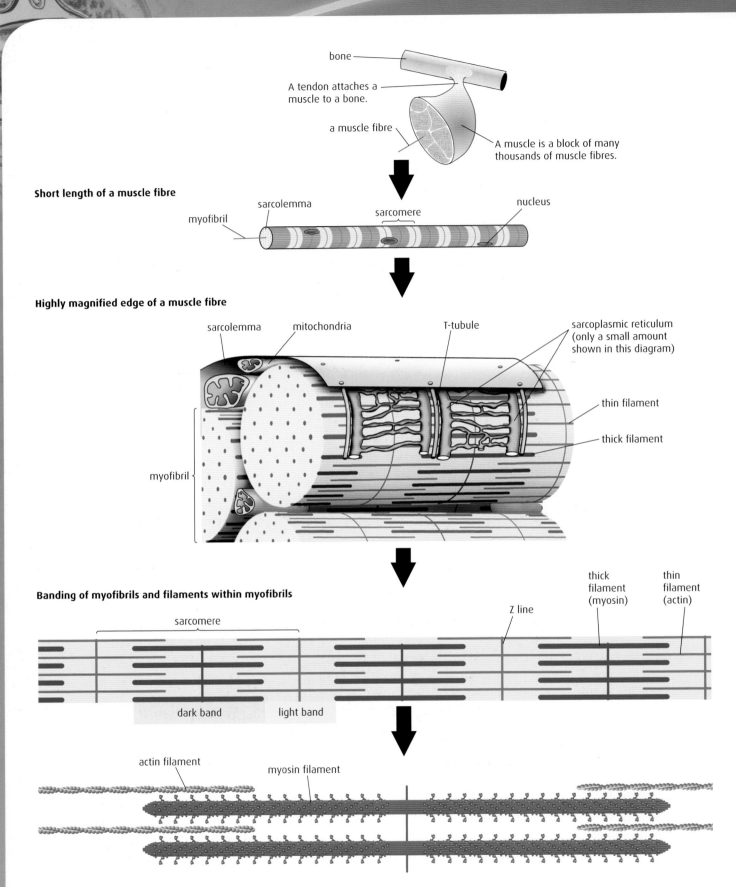

Short length of a muscle fibre

Highly magnified edge of a muscle fibre

Banding of myofibrils and filaments within myofibrils

Figure B.4 The structure of skeletal muscle.

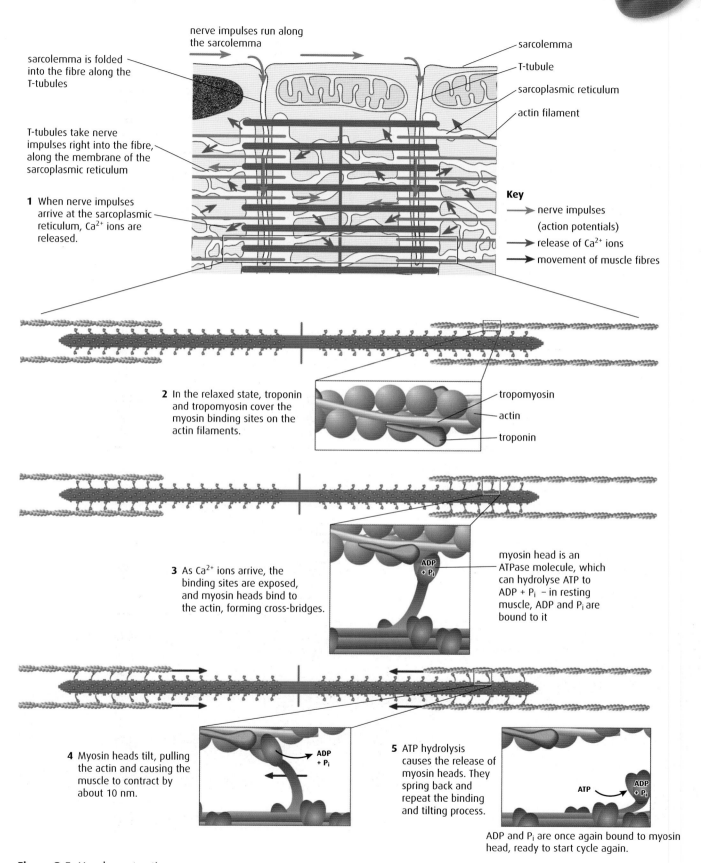

nerve impulses run along the sarcolemma

sarcolemma is folded into the fibre along the T-tubules

sarcolemma

T-tubule

sarcoplasmic reticulum

actin filament

T-tubules take nerve impulses right into the fibre, along the membrane of the sarcoplasmic reticulum

1 When nerve impulses arrive at the sarcoplasmic reticulum, Ca^{2+} ions are released.

Key

→ nerve impulses (action potentials)

→ release of Ca^{2+} ions

→ movement of muscle fibres

2 In the relaxed state, troponin and tropomyosin cover the myosin binding sites on the actin filaments.

tropomyosin

actin

troponin

3 As Ca^{2+} ions arrive, the binding sites are exposed, and myosin heads bind to the actin, forming cross-bridges.

ADP + P_i

myosin head is an ATPase molecule, which can hydrolyse ATP to ADP + P_i – in resting muscle, ADP and P_i are bound to it

4 Myosin heads tilt, pulling the actin and causing the muscle to contract by about 10 nm.

ADP + P_i

5 ATP hydrolysis causes the release of myosin heads. They spring back and repeat the binding and tilting process.

ATP

ADP + P_i

ADP and P_i are once again bound to myosin head, ready to start cycle again.

Figure B.5 Muscle contraction.

3 Now Ca^{2+} ions bind to the actin filaments, causing the troponin and tropomyosin to change shape and expose the myosin binding sites. The myosin heads bind to the actin filaments at the exposed binding sites, forming cross-bridges.

4 This causes inorganic phosphate (P_i) to be released and, as each cross-bridge forms, ADP is also released. The myosin heads bend towards the centre of the sarcomere, pulling the actin filaments inward past the myosin filaments, by about 10 nm. This produces a 'power stroke'.

5 New ATP molecules bind to the myosin heads, breaking the cross-bridges and detaching them from the actin filaments. ATP is used and the myosin heads return to the start position. If the muscle receives further stimulation, the process is repeated and the myosin heads attach further along the actin filaments.

Although the actin and myosin filaments do not change in length when a muscle contracts, the appearance of the banding patterns in the sarcomere is changed. The light bands become reduced, and as the overall length of the sarcomere decreases the dark bands take up a greater proportion of the length (Figure **B.6**).

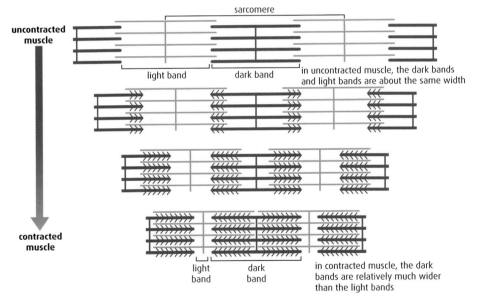

in uncontracted muscle, the dark bands and light bands are about the same width

in contracted muscle, the dark bands are relatively much wider than the light bands

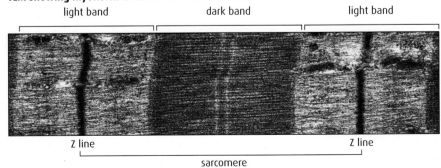

TEM showing myofibrils in an uncontracted skeletal muscle fibre

Figure B.6 When muscle contracts, the interleaved fibres slide inward, past each other. This makes the light bands appear narrower, but the dark bands remain the same width.

1 State the role of muscles in movement.

2 Outline the function of cartilage at a synovial joint.

3 Explain the role of calcium ions in muscle contraction.

B2 Training and the pulmonary system

Assessment statements

- Define 'total lung capacity', 'vital capacity', 'tidal volume' and 'ventilation rate'.
- Explain the need for increases in tidal volume and ventilation rate during exercise.
- Outline the effects of training on the pulmonary system, including changes in ventilation rate at rest, maximum ventilation rate and vital capacity.

Measuring pulmonary performance

The pulmonary system supplies oxygen for working muscles and removes from the body the waste products of respiration in these active cells. Pulmonary ventilation is the term given to the movement of air in and out of the lungs (breathing), but sports physiologists also use a number of other terms when discussing the performance of the pulmonary system during exercise.

The total volume of air in the lungs when a person has breathed in as much as possible is called the **total lung capacity**. If the person then breathes out as much as possible, the maximum volume of air that can be exhaled is called the **vital capacity**.

However hard you try, you can never expel all the air from your lungs. A small amount of air will remain in the lungs keeping them partially inflated even after a maximum exhalation. This volume is known as the **residual volume**. So the total volume of air in the lungs after a maximum inhalation (the total lung capacity) includes the vital capacity plus the residual volume.

The **tidal volume** is the volume of air that is inhaled or exhaled during normal breathing at rest. An average, healthy adult has a tidal volume of about $500\,\mathrm{cm}^3$. The number of breaths a person takes each minute is called the **ventilation rate**. Measurements of ventilation rate and tidal volume are made using an instrument called a spirometer (Figure **B.7**).

Ventilation during exercise

Figure **B.8** (overleaf) shows a graph based on a spirometer recording. Notice how the tidal volume varies with activity level – very little air is drawn into the lungs in resting conditions, but this increases rapidly as a person starts to exercise.

Total lung capacity the volume of air in the lungs after a maximum inhalation
Vital capacity the maximum volume of air that can be exhaled after a maximum inhalation
Tidal volume the volume of air that moves in or out with each inhalation or exhalation
Ventilation rate the number of inhalations or exhalations per minute

Figure B.7 A person undergoing a fitness test using a spirometer to measure pulmonary performance.

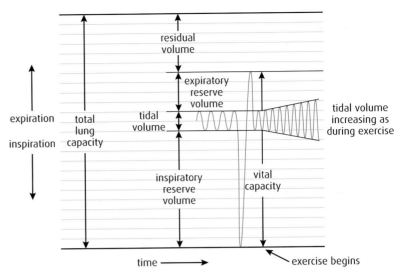

Figure B.8 A spirometer recording for a person at rest, and then starting to exercise. Each horizontal division represents 250 cm³ of air. Spirometer readings for different people vary with their level of activity.

When a person exercises, both the ventilation rate and tidal volume increase. Muscles need oxygen for aerobic respiration to produce ATP for contractions. As the rate of exercise increases and more energy is needed, the rate of oxygen consumption rises. Blood returning to the lungs also contains a higher level of carbon dioxide, produced as a result of the increased respiratory activity. An increase in ventilation rate and tidal volume draws in more fresh air to provide oxygen at a faster rate and enables the body to get rid of the additional carbon dioxide produced. The changes in ventilation are adjusted to match the body's metabolic needs.

If insufficient oxygen is supplied to the muscles, they begin to respire anaerobically, producing lactate as a waste product. Anaerobic activity cannot continue for long because it generates very reduced supplies of energy and, as lactate builds up, it causes fatigue and limits muscle action.

Effects of training on ventilation

Regular training, with repetition of specific exercises to increase fitness, has an effect on the muscles that are used and also on the cardiac and ventilation systems.

Vital capacity increases by a small amount because the intercostal muscles and diaphragm become stronger. Studies have demonstrated that the diaphragm improves its endurance capacity after training, but only by about 20%, because it is already well equipped for sustained periods of work. Other muscles involved in breathing, including the abdominal muscles, become more active and also improve their endurance capacity.

The maximum ventilation rate during exercise can increase by 10–15% as a result of training. There is also an increase in the vital capacity and development of new capillaries in the alveoli. These factors lead to a higher rate of oxygen absorption and of carbon dioxide removal. The ventilation rate at rest will decrease as a result of this improved efficiency.

B3 Training and the cardiovascular system

Assessment statements

- Define 'heart rate', 'stroke volume', 'cardiac output' and 'venous return'.
- Explain the changes in cardiac output and venous return during exercise.
- Compare the distribution of blood flow at rest and during exercise.
- Explain the effects of training on heart rate and stroke volume, both at rest and during exercise.
- Evaluate the risks and benefits of using EPO (erythropoietin) and blood transfusions to improve performance in sports.

Measuring cardiac performance

The heart and blood vessels make up the cardiovascular system, which conveys oxygen and glucose to working muscles and removes waste products from them. To measure the efficiency of the heart, physiologists consider several difference parameters.

The **heart rate** is the number of contractions of the heart each minute, while the volume of blood pumped out by the heart with each contraction is known as the **stroke volume**. The **cardiac output** is the volume of blood pumped out of the heart per minute (which is a product of the heart rate and the stroke volume). **Venous return** is the name given to the volume of blood returning to the heart each minute via the veins.

Cardiovascular system during exercise

During exercise, cardiac output increases to supply muscles with the additional oxygen and glucose they need. As respiration increases, more carbon dioxide is produced and the pH of the blood falls. If lactate is present in the blood (produced by anaerobic respiration) this also influences blood pH. Changes in pH are detected by the chemoreceptors in the aorta and carotid arteries, which send information to a control centre in part of the brain stem known as the medulla oblongata. Impulses are sent from the medulla to the sinoatrial node (pacemaker) in the heart, which stimulates increases in both the heart rate and the stroke volume.

An increase in muscle activity and cardiac output means that there is also an increase in venous return. As skeletal muscles work, they compress the veins passing through them and force blood in the direction of the heart. In this way, venous return is increased and there is a greater volume of blood in the ventricles so that cardiac output can also be greater.

Heart rate the number of contractions of the heart per minute

Stroke volume the volume of blood pumped out with each contraction of the heart

Cardiac output the volume of blood pumped out by the heart per minute

Venous return the volume of blood returning to the heart via the veins per minute

Increased blood flow	skeletal muscles, cardiac muscle, skin
Unchanged blood flow	brain
Reduced blood flow	kidneys, intestine, stomach and other abdominal organs

Table B.1 Changes in blood flow that occur during exercise.

Distribution of blood

Blood supply to organs of the body changes significantly during exercise. Blood flow to skeletal muscles and to the cardiac muscle of the heart increases to supply additional oxygen for respiration and to remove the waste products carbon dioxide and lactate. Blood flow to the skin also increases as the large surface area of the skin provides a way of removing metabolic heat generated by the muscles. The heat is lost through radiation and sweating.

Blood flow to the brain remains largely unchanged but blood flow to the abdominal organs – including the stomach, intestines and kidneys – decreases. As a result, digestion slows down and less urine is produced, ensuring that water is kept in the body during exercise. Table **B.1** summarises the changes in blood flow that occur during exercise.

Effects of training on the cardiovascular system

Cardiac muscle, which makes up the heart, responds to training in the same way that skeletal muscles of the arms or legs respond – it becomes stronger and increases in size and efficiency. Training increases both the thickness of the muscle that makes up the heart wall and the volume of the ventricles.

- A stronger heart with larger chambers can pump more blood per heart beat so the stroke volume of the heart is increased with training, both during exercise and at rest.
- The heart rate at a certain level of activity, and at rest, decreases with training because the larger volume of blood being pumped with each contraction means that fewer contractions are needed per minute to supply the body's needs.

A trained athlete has a lower heart rate than an untrained individual performing the same exercise, because the athlete's stroke volume (and therefore cardiac output) is greater. A person's maximum heart rate remains unchanged by training but maximum cardiac output becomes greater as a person's fitness improves because the stroke volume increases.

Table **B.2** summarises the changes to cardiac performance resulting from training.

	Heart rate	Stroke volume
At rest	lower than before training	greater than before training
During exercise	lower than before training	greater than before training

Table B.2 Effect of training on the cardiovascular system of a trained individual.

Erythropoietin

Erythropoietin (**EPO**) is a hormone that is naturally produced by the kidneys to stimulate red blood cell production in bone marrow. It is also used as a performance-enhancing substance by some athletes.

Red blood cells carry oxygen so an athlete who has extra cells has improved oxygen delivery to the muscles, which in turn improves physical performance. Artificially increasing the proportion of red blood cells in the blood is known as **blood doping**. It can be achieved by transfusion – an athlete stores a blood sample in advance, and then some time later, just before a competition or event, receives a transfusion of his or her own red blood cells. Alternatively, an athlete may receive an injection of EPO (which can be produced by genetic engineering) to stimulate additional red blood cell production.

By increasing the level of EPO in the body, individuals can increase the proportion of red blood cells in their blood by up to 10%, which can significantly improve performance, particularly in endurance events. Another advantage of EPO to such an athlete is that, because it is a natural substance, it is very difficult to detect in drugs tests.

The disadvantages and risks of blood doping include the increased likelihood of a blood clot (thrombosis), because the additional red blood cells increase the viscosity (thickness) of the blood. Thrombosis can cause heart attacks or a stroke. Increased blood viscosity can also cause high blood pressure, which puts strain on the heart. In endurance events, the additional cells may lead to dehydration because the ability of the blood to retain water is reduced by the presence of more red blood cells.

6 Define 'stroke volume'.

7 Compare blood flow to the intestine at rest and during exercise.

Is EPO OK?

Both professional and amateur athletes have been known to use EPO and there has been much debate about the acceptability of this practice. EPO has been used for blood doping in competitive endurance sports such as cycling, rowing and marathons. Until recently, there was no way to test for it directly but in 2000 French chemists developed a method of distinguishing pharmaceutical EPO from the natural hormone normally present in an athlete's urine. This was accepted by the World Anti-Doping Agency (WADA) and now EPO tests are conducted on both blood and urine samples at international events.

Some argue that, since it is possible to increase red blood cell counts by training at high attitude or sleeping in low-oxygen environments, it should be acceptable to achieve the same results by taking an injection of EPO.

EPO is also used therapeutically to treat patients who have kidney failure and cannot produce it naturally.

Questions to consider

1 Can the use of EPO be regarded as cheating?

2 What constitutes an acceptable level of risk for professional athletes when using substances such as EPO?

3 Is the case of EPO any different from other substances used to enhance athletic performance?

4 How might the views of medical practitioners and those of spectators differ in relation to the effects of EPO?

B4 Exercise and respiration

Assessment statements

- Define 'VO$_2$' and 'VO$_2$ max'.
- Outline the roles of glycogen and myoglobin in muscles fibres.
- Outline the method of ATP production used by muscle fibres during exercise of varying intensity and duration.
- Evaluate the effectiveness of dietary supplements containing creatine phosphate in enhancing performance.
- Outline the relationship between the intensity of exercise, VO$_2$ and the proportions of carbohydrate and fat used in respiration.
- State that lactate produced by anaerobic cell respiration is passed to the liver and creates an oxygen debt.
- Outline how oxygen debt is repaid.

VO$_2$ the volume of oxygen absorbed by the body per minute
VO$_2$ max the maximum rate at which oxygen can be absorbed by the body and supplied to the tissues

VO$_2$ and VO$_2$ max

VO$_2$ and VO$_2$ max are terms used by sports physiologists to assess oxygen uptake and consumption.

VO$_2$ is the volume of oxygen that the body absorbs each minute and supplies to the tissues. It rises as exercise increases, as shown in Figure **B.9**. VO$_2$ indicates how efficiently oxygen is being supplied to and used by muscles. As the graph levels out, the individual is reaching his or her maximum aerobic capacity, or **VO$_2$ max**. This is the maximum rate at which the person can absorb and supply oxygen to the tissues, and it varies between individuals depending on level of fitness.

Intensity of exercise can only increase above the maximum level shown on the graph in Figure **B.9** if anaerobic respiration is gradually increased and the percentage of aerobic respiration is reduced.

At lower intensity levels of exercise, both fat and carbohydrate are used as sources of energy for cell respiration. As exercise intensity increases, the use of fat as a respiratory substrate decreases and more carbohydrate is

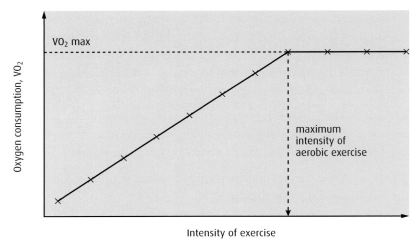

Figure B.9 Graph showing intensity of exercise against VO$_2$.

used. Anaerobic respiration uses only carbohydrate, which is more efficient as an energy source, so at VO_2 max the use of carbohydrate reaches 100% (Figure **B.10**).

Glycogen and myoglobin in muscles

For any type of aerobic exercise both oxygen and an energy source are required. The body minimises the effects of shortages of these two important components by having stores of both present in muscles.

Glycogen is a polymer of glucose, a polysaccharide, which is stored in muscle fibres and in the liver. It provides a source of energy that can be used if blood glucose levels are low. It is converted to glucose when it is needed and enables muscles to continue working during long or very intense periods of exercise.

Myoglobin is a red pigment, similar to hemoglobin, which binds to oxygen when levels of oxygen are high and releases oxygen when levels are low. Myoglobin acts as a store of oxygen that can be released as oxygen levels fall. It enables muscles to continue working aerobically for a longer period than they would otherwise be able to do.

ATP production and muscles

Muscle cells are unusual and different from other body cells because they can have widely varying energy needs. At rest, they require little ATP but when they are working hard their energy needs are very large. Muscles produce ATP in three different ways: from **aerobic respiration**, from **anaerobic respiration** or from **creatine phosphate**. All the body's cells can produce ATP from aerobic and anaerobic respiration but only muscle cells can use creatine phosphate to do so.

Creatine phosphate (CP) is stored in muscle fibres. It is produced from excess ATP when muscles are not active.

$$creatine + ATP \rightleftharpoons CP + ADP$$

Creatine is produced in the liver and kidneys and is carried to the muscles, where it is converted to creatine phosphate using excess ATP, in the

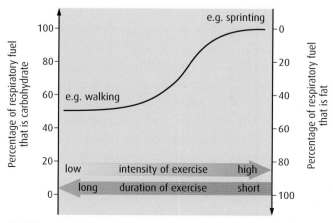

Figure B.10 Diagram to show the proportions of carbohydrate and fat used in different types of exercise.

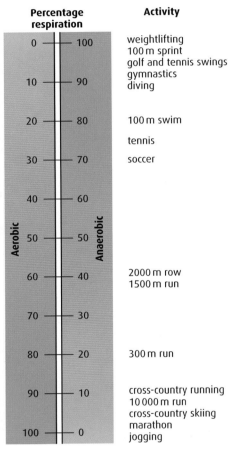

Figure B.11 The percentages of aerobic and anaerobic respiration in various sporting activities.

Percentage respiration		Activity
Aerobic	Anaerobic	
0	100	weightlifting
		100 m sprint
		golf and tennis swings
10	90	gymnastics
		diving
20	80	100 m swim
		tennis
30	70	soccer
40	60	
50	50	
60	40	2000 m row
		1500 m run
70	30	
80	20	300 m run
90	10	cross-country running
		10 000 m run
		cross-country skiing
		marathon
100	0	jogging

reaction shown above. Muscles store more creatine phosphate than ATP and this store enables them to produce enough ATP for up to 10 seconds of intense exercise, such as a 100 m sprint.

Aerobic respiration produces ATP continuously using oxygen that is brought to the muscles by the blood, or supplemented by oxygen from myoglobin. Aerobic respiration uses glucose as a source of energy, and can produce sufficient ATP for long periods of low intensity exercise such as walking or 'aerobics'.

Anaerobic respiration produces ATP for short periods of very high intensity activity, lasting between 30 seconds and 2 minutes. Stored glycogen is converted to glucose, which is converted to lactate (via glycolysis and the formation of pyruvate) during anaerobic respiration (pages **58–60**). Lactate is slowly removed and taken to the liver, but lactate is toxic and if it is present in large amounts in muscles it leads to fatigue or soreness. This can happen after a long run or swim. Anaerobic respiration is only suitable for short bursts of activity such as sprinting or high diving.

Both aerobic and anaerobic energy systems contribute ATP during exercise but in most sports one system usually contributes more (Figure **B.11**). As the intensity of exercise decreases and duration increases the percentage of ATP from aerobic respiration increases.

Dietary supplements of creatine phosphate

Creatine phosphate (CP) is used as a legal performance-enhancing supplement by some athletes. It is permitted by the governing bodies of athletics organisations but it is not recommended for young athletes under 18 years old. Studies into its effectiveness are not conclusive and there are differing views as to its overall benefits. The long-term effects of the substance are unknown.

CP is absorbed via the digestive system and so can be taken as a dietary supplement. It can lead to an increase in creatine in muscle cells in athletes whose natural levels are low but a normal diet containing meat and fish includes creatine, which is also produced by the body. It therefore seems unlikely that additional creatine is needed by many individuals. Excess creatine is excreted.

Individual performance in intense, short-term sporting activities such as sprinting and weightlifting does seem to improve when CP is taken. There is also an increase in muscle size but this may be due to increased water retention, which is caused by CP. CP supplements have no effect on performance in aerobic, endurance events such as marathon running.

If large doses of CP are taken, side-effects can include weight gain and high blood pressure due to water retention, and stomach and muscle cramps. CP supplements are dangerous for individuals with kidney conditions because any excess must be removed by the kidneys.

Lactate and oxygen debt

During anaerobic respiration, lactate is produced in muscles. An accumulation of lactate causes fatigue, which eventually prevents the muscle contracting. If there is no ATP present, the muscle may remain in a state of continuous contraction known as **cramp** until ATP production begins again. Lactate is carried from muscles to the liver where it is processed to produce pyruvate or glucose.

The oxygen needed for this processing is drawn in during the rapid period of heavy breathing that occurs just after a period of intense exercise. The amount of oxygen needed to break down lactate in the liver is known as the **oxygen debt**. The additional oxygen that is taken in is also used to 'recharge' myoglobin in the muscles.

Lactate in the liver may be broken down by oxidation to carbon dioxide and water or converted to pyruvate for use in aerobic respiration in the Krebs cycle. Alternatively, lactate may be converted to glucose, which either enters the bloodstream or is stored in the liver as glycogen.

....

8 Define 'VO_2'.

9 Outline the methods of ATP production during exercise.

10 State when glycogen is used as an energy source during exercise.

11 List possible side-effects of large doses of CP on the body.

....

B5 Fitness and training

Assessment statements

- Define 'fitness'.
- Discuss speed and stamina as measures of fitness.
- Distinguish between 'fast' and 'slow' muscle fibres.
- Distinguish between the effects of 'moderate-intensity' and 'high-intensity' exercise on fast and slow muscle fibres.
- Discuss the ethics of using performance-enhancing substances including anabolic steroids.

Fitness

There are many different definitions of **fitness**. Fitness has been described as the ability of the cardiovascular, pulmonary and muscle systems to work at their optimal efficiency, and also as the capacity to exercise without excessive fatigue with enough energy remaining for emergencies.

Fitness is the condition of the body that enables a person to perform a particular type of activity or exercise. Fitness is different for different people and for different sports or exercises. The type of fitness needed for playing football is quite different from that required by a rower, for example.

Fitness may include aspects of stamina, skill, flexibility, strength and endurance. No single activity will develop all the components of fitness. During training, a footballer might require development of speed, agility, flexibility, strength and skill. Some of these aspects will be developed by specific training while others develop as he or she plays the game.

> **Fitness** the condition of the body that enables a person to perform a particular type of action or exercise, so that he or she can function efficiently in work, leisure and sporting activities, and cope with emergency situations; fitness is improved as a result of exercise and proper nutrition

Figure B.12 Sprinters have a higher proportion of fast-twitch fibres in their muscles.

Figure B.13 Endurance events such as the marathon require more slow-twitch muscle fibres.

Speed and stamina

Speed and stamina often serve as useful measures of a person's fitness. Speed describes the rate at which an activity can be performed and is an important aspect of training for athletes such as sprinters or swimmers. Stamina is also called endurance and it is the ability to continue performing an activity for a long period of time. This quality is essential in marathon or cross-country runners.

In most cases, it is useful for an individual to include in their training regimes exercises that will develop both speed and stamina.

Fast-twitch and slow-twitch muscle fibres

Individuals are sometimes described as being 'born to run' and there is an element of truth in this statement. Most skeletal muscles are a mixture of two types of muscle fibres – **fast-twitch fibres** and **slow-twitch fibres**.

- **Fast-twitch fibres**, or fast fibres, are white in colour and can contract rapidly, although they are easily exhausted. They are larger in diameter than slow-twitch fibres and exert greater forces. Fast fibres are best suited to anaerobic activities involving speed and strength, such as sprinting (Figure **B.12**). Fast fibres have a greater oxygen need but lower myoglobin content than slow-twitch fibres.
- **Slow-twitch fibres**, or slow fibres, are red-coloured and can contract repeatedly for long periods of time. They are smaller in diameter than fast fibres and produce less force. They are best suited to aerobic activities such as long-distance running (Figure **B.13**). Slow fibres contain much myoglobin and have a rich blood supply to support their aerobic activity.

The proportions of each type of fibre found in the muscles of individuals vary and are partly determined by genetics. However, as a result of moderate intensity training such as long-distance running, the diameter of slow fibres may be increased, while high-intensity training such as sprinting can increase the development of fast fibres. Figure **B.14** shows the proportions of fast and slow fibres in some male athletes who participate in different sports.

Ethics and performance-enhancing substances

Performance-enhancing substances have been used in sporting competition for thousands of years. At the first Olympic Games in Ancient Greece more than 2500 years ago (776 BC at Olympia) it is alleged that athletes took 'monkey glands' containing the male hormone testosterone to enhance their performances. The use of EPO and creatine phosphate has already been discussed (pages **320** and **324**) and there are many other substances that can be used to enhance sporting performance.

Testosterone is a steroid hormone that has the effect of increasing body mass at puberty. Anabolic steroids, used as performance-enhancing drugs by some people, are manufactured versions of the natural hormone, which cause muscle and bone growth. Steroids have been used by both male and female athletes although they are now banned in most sports.

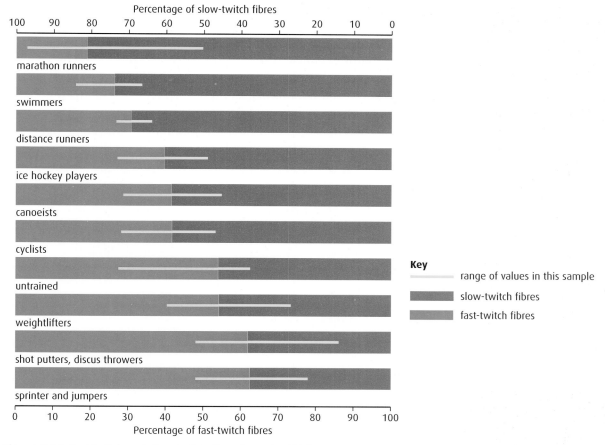

Figure B.14 Fast-twitch and slow-twitch fibres in male athletes.

Those who favour the use of performance–enhancing substances have cited the following arguments:

- They can improve performance quickly and easily so that competitors have a better chance to do well.
- Some consider that a peak performance is what an athlete is aiming for and this is just another method of improving that performance.
- Drugs can improve a competitor's mood and focus as well as their physical condition.
- Better performances are more fun for the audience at competitive events.

But there are many side–effects associated with taking performance–enhancing substances and because they have been used for many years these are well documented. Long–term health consequences recorded in individuals who use anabolic steroids include:

- liver and kidney damage
- increased risk of heart disease
- atrophy of the testes and low fertility in men
- interruption of the menstrual cycle and sterility in women
- appearance of male characteristics, such as facial hair, in women
- aggressive behaviour and depression.

In addition, athletes who do take drugs may gain an unfair advantage over those who follow the rules and do not.

Today, professional athletes are regularly tested for traces of banned substances in their bodies to try to ensure that competition is fair. Despite the ban on certain drugs, they do remain available – often through illegal means, which result in poor regulation of their content and the possibility of criminal activity in their supply.

In discussing the ethics of drug use, it is important to consider whether an enhanced performance is really desirable if it carries risks to the health of individuals as well as encouraging and supporting an illicit trade in potentially harmful substances.

12   List **three** differences between fast-twitch and slow-twitch muscle fibres.

13   Outline reasons why some athletes use anabolic steroids.

B6 Injuries

Assessment statements
- Discuss the need for warm-up routines.
- Describe injuries to muscles and joints, including sprains, torn muscles, torn ligaments, dislocation of joints and intervertebral disc damage.

Warming up

Warm-up routines are recommended by sports physiologists as a way to prepare the body for exercise or competitive sport. Warm-up routines usually include a low-intensity version of the activity to come. For example, stretches can prepare long-jumpers for their event, jogging and turning are good preparation for a footballer and lifting small weights before moving on to heavier ones is recommended.

Benefits of warm-up routines are said to include the following.
- **Improvement in performance** – warming up increases blood flow to the muscles and a greater blood flow increases the supplies of oxygen and nutrients. The respiration rate of these muscles increases gradually so that they prepare for the increased activity to come. Metabolic rate increases with increasing temperature so that warming up speeds up energy production further. And, as the muscles are warmed, the raised temperature means that hemoglobin releases a little more oxygen. The heart muscle is also prepared in this way.
- **Increased focus** – mental preparation is enhanced by a warm-up routine, so that the athlete is able to clear his or her mind, concentrate specifically on the physical activity to be undertaken, and review skills or strategy. Adrenaline and other hormones are released, which help with preparation and decrease reaction time.

- **Reduced chance of injury** – if muscles, ligaments and tendons are warmed up, they are less likely to be torn or overstretched when intense activity begins. The body becomes more supple, and when muscles, ligaments and joints are loosened in this way the athlete is less likely to suffer soreness after exercise.

Although most professional trainers recommend that athletes warm up before an event, there is little hard evidence to support its benefits. No detailed scientific studies have been carried out and the evidence available is based on reports from individuals or small groups of people. The importance of warming up is still being debated. Some argue that warming up is not necessary, citing the examples of substitute players who join a match without warming up or animals that start running at great speed without a warm up.

Injuries to muscles and joints

Muscles and joints can be damaged is various ways during extreme exertion or as a result of extraordinary movement.

- **Sprains** are stretching injuries to ligaments, which connect bones to one another at a joint. Sprains are usually caused by an unusual movement such as turning an ankle or wrist the wrong way. Ligaments may be overstretched or suffer small tears. The joint becomes swollen for a short time but healing usually occurs within two weeks.
- **Torn ligaments** occur when a joint is forced beyond its normal range of movement. Tearing may occur in the ligament itself or where it is inserted into a bone. Cruciate ligaments of the knee may be torn and cause serious pain and swelling. The joint becomes unstable and may take a long time to heal.
- **Torn muscles** are caused by excessive stretching, overload or compressive forces. Muscle fibres that tear may cause bleeding and pain and there is likely to be swelling of the affected area.

Is warming up worth it?

Consider the statements below about two different types of warm-up activity.

Static stretches involve contracting and relaxing muscles to increase flexibility and agility and help prevent injury. But static stretches can make muscles more likely to be damaged if they are stretched when they are cold. Excessive static stretching can result in a temporary loss of muscle strength.

Ballistic stretches involve bouncing or jerking movements. They are said to help the extension of muscles during exercise, increasing agility and flexibility. But this type of stretching can cause injuries to some people and many sports physiologists do not recommend it.

Questions to consider

1. Do these statements support or contradict the suggestion that warming up is a good idea?
2. Most athletes take the advice of trainers who are likely to support the idea that warming up is beneficial. Do athletes accept this advice without questioning it?
3. Why are athletes unlikely to be willing to take part in a research programme to evaluate the benefit of warming up?
4. Could the actions of athletes and their trainers in continuing to warm up without scientific evidence about its benefits be an example of the precautionary principle?

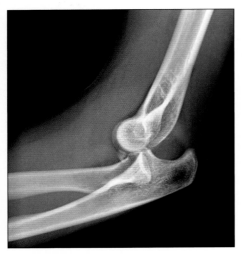

Figure B.15 Injuries such as a dislocated elbow can result from extreme or excessive movements, during an accident or sporting activity, for example.

- **Dislocation** occurs when the bones of a joint are moved out of position (Figure **B.15**). A dislocated joint also causes damage to the ligaments and tendons that normally hold the joint in place, as well as the muscles associated with it.
- **Intervertebral disc damage** can be caused by lifting heavy objects with poor lifting techniques or by abnormal movement of the back. The discs are positioned between the vertebrae and absorb the shock of the body's movements. The outer part of a disc is fibrous but the centre is soft and compressible. Over-compression of the outer wall may cause it to tear so that the inner core bulges out. If this bulge presses on a nerve, it can cause severe pain or numbness in one or both legs.

End-of-chapter questions

1 Describe the structure of striated muscle fibres. (5)

2 Explain how skeletal muscle contracts. (6)

3 Explain the need for increases in tidal volume and ventilation rate during exercise. (4)

4 Explain the changes in cardiac output and venous return during exercise. (4)

5 Evaluate the risks and benefits to an athlete of using erythropoietin (EPO). (4)

6 Outline the method of ATP production used by muscle fibres during exercise of varying intensity and duration. (2)

7 Outline how the oxygen debt is formed and repaid. (4)

8 Distinguish between fast-twitch and slow-twitch muscle fibres. (5)

9 Distinguish between a sprain, a tear and a dislocation. (5)

10 A reliable method of estimating cardiovascular fitness is by measuring the oxygen consumption of the body when the rate of heart beat is at its maximum (V_{max}) during intense exercise. This test was used to measure fitness among 71 volunteers. Two weeks later, the same individuals were asked to run for 2.1 km at two different speeds (V_{70} and V_{90}) and the power they developed during these runs was measured.

- V_{70} in which they ran at a speed where their rate of heart beat was 70% V_{max}.
- V_{90} in which they ran at a speed where their rate of heart beat was 90% V_{max}.

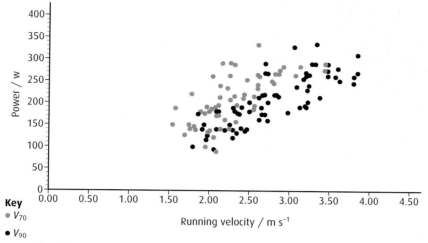

source: Leibetseder, V J et al. (2002) *Journal of Exercise Physiology*, **5** (3), p 11

a State the maximum power developed by a runner at V_{70}.   (1)

b Outline the relationship between running velocity and power developed at V_{90}.   (1)

c Compare the data for V_{70} and V_{90}.   (2)

d Suggest why measurements of V_{max} are dangerous for older people.   (1)

(total 5 marks)

© IB Organization 2009

11 During muscular activity, the heart must deliver more blood to the tissues due to increased oxygen demand. Graph 1 shows the distribution of total blood flow (cardiac output) between muscles (grey-shaded bars) and all other parts of the body (black-shaded bars) in resting men, and in both average men and top athletes doing heavy exercise. Graph 2 shows oxygen consumption by the muscles and all other parts of the body in the three groups. The value given for each bar represents the total body values.

Graph 1: Cardiac output / (litres) l min⁻¹

Graph 2: Oxygen consumption / (millilitres) ml min⁻¹

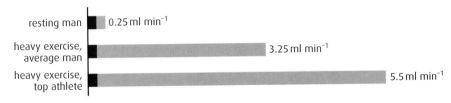

source: Schmidt-Nielsen, K (1987) *Animal Physiology: Adaptation and Environment*, Cambridge University Press, pp148–149

a Describe the relationship between exercise and total cardiac output. (1)

b **i** Calculate the percentage of cardiac output to the muscles for an average man during heavy exercise as compared to the total body value. (1)

  ii Calculate the increase in total oxygen consumption ($ml\,min^{-1}$) for a top athlete during heavy exercise as compared to a resting man. (1)

c Using the data, explain how training affects an athlete's body with respect to cardiac output and oxygen consumption. (3)

(total 6 marks)

© IB Organization 2009

Cells and energy Option C

Introduction

Photosynthesis and respiration are the key chemical reactions that enable ATP to be produced so that organisms can survive. All cells need energy to function and this comes from respiration. Respiration is a complex series of reactions, catalysed by enzymes, which release the chemical energy stored in sources such as glucose. Respiration provides cells with ATP that they can use to carry out their activities. Photosynthesis is the vital series of reactions by which plant cells build organic compounds, including glucose, from simple raw materials and light energy. An understanding of the biochemical events of respiration and photosynthesis, and how they are controlled, is crucial to understanding how cells use energy and stay alive.

C1 Proteins

Assessment statements

- Explain the four levels of protein structure, indicating the significance of each level.
- Outline the difference between fibrous and globular proteins with reference to two examples of each protein type.
- Explain the significance of polar and non-polar amino acids.
- State four functions of proteins, giving a named example of each.

Protein structure

Proteins are large, complex molecules, usually made up of hundreds of amino acid subunits. The way these subunits fit together is highly specific to each type of protein, and is vital to its function. Figure **C.1** (overleaf) illustrates the structure of the protein hemoglobin.

The first stage of protein production is the assembly of a sequence of amino acid molecules that are linked by peptide bonds formed by condensation reactions. This sequence forms the **primary structure** of a protein. There are many different proteins and each one has different numbers and types of amino acids arranged in a different order, coded for by a cell's DNA.

The **secondary structure** of a protein is formed when the polypeptide chain takes up a permanent folded or twisted shape. Some polypeptides coil to produce an α helix, others fold to form β pleated sheets. The shapes are held in place by many weak hydrogen bonds. Depending on the sequence of amino acids, one section of a polypeptide may become an α helix while another takes up a β pleated form. This is the case in hemoglobin.

The **tertiary structure** of a protein forms as the molecule folds still further due to interactions between the R groups of the amino acids and within the polypeptide chain. The protein takes up a three-dimensional

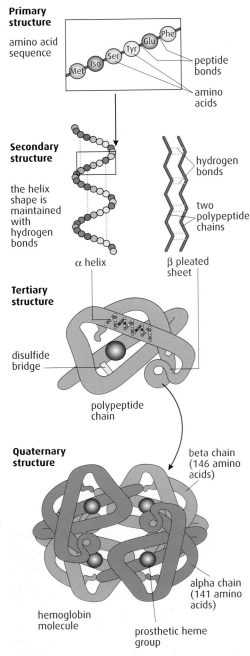

Primary structure

amino acid sequence

Met — Iso — Ser — Tyr — Glu — Phe

peptide bonds

amino acids

Secondary structure

the helix shape is maintained with hydrogen bonds

α helix

hydrogen bonds

two polypeptide chains

β pleated sheet

Tertiary structure

disulfide bridge

polypeptide chain

Quaternary structure

beta chain (146 amino acids)

alpha chain (141 amino acids)

hemoglobin molecule

prosthetic heme group

Figure C.1 The structure of hemoglobin.

shape, which is held together by ionic bonds between particular R groups, disulfide bridges (covalent bonds) between sulfur atoms of some R groups, and by weaker interactions between hydrophilic and hydrophobic side chains. Figure **C.2** shows the different types of bond involved in maintaining the tertiary structure of proteins. Tertiary structure is very important in enzymes because the shape of an enzyme molecule gives it its unique properties and determines which substrates can fit into its active site. Fibrous proteins such as collagen (Figure **C.3**) and keratin have a large helical content and a rod-like shape.

The final level of protein structure is **quaternary structure**, which links two or more polypeptide chains to form a single, large, complex protein. The structure is held together by all the bonds that are important in the previous levels of structure. Examples are collagen (which has three polypeptide chains, Figure **C.3**), hemoglobin (which has four), antibodies (which also have four) and myosin (which has six).

In addition, many proteins contain **prosthetic groups** and are called **conjugated proteins**. Prosthetic groups are not polypeptides but they are able to bind to different proteins or parts of them. For example, hemoglobin is a conjugated protein with four polypeptide chains, each containing a prosthetic heme group.

Fibrous and globular proteins

Protein molecules are categorised into two major types by their shape. **Fibrous proteins** are long and narrow and include collagen, keratin (which is found in hair and nails) and silk. Fibrous proteins are usually insoluble in water and in general have secondary structure. **Globular proteins** have a more rounded, three-dimensional shape and have either tertiary or quaternary structure. Most globular proteins are soluble in water. Globular proteins include enzymes such as pepsin, and antibodies. Myoglobin and hemoglobin are also globular proteins.

Polar and non-polar amino acids

Amino acids are divided into two groups according to the chemical properties of their side chains or **R groups** (Figure **C.4**). Polar and non-polar amino acids have different properties and their positions in a molecule affect the behaviour and function of the whole protein.

Amino acids with non-polar side chains are **hydrophobic**. Those with polar side chains are **hydrophilic**. Non-polar amino acids are found in parts of proteins that are in hydrophobic areas, while polar amino acids are in areas that are exposed to an aqueous environment such as cytoplasm or blood plasma.

For membrane proteins, the polar hydrophilic amino acids are found on the outer and inner surfaces in contact with the aqueous environment, while the non-polar hydrophobic amino acids are embedded in the core of the membrane in contact with the hydrophobic tails of the phospholipid bilayer (Figure **C.5**, page **336**). This helps to hold the protein in place in the membrane. Some integral proteins act as channels, and the pore is lined with hydrophilic amino acids to enable polar substances to pass through.

Hydrogen bonds form between strongly polar groups. They can be broken by high temperature or by pH changes.

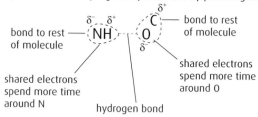

bond to rest of molecule

shared electrons spend more time around N

hydrogen bond

bond to rest of molecule

shared electrons spend more time around O

Disulfide bonds form between cysteine molecules. The bonds can be broken by reducing agents.

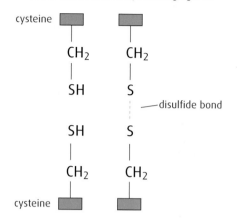

cysteine

CH_2

SH

SH

CH_2

cysteine

CH_2

S

S

CH_2

disulfide bond

Ionic bonds form between ionised amine and carboxylic acid groups. They can be broken by pH changes.

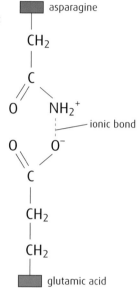

asparagine

CH_2

C

O

NH_2^+

ionic bond

O

O^-

C

CH_2

CH_2

glutamic acid

Hydrophobic interactions occur between non-polar side chains.

tyrosine

CH_2 — OH

CH_3

HC

CH_3

valine

Figure C.2 Types of bond that are important in protein structure.

General structure of an amino acid

R — This group varies in different amino acids. It is known as the R group or side chain.

H

H

N

C

C

O

OH

H

Structure of the simplest amino acid, glycine

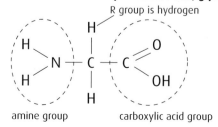

R group is hydrogen

H

H

H

N

C

C

O

OH

H

amine group

carboxylic acid group

Figure C.4 The general structure of an amino acid and the structure of glycine.

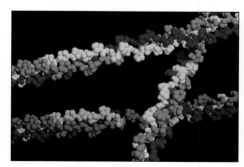

Figure C.3 The triple helix of collagen is an example of quaternary structure.

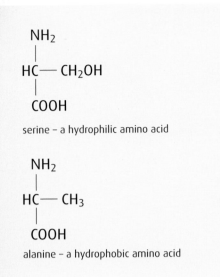

NH₂
|
HC— CH₂OH
|
COOH

serine – a hydrophilic amino acid

NH₂
|
HC— CH₃
|
COOH

alanine – a hydrophobic amino acid

Polar and non-polar amino acids are also important in enzymes, where they assist in the binding of substrates. An enzyme that acts on a polar substance (for example, amylase) has polar amino acids in its active site, whereas lipases have non-polar amino acids in the active site.

Polar amino acids on the surface of a protein increase its solubility while non-polar amino acids help a protein maintain its structure. Lipases are proteins that have polar groups on the outside so they are soluble in the gut, but non-polar groups in their active site so that lipids can bind to them.

Protein functions

Some proteins build the structure of an organism's body, some act as chemical receptors and others act as enzymes or hormones. Table **C.1** summarises some important protein functions.

Protein	Function	Comments
hemoglobin	transport	hemoglobin binds oxygen in areas of high concentration and releases it in respiring tissues
actin and myosin	movement	these proteins interact to cause the contraction of muscles
pepsin	digestion	pepsin is an enzyme that digests protein in the stomach
collagen	structural	collagen strengthens bone and is a major component of tendons, ligaments and the skin
immunoglobulin	defence	immunoglobulins act as antibodies

Table C.1 Some functions of proteins.

1 Outline the **four** levels of protein structure.

2 List **three** differences between fibrous and globular proteins.

3 List **four** functions of proteins.

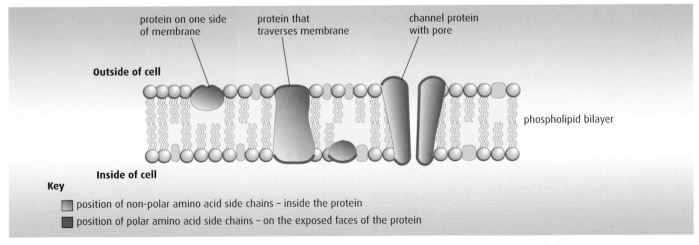

Figure C.5 In membrane proteins, polar (hydrophilic) amino acids are found on the surfaces in contact with the aqueous environment, while non-polar (hydrophobic) amino acids are embedded inside the phospholipid bilayer.

C2 Enzymes

Assessment statements

- State that metabolic pathways consist of chains and cycles of catalysed reactions.
- Describe the induced-fit model.
- Explain that enzymes lower the activation energy of the chemical reactions that they catalyse.
- Explain the difference between competitive and non-competitive inhibition, with reference to one example of each.
- Explain the control of metabolic pathways by end-product inhibition, including the role of allosteric sites.

The basics of enzyme action were introduced in Chapter **3**. It would be useful to re-read that section before beginning this topic.

Metabolic pathways

Metabolic pathways consist of chains or cycles of reactions that are catalysed by enzymes. Metabolism includes all the chemical activities that keep organisms alive. Metabolic pathways may be very complex, but most consist of a series of steps, each controlled by an enzyme. Simple pathways involve the conversion of substrates to a final product:

$$\text{substrate X} \xrightarrow{\text{enzyme 1}} \text{substrate Y} \xrightarrow{\text{enzyme 2}} \text{substrate Z} \xrightarrow{\text{enzyme 3}} \text{end product}$$

Each arrow represents the specific enzyme needed to catalyse the conversion of one substrate to the next.

Other metabolic pathways, such as photosynthesis or respiration, involve both chains of reactions, like the one above, and cycles of reactions.

Induced-fit model of enzyme action

The lock-and-key hypothesis discussed in Chapter **3** explains enzyme action by suggesting that there is a perfect match between the shape of the active site of an enzyme and the shape of its substrate. This theory was proposed in 1890 by Emil Fischer (1852–1919), who was Nobel laureate in 1902.

In 1958, research published by Daniel Koshland (1920–2007) suggested that the process is not quite this straightforward. The lock-and-key hypothesis cannot account for the binding and simultaneous change that is seen in many enzyme reactions, nor the fact that some enzymes can bind to more than one similarly shaped substrate.

A more likely explanation of enzyme action is that the shape of an enzyme is changed slightly as a substrate binds to its active site (Figure **C.6**, overleaf). The substrate causes or induces a slight change in the shape of the active site so it can fit perfectly. As the enzyme changes shape, the substrate molecule is activated so that it can react and the resulting product or products are released. The enzyme is left to return to its normal shape, ready to receive another substrate molecule.

This hypothesis is known as the **induced-fit model** of enzyme action.

Enzymes do not change the quantity of product that is formed, only the rate at which the product is formed.

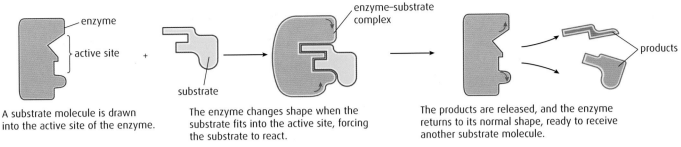

A substrate molecule is drawn into the active site of the enzyme.

The enzyme changes shape when the substrate fits into the active site, forcing the substrate to react.

The products are released, and the enzyme returns to its normal shape, ready to receive another substrate molecule.

Figure C.6 The induced-fit model of enzyme action.

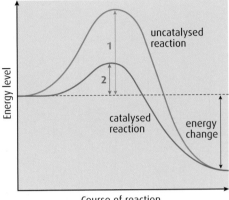

Key

1 = activation energy without catalyst

2 = activation energy with catalyst

energy
change = overall energy change after reaction – most biological reactions release more energy than they take in as activation energy and are said to be exothermic

Figure C.7 Graph to show activation energy for an exothermic reaction with and without a catalyst.

Activation energy

Enzymes work by lowering the activation energy of the substrate or substrates. In order for a metabolic reaction to occur, the substrate has to reach an unstable, high-energy 'transition state' where the chemical bonds are destabilised, and this requires an input of energy, which is called the **activation energy**. When the substrate reaches this transition stage, it can then immediately form the product. Enzymes can make reactions occur more quickly because they reduce the activation energy of reactions they catalyse to bring about a chemical change (Figure **C.7**). Most biological reactions result in the release of more energy than the activation energy and are said to be **exothermic**.

Metabolic reactions that occur in living organisms have to occur at the body temperature of the organism, which is never high enough to bring substrates to their transition state. The active site of an enzyme is very important because it can lower the amount of energy needed to reach a transition state, so the reaction can occur at the temperature of the organism.

Competitive and non-competitive inhibition

Enzyme inhibitors are substances that reduce or prevent an enzyme's activity. Some inhibitors are competitive and others non-competitive.

Competitive inhibitors have molecules whose structure is similar to that of the substrate molecule that normally binds to the active site. They compete with the substrate to occupy the active site of the enzyme, and prevent the substrate molecules from binding (Figure **C.8**). The inhibitors are not affected by the enzyme and do not form products, so they tend

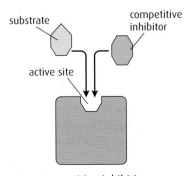

Figure C.8 Competitive inhibition.

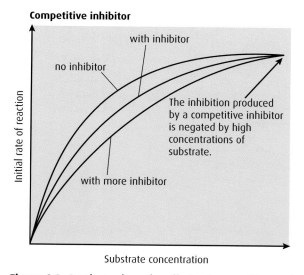

Competitive inhibitor

Initial rate of reaction

with inhibitor

no inhibitor

The inhibition produced by a competitive inhibitor is negated by high concentrations of substrate.

with more inhibitor

Substrate concentration

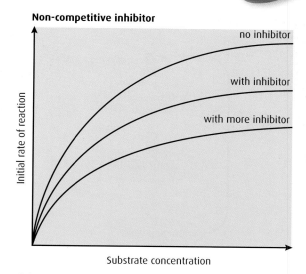

Non-competitive inhibitor

Initial rate of reaction

no inhibitor

with inhibitor

with more inhibitor

Substrate concentration

Figure C.9 Graphs to show the effects of competitive and non-competitive inhibitors on reaction rate, as substrate concentration increases.

to remain in the active site. This means that the rate of reaction is lower because the substrate cannot enter an active site that is blocked by an inhibitor. At low concentrations of substrate, competitive inhibitors have a more significant effect than at higher concentrations, when the substrate can out-compete the inhibitor (Figure **C.9**).

Non-competitive inhibitors also combine with enzymes but not at the active site. They bind at another part of the enzyme where they either partly block access of the substrate to the active site or cause a change in the shape of the enzyme so that the substrate cannot enter the active site (Figure **C.10**). Increasing the concentration of substrate in the presence of a non-competitive inhibitor does not overcome inhibition (Figure **C.9**).

Table **C.2** compares the nature and effects of competitive and non-competitive inhibitors.

Controlling metabolic pathways by end-product inhibition

End-product inhibition means that an enzyme in a pathway is inhibited by the product of that pathway. This prevents a cell over-producing a

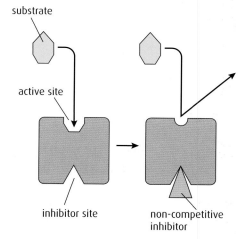

substrate

active site

inhibitor site

non-competitive inhibitor

Figure C.10 Non-competitive inhibition.

Competitive inhibitors	Non-competitive inhibitors

• structurally similar to the substrate molecule
• occupies and blocks the active site
• if concentration of inhibitor is low, increasing the concentration of substrate will reduce the inhibition
• examples include:
   – oxygen, which competes with carbon dioxide for the active site of ribulose bisphosphate carboxylase in photosynthesis
   – disulfiram, which competes with acetaldehyde for the active site of aldehyde dehydrogenase
	• structurally unlike the substrate molecule
	• binds at a site away from the active site, reduces access to it
	• if concentration of substrate is low, increasing the concentration of substrate has no effect on binding of the inhibitor so inhibition stays high
	• examples include:
	   – cyanide and carbon monoxide, which block cytochrome oxidase in aerobic respiration, leading to death

Table C.2 Comparing competitive and non-competitive inhibitors.

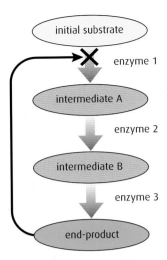

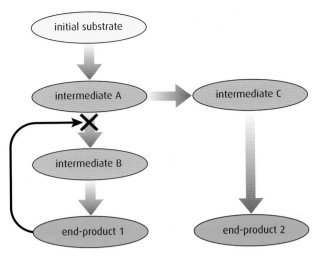

The end-product inhibits the enzyme catalysing the first reaction in the series, so all the subsequent reactions stop.

The end-product inhibits an enzyme in the pathway, which causes a different enzyme to come into play and the pathway is diverted down a different route.

Figure C.11 End-product inhibition.

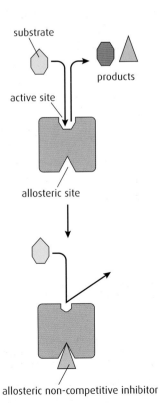

Figure C.12 Allosteric control. Allosteric inhibitors prevent the active site functioning.

substance it does not need at the time. Many products may be needed by the cell at a specific time or in specific amounts and over-production not only wastes energy but may also become toxic if the product accumulates.

In an assembly-line reaction, such as those described in Figure **C.11**, each step is controlled by a different enzyme. If the end-product begins to accumulate because it is not being used, it inhibits an enzyme earlier in the pathway to switch off the assembly line. In most cases, the inhibiting effect is on the first enzyme in a process, but in other cases it can act at a branch point to divert the reaction along another pathway.

When the end-product starts to be used up, its inhibiting effect reduces, the inhibited enzyme is reactivated and production begins again. This is an example of **negative feedback** (see page **154**).

End-product inhibition may be competitive or non-competitive. Competitive inhibition will only work if the product is a similar shape to the normal substrate and there can be an induced fit of the product or inhibitor onto the enzyme. In most cases, the product will be a different shape and therefore this has to be non-competitive inhibition. In this case, the enzyme is known as an **allosteric enzyme**, the product is called an **allosteric inhibitor** and the place where it binds to the enzyme (not the active site) is called the **allosteric site** (Figure **C.12**).

4 Outline what is meant by 'activation energy'.

5 Explain how the induced-fit model differs from the lock-and-key hypothesis for enzyme action.

6 State the difference between a competitive and a non-competitive inhibitor.

7 Outline how allosteric enzymes work.

C3 Cell respiration

Assessment statements

- State that oxidation involves the loss of electrons from an element, whereas reduction involves a gain of electrons; and that oxidation frequently involves gaining oxygen or losing hydrogen, whereas reduction frequently involves losing oxygen or gaining hydrogen.
- Outline the process of glycolysis, including phosphorylation, lysis, oxidation and ATP formation.
- Draw and label a diagram showing the structure of a mitochondrion as seen in electron micrographs.
- Explain aerobic respiration, including the link reaction, the Krebs cycle, the role of $NADH + H^+$, the electron transport chain and the role of oxygen.
- Explain oxidative phosphorylation in terms of chemiosmosis.
- Explain the relationship between the structure of the mitochondrion and its function.
- Analyse data relating to respiration.

Respiration and photosynthesis are two key biochemical pathways in ecosystems. Light energy from the Sun is trapped as chemical energy in photosynthesis and then the energy is transferred through food chains and released back to the environment as heat energy from respiration. The two pathways can be simply written as:

$$6CO_2 + 6H_2O + energy \underset{\text{respiration}}{\overset{\text{photosynthesis}}{\rightleftharpoons}} C_6H_{12}O_6 + 6O_2$$

There are a number of similarities between the two pathways, which will be examined in this chapter. The basics of photosynthesis and respiration are covered in Chapter **3**, and it would be useful to review this chapter before proceeding.

Oxidation and reduction

Cell respiration involves several **oxidation** and **reduction** reactions. Such reactions are common in biochemical pathways. When two molecules react, one of them starts in the oxidised state and becomes reduced, and the other starts in the reduced state and becomes oxidised, as shown in Figure **C.13**.

There are three different ways in which a molecule can be oxidised or reduced, as outlined in Table **C.3**. In biological oxidation reactions, addition of oxygen atoms is an alternative to removal of hydrogen atoms. Since a hydrogen atom consists of an electron and a proton, losing hydrogen atoms (oxidation) involves losing one or more electrons.

Oxidation	Reduction
loss of electrons	gain of electrons
loss of hydrogen	gain of hydrogen
gain of oxygen	loss of oxygen

Table C.3 Changes involved in oxidation and reduction.

Notation in biochemical pathways

Photosynthesis and respiration involve large organic molecules. For simplicity, these are often identified by the number of carbon atoms they contain. Thus glucose, $C_6H_{12}O_6$, is simplified to C_6. A biochemical pathway may be written as $C_3 \rightarrow C_3$ so that nothing appears to have happened but the number of oxygen and/or hydrogen atoms in the second C_3 molecule will have changed. Both photosynthesis and respiration have linear and cyclic components in their pathways. Many of the compounds involved are abbreviated to their initials.

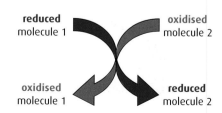

Figure C.13 Oxidation and reduction are linked processes – as one molecule is reduced another is oxidised in a redox reaction.

Oxidation and reduction occur together in biochemical reactions. As one compound loses electrons, for example, another gains. In the simple equation for respiration, glucose is oxidised as hydrogen atoms, and therefore electrons, are gradually removed from it and added to hydrogen acceptors (the oxygen atoms on the left side of the equation), which become reduced.

$$C_6H_{12}O_6 + 6O_2 \rightarrow 6CO_2 + 6H_2O + energy$$

Chemical reactions like this are referred to as **redox reactions**. In redox reactions, the reduced molecule always has more potential energy than the oxidised form of the molecule. Electrons passing from one molecule to another carry energy with them.

Respiration

Cell respiration is the controlled breakdown of food molecules such as glucose or fat to release energy, which can be stored for later use. The energy is most commonly stored in the molecule adenosine triphosphate, or ATP. The respiration pathway can be divided into four parts:

- glycolysis
- link reaction
- Krebs cycle
- electron transfer chain and chemiosmosis.

Glycolysis

Glycolysis is the first stage in the series of reactions that make up respiration. It literally means 'breaking apart glucose'. The glycolysis pathway occurs in the cytoplasm of the cell. It is anaerobic (that is, it can proceed in the absence of oxygen) and produces pyruvate and a small amount of ATP. One molecule of the hexose sugar glucose is converted to two molecules of the three-carbon molecule called pyruvate with the net gain of two molecules of ATP and two molecules of NADH + H$^+$. The process is shown in detail in Figure **C.14**.

1 The first steps are to add two phosphate groups from ATP, in a process called **phosphorylation**. A hexose bisphosphate molecule is produced. (This appears contrary to the purpose of respiration, which is to make ATP, but the two lost ATPs are recovered later.)

2 The hexose bisphosphate is now split into two triose phosphates in a reaction called **lysis**.

3 Now, another phosphorylation takes place but this time an inorganic phosphate ion, P$_i$, is used and not ATP. Two triose bisphosphates are formed. The energy to add the P$_i$ comes from an **oxidation** reaction. The triose bisphosphate is oxidised and at the same time NAD$^+$ is reduced to NADH + H$^+$.

4 There now follows a series of reactions in which the two phosphate groups from each triose bisphosphate are transferred onto two molecules of ADP, to form two molecules of ATP – this is **ATP formation**. A pyruvate molecule is also produced.

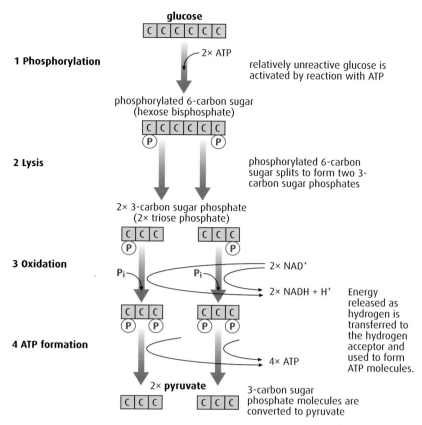

glucose

1 Phosphorylation

2× ATP

relatively unreactive glucose is
activated by reaction with ATP

phosphorylated 6-carbon sugar
(hexose bisphosphate)

2 Lysis

phosphorylated 6-carbon
sugar splits to form two 3-
carbon sugar phosphates

2× 3-carbon sugar phosphate
(2× triose phosphate)

3 Oxidation

P$_i$

P$_i$

2× NAD$^+$

2× NADH + H$^+$

Energy
released as
hydrogen is
transferred to
the hydrogen
acceptor and
used to form
ATP molecules.

4 ATP formation

4× ATP

2× **pyruvate**

3-carbon sugar
phosphate molecules are
converted to pyruvate

Figure C.14 The stages of glycolysis. Note that for each molecule of glucose, two molecules of ATP are used and four are formed, so there is a net gain of two ATPs.

NAD^+ is a hydrogen carrier that accepts hydrogen atoms removed during the reactions of respiration. During glycolysis, two hydrogen atoms are removed and NAD^+ accepts the protons from one of them and the electrons from both of them.

$$NAD^+ + 2H \rightarrow NADH + H^+$$

Note that $NADH + H^+$ must be written in this way and should not be simplified to $NADH_2$.

Four molecules of ATP are formed by converting one molecule of glucose to two molecules of pyruvate. However, two molecules of ATP were required to start the pathway and so there is a net gain of two molecules of ATP per glucose. In addition two $NADH + H^+$ are formed.

To summarise, the net products of glycolysis per glucose molecule are:

- 2 ATP
- 2 $NADH + H^+$
- 2 molecules of pyruvate.

8   List **three** ways in which a substance can be reduced.

9   What molecule is used to phosphorylate glucose at the start of glycolysis?

10 State the name of the process that splits the hexose bisphosphate molecule into two triose phosphate molecules.

11 What is used to phosphorylate each triose phosphate molecule following the above reaction?

12 In the glycolysis pathway, which molecule is oxidised during an oxidation/reduction reaction?

13 What is the name of the C_3 (three-carbon) molecule formed at the end of glycolysis?

14 What is the net gain of ATP from glycolysis per glucose molecule?

The link reaction and Krebs cycle

If oxygen is present, pyruvate formed during glycolysis moves into the mitochondrial matrix by facilitated diffusion. The structure of a mitochondrion is shown in Figures **C.15** and **C.16**.

The link reaction and the Krebs cycle pathways occur in the mitochondrial membrane. These are shown in Figure **C.17**.

1 The **link reaction** converts pyruvate to acetyl CoA using coenzyme A, and a carbon atom is removed as carbon dioxide. This called a **decarboxylation reaction**. At the same time as the carbon dioxide is removed, pyruvate is oxidised by the removal of hydrogen. The hydrogen atoms are removed by NAD^+ to form $NADH + H^+$.

2 Acetyl CoA now enters the **Krebs cycle** to continue the processes of aerobic respiration. Immediately, the coenzyme A is removed to be recycled.

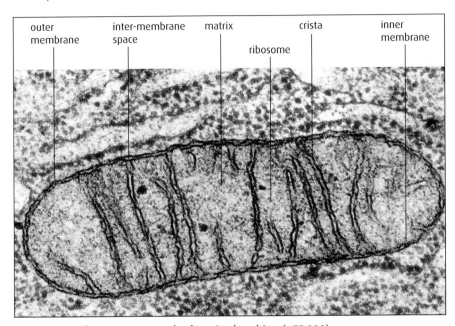

outer membrane inter-membrane space matrix ribosome crista inner membrane

Figure C.15 Electron micrograph of a mitochondrion (×72 000).

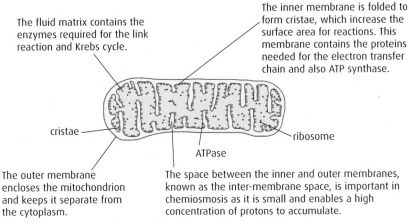

The fluid matrix contains the enzymes required for the link reaction and Krebs cycle.

The inner membrane is folded to form cristae, which increase the surface area for reactions. This membrane contains the proteins needed for the electron transfer chain and also ATP synthase.

cristae

ribosome

ATPase

The outer membrane encloses the mitochondrion and keeps it separate from the cytoplasm.

The space between the inner and outer membranes, known as the inter-membrane space, is important in chemiosmosis as it is small and enables a high concentration of protons to accumulate.

Figure C.16 Diagram of a mitochondrion in longitudinal section.

Increasing area

Just as the inner lining of the small intestine is folded to increase its surface area to absorb food, so the inner mitochondrial membrane is folded into cristae to increase its surface area. The cristae provide a large area for the enzymes and molecules used in the electron transport chain (see page **346**).

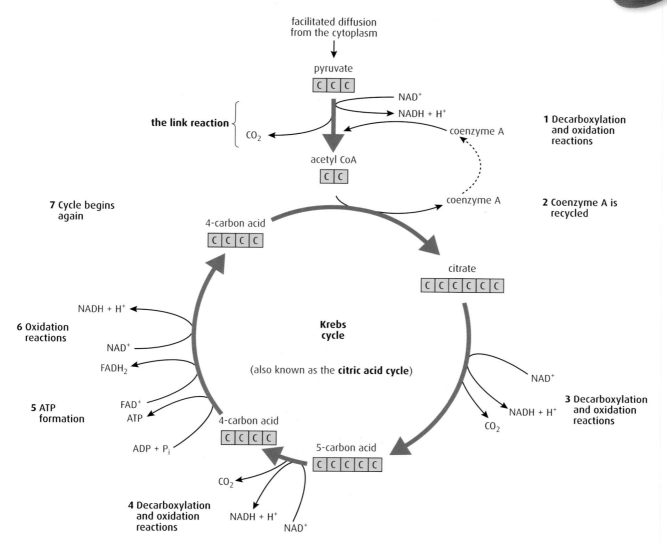

Figure C.17 The link reaction and Krebs cycle.

3 The two carbons that enter with acetyl CoA also leave as carbon dioxide from two decarboxylation reactions.

4 One molecule of ATP is formed.

5 Hydrogen is removed during oxidation reactions to the two hydrogen carriers NAD^+ and FAD^+.

6 Since the Krebs cycle is a cyclic process, what enters must eventually leave so that the cycle begins and ends with the same substances.

Because each molecule of glucose forms two molecules of pyruvate during glycolysis, each glucose molecule requires two link reactions and two rotations of the Krebs cycle. Thus, when working out the products of the cycle we must consider two sets of products. So, to summarise, the products of the link reaction and Krebs cycle, per glucose molecule, are:

- 8 molecules of $NADH + H^+$
- 2 molecules of $FADH_2$
- 2 molecules of ATP
- 6 molecules of CO_2.

Note that the correct method to show reduced FAD is $FADH_2$.

The electron transport chain, oxidative phosphorylation and chemiosmosis

Most of the ATP produced from glucose breakdown occurs in the last phase of respiration at the end of the **electron transport chain**. Reactions take place on the inner mitochondrial membrane of the cristae and in the inter-membrane space between the inner and outer membranes. The inner membrane holds molecules called **electron carriers**, which pick up electrons and pass them from one to another in a series of oxidations and reductions. The pathway is called the electron transport chain (ETC) because electrons from hydrogen are moved along it. Several protein molecules are electron carriers and the three key ones are shown in Figure **C.18**.

Electrons from NADH + H$^+$ are transferred onto the first electron carrier. As they pass through the carrier, they lose energy and this is used to pump a proton (H$^+$) from the matrix to the inter-membrane space, lowering the pH of the space. The electrons are then transferred to two further carriers and the process is repeated. As the electrons from one NADH + H$^+$ pass along the chain, a total of nine protons are pumped into the inter-membrane space. At the end of the chain, the electrons are combined with protons and oxygen atoms to make water, in the oxidative part of **oxidative phosphorylation**.

The space between the membranes is very narrow and allows for a rapid increase in the concentration of the protons that are pumped into it during the electron transfer reactions. The protons in the inter-membrane space create a concentration gradient between the space and the matrix.

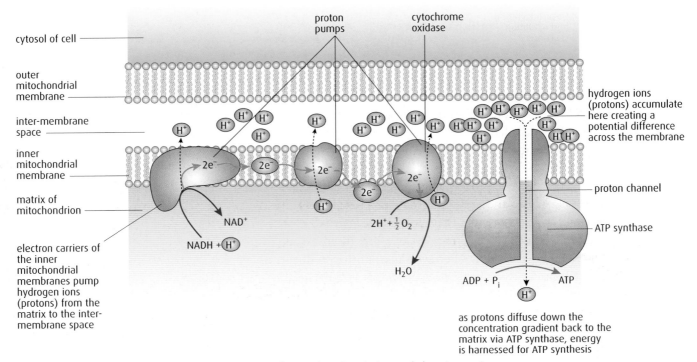

Figure C.18 The electron transport chain showing oxidative phosphorylation and chemiosmosis.

These protons can now flow passively down this concentration gradient back into the matrix, through a very large integral protein. This is called **chemiosmosis**. The large protein contains the enzyme **ATP synthase**, which joins ADP and P_i to form ATP. Three protons flowing through this enzyme results in one ATP being formed. Since the electrons from one $NADH + H^+$ pump nine protons into the inter-membrane space, each $NADH + H^+$ results in the formation of three ATP. This is the phosphorylation part of oxidative phosphorylation.

FADH$_2$ also supplies electrons to the electron transport chain but further down the chain than $NADH + H^+$, missing the first proton pump. FADH$_2$ allows the production of just two ATPs.

Overall ATP production during aerobic respiration

Together, glycolysis, the link reaction and the Krebs cycle yield 36 ATP molecules for each molecule of glucose broken down by aerobic respiration, as summarised in Table **C.4**.

Stage		ATP use	ATP yield
glycolysis	2 ATP used at the start	−2 ATP	
	2 NADH + H$^+$		+4 ATP
	ATP formation		+4 ATP
link reaction	2 NADH + H$^+$		+6 ATP
Krebs cycle	ATP formation		+2 ATP
	6 NADH + H$^+$		+18 ATP
	2 FADH$_2$		+4 ATP
net energy yield			+36 ATP

Table C.4 Summary of ATP production during aerobic respiration.

15 Where precisely do the link reaction and the reactions of Krebs cycle take place?

16 Where precisely do the reactions of the electron transport chain take place?

17 In the link reaction, is pyruvate oxidised or reduced?

18 Name the molecule that enters the Krebs cycle.

19 During one rotation of the Krebs cycle, how many molecules of carbon dioxide are formed?

20 During one rotation of the Krebs cycle, how many molecules of ATP are formed directly by the cycle?

21 What is the purpose of the folding of the inner mitochondrial membrane?

22 What is the function of the electron transport chain (ETC)?

23 What happens to the pH of the inter-membrane space as electrons move along the ETC?

Chemiosmosis

Osmosis is the passive flow of water molecules down a concentration gradient through a partially permeable membrane. Chemiosmosis is similar but instead of water moving, it is protons that pass down a concentration gradient.

As Table **C.4** shows, the net production of ATP from one molecule of glucose is, in theory, 36. Biochemists have discovered that the actual production is closer to 30 ATPs and propose that this discrepancy occurs because some protons are used to transfer ATP from the matrix to the cytoplasm. Only about 30% of the energy in a glucose molecule generates ATP.

C4 Photosynthesis

Assessment statements

- Draw and label a diagram showing the structure of a chloroplast as seen in electron micrographs.
- State that photosynthesis consists of light-dependent and light-independent reactions.
- Explain the light-dependent reactions.
- Explain photophosphorylation in terms of chemiosmosis.
- Explain the light-independent reactions.
- Explain the relationship between the structure of the chloroplast and its function.
- Explain the relationship between the action spectrum and the absorption spectrum of photosynthetic pigments in green plants.
- Explain the concept of limiting factors in photosynthesis with reference to light intensity, temperature and concentration of carbon dioxide.
- Analyse data relating to photosynthesis.

The reactions of photosynthesis

Photosynthesis is the process by which light energy is harvested and stored as chemical energy, primarily in sugars but also in other organic molecules such as lipids. It occurs in green plants, algae and some bacteria. All these organisms are known as **autotrophs**, which means they can make their own food.

Photosynthesis can be divided into two parts:

- the light-dependent reaction
- the light-independent reaction.

The light-dependent reaction produces compounds that are used in the light-independent reaction.

Both the light-dependent and the light-independent reactions take place in the **chloroplasts** of plant cells (Figures **C.19** and **C.20**). The stroma contains the enzymes required for the light-independent reaction and the stacks of thylakoid membranes increase the surface area for the light-dependent reaction.

The light-dependent reaction

The **light-dependent reaction** occurs on the **thylakoid membranes** of the chloroplast and is powered by light energy from the Sun. Each thylakoid is a flattened sac so the space in the middle is narrow. The thylakoid membranes form stacks called **grana**, which may be joined together by intergranal membranes. Light is absorbed by photosynthetic pigments such as chlorophyll, which are found on the granal membranes. There are several pigments found in plants and each one absorbs light of a slightly different wavelength. The pigments are associated with proteins that are involved in electron transport, proton pumping and chemiosmosis.

The light-dependent and light-independent reactions

Both of these reactions are part of photosynthesis and can only occur when there is sufficient light. The light-independent reactions do not have to take place during darkness.

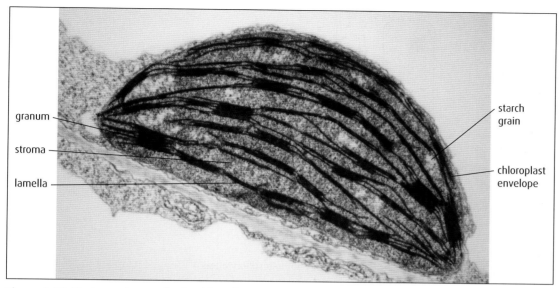

Figure C.19 Electron micrograph of a chloroplast (×20 000).

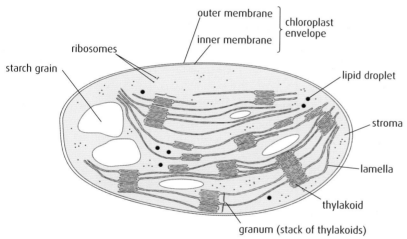

Figure C.20 Diagram of a chloroplast.

The photosynthetic pigments are combined into two complex groups called **photosystems I and II**, which absorb the light energy and use this to boost electrons to a higher energy level so that they become 'excited', as shown in Figure **C.21** (overleaf).

1 The first step in the light-dependent reaction is the **photoactivation** of photosystem II. Pigment molecules in the photosystem absorb light energy and boost electrons in a molecule of chlorophyll to a higher energy level. The electrons are accepted by a carrier protein molecule at the start of the electron transport chain.

2 Photosystem II has to replace these lost electrons and it does this by taking them from water. Water is split into electrons, protons (hydrogen ions) and an oxygen atom. Since the splitting is brought about by light energy, it is called **photolysis**. The oxygen is released as an excretory product.

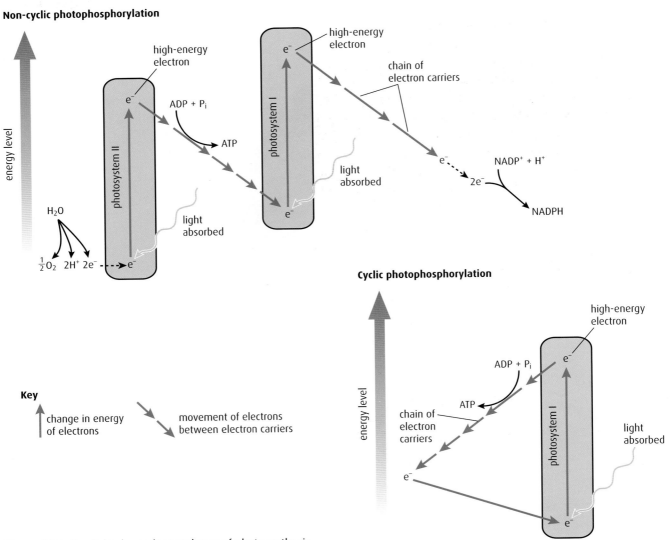

Non-cyclic photophosphorylation

high-energy
electron

high-energy
electron

chain of
electron carriers

photosystem II

photosystem I

energy level

ADP + P$_i$

ATP

e$^-$

e$^-$

light
absorbed

NADP$^+$ + H$^+$

H$_2$O

e$^-$

2e$^-$

NADPH

$\frac{1}{2}$O$_2$ 2H$^+$ 2e$^-$ → e$^-$

light
absorbed

Key

change in energy
of electrons

movement of electrons
between electron carriers

Cyclic photophosphorylation

high-energy
electron

energy level

ADP + P$_i$

ATP

chain of
electron
carriers

photosystem I

light
absorbed

e$^-$

e$^-$

e$^-$

Figure C.21 The light-dependent pathway of photosynthesis.

3 Excited electrons travel along the electron transport chain into photosystem I. As they do this, they lose energy but this is used to pump protons into the thylakoid interior (in a similar way as occurs in the electron transport chain in the mitochondrion). The thylakoid interior is small and so a proton concentration gradient builds up quickly. The protons then flow out through a large channel protein, almost identical to the one in mitochondria, which contains the enzyme ATP synthase. This time though, the formation of ATP is called **photophosphorylation** and it occurs between photosystems II and I (Figure **C.22**).

4 Absorption of light energy causes photoactivation in photosystem I, boosting more electrons to an even higher energy level. The electrons that arrive from photosystem II replace those that are displaced. The electrons at the higher energy level are combined with protons in the hydrogen carrier NADP$^+$ to form NADPH + H$^+$.

The two products of the light–dependent reaction, ATP and NADPH + H$^+$, are used to drive the light–independent reaction.

NADP$^+$ is very similar to NAD$^+$ – it simply has a phosphate group attached. An easy way to remember that photosynthesis uses NADP$^+$ is to note that they both have a letter 'P'.

Cyclic and non-cyclic photophosphorylation

When ATP is produced using energy from excited electrons flowing from photosystem II through photosystem I and on to $NADP^+$, the process is called **non-cyclic photophosphorylation**.

When light is not a limiting factor, the light-independent reactions may proceed more slowly than the light-dependent reaction, so that the supply of $NADP^+$ runs out. This means the electrons boosted up from photosystem I have no acceptor available to take them. They rejoin the electron transport chain near the start and generate more ATP for the light-independent reaction. This alternative pathway is called **cyclic photophosphorylation** (Figure **C.21**).

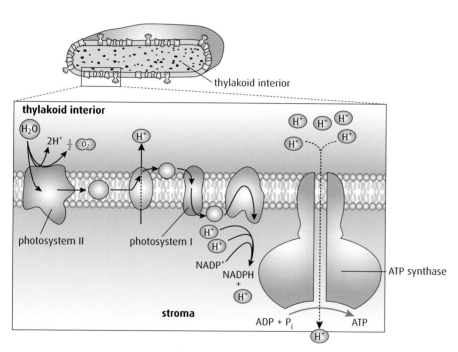

Figure C.22 Chemiosmosis in photosynthesis.

The light-independent reaction

The **light-independent reaction** occurs in the stroma of the chloroplast and is a cyclic pathway called the **Calvin cycle**. The pathway is shown in Figure **C.23** (overleaf). (Large organic molecules have been simplified to show just the number of carbon atoms they contain.) ATP and NADPH + H^+ formed during the light-dependent stage supply energy and reducing power for the Calvin cycle. The final product of the cycle is carbohydrate.

During each turn of the Calvin cycle one molecule of carbon dioxide is used so Figure **C.23** shows three cycles combined together. As this is a cycle, what goes in must leave, so three carbons enter in three molecules of carbon dioxide and three carbons leave in one molecule of triose phosphate, which can be used to form glucose or other organic compounds.

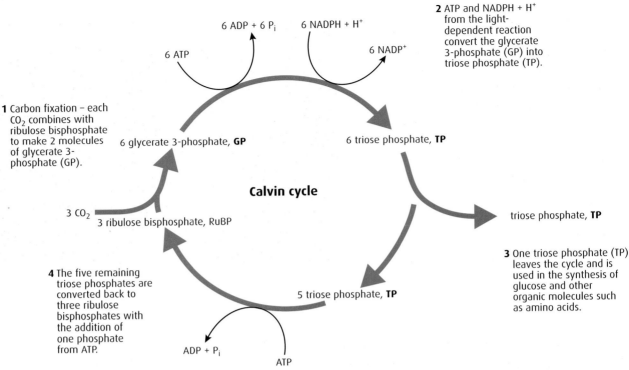

1 Carbon fixation – each CO_2 combines with ribulose bisphosphate to make 2 molecules of glycerate 3-phosphate (GP).

6 ADP + 6 P_i

6 ATP

6 NADPH + H⁺

6 NADP⁺

2 ATP and NADPH + H⁺ from the light-dependent reaction convert the glycerate 3-phosphate (GP) into triose phosphate (TP).

6 glycerate 3-phosphate, **GP**

6 triose phosphate, **TP**

Calvin cycle

3 CO_2

3 ribulose bisphosphate, RuBP

triose phosphate, **TP**

3 One triose phosphate (TP) leaves the cycle and is used in the synthesis of glucose and other organic molecules such as amino acids.

4 The five remaining triose phosphates are converted back to three ribulose bisphosphates with the addition of one phosphate from ATP.

5 triose phosphate, **TP**

ADP + P_i

ATP

Figure C.23 The light-independent pathway of photosynthesis.

1 At the start of the cycle, the acceptor molecule ribulose bisphosphate (RuBP) combines with incoming carbon dioxide from the air to form glycerate 3-phosphate (GP). This reaction is called **carbon fixation**. It is catalysed by **RuBP carboxylase**, an enzyme that is sometimes called **rubisco**.

2 The ATP and NADPH + H⁺ from the light-dependent reaction convert the glycerate 3-phosphate into triose phosphate (TP). Glycerate 3-phosphate therefore becomes reduced to triose phosphate. No more phosphate is added so the only input from ATP is energy.

3 Six molecules of triose phosphate are produced but only five are needed to reform the ribulose bisphosphate to keep the cycle going. The extra triose phosphate leaves the cycle and since it takes a phosphate with it, this is replaced in the cycle from ATP.

Six 'turns' of the Calvin cycle produces two triose phosphate molecules, which can be combined to form the final product, glucose. Some triose phosphate molecules will follow other pathways to make other organic carbohydrate molecules, such as sucrose or cellulose, or other molecules that the plant needs, such as amino acids, fatty acids or vitamins.

24 Where does the light-independent reaction take place?

25 When photosystem II loses electrons, what molecule is used to replace them?

26 Name the **two** useful products from the light-dependent reaction.

27 Name the starting acceptor molecule in the Calvin cycle, which reacts with carbon dioxide.

More questions on photosynthesis can be found in Chapter **8**, page **206**.

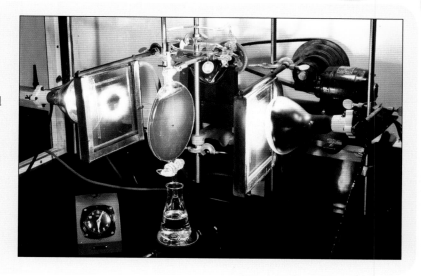

The action spectrum and the absorption spectrum

The spectrum of colours that humans can perceive is just part of the electromagnetic spectrum. The range of wavelengths in visible light is from 400 nm to about 700 nm. Light provides the energy for photosynthesis but not all wavelengths are absorbed equally by the chloroplasts. If white light is shone onto chloroplasts, the wavelengths they absorb depend on the pigments present in them. Figure **C.24** (overleaf) shows an investigation in which the pigments from chloroplasts have been extracted and form a solution. They are illuminated by light that has passed through a prism, so that the whole spectrum is visible. As the spectrum of wavelengths passes through the solution, the red and blue colours are lost, because they have been absorbed by the pigments. The green part of the spectrum is not affected, as chlorophyll does not absorb green light.

The investigation in Figure **C.24** can be made more sophisticated by filtering white light so that only a precise wavelength is shone onto the chlorophyll solution. The proportion of each wavelength that is absorbed by the solution can be measured and an **absorption spectrum**, which shows the relative amounts of each wavelength that is absorbed, can be built up. Each pigment has a characteristic absorption spectrum, as shown in Figure **C.25** (overleaf).

The rate of photosynthesis can be measured in several ways, one of which is to measure the volume of oxygen released. Rapid oxygen production indicates a high rate of photosynthesis. If the rate is measured for a range of wavelengths, a graph known as an **action spectrum** can be built up. Chlorophyll is more sensitive to some wavelengths of light than others and produces excited electrons at the highest rate at these wavelengths. The more excited electrons are produced, the faster the rate of photosynthesis. A typical action spectrum shows that blue and red light are used most efficiently.

Chlorophyll is the most important and abundant plant pigment used to capture light for photosynthesis. There are several forms of chlorophyll and each selectively absorbs certain wavelengths of light at the red and blue ends of the spectrum, while reflecting green light. Terrestrial plants and green algae contain two forms of the pigment, chlorophyll *a* and *b*, but diatoms contain a third type known as chlorophyll *c* instead of chlorophyll *b*.

Plants also contain several other pigments, including carotenoids, which are orange in colour, and anthocyanins, which are red. These pigments also selectively absorb certain wavelengths and reflect others. Absorbed light may be used in chemical reactions, and the reflected light determines the colour of the plant and can be important in attracting pollinators to flowers.

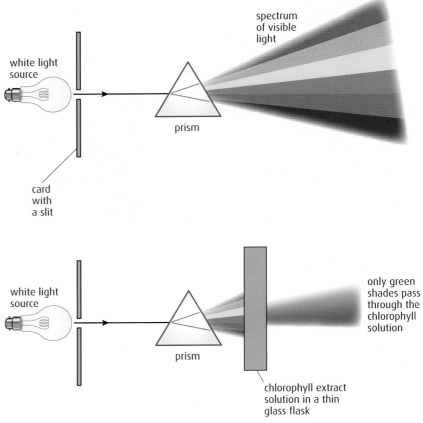

Figure C.24 Only green light passes through a chloroplast extract solution; red and blue wavelengths are absorbed.

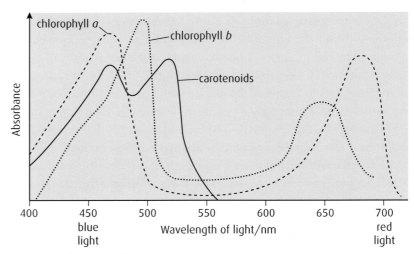

Figure C.25 Absorption spectra for photosynthetic pigments, chlorophylls *a* and *b*, and carotenoid pigments.

Figure **C.26** shows action and absorption spectra plotted on one graph. The correlation of the curves indicates that absorbed light is used in photosynthesis.

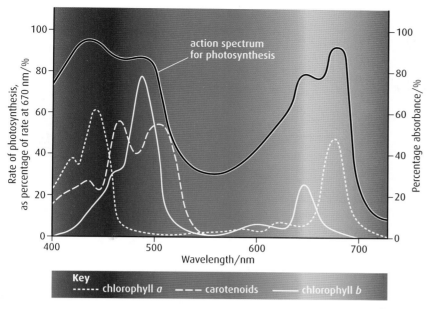

Figure C.26 Absorption and action spectra superimposed.

Absorption and action spectra vary for different species of plant. Some plants contain different pigments such as carotene and xanthophylls, which absorb wavelengths that chlorophyll cannot. These pigments, known as accessory pigments, absorb some yellow and green light and account for the photosynthesis that occurs in this range.

Limiting factors

Like all metabolic processes, the photosynthetic pathway requires a number of components to make it work. If any of these components is in short supply, it limits the rate at which photosynthesis works.

Photosynthesis requires a suitable temperature, and sufficient light energy and carbon dioxide – any one of these can become a **limiting factor** and change the rate of photosynthesis.

When one step in photosynthesis is slowed down, the whole process slows down. If light intensity is increased, the rate of photosynthesis increases until a certain point when increasing light has no further effect, as shown in Figure **C.27**.

At low light intensities, there may be a shortage of the products of the light-dependent reaction so photosynthesis is slow. At point A the plant is saturated with light and cannot photosynthesise at a faster rate even with more light. This indicates that some other factor is limiting the reaction.

Temperature affects enzymes that catalyse the reactions of photosynthesis so that if the temperature is too low the reactions may proceed very slowly and a graph of temperature versus rate of photosynthesis would look similar to Figure **C.28** (overleaf). At low concentrations of carbon dioxide there may be insufficient carbon dioxide to be fixed in the Calvin cycle. At higher carbon dioxide concentrations, another factor may limit the reaction.

Water is essential for photosynthesis but it is seldom likely to be a limiting factor since all the cells of a plant must contain it to remain alive.

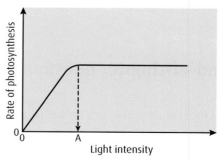

Figure C.27 Rate of photosynthesis is proportional to light intensity, until point A, when some other factor is limiting.

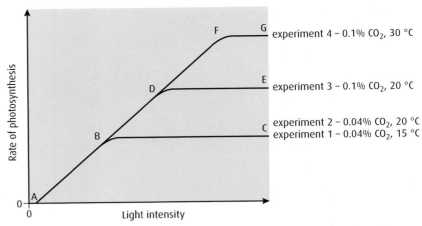

Figure C.28 The effect of temperature and CO_2 concentration on the rate of photosynthesis.

- In Figure **C.28**, experiment 1 shows that as light intensity increases so does the rate of photosynthesis between the points A and B on the graph. At these light intensities, light is the limiting factor. Between points B and C another factor has become limiting.
- In experiment 2, where the temperature has been increased to 20 °C, the line has not changed, showing that it is the carbon dioxide concentration that is the limiting factor – a change in temperature has had no effect.
- In experiment 3, raising the carbon dioxide concentration causes the rate of photosynthesis to increase to point D, but then another limiting factor comes in to play from D to E.
- In experiment 4 we see that, at the higher carbon dioxide concentration, raising the temperature causes the line to rise to F but then again another limiting factor has become limiting from F to G.

The level of carbon dioxide in the atmosphere is relatively low and carbon dioxide is frequently a limiting factor for photosynthesis. Horticulturalists increase the yield of their crops by maximising the rate of photosynthesis in their glasshouses. They do this by keeping the air inside warm with heaters, increasing the intensity of light using lamps and, in some cases, increasing the concentration of carbon dioxide.

28 If the graphs of the photosynthesis action spectrum and the chloroplast pigment absorption spectrum are superimposed what can be deduced?

29 What is meant by the term 'limiting factor'?

30 List **three** limiting factors for photosynthesis.

End-of-chapter questions

1 Protein structure can be explained in terms of four levels – primary, secondary, tertiary and quaternary structure. Outline the quaternary structure of proteins. (3)

2 Explain the reasons for a large area of thylakoid membrane in the chloroplast. (2)

3 Explain why the chloroplast contains large amounts of RuBP carboxylase. (2)

4   Outline the difference between competitive and non–competitive enzyme inhibitors.   (2)

5   Outline the differences between globular and fibrous proteins, giving a named example of each.   (3)

6   Explain the significance of polar amino acids for membrane proteins.   (2)

7   Explain how the proton gradient in the chloroplast is generated by chemiosmosis and what it is used for. (4)

8   Explain why carbon dioxide concentration is a limiting factor of photosynthesis.   (3)

9   Alcohol dehydrogenase is an enzyme that catalyses the reversible reaction of ethanol and ethanal according to the equation below.

$$NAD^+ + CH_3CH_2OH \rightleftharpoons CH_3CHO + NADH + H^+$$
$$\text{ethanol} \qquad\qquad \text{ethanal}$$

The initial rate of reaction can be measured according to the time taken for NADH to be produced.

In an experiment, the initial rate at different concentrations of ethanol was recorded (no inhibition). The experiment was then repeated with the addition of $1\,mmol\,dm^{-3}$ 2,2,2-trifluoroethanol, a competitive inhibitor of the enzyme. A third experiment using a greater concentration of the same inhibitor ($3\,mmol\,dm^{-3}$) was performed. The results for each experiment are shown in the graph below.

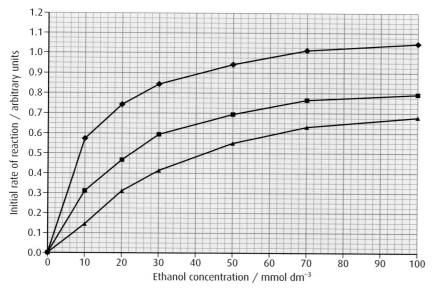

source: Taber, R (1998) *Biochemical Education*, **26**, pp 239–242

a Outline the effect of increasing the substrate concentration on the control reaction (no inhibition). (2)

b **i** State the initial rate of reaction at an ethanol concentration of $50\,\text{mmol dm}^{-3}$ in the presence of the inhibitor at the following concentrations:
$1\,\text{mmol dm}^{-3}$
$3\,\text{mmol dm}^{-3}$ (1)

ii State the effect of increasing the concentration of inhibitor on the initial rate of reaction. (1)

c Explain how a competitive inhibitor works. (3)

(total 7 marks)

10 The hydrolysis of inorganic phosphate (PPi) by phosphatase enzyme provides energy for a wide range of reactions. A phosphatase (PPase) occurs bound to thylakoid membranes. This enzyme was purified from the thylakoid membranes of spinach leaves using chromatography. The activity of the membrane-bound enzyme and the purified enzyme was measured.

The effect of the concentration of magnesium ions (Mg^{2+}) on the relative activity of these enzymes was determined using different concentrations of magnesium chloride. The concentration of inorganic phosphate used in both cases was of $1\,\text{mmol dm}^{-3}$.

Activity of phosphatase/arbitrary units	
Membrane bound	**Purified**
12 618	1215

Key

- - ◆ - - purified

■ membrane bound

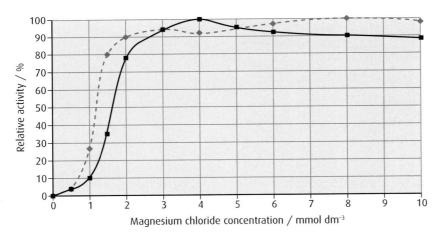

reprinted from Po-Yin Cheung *et al.* (1998) 'Thiols Protect the Inhibition of Myocardial Aconitase by Peroxynitrite', *Archives of Biochemistry and Biophysics*, vol. 350, issue 1, pp. 104–108
© 1998, with permission from Elsevier

a State the percentage of relative activity of the purified enzyme when the concentration of magnesium chloride is:

  i $1\,mmol\,dm^{-3}$

  ii $2\,mmol\,dm^{-3}$ (2)

b Outline the effect of magnesium chloride on the relative activity of the membrane-bound enzyme.   (2)

c Calculate the approximate ratio of inorganic phosphate to magnesium chloride concentration needed to achieve maximum activity in membrane–bound enzymes.   (1)

d **i**   State the difference in phosphatase activity when membrane bound and when purified.   (1)

  ii   Suggest a reason for this difference.   (1)

(total 7 marks)

© IB Organization 2009

11 The cyanobacterium *(Calothrix elenkenii)* is cultivated as a source of photosynthetic pigments for use in research and industry. The chart below shows the quantity of two of the pigments produced when exposed to a day of continuous dark, a day of 16 hours light and 8 hours dark and a day of continuous light. This was repeated in both aerobic and anaerobic conditions.

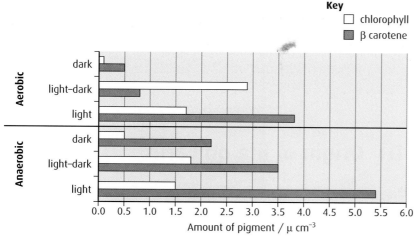

source: reprinted from Parsanna *et al.* (2002) *Journal of Plant Physiology*, Vol 161,
'Modulation of pigment...' pp 1125–1132,
© 2002, with permission from Elsevier

a Identify the light conditions that cause most chlorophyll to be made when the cyanobacterium is cultivated anaerobically.   (1)

b Calculate the percentage increase in chlorophyll grown anaerobically in the light, compared with anaerobically in the dark.   (1)

c Compare pigment production in different aerobic conditions.   (2)

d Discuss why having more than one photosynthetic pigment is an advantage to cyanobacterium.   (3)

(total 7 marks)

© IB Organization 2009

Option D Evolution

Introduction

The Earth formed around 4.6 billion years ago from a lump of molten rock. The cooling crust released carbon dioxide, nitrogen, methane, hydrogen, water vapour and ammonia, which formed the atmosphere, but there was no oxygen gas because metals in the hot rock reacted with it to form oxides. As the crust continued to cool, water vapour condensed to form the oceans. The young Earth remained sterile for the next billion (10^9) years before organic molecules began to form what could be thought of as organisms – structures that could grow and reproduce – but oxygen did not begin to appear in the atmosphere for another 1.3 billion years (Figure **D.1**).

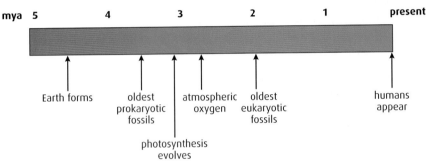

Figure D.1 Time line for the Earth.

D1 Origin of life on Earth

Assessment statements

- Describe four processes needed for the spontaneous origin of life on Earth.
- Outline the experiments of Miller and Urey into the origin of organic compounds.
- State that comets may have delivered organic compounds to Earth.
- Discuss possible locations where conditions would have allowed the synthesis of organic compounds.
- Outline two properties of RNA that would have allowed it to play a role in the origin of life.
- State that living cells may have been preceded by protobionts with an internal chemical environment different from their surroundings.
- Outline the contribution of prokaryotes to the creation of an oxygen-rich atmosphere.
- Discuss the endosymbiotic theory for the origin of eukaryotes.

The spontaneous origin of life

Prokaryotic and eukaryotic organisms alive today all have structures based on the cell. Cell structure must have originated from chemicals present on the early Earth. For this to have happened, four essential steps must have occurred.

1 Living things are made of organic molecules, so simple organic molecules such as amino acids, sugars, fatty acids, glycerol and bases must have formed.
2 Organic molecules in living organisms (such as triglycerides, phospholipids, polypeptides and nucleic acids) are large, so single molecules must have been assembled to make these more complex molecules.
3 All living things reproduce, so molecules must have formed that could replicate themselves and control other chemical reactions. This is the basis of inheritance.
4 Finally, cells have membranes, so the mixtures of these molecules must have been enclosed within membrane-bound vesicles.

Under particular conditions, certain molecules such as small polypeptides or phospholipids mixed in water collect together to form small spheres called **microspheres**. If these microspheres form from larger polypeptides along with other organic molecules, and if they become surrounded by a skin of water, they are called **coacervates**.

In the early oceans on the Earth, microspheres and coacervates formed in this way. Most would have simply broken up again, but some might have contained a mixture of chemicals that increased their survival time. They might have been able to form an internal chemical environment different from the surroundings by preferentially absorbing or ejecting certain molecules. This might have allowed new reactions inside them that could not occur in the outside surroundings. Some coacervates may have contained small molecules of RNA together with amino acids so that simple polypeptides might have been able to form. If such vesicles were able to replicate themselves in a sort of asexual reproduction, then natural selection could act on these **protobionts**, allowing them to evolve.

The origin of organic compounds

The early Earth was bombarded with debris from space (such as comets, meteorites and space dust) which could have contained organic molecules. On 28 September 1969, a meteorite fell near Murchison in Western

Theories about the origin of life

There is much speculation as to where the first organic molecules came from. Scientific theories require a hypothesis that can be tested by gathering evidence. If any piece of evidence does not fit with the theory, a new hypothesis must be put forward and more evidence gathered. It is important to recognise the difference between a scientific theory and a dogma, which is a statement of beliefs that are not subject to scientific tests. The events leading to the formation of life on Earth happened millions of years ago and many different theories have been proposed by scientists and philosophers to suggest what might have happened.

Questions to consider

1 Do you think it is possible to gather sufficient evidence to support or refute the theories about the origin of life on Earth?
2 For a scientific theory to be valid, we must also be able to test whether it is false. Is this possible in this case?

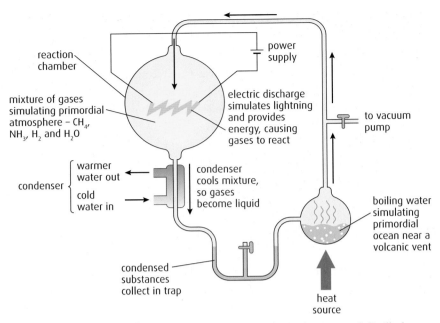

Figure D.2 The apparatus used by Urey and Miller. The flask contained distilled water, which boiled and condensed, just as it might have done on the Earth millions of years ago. The gas mixture contained methane, ammonia and hydrogen, and the electrodes produced continuous sparks to simulate lightning. After several days, the condensate became brown and was found to contain many organic compounds including several amino acids.

Australia; 100 kilograms of material were recovered from it and analysis showed that it was rich in amino acids.

In 1953, Harold Urey (1893–1981) and Stanley Miller (1930–2007) put together a simple apparatus (Figure **D.2**) and attempted to mimic the conditions that they thought existed on the early Earth. They tried to test the theory that organic molecules could have been produced when very simple molecules came together.

This investigation by Urey and Miller led to further research with different energy sources and different mixtures of gases. In 1961, John Oro showed that hydrogen cyanide and ammonia, both of which were likely to have been present on the early Earth, could react to form **adenine**, a base found in DNA and RNA, and a component of ATP. When he included sand or quartz in the mixture, complex types of amino acid were formed.

Where could organic molecules have formed?

Many scientists have suggested locations on Earth where organic compounds may have arisen naturally (for example, Figure **D.3**). These places have all the ingredients needed for the early stages of molecule formation but there are many other variables that have not been measured or considered. Much more research is necessary before a conclusion can be drawn with any certainty.

At hot springs in places such as Yellowstone Park in Wyoming, USA, mineral-rich water heated by volcanic activity comes to the surface. As water evaporates, small pools become isolated and the minerals in the

Figure D.3 The Morning Glory pool at Yellowstone National Park, USA. The first organic compounds may have been formed in conditions similar to these.

water may become so concentrated that reactions occur spontaneously. Areas like these could provide the necessary conditions for the formation of amino acids and carbohydrates.

In 1977, scientists from the Scripps Institution of Oceanography used a small deep-sea submersible vehicle called *Alvin* to go 2000 m down under the ocean to the East Pacific Rise near the Galapagos Islands where two tectonic plates are moving apart. Here they observed volcanic vents pouring out black superheated water rich in minerals and many other chemicals. Under such conditions, with very high temperatures and pressures, organic molecules could have formed. Today, they are teeming with bacteria which are the starting point of several food webs.

Using models to test scientific theories

Models are either physical or descriptive methods that can be used to test theories of scientific events. Miller and Urey's experiment (Figure **D.2**) is a physical model. The results of the experiment agree with the theory and the model has been accepted. If the results had not supported the theory and predictions, the model would have been rejected or modified. An example of a descriptive model is the lock-and-key hypothesis used to explain enzyme activity. As further evidence on enzyme action was gathered, the original model proposed by Emil Fischer (1852–1919) in 1890 was replaced by a new model, known as the induced-fit model. This was proposed by Daniel Koshland (1920–2007) in 1959.

Questions to consider

1 Does the Miller and Urey model prove how organic compounds formed on Earth?

2 If Urey and Miller's apparatus had not produced organic molecules, could their theory about the formation of organic compounds be said to be false?

3 The induced-fit model is still accepted as a description of how some enzymes work. What would have to happen for this model to be replaced?

RNA replication

RNA can replicate itself by forming a double strand using complementary base pairing with new nucleotides. The new strand can then separate off and be used as a template to build a further new strand, which will be identical to the original strand (Figure **D.4**).

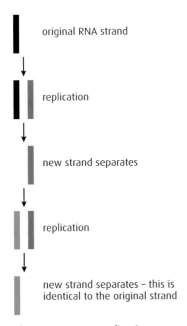

original RNA strand

replication

new strand separates

replication

new strand separates – this is identical to the original strand

Figure D.4 RNA replication.

RNA and the origin of life

Very simple, early cells would have needed a molecule that could carry some form of coded information. The information could have been instructions to form a polypeptide, or to replicate the cell. The information molecule itself may have acted like an enzyme. Some types of RNA molecule can do all of these things and so it is very likely that RNA played an important role in early cells. RNA can also be used to synthesise tRNA and rRNA, and if the enzyme reverse transcriptase is present, DNA can be synthesised from RNA. Furthermore, the building blocks of RNA (ribonucleoside triphosphates) have other functions – for example, ATP is an energy transfer molecule.

RNA molecules have several limitations. They can only catalyse a small range of reactions; enzymes are much more efficient. Also, because the structure of RNA is not strong, RNA molecules cannot become very large so they carry only a small amount of coded information. In addition, RNA replication (Figure **D.4**) is not very accurate and the mutation rate is high. Nevertheless, RNA molecules could have been important in the early world even if, in time, they were replaced with DNA and enzymes.

Prokaryotes and the atmosphere

Prokaryotes appeared around 3.5 billion years ago when Earth's atmosphere contained no oxygen. All these early organisms had to respire anaerobically and anaerobic respiration was prevalent for around a billion years. At some point around this time, a few prokaryotes, related to modern-day **cyanobacteria**, developed new light-absorbing pigments and became able to carry out an additional process – photosynthesis. They used hydrogen sulfide as their source of hydrogen and produced sulfur as their waste product. These photosynthetic prokaryotes would only have been able to survive in places where hydrogen sulfide was present.

Evidence is incomplete but most scientists agree that, around 2.8 billion years ago, changes occurred in photosynthetic pigments that seem to have allowed some of the prokaryotes to use water instead of hydrogen sulfide as their source of hydrogen. This new reaction produced oxygen as its waste product. Water was very widespread over the planet at this time so the water-using bacteria multiplied very rapidly and increased the level of oxygen in the atmosphere considerably. Oxygen 'polluted' the air and killed many anaerobic prokaryotes. Only those that were protected from it in mud or other oxygen-poor environments survived. Oxygen levels continued to rise steadily until about 1.5 billion years later, when photosynthesising eukaryotic cells appeared and the rate of increase in atmospheric oxygen rose still faster.

The endosymbiotic theory

The endosymbiotic theory is an important theory explaining how eukaryotic cells could have developed from a simple cell or prokaryote. The theory suggests that some organelles found inside eukaryotes were once free-living prokaryotes. There is evidence to suggest that prokaryotes were engulfed by larger cells, and were retained inside their membranes where they provided some advantages (Figure **D.5**).

Evidence for this theory includes the fact that two important organelles, mitochondria and chloroplasts, share many characteristics with prokaryotic cells. Both chloroplasts and mitochondria:

- contain ribosomes, which are smaller than those found in other parts of eukaryotic cells but are identical in size to those found in bacteria
- contain small circular pieces of DNA resembling bacterial plasmids in their basic structure
- have their own envelope surrounding them, on the inner membrane of which are proteins synthesised inside the organellle, suggesting that they may have used this ability long ago when they were independent organisms
- can replicate themselves by binary fission.

This evidence supports the theory that these organelles are modified bacteria that were taken in by phagocytosis, early in the evolution of eukaryotic cells, but not digested. Instead they became useful inclusions. The double outer envelope of the chloroplast or mitochondrion may have originated from the bacterial plasma membrane and the membrane of the engulfing phagocytic vesicle, together. Perhaps some of the enclosed bacteria had pigment covering their internal membranes (similar to present–day cyanobacteria). They may have used light energy to make organic molecules and release oxygen, and so became chloroplasts. Others perhaps became efficient at using the oxygen molecules for aerobic energy production, and these became mitochondria.

Aerobic respiration is very much more efficient at releasing energy from organic compounds than anaerobic respiration. This increase in efficiency, along with the process of sexual reproduction, could have been what led to a rapid evolution of life on Earth.

Critics of the endosymbiotic theory might argue that, even if prokaryotes were engulfed by larger cells, there is no certainty that they could be passed on to both daughter cells when the larger cell divided, because there is no special mechanism to ensure this. However, when a

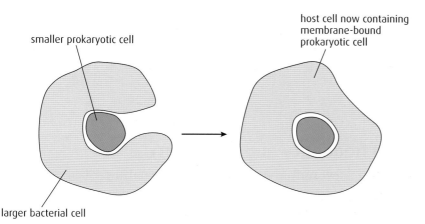

smaller prokaryotic cell

host cell now containing membrane-bound prokaryotic cell

larger bacterial cell

Figure D.5 Organelles sych as chloroplasts may have originated from free-living prokaryotes that were engulfed by larger cells.

Endosymbiosis

Symbiosis means 'life together'. Originally it was used to describe a relationship between organisms where both partners benefited, but now such a relationship is called **mutualism**. Endo means 'inside' and so **endosymbiosis** is describing a relationship taking place inside a cell.

cell divides by binary fission each daughter cell contains some cytoplasm from the parent and so at least one of the daughter cells would contain the engulfed prokaryotes. Both mitochondria and chloroplasts have retained the ability to self-replicate and so their numbers can be increased in the cytoplasm prior to cell division, which increases the chance of both daughter cells containing some. Critics also note that mitochondria and chloroplasts are not able to survive on their own if they are isolated from a cell, which they might be expected to do if they originated from free-living cells. But perhaps over time they have lost the ability to synthesise one or more essential molecules and have come to depend on the 'host' cell to provide them.

1 State **four** processes needed for the spontaneous origin of life on Earth.

2 State **three** possible locations where organic molecules could have been synthesised.

3 State **two** properties of RNA that would have allowed it to play an important role in the origin of life.

4 Outline what protobionts are and their significance to the evolution of cells.

5 Discuss the endosymbiotic theory for the origin of eukaryotic cells.

D2 Species and speciation

Assessment statements

- Define 'allele frequency' and 'gene pool'.
- State that evolution involves a change in allele frequency in a population's gene pool over a number of generations.
- Discuss the definition of the term 'species'.
- Describe three examples of barriers between gene pools.
- Explain how polyploidy can contribute to speciation.
- Compare allopatric and sympatric speciation.
- Outline the process of adaptive radiation.
- Compare convergent and divergent evolution.
- Discuss ideas on the pace of evolution, including gradualism and punctuated equilibrium.
- Describe one example of transient polymorphism.
- Describe sickle-cell anemia as an example of balanced polymorphism.

Allele frequency and evolution

In Chapter **5**, **evolution** was defined as the cumulative change in the heritable characteristics of a population. The 'heritable characteristics' referred to in this definition are all the alleles in the **gene pool** of a population. So, if the frequencies of these alleles in the gene pool do not change, then the population is not evolving. **Allele frequencies** in a population are always fluctuating, in fact, because they depend on the reproductive success of individuals. But if just a single allele shows a change in frequency over a prolonged period of time, then we can say that the population has evolved.

Defining a species

A definition is a precise description of something at a particular time. However, species are not fixed in time because they evolve, and so defining a species is difficult. In the 19th century, large numbers of organisms were collected from around the world and sent to museums, where taxonomists attempted to classify them. At this time, only physical characteristics were observed and measured. **Morphology** is still important in defining a species today, but now additional criteria are used as well. The most important defining characteristic used today is that all members of a species must have the ability to interbreed and produce fertile offspring. In addition, individuals within a species must share similar DNA profiles (Chapter **4**) and be genetically different from individuals of other species, with whom interbreeding does not normally occur.

Problems in defining species

The definition of a species as a group of actually or potentially interbreeding natural populations is helpful, but it does have some problems. For example, by this definition a species cannot include populations that can interbreed but do not do so because they are physically isolated from each other. A population of centipedes in the USA, for instance, is clearly not able to interbreed with a population in Europe, even though they would do so if they were brought together. The definition also cannot include any recently dead or fossilised specimens.

Organisms that always reproduce asexually do not technically fit the definition of a species, which says that individuals must interbreed. Further problems arise in the case of infertile individuals. Humans who are infertile could be excluded from the human species, strictly speaking, simply because they do not produce offspring!

Although the definition states that interbreeding should not happen between different species, sometimes two separate species *are* able to interbreed and produce **hybrids**. For example, among the Eastern Australian rosella parakeets the eastern rosella (*Platycercus eximius*) hybridises with the crimson rosella (*P. elegans)*. However, such hybrids are infertile (see page **371**), so the parent organisms are still considered as separate species.

Speciation

Speciation is the formation of new species from an existing population. Members of the same species and, therefore, the same gene pool can fail to reproduce as a result of a barrier that separates them. New species appear as a result of the population of a single species splitting into two or more new ones.

Gene pool all the different genes in an interbreeding population at a given time

Allele frequency the frequency of a particular allele as a proportion of all the alleles of that gene in a population

Taxonomic confusions

When only physical features were used to identify a species, some difficulties arose. Some bird species show **sexual dimorphisms**, which means that males of the species look very different from the females. Birds of paradise from New Guinea or the peacock and peahen are good examples of this. If morphology alone were used to distinguish species, males and females could be considered taxonomically separate.

Some other species have winter and summer coats. For example, *Mustela erminea* lives in northern regions of Europe and North America. In summer, its fur is brown on the back and pale underneath and its common name is the stoat. In winter, it can turn completely white and is then known by a different common name, an ermine, despite being the same species (Figure **D.7**).

On the other hand, there are some organisms that appear identical but do not interbreed, and are therefore separate species. These are called sibling species. For example, the reed warbler (*Acrocephalus scirpaceus*) and marsh warbler (*A. palustris*) in Britain look exactly the same – the species can only be distinguished by their song.

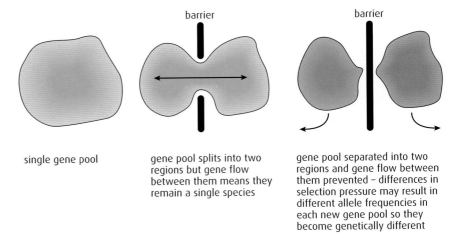

single gene pool

gene pool splits into two regions but gene flow between them means they remain a single species

gene pool separated into two regions and gene flow between them prevented – differences in selection pressure may result in different allele frequencies in each new gene pool so they become genetically different

Figure D.6 Speciation may occur when some kind of barrier divides the gene pool.

Speciation is said to be **sympatric** or **allopatric**.
- **Allopatric speciation** occurs in *different* geographical areas.
- **Sympatric speciation** occurs in the *same* geographical area.

Speciation can only occur if there is a barrier dividing the population (Figure **D.6**). The barrier may take different forms, such as geographical separation, or temporal or behavioural differences. Hybrid infertility may also cause a barrier between gene pools, though it does not lead to speciation.

Allopatric speciation

Allopatric speciation occurs when a physical barrier separates a species into two geographically isolated populations, which then develop independently under the different conditions in the two separated areas, and eventually become unable to interbreed. The barrier might be a natural feature such as a mountain range or a body of water, or it could be a result of human intervention in an environment, such as a major road system or a large conurbation.

One example of allopatric speciation resulting from a natural geographical barrier involves salamanders of the genus *Ensatina*, found on the west coast of the USA. Members of this genus all descended from a founder species that spread southward down each side of the San Joaquin Valley (Figure **D.8**). Conditions were slightly different on the east and

Figure D.7 The ermine and the stoat are both members of the species *Mustela erminea*.

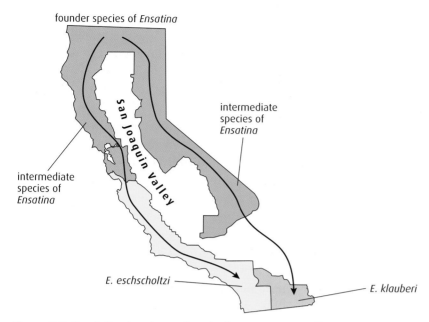

Figure D.8 Speciation in salamanders, in the San Joaquin Valley, western USA.

west sides of the valley, and the separated populations adapted to their own particular environments. The valley in between isolated them from one another. Eventually the two populations met at the southern end of the valley in Southern California but they could no longer interbreed. Two new species, *E. klauberi* and *E. eschscholtzi*, had formed.

Sympatric speciation

A gene pool may become divided without the population being geographically split. Other factors may lead to groups within the population becoming reproductively separated within the same physical environment.

Temporal and behavioural isolation

Temporal isolation occurs when the time of reproduction or behaviour of members of one population of a species is incompatible with that of another. An example is the goldenrod gall fly (*Eurosta solidaginis*) found in eastern and midwestern North America. This fly causes the formation of galls on goldenrod plants (*Solidago* sp.) (Figure **D.9**). Over most of its range, the fly lays its eggs in *S. altissima* but in some places it uses *S. gigantea* as its host. Flies associated with *S. gigantea* emerge earlier in the season than flies associated with *S. altissima* so the males and females of the two forms of fly are ready to mate at slightly different times. This suggests the beginning of a temporal barrier to interbreeding between the two populations.

The two emerging groups of flies also seem to prefer their own species of goldenrod plant and lay their eggs much more frequently in those plants. In addition, females prefer to mate with males of their own group and both of these factors indicate the development of additional behavioural barriers to interbreeding.

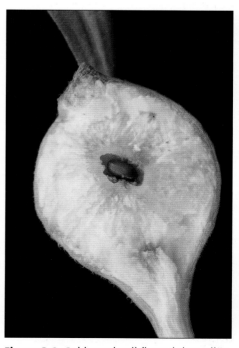

Figure D.9 Goldenrod gall fly and the gall it produces.

At the moment, the two populations can interbreed to produce fertile offspring and so are still a single species, but over time they could become separate species as the temporal and behavioural differences are reinforced and increase their separation.

Polyploidy

Another barrier between two gene pools can occur due to **polyploidy**. A polyploid organism has more than two sets of chromosomes. (Two is the normal number of sets, known as the **diploid** number ($2n$)). Polyploid organisms may have cells containing three or more sets of chromosomes, and are said to be triploid ($3n$), tetraploid ($4n$) and so on.

Polyploidy is widespread in plants but rare in animals. It occurs when sets of chromosomes are not completely separated during cell division and one cell ends up with additional chromosomes.

If the mistake occurs during mitosis and the cell fails to divide after telophase then the cell will become a tetraploid. Each chromosome will have a matching pair and will be able to undergo meiosis to form fertile gametes. A tetraploid can cross with another tetraploid to form fertile offspring in just the same way as normal plants. If a tetraploid crosses with a diploid plant they would produce triploid plants that would be sterile and unable to form gametes. In this case, polyploidy acts as a barrier between the diploid and tetraploid species. The two populations may become so different that they develop into new species.

For example, plants in the genus *Tragopogon*, a member of the sunflower family, demonstrate how speciation can occur. Three diploid species, *T. dubius*, *T. porrifolius*, and *T. pratensis*, were accidentally introduced into North America early in the 20th century. In 1950, two new species were discovered, both of which were tetraploid. Chromosome studies showed that *T. miscellus* ($4n$) was a hybrid produced by the interbreeding of *T. dubius* ($2n$) and *T. pratensis* ($2n$) whereas *T. mirus* ($4n$) was a hybrid of *T. dubius* ($2n$) and *T. porrifolius* ($2n$) (Figure **D.10**).

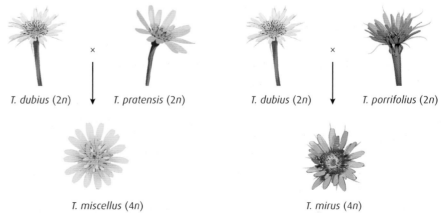

T. dubius (2n)   ×   T. pratensis (2n)   T. dubius (2n)   ×   T. porrifolius (2n)

T. miscellus (4n)   T. mirus (4n)

Figure D.10 Tetraploidy can occur through hybridisation of diploid species.

Hybrid infertility

Barriers between gene pools can also occur as a result of hybrid infertility, although this does not lead to speciation. A hybrid is the offspring of a male and female of two different species. Most plant and animal hybrids are infertile. Ligers and tigons (which are produced as a result of a cross between a lion and a tiger) and mules (which are a cross between a donkey and a horse) are all sterile and unable to produce offspring of their own. They cannot therefore lead to the development of a new species.

Comparing sympatric and allopatric speciation

A summary of the two types of speciation is shown in Table **D.1**.

Sympatric speciation	Allopatric speciation
A new species arises from an existing species that is living in the same area.	A new species arises because a physical barrier separates it from other members of an existing species.
Temporal or behavioural isolation can produce significant changes in the genetic make-up within a species so that a new species is formed.	Physical barriers may include mountain ranges, valleys or bodies of water, or human-made features such as roads, canals or built-up areas.

Table D.1 Comparison of sympatric and allopatric speciation.

Convergent and divergent evolution

As the process of speciation takes place, new species form that no longer resemble one another. When this occurs, species are said to have diverged from their common ancestor in a process known as **divergent evolution**. New species evolve as organisms exploit new habitats and reduce competition by occupying their own specific **niche**. Over generations, physical and behavioural adaptations develop through natural selection that help organisms survive and reproduce in their particular habitat. An example of divergent evolution is the **pentadactyl limb** of vertebrates (Figure **D.11**, overleaf).

Adaptive radiation is a form of divergent evolution, and occurs as new species develop from a common ancestor as they adapt to new environments. Darwin's finches on the Galapagos Islands are a good example of adaptive radiation (Figure **D.12**, overleaf). The ancestral finch species that first arrived on the islands had a small but thick beak for eating small seeds. On the various different Galapagos Islands many other food sources were available – such as buds, insects, fruits, seeds of different sizes, grubs in rotting wood. Any birds with beaks that were a slightly different shape, making them better at using a new food source, would be more likely to survive and pass on that beak shape to their offspring. The change in beak shape would be reinforced with every new generation, eventually producing different groups of birds that were well adapted to feeding on the new foods.

In other situations, organisms that have different ancestors may evolve similar characteristics, because conditions favour these particular features

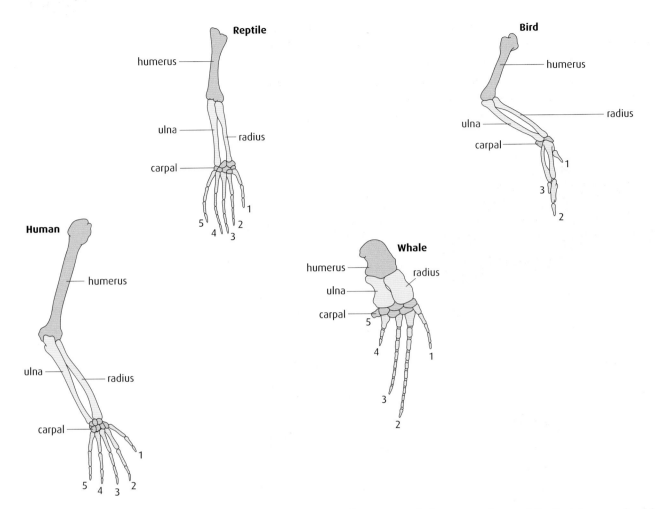

Figure D.11 The development of the pentadactyl limb demonstrates divergent evolution – many forms of the limb have evolved from a common ancestral form.

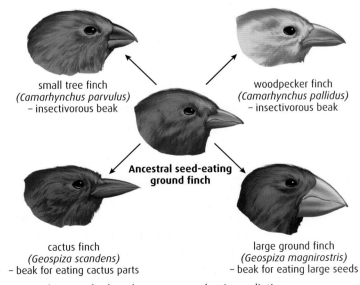

small tree finch
(Camarhynchus parvulus)
– insectivorous beak

woodpecker finch
(Camarhynchus pallidus)
– insectivorous beak

**Ancestral seed-eating
ground finch**

cactus finch
(Geospiza scandens)
– beak for eating cactus parts

large ground finch
(Geospiza magnirostris)
– beak for eating large seeds

Figure D.12 Galapagos finches demonstrate adaptive radiation.

– they make it more likely that an organisms will survive and reproduce successfully in that environment. This is known as **convergent evolution**. An example is the wing of a bat and the wing of an insect (Figure **D.13**). The wings serve similar functions but they are derived from completely different structures. Bats and insects are not closely related.

Figure **D.14** summarises the differences between convergent and divergent evolution.

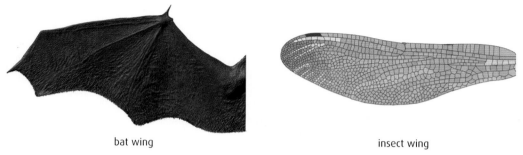

bat wing   insect wing

Figure D.13 The bat's wing is structurally very different from the insect's wing, yet they perform a similar function. This is an example of convergent evolution.

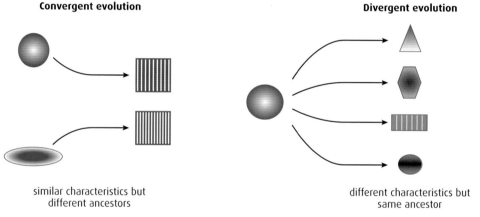

Convergent evolution

similar characteristics but
different ancestors

Divergent evolution

different characteristics but
same ancestor

Figure D.14 These diagrams show the difference between convergent and divergent evolution.

The pace of evolution: gradualism and punctuated equilibrium

Darwin viewed evolution as a slow, steady process called **gradualism**, whereby changes slowly accumulated over many generations and led to speciation. For many species, this seems to be true. A good example of gradualism is the evolution of the horse's limbs, which fossils indicate took around 43 million years to change from the ancestral form to the modern one (Figure **D.15**, overleaf).

In some cases, the fossil record does not contain any intermediate stages between one species and another. A suggested explanation is that fossilisation is such a rare event that the intermediate fossils have simply not been discovered. In 1972, Stephen J Gould (1941–2002) and Niles Eldredge (b. 1943) suggested that the fossils had not been found because

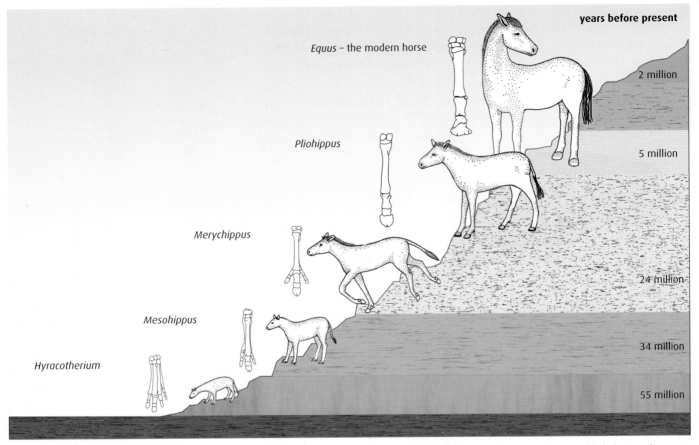

Figure D.15 Some of the many species of fossil horses and the modern horse, *Equus*. The sequence suggests a gradual change from feet with four toes to a single hoof.

they did not exist, and proposed an additional mechanism for evolution called **punctuated equilibrium**. The driving force for evolution is selection pressure, so if the selection pressure is very mild or non-existent then species will tend to remain the same – that is, in equilibrium. When there is a sudden, dramatic change in the environment, there will also be new, intense selection pressures and therefore rapid development of new species (Figure **D.16**).

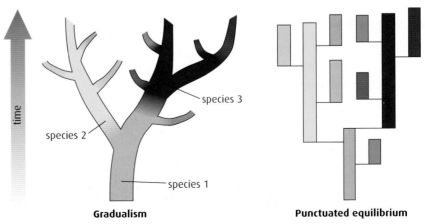

Figure D.16 A gradualism view and a punctuated equilibrium view of evolution.

A good example of intense selection pressure in modern times is the use of antibiotics, which has resulted in the appearance of resistant species of bacteria in very short periods of time. Multiple-resistant *Staphylococcus aureus* (MRSA) is an example of a bacterial pathogen resistant to several antibiotics. It has become adapted to new conditions in which there are many antibiotics in use and has developed new strategies to resist them.

Polymorphism

Polymorphism means 'many forms' and describes a situation where an allele has two different forms, which may be selected for in different environments.

If the environments are stable then the relative frequencies of the different alleles do not change and is known as a **stable polymorphism**.

If the environment changes, the frequencies of the different forms start to change and this known as a **transient polymorphism**.

Transient polymorphism

The most well-documented example of transient polymorphism is provided by the peppered moth (*Biston betularia*), and is known as industrial melanism. The peppered moth occurs in a range of forms from grey and speckled to melanic (black).

The moth is night-flying and so rests on tree trunks during the day where it needs to be camouflaged to avoid being seen and eaten by birds. The speckled form is well camouflaged on lichen-covered trees – so in clean air where lichens can grow selection pressure is for this form. Darker moths are visible and so are eaten by birds (see Figure **5.15** on page **118**).

In the mid 19th century in Britain, the Industrial Revolution resulted in a huge amount of smoke pollution close to industrial cities and caused trees trunks and stone walls to lose their covering of lichens and become blackened. Grey speckled moths were easily seen by predators in these conditions and their numbers fell. On soot-covered trees, dark moths were well camouflaged, so they survived and reproduced. In polluted regions, selection pressure favoured the melanic form and produced a temporary, transient, polymorphism as the numbers of the two forms in the population changed. From 1956 onwards, when the Clean Air Act was passed, there was less soot in the air and lichens began to grow again. The transient polymorphism moved in the opposite direction with the melanic form being selected against and the speckled form favoured.

Balanced polymorphism

When natural selection stabilises two or more alleles in a population so that their frequencies do not change, a balanced polymorphism occurs. Sickle-cell anemia provides an example of a balanced polymorphism that occurs in certain parts of the world. This human blood condition is caused by a mutation in one of the genes for the oxygen-carrying protein hemoglobin. Two alleles of the gene occur – Hb^A and Hb^S – and produce three different phenotypes.

Sudden environmental changes and evolution

65 million years ago most species of dinosaur suddenly became extinct along with millions of other species. This mass extinction may have been due to the impact of the enormous Chicxulub meteor, which caused a very sudden change in conditions on the surface of the Earth. The new conditions could have produced selection pressures that led to the rapid appearance of new species. It was long thought that it was the extinction of the dinosaurs that led to the rise of the mammals and this was supported by the existing fossil evidence. However, recent genetic analysis using data from *Genbank* (an international database of gene sequences held in the USA) has indicated that early mammals were around at least 100 million years ago, 35 million years before the dinosaur extinction. Furthermore, their evolution followed a gradualism path and not a pattern of punctuated equilibrium as the dinosaur extinction theory suggests.

- Most people have the genotype **Hb^{A}Hb^A** and have normal hemoglobin. These individuals do not develop sickle-cell anemia but they are very susceptible to malaria.
- People who are heterozygous **Hb^{A}Hb^S** have sickle-cell trait. They have some sickle-shaped cells and some normal cells, and are resistant to malaria.
- Homozygous individuals **Hb^{S}Hb^S** have sickle-shaped blood cells and are resistant to malaria but develop sickle-cell anemia, which can be fatal.

A balanced polymorphism exists in those parts of Africa where malaria is endemic. Both forms of the allele remain in the population. Heterozygotes are selected for due to their resistance to malaria but both homozygotes are selected against, because they are vulnerable to either malaria or sickle-cell anaemia. An unusually high proportion of the population are heterozygotes because of the resistance to malaria that this genotype confers.

Another example of a balanced polymorphism is seen in the cichlid fish *Perissodus microlepis*, which lives in Lake Tanganyika in Africa. These small predatory fish dart out from hiding places to bite scales off the sides of larger prey fish. *Perissodus* have developed a mouth that is angled to the side so they can attack from behind but avoid being seen (Figure **D.17**). Some of them have a mouth that is angled to the left, so they can efficiently attack the right flank of their prey. But this means that the prey fish will be watching its right flank when in *Perissodus* territory. Other fish have a mouth angled to the right and these fish can attack from the other side. If numbers of 'lefty' *Perissodus* increased, the prey fish would

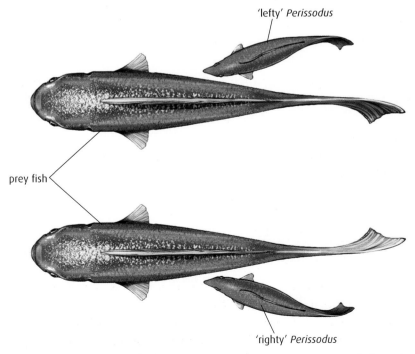

Figure D.17 The 'sidedness' of *Perissodus microlepis* is an example of a balanced polymorphism.

spend more time watching their right flank, giving 'righty' *Perissodus* an advantage. If numbers of 'righty' *Perissodus* increased, the prey fish would spend more time watching their left flank, giving 'lefty' *Perissodus* an advantage. This has resulted in a balanced polymorphism of left-angled and right-angled mouths of *Perissodus* in the lake.

6 Define 'allele frequency' and 'gene pool'.

7 List **three** difficulties with defining the term 'species'.

8 Outline the process of speciation.

9 Outline **two** ideas on the pace of evolution.

D3 Human evolution

Assessment statements

- Outline the method for dating rocks and fossils using radioisotopes, with reference to ^{14}C and ^{40}K.
- Define 'half-life'.
- Deduce the approximate age of materials based on a simple decay curve for a radioisotope.
- Describe the major anatomical features that define humans as primates.
- Outline the trends illustrated by the fossils of *Ardepithecus ramidus*, *Australopithecus* including *A. afarensis* and *A. africanus*, and *Homo* including *H. habilis*, *H. erectus*, *H. neanderthalensis* and *H. sapiens*.
- State that, at various stages in hominid evolution, several species may have coexisted.
- Discuss the incompleteness of the fossil record and the resulting uncertainties about human evolution.
- Discuss the correlation between the change in diet and increase in brain size during hominid evolution.
- Distinguish between 'genetic' and 'cultural' evolution.
- Discuss the relative importance of genetic and cultural evolution in the recent evolution of humans.

Most of our understanding of our human origins has come from looking at the remains of our fossil ancestors. Fossils record the appearance of our long-dead ancestors and their locations tell us where they may have lived, but if we can also estimate the age of the fossil, we can begin to construct a chronology of human history. Establishing the age of fossils can be done with radioactive isotopes.

Dating fossils with radioisotopes

Elements exist in different forms called **isotopes**, which each have a different number of neutrons in their atoms. Carbon exists as different isotopes – carbon-12 (^{12}C) accounts for 98% of carbon atoms, while carbon-14 (^{14}C) is found in very tiny quantities. ^{14}C is known as a **radioisotope** because it is unstable and slowly decays to stable ^{12}C. The rate of decay of any isotope is constant. For ^{14}C it is known that after 5700 years, half the unstable atoms in a sample of carbon will have decayed, so this time period is known as its **half-life**. This can be shown as a graph (Figure **D.18**, overleaf).

Half-life the time taken for half the number of atoms of a radioisotope to decay to a more stable form

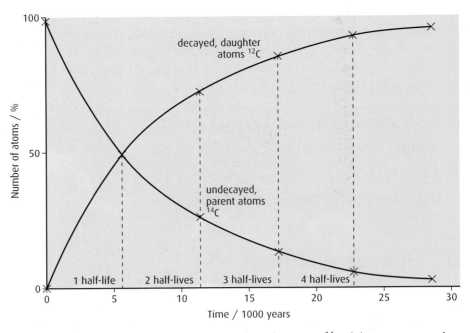

Figure D.18 Graph showing the decay of the radioisotope ^{14}C. If the percentage of remaining ^{14}C in a specimen is 50%, then one half-life has passed. If percentage is 25%, then two half-lives have passed. Carbon dating of fossil specimens with these percentages would tell us that the first fossil is around 5700 years old and the second fossil around 11 400 years old.

Carbon and potassium are used for dating fossils – ^{14}C with a half-life of about 5700 years is useful for dating fossil material between 10^3 and 10^5 years old, while ^{40}K (which decays to the inert gas argon, ^{40}Ar) has a half-life of about 1.3 billion years and is used to date very old fossil material or rocks.

All naturally occurring carbon and potassium are mixtures of isotopes of known proportions, so during its lifetime an organism will accumulate both forms in its tissues as it feeds or photosynthesises. When organisms die no more atoms are accumulated so the naturally occurring ratio will begin to change. As radioisotopes decay, their proportion in the organism will decrease and the proportion of the stable form will increase.

To date fossil material, the proportion of different isotopes is measured to assess the number of half-lives that has passed. This is known as radiocarbon dating.

Humans are primates

Taxonomy is based on shared characteristics. Humans are classified as **primates**, a group within the mammals, which includes lemurs, gibbons, monkeys and great apes. Humans share many physical and genetic characteristics with all these animals. Humans are most closely related to the great apes (orang-utan, gorillas and chimpanzees). We share the vast majority of genes with chimpanzees but the base sequences still differ in many positions. Chimpanzees are the animals most closely related to humans based on sequence comparison.

Some of the major shared characteristics are:

- long limbs and grasping hands with opposable thumbs allowing manipulation of objects
- extremely mobile joints at shoulder and hip, the ball-and-socket joints giving great flexibility of movement
- rotating forelimb, which increases the use of the hand
- retention of collar bone, which stabilises the shoulder allowing body weight to be supported by the arms when moving through trees
- forward-facing eyes and a flattened face, which permits stereoscopic vision.

Trends in the human fossil record

Hominids are a group of primates that walk on two legs. Modern humans are members of this group alive today but many other species of hominid have existed in the past, and some of them were alive at the same time. Our knowledge of these species has been gained entirely from the fossils that have been found.

The examples shown in Table **D.2** (overleaf) are only a few of the species from the human fossil record. They have been radiocarbon dated and given species names based on skull and bone fragments.

Did several hominid species live at the same time?

The data in Table **D.2** show us that, in at least two cases, different species of *Homo* lived in the same place at the same time – *H. africanus* and *H. habilis* lived in Africa at the same time, and *H. neanderthalensis* and *H. sapiens* co-existed in Europe. There is much debate about the degree to which the two species actually intermingled, but they certainly inhabited the same regions for thousands of years. At that time, their populations were small and spread over three continents so it is equally possible they never met at all.

Our understanding of human evolution is based on the fossil record but fossilisation is a rare event and discovering a fossil is also rare (see Chapter **5**).

Hominid species	Lived	Features of head, skull and brain	Reconstructed image of skull	Other features
Ardipithecus ramidus	4.4–4.3 mya (million years ago) in Ethiopia, East Africa	• foramen magnum is more ventral, indicating a trend towards bipedalism (Figure **D.19**) • brain size: unknown	few fossils of this species have been found so the description is uncertain but it seems to have been quite similar to a chimpanzee with some important hominid features	• teeth seem to be intermediate between apes and Australopithecines – incisors are small and canines are smaller and more blunt than in apes, but molars are large and ape-like
Australopithecus afarensis the most well-known specimen of this species is 'Lucy'	3.9–2.9 mya in East Africa	• ape-like face with flat nose and protruding jaws • large, tall lower jaw • brain size: 375–550 cm^3		• large molar teeth similar to *Ardipithecus ramidus*
Australopithecus africanus	3.3–2.5 mya in southern Africa	• slightly flatter face but still with large, tall lower jaw • brain size: 420–500 cm^3		• smaller canines but molars still large
Homo habilis first discovered in Olduvai Gorge in Tanzania; *H. habilis* used simple tools	2.5–1.9 mya in eastern and southern Africa	• face more flattened than *Australopithecus* • smaller lower jaw • brain size: 500–800 cm^3		• smaller teeth • hips form distinct pelvic bowl
Homo erectus specimens of *H. erectus* have been found in Europe and Asia as well as Africa so must have migrated from Africa; *H. erectus* were the first hominids to use fire	1.8–0.3 mya in Africa, Indonesia, Asia, Europe	• face further flattened • skull more rounded with large brow ridges • smaller lower jaw • brain size: 850–1100 cm^3		
Homo neanderthalensis neanderthal man	150 000–30 000 years ago in Europe, western Asia	• face further flattened but still with large brow ridges • rounded skull but lower forehead • brain size: 1200–1625 cm^3		• large teeth and jaw muscles • limbs short relative to torso • may have interbred with *H. sapiens* in Europe
Homo sapiens modern man	130 000 years ago to present	• flat face with no brow ridges • reinforced lower jaw producing a chin • rounded skull with high forehead • brain size: 1200–1500 cm^3		• smaller molars • skeleton is less robust than other ancestors

Table D.2 Some examples of hominid species, from the fossil record.

The fossil record for humans is very patchy and the six examples described in Table **D.2** are only a few of those that have been found. Over the years new fossils have been discovered, dating techniques have become more accurate, and genetic analysis has been applied to fossils where DNA has survived. Consequently, the branching pattern of the human evolutionary tree has been modified many times.

Some evolutionary paths constructed by paleoanthropologists contain 18 or 19 examples but other paleoanthropologists dispute this larger number, saying that what some describe as separate species are merely variations of the same species. With so few fossils to study it is difficult to make the distinctions clear. Figure **D.20** summarises current knowledge about how early hominid species may have been related.

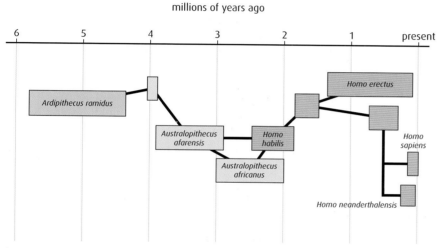

Figure D.20 Early human phylogeny – evolutionary development.

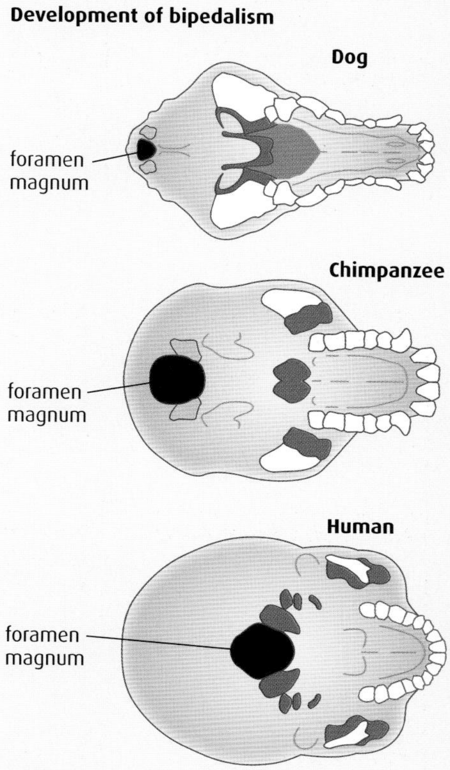

Development of bipedalism

Figure D.19 The point at which the spinal column meets the skull is the foramen magnum. A ventral foramen magnum allows for a more upright body position and bipedal walking.

Quality of evidence

Paleoanthropology as a science has only existed for about 150 years. In 1848, human remains discovered in Gibraltar were the first to be recognised as prehistoric and in 1856 more fossils were found in the Neander Valley in Germany. In 1871, Charles Darwin suggested in his book 'Descent of Man' that humans were probably descended from ape-like ancestors living in tropical jungle. This caused a great deal of controversy, but as time went on more and more fossils were discovered allowing the human evolutionary tree to be pieced together. Much of the early evidence, though, was based on poor archaeology and vital evidence was lost or ignored during excavations. The most recent discoveries are *H. georgicus* in 2002 found in Dmanisi, Georgia, and *H. floresiensis*, which was discovered on the Indonesian island of Flores in 2003. Despite the increasing number of discoveries, the quantity of evidence is still very fragmented – paleoanthropology is a data-poor science.

Questions to consider

1 What makes good evidence to support a scientific theory?
2 Is it acceptable to put forward a theory based on very little or poor evidence?
3 Should new discoveries that appear to support current theory simply be accepted or scrutinised carefully?
4 If a new discovery does not fit the current accepted theory, should it be discarded or incorporated into a new theory?
5 Do paradigm shifts in the theories weaken or strengthen the scientific case for human evolution?

Diet and brain size in hominid evolution

All the hominid fossils found fit into a sequence showing an increasing degree of adaptation to bipedalism, and increasing brain size relative to body size. Large brains require a lot of energy to enable them to function (the brain of *Homo sapiens* uses about 20% of the total energy consumed by the body) and there is evidence to correlate the increase in brain size with changes in the diets of our ancestors.

Human ape ancestors lived in northeast Africa in the Great Rift Valley. Until about five million years ago this was covered in dense forest, but movements of the Earth created a wide valley, and volcanic activity coated the plains with thick ash, which prevented growth of trees. Vegetarian tree-dwelling apes, which ate soft leaves and fruits, had to adapt or become extinct. Australopithecines adapted by developing stronger jaws and teeth to deal with tougher vegetation such as stems, tubers and roots but, as the savannah expanded, the variety of plants decreased and grazing animals started to play an important part in the diet.

Early hominids needed new strategies to access this rich source of meat, which provided an increased supply of protein, fat and energy. Natural selection favoured individuals with large brains who could develop new strategies for hunting and work in groups to kill large animals. Meat provided the nutrients to build a larger, thinking brain as well as the energy to fuel its activity.

The increase in meat in the diet shows a positive correlation with increased brain size and also with the development of more sophisticated tools for hunting. The graph in Figure **D.21** shows how hominid brain size has increased over time. A clear positive trend can be seen.

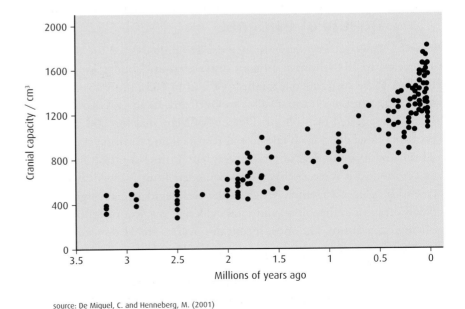

source: De Miguel, C. and Henneberg, M. (2001)
'Variation in hominid brain size: How much is due to method?' *Homo* **52**(1) pp 3–58

Figure D.21 Graph to show how hominid brain size has changed over time.

Genetic and cultural evolution

Genetic evolution of humans is the change, over millions of years, in the genome of populations. Genetic evolution occurs as a result of mutations and these may be inherited. Genetic evolution includes the change to bipedalism, changes in teeth and increase in brain size. All these features are passed on from parents to their offspring. *Homo sapiens* is the only species of human on the planet today but our evolutionary history indicates that there have been many species that have not survived (Figure **D.20**, page **381**).

Cultural evolution, on the other hand, does not involve genetic changes and can take place over very short periods of time, even within a generation. Cultural evolution involves changes in behaviour, social organisation, ideas, communication, teaching and learning. These are acquired characteristics that do not have a genetic basis, though the ability to acquire them may be genetically determined. Cultural evolution cannot result in speciation.

The rise of agriculture brought about an enormous alteration in social organisation for humans. Instead of living in small mobile hunter–gatherer groups, humans began to settle in larger fixed communities, and the rise of different religious faiths further affected these new social organisations. The invention of the printing press had a remarkable impact on communication and, in more recent history, other examples of technology such as the invention of radio, television, telephone and the internet have had a similar impact on human cultural development.

> **Evolution of language**
>
> Scientists have discovered that the evolution of language correlates to changes in genes between populations. Examining a genetic map and how genes have changed is similar to looking at a language map and how languages have changed.

10 Which radioisotope would be used for dating fossils of *Australopithecus*? Give the reason for choosing this radioisotope.

11 Discuss why the evolutionary history of humans is uncertain.

12 Discuss the relative importance of genetic and cultural evolution in the evolution of humans.

D4 The Hardy–Weinberg principle

Assessment statements

- Explain how the Hardy–Weinberg equation is derived.
- Calculate allele, genotype and phenotype frequencies for two alleles of a gene, using the Hardy–Weinberg equation.
- State the assumptions made when the Hardy–Weinberg equation is used.

The Hardy–Weinberg equation

Godfrey Hardy (1877–1947) was an English mathematician and Wilhelm Weinberg (1862–1937) was a German physician who worked independently at the start of the 20th century on modelling the frequencies of alleles in the gene pool. They concluded that if the allele frequencies in a gene pool were stable they could be calculated with a simple equation based on Mendelian genetics.

The equation that they produced can tell us how a population is changing or predict the outcome of genetic crosses. As a species evolves, the frequency of alleles in the population changes. The Hardy–Weinberg equation is used to calculate and model allele frequencies.

To do this the letters p and q are used — p represents the frequency of the dominant allele and q is the frequency of the recessive allele. If the frequencies of the alleles on chromosomes are considered, $p + q = 1$ because the chromosomes that do not have the dominant allele must have the recessive one.

Deriving the Hardy–Weinberg equation

Assume a gene has two alleles, **A** and **a**. The frequency of the dominant allele, **A**, is represented by p, and the frequency of the recessive allele, **a**, is represented by q. For example, in a population of 100 individuals there will be 200 alleles. If 170 of these are the dominant allele then the remaining 30 must be the recessive allele. Therefore:

$$p = \frac{170}{200} \times 100 = 85\%$$

$$q = \frac{30}{200} \times 100 = 15\%$$

Populations, though, are always represented by 1, so in this example p would be 0.85 and q would be 0.15. Always $p + q = 1$.

In a randomly mating population, the possible combinations of alleles can be determined from a Punnett grid.

		male allele	
		A	a
female allele	A	AA	Aa
	a	Aa	aa

Replacing the alleles with their frequencies gives:

	frequency of dominant allele, *p*	frequency of recessive allele, *q*
frequency of dominant allele, *p*	p^2	pq
frequency of recessive allele, *q*	pq	q^2

These four genotypes represent the total population, which is always 1. So:

$$p^2 + 2pq + q^2 = 1$$

This is the **Hardy–Weinberg equation**.

Conditions for the Hardy–Weinberg equation to work

The Hardy–Weinberg equation is an example of a mathematical model being used to predict and show what happens in nature. All models of this type only work if certain assumptions are made because, in reality, natural systems are very complex and have many variables that affect them.

Evolution is defined as the change in frequency of an allele in a gene pool, so if the frequency remains constant, then the population is not evolving. However, populations do evolve as a result of selection pressure, so Hardy and Weinberg listed seven assumptions in order for the equation to be applied to allele frequencies in a population that was not evolving.

1 There is no mutation that would affect the allele frequency.
2 There is no natural selection – the frequency of the alleles over time should not vary.
3 The population is large because the equation is based on proportions and percentages so as numbers increase so does the reliability of the equation.
4 All members of the population breed.
5 Mating is random between individuals who have the alleles – the equation will not work for characteristics carried on the sex chromosomes.
6 Each mating produces the same number of offspring.
7 There is no immigration or emigration to alter the allele frequencies.

Using the Hardy–Weinberg equation to calculate allele frequencies

Worked example 1

If a genetic condition is caused by a recessive allele **d** and the frequency we predict in the population for this allele is 21%, what is the frequency of the dominant healthy allele in the population?

Or, putting the question another way:

if $q = 0.21$ what is p?

$$p + q = 1$$

so $\quad p = 1 - q = 0.79$

This means that, for this gene, 79% of the gene pool is made up of the allele **D**. This gives us information about the frequency of alleles, *not* the frequency of the genotypes. We cannot say that 79% of the population is unaffected by the condition.

Worked example 2

Phenylthiocarbamide (PTC) is a compound that tastes very bitter to some people, whereas to others it is virtually tasteless. Tasting is controlled by a dominant allele (**T**). Two populations were sampled – Australian Aboriginal people and the Quecha people of Peru. Both sample sizes were 500. In the Australian sample, 245 people were non-tasters and in the Quecha sample 20 people were non-tasters. Calculate the allele frequencies in these two samples.

Step 1 Non-tasters are homozygous recessives (**tt**) and are therefore represented by q^2.

Step 2 So for Australian Aboriginals the proportion of people who are non-tasters is calculated as:

$$\frac{245}{500} = 0.49$$

so $\qquad q^2 = 0.49$

therefore $\quad q = 0.7$

The frequency of the non-tasting allele among the Aboriginal people is 0.7.

Step 3 Since $\qquad p + q = 1$

$$p = 0.3$$

The frequency of the tasting allele among the Aboriginal people is 0.3.

Step 4 In the sample of Quecha people, 20 were non-tasters, so the proportion of Quecha people who are non-tasters is:

$$\frac{20}{500} = 0.04$$

so $\qquad q^2 = 0.04$

therefore $\quad q = 0.2$

The frequency of the non-tasting allele among the Quecha people is 0.2.

Step 5 Since $\qquad p + q = 1$

$$p = 0.8$$

The frequency of the tasting allele among the Quecha people is 0.8.

Using the Hardy–Weinberg equation to calculate genotype frequencies

Worked example 3

Phenylketonuria (PKU) is a condition in humans caused by a recessive allele on chromosome 12. Newborn babies are screened for this condition because without treatment it can cause serious problems in brain development. Since it is recessive, it can only be inherited if both parents are carriers (heterozygotes). In a survey from all the maternity wards of hospitals within one state in the USA, 405 babies from a total of 200 000 babies were found to have the mutation. Use this data to determine the number of babies that were heterozygous.

Step 1 Since PKU is recessive, a baby with PKU must be homozygous recessive, with the frequency q^2.

The frequency of q^2 is $\dfrac{405}{200\,000} = 0.002\,025$.

Step 2 Therefore $q = 0.045$, therefore $p = 0.955$.

Step 3 Carriers are heterozygous and their frequency in the population is $2pq$. Using the equation:

$2pq = 2 \times 0.955 \times 0.045 = 0.08595$.

Step 4 So in a population of 200 000, there will be 0.08595 × 200 000 = 17 190 heterozygotes.

In this sample there were 17 190 babies who were heterozygous, and therefore carriers of PKU.

You can use a table like this to help you solve similar problems:

Allele frequency	recessive **a**	q	
	dominant **A**	p	
Genotype frequency	homozygous recessive **aa**	q^2	
	heterozygous **Aa**	pq	
	homozygous dominant **AA**	p^2	

Using the Hardy–Weinberg equation to calculate phenotype frequencies

Worked example 4

Some flower colours in snapdragon plants are determined by codominant alleles. Pure-breeding red flowers crossed with pure-breeding white flowers produce pink flowers. The plants die at the end of the year but grow again the next year from seeds they released.

In an investigation of phenotype frequencies, some students sowed a $100\,m^2$ greenhouse with a seed mixture that contained twice as many seeds from pure-breeding white-flowered plants as from pure-breeding red-flowered plants. Apart from maintenance, the plants were left to grow and reproduce randomly for three generations in order to allow thorough mixing of the alleles through cross-pollination.

Predict the numbers of each phenotype in a final sample of 1000 plants.

Step 1 If there were twice as many 'white' seeds as 'red' in the mixture of seeds, the frequency of the red allele $p = 0.333$ and frequency of the white allele $q = 0.667$.

Step 2 In a population:

$p^2 + 2pq + q^2 = 1$

Therefore, number of red-flowered plants in the population $= p^2 \times 1000$
$$= 0.333^2 \times 1000$$
$$= 111$$

Step 3 Number of white-flowered plants in the population $= q^2 \times 1000$
$$= 0.667^2 \times 1000$$
$$= 445$$

Step 4 Number of pink-flowered plants in the population $= 2pq \times 1000$
$$= 2 \times 0.333 \times 0.667 \times 1000$$
$$= 444$$

D5 Phylogeny and systematics

Assessment statements

- Outline the value of classifying organisms.
- Explain the biochemical evidence provided by the universality of DNA and protein structures for the common ancestry of living organisms.
- Explain how variations in specific molecules can indicate phylogeny.
- Discuss how biochemical variations can be used as an evolutionary clock.
- Define 'clade' and 'cladistics'.
- Distinguish, with examples, between 'analogous' and 'homologous' characteristics.
- Outline the methods used to construct cladograms and the conclusions that can be drawn from them.
- Construct a simple cladogram.
- Analyse cladograms in terms of phylogenetic relationships.
- Discuss the relationship between cladograms and the classification of living organisms.

Aristotle (384–322 BC) grouped organisms into plants and animals. He then divided plants into three groups based on stem shape, and animals also into three groups based on where they lived – on land, in water or in the air. A further subdivision was based on whether the animal had red blood or not. Aristotle also devised a binomial system but it was not based on evolutionary relationships.

Classifying organisms

With several million species of organism already known, and more being discovered every day, some way of grouping and organising them is essential. Classification enables scientists to identify newly found or unknown organisms, to see how organisms are related in evolutionary terms and to make predictions about the characteristics that organisms in a group are likely to have or share.

The Greek philosopher Aristotle attempted to devise a classification system 2000 years ago and many other biologists since then have added to and modified his system. Our modern biological classification began with the work of Carolus Linnaeus (1707–1778) who grouped organisms based on shared characteristics and devised the binomial system of naming organisms by their genus and species. He presented this work in his book *Systema Naturae* (1735). A natural classification such as the one devised by Linnaeus is based on identification of homologous structures that indicate a common evolutionary history. If these characteristics are shared between organisms then it is likely that they are related.

There are four main reasons why organisms need to be classified:
- to impose order and organisation on our knowledge
- to give species a clear and universal name, because common names vary from place to place
- to identify evolutionary relationships – if two organisms share particular characteristics then it is likely that they are related to each other, and the more characteristics they share then the closer the relationship
- to predict characteristics – if members of a particular group share characteristics then it is likely that other newly discovered members of that group will have at least some of those same characteristics.

Analogous and homologous characteristics

Analogous structures are those that have the same function but different evolutionary origins. **Homologous structures** have the same evolutionary origin and either the same function or a different function. Only homologous structures are useful is establishing relationships between species.

Figure **D.13** (page **373**) shows the analogous structures of the bat wing and the insect wing. Other examples of **analogous** structures include:

- the eye of a butterfly and the eye of an octopus – the butterfly's eye is composed of many different tiny lenses known as ommatidia, whereas the eye of an octopus has a cornea, iris, lens and retina; both eyes perceive light but their evolutionary origins are quite different
- the mandible of a locust and the teeth of an antelope – both structures break up food required by the organism but the mandible is formed from chitin, while mammal teeth contain dentine and are covered with enamel; the two structures are made from very different materials that are not related to one another.

Examples of **homologous** structures include:

- the forelimb of a lizard and the flipper of a dolphin – these limbs are homologous and are built on the pentadactyl limb (Figure **D.11**, page **372**); they have a common ancestry even though their functions are now different
- the sting of an ant and the ovipositor of a cricket – these have also arisen from similar structures despite having different functions in modern organisms.

The universality of DNA and protein structures

Despite the incredible complexity of life, the building components of living organisms are not only simple in structure but are also universal.

- All living organisms use DNA built from the same four bases to store their genetic information and most use the same triplet code during translation. The few exceptions include mitochondria, chloroplasts and a group of bacteria.
  (Viruses are not included, as they are not classified as organisms. However, most do use DNA, with some using RNA, as their genetic material, and most use the same triplet code.)
- Proteins are built up from amino acids and, although chemists can now synthesise any amino acid, living organisms just make use of the same 20. In most cases, if a gene from one organism is transferred into another, it will produce the same polypeptide (if the introns have been removed from it).
- Furthermore, each amino acid synthesised in the laboratory exists in two forms – the L form and the D form. In Miller and Urey's experiment (Figure **D.2**, page **362**) the amino acids produced were in both forms. But in living organisms, only the L form is found.

All these facts indicate a common origin of life and provide evidence to support the view that all organisms have evolved from a common ancestor.

Molecules, phylogeny and evolutionary clocks

Phylogenetics is the study of how closely related organisms are. The modern approach is to use molecular phylogenetics, which examines the sequences of DNA bases or of amino acids in the polypeptides of different organisms. A **phylogeny** is the evolutionary history of a group of organisms. Species that are the most genetically similar are likely to be more closely related.

We can expect that related organisms will have the same molecules carrying out particular functions and that these molecules will have similar structures. So by comparing proteins in different groups of organisms and checking them for similarities in amino acid sequences, it is possible to trace their ancestry. Chlorophyll, hemoglobin, insulin and cytochrome c, which are found in many different species, have all been studied in this way. Cytochrome c is found in the electron transport chain in mitochondria. Its primary structure contains between 100 and 111 amino acids and the sequence has been determined for a great many plants and animals.

Below are the amino acid sequences of corresponding parts of the cytochrome c from five animals. Each letter represents one amino acid. Humans and chimpanzees have identical molecules indicating that the two species are closely related. There is only one difference (shown in red) between the human cytochrome c and that of a rhesus monkey but rabbits and mice have nine differences when compared with humans, which indicates they are less closely related. This biochemical evidence supports the classification of the animals that has been made from morphological observations.

Human:

mgdvekgkki fimkcsqcht vekggkhktg pnlhglfgrk tgqapgysyt aanknkgiiw gedtlmeyle npkkyipgtk mifvgikkke eradliaylk katne

Chimpanzee:

mgdvekgkki fimkcsqcht vekggkhktg pnlhglfgrk tgqapgysyt aanknkgiiw gedtlmeyle npkkyipgtk mifvgikkke eradliaylk katne

Rhesus monkey:

mgdvekgkki fimkcsqcht vekggkhktg pnlhglfgrk tgqapgysyt aanknkgitw gedtlmeyle npkkyipgtk mifvgikkke eradliaylk katne

Rabbit:

mgdvekgkki fvqkcaqcht vekggkhktg pnlhglfgrk tgqavgfsyt danknkgitw gedtlmeyle npkkyipgtk mifagikkkd eradliaylk katne

Mouse:

mgdvekgkki fvqkcaqcht vekggkhktg pnlhglfgrk tgqaagfsyt danknkgitw gedtlmeyle npkkyipgtk mifagikkkg eradliaylk katne

Genetic changes are brought about by mutation and, provided a mutation is not harmful, it will be retained within the genome. Differences in DNA accumulate over time at an approximately even rate so that the number of differences between genomes (or the polypeptides that they specify) can be used as an approximate evolutionary clock. This information can tell us how far back in time species split from their common ancestor. A greater number of differences in a polypeptide indicates that there has been more time for DNA mutations to accumulate than if the number is smaller.

One way in which DNA molecules are compared is by hybridisation (Figure **D.22**). If a specific DNA sequence from an insect, a reptile and a mammal are compared in this way, the number of the differences between the mammal and the reptile might be found to be 40, and between the insect and the mammal 72. We can conclude that the reptile is more closely related to the mammal than the insect is. We can also estimate that the split between the insect and the mammal occurred almost twice as far back in time as that between the reptile and the mammal.

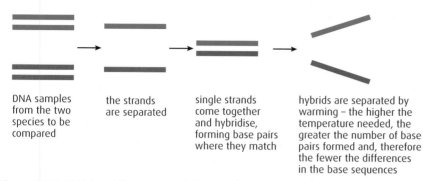

DNA samples from the two species to be compared | the strands are separated | single strands come together and hybridise, forming base pairs where they match | hybrids are separated by warming – the higher the temperature needed, the greater the number of base pairs formed and, therefore the fewer the differences in the base sequences

Figure D.22 DNA hybridisation: a technique to compare DNA from different species.

From this data we can construct a phylogenetic tree that shows the relationship between these three species (Figure **D.23**).

The phylogenetic tree in Figure **D.24** has been constructed in a similar way from DNA analysis of the dog family. It shows that the domestic dog and the grey wolf are very closely related, but the grey wolf and Ethiopian wolf are more distantly related. The black-backed jackal and golden jackal are also very distantly related.

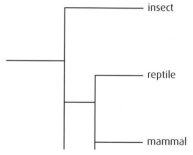

Figure D.23 Phylogenetic tree that shows the relationship between insects, reptiles and mammals.

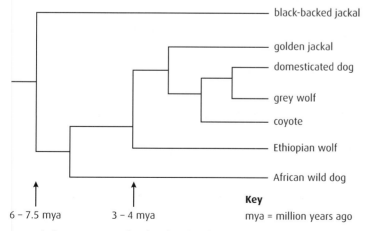

black-backed jackal
golden jackal
domesticated dog
grey wolf
coyote
Ethiopian wolf
African wild dog

6 – 7.5 mya   3 – 4 mya

Key
mya = million years ago

Figure D.24 Phylogenetic tree for the dog family.

Clades and cladistics

Cladistics is a method of classification that groups organisms together according to the characteristics that have evolved most recently. Diagrams called **cladograms** divide groups into separate branches known as **clades**.

Clade a group of organisms, both living and extinct, that includes an ancestor and all the descendants of that ancestor

Cladistics a method of classifying organisms using cladograms to analyse a range of their characteristics

One branch ends in a group that has characteristics the other group does not share. A clade contains the most recent common ancestor of the group and its descendants.

Figure **D.25** shows five organisms forming part of an evolutionary tree.

- Organisms 1, 2, 3, 4 and 5 belong to the yellow clade.
- Organisms 1 and 2 belong to the blue clade.
- Organisms 3, 4 and 5 belong to the green clade.
- Organisms 4 and 5 belong to the red clade.
- The common ancestor for each clade is shown by the coloured spot.

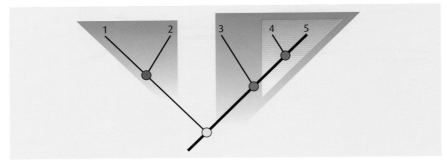

Figure D.25 A cladogram with four clades.

Constructing and analysing cladograms

In order to construct a cladogram, it is necessary to start with the group of organisms to be included and then identify the characteristics that appear to be homologous.

For example the organisms could be:

- sharks
- amphibians
- reptiles
- birds
- mammals

The selection of characteristics might be:

- vertebrae
- bony skeleton
- amniotic egg
- internal fertilisation
- hair
- placenta
- feathers

A table can be drawn, using a plus or minus to denote whether a characteristic is present or absent (Table **D.3**).

	Sharks	Mammals	Birds	Reptiles	Amphibians
Vertebrae	+	+	+	+	+
Bony skeleton	–	+	+	+	+
Amniotic egg	–	+	+	+	–
Internal fertilisation	–	+	+	+	–
Hair	–	+	–	–	–
Placenta	–	+	–	–	–
Feathers	–	–	+	–	–

Table D.3 Presence or absence of chosen characteristics for chosen organisms.

Then the table is rearranged so that there is an increasing number of plus symbols for the characteristics from left to right (Table **D.4**).

	Sharks	Amphibians	Reptiles	Birds	Mammals
Vertebrae	+	+	+	+	+
Bony skeleton	–	+	+	+	+
Amniotic egg	–	–	+	+	+
Internal fertilisation	–	–	+	+	+
Hair	–	–	–	–	+
Placenta	–	–	–	–	+
Feathers	–	–	–	+	–

Table D.4 Rearranged Table **D.3**.

Next a cladogram can be drawn (Figure **D.26**). All the organisms in this group have vertebrae, so this characteristic is placed at the base of the diagram. Then the organism with the fewest recent characteristics branches off first – the sharks, in this case. All except the sharks have a bony skeleton so the shark must branch off before this characteristic. Amphibians do not have an amniotic egg or internal fertilisation and so must branch off before these characteristics, and so on. Neither birds nor reptiles have a placenta or hair and so must branch off together. Since birds have feathers and reptiles do not this creates an additional branch.

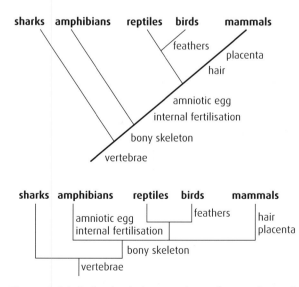

Figure D.26 A simple cladogram, drawn in two alternative formats. Each branch point is called a node.

Organism	Number of amino acid differences from human
human	0
chimpanzee	0
rhesus monkey	1
rabbit	9
mouse	9

Table D.5 Variation in the amino acid sequence of cytochrome c.

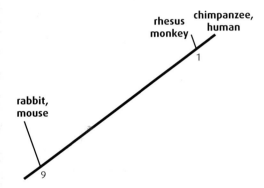

Figure D.27 A cladogram for five mammal species.

Cladograms and the classification of living organisms

Cladograms or phylogenetic trees can be produced using information from fossils, morphology, physiology and behaviour, or molecular data. In most cases, they will agree with each other, or the differences will be small. When there is uncertainty, a second cladogram, built up using a different feature can be constructed for comparison. Each cladogram can be thought of as a hypothesis about the relationships of the organisms it contains.

A disadvantage of the cladogram shown in Figure **D.26** is that gives no indication of how close or far apart the branching points are. But if molecular data are used then the cladogram can be drawn to scale based on the number of molecular differences. The cytochrome c differences given on page **390** can be tabulated as shown in Table **D.5**.

There are no differences between rabbit and mouse so they have to be drawn together at the end of a branch and the same applies to the chimpanzee and human. Rhesus monkey differs from chimpanzee and human by only one amino acid and so the branch point must be 1 unit from the end. Rabbit and mouse differ by 9 amino acids and so the branch point must be 9 units further down.

The cladogram could be simply drawn as shown in Figure **D.27**.

Biochemical analysis of other molecules or comparison of DNA sequences would be needed to complete the separation of rabbit from mouse and human from chimpanzee.

Occasionally a cladogram based on molecular data indicates an evolutionary relationship that disagrees with other or older versions. There are two possible reasons for this. First, convergent evolution can bring about morphological similarities that could be misleading, and secondly the molecular interpretation is based on the probability of change occurring at the same rate in a 'Darwinian' manner. This may not be the case as chance events could cause it to speed up or slow down and DNA analysis can be obscured by multiple point mutations which make it difficult to identify the 'true' evolution of a stretch of DNA. Nevertheless, where the different methods support each other, the evidence is more robust and where there is disagreement, it provokes scientific debate and the search for further evidence to support either one argument or the other. Cladistics is not a subjective method of classification as older methods used to be and as such it is a good example of the scientific method of studying organisms.

13 Explain the difference between homologous and analogous characteristics.

14 Outline how biochemical differences can be used to give an indication of the pace of evolution.

15 Outline the reasons why it is useful to classify organisms.

End-of-chapter questions

1 **HL** List **six** conditions that must apply for a population to be in a Hardy–Weinberg equilibrium. (3)

2 **HL** Tay-Sachs disease is a human genetic abnormality caused by a recessive allele. The condition damages the nervous system and is usually fatal by the age of four or five years. The frequency of the allele varies in different populations. In people of eastern and central European Jewish descent, the frequency of the condition is 1 in 3600 live births. Use the Hardy–Weinberg equation to calculate:

   a the frequency of the recessive allele in this population (1)

   b the frequency of the normal dominant allele in this population. (1)

   In Europe as a whole the frequency of Tay-Sachs disease in the general population is 1 in every 275 000 live births.

   c How many times more frequent is the Tay-Sachs allele in the Jewish population than it is in the European population? (1)

   (total 3 marks)

3 **HL** In a wild and randomly breeding population of the Californian dune mouse, 640 had white fur and 360 had black fur. White is dominant to black. Use the Hardy–Weinberg equation to calculate:

   a the frequency of the dominant allele (1)

   b the number of heterozygous white mice in the population. (1)

   (total 2 marks)

4 **HL** Cystic fibrosis is another human genetic abnormality that is determined by a recessive allele. In Europe the frequency of the condition is 1 in 25 000 live births. Use the Hardy–Weinberg equation to calculate:

   a the frequency of the cystic fibrosis allele (1)

   b the number of carriers in a population of 10 000 people. (1)

   (total 2 marks)

5 **HL** Why should analogous characteristics not be used when constructing a cladogram? (2)

6 **HL** Discuss how the analysis of biochemical molecules can be used to investigate the common ancestry of living organisms. (6)

7 The mechanisms of speciation in ferns have been studied in temperate and tropical habitats. One group of three species from the genus *Polypodium* lives in rocky areas in temperate forests in North America. Members of this group have similar morphology (form and structure). Another group of four species from the genus *Pleopeltis* live at different altitudes in tropical mountains in Mexico and Central America. Members of this group are morphologically distinct.

Data from the different species within each group was compared in order to study the mechanisms of speciation.

Genetic identity was determined by comparing the similarities of certain proteins and genes in each species. Values between 0 and 1 were assigned to pairs of species to indicate the degree of similarity in genetic identity. A value of 1 would mean that all the genetic factors studied were identical between the species being compared.

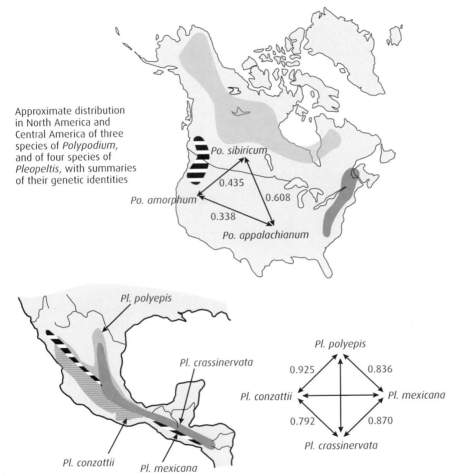

Approximate distribution in North America and Central America of three species of *Polypodium*, and of four species of *Pleopeltis*, with summaries of their genetic identities

source: Haufler, C, Hooper, E and Therrien, J (2000) *Plant Species Biology*, 15, pp 223–236

a Compare the geographic distributions of the two groups. (1)

b **i** Identify, giving a reason, which group, *Polypodium* or *Pleopeltis*, is most genetically diverse. (1)
   ii Identify the **two** species that are most similar genetically. (1)

c Suggest how the process of speciation could have occurred in *Polypodium*. (1)

d In which of the two groups have the species been genetically isolated for the longest time? Explain your answer. (2)

(total 6 marks)
© IB Organization 2009

8 Comparison of mammalian brain areas has often focused on the differences in absolute size. However, in an experiment, scientists compared the sizes of 11 different brain areas relative to the total brain size for various primate species. A *cerebrotype* was then defined for each species, which reflected the relative sizes of different brain areas. The diagram below shows the clustering of cerebrotypes within primates.

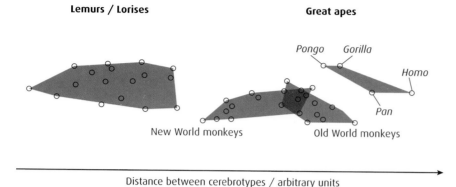

source: Clark, D A *et al.* (2001) *Nature*, 411, pp 189–193

The relationship among hominoids was constructed using the cerebrotype data and is shown below. The evolutionary trees derived from DNA sequences and bone and tooth structure (morphology) are also shown.

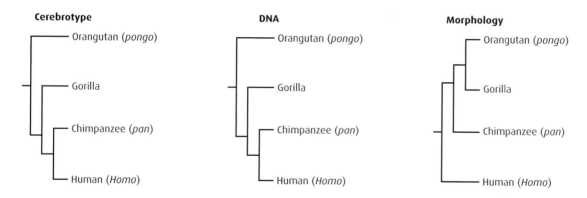

a Deduce, using the cluster diagram, which group of primates is the least related to the Great apes. (1)

b Compare the cerebrotypes of the New World monkeys and the Old World monkeys. (2)

c Explain, using the data, which evolutionary tree the cerebrotypes support. (2)

d In order to build the morphology tree, some of the fossilised bones and teeth had to be dated. Outline a method for such dating. (2)

(total 7 marks)
© IB Organization 2009

9 A comparison was made of the base sequences of genes coding for the same four proteins found in three different mammals: the cow, sheep and pig. The graph below shows the differences in base sequence expressed as a percentage.

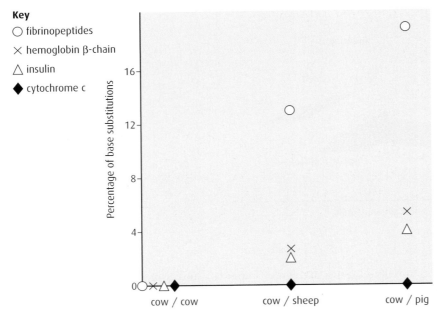

source: Goodenough, U (1978) *Genetics*, 2nd edition, Holt, Rinehart and Winston, p 759

a Identify a protein that is identical in all three mammals. (1)

b Calculate the difference in the percentage of base substitutions for the hemoglobin β–chain and fibrinopeptides when comparing the cow with sheep. (1)

c Deduce, giving a reason, whether the ancestors of pigs or sheep diverged more recently from those of cows. (1)

d Explain how the variations in these molecules can indicate the evolutionary history of these groups of mammals. (2)

(total 5 marks)
© IB Organization 2009

10 HL River dolphins live in freshwater habitats or estuaries. They have a number of features in common which distinguish them from other dolphins: long beaks, flexible necks, very good echolocation and very poor eyesight. Only four families of river dolphin have been found in rivers around the world.

River	River Dolphin Family
Amazon, Brazil	Iniidae
La Plata, Argentina	Pontoporiidae
The Yangtze, China	Lipotidae
The Indus and Ganges, India	Platanistidae

Evolutionary biologists have tried to determine how closely related these river dolphins are to one another. River dolphins are members of the group of toothed whales. Three lines of evidence were analysed producing three cladograms (family trees) for all the toothed whales. The evidence to construct these cladograms came from the morphology (form and structure) of fossil toothed whales (I), the morphology of living toothed whales (II) and the molecular sequences from living toothed whales (III).

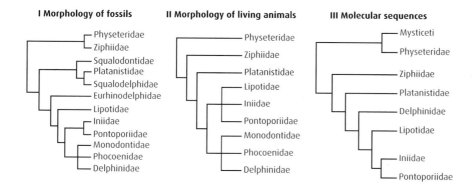

source: Hamilton, H et al. (2001) Proc R Soc Lond B, 268 pp 549–556

a Suggest a reason why there are more families present in cladogram I, produced from the morphology of fossils, than for the other cladograms. (1)

b Using only the data from cladogram III, identify which other family of river dolphins is most closely related to Platanistidae. (1)

c State what material would be used to produce cladogram III, based on the molecular sequences of living toothed whales. (1)

The tree using the data from the morphology of living animals (II) indicates that the families are more closely related than the tree using molecular sequences (III) from the same animals.

d Explain how these dolphins can look so similar when in fact they may not be so closely related. (3)

These cladograms show the species that share common ancestors but do not show how long ago they diverged from one another.

e Outline further evidence that would be needed to determine when these families of toothed whales diverged. (2)

(total 8 marks)
© IB Organization 2009

11 **HL** Molecular and radioactive dating of fossils are used to determine the phylogeny of organisms. Turtles are organisms with a long evolutionary history, making them an ideal group to study. Below is a phylogeny of some turtle genera developed using both fossil and molecular dating.

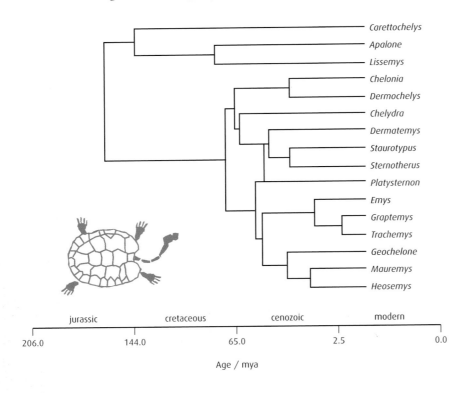

source: Near T J, Meylan P A and Shaffer H B, Assessing Concordance of Fossil Calibration Points in Molecular Clock Studies: An Example Using Turtles, *The American Naturalist* (Feb 2005), vol. 165, issue 2, pp 137–146. Copyright © 2008. University of Chicago Press

   a Identify the oldest turtle genus. (1)

   b Compare the phylogeny of *Chelonia* with *Graptemys*. (2)

   c Discuss which turtle genera are most closely related. (3)

(total 6 marks)

© IB Organization 2009

12 **HL** Below are the complete amino acid sequences of cytochrome c for five animals. The amino acids are in blocks of 10 apart from the last four.

guinea pig gdvekgkkif vqkcaqchtv ekggkhktgp nlhglfgrkt gqaagfsytd anknkgitwg edtlmeylen pkkyipgtkm ifagikkkge radliaylkk atne

grey whale gdvekgkkif vqkcaqchtv ekggkhktgp nlhglfgrkt gqavgfsytd anknkgitwg eetlmeylen pkkyipgtkm ifagikkkge radliaylkk atne

duck gdvekgkkif vqkcsqchtv ekggkhktgp nlhglfgrkt gqaegfsytd anknkgitwg edtlmeylen pkkyipgtkm ifagikkkse radliaylkd atak

alligator gdvekgkkif vqkcaqchtv ekggkhktgp nlhgligrkt gqapgfsyte anknkgitwg eetlmeylen pkkyipgtkm ifagikkkpe radliaylke atsn

bullfrog gdvekgkkif vqkcaqchtc ekggkhkvgp nlygligrkt gqaagfsytd anknkgitwg edtlmeylen pkkyipgtkm ifagikkkge rqdliaylks acsk

Use this data to calculate the number of different amino acids between the five animals – complete a copy of the table below. Then use the completed table to construct a cladogram.

	Guinea pig	Grey whale	Duck	Alligator	Bullfrog
Guinea pig					
Grey whale					
Duck					
Alligator					
Bullfrog					

(total 8 marks)

Option E Neurobiology and behaviour

Introduction

As the environment around an organism changes, it is an advantage for the organism to be able to detect those changes and respond. Most responses improve the survival chances of the organism. All living things – from the simplest unicellular protozoan, to insects, birds and mammals – respond to stimuli such as light and chemicals. Animals have a nervous system, which is an efficient way of detecting changes and transmitting information around the body. **Neurobiology** is the study of the structure and functioning of the nervous system.

Behaviour is the pattern of responses of an animal to one or more stimuli, and the study of animal behaviour is called **ethology**. Different behaviours also enable animals to develop social patterns and mating rituals.

E1 Stimulus and response

Assessment statements

- Define the terms 'stimulus', 'response' and 'reflex' in the context of animal behaviour.
- Explain the role of receptors, sensory neurons, relay neurons, motor neurons, synapses and effectors in the response of animals to stimuli.
- Draw and label a diagram of a reflex arc for a pain withdrawal reflex, including the spinal cord and its spinal nerves, the receptor cell, sensory neuron, relay neuron, motor neuron and effector.
- Explain how animal responses can be affected by natural selection, using two examples.

Stimulus a change in the environment (either internal or external) that is detected by a receptor and elicits a response

Response a reaction or change in an organism as a result of a stimulus

Reflex a rapid, unconscious response

Components of the nervous system

Receptors are the parts of a nervous system that detect a **stimulus** and initiate a nerve impulse. There are many types of receptor. In the skin, for example, there are pain, temperature and pressure receptors, and the retina contains light receptors.

Nerve impulses are carried by neurons to **effectors**, which are either muscles or glands. The effectors carry out the **response**.

This pathway usually involves the **central nervous system (CNS)** – either the brain, the spinal cord, or both.

The neuron that carries the impulse from the receptor to the CNS is called the **sensory neuron**, and the one that carries the impulse from the CNS to the effector is called the **motor neuron**. These sensory and motor neurons throughout the body make up the **peripheral nervous system (PNS)**. Within the CNS, **relay neurons** connect the sensory and motor neurons via synapses.

Sometimes, a very rapid response to a stimulus is required – for example, if you touch something that causes pain, you pull your hand away quickly, without thinking about it at all. This is called the pain withdrawal reflex, and it is an example of a **reflex action**, mediated by a rapid and simple neural pathway called a **reflex arc** (Figure E.1). The reflex arc involves the receptor cell in your finger, a sensory neuron, a relay neuron in your spinal cord, a motor neuron and the effector – the muscles of your arm that cause you to draw your hand away (Figure **E.2**).

Relay neurons also connect to neurons going up and down the spinal cord. These ascending and descending neurons carry information to and from the brain. So, for example, if you touch something painful, not only do you withdraw your hand rapidly, but information is also sent to the brain so you can remember this and not do it again.

Natural selection and animal responses

Natural selection acts on the behavioural responses of animals in just the same way as it does on other characteristics such as coat colour. One well-documented example is the migratory behaviour of a small European songbird called the blackcap (*Sylvia atricapilla*, Figure **E.3**, overleaf).

Blackcaps breed in summer, in Germany and other areas of northern and eastern Europe, and then migrate south about 1600 km to winter feeding grounds in Mediterranean regions of Spain (Figure **E.4**, overleaf). Since the 1960s, biologists in the UK have recorded increasing numbers of birds that have travelled northwest from Germany to overwinter in the UK, a distance of only 900 km. At the end of winter, these birds left the UK up to 10 days earlier than other migrants left Spain.

Modification of their migration pattern has meant that the birds travelling from the UK can quickly return to their summer breeding grounds and occupy the best nest sites. Observations of the birds have shown that they have different-shaped beaks, more suited to the food available in the UK, and also more rounded wings, which are less suitable for long migration. The 'modified migrants' also tend not to interbreed with the birds that migrate back from Spain.

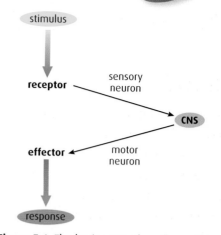

Figure E.1 The basic parts of a reflex pathway.

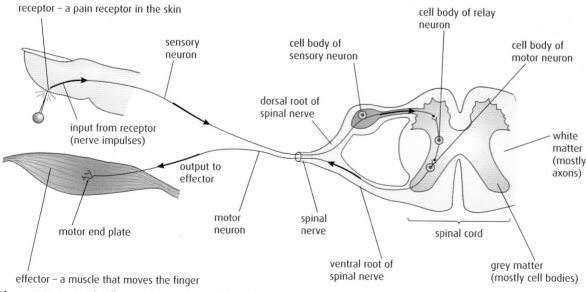

Figure E.2 A spinal reflex arc for a pain withdrawal reflex.

Figure E.3 Among European blackcaps (*Sylvia atricapilla*), birds that migrate to closer winter feeding ground appear to have a selective advantage over those who migrate longer distances.

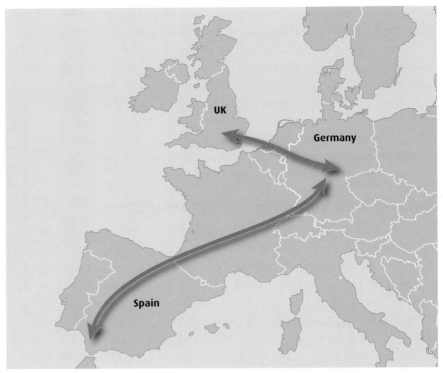

Figure E.4 Changes in migration patterns of the blackcap. Blackcaps breed in Germany in the summer and migrate about 1600 km in winter to feed in Spain. Since the 1960s, increasing numbers of birds have travelled northwest from Germany to overwinter in the UK, a distance of only 900 km.

Figure E.5 There is a selective advantage for great tits in laying eggs early, if the parents can get enough food for egg production, because when the chicks hatch they will be first to take advantage of the springtime abundance.

To study the behaviour of these birds in more detail, eggs were removed from the nests of both types of migrants and the hatchlings hand-reared. In autumn when the young birds migrated, the direction in which each bird flew was carefully observed. It was found that birds reared from eggs of south-migrating parents headed south, and those birds reared from northwest-migrating parents headed northwest. The birds had had no previous migration experience and their behaviour had not been learned from their parents. The migration patterns must be genetically determined, indicating that natural selection is operating on the behaviour of the blackcap.

A second example of how natural selection affects animals' responses can be seen in the breeding behaviour of the great tit (*Parus major*, Figure **E.5**). This European bird lays eggs at a time that is influenced by day length, and the behaviour is genetically determined. In recent years, ornithologists in the Netherlands have noted that many birds are laying their eggs earlier in the year. In general, natural selection favours early breeding because, with changes in climate, trees now tend come into leaf earlier and so small invertebrates that inhabit these trees are also available earlier. Early egg production means that there is abundant food for the birds' offspring at the time when it is needed.

The eventual extent of early breeding may in turn be limited by natural selection, because egg production is very costly and so birds' energy needs may come to restrict their laying behaviour. There may simply not be enough food around very early in the year for parents to produce eggs.

1 Define the terms 'stimulus', 'response' and 'reflex'.

2 List the components of a reflex pathway.

3 Which **two** parts of the reflex pathway are connected by a sensory neuron?

4 Which **two** parts of the reflex pathway are connected by a relay neuron?

E2 Perception of stimuli

Assessment statements

- Outline the diversity of stimuli that can be detected by human sensory receptors, including mechanoreceptors, chemoreceptors, thermoreceptors and photoreceptors.
- Label a diagram of the structure of the human eye.
- Annotate a diagram of the retina to show the cell types and the direction in which light moves.
- Compare rod and cone cells.
- Explain the processing of visual stimuli, including edge enhancement and contralateral processing.
- Label a diagram of the ear.
- Explain how sound is perceived by the ear, including the roles of the eardrum, bones of the middle ear, oval and round windows, and the hair cells of the cochlea.

Human sensory receptors

Sense organs supply the brain with the information it needs to keep us in touch with the world around us. Information is gathered by sensory receptors, which are able to absorb different types of energy from the environment and transform it into nerve impulses.

On the surface of our bodies, we have **thermoreceptors** in our skin that respond to temperature, **photoreceptors** in the retina of each eye that respond to light, and **chemoreceptors** in our noses and on our tongues that respond to chemical substances. We also have internal chemoreceptors. Those in our blood vessels detect the pH or carbon dioxide concentration of our blood and help to regulate our breathing.

Mechanoreceptors are another group of receptors, stimulated by pressure or forces. Some respond to changes in blood pressure, others to the movement of fluid in the inner ear. Whenever we move any part of our body (e.g. a leg to kick a ball, or an arm and fingers to pick up a pen) we need to know exactly where that part of the body is. We receive this information from mechanoreceptors known as stretch receptors, found in muscles. Stretch receptors respond to stretching of the muscles and allow the brain to work out the positions of all parts of the body.

The human eye

Photoreceptors in the human eye make it a very efficient light-sensitive organ. Light rays entering the eye are bent by the cornea and lens and focused onto the **retina** (Figure **E.6**). The two types of light receptor cells, arranged in a single layer in the retina, are called rods and cones.

- Cones are not very sensitive to light but three different types of cone are sensitive to three different wavelengths of light and enable us to see in colour.
- Rods are much more sensitive to light. They absorb all wavelengths of light and function well at low light intensities. In dim light, only rods cause nerve impulses to be transmitted along the optic nerve so we cannot perceive colour and the world appears in shades of grey.

Table **E.1** summarises the characteristics of rod and cone cells in the retina.

The retina also contains two layers of neurons – bipolar cells and ganglion cells (Figure **E.7**). These cells conduct the information from rods and cones to the optic nerve.

The **fovea** is an area of the retina directly behind the pupil. It contains the highest concentration of cones in the retina. When you look directly at a small object its image is focused on the fovea, which is the part of the retina that produces the most visually accurate image.

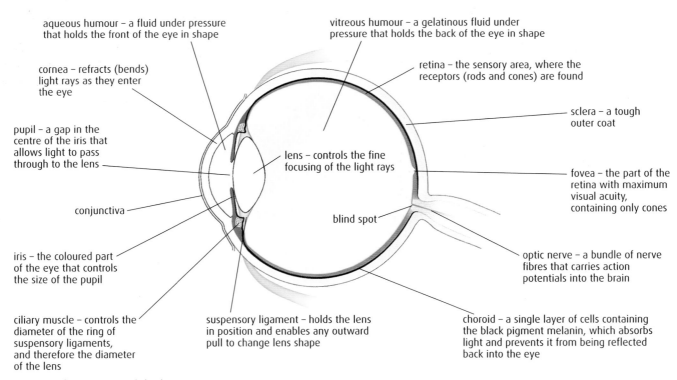

aqueous humour – a fluid under pressure that holds the front of the eye in shape

vitreous humour – a gelatinous fluid under pressure that holds the back of the eye in shape

cornea – refracts (bends) light rays as they enter the eye

retina – the sensory area, where the receptors (rods and cones) are found

sclera – a tough outer coat

pupil – a gap in the centre of the iris that allows light to pass through to the lens

lens – controls the fine focusing of the light rays

fovea – the part of the retina with maximum visual acuity, containing only cones

conjunctiva

blind spot

iris – the coloured part of the eye that controls the size of the pupil

optic nerve – a bundle of nerve fibres that carries action potentials into the brain

ciliary muscle – controls the diameter of the ring of suspensory ligaments, and therefore the diameter of the lens

suspensory ligament – holds the lens in position and enables any outward pull to change lens shape

choroid – a single layer of cells containing the black pigment melanin, which absorbs light and prevents it from being reflected back into the eye

Figure E.6 The structure of the human eye.

Rods	Cones
highly sensitive to light, work in dim light	less sensitive to light, work in bright light
one type of rod can respond to all wavelengths of light	three different cones respond to red, blue and green light so we can detect colour
groups of rods are connected to a single bipolar cell	each cone is connected to its own bipolar cell
not present in the fovea	not present at the very edge of the retina

Table E.1 Comparison of rods and cones in the human retina.

Rays of light that fall on the retina first pass through the layers of nerve fibres and neurons before reaching the light-sensitive rods and cones.

Rods are connected in groups to a single bipolar cell whereas each cone cell has its own bipolar cell. Rods are very sensitive to light and respond even in very dim light.

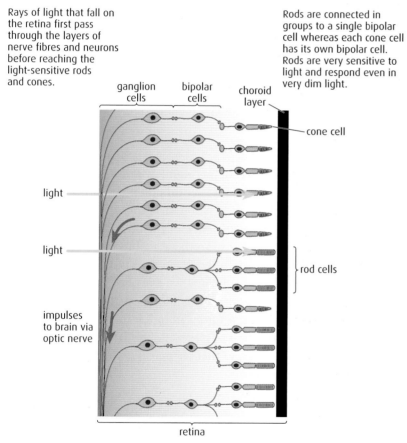

Figure E.7 The retina of the human eye.

At the point where neurons leave the eye in the optic nerve, they pass through the layer of rods and cones and this creates the 'blind spot'. We do not perceive an image when rays of light fall on the blind spot, because the light does not fall on any rods or cones here. However, the blind spot is in a slightly different position in each eye, which means each eye is able to 'fill in the gap' for the other, and we are not aware of any blank areas in our visual field.

Questions to consider

1 To what extent can the statement 'beauty is in the eye of the beholder' be related to the physiology of the eye and brain?

2 We do not know what animals actually see. Could their understanding of what they see be similar to a human's 'understanding' of an abstract impressionist painting?

3 Is it ever likely to be possible to answer these questions?

   • Does a bull really get enraged by a red cape?

   • How do bees know which flowers to visit for nectar?

   • How does a cat pounce on an insect before you are aware of it?

What do animals see and can they see in colour?

Humans have three types of cone and can see a range of colours that we call the visible spectrum. No one knows exactly what other animals see or to what extent they see in colour. We can only study the physiology of their eyes and the light-sensitive cells they contain and attempt to deduce what their brains may perceive. Colour vision and perception across the animal kingdom is the subject of ongoing research.

Of species studied so far, the best colour vision appears to be found in birds, aquatic animals and certain insects, especially butterflies and honeybees. Most mammals have weak colour vision; humans and other primates have the most advanced colour perception. Dogs have two types of cones, suggesting that they may view the world in a similar way to red–green colour-blind humans. Cats have three types of cones, but a much lower proportion of cones to rods than humans. They can distinguish blue and green but probably do not perceive red objects well. Many animals can see things that we cannot. Bees can perceive light in the ultraviolet range but do not see red well. This explains why very few wild flowers are pure red.

Visual processing

Light rays entering the eye stimulate photoreceptors that send impulses to bipolar neurons. These neurons combine impulses from groups of rods or from individual cone cells and generate action potentials in the ganglion cells. From here, nerve impulses travel along the axons of neurons in the optic nerve to the visual cortex at the back of the brain. Impulses pass via the **optic chiasma** and relay areas in the thalamus of the brain as shown in Figure **E.8**. When the impulses reach the visual cortex, they must be interpreted to produce the images we 'see'. For example, because of the way light rays pass through the retina of the eye, the image falling on the retina is both inverted and reversed from left to right. However, the images we 'see' are not inverted or reversed. This is because the brain interprets the impulses it receives, so that we perceive the world 'the right way up'. This is **visual processing**.

Contralateral processing

The brain must also coordinate the information it receives from both eyes. As we view an object, each eye receives a slightly different view of the visual field, which is detected by different regions of the retina in each eye. Axons from the region of the retina closest to the nose in each eye cross over in the optic chiasma to go to the opposite side of the brain. This means that all the information from the left visual field goes to the right visual cortex and all the information from the right visual field goes to the left visual cortex (Figure **E.8**). This is called **contralateral processing**. The visual cortex assembles all the information it receives and gives us an understanding of what we are looking at.

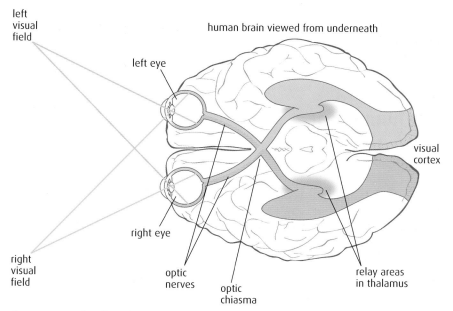

Figure E.8 Both sides of the brain work together to enable us to recognise objects. Contralateral processing allows us to work out the size of an object and its distance from us.

Edge enhancement – the Hermann grid

The Hermann grid (Figure **E.9**) is an example of an optical illusion that has been used to provide insights into the complexity of human visual processing. As you scan your eyes over the grid, grey spots appear and disappear at the intersections in your peripheral vision. The retina is able to modify the information it sends to the brain to make the edges of objects appear sharper. This is called **edge enhancement** and explains why the white lines and the black squares in the Hermann grid look sharp. However, it also produces the optical illusion.

The Hermann grid has been used as evidence to support the theory that certain receptors in the retina can influence the outputs of those around them – they can effectively 'turn off' adjacent cells by over-riding their outputs. Each ganglion cell is connected to a circular area of the retina called a **receptive field** (blue area in Figure **E.10**). Here, the ganglion cell (orange) receives an output from each of the five photoreceptors (yellow). The central photoreceptor gives an excitatory output but the other four give inhibitory output. The strength of the output is determined by how much light falls onto the photoreceptor – the more light, the stronger the output, whether excitatory or inhibitory.

If this receptive field is positioned centrally over the blue spot on the Hermann grid in Figure **E.9**, the central excitatory output is inhibited a lot by the photoreceptors at the top and bottom (where it is light) but only a little by the photoreceptors to the left and right (where it is dark). The white area therefore looks particularly 'bright' next to the dark areas – the contrast between them is enhanced.

Now consider the receptive field positioned at the purple spot on the Hermann grid. This time, there is a lot of inhibition from all four

Stereoscopic vision

Each eye captures its own slightly different view of an object and so two separate images are passed to the brain for processing. When the images arrive, they are combined into just one 'picture'. The brain unites the two images by matching up the similarities and adding in the small differences to produce stereoscopic vision. With stereoscopic vision, we can perceive where objects are in relation to us quite accurately. This is especially true when things are moving towards or away from us. We can even perceive and measure 'empty' space with our eyes and brains.

Figure E.9 The Hermann grid.

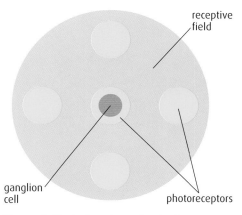

Figure E.10 A plan view of a single receptive field, viewed from inside the eye.

surrounding photoreceptors, because there are light regions to the top, bottom, left and right. This means that the final output from the ganglion cell to the brain in the purple position will be less than the final output from the ganglion cell in the blue position. The brain interprets the smaller output as 'less bright' – that is, it sees this area as grey rather than white.

The human ear

Figure **E.11** shows a diagram of a section through the human ear. It is divided into three regions – outer, middle and inner ear.

The outer ear and middle ears are separated by the ear drum, and the middle ear is separated from the inner ear by the oval and round windows. The pinna is a sound-collecting device and in many animals it can be rotated by muscles to pick up sounds from all directions. Most humans have lost the ability to use these muscles.

The Eustachian tube connects the middle ear to the back of the throat via a valve and maintains an equal pressure of air on each side of the ear drum. In the inner ear, the cochlea detects sound and the semicircular canals detect motion.

How sound is perceived

Sound is created by differences in air pressure, which produce vibrations called sound waves. Sound waves enter the outer ear canal and cause the ear drum to vibrate back and forth (Figure **E.12**, top). These movements

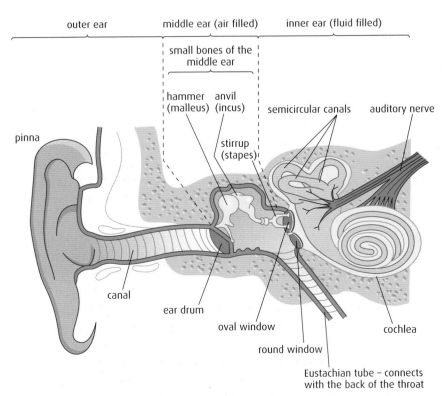

Figure E.11 Section through the human ear. Note that the pinna is not drawn to scale with the internal structures of the ear.

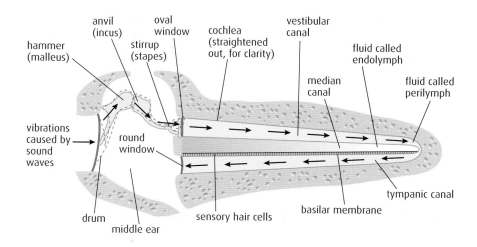

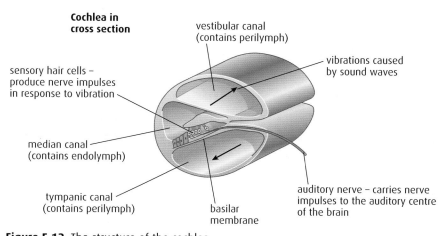

Figure E.12 The structure of the cochlea.

are transmitted to the three tiny bones in the middle ear. The ear drum is in contact with the first bone and the third bone touches the oval window. Each bone vibrates in turn so that vibrations pass via the bones to the oval window. By the time the vibrations reach the inner ear they have been amplified up to 20 times because the bones act as levers, increasing the force of the waves, and also because the oval window is much smaller than the ear drum.

Vibrations of the oval window are passed on to the fluid contained in the cochlea. The fluid cannot be compressed and can only move because the round window at the end of the coiled cochlea absorbs the pressure of the waves of fluid as they arrive.

Inside the cochlea are sensory hair cells attached to membranes, as shown in Figure **E.12**. As the fluid moves, it moves groups of hair cells, which initiate nerve impulses that are passed via the auditory nerve to the auditory centre of the brain. Different regions of the cochlea respond to different frequencies of sound. High frequencies are detected nearest to the oval window and the lowest frequencies are picked up further away. Hair cells in any one region vary in their sensitivity and this allows

A young person can detect sounds of wavelengths between 40 and 20 000 Hz but as we age, we lose the ability to detect higher frequencies. Loss of hearing is also common among rock musicians and people who work in very noisy environments without ear protection because excessive noise damages the hair cells in the cochlea. Many species can hear a different range of sounds from humans. Dogs can hear up to 40 000 Hz and bats up to 100 000 Hz.

differences in loudness to be detected. A quiet sound stimulates only a few hair cells in a particular region so few nerve impulses are sent to the brain. If the sound is louder, more hair cells are stimulated and more nerve impulses pass to the brain.

5 List **four** types of sensory receptor.

6 List **15** structures that you would label on a diagram of the eye.

7 The retina is made up of three layers of cells – photoreceptors, bipolar cells and ganglion cells. Which cell layer does light entering the eye strike first?

8 What is the function of bipolar cells?

9 List **three** differences between rods and cones.

10 Outline what is meant by 'contralateral processing'.

11 Name the region of the brain where neurons from the left eye and the right eye cross over.

12 What is meant by the term 'edge enhancement'?

E3 Innate and learned behaviour

Assessment statements

- Distinguish between 'innate' and 'learned' behaviour.
- Design experiments to investigate innate behaviour in invertebrates, including either a taxis or a kinesis.
- Analyse data from invertebrate behaviour experiments in terms of the effect on chances of survival and reproduction.
- Discuss how the process of learning can improve the chance of survival.
- Outline Pavlov's experiments into conditioning of dogs.
- Outline the role of inheritance and learning in the development of birdsong in young birds.

The study of behaviour attempts to understand many aspects of an organism's life, from its instinctive responses to more complex feeding and breeding habits. In a natural environment, two types of animal behaviour can be recognised: innate, instinctive behaviours and learned behaviours that occur as a result of experience.

Innate and learned behaviour

Innate behaviour is very often called 'instinct'. This behaviour is common to all members of a species and is genetically controlled. Innate behaviour occurs independently of the environment and is crucial to survival, helping in activities such as finding food, building a nest or escaping from danger. Short-lived species do not have time to acquire learned behaviours or skills and a high proportion of the behaviour of most invertebrates is innate. Examples of innate behaviour include the movements of dragonfly nymphs as they prepare to pupate (Figure **E.13**), movements of woodlice towards damp areas to avoid drying out, the dances performed by honeybees to communicate the direction of a food source and the mating behaviour of many bird species.

Learned behaviour, on the other hand, comes from everyday experiences. It can be very advantageous as it is much more adaptable and produces a greater range of behavioural patterns than innate behaviour. Learning can develop new skills or change existing ones, which the animal will retain in the memory. Longer-lived organisms with more developed nervous systems are likely to show a higher proportion of behaviour that is learned. Primates, big cats, wolves and many other mammals spend a long time with their parents learning social and hunting skills from them. The matriarch of an elephant herd remembers where water supplies can be found during the dry season and the routes are learned by younger members of the herd. Similarly, many monkeys and apes can remember where a particular tree will be fruiting at a certain time of the year and pass on this knowledge to their young.

Experimental study of innate behaviour

Innate behaviour of invertebrates includes the movements they make towards or way from stimuli such as food or light. Two examples of this kind of orientation behaviour that can be investigated are taxis and kinesis.

A **taxis** is when an organism moves towards or away from a directional stimulus. A choice chamber is a simple piece of apparatus that can be used to investigate taxis in small invertebrates (Figure **E.14**). It consists of a circular clear plastic box with four sections in the base, over which a piece of gauze can be stretched as a platform for small invertebrates to walk on.

The innate behaviour of woodlice can be observed and recorded using a choice chamber. The conditions under the gauze can be varied to change the humidity in each section of the chamber and the lid covered to provide different light intensities. To investigate the animals' response to light and dark, one half of the chamber can be covered with black cloth, while the other is left open. When investigating any one environmental factor, all other variables must remain unchanged.

Woodlice can be introduced to the chamber through the hole in the lid and their movements observed. In an investigation into their response to light, the woodlice begin to move from the light area into the dark side after a few minutes. The numbers of animals in each half can be counted after a fixed period of time to provide quantitative data, and the experiment repeated to obtain accurate results. Directional movement away from light is known as **negative phototaxis**. It helps woodlice to avoid bright sunny places that are likely to be dry and also ensures that they move to shelter under stones and logs away from predatory birds.

A **kinesis** is a response to a non-directional stimulus. It can be recognised as a change in the level of response to a stimulus.

To investigate the response of woodlice to humidity, a choice chamber can again be used, this time with half the chamber providing damp condition and the other half providing very dry conditions. This can be

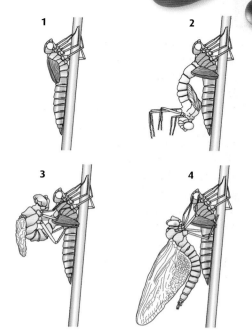

Figure E.13 A dragonfly nymph demonstrates innate behaviour.

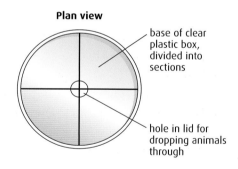

Plan view

base of clear plastic box, divided into sections

hole in lid for dropping animals through

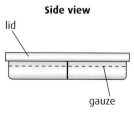

Side view

lid

gauze

Figure E.14 Plan view and side view of a choice chamber.

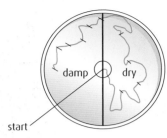

start

Figure E.15 The distance moved by the woodlouse in 10 seconds is greater in the dry half than in the damp half. The animal also changes direction more frequently.

achieved using a drying agent under the gauze in one side of the choice chamber and damp paper in the other. A single woodlouse put into the chamber moves about on the gauze and behaves differently in the different conditions. Its movements can be recorded as shown in Figure **E.15** by tracing its path on an overlay of clear acetate film. The trace can be marked at 10-second intervals, as shown, so that the speed of the woodlouse can be calculated.

The animal moves further and turns more frequently in the dry conditions. This type of behaviour is a kinesis: the rate of movement and turning depends on the level of the humidity stimulus. Woodlice live in damp environments and need an atmosphere with a high humidity. In dry conditions, they will keep moving and turn more, searching for a more humid environment.

Both of these investigations show how the innate behaviour of woodlice increases their chances of survival. The longer an animal survives, the greater the likelihood of it being able to reproduce. Since these innate behaviour patterns are genetically controlled and inherited, responses that increase survival are more likely to get passed on to offspring.

13 In each of the following, state the type of orientation behaviour that has occurred and why the behaviour helps the animals to survive.

   a A sample of 50 *Euglena*, a single-celled photosynthesising organism, was placed in a small, oblong dish and observed under even illumination under a microscope. The distribution of the *Euglena* was seen to be evenly spread over the dish. The illumination was changed so that half of the dish was illuminated and the other half was shaded. After five minutes, 48 *Euglena* were in the illuminated side and two remained in the shaded side.

   b Newly hatched female silkmoths, *Bombyx mori*, release a pheromone (scented sex hormone) called bombykol, which causes male moths to turn and fly forwards them.

   c Ten garden snails were placed at the foot of a vertical wall. After 15 minutes the snails had re-orientated themselves and climbed vertically up the wall.

   d Three human body lice were placed in a circular chamber that was divided into two parts. One half was kept at a temperature of 35 °C and the other at 30 °C. At the cooler temperature, the insects made few turns but at the warmer temperature, the insects made many random turns and travelled a greater distance in the same period of time.

   e Planaria are small flatworms that live in lakes and ponds. They have simple light-sensitive eyespots and chemoreceptors at the front of their bodies. Experiments with ten Planaria in a choice chamber showed that the animals all moved away from a source of light into a darker area. If a small piece of fish (the natural food of Planaria) was introduced into the light section of the choice chamber, five individuals moved towards it.

      How should this experiment be modified to include a control?

Learning and survival

Many animals learn from their parents or from older members of their species. Primates, in particular, show the ability to acquire new skills that help them to survive. The wild chimpanzees in the Bossou Reserve in Guinea have learned behaviours such as fishing for ants and termites in logs using sticks (Figure **E.16**), and cracking nuts open with a stone hammer and anvil. The young chimps watch other members of the troop and then try to copy them. These behaviours provide a wider range of food sources for the animals that are able to develop the necessary skills.

Many animals learn from experience or by trial and error. Caterpillars of the monarch butterfly in North America feed on a poisonous plant called milkweed. Poison is stored in the caterpillars' bodies and after pupation it is also found in the adult butterflies. If a young toad or bird catches a monarch butterfly, it quickly spits it out and avoids similar prey afterwards. Learning in this way prevents unpleasant and potentially toxic food being taken again.

Raccoons are mammals common throughout North America. Their normal habitat is forest but they have learned that human habitations are excellent sources of food, which they find in bowls of pet food, garbage cans and even kitchen cupboards. All these new food sources – along with good dens that can be found under houses, in attics and garden sheds – have improved survival rates so much that the animal has become a serious pest in some places.

Figure E.16 These chimpanzees are fishing for termites using tools that they have made.

Pavlov's dogs and classical conditioning

Ivan Pavlov (Figure **E.17**) was a Russian physiologist, psychologist and physician. In the 1890s, he studied the gastric function of dogs and tried to relate the quantity of saliva produced by the dogs' salivary glands to the stimulus of food. Salivation is a reflex response to the presence of food in the mouth but Pavlov noticed that his experimental dogs began to release saliva before they started to eat and he decided to investigate this 'psychic secretion' (Figure **E.18**, overleaf).

Just before giving the dogs food, and before they could see or smell it, he rang a bell. After repeating his experiments several times he noticed that the dogs salivated as soon as he rang the bell. They had come to associate the sound of the bell with the arrival of food. Even when Pavlov used different sound stimuli, the results were always the same. He called this modification of the dogs' behaviour **conditioning** and he used a number of specific terms to explain his results.

- Before training, the normal behaviour involved an **unconditioned stimulus** (the food) producing an **unconditioned response** (the release of saliva).
- After training, the dogs responded to the **conditioned stimulus** (the sound of a bell) and produced the **conditioned response** (the release of saliva without the appearance of food).

Figure E.17 Ivan Petrovich Pavlov (1849–1936), won a Nobel Prize for medicine and physiology in 1904.

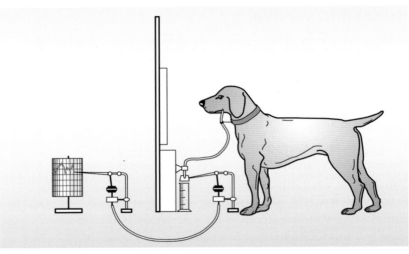

Figure E.18 One of Pavlov's experiments into classical conditioning. A tube in the dog's cheek collected saliva, and the volume collected was recorded on the kymograph drum. Pavlov used this apparatus to investigate the response of the dog's salivary glands to different types and strengths of stimuli.

Behavioural responses involving classical conditioning

Many instances of simple classical conditioning can be observed in animals, including humans.

Questions to consider

Consider the examples below and decide if the behaviour involves Pavlovian conditioning or not.

1 If you have bells in your school to mark the end of each lesson, watch what the other students do as soon as the bell rings at the end of a class. It is likely that they start to pack up their books and pens, even if the teacher is still talking.

2 As you walk past a house, a dog in the garden starts to bark at you.

3 A homeowner puts out food for the birds first thing every morning. Early in the morning birds start to gather in the trees near the bird table.

4 A sheepdog runs in particular directions or lies down when his owner makes specific whistles.

5 A chicken kept in a battery farm cage for a year will start to scratch and peck at the ground when released into a farmyard.

The development of birdsong

Birds sing to defend their territories and to attract mates in courtship rituals. It is usually male birds that sing so a male bird's song is crucial to both its survival and reproductive success. A bird's song is a long and complex series of notes, which can be analysed using acoustic spectroscopy. Different species have quite different songs, but within a species it appears that, although the basic song is the same for all members of the species, variations do develop. Young birds are born with an innate ability to sing a basic song but learn details of their species' song from their fathers. Variations in the song gradually appear and over generations these variations can build up to form local 'dialects'.

One bird that has been extensively studied is the North American white-crowned sparrow (Figure **E.19**). An immature male bird inherits the ability to sing a basic song called a 'template'. However, even before it is able to sing, a young bird listens to its father singing close to the nest and it uses what it hears to upgrade its own basic template. When the young bird starts to sing its own song, it matches what it hears to this upgraded template. A hand-reared bird that never hears adult birds sing is deprived of this learning process and is unable to produce a proper song when it matures. The sonograms of wild and hand-reared birds are shown in Figure **E.20**. A male who does not sing properly will be unable to mate and will remain a bachelor.

Figure E.19 A male North American white-crowned sparrow in song.

Wild male white-crowned sparrow

adult male white-crowned sparrow song

The young bird uses the adult song to modify its basic template. At around 150 days old, the juvenile bird starts to sing and gradually matches what he hears to the modified template.

At about 200 days, the bird's song matches what he heard as a youngster.

Hand-reared male white-crowned sparrow

At around 150 days, the juvenile bird reared in isolation begins to sing and matches what it hears to its basic, unmodified template.

At about 200 days, the full song has developed but is not as mature and complex as the song of a wild bird.

data from Peter Marler, Animal Communication Laboratory, Section of Neurobiology, Physiology and Behavior, University of California, Davis, CA 95616, USA

Figure E.20 Sonograms of North American white-crowned sparrows.

14 In what ways might learning improve an organism's chances of survival? Give **two** examples.

15 Give **one** example of a taxis and **one** example of a kinesis.

16 How is innate behaviour different from learned behaviour?

E4 Neurotransmitters and synapses

Assessment statements

- State that some pre-synaptic neurons excite post-synaptic transmission and others inhibit post-synaptic transmission.
- Explain how decision-making in the CNS can result from the interaction between the activities of excitatory and inhibitory pre-synaptic neurons at synapses.
- Explain how psychoactive drugs affect the brain and personality by either increasing or decreasing post-synaptic transmission.
- List three examples of excitatory and three examples of inhibitory psychoactive drugs.
- Explain the effects of THC and cocaine in terms of their action at synapses in the brain.
- Discuss the causes of addiction, including genetic predisposition, social factors and dopamine secretion.

Inhibitory and excitatory synapses

The structure of synapses was discussed in Chapter **6**. The most important parts of any synapse are the pre-synaptic membrane, the neurotransmitter it releases and the receptors on the post-synaptic membrane that are stimulated by it (Figure **E.21**).

The synapses discussed in Chapter **6** are **excitatory synapses**. When a neurotransmitter is released from the pre-synaptic membrane, the post-synaptic membrane is depolarised as positive ions enter the cell and stimulate an action potential.

But there are many different synapses in the body and many different neurotransmitters. Some pre-synaptic neurons release neurotransmitters that inhibit the post-synaptic neuron by increasing the polarisation of its membrane (hyperpolarisation), therefore making it harder to depolarise the membrane and trigger an action potential. Post-synaptic transmission is therefore inhibited at these **inhibitory synapses**.

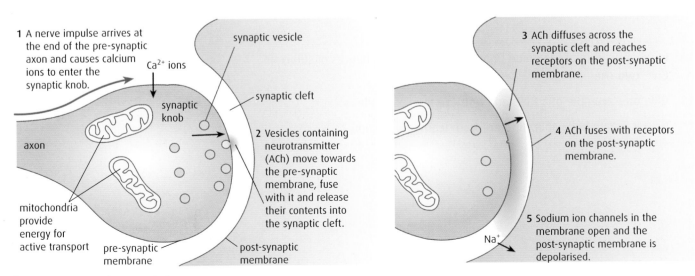

1 A nerve impulse arrives at the end of the pre-synaptic axon and causes calcium ions to enter the synaptic knob.

Ca²⁺ ions

synaptic vesicle

synaptic cleft

synaptic knob

axon

2 Vesicles containing neurotransmitter (ACh) move towards the pre-synaptic membrane, fuse with it and release their contents into the synaptic cleft.

mitochondria provide energy for active transport

pre-synaptic membrane

post-synaptic membrane

3 ACh diffuses across the synaptic cleft and reaches receptors on the post-synaptic membrane.

4 ACh fuses with receptors on the post-synaptic membrane.

5 Sodium ion channels in the membrane open and the post-synaptic membrane is depolarised.

Na⁺

Figure E.21 Synaptic transmission.

Decision making in the CNS

Synapses are the places where action potentials are passed from one neuron to the next. Some post-synaptic neurons are stimulated by many different pre-synaptic neurons, some excitatory and some inhibitory (Figure **E.22**). The balance of stimuli from these many pre-synaptic neurons can either excite or inhibit the post-synaptic neuron, giving a range of possible outcomes. The neuron may receive more stimulatory impulses overall so that it fires an action potential, or it may receive mainly inhibitory impulses so that it does not. The balance of the impulses provides an arrangement that allows us to make decisions about the actions we take.

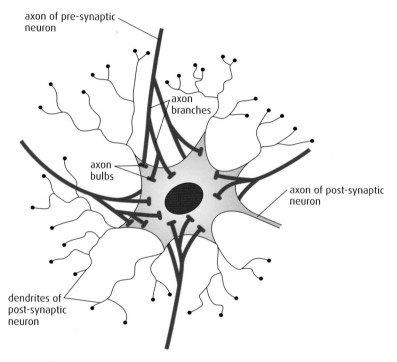

Figure E.22 Some of the neurons that form synapses with the post-synaptic neuron are inhibitory and prevent an action potential. Others stimulate the propagation of the impulse.

Psychoactive drugs

Psychoactive drugs are chemical substances that affect the way the brain transmits impulses at synapses. They are capable of altering the functioning of the brain and a person's personality.

Drugs act in different ways.

- Some have similar structures to neurotransmitters and so either block receptors, preventing a response, or have the same effect as the neurotransmitter but are not removed so that the response is prolonged.
- Some prevent neurotransmitters being released.
- Some increase the release of neurotransmitters.
- Some prevent neurotransmitters being broken down and so prolong their effects.

Sometimes you may see neurotransmitters described as being 'excitatory' or 'inhibitory', but this is not strictly accurate. The neurotransmitter itself simply activates receptors on the post-synaptic membrane, and it is these receptors that determine whether the effect will be excitatory or inhibitory. For some neurotransmitters, such as glutamate, the most important receptors all have excitatory effects and increase the probability of an action potential occurring in the post-synaptic cell. For other neurotransmitters, such as GABA, the important receptors all have inhibitory effects. And some neurotransmitters, such as acetylcholine, are received by both excitatory and inhibitory receptors.

Cholinergic and adrenergic synapses

Two of the most important neurotransmitters in the nervous system are acetylcholine and noradrenalin. Synapses are divided into two types, defined by which of the two neurotransmitters they use.

Cholinergic synapses use acetylcholine and are found in the parasympathetic nervous system (Section **E5**). Nicotine increases transmission at these synapses and has a calming effect on mood.

Adrenergic synapses use the neurotransmitter noradrenalin and are found in the sympathetic nervous system. Noradrenalin is crucial to the 'fight or flight' response. Amphetamines stimulate these synapses and produce feelings of alertness and euphoria.

Excitatory drugs

Some psychoactive drugs are excitatory – that is, they promote the transmission of impulses at excitatory synapses or inhibit transmission at inhibitory synapses. Examples of excitatory drugs include:

- cocaine
- amphetamines
- nicotine.

The effects of these substances are summarised in Table **E.2**.

Excitatory drug	Mode of action	Effects
nicotine	<ul><li>acts at synapses that use the neurotransmitter acetylcholine</li><li>is not broken down by the enzyme acetylcholinesterase, which breaks down acetylcholine</li><li>remains in the synapse, binding to the same receptors on the post-synaptic membrane as acetylcholine</li><li>increases levels of dopamine in the brain, which stimulates synapses in 'reward' pathways, giving feelings of pleasure and well-being</li></ul>	<ul><li>produces feelings of pleasure, in same way as cocaine and amphetamines, although to a lesser degree</li><li>strongly addictive because effects wear off quickly, so users must dose themselves frequently to maintain pleasurable sensations and prevent withdrawal symptoms</li><li>has a calming effect, despite being an excitatory drug, possibly because it reduces agitation caused by cravings and withdrawal symptoms</li></ul>
cocaine	<ul><li>stimulates transmission at brain synapses that use dopamine</li><li>leads to a build up of dopamine in the synapse by blocking its return to the pre-synaptic neurons</li><li>causes continuous transmission of impulses in 'reward' pathways, giving feelings of pleasure and well-being</li></ul>	<ul><li>produces feelings of increased energy, confidence and euphoria often mixed with restlessness and anxiety</li><li>highly addictive, with users seeking to maintain feelings and 'highs' induced by dopamine</li><li>as it wears off, feelings of euphoria turn into depression, and the user may 'crash', losing all energy and sometimes sleeping for long periods</li><li>prolonged use can cause long-lasting mental health problems such as depression, anxiety, paranoia and delusions</li></ul>
amphetamines	<ul><li>stimulate transmission at synapses that use noradrenalin</li><li>have similar effects to cocaine but are longer-lasting</li><li>cause the release of neurotransmitter into the synapse and prevent it being broken down</li><li>increase the concentration of dopamine present</li></ul>	<ul><li>produce feelings of euphoria and high levels of energy and alertness</li><li>may cause hyperactivity and aggression in some people</li></ul>

Table E.2 Effects of excitatory drugs.

Inhibitory drugs

These drugs increase transmission at inhibitory synapses or suppress transmission at excitatory synapses. Examples of inhibitory drugs include:

- benzodiazepines
- alcohol
- THC.

Their effects are summarised in Table **E.3**.

Inhibitory drug	Mode of action	Effects
benzodiazepines	• bind to the same post-synaptic receptors as GABA, the main neurotransmitter at inhibitory synapses • cause hyperpolarisation of post-synaptic membranes so that they are more difficult to stimulate	• reduce anxiety, cause relaxation and can induce sleep • used therapeutically to treat anxiety, insomnia and seizures
THC (tetrahydrocannabinol – the most important psychoactive substance in cannabis)	• affects receptors in cells in the cerebellum and cerebral hemispheres that use the neurotransmitter anandamide • similar in structure to anandamide and binds to the same receptors, known as cannabinoid receptors • causes hyperpolarisation of post-synaptic membranes so that they are more difficult to stimulate	• induces feelings of relaxation and affects coordination • causes panic and paranoia in some users • can interfere with short-term memory and learning, as many cannabinoid receptors are found in areas of the brain concerned with memory
alcohol	• increases the binding of GABA to receptors in post-synaptic membranes • causes hyperpolarisation of post-synaptic membranes so that they are more difficult to stimulate • decreases the action of the neurotransmitter glutamate, which stimulates post-synaptic neurons	• in small quantities, affects behaviour by reducing inhibitions • in larger quantities, can cause a lack of coordination, slurred speech, loss of balance and, in some cases, aggressive behaviour

Table E.3 Effects of inhibitory drugs.

What causes addiction?

Addiction is a chemical dependence on a psychoactive drug. Many different factors are involved in addiction as the body becomes tolerant of a drug, needing more and more of it to produce the same effects.

Three factors seem to be common to all addictions, whether drugs have been taken for therapeutic reasons or recreation.

Social factors

Peer pressure can influence young people to experiment and drug-taking behaviour can be associated with a need to belong to a group.

Culture also affects whether drug use is acceptable. In some cultures, cigarette smoking is freely accepted and in others alcohol is used to celebrate at social events. The use of opium, for example, has a long history. In Homer's *Odyssey*, written around 800 BC, opium is referred to as a '*drug that had the power of robbing grief and anger of their sting*' and in the 1850s Chinese immigrants who helped build the railways in the USA smoked opium as an integral part of their culture to relieve stress and exhaustion. Today, drug addiction is often linked to factors such as poverty or poor family circumstances, which can increase the chances of an individual starting to use drugs. However, certain drugs (such as cocaine) may be used by more affluent members of society.

Dopamine secretion

Most drugs that cause addiction are those involving the 'reward' pathway and the release of the neurotransmitter dopamine. Users of addictive drugs find it hard to give them up because of the feelings of well-being that are induced by dopamine. As dopamine receptors are repeatedly stimulated, they become desensitised so that more and more of the drug is required to produce the same feelings.

Genetic predisposition

Relatively few people become addicted to drugs although many are exposed to them. The tendency to become addicted has been shown to be more common in some families and groups than others. Research on identical twins also supports this view. This evidence seems to indicate that some individuals are more likely to carry genes that predispose them to addiction than others.

17 How does THC affect synapses in the brain?

18 List **three** causes of addiction to psychoactive drugs.

19 Outline the effect of inhibitory drugs at a synapse.

E5 The human brain

Assessment statements

- Label, on a diagram of the brain, the medulla oblongata, cerebellum, hypothalamus, pituitary gland and cerebral hemispheres.
- Outline the functions of each of the parts of the brain listed above.
- Explain how animal experiments, lesions and FMRI (functional magnetic resonance imaging) scanning can be used in the identification of the brain part involved in specific functions.
- Explain sympathetic and parasympathetic control of the heart rate, movements of the iris and flow of blood to the gut.
- Explain the pupil reflex.
- Discuss the concept of brain death and the use of the pupil reflex in testing for this.
- Outline how pain in perceived and how endorphins can act as painkillers.

The structure and function of the brain

The brain is the most complex organ in the body (Figure **E.23**). It consists of billions of neurons and hundreds of thousands of different connections, which are responsible for learning, memory and our individual personalities. Each part has a particular function, regulating some automatic processes, such as heart beat and balance, and controlling our speech and ability to reason.

- The **cerebral hemispheres** are the coordinating centre for learning, memory, language, and reasoning. These regions receive information from the sense organs and coordinate and organise motor functions.
- The **hypothalamus** controls the autonomic nervous system. It coordinates the endocrine and nervous systems by regulating the secretions of the pituitary gland.
- The **cerebellum** coordinates movement, posture and balance.

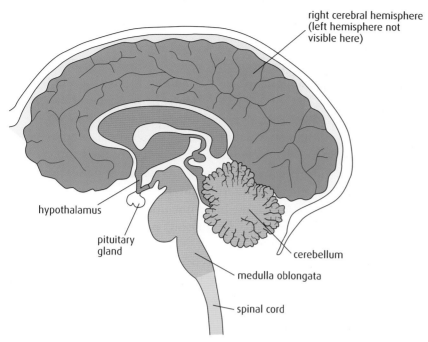

right cerebral hemisphere (left hemisphere not visible here)

hypothalamus

pituitary gland

cerebellum

medulla oblongata

spinal cord

Figure E.23 The human brain.

- The **medulla oblongata** (brain stem) controls automatic and homeostatic activities such as breathing, swallowing, digestion and heart rate.
- The **pituitary gland** has two parts – the posterior lobe stores and releases the hormones oxytocin and ADH from the hypothalamus, while the anterior lobe produces and secretes seven hormones, including FSH and growth hormone, which regulate many of the body's functions.

Investigating brain function

Investigating the brain is a difficult and complex task. Until the arrival of scanning machines, it was difficult to study a living human brain and directly observe its activities.

Animal experiments have yielded valuable information but there are ethical issues involved, particularly when primates, whose brains are most likely to be similar to the human brain, are used. Some procedures involve removing parts of the skull or carrying out experiments on the brain that result in different behaviours. Such experiments may cause distress to the subject animals, which some scientists find objectionable.

Brain lesions − injuries to a specific part of the brain − have provided more direct insights into the functioning of the human brain. Strokes and accidents can damage just one area of the brain and give information about what the area controls.

One well-documented case of brain injury was that of Phineas Gage in 1848. Gage was a construction worker who survived an accident that sent a large metal pin through his skull and destroyed the left frontal lobe of his brain (Figure **E.24**). Although he physically recovered from the injury and lived for a further 12 years, his personality was completely changed – to the extent that his friends no longer knew him.

Further information has come from people who have had surgical treatment for epilepsy that involves cutting the corpus callosum, a band of neurons linking the left and right cerebral hemispheres of the brain. Roger Sperry (1913–1994), a psychobiologist who won the Nobel prize in 1981, and his co-workers carried out 'split-brain' studies on these patients. Sperry discovered that the two sides of the brain can operate almost independently. In a normal brain, the stimulus entering one hemisphere is quickly transferred through the corpus callosum to the other hemisphere so that the brain functions as one. But if the two hemispheres cannot communicate a person's perception of the outside world is changed.

Sperry's work showed that the two halves of the brain have different functions. The left hemisphere of the brain specialises in communication and if a lesion affects this side of the brain, a person may be unable to speak. Damage to the right hemisphere of the brain, which is particularly good at interpreting sensory information and enabling us to understand what we see or hear, may result in a person failing to recognise someone they know well.

Functional magnetic resonance imaging

Since the 1990s, functional magnetic resonance imaging (FMRI) scans have been a key source of new information on brain function. This scanning technique monitors blood flow to different areas of the brain as a subject carries out different tasks. As a region of the brain becomes active, more blood flows to it. Subjects in FMRI experiments are asked to remain still in the scanner as they respond to stimuli or undertake different activities. The scans reveal which areas of the brain are active and help to show how it is working (Figure **E.25**).

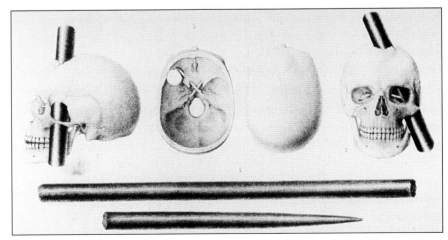

Figure E.24 The skull of Phineas Gage. The fact that his personality changed following the damage to his temporal lobe but he was able to carry on living a fairly normal life, tells us that the temporal lobe is important in coordinating a person's behaviour and reasoning, but not in controlling body functions.

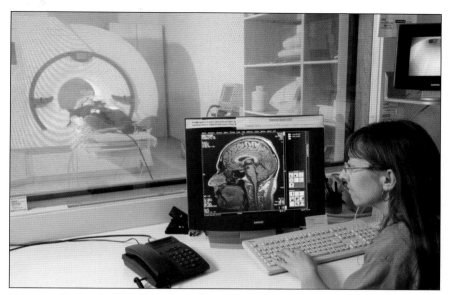

Figure E.25 A patient undergoing an FMRI scan.

FMRI scans can reveal Parkinson's disease, tumours and injuries to the brain. But it is important that the images are interpreted carefully. There may be activity in an area of the brain associated with a particular task but correlation does not imply cause. Many brain processes are complex and not confined to one area alone.

Sympathetic and parasympathetic control

The **peripheral nervous system** (**PNS**) consists of all the nerves that do not form the central nervous system (brain and spinal cord). The PNS comprises the sensory neurons, which carry impulses to the CNS, and the **autonomic nervous system**, which is involuntary and regulates internal processes (such as activities of the glands and digestive system, and blood flow) without our awareness (Figure **E.26**, overleaf).

The autonomic nervous system is subdivided into two parts: the **sympathetic nervous system** and the **parasympathetic nervous system**. Both receive impulses from the brain but have opposite effects on the body. The sympathetic system causes responses that are important in an emergency – the so-called 'fight or flight' responses. It is excitatory in its effects. The parasympathetic system controls events in non-urgent, relaxed situations and is inhibitory in its effects. Table **E.4** (overleaf) compares the actions of the two systems on some vital functions.

The pupil reflex

The pupil reflex is a constriction of the pupils caused by contraction of the circular muscles in the iris. It occurs when bright light shines into the eye. The rapid, reflex action protects the retina from excess light, which could damage it. Unlike the majority of reflexes, it is controlled by the brain instead of the spinal cord. When light stimulates photoreceptors in the retina, impulses pass along the optic nerve to the medulla oblongata.

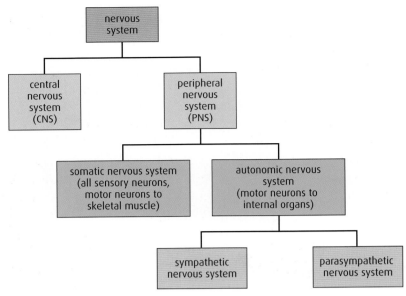

Figure E.26 The components of the human nervous system.

Organ	Effect of parasympathetic system	Effect of sympathetic system
eye	causes contraction of circular muscles of the iris, which constricts the pupil	causes contraction of radial muscles of the iris, dilating the pupil
heart	heart rate is slowed down and stroke volume is reduced as the body is relaxed	heart rate is increased and stroke volume increased so that more blood can be pumped to muscles
digestive system	blood vessels are dilated, increasing blood flow to the digestive system	blood flow to the digestive system is restricted as blood vessels constrict

Table E.4 Comparison of the effects of the parasympathetic and sympathetic nervous systems on three organs.

Motor impulses are sent from the medulla oblongata to the muscles of the iris. Circular muscles are stimulated to contract and radial muscles relax.

Figure E.27 shows how the sympathetic and parasympathetic nervous systems control the dilation and constriction of the pupils.

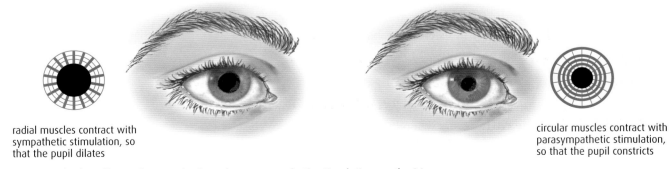

radial muscles contract with sympathetic stimulation, so that the pupil dilates

circular muscles contract with parasympathetic stimulation, so that the pupil constricts

Figure E.27 The effects of sympathetic and parasympathetic stimulation on the iris.

Brain death

Life-support machines in a modern hospital can take over the roles of vital organs such as the heart or lungs when a person is seriously ill or injured in an accident. They keep a person's body functioning without the need for impulses from the brain and can provide time for an organ to recover so that the person may regain full health. The patient may even be unconscious or in a coma because of damage to the brain, which can recover in time. But a patient with severe damage to the medulla oblongata (brain stem) is unlikely to recover because this region controls breathing, heart rate and all the automatic, vital functions of life. The legal definition of 'brain death' is based on the activity of the brain stem. If this is permanently damaged, the brain is regarded as having lost neurological function so that consciousness and spontaneous breathing will never be possible.

Doctors test the activity of the brain stem to determine whether to continue life support. The lack of a pupil reflex is a key indicator of brain death – the doctor shines a light into the patient's eye, and observes whether or not the pupil constricts. If not, the patient is likely to be considered brain dead. However, a number of other reflex actions such as eye movement and the blinking reflex are also always checked.

Perception of pain

Pain reflexes (Figure **E.2**, page **403**) occur as a result of stimulation of pain receptors in the skin and other organs. Impulses are carried from these free nerve ends to the sensory areas of the cerebral cortex, where messages are interpreted so we perceive pain and make suitable responses. Pain is an important feeling because it warns of damage to the body and enables us to take action to protect ourselves.

Excessive pain can be debilitating and, in some situations, the pituitary gland releases **endorphins**, which are neurotransmitters with pain-relieving properties. Endorphins block the transmission of pain impulses to the cerebral cortex by binding with opiate receptors at synapses in the brain. Morphine and heroin mimic endorphins and bind to the same receptors. Endorphins are released at times of stress, after accidents or injuries and can induce a feeling of well-being. Endorphins not only work as natural pain relievers, but also produce a so-called 'runner's high' after physical exercise.

Immediately after a road accident, a person may feel no pain and may sometimes even be able to move themselves away, despite serious injuries. Endorphins and adrenalin override the feelings of pain for a short time so that the person can quickly escape from danger.

20 Outline the function of the medulla oblongata.

21 What is the importance of the medulla oblongata in determining brain death?

22 Outline how FMRI scans have been used to identify the functions of different parts of the brain.

E6 Further studies of behaviour

Social organisation

Social organisation is a feature of many species in which animals live together in groups. Some animals live in large well-organised colonies while others form looser cooperative groups for part of their lives. Social organisation provides protection from predators, opportunities for division of labour among the group and support in finding food.

Rhesus macaques (*Macaca mulatta*)

Rhesus macaques live in central, south, and southeast Asia, in large mixed groups of males and females that contain between 10 and 80 individuals. Females are born and remain in the same group all their lives. The group also includes males that emigrate from their mothers' groups at the beginning of the breeding season, and may be attached to several groups during their lives.

Female macaques form hierarchies within the group. High-ranking females have greater access to feeding sites because they displace lower-ranking females and they are less likely to be disturbed during feeding. But low-ranking females do not eat less than high-ranking females. Macaques have cheek pouches and store as much as they can in them before moving away from the group to eat.

Mothers are responsible for care of the infants, although the job may be shared with close female relatives. Young receive food and are taught skills by their mothers. As young macaques grow up in the group, they learn the social, foraging and fighting skills that will influence their success as adults.

Adult males cooperate to protect the young and are responsible for the group's pattern of movement, including where to forage and sleep. Dominance and rank among males is not stable over a lifetime. Immature males inherit the rank of their mothers, but as they mature, this changes. Once a male attains dominant status, he holds this rank for about two years before being displaced.

The whole group benefits from cooperation and a social arrangement that makes it possible to forage and share food, while protecting and nurturing the young animals. Working together, the group can also keep away predators and individuals from other groups. Figure **E.28** shows some rhesus monkeys in their natural habitat.

Figure E.28 In rhesus macaques, behaviour like grooming has not only a practical role in ridding animals of parasites, but also a social role, helping to maintain the coherence of the group.

Honey bees

Honey bees (*Apis mellifera*) are social animals that live in large, well-organised colonies. No member of the group can survive without the others. Bee colonies contain up to 60 000 individuals. They may build nests in hollow trees or hives provided by a bee keeper. Each member of the colony has a specific role and belongs to one of the three **castes**.

- The **queen** is a fertile female, and lays eggs. She produces pheromones controlling the activities of the colony and preventing other females becoming fertile. A queen may live for up to two years.
- **Drones** are fertile males, and mate with virgin queens.
- **Workers** are sterile females that carry out all the work of the hive. They live for about six weeks and gather nectar and pollen, make wax combs for storing honey and feed and protect the larvae.

When a colony becomes too large, the old queen leaves the nest followed by a number of workers. They form a large swarm and find a suitable site to establish a new colony. A new queen will remain behind to re-establish the old nest, but worker bees drive out the drones at the end of the season.

Natural selection and colonies

In colonial animals, such as the honey bee, natural selection does not operate at the level of the individual since most animals in the colony are not able to reproduce. Instead natural selection acts on the whole colony. Selection pressure favours genes that keep the colony functioning efficiently. These may include genes that promote social organisation or care of the young, or those that produce effective pheromones to ensure workers work together.

Altruism

Altruistic behaviour is 'unselfish' behaviour – it does not directly benefit the individual itself, but benefits another individual, which may be genetically related. Altruistic behaviour may decrease the individual's chance of survival and reproduction, but increase the number of offspring produced by another animal. Two good examples of species that demonstrate altruistic behaviour are the naked mole rat (*Heterocephalus glaber*) and the Florida scrub jay (*Aphelocoma coerulescens*).

Naked mole rats (Figure **E.29**) live in East Africa. They build tunnels, which contain colonies of about 80 animals. Only one dominant female, the 'queen', reproduces. This means that all the members of the colony are genetically related to one another, and have many of the same genes. Some mole rats in the colony act as workers – they dig tunnels, gather food and build the nesting chamber. Other workers remain in the nesting chamber to keep the queen and her offspring warm. These 'guards' also defend the colony against predators such as snakes and may fight to the death in an effort to prevent the colony from being harmed. The sexual behaviour of all the worker animals is suppressed by the queen (probably through the production of hormones) and males only become sexually active when she is ready to mate.

Figure E.29 Naked mole rats sleep together, surrounding the breeding queen. Their body heat keeps the nesting chamber at the correct temperature.

The division of tasks in this way improves the chances of survival, and of passing on genes to the next generation, for all the members of the colony. The workers cannot have direct offspring of their own, but their behaviour increases the survival chances of other offspring, which share many of their genes.

Florida scrub jays show altruistic behaviour for part of their lives. The fledged offspring of a breeding pair of birds often help with the feeding of the next brood. They also defend the family territory and watch for predators, sacrificing their own chance to reproduce until the next season. Nests with helpers are more successful and produce larger numbers of offspring than those without a helper. As the helpers share genes with the new young brood, their altruistic behaviour increases the chance that the shared genes will pass to future generations.

Evolution favours behaviour that increases the flow of alleles to the next generation. So, in helping kin (close genetic relatives), an altruist may increase the reproductive success of its relatives sufficiently to compensate for the reduction in its own genetic contribution to the next generation.

Foraging behaviour

Efficient feeding behaviour is essential for survival and reproduction. But in hunting or foraging there is a cost in terms of the energy needed to find, catch and consume food, which has to be balanced with the benefit an animal gains from the food. Animals are able to change and balance their behaviour to ensure that the overall benefit is greater than the costs.

The blue gill sunfish (*Lepomis macrochirus*) is a well-studied species that feeds on water fleas (*Daphnia* sp.) and other small pond invertebrates. Table **E.5** shows how the foraging behaviour of the blue gill sunfish varies depending on the amounts of *Daphnia* available. When there is a low density of prey available, the fish consume all sizes of *Daphnia* but at medium densities, they consume only middle-sized or larger prey. When food is abundant they actively select only the largest *Daphnia*. Feeding on small numbers of large prey takes less energy than catching large numbers of small prey, if they are nearby. If the density of food is low, the fish will eat whatever they can rather than go hungry.

Starlings (*Sturnidae* sp.) feed their young on crane fly larvae, which burrow in grassy areas. The birds probe the soil and extract larvae. As their beaks become filled with insects to take back to their nests, foraging becomes less efficient. However, a full beak means fewer trips back to the nest. The optimum number of larvae a bird will carry depends on the distance between the foraging area and the nest. The greater the distance, the larger the number of larvae the bird carries in its beak.

Mate selection and exaggerated traits

The elaborate tail of the peacock (*Pavo cristatus*) has fascinated biologists for many years (Figure **E.30**). Why did such an elaborate and impractical structure evolve and what purpose does it serve?

Density of *Daphnia* in pond habitat	Sizes of *Daphnia* selected as prey by blue gill sunfish
low	all
medium	middle-sized or large
high	largest

Table E.5 The foraging behaviour of the blue gill sunfish depending on the amount of prey available.

Figure E.30 Females prefer males with longer tails and more eye spots, so males with these features have more reproductive success, and are more likely to pass on their genes to the next generation.

In the 1980s, research carried out by Malte Andersson revealed that on the prairies where long-tailed widow birds live, males with tails up to 1.5 m long court females by jumping in the air. In their open habitat, they can be seen more than a kilometre away. In his research, Andersson shortened the tails of some birds and lengthened those of others and discovered that female birds preferred long-tailed birds. Not only that, the females especially chose those males whose tails had been artificially lengthened.

In the 1990s, Marion Petrie studied a group of male peacocks. She discovered that females not only preferred males with long tails but also selected those with more eye spots on their tails.

It is clear that females of these species prefer males with large and attractive tails but the reasons for this are not fully understood. Females may prefer such males because they are likely to produce attractive (and therefore reproductively successful) male offspring, or because an attractive tail is a sign of good health. There is evidence that the number of eye spots is correlated with the numbers of B- and T-cells (disease-fighting white blood cells) the peacock produces, which is a sign of a strong immune system. There are many unanswered questions but the facts remain that females select their mates on the basis of their large, attractive tails and that this exaggerated feature does not reduce a male's chance of survival.

'Does the male (peacock) parade his charms with so much pomp and rivalry for no purpose?'

Charles Darwin

Rhythmical activity and its adaptive value

Rhythms of life help animals in the search for food and in reproductive success. These strategies ensure they or their gametes are in the right place at the right time to survive well.

Corals have many reproductive strategies, but nearly all large reef-building species release millions of gametes once a year, in a perfectly timed mass-spawning. This annual event provides a chance for genetic mixing and the dispersal of offspring over great distances. The enormous numbers of gametes together at the same time also maximise the chances of fertilisation, and overwhelm predators with more food than they can possibly consume. The signal to start spawning is probably linked to water temperature, lunar and tidal cycles and day length.

Some animals, such as the red deer (*Cervus elaphus*), have annual cycles for reproduction. Deer mate in the autumn when males challenge one another and fight. The winning stag gathers and mates with a harem of females. Female deer are pregnant during the winter months and give birth to their young in the spring. The advantage of this strategy is that fresh green food is available for both the mothers as they lactate and for the young as they grow. Animals that adopt this annual rhythm are more likely to have reproductive success, and so pass on their genes to the next generation.

Many other species have diurnal or daily patterns of activity. Some animals forage at night and sleep during the day, others do the opposite. The Syrian hamster (*Mesocricetus auratus*) is a nocturnal rodent that lives in underground burrows. It feeds on seeds, roots and vegetable matter and has a good sense of smell. Being active at night helps it to avoid predators as it rests unseen in its burrow or nest hole during the day.

23 Describe what is meant by 'social behaviour'

24 Outline an example in which foraging behaviour leads to optimal food intake.

25 Outline how mate selection can lead to some exaggerated features in animals.

End-of-chapter questions

1 Outline a spinal reflex using the pain withdrawal reflex as your example. (3)

2 Outline what is meant by the term 'contralateral processing'. (2)

3 Outline the role of hair cells in the cochlea in the processing of sound. (3)

4 Distinguish between innate and learned behaviour. (2)

5 Distinguish between taxis and kinesis. (2)

6 Discuss how learning may improve survival chances. (3)

7 Outline Pavlov's experiments on conditioning in dogs. (3)

8 Explain how a pre-synaptic neuron can inhibit a post-synaptic neuron. (2)

9   Outline the behavioural effects of THC (tetrahydrocannabinol).   (2)

10 Discuss the roles of genetic predisposition and dopamine secretion in addiction.   (4)

11 **HL** Outline the functions of the hypothalamus and pituitary gland.   (4)

12 **HL** Explain the role of the sympathetic and parasympathetic systems in the body, using the control of the heart rate to illustrate your answer.   (6)

13 **HL** Discuss how the pupil reflex is used to test for brain death.   (4)

14 **HL** Describe how honey bees show social organisation.   (3)

15 The antennae of the American cockroach (*Periplaneta americana*) are very sensitive to touch. Tapping an antenna causes a quick turning and running response.

The figures below summarise the results of touch trials. The cockroach in Figure A is shown by a symbol in the centre to indicate orientation; the circle represents its head. The cockroach was tapped on one of its antennae and the path of the cockroach's movement was plotted.

The circular histogram in Figure B shows the initial angle of turn for cockroaches tapped on the left antenna. The arrow points to the mean angle of turn. Figure C shows the response time (the time between touch and actual movement) for 215 trials.

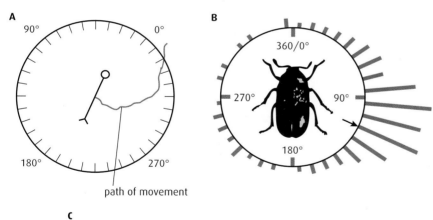

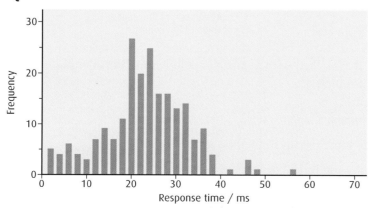

Ye and Comer (1996) *Journal of Neuroscience*, **16**, pp 5844–53 © 1996 by the Society for Neuroscience

a **i** State the mean angle of turn. (1)

The circular histogram in Figure B can be divided into four 90° quadrants, starting at 0°.

  ii Identify the quadrant which scored the lowest number of cockroach runs. (1)

b **i** State the response time with the greatest frequency. (1)
  ii State the range of response times. (1)
  iii Suggest **one** reason for the variation in response time. (1)

c Using Figure A, deduce, giving a reason, which antenna was tapped. (1)

d Discuss the survival value of the behaviour of cockroaches demonstrated by this investigation. (2)

(total 8 marks)
© IB Organization 2009

16 To move in the correct direction, wandering spiders (*Cupiennius salei*) depend on slit sense organs in their exoskeletons. In an experiment to show the importance of these organs, two groups of 32 spiders were used. One group had their slit sense organs intact and the other group had them temporarily damaged. Both groups were temporarily blinded so that so they could not see where they were going.

The spiders were briefly presented with a housefly, which was then removed. The spiders were placed in the centre of a grid and the starting angle that each spider took to find the housefly again was recorded, with 0° leading directly to the housefly and 180° being in the opposite direction to the housefly.

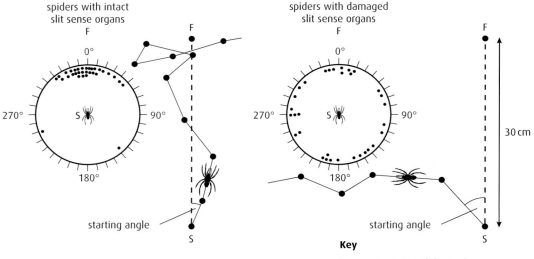

modified from Zill, S and Seyfarth, E (1996) *Scientific American* (July), pp 70–74

Key
S = starting point of the spider
F = position of the housefly

a Calculate the percentage of spiders that walked with a starting angle within 30° in either direction of the housefly in the two groups of spiders:
  i spiders with intact slit sense organs (1)
  ii spiders with damaged slit sense organs (1)

b Compare the effect of damaging the sense organs in the two groups of spiders. (2)

c Discuss whether the spiders were showing innate or learned behaviour in this experiment. (3)

(total 7 marks)
© IB Organization 2009

17 Experiments were done to see if honeybees could learn to associate a reward of sugar solution with a specific colour. Small plates were placed on a table and different wavelengths of light were used to illuminate them. Two plates, each illuminated with a different colour, were presented at one time. Only one contained a sugar solution as a reward. Bees were tested individually to find whether they chose the plate with the reward with each successive trial. Eight trials were conducted at eleven different wavelengths. The results are shown in the graph below. The bold line represents the results of the first trial.

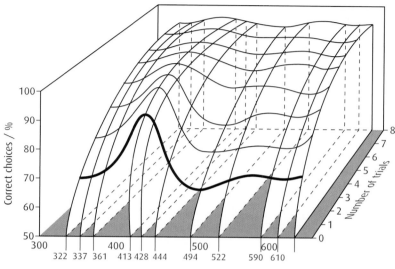

source: Carew, T J (2000) *Behavioural Neurobiology*, Sinauer Associates Inc, p 279

a State the relationship between the number of trials and the percentage of correct choices at any given wavelength. (1)

b Identify the wavelength at which the bees learned most quickly. (1)

c Compare the percentage of correct choices made by the bees on the second trial, at wavelengths of 322 nm and 494 nm. (1)

d Suggest a method based on this experiment to test the long-term memory of bees. (2)

(total 5 marks)

© IB Organization 2009

18 To determine whether birdsong is innate or learned, songs of birds raised naturally were compared with the songs of those raised in isolation. Two species, the swamp sparrow (*Melospiza georgiana*) and the song sparrow (*Melospiza melodia*), were studied. The number of different songs the birds sang, the average number of syllables in the notes, the average length of the songs and the total number of notes were recorded.

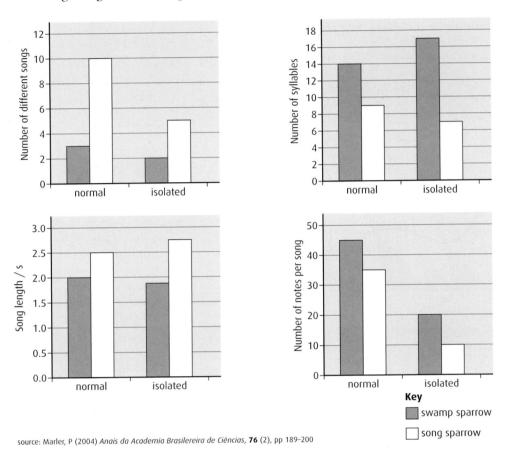

source: Marler, P (2004) *Anais da Academia Brasilereira de Ciências*, **76** (2), pp 189–200

a Calculate the difference in the number of notes per song between the normal and isolated swamp sparrows. (1)

b Compare the song length of both species of sparrow. (2)

c Define the term 'innate behaviour'. (1)

d Discuss whether the results for the song sparrow support the hypothesis that birdsong is innate. (3)

(total 7 marks)

© IB Organization 2009

Microbes and biotechnology Option F

Introduction

Microbes, so called because of their small size, have a vital role to play in all ecosystems. They recycle waste, fix nitrogen and can be used by humans to make bread, cheese, yoghurt, tofu, kvas and beer. Genetically modified bacteria also produce human proteins such as insulin and growth hormone. It has been estimated that microbes account for almost half the biomass on Earth.

Although the majority of microbes are harmless, a few species do cause disease or serious illness. Influenza, polio and HIV are viral diseases and bacteria cause tuberculosis, cholera and leprosy.

Microbes are difficult to classify because of their small size and in the last 30 years our understanding of their similarities and differences has changed as new techniques have helped in our study of their structure and biochemistry.

F1 Diversity of microbes

Assessment statements

- Outline the classification of living organisms into three domains.
- Explain the reasons for the reclassification of living organisms into three domains.
- Distinguish between the characteristics of the three domains.
- Outline the wide diversity of habitat in the Archaea as exemplified by methanogens, thermophiles and halophiles.
- Outline the diversity of Eubacteria, including shape and cell wall structure.
- State, with one example, that some bacteria form aggregates that show characteristics not seen in individual bacteria.
- Compare the structure of the cell walls of Gram-positive and Gram-negative Eubacteria.
- Outline the diversity of structure in viruses including: naked capsid *versus* enveloped capsid; DNA *versus* RNA; and single-stranded *versus* double-stranded DNA or RNA.
- Outline the diversity of microscopic eukaryotes, as illustrated by *Saccharomyces*, *Amoeba*, *Plasmodium*, *Paramecium*, *Euglena* and *Chlorella*.

Classification of living organisms into three domains

In Chapter **5**, you learned that all living organisms are classified into five kingdoms. In the past, it was commonly agreed by scientists that the organisms in the five kingdoms could be separated into two groups, based on their structures:

- **prokaryotes**, with little cellular organisation and no organelles such as the nucleus
- **eukaryotes**, which contain organelles including a nucleus

Modern molecular biology has provided more information about the prokaryotes and led to a change in they way they are classified. Studies of the base sequences of ribosomal RNA have revealed flaws in the old system. Ribosomal RNA evolves very slowly, so it is useful for looking at ancient lines of organisms. New data on the sequences of RNA has shown that the prokaryotes should be split into two distinct groups – the Archaea and the Eubacteria, which are separate from the eukaryotes. The eukaryotes are still grouped as they were before and are known as the Eukarya. These three new groups are called **domains** and were first suggested about 30 years ago. As the Archaea and Eubacteria have been studied in more detail, work on other structures and molecules have confirmed what is known as the three-domain model (Figure **F.1**).

A summary of some of the distinguishing features of the three domains is shown in Table **F.1**.

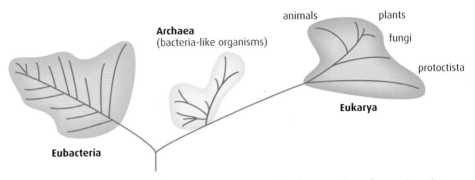

Figure F.1 A possible phylogenetic tree supporting the grouping of organisms into three domains.

	Archaea	Eubacteria	Eukarya
Ribosome analysis	70S	70S	80S
Introns within genes	some	no	yes
Plasmids	few	many	absent
Cell membrane lipids	ether bonds with some branched hydrocarbons	ester bonds, unbranched hydrocarbons	ester bonds, unbranched hydrocarbons
Cell wall containing peptidoglycan	no	yes	no
Membrane bound organelles	no	no	yes
Species with histones	few	no	all

Table F.1 Characteristic features of the three domains.

Habitats of the Archaea

The Archaea (**Archaebacteria** or ancient bacteria) inhabit some of the most extreme environmental conditions on the planet and those that reflect the conditions present in the early part of the Earth's existence. Three different groups of Archaeabacteria are identified from their metabolism and habitats.

- **Thermophilic bacteria** have evolved to survive at temperatures in excess of 70 °C and up to 100 °C in some cases. They inhabit hot, sulfurous springs in volcanic regions and hydrothermal vents on the ocean floor. One species, *Thermus aquaticus*, provides the enzyme DNA polymerase, vital for use in the polymerase chain reaction for amplifying copies of DNA.

- **Halophilic bacteria** live in very salty environments like tidal mud flats and inland lakes (such as the Dead Sea) where the Sun has evaporated much of the water. They are also found in salt mines.
- **Methanogenic bacteria** are anaerobes found in the gut of ruminants (cows and sheep) and termites as well as in waste landfills, sewage works, paddy fields and marshland. They produce methane as a waste product of respiration. Methane is a major greenhouse gas.

Diversity of the Eubacteria

Eubacteria evolved at the same time as the Eukarya, yet still possess primitive features. They have no internal organelle structure and often reproduce by simple binary fission. They are divided into groups based on their shapes (e.g. **bacillus**, **coccus**), as shown in Figure **F.2**.

Bacterial aggregates

Most bacteria live as single cells but some (such as *Streptococcus mutans*, which occurs widely in the mouth) form aggregates or groups of cells that are connected together (Figure **F.2**). *S. mutans* forms a layer known as a **biofilm** on teeth, at the junction with the gums. The bacteria convert sucrose to a glue-like, extracellular polysaccharide that allows the bacteria to stick to each other and form plaque. Together with the acid produced by bacterial metabolism, plaque leads to tooth decay. Other species of bacteria that form aggregates include some species of *Vibrio* that live in the epidermis of sea anemones, and others that produce bioluminescence in the light organs of the squid when they are assembled in large enough groups.

> **Aggregate** a group of bacteria that live together, which has characteristics not seen in individual bacteria; the sea water bacterium *Vibrio fischeri* does not emit light on its own, but in an aggregate the bacteria become bioluminescent

Gram-positive and Gram-negative Eubacteria

As well as being recognised by their shape, bacteria can be separated into two main types by the structure of their cell walls. The Gram staining method is a useful way of differentiating these two types. Gram–negative

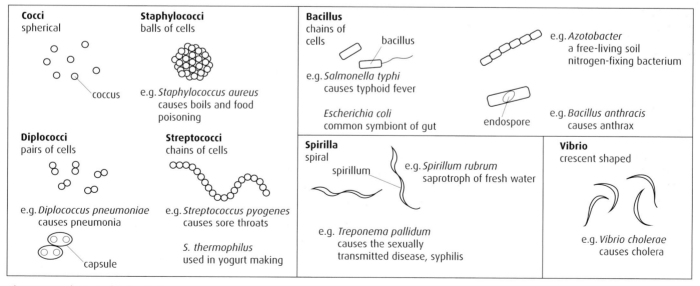

Figure F.2 Shapes of Eubacteria.

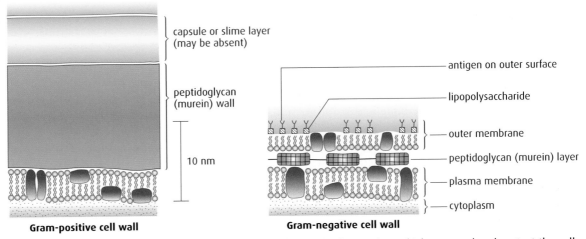

Figure F.3 Peptidoglycan consists of sugar molecules joined to polypeptides, which surround and protect the cell.

bacteria do not retain the colour when the dye crystal violet is added. Gram-positive bacteria retain the dye and appear purple, even when washed in a decolourising solution. These results are explained by the difference in structure of the cell walls – Gram-positive bacteria have large amounts of peptidoglycan in their cell walls whereas Gram-negative bacteria do not (Figure **F.3**).

The main differences between Gram-positive and Gram-negative bacteria are outlined in the Table **F.2**.

Gram-positive	Gram-negative
thick cell wall	thin cell wall
several layers of peptidoglycan connected by peptide bridges	layer of peptidoglycan sandwiched between inner and outer layer
no outer layer	outer layer contains lipopolysaccharide (LPS) and protein

Table F.2 Differences between Gram-positive and Gram-negative bacteria.

Diversity of structures in viruses

Viruses differ widely in their shape and appearance but all virus particles contain nucleic acid and are surrounded by a protective protein coat called a **capsid** (Figure **F.4**). The capsid is made from proteins encoded by the viral genome and its shape varies depending on the type of virus. Viruses are not considered to be living organisms because they cannot reproduce independently; they need a living a host cell in order to do so.

Viruses are classified using features of their capsids and genetic material:

- **capsids** – some have naked capsids with the protein coat having no membrane or envelope surrounding it, while others have enveloped capsids with a lipid bilayer surrounding them
- **nucleic acid** – some viruses contain DNA, while others have RNA. It can be either single or double stranded.

Viruses and viroids

Viruses (also called virus particles or virions) are very small and consist of nucleic acids and protein capsids. Viroids are even smaller, about 80 times smaller than a typical virus. They were discovered and given their name by Theodor Diener, an American plant pathologist, in 1971. Viroids consist only of RNA and contain no protein at all. They have circular molecules of RNA with only a few hundred nucleic acid bases – the smallest known has only 220 whereas viruses contain at least 2000 bases. Viroids cause a number of plant diseases.

Polyhedrons

Capsomeres arranged into multifaceted shapes.
The herpes virus has 162 capsomeres and has an envelope as a protective coating.

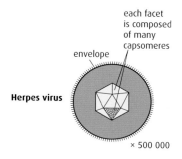

each facet is composed of many capsomeres

envelope

Herpes virus

× 500 000

Complex

More complex structure than other groups. Vaccinia (smallpox) virus has outer double membrane and inner core with DNA. Many bacteriophages (viruses that attack bacteria) are complex.

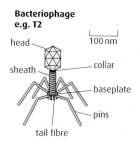

Bacteriophage e.g. T2

100 nm

head
sheath — collar
— baseplate
— pins
tail fibre

Helices

Conical capsomeres arranged helically in capsid in which RNA is embedded, forming a nucleocapsid.

Tobacco mosaic virus

helical RNA – fits into groove surrounded by protein

nucleocapsid

20 nm

Vaccinia virus

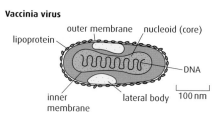

outer membrane   nucleoid (core)
lipoprotein

DNA

inner membrane   lateral body   100 nm

Figure F.4 Most viruses are geometric in shape and may be spheres, cylinders or polygons. The capsid is made up of units called capsomeres. When combined with the enclosed nucleic acid, the capsid is called a nucleocapsid.

The diversity of microscopic eukaryotes

The microscopic eukaryotes are a diverse group of organisms. Using a microscope, it is possible to see the variety in their structure. They also vary in their methods of nutrition and of movement. Table **F.3** summarises the differences found in the group. The structures of the organisms listed in the table are shown in Figure **F.5**, overleaf.

Organism	Cell structure	Nutrition	Movement
Saccharomyces sp. (yeast)	cell wall made of chitin	heterotrophic, absorbs small molecules saprotrophically and feeds on sugars	non-motile
Amoeba	no cell wall	heterotrophic, feeds on other organisms	moves using amoeboid movement
Plasmodium (malarial parasite)	no cell wall	parasitic, some of its life cycle occurs in human cells	moves by gliding
Paramecium	no cell wall	heterotrophic, takes in food by endocytosis	moves in a swimming motion using cilia
Euglena	no cell wall	autotrophic and heterotrophic, contains chlorophyll	moves by whipping its flagellum
Chlorella (single-celled green alga)	cell wall made of cellulose	autotrophic, photosynthesises using a chloroplast	non-motile

Table F.3 Differences between types of eukaryotic organisms.

1 What are the key characteristics used to classify organisms into three domains?

2 Outline the habitats in which the Archaea may be found.

3 Outline the mode of nutrition of *Saccharomyces*, *Euglena* and *Chlorella*.

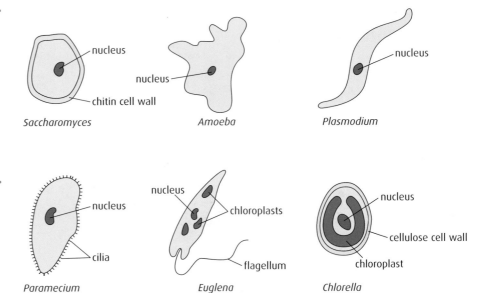

Figure F.5 Basic structures of the microscopic eukaryotic organisms listed in Table **F.3**.

F2 Microbes and the environment

Assessment statements

- List the roles of microbes in ecosystems, including producers, nitrogen fixers and decomposers.
- Draw and label a diagram of the nitrogen cycle.
- State the roles of *Rhizobium, Azotobacter, Nitrosomonas, Nitrobacter* and *Pseudomonas denitrificans* in the nitrogen cycle.
- Outline the conditions that favour denitrification and nitrification.
- Explain the consequences of releasing raw sewage and nitrate fertiliser into rivers.
- Outline the role of saprophytic bacteria in the treatment of sewage using trickling filter beds and reed bed systems.
- State that biomass can be used as raw material for the production of fuels such as methane and ethanol.
- Explain the principles involved in the generation of methane from biomass, including the conditions needed, organisms involved and the basic chemical reactions that occur.

The roles of microbes in ecosystems

Many microbial organisms have important roles in ecosystems. We can identify three main areas that benefit all other organisms living on Earth.

Producers

Many microbes contain chlorophyll and are photosynthetic. The organic material they produce can be used as a source of food for other organisms and they produce oxygen as a waste product. The cyanobacteria, also known as blue–green bacteria, are found in the sea, in fresh water and in saline lakes. They are even found in the soil crusts of arid areas.

Nitrogen fixers

These bacteria possess the enzyme nitrogen reductase, which enables them to convert nitrogen gas into ammonia. Plants of the Leguminosae family, which includes clover, peas, beans, lucerne and lupins, contain nitrogen-fixing bacteria in specialised nodules in their roots. These plants are very important in crop rotation, because the bacteria add nitrogen-containing minerals to the soil.

Decomposers

These are saprophytic bacteria and fungi that secrete hydrolytic enzymes into their surrounding environment and break down organic compounds in dead organisms. They release inorganic nutrients that can be taken up by plants. Decomposers are an important part of several mineral cycles.

The nitrogen cycle

Many bacteria are important in the nitrogen cycle. Nitrogen is an essential part of amino acids and the action of bacteria ensure that it is recycled in the environment (Figure **F.6**).

Although nitrogen gas (N_2) is inert and unreactive, many important compounds contain nitrogen. Ions of some of these compounds are:

NO_2^-	nitrite
NO_3^-	nitrate
NH_4^+	ammonium

Key

→ nitrogen fixation
→ nitrification
→ decomposition and ammonification by decomposers
→ other processes

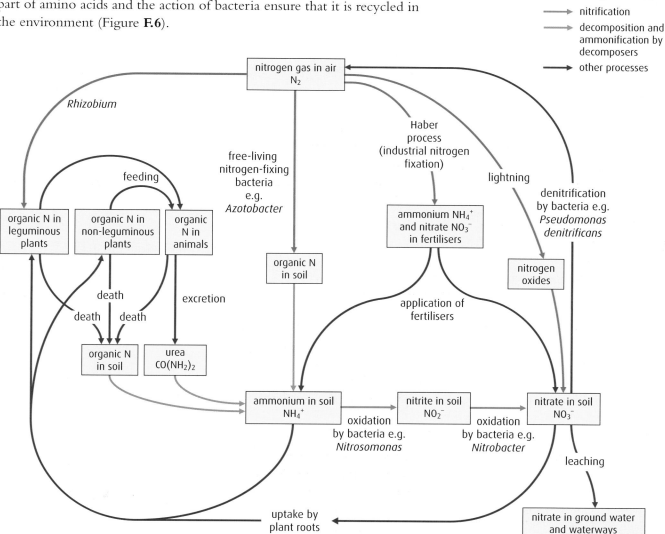

Figure F.6 The roles of different bacteria in the nitrogen cycle.

Figure F.7 *Rhizobium* nodules on the roots of a bean plant.

The nitrogen cycle and soil fertility

Plants absorb the nitrogen they need to grow in the form of nitrates. Fertile soil contains nitrates, which can be absorbed through plant roots.

Good for plant growth are:

- nitrogen fixation, which converts nitrogen gas to useful nitrates
- nitrification, which converts ammonia to useful nitrates.

Bad for plant growth is:

- denitrification, which converts useful nitrates to nitrogen gas (which plants cannot use).

Nitrogen fixation

Nitrogen fixation may be carried out by the free-living organism *Azotobacter*, which lives independently in soil. It is also carried out by *Rhizobium*, which invades the roots of legumes to form nodules in a mutualistic relationship (Figure **F.7**). The ammonia formed by both organisms reacts with organic acids to form amino acids. For example, pyruvate (pyruvic acid) reacts with ammonia to form the amino acids alanine, valine and leucine.

Nitrogen is also fixed in industrial processes such as the Haber process used for the production of fertilisers and by lightning during thunderstorms.

Nitrification

Nitrification is the oxidation of ammonia to nitrate. This is carried out in the soil by *Nitrosomonas*, which uses oxygen to convert ammonia to nitrite, and also by *Nitrobacter*, which also uses oxygen and converts nitrite to nitrate. This is an important part of the cycle because both ammonia and nitrite are toxic to plants. Plants can only absorb nitrates through their roots.

Nitrification is favoured by neutral pH, warmth and well-aerated soil, as it is an oxidative process.

Denitrification

Denitrification is the conversion of useful nitrate in the soil to nitrogen. *Pseudomonas denitrificans* completes the cycle by converting nitrite and nitrate into gaseous nitrogen. This reduces the fertility of the soil.

Denitrification is favoured by anaerobic conditions, found in compacted or waterlogged soils, with a high nitrogen input.

The pollution of waterways

Raw sewage

Raw sewage produced by human activity is high in nitrates and phosphates and also contains many pathogens. If it is released into rivers and streams that are used for drinking water or bathing, diseases such as cholera and typhoid can easily be spread.

Nitrate and phosphates in sewage also cause ecological problems if raw sewage leaks into rivers and streams. In time, the river may recover as long as no other pollution occurs.

1 Saprotrophic bacteria and fungi feed on the organic material in the raw sewage as a source of nutrients, and multiply. These aerobic organisms use up a large amount of oxygen and reduce its concentration in the water. They are said to have a high **biochemical oxygen demand** (BOD).

2 When the oxygen level drops, river organisms, including fish and many invertebrates that are highly dependent on high oxygen levels, die or move to another unpolluted areas if they can.

3 Death and decay of the sensitive organisms leads to a build up of ammonia, phosphate and minerals.

4 Ammonia is converted to nitrate and with this increased concentration of nutrients, algae reproduce rapidly. This is known as **eutrophication**.

5 In time, the increased photosynthesis by the large amounts of algae that use the nitrate to grow restores the levels of oxygen, so the river returns to normal.

6 If the algae produce an **algal bloom** and then die and decay, this may cause a cycle of events that reduce oxygen concentration again and lead to the death of other organisms, so that the river takes longer to recover. If the algae do not die, then the river can recover from sewage pollution, although this may be several kilometres downstream.

Nitrate fertilisers in rivers

Farmers are sometimes blamed for causing eutrophication through inappropriate use of fertilisers, which are high in nitrates and phosphates. Excess fertiliser can run off the land and flow into rivers.

1 Nitrates and phosphates are very soluble and cause algae in water to proliferate.

2 If algae grow very rapidly, they may form an algal bloom, which deprives other plants of light so that they die. Saprotrophs decompose the dead plants and decrease levels of oxygen in the water, as there is a high BOD.

3 Oxygen-dependent organisms become threatened, and die or move away. In many countries, fertiliser use is controlled, and in modern farming the requirements of crop plants are closely monitored. It is difficult to blame farmers if, for example, it rains heavily after fertiliser is applied, so much of it passes through the soil to ground water, before crop plants have absorbed it.

The treatment of sewage

Saprotrophic bacteria play an important role in the treatment of sewage using trickle filter beds and reed bed systems.

Sewage treatment is very important for human health and different methods are used in different countries. Inorganic material is removed first and then bacteria are used to break down and remove the organic material.

Trickle filter beds

A trickle filter bed consists of a large tank containing a layer of gravel or clinker, which provides a large surface area on which a film of saprotrophic bacteria can grow (Figure **F.8**). Raw sewage is sprayed onto the rocks while keeping the environment well aerated. The sprayer is

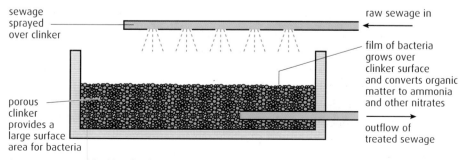

sewage sprayed over clinker

raw sewage in

film of bacteria grows over clinker surface and converts organic matter to ammonia and other nitrates

porous clinker provides a large surface area for bacteria

outflow of treated sewage

Figure F.8 A trickle filter bed.

usually turned in a circle over the rocks so there is even coverage. The bacteria feed on the organic material in sewage and break it down to simple inorganic compounds such as nitrates and phosphates.

The effluent is sent to a second tank where the bacteria sink to the bottom as sludge and are removed. One problem with this system is that the purified water may contain relatively high concentrations of nitrate and phosphate.

Reed beds

A reed bed system can also be used to treat sewage (Figure **F.9**). Reeds are grown on sand or gravel medium, which maintains an oxygenated area for the roots of the plants and the saprotrophic bacteria in the medium. Sewage flows into the reed bed and the bacteria break down organic material to nitrates and phosphate, which can be taken in by the plant roots. The nutrients provided for the reeds enable them to grow; they are later harvested and composted for fertiliser. While this system solves the problem of high levels of nitrates and phosphate in the purified water, reed beds must be large to be effective as they can only cope with a limited flow of sewage.

Biomass for fuel

Biomass in the form of wood and agricultural waste, such as straw and animal manure, already provides a useful source of fuel. Now many countries are looking at the use of **biofuels** to reduce their dependence on fossil fuels. Biofuels are produced by converting biomass into ethanol or methane. This is done in bioreactors, either on a large industrial scale or on a domestic scale at a farm or in a village. A simple, small scale bioreactor is shown in Figure **F.10**.

Methane produced from animal manure and agricultural waste is known as biogas. Manure and straw are fed into the bioreactor, where they decompose anaerobically as different groups of bacteria present in the manure break down the organic material. The slurry that remains is a useful fertiliser.

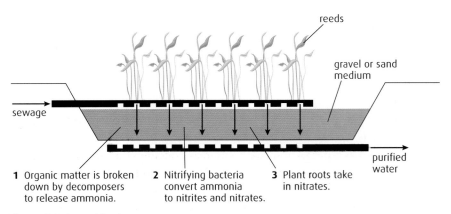

1 Organic matter is broken down by decomposers to release ammonia. **2** Nitrifying bacteria convert ammonia to nitrites and nitrates. **3** Plant roots take in nitrates.

Figure F.9 A reed bed.

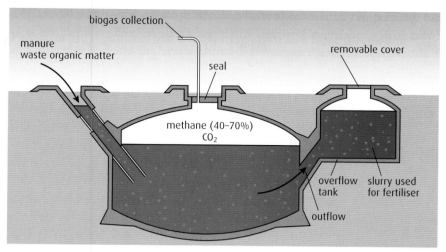

Figure F.10 Cross-section of a biogas reactor.

Three groups of bacteria produce the enzymes that digest organic material, and each stage breaks down the complex carbohydrates, fats and proteins into simpler compounds.

- Organic material is first converted to organic acids and ethanol by anaerobic, **acidogenic bacteria**, which occur naturally in manure.
- **Acetogenic bacteria** then use the organic acids and alcohol to produce acetate, carbon dioxide and hydrogen.
- Finally, **methanogenic bacteria** produce methane either from carbon dioxide and hydrogen or by breaking down acetate:

carbon dioxide + hydrogen → methane + water
$$CO_2 + 4H_2 → CH_4 + 2H_2O$$

acetate → methane + carbon dioxide
$$CH_3COOH → CH_4 + CO_2$$

The sequence of these processes is shown in Figure **F.11**.

The biogas that is produced contains up to 70% methane and about 30% carbon dioxide. Biogas can be used to produce electricity or burned directly as a renewable fuel, and the by-products of the reactions can be used as fertiliser.

The production of biofuels has the advantage of being **sustainable** because plants regrow each season. In addition, it makes use of the methane gas that is naturally produced by the anaerobic digestion of organic matter. Methane is a potent greenhouse gas, partly responsible for global warming.

Worldwide, a range of fuels is now produced from biomass on a large scale. Bioethanol can be used as a fuel for vehicles in its pure form, but it is usually used as a petrol additive to increase octane and improve vehicle emissions. Bioethanol is widely used in the USA and in Brazil. Biodiesel made from oils and fats is most often used as a diesel additive to reduce levels of emissions, and is the most common biofuel used in Europe. In 2008, biofuels accounted for almost 2% of the world's transport fuel.

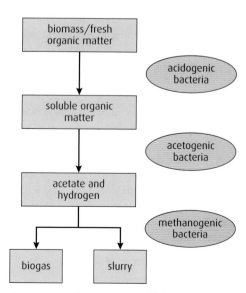

Figure F.11 Three groups of bacteria digest organic waste to produce methane.

4   Give some examples of the roles of microbes in ecosystems.

5   Distinguish between the terms 'denitrification', 'nitrification' and 'nitrogen fixation'.

6   Explain the part played by saprotrophic bacteria in sewage treatment.

F3 Microbes and biotechnology

Assessment statements

- State that reverse transcriptase catalyses the production of DNA from RNA.
- Explain how reverse transcriptase is used in molecular biology.
- Distinguish between 'somatic' and 'germ line' therapy.
- Outline the use of viral vectors in gene therapy.
- Discuss the risks of gene therapy.

Reverse transcriptase and its use in molecular biology

The enzyme **reverse transcriptase** was discovered in 1970 in a group of viruses known as **retroviruses**, which includes HIV and feline leukaemia virus. These viruses contain RNA as their genetic material. Reverse transcriptase is produced when a retrovirus invades a host cell. It enables the virus to transcribe RNA into a single strand of DNA, using nucleotides from the host cell. The new **complementary DNA (cDNA)** is then converted to double-stranded DNA using the enzyme DNA polymerase. The original RNA is degraded and the double-stranded DNA is inserted into the host's chromosomes (Figure **F.12**).

Reverse transcriptase is widely used in genetic engineering. Molecular biologists are able to produce therapeutic proteins such as insulin and growth hormone by inserting the genes that code for them into the genetic material of bacteria. The bacteria then produce large amounts of the required protein as they grow and multiply.

However, eukaryotic chromosomes contain non-coding regions of DNA known as **introns** (page **177**) within their genes. If a genetic engineer wants to produce a protein from a particular gene, these introns must be removed. In normal cells, mRNA produced from the DNA undergoes an editing process known as **post-transcriptional modification** to remove the introns. This process occurs in the nucleus. The cell uses only this modified, **mature mRNA** to make its proteins.

Bacteria are unable to remove introns, as they cannot perform post-transcriptional modification of mRNA. This means that eukaryotic DNA cannot be used directly to genetically modify bacteria. Instead, genetic engineers collect mature mRNA from eukaryotic cells that produce the required proteins and use the enzyme reverse transcriptase to produce

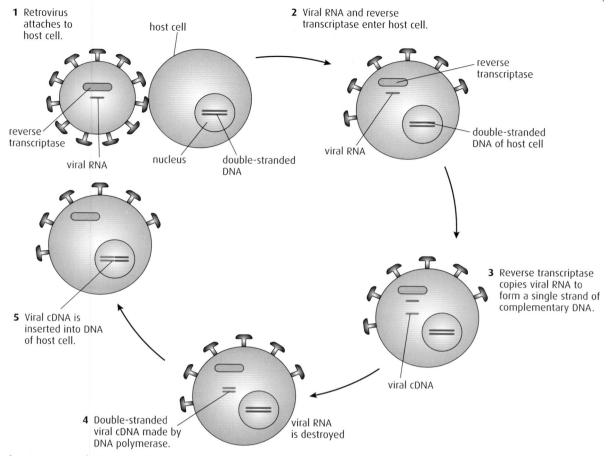

1 Retrovirus attaches to host cell.

host cell

reverse transcriptase

viral RNA

nucleus

double-stranded DNA

2 Viral RNA and reverse transcriptase enter host cell.

reverse transcriptase

viral RNA

double-stranded DNA of host cell

3 Reverse transcriptase copies viral RNA to form a single strand of complementary DNA.

viral cDNA

5 Viral cDNA is inserted into DNA of host cell.

4 Double-stranded viral cDNA made by DNA polymerase.

viral RNA is destroyed

Figure F.12 Viral invasion of a host and DNA production.

DNA from it. This DNA does not have intron sequences, since it is copied from the mature RNA, and can therefore be incorporated into bacterial DNA for protein production.

The stages in the process are shown in Figure **F.13** (overleaf).

Gene therapy

The technique of **gene therapy** involves treating genetic conditions by introducing genes into human cells so as to alter the genome. If defective genes can be replaced with fully functioning genes, it may be possible to treat certain genetic conditions.

- **Somatic cell gene therapy** means treating body cells to replace defective genes. One condition that has been considered for such treatment is the inherited disease cystic fibrosis (CF). CF is caused by a defective transporter protein in plasma membranes. The normal transporter protein moves chloride ions across the membrane and CF patients suffer with a sticky mucus in many of their secreting glands, including the lungs and digestive system, because their plasma membranes are unable to do this. One treatment for CF that has been tried is to insert the normal gene for the transporter protein into cells of the lungs via a vector. Unfortunately, this only treats the problem in one area of the body and CF patients will still pass on the defective gene to their children.

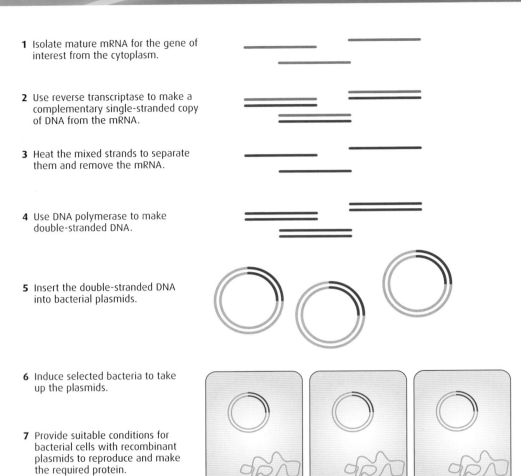

1 Isolate mature mRNA for the gene of interest from the cytoplasm.

2 Use reverse transcriptase to make a complementary single-stranded copy of DNA from the mRNA.

3 Heat the mixed strands to separate them and remove the mRNA.

4 Use DNA polymerase to make double-stranded DNA.

5 Insert the double-stranded DNA into bacterial plasmids.

6 Induce selected bacteria to take up the plasmids.

7 Provide suitable conditions for bacterial cells with recombinant plasmids to reproduce and make the required protein.

Figure F.13 The use of reverse transcriptase in genetic engineering.

The plasmids used in genetic engineering are 'marked' by the inclusion of antibiotic resistance genes. This makes it easy for biotechnologists to select them.

- **Germ line gene therapy** means treating gametes or the tissues that are responsible for making them. This treatment would not alter the disease in the individual, as they would still have the defective gene in their body cells. However, it would prevent the defective gene from being passed on to the person's children. In the future, it may be possible to use germ line therapy to treat single-gene conditions such as hemophilia but, at present, there is international agreement to ban germ line therapy on ethical grounds. Many people openly disagree with research in this area because of its unknown effect on future generations.

Viral vectors in gene therapy

Viruses are very efficient at entering the cells of organisms and as **vectors** provide a powerful means for the delivery of therapeutic genes into cells. Some viruses are even able to incorporate the genes they carry into the cells they enter.

Before a virus can be used, it must be modified so that it will enter but not replicate inside a target cell. Viral genes that are involved in replication are removed or inactivated. Deletion of these genes also allows non–viral genetic material to be inserted and these viruses are then known as vectors.

Retroviruses are the most frequently used vectors. These single-stranded RNA viruses enter target cells via specific receptors and their RNA is converted into DNA and integrated into the genetic material of the cell, where it remains for the life of the cell. Integrated genes are also passed on when the cell divides.

There has been some success in treating a condition called severe combined immune deficiency (SCID) using retroviruses. Children who suffer from SCID have no immune system because a gene mutation prevents their cells producing the enzyme ADA (Figure **F.14**). Substrates for ADA build up in cells and are very toxic to developing lymphocytes. These cells fail to mature and the patient is left without a working immune system. Stem cells from bone marrow or umbilical cord blood (see pages **16–17**) can be taken out of the body and treated with viral vectors that transfer a normal copy of the ADA gene to them. If the treated cells are returned to the bone marrow, the replacement genes can begin to produce ADA. Bone marrow and stem cell transplants now save up to 80% of SCID patients.

Figure F.14 Without treatment, some SCID patients must live in a sterile 'bubble' to protect them from infection.

Gene therapy

Gene therapy involves modification of genetic material in the cells of a patient in order to bring about a therapeutic effect. Modification is usually achieved by introducing DNA, using viral vectors or other means. Although gene therapy is still in its infancy in medical treatments, discussion of the ethical issues involves principles that apply to all clinical medicine. How are subjects selected for gene therapy trials? How can the safety of individuals who take part in the trials be safeguarded, and do scientists involved in the trials have a conflict of interest between wanting to conduct their research and the best interests of their patients?

In 2007, a 36-year-old woman with rheumatoid arthritis died while participating in a clinical trial for gene therapy. Some experts say she shouldn't have received such an unpredictable, potentially dangerous treatment at all. She was able to lead a full and active life with existing drugs keeping her disease under control. Soon after the experimental treatment a sudden infection caused her organs to fail and there is a suspicion that her death was linked to the therapy. Is it ethical to test unknown therapies on patients whose ailments are not life-threatening?

In the future, new therapies based on genetic engineering, such as DNA vaccines, could potentially benefit a great number of people worldwide. This is in contrast to early developments of genetic engineering in medicine, which were largely beneficial for the health problems of rich countries. Priorities in medical research do raise troubling issues of social ethics.

Questions to consider

1 Can 'good' and 'bad' uses of gene therapy be distinguished?
2 Who decides which traits are normal and which constitute a disability or disorder worthy of gene therapy treatment?
3 At present, the high costs of gene therapy make it available to only a few people. Can costs and benefits of treatments be evenly balanced in society?
4 How can the safety of patients be considered in treatments that are new or experimental?
5 Are there conflicts of interest between patient safety and the need to conduct research?

The risks of gene therapy

At present, gene therapy is at a very early stage of development and much more research is needed before it can be used in routine treatments. There are many risks associated with gene therapy, some of which are listed below.

- If a virus vector integrates the therapeutic gene in the wrong place in the host DNA it can cause an existing gene to malfunction.
- Retroviruses can turn on cancer-causing genes.
- Virus vectors may revert to a pathogenic form of the virus.
- Viral proteins may trigger an immune response.
- Therapeutic genes may not be expressed, or if they are there is no guarantee that the correct quantity of protein will be produced.
- If the virus does not integrate the therapeutic gene into the host DNA, treatment must be repeated.
- A virus vector may be transferred from person to person with unforeseen outcomes.

7   Outline the role of the enzyme reverse transcriptase in gene technology.

8   Outline some of the risks associated with gene therapy.

F4 Microbes and food production

Assessment statements

- Explain the use of *Saccharomyces* in the production of beer, wine and bread.
- Outline the production of soy sauce using *Aspergillus oryzae*.
- Explain the use of acids and high salt or sugar concentrations in food preservation.
- Outline the symptoms, method of transmission and treatment of one named example of food poisoning.

The production of bread, wine and beer

People have been making use of microorganisms in the production of food for thousands of years. Bread, made from wheat, has been a staple food since the beginnings of agriculture. Without knowing what the organism was, people have used several yeast species (*Saccharomyces* spp.) to make bread, wine and beer since ancient Egyptian times. The simple, single-celled fungus was identified by Louis Pasteur in the late 19th century. *Saccharomyces* species metabolise sugars aerobically to form carbon dioxide and water, while in anaerobic conditions they ferment sugars to produce ethanol and carbon dioxide. It is the anaerobic pathway that is important in food production.

glucose (or other sugar) → ethanol + carbon dioxide

In bread making, yeast converts the sugar in wheat dough to carbon dioxide and ethanol. As bread is made, it is left to rise in a warm place, allowing the yeast time to feed on sugars and reproduce at their optimum temperature. Carbon dioxide produced by the yeast makes the bread rise as the gas becomes trapped between the gluten fibres of the wheat. Kneading the dough stretches the gluten and increases its elasticity so that it can retain the carbon dioxide more easily. When bread is baked, the yeast cells are killed and the ethanol they have produced evaporates.

In beer making, grains of barley or other cereals provide the glucose that is fermented by yeast. Barley is mixed with water, which starts the process of germination and releases enzymes, turning the seeds' store of starch into maltose and glucose. Then the seeds are dried so that they do not germinate and develop any further. This process is known as malting. Malted barley is mixed with water, yeast and hops, which add flavour. The yeast respires anaerobically to ferment the sugars from the barley into alcohol and carbon dioxide. Fermentation ends when the sugars are used up and the beer contains between 2% and 6% alcohol (ethanol).

Wine making uses crushed grapes as a source of sugar. Grapes are mixed with yeast in fermentation tanks, where fermentation continues for several months. Alcohol remains in the wine but carbon dioxide escapes from the tank. The species of yeast used in wine making can tolerate alcohol concentrations up to 15% but they are eventually killed by the alcohol. Yeast cells are allowed to settle out of the mixture before the wine is bottled. Different types of wine are produced using different grapes and species of yeast, which give each one a characteristic taste.

The manufacture of soy sauce

Soy sauce is an important ingredient of many oriental cuisines. Crushed soya beans and wheat are mixed with the fungus *Aspergillus oryzae*, which ferments the mixture. In the traditional process, fermentation can last many months.

1 Soya beans are soaked and then boiled.
2 The resulting mash is mixed with flour from roasted wheat.
3 A culture of the fungus *Aspergillus oryzae* is added.
4 The mix is incubated at 30 °C for three days. During this time, the fungus produces amylase, which digests starch in the wheat, and proteases, which digest protein in the soya beans.
5 The mixture is heavily salted and incubated in deep tanks for 3–6 months. After this time, the mixture contains alcohol, organic acids, sugars and amino acids. It is left to age for 4–5 months.
6 The solids are filtered off and the liquid is collected.
7 The liquid is pasteurised, re-filtered and bottled.

This process is summarised in Figure **F.15** (overleaf).

Food preservation

To preserve fresh food, it must be kept free from bacterial or fungal attack. Traditional methods of preserving food use acids, salt or sugar to prevent microbes growing in the food and making it decay or 'go off'.

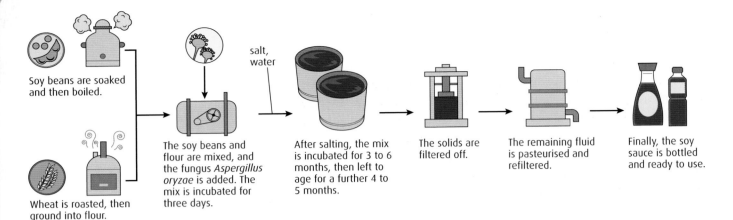

Soy beans are soaked and then boiled.

Wheat is roasted, then ground into flour.

The soy beans and flour are mixed, and the fungus *Aspergillus oryzae* is added. The mix is incubated for three days.

salt, water

After salting, the mix is incubated for 3 to 6 months, then left to age for a further 4 to 5 months.

The solids are filtered off.

The remaining fluid is pasteurised and refiltered.

Finally, the soy sauce is bottled and ready to use.

Figure F.15 The production process of soy sauce.

Irradiation

Irradiation with gamma rays can preserve food, by killing most of the microbes in it. There is little effect on the food itself. The strawberries in Figure **F.16** were picked on the same day and kept in the same conditions. The fruit on the left was irradiated but those on the right were not.

Figure F.16 Irradiated soft fruits like strawberries stay fresh for longer because microbes that would cause decay are eradicated.

Acids

Pickling is a way of preserving food using vinegar, which contains ethanoic (acetic) acid. The low pH of vinegar stops bacteria and fungi from growing. Fruit or vegetable pickles are flavoured with spices and are widely used in cooking to add flavour and texture to other foods. In some cultures, the pickling of small onions, cucumbers and cabbage is popular.

Milk is also preserved by acid in the form of yoghurt. Lactic acid bacteria convert lactose in the milk to lactic acid, which prevents other microbes growing in the milk and preserves it.

Salt and sugar

High salt or sugar concentration kills microbes because of its osmotic effect. A strong salt or sugar solution draws water out of the cells of bacteria or fungi and kills them. Salting meat and fish was a common method of preservation used on long sea voyages in the past; today, refrigeration and freezing are used instead.

Honey keeps well because it is naturally high in sugar. Fruits and vegetables prepared in jams and jellies are also preserved by added high concentrations of sugar.

Food poisoning

Most food-borne illness is caused by single-celled bacteria. Bacteria such as *Campylobacter jejuni* may grow in food that has not been stored or cooked properly and cause outbreaks of food poisoning. Food poisoning is caused by bacterial toxins, which harm the tissues of the stomach and intestines.

Bacteria may grow in food and produce toxins before the food is eaten. Once formed, these toxins may survive high temperatures, so that even if the bacteria themselves are killed by cooking, the toxins remain. Alternatively, bacteria can be taken into the gut as food is eaten. *Campylobacter* invades the lining of the intestine where it grows and produces toxins that cause the symptoms of food poisoning. Pain, vomiting, diarrhoea and a high temperature may develop 3–5 days after contaminated food has been eaten.

Campylobacter jejuni is found in raw meat and particularly in poultry. Chicken is most often implicated as the source of *Campylobacter* infection although the bacteria are regularly found in turkey, duck, other meat and unpasteurised dairy products.

Campylobacter is killed by thorough cooking, so it is important never to eat undercooked chicken. Good food hygiene when handling raw poultry prevents the spread of bacteria to other foods. Chicken should always be stored in a refrigerator at less than 4 °C to prevent bacteria reproducing. Chopping boards used to cut raw meat should be thoroughly washed before being used for other foods and hand washing after touching raw meat will prevent bacteria being transferred to other people or foods.

In recent decades, there has been an increase in reported cases of food poisoning worldwide. Food scientists think that several factors have led to this.

- Food poisoning bacteria may have developed more virulent strains.
- Fast food has become more popular, and there is less opportunity to observe good hygiene standards by washing hands before and after eating.
- Some fast food outlets may have poor hygiene and keep meat warm for long periods of time – ideal conditions for bacterial infection and growth.
- Greater public awareness may have led to more cases of food poisoning being reported.

9 Explain why high levels of salt or high concentrations of sugar help in the preservation of foods.

10 Give **one** example of an organism that causes food poisoning and explain how it is transmitted.

F5 Metabolism of microbes

Assessment statements

- Define the terms 'photoautotroph', 'photoheterotroph', 'chemoautotroph', and 'chemoheterotroph'.
- State one example of a photoautotroph, photoheterotroph, chemoautotroph and chemoheterotroph.
- Compare photoautotrophs with photoheterotrophs in terms of energy sources and carbon sources.
- Compare chemoautotrophs with chemoheterotrophs in terms of energy sources and carbon sources.
- Draw and label a diagram of a filamentous cyanobacterium.
- Explain the use of bacteria in the bioremediation of soil and water.

Microbe metabolism

Microbes have a varied range of metabolic processes that enable them to use different sources of energy and carbon. Microbes are divided into four groups based on their methods of metabolism: **photoautotrophs**, **photoheterotrophs**, **chemoautotrophs** and **chemoheterotrophs** (Table **F.4**, overleaf).

Method of metabolism	Energy source to generate ATP	Carbon source used to obtain organic compounds	Example
photoheterotrophic	light	organic compounds	An example of a photoheterotroph is *Heliobacter*. These bacteria are found in waterlogged soils and paddy fields. They are able to fix nitrogen so they are probably important in soil fertility.
chemoheterotrophic	chemical reactions	organic compounds	Fungi such as the yeast *Saccharomyces* are chemoheterotrophic microbes. These organisms cannot photosynthesise, so must use organic material as an energy source. They respire or ferment sugars to make ATP. Most bacteria are chemoheterotrophs.
photoautotrophic	light	inorganic carbon dioxide	An example of a photoautotroph is *Anabaena*, a cyanobacterium (filamentous blue–green bacterium) found in freshwater plankton and on grass (Figure **F.17**). It fixes nitrogen and forms symbiotic relationships with some plants.
chemoautotrophic	chemical reactions	inorganic carbon dioxide	*Nitrobacter*, a nitrifying bacterium found in the soil (Figure **F.6**, page **443**), is an example of a chemoautotroph. Others include the sulfur-oxidising Archaea that live in hostile environments such as deep sea vents.

Table F.4 Different types of microbe metabolism.

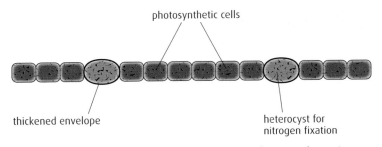

photosynthetic cells

thickened envelope

heterocyst for nitrogen fixation

Figure F.17 The structure of *Anabaena*, a photoautotrophic cyanobacterium.

Photoautotroph microbe that uses light energy to create ATP and to produce organic material from simple inorganic materials

Photoheterotroph microbe that uses light energy to generate ATP but which gets the organic compounds it needs from other organisms

Chemoautotroph microbe that uses energy released from chemical reactions to generate ATP and which makes its own organic material from simple inorganic materials

Chemoheterotroph microbe that uses the chemical energy released from chemical reactions to generate ATP and obtains organic compounds from other organisms

Bioremediation

Bioremediation is the process that uses microbes to treat areas of land or sea that have been contaminated by pesticides, oil or solvents.

Crude oil spills from tankers at sea contain many chemicals that harm the marine environment and seashore. Many different microbes are able to oxidise harmful hydrocarbons and break down the oil. To increase the numbers of bacteria and speed up the bioremediation process, nitrate and phosphate fertilisers are added to encourage the decomposition of the crude oil by the bacteria. Bioremediation like this can halve the time it takes to clean up an oil spill.

On land, bioremediation has been used to remove pesticide residues, heavy metals such as selenium, and solvents. Bioremediation often happens very slowly as bacteria in the environment break down toxic substances. To speed up the process, the supply of nutrients is enhanced by adding inorganic fertilisers. Spreading out polluted soils can stimulate faster growth of bacteria.

Several species of bacteria have been found to contain the enzyme nitro-reductase, which gives them the ability to break down explosives such as TNT (2,4,6-trinitrotoluene). These species can be used to clean up contaminated land. Over the last century, large quantities of explosives have been manufactured for military and industrial use. Many are highly resistant to biodegradation and large areas of land are contaminated with residues from their manufacture and storage. Incineration of affected soil is very expensive, so bioremediation is an attractive alternative.

In Australia, two species of bacteria, *Pseudomonas* sp. and *Azospirillum* sp., have been isolated from contaminated soils around disused sheep dips. These bacteria have been shown to be capable of breaking down organophosphate pesticides, which remain in the soil and pose a significant threat to the environment and public health. The bacteria are being used to develop a more general bioremediation strategy for the removal of the pesticides.

11 State the difference between a photoautotroph and a photoheterotroph, and give **one** example of each.

12 What is meant by the term 'bioremediation'?

F6 Microbes and disease

Assessment statements

- List six methods by which pathogens are transmitted and gain entry to the body.
- Distinguish between 'intracellular' and 'extracellular' bacterial infection using *Chlamydia* and *Streptococcus* as examples.
- Distinguish between endotoxins and exotoxins.
- Evaluate methods of controlling microbial growth by irradiation, pasteurisation, antiseptics and disinfectants.
- Outline the mechanism of the action of antibiotics, including inhibition of synthesis of cell walls, proteins and nucleic acids.
- Outline the lytic life cycle of the influenza virus.
- Define 'epidemiology'.
- Discuss the origin and epidemiology of one example of a pandemic.
- Describe the cause, transmission and effects of malaria, as an example of disease caused by a protozoan.
- Discuss the prion hypothesis for the cause of spongiform encephalopathies.

The transmission of pathogens

A **pathogen** is a disease-causing agent or microbe, so the study of disease is called **pathology**. For a pathogen to be successful, it must transfer from one person to another and gain entry into a new host. The human body is protected by a tough outer layer of skin, mucous membranes, cilia, tears and oil glands but even so, pathogens have a variety of ways to infect people (Table **F.5**, overleaf).

Route of transmission of pathogen	Mode of entry of pathogen	Examples
airborne, usually through droplets of mucus from a sneeze (Figure **F.18**), cough or talking	breathed in via the respiratory system	influenza, tuberculosis
in water or food	mouth	cholera, dysentery
wounds such as a cut or scratch	bacteria and viruses can enter once the protective skin barrier is broken	tetanus, schistosomiasis, rabies
indirect contact with objects such as cups or toys that have been in contact with a source of infection	pathogens may enter via the mouth or skin	conjunctivitis
used syringes from infected people	injection into veins	HIV, hepatitis
animal vectors, such as mosquitoes or fleas	skin is punctured by biting insects	malaria, dengue fever, bubonic plague
direct person-to-person contact, or exchange of body fluids	sexual intercourse transfers pathogens directly into another person's body	syphilis, HIV

Table F.5 The ways in which pathogens cause and spread infections.

If a person is infected by a pathogen, one of three things may happen.

- The person's immune system may fight the infection and kill it.
- The microorganism may remain in the body in such a way as to be invisible to the immune system.
- The person may die of the infection, so the microorganism may die too.

Intracellular and extracellular infections

Once inside a human, a pathogen can survive in two different ways. Some survive in body fluids without actually invading cells, causing **extracellular infection**. Others invade and live inside host cells, causing **intracellular infection**. Table **F.6** compares common examples of these two types of infection.

Figure F.18 Sneezes spread diseases in droplets of mucus.

Streptococcus – an extracellular pathogen	Chlamydia – an intracellular pathogen
lives in the body, but outside cells	lives inside cells
produces toxins	does not produce toxins
harms or kills cells	does not harm cells (during dormant phase)
detected by the immune system	not detected by the immune system

Table F.6 Comparison of an intracellular and extracellular pathogen.

Extracellular infection

Streptococcus is a typical example of an extracellular bacterium. It is a very common pathogen and it has been estimated that 5–15% of humans harbour the bacterium without having any symptoms. It is found on the skin and in the upper respiratory tract, often causing minor infections such as impetigo or 'strep throat'. *Streptococcus* spreads by direct person-to-person contact or through the air by sneezing or coughing. Usually, symptoms are mild and need no treatment although sometimes a doctor may prescribe antibiotics. On rare occasions, *Streptococcus* can penetrate further into the blood or deeper layers of skin where it causes more serious infections including some that are life-threatening. All extracellular bacteria secrete exotoxins (see below), which cause symptoms such as fever, rashes or a sore throat. *Streptococcus* also secretes substances called **invasins**, which digest host cells. Invasins are enzymes that degrade tissues and the materials holding tissues together, so the bacterial infection can spread. *Streptococcus* triggers the immune system to produce antibodies, which fight the infection.

Intracellular infection

Chlamydia is an example of an intracellular bacterial infection. It is one of the commonest sexually transmitted diseases, and often remains untreated because infected people have no symptoms, or symptoms that are non-specific. Once a person becomes infected, the organism invades and lives inside the epithelial cells lining the genital tract. When the bacterium reproduces it ruptures the host cell membrane and re-enters the genital tract, ready to invade other cells. Intracellular bacteria are hidden inside body cells and do not produce any toxins, so the immune system is unaware of their presence and symptoms do not develop. *Chlamydia* does not damage cells when it is inside them, but long-term consequences of the infection include pelvic inflammatory disease and infertility.

Endotoxins and exotoxins

Toxins are harmful substances produced by pathogens.

Endotoxins are substances known as lipopolysaccharides found in the outer layer of cell walls of Gram-negative bacteria. They are immunogenic and stimulate an inflammatory response in the infected person. This gives rise to fever and aching.

Exotoxins are secreted by bacteria and may act at areas distant from the site of bacterial infection. Exotoxins are usually proteins, often enzymes, which act directly on host cells. Some are very specific – for example, *Clostridium tetani* (the bacterium that causes tetanus) acts on neurons to produce muscular spasms. *Cholera* bacteria produce an exotoxin that damages cells in the intestine causing fluid loss from the ileum (small intestine) and diarrhoea.

Controlling microbial growth

Microbial growth can be controlled either by killing the microorganisms or by slowing down their growth. **Bactericides** are substances that kill bacteria, while **bacteriostatic** substances inhibit their growth.

Irradiation

Various parts of the electromagnetic spectrum kill bacteria.

- Gamma irradiation kills by breaking down nucleic acids and interfering with cell division. This method is often used in treating packaged food such as tinned products and soft fruits (Figure **F.16**, page **454**), and for sterilising medical equipment.
- Microwaves kill bacteria by heating them to a point where macromolecules, especially proteins, denature and the cells boil.
- Ultraviolet (UV) light kills bacteria but their spores may still be active.

Pasteurisation

Pasteurisation is the heat-treatment method discovered by Louis Pasteur (1822–1895) in the 19th century. A temperature is chosen that is **bactericidal** for pathogenic bacteria, so these bacteria are killed. Food such as milk is then safe to consume but retains its flavour and consistency. The pasteurisation temperature is only **bacteriostatic** to non-pathogenic bacteria so that their growth is inhibited but some bacteria remain. Pasteurised milk will eventually turn sour through the action of acid-producing bacteria that remain in it. However, keeping milk cold will extend its life for several days. For milk and milk products, a temperature of over 65 °C is bactericidal but to sterilise milk for yoghurt production and kill all the bacteria it contains, a temperature of about 95 °C is necessary.

Antiseptics and disinfectants

Both antiseptics and disinfectants are used to kill bacteria on contact.

Antiseptics are used on the skin, often at a cut or wound, or before surgery. Common antiseptics are iodine and alcohol, which are not very toxic to skin and are not readily absorbed. A few antiseptics are bacteriostatic and just prevent bacterial growth.

Disinfectants are not used on the skin because they can damage living tissues and are also toxic to humans. They are used on hard surfaces such as kitchen floors, work tops, medical equipment and drains, which must be kept free of pathogenic bacteria. Common disinfectants include phenol, chlorine-containing bleaches and detergents. Disinfectants kill microbes because they oxidise components of the bacterial cell wall, causing the cells to break apart.

Antibiotics

In 1928, Sir Alexander Fleming (1881–1955) was working at St Mary's hospital in London. He had been growing *Staphylococcus* sp. on media in agar plates and he noticed that in one plate there was a contaminating fungus. He was surprised to see that the fungus had not only stopped the bacterial growth but had killed it. He sampled the fungus and discovered that it was from the *Penicillium* genus. Howard Florey and Ernst Chain took up Fleming's work and purified the active, antibiotic ingredient from the fungus, which was called penicillin. Tests on humans demonstrated that it was active against bacterial infections. Production of penicillin began in America in the 1940s, and it became the first widely available **antibiotic**.

Antibiotics are part of a range of antimicrobial drugs, derived from bacteria and fungi. They are produced naturally by microorganisms to inhibit competitor microbes around them although many are now synthesised in the laboratory.

All antibiotics interfere with bacterial metabolism but different antibiotics work in different ways.

- Some damage bacterial cell walls. For example, the synthesis of new cell wall components (such as peptidoglycan) during cell division may be inhibited.
- Some inhibit protein synthesis by blocking transcription of DNA into mRNA, or by blocking translation of mRNA into protein on ribosomes.
- Some inhibit bacterial enzymes that are vital for their cell metabolism.
- Some inhibit DNA replication, so cell division cannot take place.

Some examples of antibiotic action are shown in Table **F.7**.

Antibiotics	Mode of action
penicillin, cephalosporin	cell wall damage
tetracycline, streptomycin, chloramphenicol	block protein synthesis
sulfanilamide	inhibits vital enzymes
rifampin (also known as rifampicin)	inhibits DNA replication

Table F.7 Antibiotics and their modes of action.

Unfortunately, many pathogenic bacteria evolve drug resistance, so an antibiotic may become inactive against them. In such cases, new or different antibiotics have to be used. Pharmaceutical companies are constantly researching new antibiotics and other ways of combating bacterial infections.

The life cycle of the influenza virus

Influenza is a typical virus, which must infect a living cell in order to reproduce. Once inside a cell, the virus takes over the machinery of the cell to manufacture many copies of itself, which may go on to infect other cells in the infected organism. Influenza viruses reproduce in what is known as the **lytic** life cycle.

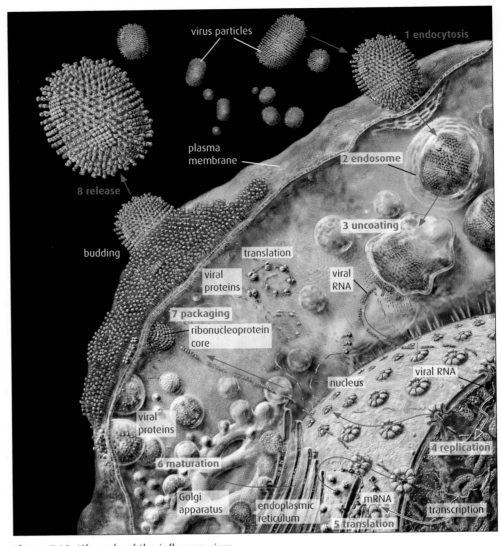

Figure F.19 Life cycle of the influenza virus.

Many types of virus fill up their host cells with new viruses as they use the cell's metabolism to reproduce. When the cell is full of up to 200 viruses, it bursts (**lyses**) thus giving the lytic cycle its name. Some viruses, including influenza, escape the host cell without bursting the cell membrane. New viruses bud off from infected cells, taking portions of the membrane with them. The virus' reproduction is still the same in all other ways as the lytic life cycle, so they are still included in this category.

1 The virus attaches to receptors on the cell surface.
2 The virus particle forms an endosome, coated with some of the cell membrane, as it enters the cell by endocytosis.
3 Once inside the cell, it loses its envelope, and viral RNA is released.
4 Viral RNA travels to the nucleus where copies of the RNA and complementary mRNA are produced.
5 Some of mRNA moves to the cytoplasm where it is translated into viral protein on the rER of the host cell.
6 Some of the proteins are modified in the Golgi apparatus and become incorporated in the outer membrane of the cell. Others move back inside the nucleus to surround the viral RNA and form new viruses.
7 New viruses move to the outer cell membrane where they recognise the inserted viral proteins. They bud off from the membrane, surrounded by the viral proteins.
8 Released viruses infect other cells or transfer to a new host in droplets that are sneezed or coughed out.

Epidemiology

Information from epidemiological studies is used to plan strategies to prevent illness at a national and global level, and as a guide for the management of patients who already have diseases. **Epidemiology** is very important in public health and preventive medicine and most governments have strategies in place for dealing with outbreaks of serious communicable diseases.

Pathogenic organisms do not recognise national boundaries, so it is important that epidemiological research is conducted at the international level. Organisations such as the Centers for Disease Control (CDC) in the USA and the World Health Organization (WHO) in Switzerland collect data on diseases such as malaria, influenza and HIV.

Pandemics

Several disease-causing organisms have the ability to spread rapidly across countries and continents, resulting in a **pandemic**. Historically, the bubonic plague pandemic devastated the whole of Europe in the Middle Ages, and it is estimated that a third of the population of Europe died as a result. In modern times, influenza has erupted as a pandemic several times. The worst outbreak to date was in 1918 when between 20 and 40 million people died worldwide. Many epidemiologists think that the world is due for another influenza pandemic, so this is why new infections such as 'bird flu' and 'swine flu' are always closely monitored.

The 1918 pandemic of influenza was known as 'Spanish flu'. The factors involved in producing the pandemic include:

- The causative agent, the influenza virus, mutated to a new strain that was not recognised by the immune system, so people had little natural immunity.
- The pathogen spread easily from person to person. In 1918, the First World War was ending and many people were moving across countries as soldiers returned home.
- The mortality rate was very high, but the course of the disease was long enough for the pathogen to spread to other people before it caused the death of its host.
- Influenza virus is more likely to produce a pandemic because it contains single-stranded RNA, which can easily mutate. It is likely that the 'Spanish flu' virus mutated by exchanging pieces of RNA with other viruses.

On scientific and medical advice, public health departments tried to contain the pandemic in various ways.

- Face masks were worn in public places, as it was realised that the virus was transmitted by droplets in air.
- Public gatherings in places such as cinemas and theatres were banned.
- In some countries, schools were closed.
- The use of disinfectants and sterilisation of equipment became common in hospitals.

Epidemiology the study of the occurrence, distribution and control of disease

Viruses and receptors

Some viruses are very specific and only recognise certain receptors on the surface of a cell. Cells without them cannot be infected.

The HIV virus uses a receptor known as CD4 to gain entry to host T-cells and only T-cells are affected by the virus. HIV virus attaches to CD4 using a protein in its capsid. The binding to CD4 allows the virus to bind to two other surface receptors on the cell. HIV infection reduces the number of T-cells that have CD4 receptors. A count of the number of CD4 receptors is used to decide on treatments for HIV-infected patients.

Epidemics and pandemics

An epidemic is a widespread outbreak of an infectious disease where many people in a community are infected at the same time.

A pandemic is an epidemic that is geographically very widespread and may occur throughout a region or throughout the world.

- In hospitals, infected people were placed in quarantine and separated from other patients.
- People were educated about hygiene and hand washing to prevent the spread of viruses.

In 1920, the pandemic came to an end as the number of new cases fell dramatically. This may have been due to the preventive measures, to natural immunity building up in the population, or to further mutation in the virus – or to a combination of all of these factors.

Today, immunisation is used to help prevent pandemics. But this is difficult with the influenza virus because of its rapid mutation rate. For each new strain, a new vaccine is needed and this may take several months to manufacture. In the meantime, the disease may have spread to epidemic or pandemic proportions.

Modern forms of transport make the spread of a disease much quicker than ever before. This is why airports often have screening measures in place. During the 'swine flu' outbreak, in 2008–2009, many airports had infrared cameras to check for any passengers with high temperatures that might suggest an influenza-type fever.

Malaria

Malaria is a major health problem in the tropics, affecting 300 million people each year in equatorial Africa, Central and South America and the Middle East. It is caused by the protozoan parasite *Plasmodium* spp. (Figure **F.20**). Four different species cause malaria, and produce either

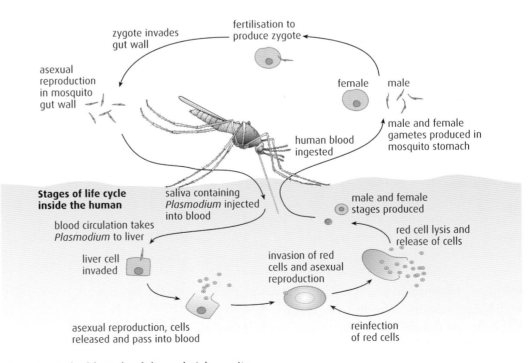

Stages of life cycle inside the mosquito

fertilisation to produce zygote

zygote invades gut wall

asexual reproduction in mosquito gut wall

female   male

male and female gametes produced in mosquito stomach

human blood ingested

Stages of life cycle inside the human

saliva containing *Plasmodium* injected into blood

male and female stages produced

blood circulation takes *Plasmodium* to liver

red cell lysis and release of cells

liver cell invaded

invasion of red cells and asexual reproduction

asexual reproduction, cells released and pass into blood

reinfection of red cells

Figure F.20 The life cycle of the malarial parasite.

acute or chronic symptoms. The parasite is spread from person to person by a vector, the female *Anopheles* sp. mosquito, when she feeds on blood. *Plasmodium* reproduces in the intestine of the mosquitoes and releases cells called sporozoites, which travel to the insect's salivary glands. Males of the species feed only on plant nectar and so do not carry the parasite.

When a *Plasmodium*-carrying mosquito bites, it injects saliva to prevent the blood clotting and the sporozoites are injected with it into its host's bloodstream. They travel to the liver where they continue to develop and multiply inside hepatic cells. Once mature, they change their form and invade red blood cells (Figure **F.21**), multiplying inside them until they burst out into the plasma, where they can invade more red blood cells. Some develop into male and female forms that can infect new mosquitoes. If a non-infected mosquito bites the malaria sufferer, *Plasmodium* is taken up with the insect's meal and transferred to its intestine. Sexual reproduction takes place and *Plasmodium* migrates to the salivary glands ready to infect a new person (Figure **F.20**).

Mosquitoes breed in any warm, still, stagnant water, so places like marshes, rainwater tanks, water collecting in rubbish such as car tyres and cans are all used by the mosquito.

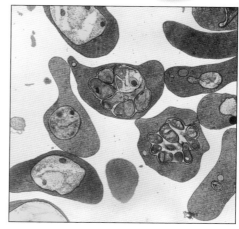

Figure F.21 Coloured transmission electron micrograph of a section through some red blood cells infected with the malarial parasite.

Symptoms of malaria

Infected people suffer from periods of fever, sweating and chills. Anemia also develops as the red blood cells are damaged. Symptoms peak when red blood cells burst, which may happen in a recurring cycle in chronic malaria.

In acute malaria, damaged red blood cells may block capillaries and lead to organ failure and fever may increase to a level at which coma and convulsions result in death.

Treatment and prevention

Malaria can be prevented if mosquitoes are killed by draining swamp areas or spraying insecticides. Mosquitoes feed mostly during the night so mosquito nets keep insects away from people while they are sleeping (Figure **F.22**, overleaf).

Malaria can be prevented with anti-malarial drugs and treated if drugs are administered soon enough after infection. In some parts of the world, *Plasmodium* has become resistant to many of the anti-malarial drugs available, so new methods of treatment and vaccines are being investigated.

Transmissible spongiform encephalopathies

Transmissible spongiform encephalopathies (TSEs) are a group of incurable diseases that affect a variety of mammals especially cattle, sheep, goats and humans. Bovine spongiform encephalopathy (BSE, also known as mad cow disease) in cattle, Creutzfeldt-Jacob disease (CJD) in humans and scrapie in sheep are the most well known examples of TSEs. The brains of infected animals develop lesions and a sponge-like appearance causing a lack of coordination, premature aging, dementia and death.

Figure F.22 Sleeping under a mosquito net can protect against being bitten by mosquitoes.

In 1996 a new form of CJD was reported, and named variant Creutzfeldt-Jacob disease (vCJD). Whereas the classic form of the disease affected older people, vCJD affects younger people. Similarities observed between the strain of the agent responsible for vCJD and those of BSE and other TSEs are consistent with the hypothesis that vCJD is due to the same agent that causes BSE in cattle.

Infection occurs when meat from a TSE animal is eaten. The bovine form (BSE) was first diagnosed in the 1980s. It appears that the much older disease scrapie had crossed the species barrier from sheep to cows. The origin of the outbreak of was probably animal feed contaminated with infected carcasses. When humans ate beef from an animal with BSE, the disease was passed to them.

The cause of TSEs: the prion hypothesis

The agent that transmits TSEs is highly stable, resisting freezing, drying and heating at normal cooking temperatures. Enzymes that digest DNA and RNA do not have any effect on it and it is not denatured by chemical treatments. This suggests it is not cellular or viral in form. The exact nature of the infectious agent is in debate. The most widely held view is that it is an abnormal **prion** protein. Normal prion protein (PrP) occurs in the brain on the surfaces of neurons, but its function is still unclear. In TSEs, a mutation in the gene responsible for making PrP causes cells to produce an abnormal form of prion known as PrP^{Sc}. This has the ability to convert PrP into more PrP^{Sc} in a chain reaction. The abnormal form builds up in the brain creating the sponge-like appearance.

Eating beef products from cattle infected with BSE may be the way that PrP^{Sc} enters the human body. This hypothesis is supported by a parallel example in the occurrence of a TSE called kuru in Papua New Guinea in the 19th and early 20th century. This seems to have been transmitted when tribe members ate tissue of affected people during ritual

Accepting the unexpected

The transmission of BSE did not fit any known theory for disease transmission at the time when the first cases occurred. There are still uncertainties about how prions, if they are responsible for spongiform encephalopathies, are passed from species to species.

Stanley Prusiner discovered prions, which he described as a class of infectious self-reproducing pathogens. He proposed that prions were composed primarily or solely of protein but, as he writes below, gaining acceptance of his work was not easy.

'I had anticipated that the purified scrapie agent would turn out to be a small virus and was puzzled when the data kept telling me that our preparations contained protein but not nucleic acid. When everything seemed to be going wrong, including the conclusions of my research studies, it was the unwavering, enthusiastic support of a few of my closest colleagues that carried me through this very trying and difficult period.

As the data for a protein and the absence of a nucleic acid in the scrapie agent accumulated, I grew more confident that my findings were not artefacts and decided to summarise that work in an article that was eventually published in the spring of 1982. Publication of this manuscript, in which I introduced the term 'prion', set off a firestorm. Virologists were generally incredulous and some investigators working on scrapie and CJD were irate. The term prion, derived from 'protein' and 'infectious', provided a challenge to find the nucleic acid of the putative 'scrapie virus'. Should such a nucleic acid be found, then the word prion would disappear! Despite the strong convictions of many, no nucleic acid was found; in fact, it is probably fair to state that Detlev Riesner and I looked more vigorously for the nucleic acid than anyone else.

While it is quite reasonable for scientists to be sceptical of new ideas that do not fit within the accepted realm of scientific knowledge, the best science often emerges from situations where results carefully obtained do not fit within the accepted paradigms'.

from Stanley B. Prusiner – Autobiography. Nobelprize.org © The Nobel Foundation

Questions to consider

1 How are theories to explain such unexpected events developed?

2 How do scientists communicate their hypotheses and discoveries and how is a consensus eventually reached?

3 Prusiner's work eventually led to a paradigm shift in the scientific world and in 1997 he was awarded a Nobel Prize in Physiology and Medicine for his prion research. What does the term 'paradigm shift' mean?

cannibalistic feasts. Also, animals that are infected with PrP^{Sc} do develop TSE and abnormal prions can induce normal proteins to change shape. The prion hypothesis is the best explanation of the current observations of TSEs, although it does not explain how new forms of the disease arise.

Another possible cause is a virus–like agent (or virino). In this case, the infecting agent would contain RNA or DNA, capable of undergoing mutations – but, as yet, no nucleic acids have been found in the infecting agent. On the other hand, a virino could explain the presence of multiple strains of the BSE agent.

13 How do *Chlamydia* and *Streptococcus* differ in the way they infect the human body?

14 Outline the different ways that are used to control microbial growth in everyday life.

15 Describe how malaria is transmitted and outline its effects on the body.

End-of-chapter questions

1 Outline the production of soy sauce. (4)

2 Distinguish between 'somatic therapy' and 'germ line therapy'. (2)

3 The drive for healthier eating has led to an increase in the demand for natural food additives such as colours and preservatives. An essential oil (OEO) extracted from oregano, a herb used in cooking, has been shown to have anti-microbial properties. However, it has a strong flavour and so investigations were carried out on two of its principle components, thymol and carvacrol, on two bacteria, *Pseudomonas aeruginosa* and *Staphylococcus aureus*. Both thymol and carvacrol are nearly tasteless.

The graphs below show the extracellular concentrations of phosphate and potassium ions in samples of *S. aureus* with and without OEO.

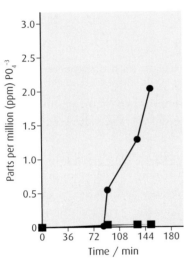
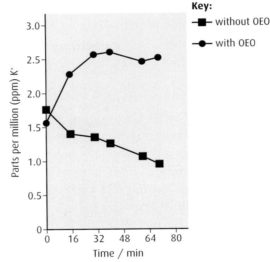

Key:
- without OEO
- with OEO

source: Lambert, R J W, Skandamis, P N, Coote P J and Nychas, G-J E (2001) 'A study of the minimum inhibitory concentration and mode of action of oregano essential oil, thymol and carvacrol', *Journal of Applied Microbiology*, **91**, 453–462

a Compare the extracellular concentrations of potassium ions with and without treatment with oregano essential oil in *S. aureus*. (2)

b Explain why the effects of thymol and carvacrol will kill the cells. (2)

c The normal cytoplasmic concentration of potassium ions is about 2 ppm. Deduce the mechanism of transport of K^+ into the cell. (2)

Ethidium bromide (EB) is a substance that can be detected by a particular laser microscope. EB is unable to pass through the cell membrane of a healthy cell. Cultures of *P. aeruginosa* and *S. aureus* were cultured in a nutrient medium containing EB with and without OEO, thymol and carvacrol and samples observed under the laser microscope.

	Percentage of cells of *P. aeruginosa* containing EB / %	Percentage of cells of *S. aureus* containing EB / %
Control culture	3	1
+ thymol	90	92
+ carvacrol	85	89
+ carvacrol + thymol	87	90
+ OEO	88	89

d Explain the effect of thymol and carvacrol on the bacterial cells. (1)

e Evaluate the use of thymol and carvacrol as a food preservative. (2)

(total 9 marks)

© IB Organization 2009

4 Many microbes are pathogenic and cause disease in other organisms. They can be used as a biological control agent rather than using a chemical pesticide.

a State **one** advantage of using a biological control agent rather than a chemical pesticide. (1)

The beetle *Melolontha melolontha* is a serious pest in hazelnut orchards of northern Turkey. The larvae eat roots, resulting in a reduced harvest. Soil samples from a wide range of environments were collected and fungal species that kill insect larvae cultured from them. Seven strains were selected to test against larvae of *M. melolontha*.

Solutions of spores of each fungal strain were made up. Beetle larvae were dipped in the solution for 2–3 seconds and then placed on moist sand at a constant temperature. Dead larvae were removed and kept separately on moist sand to see if the fungus started to grow on them. After 15 days the percentage of dead larvae was determined. The bars show the standard deviation.

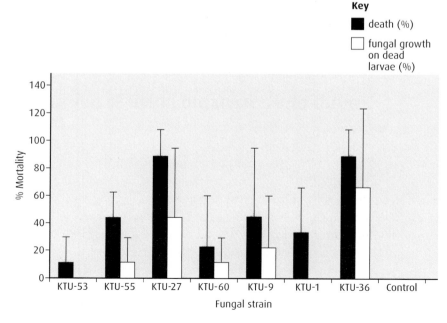

source: adapted from Sevim *et al.* (2010) BioControl, **55**, pp. 279–297, fig. 6

b Identify the fungal strain that caused the lowest death count. (1)

c Evaluate which fungal strain would be the best one to use in a field trial. (2)

d Measure the standard deviation for death in fungal strain KTU–55. (1)

e Suggest what treatment would have been given to the control larvae. (1)

(total 6 marks)

Ecology and conservation Option G

Introduction

Understanding ecology and conservation enables us all to appreciate the delicate web of interactions between organisms in different ecosystems and different parts of the world. Where organisms can live is influenced by climate and other abiotic conditions as well as by the other organisms in the ecosystem. All ecosystems are found in one of seven biomes, which are defined by their own climatic conditions and vegetation. As human populations increase and encroach further into these areas, organisms are being lost and the Earth's biodiversity is decreasing. Conservation of threatened species and protection of important ecosystems can be achieved if there is international cooperation and understanding.

G1 Community ecology

Assessment statements

- Outline the factors that affect the distribution of plant species, including temperature, water, light, soil pH, salinity and mineral nutrients.
- Explain the factors that affect the distribution of animal species, including temperature, water, breeding sites, food supply and territory.
- Describe one method of random sampling, based on quadrat methods, that is used to compare the population sizes of two plant or two animal species.
- Outline the use of a transect to correlate the distribution of plant or animal species with an abiotic variable.
- Explain what is meant by the niche concept, including an organism's spatial habitat, its feeding activities and its interactions with other species.
- Outline the following interactions between species, giving two examples of each: competition, herbivory, predation, parasitism and mutualism.
- Explain the principle of competitive exclusion.
- Distinguish between 'fundamental' and 'realised' niches.
- Define 'biomass'.
- Describe one method for the measurement of biomass of different trophic levels in an ecosystem.

It is almost impossible for an organism to live in isolation. Organisms interact to provide one another with food and shelter and each one influences the distribution of others. Only in highly inhospitable places, like hot springs, do species exist alone, and these are simple organisms such as bacteria that have evolved to survive in these extreme conditions. Even at the bottom of the oceans, where hot vents release geothermal energy from below, there are interactions between organisms.

Factors affecting the distribution of plant species

Organisms are said to live in communities. A **community** may be described by the geographical area in occupies (a lake community, for example), or by the dominant plant species present (coniferous forest, for instance). The organisms present in a community depend on the other organisms living there, as well as on the non-living, **abiotic** aspects, such as soil or climate. The distribution of plants in communities depends on a number of these abiotic factors.

Temperature

No plant can survive freezing conditions for very long because, to grow and reproduce, plants must carry out chemical reactions within their cells that require enzymes. In arctic climates, plant growth is often very slow because enzymes work slowly at the low temperatures, but seasonal because the rate of growth picks up during the relatively short summer. In tropical areas, like rainforests, growth is usually rapid because temperatures are warm, and continuous because there is little seasonal variation in temperature.

Water

All plants require water. It is the universal solvent in their cells, the substrate for photosynthesis, and their transport medium. However, many plants have evolved a variety of mechanisms to survive periods of drought. Some remain dormant, some (such as cacti and succulent plants) store water, and others complete their life cycle in a brief rainy season.

Light

Plants need light for photosynthesis. Many use the changing day lengths of the different seasons to trigger flowering. Where light intensity is high, as in a desert, plants have evolved mechanisms to prevent damage to their chlorophyll, such as dense spines or white hair that reflects light (Figure **G.1**).

Where light levels are low, as they are at ground level in a deciduous forest in the northern hemisphere, some plants grow and complete their annual life cycle in the early part of the year, before overshadowing trees have come into leaf.

Soil pH

Most plants prefer a pH of 6.5–7.0 because nutrients are easily available in this range. Some soils are slightly alkaline because they are based on chalk. Chrysanthemum and lavender are two examples of plants that tolerate alkaline soils well and are found in chalky areas. Other soils are acidic; beech, spruce and camellia can grow here. Peat bogs are very acidic because they are composed of decomposing organic material. Very few plants can grow here, although heathers can survive in acid soils.

Salinity

Saline (salty) soils present a particular problem to plants, because they make it difficult for them to take up water and minerals. Some plants

Figure G.1 The spines and hairs on a cactus help to deflect harmful ultraviolet rays in sunlight.

Figure G.2 The sundew (*Drosera rotundifolia*) is a carnivorous plant that attracts, kills and breaks down insects, for their protein. In this way, it can absorb amino acids and use these to make plant protein and other nitrogenous compounds.

absorb salt in the soil, secrete it in their leaves and then drop these leaves to remove the salt. A few plants, such as marram grass and lyme grass, can survive in saline conditions.

Mineral nutrients

Soils that are rich in minerals can support a diverse community of plant species, including trees and shrubs. Plants that survive in mineral-poor soils often have special adaptations to supplement their needs. Carnivorous plants such as sundew and Venus flytraps live in very peaty soils that are deficient in nitrogen (Figure **G.2**).

Factors affecting the distribution of animal species

Just as for plants, the distribution of animals is affected by the abiotic factors in their environment.

Temperature

Animal enzymes are influenced by temperature in much the same way as those of plants. However, animals have the advantage that they can move to avoid the harshest of conditions. In hot, arid areas like deserts, many animals avoid the heat of the day and burrow underground. The jerboa (*Jaculus jaculus*) has long legs that keep its body off the hot sand and its ears have a large surface area, enabling the animal to lose heat efficiently (Figure **G.3**). Birds and mammals can control their internal temperatures but other species use behaviour and other adaptations to maintain theirs.

Some animals, such as the hedgehog, hibernate to overcome the rigours of cold winters. Many bird species migrate during wintry seasons to warmer climates.

Figure G.3 The jerboa.

Water

Most animals need to drink water to survive. Very few have evolved to be independent of water. Some desert animals like the jerboa (Figure **G.3**) have done this, however. Jerboas eat seeds and, as the stored carbohydrate is respired in their cells, it produces all the water these animals need – they do not actually drink any liquid water.

Lack of water in certain seasons may change the distribution of animals. Herds of wildebeest and zebra in Africa undertake huge migrations to find new supplies of water and, therefore, vegetation. Carnivorous species often follow these herds, which are their source of food.

Breeding sites

Animals need to find appropriate sites to express mating behaviour and then rear young. These sites may be chosen for safety away from predators, or because they provide rich feeding grounds so the young may benefit. Different species have their own requirements. Many frogs and toads live almost entirely on land but must return to water to breed.

Food supply

Unlike plants, which are autotrophic, animals need a source of food. Herbivores need plants and carnivores need other animals to feed on. The availability of food will determine the distribution of different types of animal. Some animals are restricted to a particular area because it supplies their food – so, for example, rabbits are usually found on grasslands. Others, such as lions, have huge territories and may cover many kilometres searching for food. Animals that have a varied diet are generally more successful and have a wider choice of habitats. If one source of food becomes scarce, they can move on to another.

Territory

Herbivores that exist in large herds, such as wildebeest, graze on large areas of grassland and, when the dry season arrives, they migrate to find fresh grass. Some birds, such as the European robin, live in smaller numbers or singly and have less need for space but males defend their territories vigorously because they contain food and a nesting area. Carnivores, such as wolves, that live in packs require a large area to hunt in. They may mark their territory with scent and defend it from other packs. Others, like eagles and other raptors, live solitary lives and have a large hunting territory because their prey is hard to find.

Random sampling of communities

When ecologists want to understand the distribution of a species or to compare the distribution of one species with another in a different location, it is usually impossible to do so by a direct counting method. In most cases, ecologists take a sample of the population and, if the sample is random, it should provide a good representation of the whole population. Random sampling assumes that every organism has an equal chance of being sampled. There are a number of methods available to sample not only what species are present, but how many.

Quadrats

One of the simplest and easiest sampling techniques involves using a quadrat (Figure **G.4**). A **quadrat** is a square made of metal or wood that is placed on the ground so that the organisms present inside the square can be counted.

The size of the quadrat will largely be determined by what is being measured. To estimate the number of different trees in a wood may require quadrats of 10 m by 10 m, but a 1 m quadrat would be the best size for studying wild flowers in grassland. Very small 10 cm quadrats might be used for sampling lichens on walls or tree trunks.

If you just place a quadrat on the ground, you introduce personal bias, because even without meaning to you might place it in a spot that you think will be more interesting, perhaps, or easier to work in. To ensure that your sampling within the survey area is completely random, you should follow these steps.

1 Divide the area to be surveyed into a grid of 1 m squares. Each square can be identified within the grid by numbered coordinates. For example, the square in column 3 (from the left) and row 4 (from the bottom of the grid) would be (3,4) (see Figure **G.5**).

2 Use a random number generator programme or table to choose which grid squares to use. For example, in a grid of 9 m by 9 m, the randomly generated numbers 7 and 2, 6 and 0, and then 3 and 8 would select squares (7,2), (6,0) and (3,8).

3 Now put a quadrat on each of the selected squares in turn, and count the number of individuals of the species being sampled that occur within the quadrat.

4 Finally, find the average number of individuals found in 1 m^2, and multiply this by the total number of squares in the survey area to obtain an estimate of the numbers present in the whole area.

Figure G.4 Using a quadrat to sample a shoreline community.

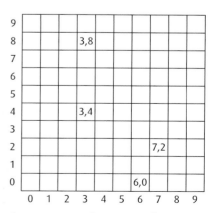

Figure G.5 To select a part of an area to sample with a quadrant, divide the area into a grid of squares, then randomly select a column and a row number.

The number of quadrats that are counted can be determined in one of two ways. To compare populations of a species in two areas, it may be appropriate to sample 5% of the quadrats in each survey area grid. Or, if you are studying the number of different species present in your survey area, you might continue to count quadrats until, after five consecutive samples, no new species is found.

Transects

Another commonly used sampling method in ecology is a transect. A **transect** can show the distribution of a species in relation to a particular abiotic factor or it can give an idea of successions or changes in communities of organisms across a habitat (Figure **G.6**). Transects can be used to sample the distribution of plants on a beach or in a field or to study the different vegetation or the changing plant distributions as soil or moisture varies. Transects provide a method of systematic, rather than random, sampling.

To take samples along a transect, follow these steps.

1   Stretch a tape or rope from a fixed point for a selected distance across the changing habitat you are interested in. If you are studying a salt marsh or sand dunes above a beach, a distance of 100 m would be appropriate.
2   At intervals of 10 m, or another suitable distance, along the tape put down a quadrat and count the organisms inside it. A series of samples like this provides information about the changes in density and community composition along the transect.
3   Measure the abiotic factor of interest – such as temperature, salinity, soil pH or light intensity – at each quadrat location.

The best type of transect to carry out depends on the terrain and on the organisms present. It may be better to carry out a point transect, where organisms are recorded at specific sampling points along the tape. On the other hand, a continuous 'belt' transect where all species in a 1 m zone along the transect are recorded, might be more helpful in providing a detailed picture of the area.

Niches and habitats

A **niche** is the particular environment and 'lifestyle' that is adopted by a certain species. It is the place where the organism lives and breeds, and includes its food and feeding method, as well as its interactions with other species. A niche is unique to each species because it offers the exact conditions that the species needs or has become adapted to.

A **habitat** is a wider area offering living space to a number of organisms, so a habitat comprises a number of niches and includes all the physical and abiotic factors in the environment. An example might be a woodland habitat, which contains niches for a huge variety of species, from burrowing invertebrates at ground level to nesting birds in the tree canopy.

Figure G.6 These students are using a transect line to survey the plants in a grassy area. A quadrat is placed at measured intervals along the transect line and the plants at each location are counted and recorded. In this way, the plant population can be estimated from a series of samples in a few areas.

Spatial habitat

Every organism has its own space in an ecosystem, which is known as its spatial habitat. The surroundings are changed by the presence of the organism – for example, a woodpecker lives inside hollow trees, adapting them to provide nesting places and shelter, while a rabbit burrowing underground affects the soil and plant species growing there.

Feeding activities

As an organism feeds within its niche, it affects the other organisms that are present. For example, an owl feeding on mice in woodland helps to keep the population of mice at a stable level, and rock limpets grazing on small algae control the degree of algal cover.

Interaction between organisms

Organisms interact with other organisms living in the same area. The interactions include competition, herbivory, predation, parasitism and mutualism. Almost all organisms influence the lives of others.

Competition

Competition occurs when two organisms require the same resource. As one uses the resource, less is available to the other so there is competition for a limited supply. If a pride of lions kills an antelope, they must protect this source of food from scavenging hyenas and vultures that will compete with them for the prey.

Plants also compete for resources such as light and space. Fast-growing birch trees quickly become established in areas of cleared land, but they require high light levels. Slower-growing species such as oak begin to grow up around them and for a while, they form a mixed woodland. Eventually the birch trees are over-shadowed and out-competed by the more dominant oaks.

Competitive exclusion

Loss of habitat, often caused by human activities such as farming or deforestation, severely limits vital resources such as food, water and breeding sites for the species that live there. When two different species require the same limited resources in the same area, they may find themselves in competition for the same niche. If they are prey species, they may become susceptible to the same predators as well. The principle of **competitive exclusion** states that no two species can occupy the same niche. The species cannot exist together because one will come to dominate and exclude the other. The oak and birch trees described above are an example of competitive exclusion. Both compete for soil resources and light but eventually the oak shades out the light and the birches die off.

In 1934, a classical study on competition was conducted by G F Gause (1910–1986), a Russian ecologist. He experimented with two species of *Paramecium*, a large protozoan that is common in fresh water – *P. aurelia* and *P. caudatum*. If the two species were allowed to grow in separate cultures on a food source of bacteria, both species grew well. When the two species were cultured together with an identical food source, *P. aurelia* survived while *P. caudatum* died out (Figure **G.7**). Both species had similar needs in the culture but *P. aurelia* had an advantage that enabled it to outgrow *P. caudatum*.

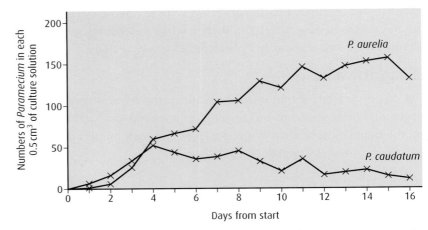

Figure G.7 Over the 16-day culture period, the population of *P. aurelia* increased while *P. caudatum* declined. *P. caudatum* was competitively excluded by *P. aurelia*.

Herbivory

A single plant may provide leaves for herbivorous animals, fruits and seeds for birds, and roots for burrowing animals. The horse chestnut leafminer (*Cameraria ohridella*) is a moth that lays its eggs on horse chestnut leaves. As the larvae hatch, they burrow inside to feed on the tissues of the leaf. The nuts from the horse chestnut tree also provide food for squirrels and deer. Other leafminer species feed on different tree species around the world, such as oak, birch and holly.

Predation

A well-studied example of **predation** is that of the Canadian lynx, which feeds on the arctic hare. The numbers of the **predator** and prey fluctuate over the years with changes in the hare population being followed by corresponding changes in the numbers of lynx (Figure **G.8**).

The largest predatory fish is the spectacular great white shark (*Carcharodon carcharias*). Its prey include dolphins, porpoises and seals.

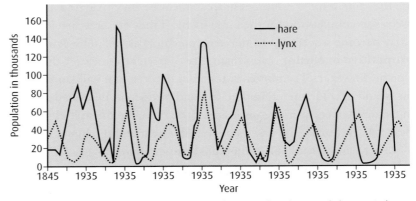

Figure G.8 Changes in the populations of the Canadian lynx and the Arctic hare over time.

Parasitism

Parasites are organisms that live entirely on or in a **host** species and cannot survive without it.

Exoparasites, such as fleas and ticks, live on the outside of a host. One economically important example is the southern cattle tick (*Boophilus microplus*), which lives on cattle, feeding on their blood and weakening the animals. It causes significant losses to farmers all over the world.

Endoparasites, such as tapeworms, roundworms and malarial parasites, live inside their host (Figure **G.9**). One example, the barber's pole worm (*Haemonchus contortus*) is a roundworm that lives in the stomachs of sheep in warm, humid climates all over the world. It causes anemia and progressive weakness as it feeds on blood in the sheep's stomach. If present in large numbers, this parasite can kill young animals.

Mutualism

Sometimes two organisms co-exist and benefit each other, forming what is known as a **mutualistic relationship**.

Lichens such as common orange lichen (*Xanthoria parietina*), which grows on twigs and branches, are the result of a union between a fungus and an alga. The alga carries out photosynthesis and provides sugars for both organisms. The fungus protects the alga from intense sunlight and drying out and absorbs minerals for the benefit of both organisms.

Another mutualistic relationship occurs between the Egyptian plover (*Pluvianus aegyptius*) and the Nile crocodile. The bird feeds on parasites and food particles left around the crocodile's mouth, keeping its teeth clean and healthy. The crocodile openly invites the birds to hunt on its body, even allowing them to enter its mouth.

Fundamental and realised niches

We have described a 'niche' as the special space and 'lifestyle' inhabited by a particular plant or animal. This is the **fundamental niche** for that species. It is the potential mode of existence of the species, given its adaptations.

Often the environment will change through natural phenomena, competition or human intervention. So a species may find that its niche becomes more restricted or begins to overlap with that of another species. This more restricted life pattern is known as the **realised niche**. The realised niche is the actual mode of existence of a species resulting from its adaptations as well as competition from other species. A realised niche can only be the same size as or smaller than the fundamental niche.

Biomass

Biomass is biological material, living or dead, that can be used as an energy source. Since living material also contains water, which is not organic and does not contain energy, biomass is usually measured as dry mass of organic matter in organisms.

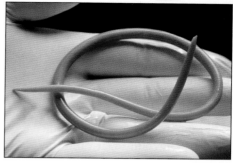

Figure G.9 This roundworm (*Ascaris lumbricoides*) is a parasite of the human intestine. Female roundworms can lay up to 200 000 eggs per day, which are excreted in the faeces and ingested by a new host through contaminated water or food. Infection causes abdominal pain, vomiting and diarrhoea.

Biomass the total amount of living, or recently living, material in a given habitat, population, or sample; it is usually expressed in dry mass (after removal of all water from the sample) per unit area of land or unit volume of water

Biomass does not include biological material that has been changed over time into coal or oil. There is much interest currently into using biomass as fuels in place of fossil fuels, because they are renewable. Plants such as perennial grasses, hemp and sugar cane are undergoing trials as sources of industrial biomass.

Measuring biomass

Measuring biomass is not easy, and may be quite destructive. In a terrestrial ecosystem, a sample area that is representative of the whole area must be chosen. This may be relatively straightforward for studying the biomass of plants, but trapping and measuring the animal life might prove difficult. The presence or absence of some plants or animals might be seasonal, and there might be population explosions at certain times of year.

To measure the biomass of a forest, you would need to follow these steps.

Trophic level 1 (producers)

- Select one or more areas to study, using the same random sampling method used in population studies with quadrats.
- Choose a small area and measure the height and diameter of all the trees and shrubs.
- In this small area, cut down all vegetation to ground level and dry the specimens of each type of tree and shrub in an oven at 90 °C.
- Measure the dry mass of each specimen using an accurate electronic balance.
- Use the masses found for the dried specimens, along with their original height and diameter measurements, to construct tables showing the biomass contained in fresh specimens of particular dimensions, for each plant species.
- Sample other areas in the forest by measuring the heights and diameters of all the plants present and using your tables to calculate their biomass.

Other trophic levels (consumers)

- Set a variety of traps in a measured area to capture the different types of animals present.
- Sort the organisms into trophic levels.
- Dry and weigh a sample of each species caught and calculate the biomass (or use published data to provide this information).
- Estimate the total population of each species in the sample area.
- Use this information to calculate the total biomass of each trophic level, multiplying the average biomass for each sampled species by the number in the population.
- Carefully release the unused, captured animals back into the ecosystem.

The combined data – biomass of plant life and of animal life – can then be used to calculate the biomass of the entire ecosystem.

Clearly this procedure is not ideal because it destroys wildlife as results are obtained. Such interference with an ecosystem may be harmful to its survival. In addition, a single set of measurements may not reflect seasonal or annual changes, so repeats are necessary, and this causes further destruction. Ecologists often use tables providing previously calculated information on organisms to estimate biomass and so avoid the need to destroy plants and animals, which can instead simply be counted.

1   Outline **three** factors that affect the distribution of animals and why they are important.

2 Outline how you would use a transect to compare **two** populations of plants in a grassy meadow.

3 Define 'biomass'.

4 Define the term 'competitive exclusion'.

5 Outline what is meant by the 'niche concept', referring to a named ecosystem.

G2 Ecosystems and biomes

Assessment statements

- Define 'gross production', 'net production' and 'biomass'.
- Calculate values for gross production and net production using the equation:
  gross production − respiration = net production.
- Discuss the difficulties of classifying organisms into trophic levels.
- Explain the small biomass and low numbers of organisms in higher trophic levels.
- Construct a pyramid of energy, given appropriate information.
- Distinguish between 'primary' and 'secondary' succession, using an example of each.
- Outline the changes in species diversity and production during primary succession.
- Explain the effects of living organisms on the abiotic environment, with reference to the changes occurring during primary succession.
- Distinguish between 'biome' and 'biosphere'.
- Explain how rainfall and temperature affect the distribution of biomes.
- Outline the characteristics of six major biomes.

Energy in ecosystems

Plants are the primary source of energy in nearly all ecosystems. They carry out photosynthesis and use energy in sunlight to build carbohydrates. They use these carbohydrates, and minerals from the soil, to make all the proteins, lipids and nucleic acids they need to grow. These processes are not 100% efficient and not all of the energy of the sunlight is used. Some is reflected at the leaf surface, some goes right through leaves without being used, and some is lost when plants respire carbohydrate for energy. When herbivores feed, the energy transferred from plant to herbivore is also not 100% efficient. Not all of the plant material is eaten, not all the material is absorbed in the gut, and some energy is lost in movement and respiration. The same is true for carnivores eating prey animals. Only about 10% of the energy in producers is passed to herbivores and a similar low percentage of energy is passed from herbivores to carnivores (Figure **G.10**, overleaf).

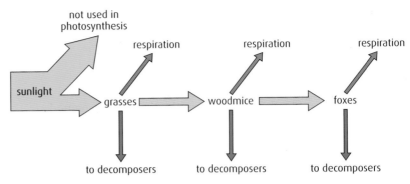

Figure G.10 Energy losses in a food chain.

Ecologists show the availability of energy in an ecosystem in diagrams known as **pyramids of energy**. Each layer of the pyramid represents the organisms at each trophic level, so layer 1 includes all the primary producers, layer 2 all the primary consumers and so on (Figure **G.11**). It is also possible to construct pyramids of numbers and biomass.

Gross production and net production

A pyramid of energy shows energy flow in an ecosystem. The lowest bar of the pyramid represents **gross primary production**, the total amount of energy that flows through the producers. It is measured in kilojoules of energy per square metre per year ($kJ\,m^{-2}\,y^{-1}$).

Net primary production is the amount of energy available to herbivores from producers after subtracting the energy used by the plants for respiration.

This can be represented as:

net production = gross production − energy lost in respiration

Similar calculations can be carried out for each trophic level and the data used to construct pyramids of energy like the one shown in Figure **G.11**.

Gross production the total amount of energy used by plants to make carbohydrates during photosynthesis
Net production the amount of energy in plants that is available to herbivores, per square metre, per year, after some energy has been lost through respiration

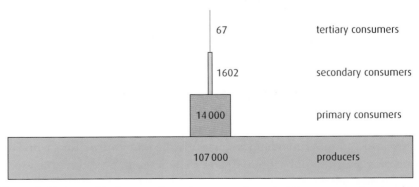

Figure G.11 Pyramid of energy for a river ecosystem. Each bar represents a trophic level and the width of the bar indicates how much energy it contains. Energy is measured in $kJ\,m^{-2}\,y^{-1}$. Only a small percentage of the energy in each level is transferred to the next.

Problems with trophic levels

grass → rabbit → fox

In a simple food chain, such as the one shown above, grass is the primary producer, the rabbit is the primary consumer and the fox is the secondary consumer, so each organism is said to occupy a separate trophic level. In practice, simple food chains rarely exist – foxes do not feed exclusively on rabbits – so more complicated food webs are constructed.

In the example of a food web shown in Figure **G.12**, several of the organisms do not occupy a single trophic level because they have a varied diet. The fox could be said to be a primary consumer because it eats fruit. It could also be classed as a secondary or tertiary consumer because it eats both rabbits (primary consumers) and great tits (secondary consumers). In addition, food chains and webs usually contain organisms that feed on dead material. These are the detritivores and saprotrophs, together known as decomposers, which do not fit into a particular trophic level.

To overcome the difficulty of categorising organisms like these, animals are often classified according to their main food source.

As one moves up a food chain or food web, energy is lost at each trophic level through respiration and waste. As we have seen, and as Table **G.1** (overleaf) confirms, the efficiency of transfer from one level to the next is only about 10%. This is why ecosystems rarely contain more than four or five trophic levels. There is simply not enough energy to support another level. This is demonstrated in a pyramid of biomass, which shows decreasing amounts of biomass at each level (Figure **G.13**, overleaf).

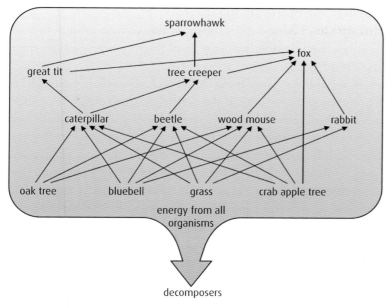

Figure G.12 A woodland food web.

Pyramids of biomass are constructed from measurements taken at one point in time during the year. Some pyramids of biomass do not have a pyramid shape because at certain times of year there may be a population explosion of a particular organism. For example, the population of green algae in a pond in a temperate region of the northern hemisphere will be low in February, very high in May but low again in July. In other examples, the biomass of a trophic level is greater than the one below for a short while. However, this situation changes with the season or as predators take their toll.

Trophic level	Organism	Energy (kJ m^{-2} y^{-1})	Energy transferred
1	cedar tree	837	
2	beetle	82	9.8%
3	wood warbler	8.4	10.2%
4	sparrow hawk	0.8	9.5%

Table G.1 Energy transfers at each trophic level in a coniferous forest food chain.

2 — secondary consumers

20 — primary consumers

5319 — producers

Figure G.13 Pyramid of biomass for a woodland ecosystem, showing the biomass at each trophic level of the ecosystem. Biomass decreases at each level so that there is very little to be transferred to trophic level 4. Biomass is measured as dry mass in g m^{-2}.

6 **a** Construct a pyramid of energy for the food chain described in Table **G.1**.

b What would a pyramid of numbers look like for this food chain?

Succession

Succession is the change in an ecosystem over time. It includes **abiotic (non-living)** and **biotic (living) factors**.

Primary succession begins when an area of bare ground or rock is colonised for the first time. In many cases the first organisms to appear are lichens (Figure **G.14**).

Lichens are able to slowly break down rock, dissolve the minerals, and use them for growth. As some of the lichens die, they decompose and soil is created. Lichens grow very slowly, so this process may take many years. Once soil is formed, simple green plants such as mosses and liverworts can become established and grow. Later, as these plants die and decompose, more soil forms and seeds from other plants are able to germinate. Gradually the soil becomes deeper and its structure improves as more organic matter binds mineral particles together. The soil is able to hold more water and as roots grow through it they protect it from erosion. Minerals locked in the soil enable larger plants such as shrubs and trees to become established so that production and biomass both increase.

A typical sequence of succession, which might occur over a period of 100–200 years, is shown here:

Figure G.14 Lichens are a mutualistic union of an alga and a fungus. The fungus absorbs nutrients while the alga photosynthesises to produce food for the lichen.

bare rock → lichens → mosses and liverworts → grasses and small shrubs → fast growing trees → slower growing trees
(bryophytes)

Secondary succession occurs where there has been a land clearance, perhaps by fire or landslip. An ecosystem has been established but is replaced as conditions have changed. Soil is already present so secondary succession is usually much quicker than primary succession and a variety of plants such as annual grasses and low-growing perennials can colonise rapidly.

Over time, a sequence of colonisation takes place. Some plants thrive, and are then replaced by others as the abiotic environment changes. The exact sequence depends on local conditions but eventually a stable community, known as the **climax community**, develops.

Case study: Surtsey

Surtsey is an island that formed as a result of volcanic activity off the coast of Iceland in 1963 (Figure **G.15**). For the first 20 years after it was formed, the sands and lava of Surtsey were quite barren and soil development was poor. Mosses and lichens were found early on the island but few other species are adapted to such conditions. Shore plants that grow on sandy beaches were the first pioneers to colonise Surtsey and were characteristic of the vegetation during the first decades.

The first higher plant species found on Surtsey was sea rocket (*Cakile arctica*, Figure **G.16**, overleaf) in 1965 and in the following year sea lyme grass (*Leymus arenarius*) was found. In 1967, these species were joined by the oyster plant (*Mertensia maritima*).

Between 1977 and 1979, sea lyme grass and oyster plant started seeding and spreading throughout the sands and pumices of the island. Sea lyme grass is a hardier species and is now one of the most common species present on Surtsey.

The first birds to nest on Surtsey were the fulmar (*Fulmarus glacialis*) and the black guillemot (*Cepphus grille*, Figure **G.17**, overleaf) in 1970. In 1974, they were joined by the great black-backed gull (*Larus marinus*), in 1975 by the kittiwake (*Rissa tridactyla*).

Figure G.15 Scientists have observed and studied the natural progress of primary succession on the new land of Surtsey.

Figure G.16 Sea rocket is a pioneering plant, one of the first to appear in the primary succession on Surtsey.

Figure G.17 Black guillemots began to nest on Surtsey in 1970.

Dwarf willow (*Salix herbacea*) was discovered in 1995 and was the first willow species to colonise the island. The improved soil conditions following the gull colonisation are probably the main reason for this invasion of willows on Surtsey.

Northern green orchid (*Platanthera hyperborean*) and lady's bedstraw (*Galium verum*) were found for the first time in the summer of 2003 and both these plants were found in lush vegetation in the gull colony where bird droppings have acted as a natural fertiliser. They are both examples of species that colonise land where vegetation has been developing for some time.

Since 1963, the primary production and biomass of all species have increased significantly as stages of succession have taken place.

How living organisms influence the abiotic environment

Over time, an area that has been colonised as a result of a primary succession changes. The amount of soil increases, and so too does the diversity of plants, animals and other species. Some of the changes to the abiotic environment that result from the increasing presence of living organisms during primary succession are summarised below.

- Organic matter is released by plants and other organisms when they die and their tissues are broken down by decomposers. Animals also release organic matter in the form of faeces. This material forms humus in the soil, which provides a medium for plant growth.
- Soil depth increases as more organic matter accumulates and binds mineral fragments together.
- Soil structure improves as moisture and minerals are retained in it by the humus.
- Erosion is prevented as plant roots stabilise the ground.
- Minerals are recycled so that more nutrients are retained in the developing ecosystem, rather than being leached away by rainwater.

Biomes and the biosphere

The **biosphere** is that part of the planet and atmosphere that can support life. Satellite images show the abundance of life in certain parts of the world, especially in the tropics (regions near the equator). This is because there is warmth and copious rainfall, so many species of plants grow here. **Biomes** are divisions of the biosphere and are defined by their climate and topography. Rainfall and temperature are the two most important factors that determine the appearance of a biome (Figure **G.18**).

Some important world biomes are described below.

Deserts

A desert is characterised by hot, dry daytime conditions with cold nights. Rainfall may be sparse throughout the year, or occur in a short wet season. Deserts are sometimes defined as areas experiencing less than 250 mm of precipitation per year. Cacti and other succulent plants can survive because they have water storage organs, reduced leaf surface area and waxy cuticles. Annual plants grow and reproduce after a wet period and then remain dormant as seeds until the next rain.

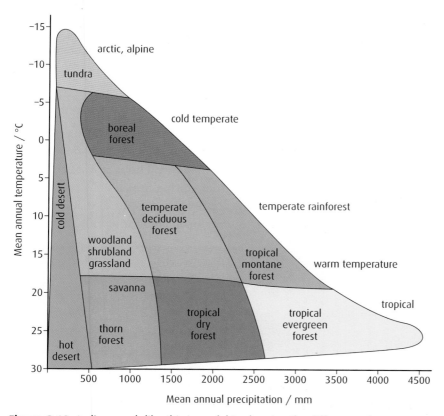

Figure G.18 A climograph like this is useful in showing the differences between biomes because it illustrates the rainfall and temperature of a particular region.

Grasslands

Grasslands generally have cold winters and warm or hot summers. Rainfall is usually seasonal and drought is common. Fires occur in the dry summers, preventing the establishment of trees and shrubs. Prairie grasses have long roots so they can access water deep below the surface, and thereby tolerate drought. Grasses and other herbs that can withstand grazing dominate the vegetation (Figure **G.19**).

Figure G.19 The prairie grasslands of South Dakota, USA.

Shrublands

Shrubland is also called chaparral, maquis or dry heathland (Figure **G.20**). Winters in shrubland biomes are mild and wet, while summers are hot, which makes the areas susceptible to seasonal fires. Drought resistant shrubs dominate and these can burn and die back during fires, leaving roots surviving in the ground. Some of these plants produce seeds that only germinate after a fire, when there is more open land for them to grow.

Figure G.20 Shrubland in the Valle delle Luna on Sardinia, Italy.

Temperate deciduous forests

Temperate forests are cold in winter and warm in summer. Rainfall is spread throughout the year, falling as snow in winter. Most trees lose their leaves in autumn, so freezing conditions in winter do not affect transpiration. The relatively long summers encourage a variety of shrubs and flowers to grow on the forest floor. Many of these flower early in spring before the tree canopy reduces light levels.

Tropical rainforests

Tropical forests are warm or hot all year round. Rainfall is high falling throughout the year. This biome supports the greatest number and diversity of plants, ranging from epiphytes like orchids and bromeliads to large fast-growing trees. Growth is continuous and rapid.

Tundra

Tundra is cold all year. In summer, the upper layer of soil thaws to allow some low-growing plants to flourish. These are shallow rooted because the lower levels of soil, known as the permafrost, are permanently frozen. Only mosses, lichen and a few grasses and shrubs can survive here (Figure **G.21**). Rainfall is low, occurring mostly in the brief summer.

7 State the difference between primary and secondary succession.

8 Name the key factors used to define biomes.

9 Define 'net production'.

10 Outline the characteristics of tundra, tropical rainforests and temperate deciduous forest.

Figure G.21 Tundra in the Cascade Mountains, Washington, USA.

G3 Impacts of humans on ecosystems

Assessment statements

- Calculate the Simpson diversity index for two local communities.
- Analyse the biodiversity of the two local communities using the Simpson index.
- Discuss reasons for the conservation of biodiversity using rainforests as an example.
- List three examples of the introduction of alien species that have had significant impacts on ecosystems.
- Discuss the impacts of alien species on ecosystems.
- Outline one example of biological control of invasive species.
- Define 'biomagnification'.
- Explain the cause and consequences of biomagnification, using a named example.
- Outline the effects of ultraviolet (UV) radiation on living tissues and biological productivity.
- Outline the effect of chlorofluorocarbons (CFCs) on the ozone layer.
- State that ozone in the stratosphere absorbs UV radiation.

The Simpson diversity index

Biodiversity is a relatively modern term that simply means 'the variety of life on Earth'. One of the best ways to assess the health of an ecosystem is to measure the variety of species living there. The Simpson diversity index allows us to quantify the biodiversity of a habitat. It takes into account both the number of different species present (the species 'richness' of the habitat) and the abundance of each species. If a habitat has similar population sizes for each species present, the habitat is said to have 'evenness'.

Simpson's diversity index gives us a measure of both richness and evenness. It is calculated with the formula:

$$D = \frac{N(N-1)}{\Sigma n(n-1)}$$

where D is the diversity index

N is the total number of organisms in the habitat

n is the number of individuals of each species

The value of the Simpson diversity index is best illustrated by comparing two habitats. Two ponds might contain species of insects in the numbers shown in Table **G.2**.

	Species					Total number of organisms
	Water boatmen	Water measurers	Pond skaters	Whirligig beetles	Water spiders	
Number of organisms in pond A	43	18	38	3	1	103
Number of organisms in pond B	26	18	29	11	5	89

Table G.2 Numbers of different insect species found in two separate ponds.

Using the formula, we can calculate that for pond A:

$$\text{Simpson diversity index } D = \frac{(103 \times 102)}{43(43-1) + 18(18-1) + 38(38-1) + 3(3-1) + 1(1-0)}$$
$$= \frac{10\,506}{3525}$$
$$= 2.98$$

For pond B:

$$\text{Simpson diversity index } D = \frac{(89 \times 88)}{26(26-1) + 18(18-1) + 29(29-1) + 11(11-1) + 5(5-1)}$$
$$= \frac{7832}{1898}$$
$$= 4.13$$

Although there are fewer organisms in pond B, the individual populations are more even, so the community is not dominated by one or two species. We conclude that pond B is more biodiverse. It is instructive to alter some of the figures and see what effect this has on the value of D. An advantage of the index is that you do not need to know the name of every different species – it must simply be distinguished as a separate species. Calculating the Simpson diversity index at intervals over time can give a good indication of the health of an ecosystem and whether conservation measures might be valuable.

Conservation of biodiversity

In the last 50 years, the importance of biodiversity has come to the forefront of science. Species are not evenly distributed on Earth – biodiversity is far richer around the tropics, and areas containing rainforest are among the most diverse on the planet. People have come to realise that there are many compelling reasons for conserving the biodiversity of the rainforests.

Economic reasons

Many plant and animal species have yet to be discovered and named. It is only in recent years, since the invention of inflatable walkways, that the canopy layer of rainforests has been explored. New species of plants are being discovered that may contain valuable medicinal compounds. Many of the plants are wild examples of cultivated plants and may hold valuable genetic resources. A number of the countries that contain rainforests are developing countries and eco-tourism is a valuable source of income for them. People in developed countries want to visit rainforests to experience the wonder of the plants and animals living there.

Ecological reasons

Rainforests create climate. The huge transpiration rate of rainforests creates clouds, which give rise to rainfall. Cutting down forests reduces the amount of carbon dioxide being absorbed, because rainforest conducts photosynthesis at a faster rate than the farmland that often replaces it. In addition, trees lock up considerable amounts of carbon dioxide during their growth, as lignin and cellulose. Cutting down and burning trees releases carbon dioxide back into the atmosphere, adding to the greenhouse effect.

Clearing rainforests for logging or farming changes the way sunlight is reflected by the Earth's surface. Strong sunshine reaches ground that was previously shaded. Much of this is reflected as infrared radiation, heating up the atmosphere. Exposed soil can soon erode, which leads to flooding and silting up of rivers.

Ethical reasons

Indigenous peoples will be displaced if the rainforest is not conserved. These people often hold and use old remedies for diseases using the plants from their locale. If we lose these people, we lose this knowledge and cultural history. We should also question whether humans have the right to destroy the organisms that live in the rainforests.

Aesthetic reasons

Many people have been inspired to create art, music and written accounts of the rainforests and their beauty. Once destroyed, these natural areas are impossible to replace.

Interfering with ecosystems

There have been many occasions throughout history when an organism has been introduced from one ecosystem to another, either:
- deliberately
- accidentally
- for biological control of a pest organism.

Many plants, collected in distant regions, have been deliberately introduced to domestic gardens because of their attractive flowers or exotic foliage. Orchids, bamboos and rhododendrons are now seen all over the world but most were introduced following plant-collecting expeditions in the 19th and 20th centuries.

Much of the time, introduced species create no problems. However, in some cases, an introduced species finds the new conditions so advantageous that it becomes **invasive**. It grows rapidly and becomes a threat to native species, which it out-competes and eventually eliminates. One such example is Japanese knotweed (*Fallopia japonica*), which was **deliberately** introduced into European gardens in the nineteenth century for its attractive flowers. It reproduces vegetatively and even short sections of root can re-grow to become whole new plants. This plant now covers huge areas of land in Europe. It can be controlled with herbicides, but there is a problem using these chemicals near rivers, as the herbicide gets into the waterway and upsets its ecological balance, harming plant and animal life.

The zebra mussel (*Dreissena polymorpha*) is a small freshwater species, originally native to lakes in southeast Russia. It has been **accidentally** released in many other areas, probably carried in ballast water of cargo ships. It has become an invasive species in many different countries. Zebra mussels are now found in the Great Lakes of the USA where they grow on docks and boats. They have spread into streams and rivers and block water pipes and interfere with water supplies (Figure **G.22**). In some areas, they have out-competed all other freshwater mussels because they grow in dense clumps. Zebra mussels are also believed to be the source of deadly avian botulism poisoning that has killed tens of thousands of birds in the Great Lakes since the late 1990s. On the other hand, zebra mussels are thought to be partly responsible for the increase in the population of bass and yellow perch in the lakes. Zebra mussels are filter feeders and remove pollutants from lake water which becomes clearer as a result. Algae deep under the water receive more light and grow more vigorously, providing habitats and food for the fish.

Another example of a deliberately introduced species is the prickly pear cactus (*Opuntia* sp.), which was introduced to Australia as a source of cattle feed. The prickly pear rapidly grew out of control. At its height, it was spreading at a rate of 400 000 hectares per year. The dry, hot climate of Australia was ideal for this plant and there were no native animals that would eat it. Scientists conducted research to find a natural predator in its homelands of the USA and Mexico. There it is eaten by a caterpillar of the cactus moth (*Cactoblastis cactorum*). This was also deliberately introduced into Australia and now keeps the plant under control. This is an example of successful **biological control.**

A separate, far less successful attempt at biological control has proved disastrous for much of the wildlife of Australia. The Puerto Rican cane toad was introduced into Queensland in 1935 in an attempt to control sugar cane beetles, which were causing huge losses to cane growers in the north of Australia. In their native regions of Central and South America,

Figure G.22 Masked workers use a water jet to clear zebra mussels clogging the walls of the pump room of Detroit Edison's power station in Michigan, USA. Not only do zebra mussels encrust water pipes and pump rooms, but they also excrete a corrosive substance.

cane toads are controlled by a number of predators, particularly snakes. In Australia, potential predators were not adapted to deal with the cane toad's skin, which produces dangerous toxins, so the toad population has grown out of control – so much so that they have spread from Queensland to Northern Territory and New South Wales, wiping out the native amphibians, which breed more slowly and later in the season than the cane toad. The toads also failed to control the beetle, preferring to eat small rodents, insects, and even dog food.

The introduction of alien species described above are summarised in Table **G.3**.

Species	Reason for introduction
Japanese knotweed	deliberately planted in European gardens
zebra mussels	accidentally introduced into USA
cane toad	deliberately introduced to control sugar cane beetles in Australia (unsuccessful)
cactus moth	deliberately introduced to control prickly pear cactus in Australia (successful)

Table G.3 Several species that have been introduced into new ecosystems.

Any programme to introduce an alien species as a means of biological control must take the following into account.

- The new species may compete with native organisms and reduce their populations.
- This in turn may affect other species within a habitat.
- The introduced species may feed on native organisms, affecting local food chains and webs.
- The combined effect may be that a native species becomes extinct.

The danger of predation by an introduced species is well demonstrated by the effect of rats on the bird population of New Zealand. Rats probably arrived on the islands of New Zealand with early European explorers in the 1800s. Many bird species, particularly flightless birds native to the region, became extinct as a result of predation by the rats, which fed on eggs, young and adult birds. Some bird species did survive on outlying islands, but as rats reached them, they too were affected. Conservation programmes launched in the 1980s have attempted to eradicate rats and reintroduce some native species to these islands (Figure **G.23**).

Biomagnification

Some chemicals used in the environment as pesticides are taken into living organisms but then accumulate in their body tissues because the organism cannot excrete them very well. Insecticides such as DDT and dieldrin are well-studied examples of the way toxic chemicals can accumulate in the environment. This is **biomagnification**.

Small quantities of these substances, used to control insect pests, may be taken up by plants, or deposited on the surface of their leaves. The plants may be unaffected, but when primary consumers feed on the sprayed

Biomagnification the process that leads to accumulation of chemical substances in food chains; the chemical substances become more concentrated at each trophic level

Figure G.23 The South Island Saddleback (*Philesturnus carunculatus*) was saved from extinction when individuals were transferred to rat-free islands off the coast of New Zealand, where they were able to become established and breed.

plants they take in a far greater quantity of the toxin. The chemical remains in the bodies of the primary consumers and if a secondary consumer feeds on a number of these animals, it accumulates an even greater amount of the chemical.

DDT is an organochlorine (OC) insecticide that was widely used to kill mosquitoes that carry the malarial parasite. It is stored in the fatty tissues of animals that have ingested it. It is now known that it is not readily biodegradable and can remain in the environment for up to 15 years.

A survey of numbers of peregrine falcons in Europe in the early 1960s showed that they were in decline. Their bodies contained high levels of DDT, which was causing the shells of the bird's eggs to be thinner than normal. As a female tried to incubate the eggs, they broke under her body. This effect was also reported in many other parts of the world in a variety of wild bird populations. Even penguins in Antarctic regions were found to have the chemical in their bodies.

Although the original concentration of DDT used in insecticide sprays was low, at about 3×10^{-6} ppm (parts per million), the chemical was running into waterways and being taken up by microscopic plants in rivers and lakes. As these plants were eaten by microscopic animals, the DDT became more concentrated. It was found that small fish feeding on the microscopic animals had accumulated about 0.5 ppm in their body fat and fish-eating water birds, such as the osprey, had about 25 ppm of DDT in their bodies (Figure **G.24**, overleaf).

DDT was a successful insecticide because it remained effective for a long time without breaking down, but its damage to the environment was considerable. From the 1970s, it has been banned in many countries

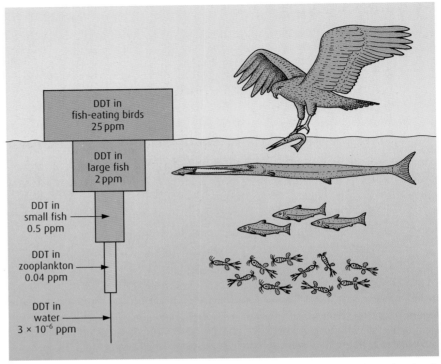

Figure G.24 An example of how DDT concentrations increase up the trophic levels of an estuarine food chain.

and wild bird populations are recovering. Heavy metals and industrial chemicals such as PCBs (polychlorinated biphenyls) that are also released into the environment remain a problem for living organisms as these accumulate in a similar way.

The effects of ultraviolet radiation

Ultraviolet (UV) rays reaching the Earth can cause problems for a range of living organisms.

Fair-skinned people are warned of the effect of too much UV radiation on exposed skin and advised to protect themselves with sun-block creams to prevent sunburn. Overexposure can be extremely harmful to health because UV rays cause mutations in DNA, and are linked to various types of skin cancer such as malignant melanoma and non-lethal carcinomas. Long-term exposure is also a risk factor for cataracts in the eyes.

Plants can also suffer from UV radiation. Not only is their DNA likely to be damaged, UV radiation also affects photosynthesis. The photosynthetic pathways are inhibited, resulting in lower productivity in exposed plants. DNA damage restricts plant growth so that both biomass and net productivity decrease. Many plants that grow at high altitude, such as in the Andes mountains, have evolved mechanisms to screen themselves from the intense radiation, but floating aquatic plants seem to be very susceptible to UV light. Since plants play such a fundamental role as producers in food chains, decreased photosynthesis has the potential to affect a whole ecosystem.

CFCs and the ozone layer

Most of the UV radiation reaching the atmosphere from the Sun is absorbed by the **ozone layer,** which is a layer of gas, about 20 km thick, sandwiched between the stratosphere above and the troposphere below. At this altitude, oxygen in the atmosphere breaks down and reacts with other oxygen molecules to form ozone (O_3). In 1985, research showed that the ozone layer was getting thinner and that 'holes' were appearing in it over Antarctica. It is now generally agreed that chlorofluorocarbons (CFCs) were the cause. These gases are used in refrigerants, in aerosols and to make polystyrene packing. Once released, they break down in the upper atmosphere to form atoms of chlorine, which react with ozone to form oxygen and chlorine monoxide (ClO). A chain reaction then occurs as ClO reacts with more ozone molecules to form more oxygen gas and chlorine. A chlorine atom can react with and destroy many ozone molecules and gradually the concentration of ozone decreases. Today, action has been taken in many countries to phase out the use of CFCs.

Chlorine and ozone undergo a chain reaction:

$$Cl + O_3 \rightarrow ClO + O_2$$

$$ClO + O_3 \rightarrow Cl + 2O_2$$

11 Give an example of an alien species that has been introduced into an ecosystem and outline the effects the species has had on the ecosystem.

12 Define 'biomagnification'.

G4 Conservation of biodiversity

Assessment statements

- Explain the use of biotic indices and indicator species in monitoring environmental change.
- Outline the factors that contributed to the extinction of one named animal species.
- Outline the biogeographical features of nature reserves that promote the conservation of diversity.
- Discuss the role of active management techniques in conservation.
- Discuss the advantages of *in situ* conservation of endangered species (terrestrial and aquatic nature reserves).
- Outline the use of *ex situ* conservation measures, included captive breeding of animals, botanic gardens and seed banks.

Biotic indices and indicator species

Certain species are very sensitive to environmental changes such as pollution from toxic gases in the atmosphere or chemicals in water. These organisms are called **indicator species** because their presence or absence tells us about the environmental conditions present in a way that direct measurements of abiotic factors cannot.

Lichens and bryophytes (mosses) are very sensitive to air pollution. Leafy species of lichen can only survive in areas with the highest quality of clean air, so by studying the lichens present in an area we can obtain a measure of air quality. Lichens vary considerably from most plants in their ability to tolerate pollutants such as sulfur dioxide in their environment because they have no waxy cuticle as the majority of terrestrial plants do. Without this protection, lichens absorb and accumulate various pollutants, including metal ions in airborne dust.

Water quality in rivers and lakes can be measured in a similar way. Some invertebrates can survive in polluted water, while others cannot (Figure **G.25**). Water that is polluted by sewage effluent is usually low in oxygen because bacteria in the water feed on the organic material and respire aerobically, using up the oxygen. Active invertebrates such as stonefly nymphs, mayfly larvae and flatworms are very sensitive to this kind of pollution because they require a lot of oxygen. So if these organisms are abundant, it is a good indication that water is clean. On the other hand, bloodworms (midge larvae of *Chironimus* sp.), sludge worms and leeches are more tolerant, and the presence of these organisms in large numbers is an indication of polluted water.

Chironimus larvae can tolerate low levels of oxygen and so indicate high levels of pollution.

The presence of water boatmen indicates moderately polluted water.

Mayfly nymphs are an indicator of clean, unpolluted water.

Figure G.25 The presence of particular organisms can indicate how polluted a body of water is.

To gather data for a **biotic index** of a river or lake, the habitat is surveyed and samples of the organisms present are collected. The number and type of the species present is recorded. The number of each organism found is multiplied by a 'sensitivity factor', which indicates its ability to tolerate pollution. A greater value is given to intolerant species, which require clean water, and a calculation is performed resulting in a figure for the overall cleanliness of the water. A high number of sensitive species gives a high biotic index score but if many species that are very tolerant to pollution are found the index will be low. For example, the index for the River Trent in the UK gives values between 0 and 15 at different points along its length. Zero indicates very polluted water, whereas 15 indicates very clean water.

Using a biotic index for a freshwater habitat

The Trent Biotic Index was developed for the River Trent in the UK, and most modern systems have evolved from this. Two commonly used systems are the Biological Monitoring Working Party System (BMWP), used mainly in Great Britain, and the Belgian Biotic Index Method.

The Biological Monitoring Working Party System

The advantages of this system are that the invertebrate organisms need to be identified only to family level and that it can be used internationally. Each family is assigned a score from 1 to 10 (excluding 9) depending on their pollution tolerance, 10 being the most intolerant. Some example organisms are listed in Table **G.4**.

Example organisms	Score
caddis flies	10
crayfish, dragonflies, damselflies	8
mayfly, tube-making caddis flies	7
small air-breathing snails, amphipod crustaceans	6
pondskaters, water striders, creeping water bugs	5
small mayflies, freshwater leeches, alderflies	4
valve snails, bladder snails	3
non-biting midges	2
segmented worms	1

Table G.4 Some of the families in the nine different classes of pollution tolerance (common names have been used for simplicity).

All parts of the stream, river or lake are sampled. The sides, centre and areas among vegetation are all included and the invertebrates are collected and sorted into their families. Each is assigned a score from the table. The number of individuals in each family is not important. The results are added together to give a BMWP score.

The efficiency of sampling and sample size are taken into account using the Average Score Per Taxon (ASPT). ASPT is the BMWP score divided by the number of families (taxa) in the sample, which gives an idea of the diversity of the community. The overall water quality is assessed by looking at the BWMP and ASPT scores, as summarised in Table **G.5**.

BMWP		ASPT	
Score	Water quality	Score	Water quality
>150	very good biological quality	>4.4	very good
101–150	good biological quality	4.81–4.4	good
51–100	fair biological quality	4.21–4.8	fair
16–50	poor biological quality	3.61–4.2	poor
0–15	very poor biological quality	<3.61	very poor

Table G.5 BMWP and ASPT scores related to water quality.

Worked example 1

Samples taken from two streams are recorded and given scores as shown in the table.

Stream 1		Stream 2	
Family	**Score**	**Family**	**Score**
pondskaters	5	bladder snails	3
pulmonate snails	6	midge larvae	2
water striders	5	marsh snails	3
creeping water bugs	5	valve snails	3
leeches	4		
air-breathing snails	3		
alder flies	4		
midge larvae	2		

The total BMWP scores are 34 for stream 1 and 11 for stream 2. The ASPT scores are calculated using

$$\text{ASPT} = \frac{\text{BMWP}}{\text{number of families}}$$

So for stream 1

$$\text{ASPT} = \frac{34}{8} = 4.3$$

and for stream 2

$$\text{ASPT} = \frac{11}{4} = 2.8$$

Looking up these scores in Table **G.5** (page **499**), we can see that the water quality of stream 1 is poor by the BMWP score, but fair by the ASPT. Stream 2 scores very poor on both scales.

Factors contributing to extinction

As the numbers of a species dwindle and few members are left to reproduce, populations of endangered plants and animals edge closer to **extinction**. Although extinction has always been part of the evolution of ecosystems as organisms compete for survival, the rate of extinction is probably higher today than it has ever been before. Many of the causes of extinction result from human activities and some scientists estimate that half of all species present on Earth today may be extinct by the end of the century.

The dodo was a flightless bird that lived on the island of Mauritius (Figure **G.26**). As with many animals that have evolved in isolation from significant predators, the dodo was entirely fearless of people, and this, in combination with its inability to fly, made it easy prey for humans. When explorers and settlers first arrived on Mauritius, they also brought with them animals that had not existed on the island before. Their dogs, pigs, cats and rats plundered the dodo nests, while humans destroyed the forests where the birds made their homes. The last record of a living dodo was in the middle of the 17th century.

Features of effective nature reserves

As people have become more aware of the need to conserve species, many governments have set aside land or protected areas of the country to provide an area where organisms are protected. When new nature reserves are planned, many factors need to be taken into account to ensure they are successful in promoting conservation of diversity.

Size

Large reserves work better than small ones. Small reserves can only support small population numbers, so there is a risk that inbreeding will occur and the genetic diversity of species will diminish. In a small reserve, there is always a risk that a natural disaster such as flooding or a forest fire will wipe out all the organisms of a species. This is less likely to happen in a large reserve. Edge effects are also less significant in large reserves than in small ones.

Edge effects

The centre of a nature reserve is likely to have different features from the areas at the edge. A woodland reserve has more light, more wind and less moisture at the edge than at the centre. Organisms that live in the centre of the wood will be protected from the influence of other organisms, such as farm animals or human activity, outside the reserve. This is not so for organisms living close to the edge, which may be disturbed by or even compete with organisms outside the reserve. Small reserves have more edge per hectare than large ones, so edge effects have a greater impact on the overall ecosystem in smaller reserves.

One well-studied example of an edge effect involves the brown-headed cowbird of northern and western USA. This bird is a notorious brood parasite, laying its eggs in the nests of other birds at the edge of forests. It feeds in open areas where insects are abundant. As forests have become fragmented, due to urbanisation and farming, more forest edges have become available. The brown-headed cowbird population has increased so much that, in recent decades, many land managers and conservationists have argued that brown-headed cowbirds are a major threat to North American songbird populations.

Wildlife corridors

If it is impossible to create a large nature reserve, good planning may make it possible to link two smaller areas through a corridor. These are often built under busy roads or railway lines, so that organisms have, in effect, a larger area to colonise. A corridor is not ideal because animals using it may be exposed to dangers from outside the reserve. In addition, dangerous or venomous creatures using the corridor may come into closer contact with humans than they would do in a large reserve.

Figure G.26 The dodo became extinct because every aspect of its lifestyle was compromised after the arrival of settlers in its native Mauritius.

Active management in conservation

A newly created nature reserve must be actively managed so that local species are encouraged and any areas that have been damaged by human interference can be restored. Without management, some species could dominate and threaten the existence of other important organisms. A well thought-out policy should seek to conserve the local ecosystem, while at the same time allowing access for scientists and visitors. It is important to know which species are present and what size their populations are. Only then is it possible to undertake positive measures to restore and conserve the area.

Restoration

Restoring an area of land to a natural state may be extremely time-consuming and expensive. In 2004, a six-year restoration programme was started on Montague Island in New South Wales, Australia. The island had become covered with kikuyu grass (*Pennisetum clandestinum*) and other non-native plants that had been planted in the 1900s to help stabilise the sandy soil and provide food for grazing animals. The kikuyu grass had spread to such an extent that it had displaced seabird nesting areas and was responsible for the death of significant numbers of the native little penguins, which became trapped or strangled in the grass. The grass was also a significant threat to other bird species such as the shearwaters and crested terns that nest on the island. Management techniques included clearing the grass by controlled burning and spraying with herbicide, followed by re-vegetation of the island with native plant species.

Through the 20th century, large areas of Snowdonia National Park in North Wales, UK, had become overgrown with rhododendron, which flourished in the wet climate. This plant had been introduced widely in the 19th century as a garden shrub because of its very showy flowers. To restore the land, the thick branches had to be cut and the roots pulled out to prevent re-growth (Figure **G.27**). Rhododendron forms an association with certain soil fungi which prevent the germination of seeds of many other plants. So, even when the ground had been cleared, it had to be left for some time until these fungi died.

Conserving threatened species

Restoring an area to its original state should benefit native species of plants and animals. However, if population numbers are very low, more active intervention may be required. Each nature reserve will have its own unique solutions to conservation problems. At Belsize Wood Nature Reserve, a small woodland reserve near the centre of London in the UK, nesting boxes for birds and bats have been put in place, because the number of mature trees providing suitable natural nesting sites is low. In a wetland nature reserve, nesting platforms that float on lakes can be beneficial and offer some protection against predators for nesting birds. At Sungei Buloh Wetland Reserve in Singapore, sluice management allows the control of water levels in the ponds. At any one time, the water level

Figure G.27 Conservation workers clearing the land of invading rhododendron plants.

in at least one pond is kept low to expose the mudflats for shorebirds to feed and roost (Figure **G.28**).

Protection, access and funding

Members of the public may question the funding and existence of a nature reserve if access is denied to them. This is a difficult issue, as the more people that visit a nature reserve, the more chance there is of habitats being damaged or destroyed. On the other hand, visitor access can have positive outcomes, if public awareness and knowledge of wildlife is improved. Usually, special trails or walkways are built at reserves to ensure that observers can visit safely without compromising the surrounding habitats (Figure **G.28**). Legislation can also protect nature reserves from development and industrial activities.

In situ conservation

In situ **conservation** protects species within their normal habitat. This makes sense because each species has evolved to adapt to a particular environment. *In situ* conservation protects species in their own habitats by maintaining the environment. This can involve removal of invasive species, such as the kikuyu grass on Montague Island or rhododendron plants in North Wales, or protecting certain species from predators. Provided there are sufficient numbers in the population, *in situ* conservation should provide sufficient genetic diversity for a population to be sustained.

Ex situ conservation

Ex situ **conservation** involves preserving a species whose numbers are very low in a **captive breeding programme** in a zoo or **botanic garden** to prevent it dying out.

Figure G.28 The habitat is carefully managed at Sungei Buloh Wetland Reserve in Singapore. There are a number of trails through the wetland, but the highlight is this 500 m boardwalk that takes visitors right to the centre of the reserve.

In situations where *in situ* conservation is difficult or inadequate, *ex situ* conservation must be used. This is not ideal, because an organism behaves differently outside its natural habitat. However, it does give rise to the opportunity for captive breeding using scientific knowledge and modern technology. Techniques such as artificial insemination and embryo transfer may be used if animals fail to breed normally, and embryos can be preserved for later use. Difficult pregnancies can be monitored and the young cared for by staff.

An *ex situ* breeding programme has proved invaluable for the Arabian oryx. This animal, once almost extinct in the wild, has been successfully bred in a number of zoos in USA and Europe. The DNA from the few remaining animals was compared and animals specially selected for breeding so that genetic diversity was maintained as far as possible. Studying the behaviour of captive animals is key to breeding programmes. Some species with complex behaviours such as the giant panda from China are very challenging to breed in captivity, but the centre at Chengdu in China has been very successful.

Plants are more straightforward to maintain in an *ex situ* situation. Botanic gardens can supply the correct environmental conditions for different plants and computer-controlled glasshouses can maintain the temperature and humidity that each requires. Many countries maintain 'national collections' of a variety of species including native plants, exotic genera and important food plants.

There are also **seed banks** for many of the world's staple crops such as rice or maize. These preserve varieties of important crops, called **landraces**, which may be useful in the future to produce new varieties of food plants. At the Millennium Seed Bank at Wakehurst Place in England, seeds are kept in cool, dark conditions which prevent germination, and can be stored for many decades. The Svalbard Global Seed Vault, on the Norwegian island of Spitsbergen, holds duplicate samples of seeds held in genebanks worldwide, in an underground cavern.

13 Outline how indicator species are used to monitor an environment such as a river.

14 What are the features of nature reserves that enable them to conserve diversity?

15 Outline the techniques used in a captive breeding programme.

G5 Population ecology

Assessment statements

- Distinguish between 'r-strategies' and 'K-strategies'.
- Discuss the environmental conditions that favour either r-strategies or K-strategies.
- Describe one technique used to estimate the population size of an animal species based on a capture–mark–release–recapture method.
- Describe the methods used to estimate the size of commercial fish stocks.
- Outline the concept of maximum sustainable yield in the conservation of fish stocks.
- Discuss international measures that would promote the conservation of fish.

r-strategies and K-strategies

Organisms have many different means of reproduction, which result in different patterns of population growth. If the environment is unstable, it may be better to produce many offspring quickly, but in a stable situation, long-lived organisms that produce few offspring are likely to be more prevalent. r-strategies and K-strategies have been defined as the extreme ends of a spectrum of patterns of reproduction.

r-strategies

Species that follow an r-strategy have a relatively short lifespan, during which they reproduce once and produce large numbers of offspring. They are unlikely to care for their young, and the offspring are very likely to be small and reach maturity quickly. Many invertebrates, such as insects, follow an r-strategy. Pest species of plants are also likely to be r-strategists, seizing opportunities occuring as a result of environmental disturbance. Weeds produce many seeds, only a few of which survive but which are able to take advantage of unstable habitats such as wasteland. Seeds of these plants are usually light and spread by air currents (Figure **G.29**). So, r-strategy plants can spread rapidly over large distances.

Frogs and many species of fish also reproduce using an r-strategy. Few of their young survive to adulthood because both eggs and young are eaten by predators. Adults do not invest time and energy in their young: on this large scale, this would not be possible, so only small numbers survive to produce the next generation. If all the offspring did mature to reproduce, there would be a huge over-expansion of the population, but this is very unlikely to occur.

K-strategies

Animals and plants that adopt a K-strategy take longer to reach maturity and produce few offspring, but they reproduce several times during adult life. In the animal kingdom, this behaviour is common among the vertebrates: gorillas, deer and elephants are all K-strategists (Figure **G.30**). The young are relatively weak and helpless, so parental care is common. Often it is not confined to the immediate parents. Elephants care for all

Figure G.29 Dandelions seeds are produced in huge numbers and are carried on the wind.

Figure G.30 Gorillas give birth to a single young about once every four years.

the young in their herd and most pack animals keep the young in the centre of their group, so they do not stray and get picked off by a predator.

Some plants can be said to use a K-strategy. The coco de mer palm (*Lodoicea maldivica*) from the Seychelles islands produces the largest palm nut. One nut may weigh up to 20 kg and take seven years to mature on the palm tree. As this represents a large investment by the plant, individual trees produce very few of these nuts at a time.

r-strategies and K-strategies are two extremes of reproductive pattern and many organisms have adopted schemes somewhere in between. Many birds and reptiles produce more eggs than would be expected of a strict K-strategist, which allows for losses in the young through predation, lack of food or disease. Other organisms can switch between r-strategies and K-strategies depending on environmental conditions.

In a stable environment, K-strategies are beneficial. An organism can invest in the next generation because conditions are favourable for its survival. Food is plentiful, and predation and disease are low or manageable. However, if the environment changes through drought, famine or disease, the few offspring may die and a new generation is lost. In these circumstances, r-strategies become beneficial. Producing large numbers of offspring means that a few may survive these new environmental conditions and become the adults of the next generation.

Estimating numbers in animal populations

The most common method of estimating population size is the 'capture–mark–release–recapture' technique (Figure **G.31**). It is used for populations where individuals are mobile and move freely in their habitat.

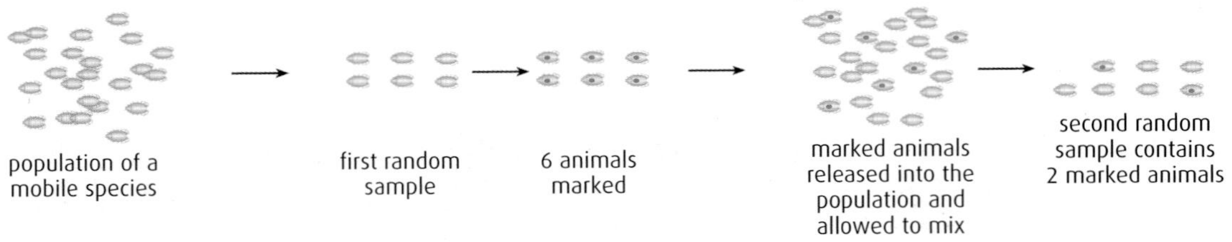

population of a mobile species

first random sample

6 animals marked

marked animals released into the population and allowed to mix

second random sample contains 2 marked animals

$$\text{estimated population size} = \frac{\text{number in first sample} \times \text{number in second sample}}{\text{number of marked animals in second sample}}$$

$$\text{estimated population size} = \frac{6 \times 7}{2}$$

estimated population size = 21

Note: This method only produces results of acceptable accuracy if the numbers in the samples are larger than shown here. At least 20 animals should be sampled.

Figure G.31 Capture–mark–release–recapture technique for estimating population size.

1 A sample of the population is collected by netting or trapping or another suitable method. The sample must be as large as possible and the trapping method must not harm the animals.
2 The number of organisms in the sample is counted and recorded.
3 Each of the captured animals is inconspicuously marked in some way – for example, with non-toxic paint for invertebrates or by trimming a concealed area of fur for small mammals.
4 The animals are returned to the wild and left for long enough to mix with the rest of the population.
5 A second sample of the population is collected after this time.
6 The number of marked and unmarked individuals in the second sample is counted.

The population size is calculated using the Lincoln Index formula:

$$\text{total population } P = \frac{\text{number of animals in first sample} \times \text{number of animals in second sample}}{\text{number of marked animals in second sample}}$$

or

$$P = \frac{(n_1 \times n_2)}{n_3}$$

where

P is the total population
n_1 is the number of organisms caught originally
n_2 is the number caught in the second sample
n_3 is the number of marked individuals in the second sample

This method depends on a number of factors, which need to be taken into account.

- Marking the organisms must not harm them or cause them to be conspicuous to predators. That is, the marking itself must have no effect on the population size.
- There should be minimal **immigration** to or **emigration** from the population.
- The measurements must be conducted within a single life cycle, so there are no changes to the population through births or deaths.

The capture–mark–release–recapture technique is most appropriate for invertebrates such as woodlice, snails and ladybirds or small mammals, such as mice, with a limited territory. Sampling organisms with a large territory, or those where the population is small, is not accurate using this method.

Estimating the size of commercial fish stocks

The commercial fishing industry is of enormous importance worldwide. Fish provide what should be a renewable source of food, but catching fish has become an industrial process, involving technology such as the use of sound waves to track shoals of fish, and large-scale machinery including huge trawling nets. Many species are in danger of being over-fished, as their populations are reduced to unsustainable levels. In some species, the numbers of adult fish available to breed is too low to replace the animals removed by fishing. There is a pressing need to monitor fish populations so that the industry can survive.

The International Council for Exploration of the Sea (ICES) is an organisation that monitors harvests in the North Atlantic. Fish are not easy to count because they move over long distances. The usual method to estimate a population involves collecting data from landings at fish markets, from the numbers of fish discarded from fishing boats, and from targeted surveys with research vessels.

- The numbers of fish of different ages are recorded to give an idea of the age distribution in the population. The age of individual fish is a useful indicator of fish stocks. Too few young ones indicate that the fish are not spawning sufficiently to replace caught fish, and too few large fish indicates that over-fishing is occurring.
- Fish age can be estimated by the length and weight of individuals. A more accurate method is to measure the rings in the ear bones. As fish grow, the number of rings increases and these can be measured using a microscope.
- The data collected from catches and age estimation can be used to deduce spawning rates and survival of different species.
- Research vessels can use echo sounding to estimate the sizes of fish shoals in some locations.

ICES offers advice on over 130 species of fish and shellfish. Using the advice from this and other similar organisations, scientists can work out the health of a particular fish population and whether it is being over-fished.

Maximum sustainable yield

The **maximum sustainable yield** is the largest proportion of fish that can be caught without endangering the population. How this figure is arrived at is debatable, and many countries have different views on the issue, often clouded by vested interests. At extremes, if the fish population is very small, there will be few adults to produce young, and if the population is large, competition for food will slow growth. The ideal, then, is to fish at a level that maintains the maximum yield by allowing fish stocks to replenish at the optimum rate. Fish are a renewable resource and can always be available for food if they are only taken in a way that allows them to survive and reproduce their numbers.

International measures to conserve fish

In recent years, there have been several alarming reports on declining fish populations worldwide (Figure **G.32**). In 2003, 29% of open-sea fisheries were in a state of collapse, defined as a decline to less than 10% of their original yield.

Populations of fish must be monitored and quotas or closed seasons put in place to reduce fishing during the breeding seasons. If net sizes are monitored and controlled, smaller immature fish can be left in the water to breed.

Bigger vessels, bigger nets and new technology for locating fish are not improving catches, simply because there are fewer fish to catch. Experiments carried out in small contained ecosystems show that

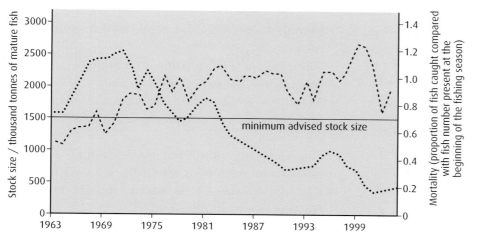

Figure G.32 Stocks and fishing mortality in North Sea cod between 1963 and 2004. The population of North Sea cod has fallen greatly since the end of the 1960s, almost certainly as a direct result of over-fishing. The horizontal line shows the minimum stock size that has been calculated will allow the cod population to be maintained at a viable level.

reductions in biodiversity bring decreases in the size and sustainability of fish stocks. Where fishing is banned or regulated, biodiversity can improve and fish populations may be restored relatively rapidly. This means protecting not only fish populations but also other organisms within a marine ecosystem. International cooperation is essential if measures like these are to be successful.

The International Union for the Conservation of Nature (IUCN) supports scientific research and helps governments to develop and implement policies, laws and best practice. They currently work with 140 different countries on a variety of issues, including marine biodiversity conservation.

The European Union (EU) has enacted several measures to try to ensure a sustainable fishing industry. This includes restricting sizes of nets, a ban on drift nets (which catch many different species together) and the imposition of quotas for different fish. If a trawler nets more than the quota, it has to return the excess to the sea. While this sounds reasonable and sensible, in practice it does not work. When bony fish are brought to the surface, their swim bladders are destroyed and the fish die. So returning them to the sea does not help the fish population.

16 Compare r-strategies and K-strategies adopted by different species.

17 **a** Describe how the 'capture–mark–release–recapture' method is used to estimate the size of a population of small invertebrates.
   b What are the limitations of this method?

18 Outline what is meant by 'maximum sustainable yield' of fish stocks.

Conservation of fish and international cooperation

Why is it difficult to ensure that fishing is regulated to the benefit of fishermen, consumers and the environment? Consider the following statements and discuss the problems that arise as international negotiators attempt to interpret and apply scientific data.

- Data on fish stocks is difficult to obtain and there is no common view on what is a sustainable population.
- It is difficult to enforce fishing regulations. Authorities may be active in one region but unable to control actions of other countries that ignore the rules.
- Politicians are under pressure from fishing communities not to limit fish catches.
- As fisheries go out of business due to declining stocks, it is not easy to limit the activities of those that remain.
- Fish are mobile animals and can be caught thousands of miles from where they are bought. Can ethical consumers be sure that the fish they buy is from a sustainable stock?

End-of-chapter questions

1   Explain **two** factors that affect the distribution of animal species.   (4)

2   Describe **one** method of sampling using a quadrat and state what it would be used for.   (4)

3   Explain what is meant by 'niche concept'.   (4)

4   Outline **one** named example of competition and **one** named example of parasitism.   (4)

5   Discuss the difficulty of classifying organisms into trophic levels, using named examples.   (4)

6   Explain the effects of organisms on the abiotic environment during primary succession.   (4)

7   Discuss **two** reasons for the conservation of rainforest biodiversity.   (4)

8   Explain the cause and consequences of biomagnification, using a named example.   (5)

9   **HL** Explain the use of biotic indices and indicator species in monitoring environmental change.   (5)

10 **HL** Discuss the advantages of *in situ* conservation of endangered species.   (3)

11 **HL** Discuss the environmental conditions that favour a K-strategy.   (3)

12 **HL** Outline the concept of maximum sustainable yield in the conservation of fish stocks.   (3)

13 In the south-west of the USA, dams were built across rivers in the early 1900s to stop natural flooding. As a result, a non-native tree called the salt cedar (*Tamarix ramosissima*) gradually replaced the native cottonwood (*Populus deltoides*) as the dominant woody species. Flooding is being re-established to reverse the invasion of *Tamarix*.

Studies were done to investigate the relative competitive abilities at the seedling stage using different densities of the two species. Seedlings were grown in pots at different densities and mixtures of the two species. A three-dimensional model was developed to show the effect of the densities of each species on *Populus* mass (graph A) and height (graph B). Densities represent the number of seedlings per 20 cm diameter pot.

Graph A:
Effect of seedling densities
on *Populus* mass

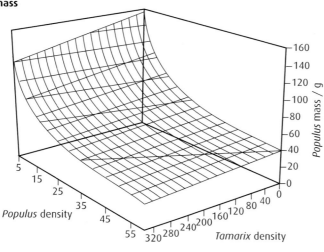

Graph B:
Effect of seedling densities
on *Populus* height

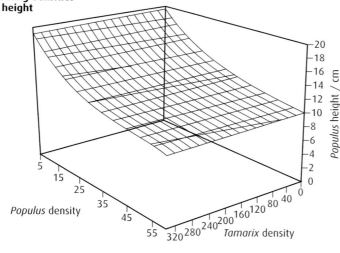

source: Sher A, Marshall D and Gilbert S (2000) *Conservation Biology*, **14**, pp 1744–54

a Considering the pots where *Populus* is growing without *Tamarix*, describe the change in mass and height of *Populus* with increased density of *Populus* seedlings. (3)

b Describe how *Tamarix* density affects *Populus* height. (1)

c Suggest two factors that could have allowed *Tamarix* to dominate in non-flood conditions. (2)

(total 6 marks)
© IB Organization 2009

14 Sea water temperature has an effect on the spawning (release of eggs) of echinoderms living in Antarctic waters. Echinoderm larvae feed on phytoplankton. In this investigation, the spawning of echinoderms and its effect on phytoplankton was studied.

In the figure below, the top line indicates the number of larvae caught (per 5000 litres of sea water). The shaded bars below show when spawning occurred in echinoderms.

The concentration of chlorophyll gives an indication of the concentration of phytoplankton. Note that the seasons in the Antarctic are reversed from those in the northern hemisphere.

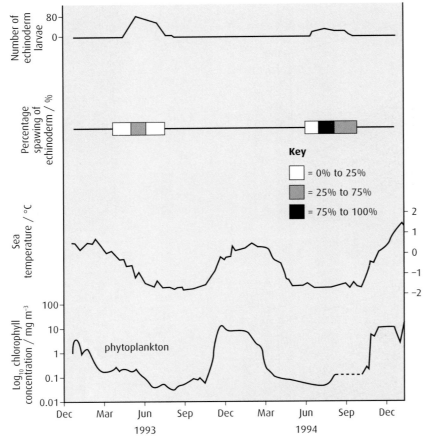

source: adapted from Stanwell-Smith and Peck (1998) *Biological Bulletin*, **194**, pp 44–52

a State the trophic level of echinoderm larvae. (1)

b Identify the period during which the spawning of echinoderms lies between 25% and 75%. (1)

c Explain the relationship between the seasons and the concentration of phytoplankton. (2)

d i Outline the effect of sea water temperature on echinoderm larvae numbers. (2)
   ii Using the data in the figure, predict the effect of global warming on echinoderm larvae numbers. (2)

(total 8 marks)

© IB Organization 2009

15 Conservationists identified 24 wilderness zones in the world. A wilderness is defined as an area greater than 10 000 km^2 with a human population of less than five inhabitants per km^2 and is mostly unspoiled, therefore retaining its natural condition. Various activities threaten the biodiversity of these wilderness zones. Each wilderness zone was identified as belonging to one of six major biomes. The chart below shows the number of wilderness zones belonging to each biome and the number under threat.

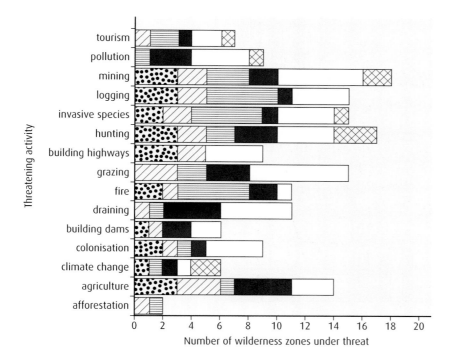

Key biomes and number of wilderness zones within each biome

- tropical humid forests (3)
- tropical dry forests and grasslands (3)
- temperate forests (5)
- wetlands (4)
- deserts (7)
- tundra (2)

Mittermeier, R A *et al.* (2003) 'Wilderness and biodiversity conservation', *PNAS* (2 Sep 2003), vol 100, issue 18, Fig 2 © 2003 National Academy of Sciences, USA

a State how many of the activities threaten **all** of the biomes. (1)

b Identify **one** activity that threatens all desert wilderness zones. (1)

c Compare the effects of pollution and climate change on the biomes. (3)

d Suggest how fire affects biodiversity. (1)

(total 6 marks)

© IB Organization 2009

16 The biodiversity of Costa Rican salamanders was studied over a range of altitudes. The salamanders belong to three genera: *Nototriton, Oedipina* and *Bolitoglossa*. *Nototriton* includes very small animals (less than 40 mm), *Oedipina* has an average size of 60 mm and *Bolitoglossa* is a diversified genus including *B. pesrubra*, which is less than 65 mm, and *B. nigrescens*, which is about 95 mm.

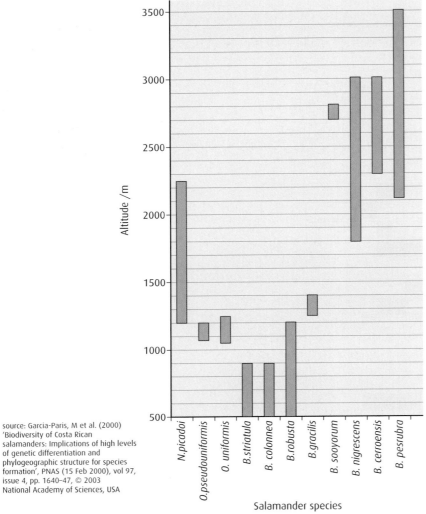

source: Garcia-Paris, M et al. (2000)
'Biodiversity of Costa Rican
salamanders: Implications of high levels
of genetic differentiation and
phylogeographic structure for species
formation', PNAS (15 Feb 2000), vol 97,
issue 4, pp. 1640–47, © 2003
National Academy of Sciences, USA

a Identify the range of altitude at which *B. cerroensis* can be found. (1)

b Identify the altitude at which the greatest diversity of salamanders can be found. (1)

c Compare the distribution of *Bolitoglossa* and *Oedipina*. (2)

d Evaluate the evidence provided by the data for altitude as a factor in the ecological niches of the salamanders. (3)

(total 7 marks)

© IB Organization 2009

Further human physiology Option H

Introduction

Human physiology involves examining not only the structures of the human body but also how they work together in harmony. Nerves and hormones work together under the control of the brain to ensure that the heart beats at the correct rate, that digestion is completed by all the right enzymes produced at the right times, and that our breathing rate matches our activity level. After digestion, nutrients are processed, stored or disposed of so that our cells have the resources they need to live, grow and repair themselves. If an emergency arrives, the body is prepared; and if we should move to a high altitude, our physiology will be modified so that we adapt to the different conditions.

H1 Hormonal control

Assessment statements

- State that hormones are chemical messengers secreted by endocrine glands into the blood and transported to specific target cells.
- State that hormones can be steroids, proteins and tyrosine derivatives, with one example of each.
- Distinguish between the mode of action of 'steroid hormones' and 'protein hormones'.
- Outline the relationship between the hypothalamus and the pituitary gland.
- Explain the control of ADH (vasopressin) secretion by negative feedback.

The body is under the control of two systems: the nervous system and the endocrine system. These are mostly independent of one another but there are situations in which the two work together to control activities such as heart rate (outlined in Chapter **6**).

The chemical forms of hormones

Hormones are chemical substances that are secreted directly into the bloodstream from endocrine glands found throughout the body (Figure **H.1**, overleaf).

Since hormones circulate in the bloodstream, they come into contact with all cells in the body but only cells that have specific, genetically determined receptors will respond. These target cells have receptors on the plasma membrane that recognise and bind to the hormone. Different hormones have different chemical structures and can be divided into three categories as shown in Table **H.1** (overleaf).

How hormones control cells

Protein hormones and steroid hormones control their target cells in different ways. Protein hormones bind to a surface receptor, very often a glycoprotein, but do not enter the cell. Instead, the binding process

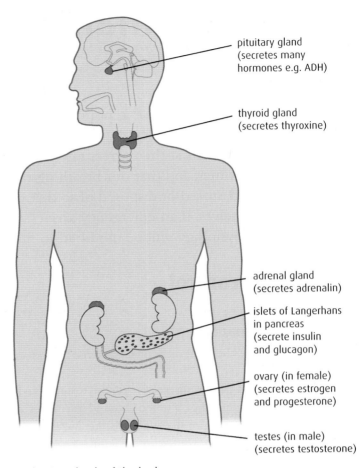

Figure H.1 Endocrine glands of the body.

pituitary gland
(secretes many
hormones e.g. ADH)

thyroid gland
(secretes thyroxine)

adrenal gland
(secretes adrenalin)

islets of Langerhans
in pancreas
(secrete insulin
and glucagon)

ovary (in female)
(secretes estrogen
and progesterone)

testes (in male)
(secretes testosterone)

Chemical form of hormone	Examples
steroids derived from cholesterol	testosterone, progesterone
proteins	insulin, FSH, LH
tyrosine derivative	thyroxine – each thyroxine molecule has four iodine atoms

Table H.1 The different chemical forms of hormones.

triggers the release of a second messenger chemical from the cytoplasmic side of the cell membrane and this messenger controls the activity of the cell. This may be achieved by regulating the activity of a specific enzyme in the cell, either activating it or inhibiting it.

Steroid hormones do enter the cell, since they can easily pass through the plasma membrane. They bind to a specific receptor in the cytoplasm forming a hormone–receptor complex, which is transported through a nuclear pore (Figure **H.2**) into the nucleus. Here, the hormone regulates the process of transcription of one or more specific genes.

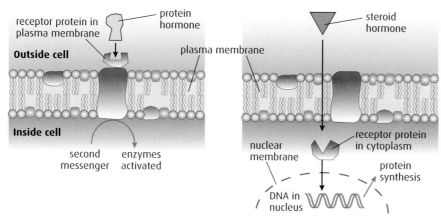

Figure H.2 The modes of action of protein and steroid hormones.

The hypothalamus and the pituitary gland

The **hypothalamus** is a small area of the brain that monitors hormone levels and indirectly controls functions including body temperature, hunger and sleep. It links the hormonal and nervous systems and secretes releasing hormones that regulate the hormones of the anterior pituitary gland. It has a range of receptors of its own, which allow it to act independently, but it also receives information from other parts of the brain.

The **pituitary gland**, situated just below the hypothalamus (Figure H.3), is made up of two different parts – the anterior and posterior lobes. The posterior lobe develops from the brain and has neurons connecting it directly to the brain. The anterior lobe develops separately and has no direct neural connection with the brain.

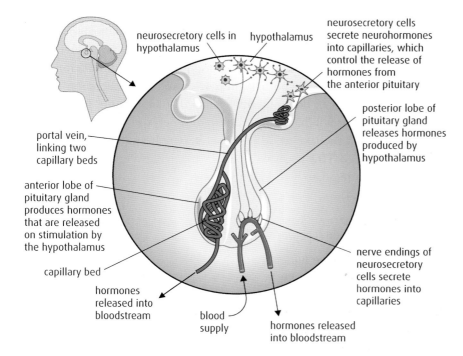

Figure H.3 The hypothalamus and pituitary gland.

The hypothalamus has to communicate with each lobe of the pituitary gland in a different way.

- The hypothalamus contains the cell bodies of many **neurosecretory cells**, which have their terminal ends in the posterior lobe of the pituitary. A neurosecretory cell is simply a neuron that has been modified to secrete and store a large quantity of hormone at the terminal end of the cell body. Surrounding the terminal ends of the neurosecretory cells is a capillary network so that when the cells receive the appropriate information they can release the hormone directly into the blood. Two examples of posterior lobe hormones released in this way are antidiuretic hormone (ADH) and oxytocin.

- Control of the anterior lobe of the pituitary is regulated by another set of neurosecretory cells in the hypothalamus. These cells end in a different capillary bed just above the pituitary gland. The blood from these capillaries flows into a portal vein, which passes into capillaries within the anterior lobe of the pituitary. These neurosecretory cells secrete releasing hormones (RH), which control the release of the hormones from the cells of the anterior lobe. One example is gonadotrophin releasing hormone (GnRH), which controls the release of follicle stimulating hormone (FSH) and luteinising hormone (LH).

The control of ADH secretion

Antidiuretic hormone (ADH) (also known as vasopressin) is used in the homeostatic regulation of blood plasma concentration. ADH is produced by neurosecretory cells in the hypothalamus and stored in their nerve endings in the posterior pituitary gland. Osmoreceptors in the hypothalamus detect when blood concentration rises above the normal level. This triggers the release of ADH, which travels in the blood to target cells in the collecting ducts of the kidneys. ADH causes the reabsorption of water from the ducts into the blood (Chapter **11**). As more water enters the blood, the concentration of blood plasma falls, stimulation of the osmoreceptors in the hypothalamus ceases, and ADH secretion stops. ADH is quickly broken down by the liver so that after about 20 minutes more than half of it will have been removed. When the concentration of plasma falls and the level of ADH falls, larger volumes of more dilute urine are produced. This negative feedback mechanism enables the hypothalamus to regulate blood plasma concentration within narrow limits (Figure **H.4**).

1   List the **three** chemical forms of hormones.

2   State which hormone type:
    a   enters the cell directly
    b   binds to a cell surface receptor.

3   Describe the negative feedback pathway involving ADH.

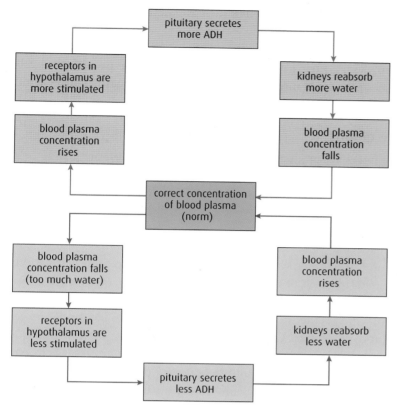

Figure H.4 Control of blood plasma concentration is an example of a negative feedback pathway.

H2 Digestion

Assessment statements

- State that digestive juices are secreted into the alimentary canal by glands, including salivary glands, gastric glands in the stomach wall, the pancreas and the wall of the small intestine.
- Explain the structural features of exocrine gland cells.
- Compare the composition of saliva, gastric juice and pancreatic juice.
- Outline the control of digestive juice secretion by nerves and hormones using the example of secretion of gastric juice.
- Outline the role of membrane-bound enzymes on the surface of epithelial cells in the small intestine in digestion.
- Outline the reasons for cellulose not being digested in the alimentary canal.
- Explain why pepsin and trypsin are initially synthesised as inactive precursors and how they are subsequently activated.
- Discuss the roles of gastric acid and *Helicobacter pylori* in the development of stomach ulcers and stomach cancers.
- Explain the problems of lipid digestion in a hydrophilic medium and the role of bile in overcoming this.

Secretion of digestive juices

The food we eat is composed of many different molecules and many of these are macromolecules, which cannot pass through the walls of the alimentary canal into the bloodstream. As ingested food passes along the alimentary canal, it is mixed with enzymes and other digestive juices which break down macromolecules such as starch and protein into a form in which they can be absorbed.

Salivary glands in the mouth secrete saliva containing the enzyme salivary amylase. Gastric glands in the stomach wall, the pancreas and cells in the wall of the small intestine all produce further digestive juices which are added to food as it travels along the alimentary canal.

Exocrine glands

Digestive juices are produced in **exocrine glands**. These are glands whose secreted products are carried via ducts to the alimentary canal. Cells of an exocrine gland are arranged in a single layer around small ducts that carry away the digestive juices they produce. One group of exocrine cells arranged around a duct is called an **acinus** (Figure **H.5**) and one exocrine gland contains many acini. The small ducts join together to form one larger duct, which carries the secretions to their destination.

Exocrine gland cells of the digestive system produce enzymes that are proteins and so the cells contain an extensive rough endoplasmic reticulum, which is the site of protein synthesis. Also visible inside the cells are numerous ribosomes, Golgi apparatus for packaging and processing the enzymes, and large number of vesicles, which store enzymes before they are secreted by exocytosis into the ducts of the gland. Exocrine cells also contain a clearly visible nucleolus in the nucleus for the production of ribosome subunits, and numerous mitochondria to produce ATP for protein synthesis (Figure **H.6**).

Saliva, gastric juice and pancreatic juice

Digestive juices contain many different enzymes and other substances that assist with digestion. The contents of the secretions of three exocrine glands are summarised in Table **H.2**.

Pepsin and trypsin are protease enzymes that digest protein and are therefore potentially harmful to the cells that produce them and

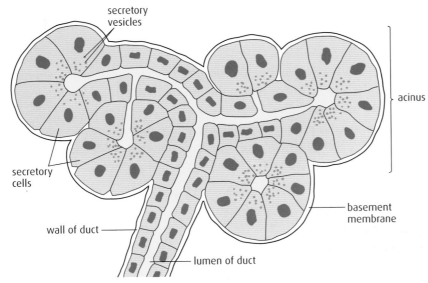

Figure H.5 A group of acini in exocrine tissue of the pancreas.

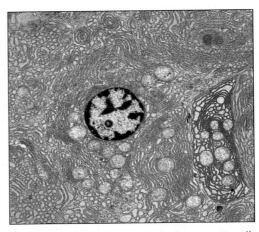

Figure H.6 Electron micrograph of pancreatic cell showing rough endoplasmic reticulum and many mitochondria.

Saliva from salivary glands	Gastric juice from glands in the stomach wall	Pancreatic juice from exocrine cells in the pancreas
water and mucus	water and mucus	water
salivary amylase	pepsin secreted as pepsinogen	pancreatic amylase trypsin secreted as trypsinogen pancreatic lipase carboxypeptidase chymotrypsin
	hydrochloric acid	hydrogencarbonate (HCO_3^- ions)

Table H.2 The contents of saliva, gastric juice and pancreatic juice.

structures that they come into contact with. In order to prevent damage to the proteins in body cells, both these enzymes are secreted as inactive precursors: pepsinogen and trypsinogen respectively. These are converted to their active form where they are needed, after secretion.

- Pepsinogen is converted to pepsin in the stomach when in the presence of hydrochloric acid, which is secreted by different cells in the stomach lining. The inner lining of the stomach is protected from both hydrochloric acid and pepsin by a thick layer of mucus.
- Trypsinogen is activated by the enzyme enterokinase (or enteropeptidase), which converts trypsinogen to trypsin. The activating enzyme is secreted by the walls of the small intestine when food enters from the stomach.

Control of secretion of digestive juices

The production of digestive juices requires energy, and large numbers of mitochondria are present in exocrine cells to provide this. To avoid wasting both enzymes and energy, the body controls the secretion of digestive juices so that they are released at the correct time when food is present in the alimentary canal.

Experience tells us that the sight or smell of food stimulates the production of saliva, and the nerve impulses that cause this response also stimulate the release of gastric juice in the stomach. Both responses are reflex actions. As food enters the stomach, more gastric juice is released as touch and stretch receptors in the stomach wall send impulses to the brain. Chemoreceptors in the lining also send impulses and the brain continues the stimulation of the gastric glands. In addition, impulses pass to the endocrine glands in the stomach wall that release the hormone gastrin. Gastrin stimulates gastric glands to produce more hydrochloric acid and continue the production of gastric juices.

Membrane-bound digestive enzymes

Enzymes that form part of the digestive juice poured into the alimentary canal are mixed with ingested food passing along it. Movements of the muscles of the intestine walls squeeze food along and mix it with digestive juices as it travels. Enzymes and food travel together, and digestion proceeds in the process.

Not all enzymes are mixed with food in this way. Some remain bound to the membranes of cells forming the inner lining of the small intestine. These enzymes are not swept away by the passage of food and remain in place on the surface of the villi and microvilli where they make contact with their substrate molecules. Membrane-bound enzymes remain in place much longer than enzymes that are released. They digest their substrates at the cell membrane and products can be absorbed immediately. Although the cells of the villi are worn away as food passes by, the enzymes remain attached to the membranes and continue to work as they are mixed into the food in the small intestine. Maltase, an enzyme that hydrolyses the carbohydrate maltose to two molecules of glucose, is an example of a membrane-bound enzyme.

Cellulose

Humans cannot digest cellulose, which makes up the walls of plant cells. Cellulose is a complex carbohydrate requiring the enzyme cellulase to catalyse its digestion. Humans and other mammals are unable to produce this enzyme. Herbivorous mammals such as cows retain large numbers of mutualistic bacteria in their digestive systems to produce the necessary cellulase. Other mammals, such as rabbits, retain cellulose-producing bacteria in their appendix and pass food twice through their digestive systems. These herbivores are able to extract energy from plant material but as humans do not have any source of cellulase, cellulose (also known as fibre) passes undigested out of the body in faeces.

Digestion of lipids

Lipids are water-insoluble molecules and present a problem for digestion in the intestine where the medium is aqueous and most enzymes are water-soluble. Lipids are hydrophobic molecules and tend to coalesce into droplets when in water. Water-soluble lipase, the enzyme that digests lipid, cannot enter the droplets, which have a relatively small surface area in relation to their volume. Lipase can only hydrolyse the outer lipid molecules and the internal areas of the droplet remain undigested.

In the intestine this problem is solved by the addition of **bile**. Bile is produced in the liver and stored in gall bladder, which releases it along the bile duct into the small intestine. Bile contains mostly cholesterol, bile acids (also called bile salts), and bilirubin (a breakdown product of red blood cells). Bile salts are molecules with both hydrophilic and hydrophobic areas and so are soluble in both water and lipid. They tend to aggregate around fat droplets, breaking them up and coating lipid molecules to prevent the formation of large droplets. This process is called **emulsification** (Figure **H.7**)

Emulsification produces many small fat droplets, which have a much larger total surface area for enzymes to work on than one large droplet. Emulsification speeds up the digestion process so that lipids can be completely digested in the small intestine.

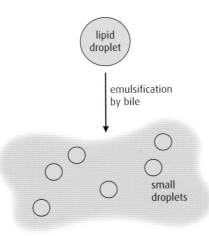

Figure H.7 Bile breaks down large droplets of lipids into smaller ones.

Helicobacter pylori and stomach ulcers

Helicobacter pylori is a spiral-shaped bacterium that is able to grow in the human stomach. Unlike other bacteria, it can tolerate acidic conditions and survives well at pH values similar to those in the stomach. The organism was brought to the attention of the medical profession in the 1980s by two Australians, Dr Barry Marshall and Dr Robin Warren who isolated it from the stomach linings of patients who were suffering from stomach ulcers and inflammation of the stomach lining (gastritis). Marshall and Warren proposed that *H. pyloric* caused these symptoms. Until this time, stomach ulcers were thought to be caused by the excess secretion of acid, which caused damage to the stomach lining. Ulcers were associated with a stressful lifestyle, which was said to cause excess production of gastric juice. Since the 1980s, plenty of evidence has been gathered to support the hypothesis proposed by Marshall and Warren.

- Ulcers used to be treated with antacid treatments, which relieved the symptoms for relatively short periods of time. Today, antimicrobial drugs that kill bacteria and remove *H. pylori* infection provide long-term relief of symptoms and cure ulcers.

- *H. pylori* is regularly found in patients with both gastritis and ulcers. Many strains of the bacterium produce toxins that cause inflammation of the stomach lining. Patients who are infected for many years with these strains are also more likely to develop stomach cancer than non-infected people.

Stomach cancer occurs far more frequently in patients with *H. pylori* than in non-infected people so the bacterium seems to increase the risk of stomach cancer. But millions of people are infected with these bacteria and most of them do not get stomach cancer so there must be other factors at work. *H. pylori* has not been established as the cause of stomach cancer. It can cause an inflammatory condition called severe chronic atrophic gastritis (SCAG) and this can lead to stomach cancer. People with SCAG have an increased risk of cancer in both the upper and lower parts of the stomach. So, while *H. pylori* is a significant risk factor in stomach cancer, other factors such as age, diet (particularly if it is high in salted or smoked foods and low in fruits and vegetables), pernicious anemia and a family history of stomach cancer, are also important.

4 Outline the differences between the composition of saliva and that of pancreatic juice.

5 Outline the role of enzymes that are bound to the surfaces of cells in the small intestine.

6 Why is there a problem digesting lipids in an aqueous environment?

A paradigm shift

'No one believed it,' Staffan Normark, a member of the Nobel Assembly at the Karolinska institute, said at a news conference.

The discovery of *Helicobacter pylori* is an example of a paradigm shift. This term was first used by an American philosopher Thomas Kuhn in his book *The Structure of Scientific Revolutions* (1962). It describes a change in assumptions within a ruling scientific theory. A paradigm shift occurs when there are a significant number of anomalies that counter the accepted paradigm – in this case, the belief that bacteria could not survive in the stomach and that ulcers were caused by excessive acid production. The accepted theory is thrown into a state of crisis until a new paradigm is formed and gains its own followers. For a time, an intellectual 'battle' will occur between the followers of the old and new paradigms.

For some time after Marshall and Warren's initial discovery of *H. pylori* in their patients, the well-established idea that bacteria could not survive in acid conditions persisted, despite evidence to the contrary. The men's proposed hypothesis was outside the mainstream view of the time (even though there had been some anecdotal and published evidence regarding antibiotic treatment of ulcers), and Marshall and Warren had to persevere in the face of considerable scepticism. They tested their theory, gathered evidence to support it, published their results and eventually they overturned the prevailing notion that ulcers were caused by stress and diet, based on the evidence of their experiments. Marshall even decided to deliberately infect himself with the bacterium in 1985 in order to show from his own experience that it caused stomach inflammation, a potential precursor of an ulcer. Their persistence paid off and the two men were awarded Nobel Prize for medicine in 2005 for showing that bacterial infection was to blame for painful ulcers in the stomach and intestine.

Questions to consider

1 Marshall and Warren used themselves as experimental subjects to provide evidence to support their hypothesis. Do you think there is a case for carrying out research on human subjects?
2 Discuss the ethical implications of doing research on humans.

H3 Absorption of digested foods

Assessment statements

- Draw and label a diagram showing a transverse section of the ileum as seen under a light microscope.
- Explain the structural features of an epithelial cell of a villus as seen in electron micrographs, including microvilli, mitochondria, pinocytotic vesicles and tight junctions.
- Explain the mechanism used by the ileum to absorb and transport food including facilitated diffusion, active transport and endocytosis.
- List the materials that are not absorbed and are egested.

Structure of the small intestine

Absorption of digested food occurs in the ileum, which is part of the small intestine. The structure of this region is related to its function. For example, the surface area provided for absorbing food is increased enormously by folding of its inner lining into structures known as villi (Figure **H.8**). Each villus contains capillaries and a lacteal to transport absorbed molecules.

The inner lining of the small intestine is known as the intestinal mucosa. It is this layer that is responsible for absorbing food. The longitudinal and circular muscles in the intestine wall contract to move food along.

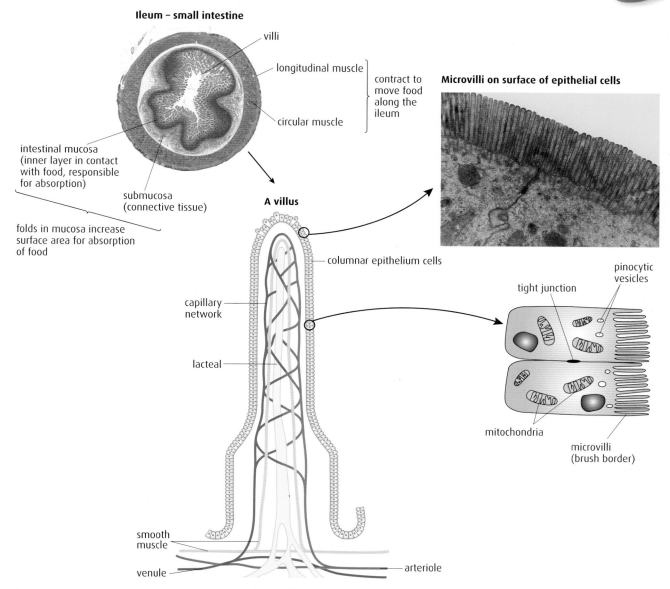

Figure H.8 The structure and microstructure of the small intestine.

Structure of a villus

Each fold of the intestinal mucosa is known as a **villus** and each villus also has many tiny projections known as **microvilli** (see also Chapter **6**) These structures produce a very large surface area for the absorption of digested materials.

Digested material must pass through the epithelial cells of the microvilli in order to reach a capillary or lacteal vessel. Cells of the microvilli contain structures that are vital to the processes of absorption.

The cells have many mitochondria indicating that some absorption occurs using active transport, and requires energy. In addition, many vesicles are present and these structures show that some materials are taken in from the intestine by the process of **pinocytosis**.

The epithelial cells are linked together by **tight junctions**, which seal each cell from the adjacent cell. The two adjacent membranes share some proteins and the tight junction between them prevents materials moving between cells. Most molecules are forced to pass straight through the cells from the lumen of the small intestine and into capillaries on the other side.

Digested molecules are small enough to pass through the epithelial cells and into the bloodstream. Movement can occur by a number of means.

- **Simple diffusion** can occur if molecules are small and can pass through the hydrophobic part of the plasma membrane.
- **Facilitated diffusion** occurs in the case of molecules such as fructose, which are hydrophilic. Protein channels in the epithelial cell membrane enable these molecules to move, provided they are small enough and there is a concentration gradient, which permits diffusion.
- **Active transport** is used to transport molecules that do not have a sufficiently high concentration gradient to pass by diffusion. Glucose, amino acids and mineral ions are all absorbed by this method. Mitochondria produce the ATP needed for active transport by the membrane pumps.
- **Pinocytosis** also draws in small drops of liquid from the ileum. Each droplet is surrounded by small sections of membrane that invaginate to form a vesicle. The vesicles are taken into the cytoplasm where their contents can be released.

Undigested material

Materials such as cellulose, which cannot be digested or absorbed, pass right through the intestine and are egested as part of the solid waste, or **faeces**. Faeces contain not only cellulose but also lignin from plant cell walls and bacteria that live in the digestive system and are carried through it. Cells of the intestine wall that are worn away as food travels past them also form part of the faeces, as well as bile pigments containing material from the breakdown of red blood cells, which give the faeces their familiar colour.

....

7 What are the roles of pinocytotic vesicles and tight junctions in absorption?

8 List **three** materials that are egested, not absorbed.

....

H4 Functions of the liver

Assessment statements

- Outline the circulation of blood through the liver tissue, including the hepatic artery, hepatic portal vein, sinusoids and hepatic vein.
- Explain the role of the liver in regulating levels of nutrients in the blood.
- Outline the role of the liver in the storage of nutrients, including carbohydrate, iron, vitamin A and vitamin D.
- State that the liver synthesises plasma proteins and cholesterol.
- State that the liver has a role in detoxification.
- Describe the process of erythrocyte and hemoglobin breakdown in the liver, including phagocytosis, digestion of globin and bile pigment formation.
- Explain the liver damage caused by excessive alcohol consumption.

Circulation of blood through the liver

The liver is the largest internal organ in the body and makes up 3–5% of our body weight. It is situated just below the diaphragm and has many important roles including storage of nutrients, production of bile and detoxification of poisons.

The liver is an unusual organ because it is supplied by two large blood vessels (Figure **H.9**). The first is the hepatic artery, a branch of the aorta, which carries oxygenated blood to the liver, and the second is the hepatic portal vein, which carries blood from the intestine. Blood in the hepatic portal vein is rich in nutrients that have been absorbed by capillaries in the small intestine. 20% of the total volume of blood in the body flows through the liver at any time.

The liver is divided into **lobules**, which are rows of **hepatocytes** (liver cells) arranged in a circular pattern around a central vein (Figure **H.10**, overleaf). Between the rows of cells are **sinusoids**, which are a type of blood capillary that is much larger than the capillaries of other tissues. Blood from branches of both the hepatic portal vein and the hepatic artery flows along the sinusoids. The endothelial cells that line the sinusoids are very thin and well spaced. These structural features help with absorption of substances into the surrounding hepatocytes (Figure **H.10**).

Attached to the walls of the sinusoids are numerous phagocytes called Kupffer cells, which remove bacteria and damaged red blood cells. Red blood cells are broken down inside the Kupffer cells. Blood from the sinusoids flows into the central veins, which unite to form the hepatic vein. The hepatic vein leaves the liver and joins the vena cava.

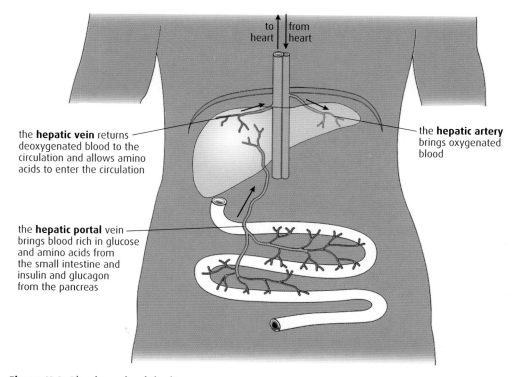

to heart | from heart

the **hepatic vein** returns deoxygenated blood to the circulation and allows amino acids to enter the circulation

the **hepatic artery** brings oxygenated blood

the **hepatic portal** vein brings blood rich in glucose and amino acids from the small intestine and insulin and glucagon from the pancreas

Figure H.9 Blood supply of the liver.

Bile

Small channels called bile canaliculi pass between the rows of hepatocytes. Bile is produced in the hepatocytes and secreted into these channels, which connect to form the bile duct. Bile contains bile salts, which are important in the digestion of lipids in the intestine, and bile pigments, which are derived from the breakdown of hemoglobin. Bile is stored in the gall bladder and released when food enters the small intestine.

Vitamin D

Vitamin D is made in the skin when exposed to sunlight. People who live in areas close to the Poles, where there is little sunlight and the temperature is very cold, cover most of their skin during winter. In this situation, the liver is able to release vitamin D that has been stored during the warmer, summer months when more skin is exposed to sunlight. However, sunlight contains ultraviolet rays that can cause skin cancer, and so a balance is needed between exposure, to synthesise vitamin D, and protection from the damaging UV.

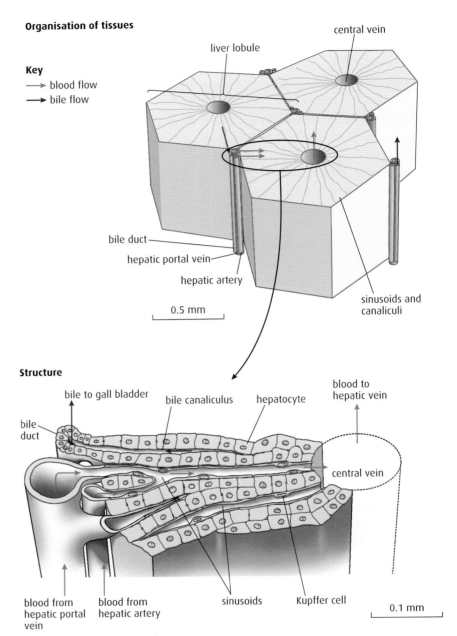

Organisation of tissues

Key
→ blood flow
→ bile flow

liver lobule
central vein
bile duct
hepatic portal vein
hepatic artery
sinusoids and canaliculi
0.5 mm

Structure

bile to gall bladder
bile canaliculus
hepatocyte
blood to hepatic vein
bile duct
central vein
blood from hepatic portal vein
blood from hepatic artery
sinusoids
Kupffer cell
0.1 mm

Figure H.10 Structure of a liver lobule.

Storage and regulation of nutrients by the liver

The liver plays a key role in homeostasis. It regulates blood sugar levels and is able to store lipids, iron (from the breakdown of hemoglobin) and the fat-soluble vitamins A and D. The liver also synthesises cholesterol and plasma proteins. Absorbed nutrients are carried in the blood directly from the intestine to the liver in the hepatic portal vein. The blood that leaves the liver contains regulated amounts of nutrients.

One of the most important roles of the liver is to maintain the correct level of glucose in the blood. After a meal containing carbohydrate, the glucose level in the blood will rise, but during exercise it will fall as glucose is respired by the muscles. The liver helps to balance out these fluctuations by storing glucose as glycogen in the hepatocytes when levels are high and breaking down and reconverting the glycogen to glucose when the level falls. Two pancreatic hormones (insulin and glucagon) control this process. **Insulin** stimulates the hepatocytes to take up glucose and convert it to glycogen. **Glucagon** is released when levels are low and stimulates hepatocytes to convert glycogen back to glucose.

Synthesis and detoxification

Plasma proteins, found in the blood, play an important part in blood homeostasis. They are key to regulating the osmotic balance of body fluids and regulate the movement of water between plasma and tissue fluid, as well as affecting ultrafiltration in the kidney. The plasma proteins synthesised by hepatocytes include globulins and albumen and the blood-clotting protein, fibrinogen.

Hepatocytes also synthesise cholesterol, which is essential in membrane structure and is the precursor for several other molecules including the steroid hormones testosterone, estrogen and progesterone. Cholesterol is found in many of the foods we eat but all the cholesterol required by the body is made by the liver.

The liver has an essential role in **detoxification**. Hepatocytes absorb toxins and convert them into non-toxic or less toxic products. Some of the toxins are by-products of metabolic reactions (such as lactate from anaerobically respiring muscles or hydrogen peroxide produced by processes including fatty acid metabolism). These toxins are broken down by the enzyme catalase. Other toxins that the liver processes are ingested substances such as alcohol, food additives or pesticides.

Alcohol and the liver

Alcohol, absorbed from the gut, passes straight to the liver in the hepatic portal vein and is absorbed by the hepatocytes. Hepatocytes remove and detoxify the alcohol, but if it is present in large amounts, blood may have to flow through the liver many times before all the alcohol can be absorbed. This makes the liver very susceptible to damage by alcohol. If large quantities are consumed, fatty deposits begin to build up in the liver lobules, replacing damaged cells, and reducing liver function (Figure **H.11**). The liver can become inflamed, a condition known as alcoholic hepatitis and symptoms include nausea and jaundice. In jaundiced individuals, skin becomes yellow as a result of the liver's inability to metabolise and excrete the pigment bilirubin, which accumulates in the body. In the longer term, the liver may become permanently damaged as scar tissue develops in place of damaged blood vessels and hepatocytes. This is called **cirrhosis** of the liver. These areas of the liver are no longer able to function efficiently and if cirrhosis is extensive, liver failure can be the result. Liver damage like this is fatal unless it can be replaced by a transplant.

Cholesterol

The liver can regulate the amount of cholesterol in the blood. If there is sufficient, the liver may stop its synthesis of cholesterol, in a negative feedback process. Excess cholesterol is excreted in the bile, but high levels in bile can cause deposits in the gall bladder called gallstones, which obstruct the bile duct. Excess cholesterol in the blood can contribute to blockages in the walls of certain arteries and lead to cardiovascular disease.

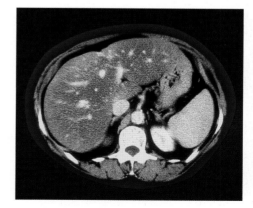

Figure H.11 This is an MRI scan of a person suffering from a fatty liver. The fat deposits can be seen as blue patches in the liver (purple).

Alcohol is very widely consumed and there are major health concerns with the rise of 'binge drinking' in young people. Binge drinking is the consumption of large amounts of alcohol in a short period of time. There is a well-established correlation between excessive alcohol consumption and liver disease, as well as the longer-term problems of alcohol addiction.

Erythrocyte and hemoglobin breakdown

Red blood cells survive in the bloodstream for about 120 days before they must be replaced with new cells from the bone marrow. At the end of their lives, red blood cells may break into fragments as their membranes become weakened and thus release free hemoglobin into the bloodstream. Cell fragments and hemoglobin are taken up by the Kupffer cells in the sinusoids of the liver and the component parts of hemoglobin are broken down for recycling or excretion. This is shown in Figure **H.12**.

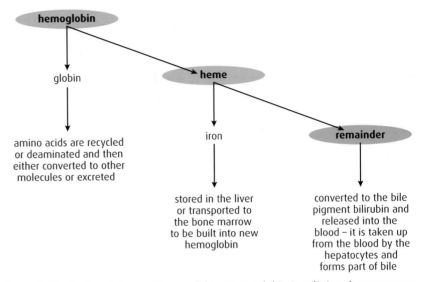

Figure H.12 The breakdown of hemoglobin. Hemoglobin is split into heme groups and globins. Globins are hydrolysed to amino acids, which can be re-used. Iron is removed from the heme group and either stored or recycled. The remaining part of the molecule becomes part of bile.

9 Outline **three** important roles of the liver.

10 Outline the stages in the breakdown of red blood cells and the fate of the products.

11 Name the main blood vessels that enter and leave the liver.

H5 The transport system

Assessment statements

- Explain the events of the cardiac cycle, including atrial and ventricular systole and diastole, and heart sounds.
- Analyse data showing pressure and volume changes in the left atrium, left ventricle and the aorta, during the cardiac cycle.
- Outline the mechanisms that control the heart beat, including the roles of the SA (sinoatrial) node, AV (atrioventricular) node and conducting fibres in the ventricular walls.
- Outline atherosclerosis and the causes of coronary thrombosis.
- Discuss factors that affect the incidence of coronary heart disease.

The cardiac cycle

The **cardiac cycle** describes the events that go to make up one heart beat. The heart rate, normally about 70 beats per minute, is a measure of the frequency of the cardiac cycle. The structure of the heart has been discussed in Chapter **6**, but the key structures that are important in the cardiac cycle are the muscles of the walls of the atria and ventricles, the atrioventricular and semilunar valves (Figure **H.13**), the sinoatrial node (SAN) or pacemaker and the atrioventricular node (AVN).

Contraction of the heart is called **systole** and relaxation is known as **diastole** (Figure **H.14**, overleaf). Atria and ventricles always contract separately, with contraction of the two atria being followed by contraction of the two ventricles. The four valves, two in the heart and two in the main arteries, keep blood flowing in one direction. As these valves close,

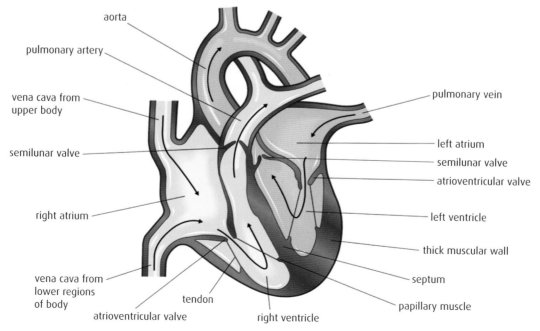

Figure H.13 The heart.

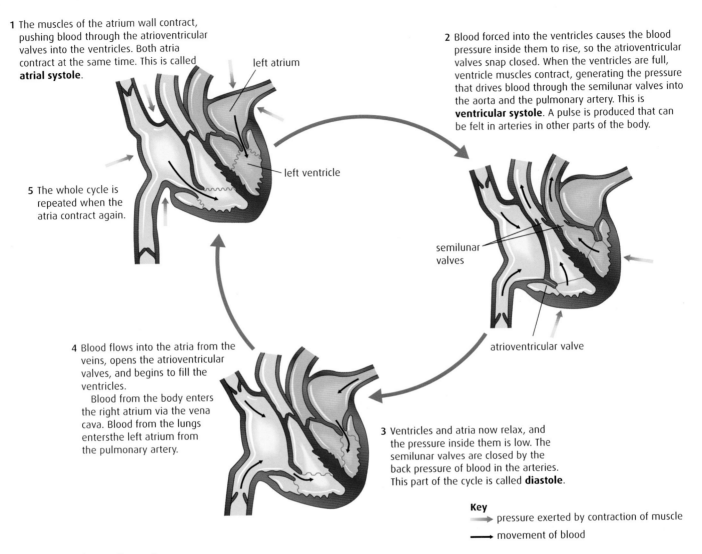

1 The muscles of the atrium wall contract, pushing blood through the atrioventricular valves into the ventricles. Both atria contract at the same time. This is called **atrial systole**.

left atrium

left ventricle

5 The whole cycle is repeated when the atria contract again.

2 Blood forced into the ventricles causes the blood pressure inside them to rise, so the atrioventricular valves snap closed. When the ventricles are full, ventricle muscles contract, generating the pressure that drives blood through the semilunar valves into the aorta and the pulmonary artery. This is **ventricular systole**. A pulse is produced that can be felt in arteries in other parts of the body.

semilunar valves

atrioventricular valve

4 Blood flows into the atria from the veins, opens the atrioventricular valves, and begins to fill the ventricles.
   Blood from the body enters the right atrium via the vena cava. Blood from the lungs entersthe left atrium from the pulmonary artery.

3 Ventricles and atria now relax, and the pressure inside them is low. The semilunar valves are closed by the back pressure of blood in the arteries. This part of the cycle is called **diastole**.

Key
→ pressure exerted by contraction of muscle
→ movement of blood

Figure H.14 The cardiac cycle.

they produce the characteristic 'lub–dub' or heart sounds that can be heard through a stethoscope. The two sides of the heart work together so that the 'lub' sound is made as the two atrioventricular valves flap shut and the 'dub' sound is the closing of the two semilunar valves.

As the heart beats, the pressure and volume in each of its four chambers change and these changes can been seen on graphs such as the one shown in Figure **H.15**.

At the end of the cardiac cycle, both atria and ventricles are in diastole (relaxed). Blood has been pumped out of the ventricles and blood is re-entering the atria from the pulmonary veins and vena cava. The pressure in the atria is slightly greater than in the ventricles so blood flows through the atria via the atrioventricular valves and into the ventricles. Blood pressure in the arteries is higher than that in the ventricles so the semilunar valves remain closed.

When the ventricles are approximately 70% full a new cardiac cycle begins. It starts with contraction of the walls of the atria, **atrial systole**.

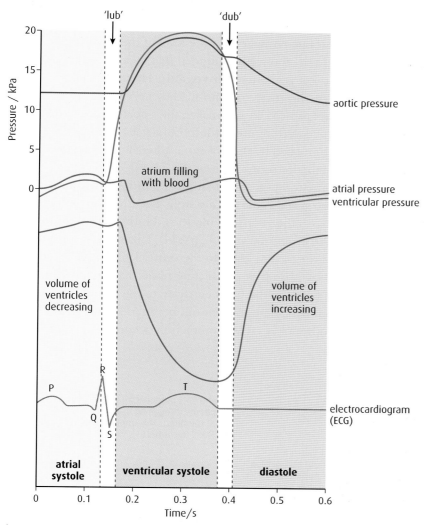

Figure H.15 Pressure and volume changes in the heart during the cardiac cycle.

Blood is pumped through the atrioventricular valves, filling the ventricles to capacity. The thin walls of the atria do not generate much pressure, but after the contraction is complete, most of the blood from the atria has entered the ventricles.

As **ventricular systole** begins, it produces sufficient pressure to snap the atrioventricular valves closed and produce the first heart sound. As the ventricles contract, pressure inside the chambers rises so that it becomes greater than the pressure in the arteries (the pulmonary artery and aorta) that leave the heart. This pressure forces the semilunar valves open and blood is pumped out of the ventricles into the arteries. At the end of ventricular systole, blood pressure in the ventricles is lower than that in the arteries and the back pressure forces the semilunar valves shut, causing the second heart sound.

When pressure in the ventricles falls below that in the atria, the atrioventricular valves re-open. Blood from the veins flows passively through the atria and into the ventricles. All four chambers of the heart return to diastole and the cycle begins all over again.

Control of the heart beat

An individual's heart rate changes with the level of their activity, emotions or stress. Heart muscle is unique in that it can contract without stimulation – it is said to be **myogenic**. However, under normal circumstances, heart rate is controlled by nervous or hormonal stimulation. Impulses pass to the pacemaker, the sinoatrial node (SAN), in the left atrium via nerves from the medulla oblongata in the brain. The pacemaker is also stimulated by the hormone adrenalin (epinephrine).

The pacemaker initiates contraction of the heart. Cells in the pacemaker produce action potentials that spread through the muscle cells in the walls of the atria and cause atrial systole. The impulses are prevented from passing directly to the ventricles but they do stimulate a group of cells known as the atrioventricular node (AVN). This node is situated in the lower part of the atrium, close to the ventricles. The AVN sends out impulses down two bands of conducting fibres that run down the centre of the heart, between the two ventricles, to the base of the heart (Figure **H.16**). From here, fibres branch out between the cells of the thick ventricular walls. As impulses arrive, contraction occurs in the muscles of the ventricle walls.

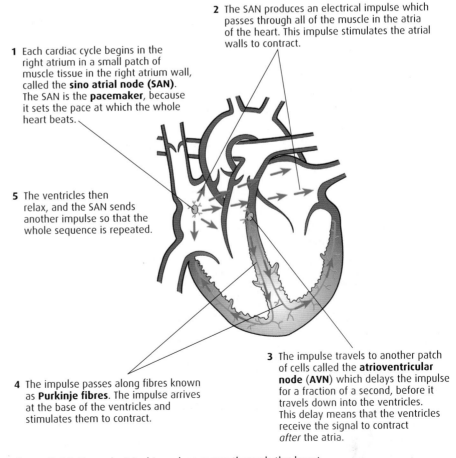

1 Each cardiac cycle begins in the right atrium in a small patch of muscle tissue in the right atrium wall, called the **sino atrial node (SAN)**. The SAN is the **pacemaker**, because it sets the pace at which the whole heart beats.

2 The SAN produces an electrical impulse which passes through all of the muscle in the atria of the heart. This impulse stimulates the atrial walls to contract.

5 The ventricles then relax, and the SAN sends another impulse so that the whole sequence is repeated.

4 The impulse passes along fibres known as **Purkinje fibres**. The impulse arrives at the base of the ventricles and stimulates them to contract.

3 The impulse travels to another patch of cells called the **atrioventricular node (AVN)** which delays the impulse for a fraction of a second, before it travels down into the ventricles. This delay means that the ventricles receive the signal to contract *after* the atria.

Figure H.16 How electrical impulses move through the heart.

Heart rate is speeded up during exercise as a rise in carbon dioxide and a fall in the pH of the blood causes impulses to be sent from the medulla in the brain via the sympathetic nerve to the SAN. When exercise stops and blood pH returns to normal, impulses pass via the vagus nerve, which slows the heart rate down. Increasing levels of adrenalin, the 'fight or flight' hormone, are produced at times of stress or anxiety. Adrenalin stimulates the SAN to increase the heart rate.

Coronary heart disease

Heart muscle works throughout our lives and never rests. It requires constant supplies of blood, which carries oxygen and nutrients to it. Three large coronary arteries branch from the aorta and supply heart muscle with oxygen-rich blood (Figure **6.5**, page **136**). If any of the three arteries is blocked, an area of the heart will receive less oxygen and cells in that region may stop contracting or even die. A blockage in a coronary artery or one of its branches is known as a **coronary thrombosis** or heart attack.

The cause of coronary heart disease (CHD) is often damage to the arteries. One serious cause of damage is **atherosclerosis**. Atherosclerosis is a slow degeneration of the arteries caused by a build-up of material known as **plaque** inside them. Plaque becomes attached to the smooth endothelium lining an artery and can accumulate over many years. Few people suffer from any symptoms before middle age. Fibrous tissue in the lining may become damaged and thickened so that lipids, cholesterol (released from low-density lipoproteins) and cell debris accumulate. Calcium may also be present, making the artery hard and inflexible. Over time, the diameter of the artery becomes restricted so that blood cannot flow along it properly, and it loses elasticity (Figure **H.17**). As the rate of flow slows down, blood may clot in the artery, further restricting the movement of blood along it. Clots may also break free and travel to block another smaller artery elsewhere in the body. If this artery is in the brain, the clot may cause a stroke.

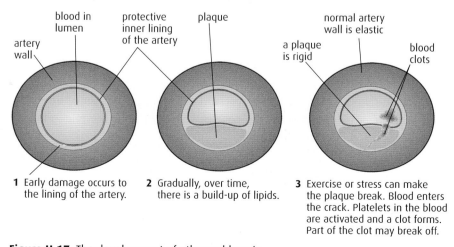

1 Early damage occurs to the lining of the artery.

2 Gradually, over time, there is a build-up of lipids.

3 Exercise or stress can make the plaque break. Blood enters the crack. Platelets in the blood are activated and a clot forms. Part of the clot may break off.

Figure H.17 The development of atheroschlerosis.

Risk factors associated with CHD

The incidence of heart disease varies from country to country and between individuals. Some factors associated with the likelihood of developing CHD are related to a person's environment. By making personal choices about lifestyle, it is possible to lower the risk of developing CHD. Other factors that increase the risk cannot be controlled. For example, the risk of CHD is affected by:

- **genetic factors** – CHD tends to occur more frequently in some families than others with similar lifestyles
- **the person's sex** – men are more likely to have CHD than women
- **the person's age** – CHD is more prevalent in older people.

Lifestyle factors that increase the risk of CHD include:

- **smoking** – smokers are significantly more likely to suffer from CHD than non-smokers
- **lack of exercise** – a lifestyle involving little physical activity may contribute to obesity and high blood pressure
- **high blood pressure** – causes strain on the heart, which has to work harder to pump blood
- **obesity** – increases the work of the heart; people who are overweight are also more likely to have high blood pressure and high cholesterol levels in their blood
- **diet** – there have been many claims that diet can increase the risk of CHD; for example, there is a positive correlation between intake of saturated fat and CHD, but cause and effect have not been proven. Reliable evidence suggests that in countries where many high-fat foods, animal products and processed foods are eaten, there is likely to be a high incidence of CHD. Since all fatty acids are high in energy, an excess of these foods in the diet can also lead to obesity, which places a further strain on the heart.

There is some correlation between CHD and blood cholesterol levels. Reducing the amount of cholesterol in the diet can reduce blood cholesterol levels to a certain extent. But while LDL cholesterol (low-density lipoprotein) is associated with an increased risk of CHD, HDL cholesterol (high-density lipoprotein) is correlated with a reduced risk. So it is difficult to predict the effect of reducing dietary cholesterol on risk with any certainty.

Many aspects of lifestyle are inter-related and it is very difficult to isolate a single factor that can be said to cause CHD. Research focusing on just one aspect of risk may underestimate the contribution of other important factors. If a person changes one aspect of their lifestyle, other risk factors may become important.

12 Outline the risk factors for coronary thrombosis.

13 Describe what happens to the chambers of the heart during atrial systole, ventricular systole and diastole.

14 What is meant by the term 'myogenic'?

H6 Gas exchange

Assessment statements

- Define 'partial pressure'.
- Explain the oxygen dissociation curves of adult hemoglobin, fetal hemoglobin and myoglobin.
- Describe how carbon dioxide is carried by the blood, including the action of carbonic anhydrase, the chloride shift and buffering by plasma proteins.
- Explain the role of the Bohr shift in the supply of oxygen to respiring tissues.
- Explain how and why ventilation rate varies with exercise.
- Outline the possible causes of asthma and its effects on the gas exchange system.
- Explain the problem of gas exchange at high altitudes and the way the body acclimatises.

Oxygen dissociation curves

The oxygen content of air is measured as a **partial pressure**. In a mixture of gases, each component gas exerts a pressure (the partial pressure) in proportion to its percentage in the mixture. It is calculated as follows:

For normal dry air at sea level, atmospheric pressure is 101.3 kPa. The partial pressure of oxygen, which makes up 21% of the air, is:

$$\frac{21}{100} \times 101.3\,\text{kPa} = 21.3\,\text{kPa}$$

The partial pressures of other gases in dry air at sea level are shown in Table **H.3**.

> **Partial pressure** the proportion of the total pressure that is due to one component of a mixture of gases

Gas	Approximate percentage composition/%	Partial pressure/kPa
oxygen	21	21.3
carbon dioxide	0.0035	negligible
nitrogen	79	80.0

Table H.3 The partial pressures of gases in dry air at sea level. At high altitude, the pressure of air falls but the percentage of oxygen in the air remains approximately the same. At 5000 m, the partial pressure of oxygen is 11.5 kPa; at 10 000 m, it falls to just 5.5 kPa.

Oxygen is transported from the lungs to respiring tissues bound to the hemoglobin molecules that fill red blood cells. Each hemoglobin molecule can bind four oxygen molecules via the iron in the heme groups it contains (Figure **H.18**). When hemoglobin comes into contact with normal air, containing approximately 21% oxygen, it binds readily with oxygen molecules and becomes almost 100% saturated.

It follows that in an area of the body where there is a lot of oxygen (a high partial pressure), such as the lungs, most hemoglobin molecules will be carrying the maximum amount of oxygen and will be fully saturated. However, in areas where the oxygen level is lower, fewer

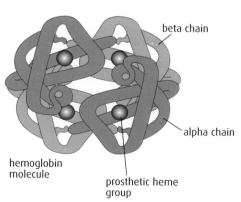

Figure H.18 Hemoglobin is a protein that has quaternary structure. It consists of four subunits bound together – two α and two β units – each of which contains an iron-containing heme group.

hemoglobin molecules carry their maximum complement of oxygen and the hemoglobin may be only 50% saturated. As blood travels from the lungs to actively respiring tissues, the amount of oxygen bound to hemoglobin changes as the partial pressure of oxygen decreases. Hemoglobin readily releases oxygen where the partial pressure is lower, so it acts as an oxygen delivery service for respiring cells. Figure **H.19** shows the percentage saturation of hemoglobin at different oxygen concentrations and is known as an **oxygen dissociation curve**.

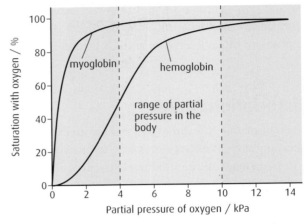

Figure H.19 Dissociation curves for hemoglobin and myoglobin. The curves are constructed using the normal range (at sea level) of partial pressure of oxygen in the body. The partial pressure of oxygen in alveolar air is about 14 kPa due to the presence of water vapour, which forms about 6% of alveolar air.

The steep S-shape of the dissociation curve shows how the affinity of hemoglobin changes at different partial pressures of oxygen. At a partial pressure of 10 kPa, which might be found in the lungs, hemoglobin is 95% saturated. At a partial pressure of 4 kPa, found in the tissues, hemoglobin does not bind with oxygen and will release it, so saturation falls to only about 50%. About half of the oxygen collected by hemoglobin in the lungs is released at this low partial pressure to supply the needs of actively respiring cells.

Myoglobin is another oxygen-binding protein found in muscle cells. Each myoglobin molecule has only one heme group and can bind to just one oxygen molecule. It is used to store oxygen, which is released as oxygen supply falls and the muscles begin to respire anaerobically. The dissociation curve for myoglobin (Figure **H.19**) is to the left of the curve for hemoglobin. At almost all partial pressures of oxygen, myoglobin remains saturated. It is still fully saturated with oxygen at partial pressures well below those that cause hemoglobin to release oxygen, and myoglobin can hold onto oxygen until the partial pressure falls extremely low. It provides a 'reserve supply' of oxygen during vigorous activity because oxygen is only released when the partial pressure falls to 1 or 2 kPa, so muscles can continue to respire aerobically for longer.

Sigmoid curve

The sigmoid shape of a dissociation curve is due to the allosteric effect that occurs when the first molecule of oxygen binds to hemoglobin. Once the first oxygen molecule has bound to one of the heme groups in hemoglobin, the shape of the molecule changes making it much easier for other oxygen molecules to bind. The steep slope of the curve shows that as the partial pressure of oxygen rises, hemoglobin readily becomes saturated.

The molecular structure of hemoglobin in the blood of a fetus is different from that of an adult. The dissociation curve for fetal hemoglobin lies to the left of the adult curve for all partial pressures of oxygen (Figure H.20). This tells us that fetal hemoglobin has a higher affinity for oxygen than maternal (adult) hemoglobin, whatever the concentration of oxygen. In the capillaries of the placenta, the partial pressure of oxygen is low. Here the mother's adult hemoglobin releases oxygen, which is easily picked up and bound to fetal hemoglobin. At a partial pressure of 4 kPa, the mother's hemoglobin is only 50% saturated, but fetal hemoglobin becomes approximately 70% saturated. The fetal hemoglobin carries the oxygen to the baby's body and releases it into the respiring fetal tissues.

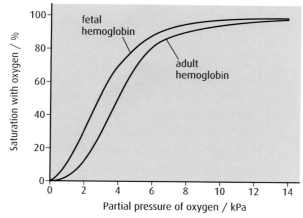

Figure H.20 Dissociation curve of adult hemoglobin and fetal hemoglobin.

Transport of carbon dioxide in the blood

Carbon dioxide produced during aerobic respiration is carried back to the lungs by the blood. It diffuses into capillaries close to respiring cells and is transported in one of three ways.

- About 70% of carbon dioxide enters red blood cells and is converted to HCO_3^- (hydrogencarbonate) ions.
- About 7% remains in the blood and is transported dissolved in plasma.
- The remainder is bound to hemoglobin.

Carbon dioxide reacts with water to form carbonic acid, which dissociates to form hydrogencarbonate ions and hydrogen ions:

$$CO_2 + H_2O \rightarrow H_2CO_3 \rightleftharpoons H^+ + HCO_3^-$$

The hydrogen ions bind to plasma proteins and this process has a buffering effect, preventing an excessive fall in pH in the blood. This reaction in the plasma is slow, but most of the carbon dioxide (about 70%) diffuses into the red blood cells where the reaction is catalysed by the enzyme carbonic anhydrase.

The hydrogencarbonate ions that are formed move out of the red blood cells via special protein channels by facilitated diffusion. Hydrogencarbonate ions are exchanged for chloride ions, so the balance of charges on each side of the membrane is maintained. This is known as the **chloride shift** (Figure **H.21**).

The hydrogen ions remaining in the red blood cells bind reversibly to hemoglobin and prevent the pH of the cell falling, a process known as pH buffering.

Some carbon dioxide binds to hemoglobin. Each hemoglobin molecule can combine with one carbon dioxide molecule to form carbaminohemoglobin but as it does so, it must release its oxygen. As carbaminohemoglobin is formed, oxygen is released into actively respiring tissues, just where it is needed. When red blood cells reach the lungs, the carbaminohemoglobin releases carbon dioxide, which is exhaled and hemoglobin is available again to collect oxygen. About 20% of carbon dioxide produced by respiration is carried in this way. As hydrogen ions and carbon dioxide bind to hemoglobin they cause the Bohr shift, which is described below.

The Bohr shift

The affinity of hemoglobin for oxygen is not only affected by the partial pressure of oxygen, but also reduced in the presence of high carbon dioxide concentrations. As the partial pressure of carbon dioxide rises, the ability of hemoglobin to combine with oxygen falls and so the dissociation curve moves to the right. This effect is known as the **Bohr shift**. It is

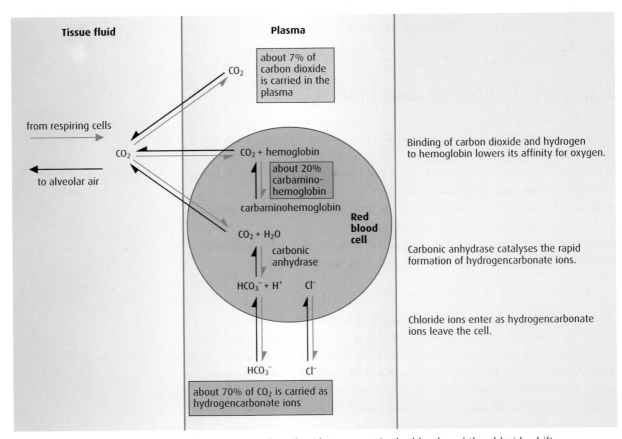

Figure H.21 Carbon dioxide transport in the blood, and the chloride shift.

caused when hydrogen ions produced from carbonic acid combine with hemoglobin. Figure **H.22** shows the effect of two different partial pressures of carbon dioxide on the dissociation curve. In an environment where the partial pressure of carbon dioxide is high, such as in actively respiring tissue, the curve moves to the right – which means that, at any given oxygen partial pressure, oxygen is more likely to dissociate from hemoglobin if the partial pressure of carbon dioxide is high. This effect promotes the release of oxygen in active tissues where respiration is producing high levels of carbon dioxide, so cells receive the oxygen they need.

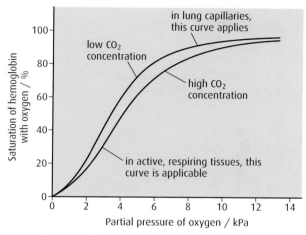

Figure H.22 The effect of carbon dioxide concentration on hemoglobin saturation: the Bohr shift.

Ventilation rate and exercise

When a person exercises, their ventilation rate and tidal volume (depth of breathing) increase. Muscles need oxygen for aerobic respiration and as the rate of exercise increases, so does the rate of oxygen consumption. Blood returning to the lungs also has a higher level of carbon dioxide, produced as a result of the increased activity. An increase in ventilation rate and tidal volume draws in more fresh air to maintain the concentration gradient between the alveolar air and the blood. Thus oxygen can be absorbed at a faster rate and the body can get rid of the additional carbon dioxide produced. These changes in ventilation are adjusted to match the body's metabolic needs.

Ventilation rate is controlled by the breathing centre of the medulla oblongata in the brain stem, which receives nerve impulses from sensory cells in different parts of the body. The breathing centre responds to match ventilation rate to activity levels (Figure **H.23**, overleaf). Chemoreceptors in the inner wall of the aorta and carotid arteries respond to an increase in carbon dioxide in the blood. This excess carbon dioxide forms carbonic acid that cannot be buffered and so the pH of the blood falls. Impulses are passed to the medulla, which increases the ventilation rate by sending motor impulses to the intercostal muscles and diaphragm to increase their rate of contraction. The breathing centre contains similar chemoreceptors, which also respond to deviations of blood pH from the normal level.

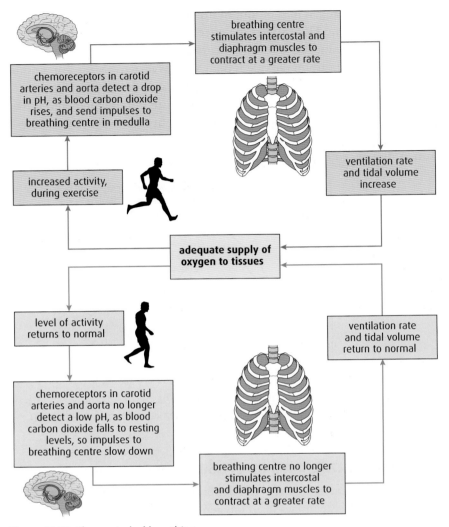

Figure H.23 The control of breathing.

An increase in ventilation rate causes carbon dioxide to be removed from the body at a faster rate and blood pH returns to its normal level of about 7.4.

After exercise, as the level of carbon dioxide in the blood falls, ventilation rate decreases.

Asthma

Asthma is a condition affecting the walls of the bronchi, which constrict, making ventilation difficult and restricting the amount of oxygen that can enter the body. Asthma is an allergic reaction and different substances can trigger an attack in different people. Common allergens include dust mites, pollen, fungi, animals and some foods. Asthma may also be caused by stress or exposure to cold conditions in some sufferers. During an attack, bronchi become swollen and inflamed, narrowing the airways and making ventilation difficult. Smooth muscles in the walls of the bronchi also contract and restrict airflow still further. Restricted ventilation means that less air is drawn into the lungs and makes gas exchange difficult. Excess carbon dioxide in the body causes an increase in breathing rate as the body struggles to remove it.

Gas exchange at high altitude

At high altitude, the percentage of oxygen in the air is the same as it is as sea level, but because air pressure is lower, the partial pressure of oxygen is reduced. At these lower partial pressures, hemoglobin does not become fully saturated with oxygen so that when a person moves suddenly from low to high altitude they may experience 'altitude sickness'. Symptoms include headache, nausea, dizziness and breathlessness as well as an increased heart rate. Altitude sickness can be avoided by travelling to high altitude gradually over a period of days so that the body has the opportunity to acclimatise.

During acclimatisation, the body adjusts both the ventilation and circulatory systems to cope with the lower oxygen availability. Ventilation rate increases temporarily and adjustments to the circulatory system ensure that the rate of oxygen delivery to the tissues increases. Over a period of weeks, the number of red blood cells and thus the concentration of hemoglobin steadily increase and the density of capillaries in the lungs and muscles also rises. After long periods at high altitude, the size of the lungs and the tidal volume increase so that the volume of air breathed can be 25% greater than at sea level. Once these adjustments have been made, heart and ventilation rates can return to their previous levels. People who live permanently at high altitude have a larger lung capacity and surface area for gas exchange, as well as a greater concentration of myoglobin in their muscles. Animals from high-altitude environments, such as llamas and vicunas, are also adapted to cope with the lower oxygen availability.

Some athletes choose to train at high altitude to develop increased levels of red blood cells and myoglobin. These adaptations are retained for a short time when they return to sea level and can improve athletic performance.

15 Define 'partial pressure'.

16 What is meant by the term 'Bohr shift' and why is it important in supplying oxygen to respiring tissues?

17 How does asthma affect the gas exchange system?

End-of-chapter questions

1 Explain the control of ADH (vasopressin) secretion. (5)

2 Distinguish between the mode of action of steroid and protein hormones. (2)

3 Explain why pepsin is initially synthesised as an inactive precursor and how it is subsequently activated. (3)

4 Explain how the body overcomes the problem of lipid digestion in the alimentary canal. (3)

5 a Describe how active transport is used by the ileum to absorb food. (3)

  b Explain how the structural features of the epithelium cells of a villus are related to their function. (5)

6 Outline how blood is brought to the liver, circulates through the liver, and then leaves the liver. (4)

7 a Describe the process of erythrocyte and hemoglobin breakdown in the liver. (5)

  b Outline the role of the liver in the storage of nutrients. (2)

8 Explain the events of the cardiac cycle including systole, diastole and heart sounds. (6)

9 a Define the term 'partial pressure'. (1)

  b Outline how the body acclimatises to high altitudes. (3)

10 The effect on metabolism and performance of different types of meals before exercise was tested for twelve competitive cyclists. The cyclists ingested either high-fat or high-carbohydrate meals before the start of exercise.

The test consisted of:
- 1 hour of cycling at half peak power (pre-load)
- followed by five × 10-minute incremental increases in intensity (load)
- a 50 km time trial.

The concentration of various hormones in the blood plasma of the cyclists was measured. The graphs below indicate the change in insulin and glucagon levels before and during the cycling test.

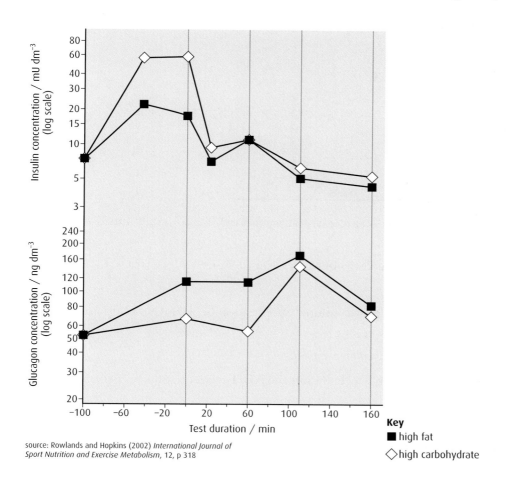

source: Rowlands and Hopkins (2002) *International Journal of Sport Nutrition and Exercise Metabolism*, 12, p 318

Key
■ high fat
◇ high carbohydrate

a Describe the changes in insulin concentration during the course of the exercise period for those cyclists who ate a high-carbohydrate meal. (2)

b Compare the changes in insulin and glucagon concentration during the pre-load and incremental test period. (2)

c Using the data provided, outline how the changes illustrate negative feedback of insulin and glucagon. (2)

(total 6 marks)
© IB Organization 2009

11 Plasma solute concentration, plasma antidiuretic hormone (ADH) concentration and feelings of thirst were tested in a group of volunteers. These graphs show the relationship between intensity of thirst, plasma ADH concentration and plasma solute concentration.

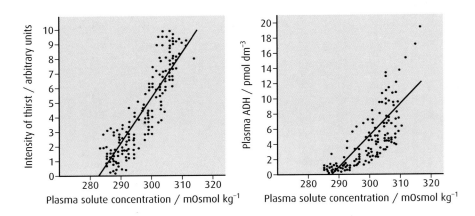

source: adapted from Thompson, C T, *et al.* (1986) *Clinical Science London*, 71, p 651

a Identify the plasma ADH concentration at a plasma solute concentration of $300\,\text{mOsmol kg}^{-1}$ using the line of best fit. (1)

b Compare intensity of thirst and plasma ADH concentration. (1)

c Outline what would happen to plasma solute concentration and ADH concentration if a person were to drink water to satisfy his/her thirst. (2)

d State **two** reasons why a person's plasma solute concentration may increase. (2)

(total 6 marks)

© IB Organization 2009

12 Reduced risk of type II diabetes has been associated with coffee consumption. A compound called C-peptide is found in the bloodstream when insulin is released. Increased C-peptide levels are associated with type II diabetes.

The following study investigated the effect of coffee consumption on blood plasma concentration of C-peptide in women. The subjects were grouped according to their weight and their level of coffee consumption. The study investigated both total coffee consumption (caffeinated and decaffeinated coffee) and consumption of caffeinated coffee.

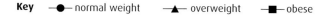

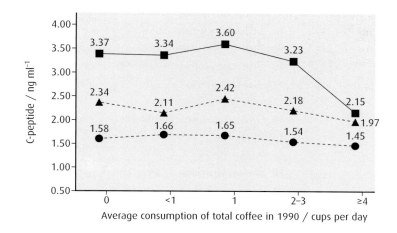

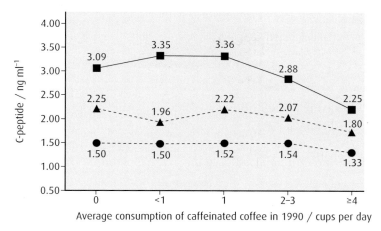

source: Tianying Wu *et al.* (2005) *Diabetes Care*, 7, p 1390. Copyright © 2005 American Diabetes Association. From *Diabetes Care*, Vol. 28, 2005: 1390–1396. Reprinted with permission from The American Diabetes Association

a Describe the relationship between C-peptide concentration and total coffee consumption. (2)

b Compare the effect on C-peptide concentrations in women who drink more than four cups of caffeinated coffee per day with those who drink no caffeinated coffee. (2)

c Using the data provided, suggest advice that could be given to women in order to reduce the incidence of type II diabetes. (2)

(total 6 marks)

© IB Organization 2009

Answers to short-answer questions

Chapter 1

1 the graph on the left

2 2.2 mm

3 Yes, because 4.02 > 2.09, which is the critical value at 20 df.

4 No, because 1.82 < 2.04, which is the critical value at 30 df.

5 Yes, pollution has an effect on the density of branching coral. This is very certain because the *t*-value of 4.5 is much greater than the critical value or 2.05 at 28 df.

Chapter 2

1 As surface area increases, ratio of surface area to volume decreases.

2 10 cells

3 For example:
   nerve cells work with muscles to co-ordinate flight
   lungs and vocal cords produce song
   petals and nectaries attract insects
   petals and anthers work together to achieve pollination.

4 any of: treatment of leukemia; treatment of Alzheimer's disease; treatment of diabetes

5 Each specialised cell differentiates to carry out its function, e.g. producing insulin, absorbing food, photosynthesis. Genes not relating to this function are switched off.

6 1000 μm or 1 mm

7 Eukaryotic cells have a nuclear envelope, organelles such as mitochondria, and DNA that is associated with protein. Prokaryotes do not.

8 a The cell wall is made of cellulose and surrounds a plant cell, whereas a plasma membrane surrounds both plant and animals cells.

   b Pili are used to connect a bacterium to other bacteria and pull the cells together. A flagellum enables a cell to move.

9 any two of:
   enable communication between plant cells
   help cell to resist osmotic pressure
   enable cell adhesion
   support the cell membrane
   maintain cell shape

10 Binary fission occurs in prokaryotes when a cell divides into two genetically identical cells.

11 Simple diffusion is the movement of molecules across a permeable membrane from a higher to a lower concentration. Facilitated diffusion involves the movement of larger molecules or ions through specific integral protein channels in a membrane. Both are passive processes.

12 'Fluid' because phospholipids and proteins can move and occupy any position in the membrane, which can break and reform. 'Mosaic' because the surface view of a membrane resembles a mosaic made of many small separate parts.

13 Fatty acids are hydrophobic (water-hating) and always orientate away from water.

14 Integral proteins are partially or completely embedded in the plasma membrane. Peripheral proteins are attached to its surface.

15 diffusion, facilitated diffusion, protein pumps, osmosis, phagocytosis, exocytosis

16 phagocytosis and protein pumps

17 enzymes, protein channels, cell recognition, hormone binding sites, electron transport

18 G_1, S, G_2, mitosis, cytokinesis

19 a G_2
    b cytokinesis

20 tumour formation

21 growth, transcription, translation, metabolism, protein synthesis and DNA replication

22 prophase, metaphase, anaphase, telophase

23 Mitosis is found in growth, repair and asexual reproduction.

Chapter 3

1 Water has a high specific heat capacity and energy is needed to break bonds between its molecules. It evaporates below its boiling point as energy is used to break hydrogen bonds.

2 A high concentration would cause water absorption by osmosis.

3 Hydrolysis is the separation of two molecules by the addition of water, whereas condensation is the joining of two molecules with the loss of water.

4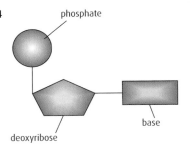

5 on ribosomes/rER in the cytoplasm

6

DNA	RNA
double stranded	single stranded
contains bases A, C, G and T	contains bases A, C, G and U
sugar = deoxyribose	sugar = ribose

7 specific pairing of base A with T or U and base C to G

8 a protein molecule that catalyses a biochemical reaction

9 Enzymes and proteins are both built from amino acids, but many proteins do not catalyse biochemical reactions, which enzymes do.

10 The optimum temperature for enzyme activity is the temperature at which the enzyme works at its maximum efficiency.

11 Because the reaction may be limited by the number of active sites available on the enzymes or by the temperature of the reactants.

12 ATP and lactate

13 in the mitochondria

14 in the cytoplasm

15 red and/or blue

16 It would not grow well and might become thin and weak.

17 the splitting of water by light

18 red and blue /all colours except green

19 directly by measuring oxygen production or carbon dioxide release and indirectly by measuring the increase in biomass

Chapter 4

1 438 nucleotides

2 a DNA and protein
  b Prokaryotes do not have protein associated with their DNA.

3 a a heritable factor that controls a specific characteristic
  b one specific form of a gene, differing from other alleles by one or a few bases only and occupying the same gene locus as other alleles of the gene
  c the whole of the genetic information of an organism
  d a change in the sequence of bases in a gene

4 the replacement of a base in a gene with a different base

5 a C–A–C
  b The normal amino acid is glutamic acid, and the amino acid as a result of mutation is valine.
  c The altered amino acid causes the hemoglobin molecule to fold differently, and the red blood cells become sickle shaped in low oxygen concentration. Sickle cells carry less oxygen, leading to anemia.

6 D

7 a anaphase I
  b prophase I or II
  c anaphase II
  d metaphase II
  e prophase
  f anaphase I

8 chromosomes with the same genes but not necessarily the same alleles

9 The number of chromosomes is halved.

10 4 cells

11 a nucleus that contains three copies of one chromosome instead of two

12 Down's syndrome

13 any two of: banding pattern; position of centromere; length

14 diploid

15 a the alleles possessed by an organism
  b the characteristics of an organism
  c an allele that has the same effect on the phenotype whether in homozygous or heterozygous state
  d an allele that only has an effect on the phenotype in the homozygous state
  e the specific position of a gene on a homologous chromosome
  f having two identical alleles at a gene locus
  g having two different alleles at a gene locus
  h an individual that has one copy of a recessive allele that causes a genetic condition in individuals that are homozygous for this allele
  i testing a dominant phenotype to determine whether it is heterozygous or homozygous

16 a red
  b red
  c yellow

17 a **R**
  b **r**
  c **R** and **r**

18

		gametes from green parent	
		Ⓖ	ⓖ
gametes from green parent	Ⓖ	**GG** green	**Gg** green
	ⓖ	**Gg** green	**gg** purple

19 a 2
  b 2
  c 1

20 blood group O

21 colour blindness and hemophilia

22 ●

23 co-dominant

24 carrier

25 to amplify small quantities of DNA

26 their size and charge

27 any two of: paternity testing, forensic examination of crime scenes, animal pedigree testing

28 the fact that the code is universal

29 plasmids

30 restriction enzyme and DNA ligase

31 mammary gland cell and egg cell

Chapter 5

1 **a** trophic level 3/secondary consumer
  b trophic level 4/tertiary consumer

2 **a** a group of organisms that can interbreed and produce fertile offspring
  b the environment in which a species normally lives, or the location of a living organism
  c a group of organisms of the same species which live in the same area at the same time
  d a group of populations of different species living and interacting with each other in an area
  e a community and its abiotic environment
  f the study of relationships between living organisms and between organisms and their environment

3 An autotroph makes its own food/organic compounds; a heterotroph takes in organic materials as food.

4 A consumer ingests other organic matter that is living or recently dead; a detritivore is an organism that ingests non-living organic matter; a saprotroph lives on or in non-living organic matter and absorbs digested food.

5 any food chain that starts with a producer

6 the transfer of nutrients and energy

7 a series of interlinking food chains

8 the Sun

9 the position of an organism in a food chain

10 not consumed; heat; excretion

11 $2000\,\text{J}\,\text{m}^{-2}\text{y}^{-1}$

12 bacteria and fungi

13 Energy enters and leaves the ecosystem but nutrients cycle within the ecosystem.

14 any three of: plants, animals, bacteria, fungi

15 photosynthesis

16 any three of: carbon dioxide; water vapour; methane; oxides of nitrogen; fluorocarbons

17 burning fossil fuels in factories and vehicles; rice farming; cattle farming; rainforest destruction; CFCs from refrigerants

18 Humans should not undertake any activity which has the potential to make a large change without first proving that it will not do harm.

19 any three of: melting ice caps; loss of algae as sea ice melts; loss of habitats of mammals such as polar bears and walruses; caribou falling through the ice; less feeding time for polar bears

20 increase in food supply; reduction in predators and disease; more births and immigration

21 birth + immigration = death + emigration

22 a cumulative change in the heritable characteristics of a population

23 It produces variation in a population.

24 competition for resources

25 survival of the fittest

26 resistance to antibiotics in bacteria; change in phenotype of the peppered moth

27 kingdom; phylum; class; order; family; genus; species

28 genus and species

29 conifers/Coniferophyta

30 Bryophyta

31 Arthropoda

32 Annelida

33 'Large' is a subjective term and not suitable for use in a key.

Chapter 6

1 because large molecules cannot pass through the intestine wall and be absorbed by cells

2 Absorption is the uptake of nutrients into blood or cells; assimilation is the use of absorbed molecules by the body.

3 Enzymes speed up chemical reactions so that food can be digested as it passes through the intestine.

4 It provides a large surface area/microvilli, has a rich blood supply for absorption, and the diffusion distance between the intestine and the blood is very small.

5 vena cava, right atrium, atrioventricular valve, right ventricle, semilunar valve, pulmonary artery, lung capillaries, pulmonary vein, left atrium, atrioventricular valve, left ventricle, semilunar valve, aorta

6 any five of: glucose; hormones; carbon dioxide; antibodies; urea; amino acids

7 Arteries must resist higher blood pressure than veins.

8 to supply additional oxygen to working muscles and to carry away the carbon dioxide they produce

9 red blood cells, white blood cells, plasma, platelets

10 an organism or a virus that causes disease

11 a protein that provokes an immune response

12 Helper T-cells stimulate B-cells to produce antibodies.

13 Phagocytes engulf bacteria and cell fragments whereas lymphocytes secrete antibodies.

14 atmosphere, nasal passages or mouth, trachea, bronchi, bronchioles, alveolus

15 rich blood supply, large surface area, short diffusion distance

16 diaphragm and intercostal muscles (external)

17 Gas exchange is the exchange of oxygen and carbon dioxide between the alveoli and the blood; ventilation is the movement of air into and out of the lungs.

18

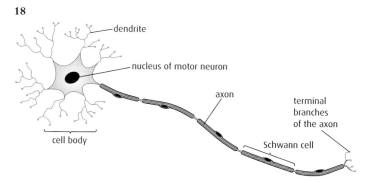

19 the depolarisation and repolarisation of a nerve cell membrane

20 calcium ions enter the pre-synaptic neuron, vesicles fuse with the pre-synaptic membrane, neurotransmitter is released into synaptic cleft, neurotransmitter binds to receptor on post-synaptic membrane, post-synaptic membrane is depolarised

21 Negative feedback causes any deviation from the normal level of a variable to be corrected so that the level returns to normal.

22

Type I	Type II
early onset	late onset
controlled by insulin injection	can be controlled by change in diet
pancreas produces no insulin	insulin is produced but in insufficient quantities
can be caused by autoimmune disease	caused by obesity, age or genetic factors

Chapter 7

1 The two strands of DNA in the double helix run in opposite directions.

2 consists of two twists of DNA wound around eight histone proteins, which are held in place by an additional histone

3 5' to 3'

4 because DNA replication can only occur in a 5' to 3' direction

5 a section of mRNA that is transcribed but not translated

6 Transcription is the production of mRNA from DNA; translation is the production of a polypeptide from mRNA.

7 The sense strand has the same base sequence as mRNA (with thymine instead of uracil). The antisense strand is the one that is transcribed to produce mRNA.

8 The promoter region contains specific DNA sequences that are the initial binding site for RNA polymerase during transcription.

9

peptide bond

$$H_2N - \underset{\underset{H}{|}}{\overset{\overset{R}{|}}{C}} - CO - HN - \underset{\underset{H}{|}}{\overset{\overset{R}{|}}{C}} - COOH$$

10 It is used in the cell; it is not exported for use elsewhere.

11 primary – the sequence of amino acids

secondary – folded or twisted structure of the polypeptide chain
tertiary – three dimensional structure formed by bonds between R groups
quaternary – two or more polypeptide chains linked together

12 Fibrous proteins have long and narrow molecules, are insoluble in water and usually have secondary structure. Globular proteins have a more rounded shape, are soluble in water and have tertiary structure.

13 any four of: antibodies; enzymes; some hormones; movement; transport

14 the amount of energy required to destabilise chemical bonds so that a chemical reaction can occur

15 The induced-fit model suggests that an active site can change its shape as a substrate approaches. The lock–and–key hypothesis suggests that an active site has a permanent shape that can accommodate the substrate.

Chapter 8

1 gain of electrons, loss of oxygen, gain of hydrogen

2 phosphate from ATP

3 lysis

4 phosphate (P_i)

5 triose phosphate

6 two molecules of ATP

7 in the matrix of mitochondria

8 on the membranes (cristae) of mitochondria

9 oxidised

10 acetyl CoA

11 two

12 one

13 to provide a large surface area for the enzymes involved in respiration

14 to pump hydrogen ions into the inter-membrane space and create a diffusion gradient, which enables ATP to be produced

15 the pH decreases

16 three

17 ATP synthase

18 in the stroma of the chloroplast

19 in the grana (thylakoid membranes) of the chloroplast

20 photoactivation

21 green

22 to boost electrons to a higher energy level

23 water

24 photolysis

25 oxygen

26 ATP and NADPH$^+$

27 ribulose bisphosphate

28 glycerate 3-phosphate (GP)

29 triose phosphate (TP)

30 photophosphorylation

31 cyclic photophosphorylation

32 The plant uses the absorbed light for photosynthesis.

33 If a component needed for photosynthesis is in short supply, it will inhibit the process.

34 light, temperature and carbon dioxide concentration

Chapter 9

1 Monocotyledons have parallel venation, a vascular system throughout the stem and floral organs in multiples of three. Dicotyledons have veins in net-like arrangement, vascular tissue around the edges of the stem and floral organs in multiples of four or five.

2 The presence of auxin on the shaded side of a shoot causes the shoot to bend towards a source of light as cells on the shaded side elongate.

3 Apical meristems occur at the end of a shoot and growth here results in a taller plant. Growth at lateral meristems causes thickening of a stem or growth of side shoots.

4

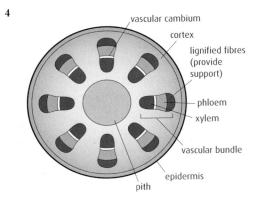

vascular cambium
cortex
lignified fibres (provide support)
phloem
xylem
vascular bundle
epidermis
pith

5 thickened cellulose cell walls, cell turgor and lignified xylem

6 Xylem is composed of dead cells whose walls are thickened with lignin, whereas phloem is made of living cells and adjacent companion cells. Both xylem and phloem are found in vascular bundles in the stem and leaves. The xylem carries water and salts up the plant, whereas phloem carries sugars, vitamins and other nutrients both up and down.

7 water and mineral salts

8 Mineral ions enter the root hair cells by active transport if their concentration in the soil is lower than that in the cells. If the concentration of the ions is higher in the soil than in the cells, they may enter by mass flow or by facilitated diffusion.

9 Root hairs increase the surface area for absorption of substances from the soil into the root of a plant.

10 Transpiration is increased by an increase in temperature, wind or light intensity and by a decrease in humidity.

11 Germination requires activation of enzymes to digest food reserves and initiate respiration. All enzyme-controlled reactions are temperature-sensitive and so a suitable temperature (which varies from species to species) is needed for germination.

12 Pollination is the transfer of pollen from anthers to stigma whereas fertilisation is the fusion of the male and female gamete in the ovary.

13 anthers and filaments (together known as the stamen)

14 Seeds that germinate at some distance from the parent plant do not have to compete with it for water, light or nutrients and so are more likely to survive.

Chapter 10

1 four

2 **Ttrr**: **Tr** and **tr** in a ratio of 1:1
HhGg: **HG**, **Hg**, **hG** and **hg** in a ratio of 1:1:1:1

3 Punnett grid

4 members of the F_1 generation

Chapter 11

1 One member of the pair causes flexing of a joint and the other causes extension of it.

2 Cartilage reduces friction between two bones in a joint and synovial fluid acts as a lubricant.

3 A hinge joint (e.g. the elbow joint) moves in one direction whereas a ball-and-socket joint can allow movement in a circle.

4 Actin is made up of thin fibres whereas myosin fibres are thicker. Each type of filament is arranged in bands that alternate in skeletal muscle. The lighter bands of thin myosin alternate with darker bands of thicker myosin, which produces the striped appearance.

5 ATP provides the energy for muscle contraction. ATP molecules bind to myosin heads; the energy from the ATP breaks cross-bridges and detaches the myosin heads from the actin filaments.

6 Excretion is the removal from the body of waste products produced as a result of metabolic activity. Osmosregulation is the maintenance of the correct level of water in the body.

7

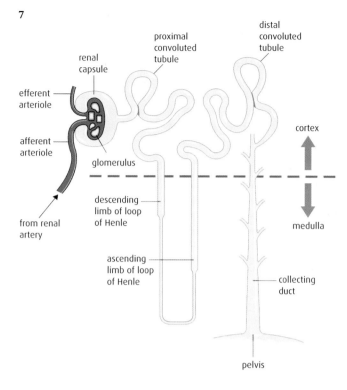

8 The descending limb of the loop of Henle is permeable to sodium and chloride ions, which leave the tubule and are concentrated in the medulla region of the kidney. The high level of salt in the medulla causes water to enter the capillaries in the medulla from the descending limb, increasing the concentration of the solution in the loop of Henle.

9 The afferent arteriole is wider in diameter than the efferent arteriole. This causes a build-up of pressure in the glomerulus that enables ultrafiltration of molecules.

10 Microvilli increase the surface area of the cells in the proximal convoluted tubule, which is the region where useful molecules are reabsorbed into the bloodstream from the kidney tubule. The large surface area ensures this process occurs efficiently.

11 capillary endothelium, basement membrane, cell of Bowman's capsule wall

12 ADH influences the permeability to water of the cell wall in the collecting duct. If ADH is released, the collecting duct is more permeable and water is taken back into the blood so that more concentrated urine is produced.

13 A diabetic person cannot regulate the amount of glucose in their blood. If blood glucose is very high, glucose cannot be reabsorbed from the kidney tubule and passes out of the body in the urine.

14 Sertoli (or nurse) cells protect developing sperm providing protection from attack by the male immune system.

15 Testosterone stimulates secondary spermatocytes to mature into sperm cells.

16 An ovum must contain sufficient nutrients to provide fuel for the first few divisions after fertilisation. Unequal cell division during oogenesis produces one large cell that contains these nutrients and three small polar bodies that do not become gametes.

17 The prostate gland produces about 30% of seminal fluid. Its secretions are alkaline and help sperm to survive the acidic conditions in the vagina.

18 Spermatogenesis produces four gametes, begins at puberty and continues throughout a man's life and produces sperm continuously, whereas oogenesis produces one gamete, occurs from puberty to menopause and produces one gamete each month.

19 The amnion forms a protective, fluid-filled sac around the fetus that protects it from pressure and allows it to move.

20 Oxytocin stimulates the contraction of the muscles in the wall of the uterus. It works by positive feedback so that more hormone is produced as the muscles contract more strongly.

Option A

1 Volunteers were deprived of foods containing vitamin C but each given identical quantities of L-ascorbic acid so that there was no variation between them at the start of the experiment.

2 Essential amino acids cannot be synthesised in the human body and must be taken in as part of the diet. Non-essential amino acids are made in the body.

3 Phenylketonuria is caused by a lack of the enzyme that processes phenylalanine (an amino acid). It is treated with a low-protein diet that must avoid milk, nuts and meat (these contain phenylalanine).

4 Vitamins are organic compounds whereas minerals are inorganic ions. Vitamins are made in plants and animals but minerals are derived from the abiotic environment.

5 Rebound malnutrition occurs when high levels of vitamin C are taken for a period of time and then reduced. The body continues to excrete vitamin C, leading to a shortage.

6 A shortage of iodine leads to a shortage of thyroxine and goitre. In babies and young children, iodine deficiency disorder (IDD) results in poor development of the nervous system and even cretinism. Iodine supplements given to pregnant women and children are inexpensive and prevent both conditions.

7 Diets rich in fats can lead to obesity, heart disease and type II diabetes.

8 lack of exercise; excessive consumption of processed and high-sugar foods; large portions

9 fertility problems; loss of hair and muscle mass; low blood pressure; kidney damage; withdrawal of calcium from bones and teeth

10 Human milk contains human butterfat while artificial milk has oil added from plant sources.
Human milk contains human whey and casein, artificial milk contains bovine whey and casein or soy proteins.
Human milk contains antibodies, hormones and enzymes; artificial milk does not.

11 glucose present in the urine; high glucose level in the blood; thirst; need to urinate frequently; tiredness

12 The distance that food has to travel from the site of production to the consumer who will eat it.

OPTION B

1 Muscles contract to pull bones into new positions.

2 Cartilage covers the ends of bones and reduces friction as they slide past one another.

3 Calcium ions are released as the sarcoplasmic reticulum receives an impulse. They bind to the actin filaments to expose the myosin binding sites as the muscle contracts.

4 the number of inhalations or exhalations per minute

5 The maximum ventilation rate can increase.

6 the volume of blood pumped out by each contraction of the heart

7 Blood flow to the intestine is lower during exercise than at rest.

8 The volume of oxygen absorbed by the body per minute.

9 aerobic respiration; anaerobic respiration; from creatine phosphate (in muscles only)

10 Glycogen is used when blood glucose levels are low.

11 weight gain; high blood pressure; water retention; muscle cramps

12 fast twitch fibres – white in colour; contract rapidly; easily exhausted
slow twitch fibres – red in colour; contract repeatedly for long periods of time; produce less force than fast twitch

13 cause muscle and bone growth; improve performance quickly; improve mood and focus

OPTION C

1 primary – the sequence of amino acids
secondary – folded or twisted structure of the polypeptide chain
tertiary – three dimensional structure formed by bonds between R groups
quaternary – two or more polypeptide chains linked together

2 Fibrous proteins have long and narrow molecules, are insoluble in water and usually have secondary structure. Globular proteins have a more rounded shape, are soluble in water and have tertiary structure.

3 any four of: antibodies; enzymes; some hormones; movement; transport

4 the amount of energy required to destabilise chemical bonds so that a chemical reaction can occur

5 The induced-fit model suggests that an active site can change its shape as a substrate approaches. The lock-and-key hypothesis suggests that an active site has a permanent shape that can accommodate the substrate.

6 A competitive inhibitor competes with the substrate for the active site of an enzyme. A non-competitive inhibitor interacts with another site on the enzyme.

7 Allosteric enzymes change between active and inactive shapes as a result of the binding of substrates at the active site, and of regulatory molecules at other sites.

8 gain of electrons, loss of oxygen, gain of hydrogen

9 phosphate from ATP

10 lysis

11 phosphate (P_i)

12 triose phosphate

13 pyruvate

14 two molecules of ATP

15 in the matrix of mitochondria

16 on the membranes (cristae) of mitochondria

17 oxidised

18 acetyl CoA

19 two

20 one

21 to provide a large surface area for the enzymes involved in respiration

22 to pump hydrogen ions into the inter-membrane space and create a diffusion gradient, which enables ATP to be produced

23 the pH decreases

24 in the stroma of the chloroplast

25 water

26 ATP and $NADPH^+$

27 ribulose bisphosphate

28 The plant uses the absorbed light for photosynthesis.

29 If a component needed for photosynthesis is in short supply, it will inhibit the process.

30 light, temperature and carbon dioxide concentration

OPTION D

1 formation of simple organic molecules; assembly of these molecules into large ones; ability of molecules to reproduce themselves; cell membranes to separate reactions

2 any three of: hot springs; in superheated water under the sea; sulfur lakes; volcanic vents

3 RNA can replicate itself; RNA can act as an enzyme; it can be used to synthesise tRNA and in some cases DNA.

4 coacervates with small molecules of RNA, amino acids and maybe polypeptides, with the capacity to reproduce

5 Evidence that supports the theory of endosymbiosis: mitochondria and chloroplasts are similar in size to prokaryotes; they contain DNA and have double membranes; they can replicate themselves. But there is no evidence that prokaryotes inside larger cells could be passed on and organelles cannot replicate outside a cell when isolated, which does not support the theory.

6 allele frequency – the frequency of an allele as a proportion of all the alleles of that gene in a population

gene pool – all the different genes in an interbreeding population at a given time

7 The definition cannot include all members of a species who might interbreed but are separated spatially; it cannot include organisms that reproduce asexually; some separate species can interbreed to produce hybrids.

8 New species arise when a population is separated into two parts by a physical barrier, a temporal barrier or by behavioural differences, or when two populations become geographically separated.

9 Gradualism proposes that small changes accumulate over many generations and lead to speciation.

Punctuated equilibrium suggests that a sudden change in the environment will lead to a rapid development of new species.

10 ^{14}C, because it has a half-life of 5700 years

11 There are very few human fossils to study and these are widely spaced across the world. It is difficult to deduce direct links between them.

12 Only genetic evolution can lead to the formation of new species. Genetic evolution can be studied with objective biochemical tests and analyses, whereas cultural changes are more subjective and may take place over a very short time.

13 Homologous characteristics have the same evolutionary origin but not necessarily the same function; analogous characteristics have the same function but different evolutionary origins.

14 Mutations can happen at varying rates, but changes in biochemistry can provide an estimate of the timescale of evolutionary changes. The greater the number of observed differences, the greater the time between the divergence of two organisms from a common ancestor.

15 Classification enables us to organise and order knowledge, to deduce evolutionary relationships, to identify new species and make predictions about a new species' characteristics.

OPTION E

1 stimulus: a change in the environment, detected by a receptor that causes a response

response: a reaction in an organism as a result of a stimulus

reflex: a rapid, unconscious response

2 receptor; sensory neuron; relay neuron; motor neuron; effector

3 receptor, relay neuron

4 sensory neuron, motor neuron

5 thermoreceptors, photoreceptors, chemoreceptors, mechanoreceptors

6 iris, pupil, lens, conjunctiva, retina, fovea, blind spot, optic nerve, ciliary muscle, choroid layer, vitreous humour, aqueous humour, cornea, suspensory ligament, sclera

7 ganglion cells

8 Bipolar cells connect ganglion cells to either rod or cone cells.

9 Any three of the following differences. Rods are rod-shaped, cones are cone-shaped. Rods are very sensitive to light and work in dim light, cones are less sensitive and work in bright light. One type of rod responds to all wavelengths of light but there are three types of cone cell, each of which responds to a different wavelength. Groups of rods are connected to a single bipolar cell, each cone is connected to one bipolar cell.

10 Each eye receives a slightly different view of the world, which is detected by different areas of the retina. Information from the left visual field goes to the right visual cortex in the brain and information from the right visual field goes to the left visual cortex. The visual cortex assembles the information so we recognise what we see.

11 optic chiasma

12 The brain is able to modify images so that the edges of objects appear sharper.

13 a *Euglena* shows positive phototaxis: it moves towards light in order to photosynthesise.

b Male moths respond with positive chemotaxis. This behaviour enables them to mate and reproduce.

c Snails respond with negative geotaxis. They move away from gravity, which enables them to climb up to find leaves for food.

d Lice respond to temperature by kinesis. The temperature of the surface of human skin is about 30 °C. At other temperatures, they change their rate of movement until they are in more suitable conditions. Slow movement indicates that the organism is in conditions most suitable for survival.

e Planaria move away from light in a negative phototaxis response. In their natural habitat, this behaviour would move them to hidden areas under stones or leaves, away from predators. The response to food is a positive chemotaxis, so the animals obtain food.

The experiment with food should be conducted either in a constant source of light or in darkness so that only one variable is investigated.

14 any two of: to learn new skills for catching food; to avoid harmful foods; to find new places to nest or hide

15 taxis: woodlice move away from light; male moths move towards pheromones released by female moths

kinesis: response of woodlice to humidity

16 Innate behaviour is the same in all members of a species and is genetically determined. Learned behaviour varies among members of a species and comes from experience.

17 THC causes hyperpolarisation of post-synaptic membranes so that they are more difficult to stimulate.

18 social pressures; genetic predisposition; feelings of pleasure influenced by the release of dopamine

19 Inhibitory drugs increase transmission of impulses at inhibitory synapses or suppress transmission at excitatory synapses.

20 controls automatic activities such as breathing, swallowing and heart rate

21 If the medulla is permanently damaged and inactive, a person cannot control the basic, automatic activities needed for life. Consciousness and independent breathing are not possible.

22 FMRI scans reveal blood flow to different areas of the brain and indicate activity in that region as a subject performs different tasks.

23 Social behaviour is seen in species that live together in groups, and helps them to protect themselves from predators or enables them to divide the tasks in the group between its members.

24 Blue gill sunfish will consume all sizes of *Daphnia* when there is a low prey density, but if food is abundant they select large prey.

25 Male peacocks have developed exaggerated tails, which are preferred by females.

OPTION F

1 analysis of ribosomes; presence/absence of introns; presence/absence of plasmids

2 sulfurous springs; salty environments; the guts of ruminants

3 *Saccharomyces*: heterotrophic saprotroph
Euglena: autotrophic (photosynthesises) and heterotrophic
Chlorella: autotrophic (photosynthesises)

4 producers; fixation of nitrogen; decomposers.

5 denitrification: conversion of nitrate to nitrogen
nitrification: conversion of ammonia to nitrate
nitrogen fixation: conversion of nitrogen gas to ammonia and other nitrogen compounds

6 Saprotrophic bacteria feed on organic matter in sewage and convert it to inorganic compounds such as nitrates and phosphates.

7 Reverse transcriptase is produced when a virus invades a host. It converts viral RNA to DNA which is inserted into the host's chromosome. It is used to insert useful genes into bacteria which express the genes and produce substances such as insulin or growth hormones for medical use.

8 Therapeutic genes may be inserted in the wrong place; retroviruses used as vectors might become cancer-causing; viral protein might trigger an immune response; therapeutic genes may not be expressed.

9 High salt or sugar concentrations affect the osmotic potential of spoilage organisms so they cannot function and food is therefore preserved.

10 *Campylobacter* or *Salmonella*. Both are transmitted to humans through undercooked meat. Transmission to other food products can occur through poor food hygiene, if kitchen equipment is not cleaned properly or hands are not washed.

11 photoautotroph: uses light energy to produce organic materials from inorganic substances, e.g. *Anabaena*
photoheterotroph: uses light energy to generate ATP but obtains organic material from other organisms, e.g. *Heliobacter*

12 use of microbes to treat areas that have been contaminated with pesticides, oil or solvents

13 *Chlamydia* is an intracellular infection that lives inside epithelial cells but does not kill them during the dormant phase. *Streptococcus* is an extracellular bacterium that lives on the skin and in the upper respiratory tract. It produces toxins that kill or harm cells.

14 bactericides kill bacteria, e.g. irradiation, pasteurisation; bacteriostatic treatments inhibit bacterial growth, e.g. antiseptics

15 Transmitted to humans in the saliva of a female *Anaopheles* sp. mosquito. The parasite enters the blood, causing fever, sweating and chills as it completes its life cycle. Red blood cells may burst and lead to blocked capillaries and organ failure.

OPTION G

1 any three of:
temperature: suitable temperature is essential for enzyme activity;
light: essential for photosynthesis;
water: essential for photosynthesis and transport of dissolved substances;
breeding sites: essential for animals, must be safe and within reach of food;
food supply: animals need a source of food to survive

2 set out transect line in the two areas; sample chosen species of plant at regular intervals (interval depends on the length of the transect); record and compare the frequency of occurrence of the species in two sites

3 Biomass is biological material, living or dead, which can be used as an energy source.

4 Competitive exclusion occurs if two different species require the same resource which is in short supply. No two species can occupy the same niche, so one will dominate and exclude the other.

5 A niche is a particular environment and lifestyle inhabited by a species. For example, the niche of a rabbit is an underground burrow in grassland.

6 a

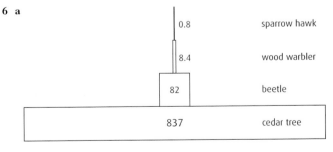

b

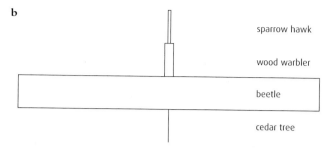

sparrow hawk

wood warbler

beetle

cedar tree

7 Primary succession occurs when an area of bare ground is colonised for the first time, whereas secondary succession occurs where land has been cleared (either naturally or by human intervention) and then re-colonised.

8 Biomes are areas of the world which are defined mainly by their rainfall and temperature.

9 Net production is the amount of energy in plant matter that is available to herbivores per square metre per year, after respiration losses have been deducted.

10 Tundra is cold all year; rainfall is low, only mosses, lichen and a few grasses can grow well.
Tropical rainforests are hot all year with high rainfall. Vegetation is dominated by many tress that grow continuously. Biodiversity is high.
Temperate deciduous forests are cold in winter and warm in summer with rainfall throughout the year. Trees lose their leaves in winter.

11 Cane toad introduced to Queensland, Australia: competes with native amphibian species and has severely reduced their numbers. The toad's poisonous skin deters potential predators and the toad feeds on rodents and insects, upsetting natural food chains.

12 Biomagnification is the process that leads to the accumulation of chemical substances in food chains so that they become more concentrated at higher trophic levels.

13 Indicator species are very sensitive to changes in their environment and can give information about the condition of an ecosystem by their presence or absence.

14 Nature reserves provide the conditions needed for species to survive when their natural habitat is restricted or destroyed. They must be a suitable size and be protected and funded so that these conditions can be maintained.

15 Captive breeding uses animal breeding in zoos to increase species numbers. Artificial insemination or embryo transfer may be used, genetic diversity can be monitored. Plants can be bred in greenhouses, which provide the correct environmental conditions. Selected seed from seed banks may be used.

16 r-strategy: organisms produce large numbers of offspring, do not care for their young who reach maturity quickly
K-strategy: organisms produce few offspring, animals care for their young for long periods and the young take a long time to become mature

17 A sample of organisms is captured, marked and released. Later a second sample is taken and the proportion of marked individuals noted. The proportion marked in the second sample is assumed to be the same as the proportion of the total population that was originally marked. Limitations: only useful for mobile small animals with limited territories; assumes there is no immigration or emigration; not useful for very small populations.

18 Maximum sustainable yield is the largest proportion of fish in a population that can be caught without endangering the population by ensuring there are sufficient fish to re-stock the population.

OPTION H

1 steroids; proteins; tyrosine derivatives

2 a steroid
b protein

3 osmoreceptors in the hypothalamus stimulated if concentration of blood plasma rises above normal; pituitary gland releases ADH; cells in the collecting duct of the kidney reabsorb more water from the kidney tubule; concentration of the blood plasma falls; stimulation of osmoreceptors decreases

4 Saliva contains mucus, amylase and water; pancreatic juice contains water, pancreatic amylase, trypsinogen, lipase and carboxypeptidase.

5 enzymes are not swept along the intestine; remain in place much longer; contact their substrates at the membrane; products are absorbed immediately; as membranes are detached the enzymes continue to work in the lumen of the intestine

6 Lipids are hydrophobic and not water soluble, but in the gut enzymes work in aqueous solution.

7 Vesicles enclose and engulf liquid containing products of digestion from inside the gut. Tight junctions ensure the absorbed molecules pass through intestine cells to the blood and not to adjacent cells.

8 cellulose; lignin; bacteria

9 any three of: storage of iron and some vitamins; detoxification; bile production; regulation of blood sugar level; storage of glycogen

10 Hemoglobin is separated into globin and heme. Globin is hydrolysed to amino acids, which are reused. Iron is removed from the heme group and stored, and the remaining part of the molecule is converted to bilirubin and becomes part of bile.

11 enter: hepatic artery and hepatic portal vein; leave: hepatic vein

12 genetic predisposition; age; sex; lifestyle choices: smoking, lack of exercise and obesity increase the risk

13 atrial systole: atria contract to force blood into the ventricles
venticular systole: the ventricles contract; atrioventricular valves close, right ventricle forces blood into the pulmonary artery and left ventricle forces blood into the aorta
diastole is the relaxation of the chambers of the heart, semilunar valves close and heart begins to refill with blood from the veins

14 the contraction of the heart muscle in the absence of a stimulus

15 the proportion of the total pressure of a gas mixture that is due to one component of the mixture

16 The affinity of hemoglobin for oxygen is reduced in the presence of carbon dioxide, so in respiring tissue where carbon dioxide pressures are higher, oxygen is released to supply the tissue.

17 Bronchi walls constrict so ventilation is difficult; oxygen reaching the lungs is reduced; gas exchange is more difficult as the diffusion gradient across the alveoli decreases; additional carbon dioxide in the blood stimulates an increased ventilation rate.

Answers to end-of-chapter questions

Chapter 1

1 C (1)
2 A (1)
3 D (1)
4 D (1)
5 B (1)
6 68% fall within ±1 standard deviation of the mean (1)
and 95% fall within ±2 standard deviations of the mean. (1)
7 Calculation of the standard deviations of the two sets of data shows that the data for the first set of dandelions is much more widely spread than the data for the second set of dandelions. (For the first set the standard deviation is 11.4% of the mean and for the second set it is 20.6%.) There was much greater variation in the length of the dandelion leaves from the wasteland. The growth of dandelions in the two areas is definitely very different. (2)
8 The second set of data was much more spread out than the first set. (For the first set of data the standard deviation was 3.8% of the mean whereas for the second set it was 6.2% of the mean.) There was much greater variation in the number of eggs laid by salmon in the River Gaula compared to the River Namsen. (2) (Notice though that the standard deviations are almost the same. In cases like this it is useful to calculate the %.)
9 a The data shows a clear positive correlation. (1)
   b It is known that elephants are herbivores and eat grass and the bark and leaves of trees so they may push trees over in order to get at the leaves. It would therefore seem that there could be a causal relationship between the sets of data but field observations would need to be carried out to verify this. (2)
10 The calculated value of *t*, 3.55, is greater than the critical value for 28 degrees of freedom, 2.05, and so the conclusion is that the 'buriers' remove more dung than the 'rollers'. The probability is between 0.1% and 0.01% and so the conclusion can be stated with confidence because we can be more than 99.9% certain that the 'buriers' remove more dung than the 'rollers'. (3)

Chapter 2

1 B (1)
2 D (1)
3 hydrophilic head groups point outward;
hydrophobic tails form a lipid bilayer;
forms a (phospholipid) bilayer;
ions and polar molecules cannot pass through hydrophobic barrier;
helps the cell maintain internal concentration and exclude other molecules (2 max)

4 small cells have larger ratio (than larger cells) / ratio decreases as size increases;
surface area / membrane must be large enough to absorb nutrients / oxygen / substances needed;
surface area / membrane must be large enough to excrete / pass out waste products;
need for materials is determined by (cell) volume;
cell size is limited (by surface area to volume ratio) / cells divide when they reach a certain size;
reference to diffusion across / through membrane / surface area (3 max)
5 a active transport requires energy, facilitated diffusion does not;
active transport moves substances against a concentration gradient, facilitated diffusion cannot (2)
   b exocytosis uses (membrane-bound) vesicles to transport molecules;
vesicles fuse with plasma membrane to release molecules outside the cell (2)
6 a as the diameter of the molecule increases the permeability / relative ability to move decreases (*accept converse*);
the relationship is logarithmic / non-linear / negative;
for molecules above 0.6 (±0.1) nm relative ability to move changes little / for molecules below 0.6 (±0.1) nm relative ability to move changes rapidly (2 max)
   b 'U-1' rule applies.
      i 10 mmol dm^{-3} cells h^{-1} (*accept values within ±5*) (1)
      ii 370 mmol dm^{-3} cells h^{-1} (*accept values within ±10*) (1)
   c i glucose uptake in facilitated diffusion levels out whereas uptake in simple diffusion does not level out / continues to rise;
glucose uptake increases in both;
glucose uptake is higher in facilitated diffusion (than in simple diffusion);
glucose uptake in simple diffusion is constant / linear whereas in facilitated diffusion uptake increases rapidly at the beginning / increase is not constant (3 max)
      ii little / no change in glucose uptake;
most / all (protein) channels in use (2)
(total 9 marks)
© IB Organisation 2009

7 a mitochondrion (1)
   b crista (1)
   Award 1 mark for each of the following, up to 3 max.
   folded membrane;
   provides large surface area;
   for electron transfer chain / site of ATP synthesis;
   moves protons to inter-membrane space from matrix (3 max)
(total 5 marks)
© IB Organisation 2009

Chapter 3

1 B   (1)

2 D   (1)

3 condensation;
   involves the removal of water to join monosaccharides
   together / equation to show this;
   catalysed by enzymes;
   consists of many monosaccharides linked (glycosidic linkages)
   to make polysaccharide   (2 max)

4 enzymes are specific for their substrate / lock–and–key model /
   energy requirements for reactions with substrates vary;
   each step of the pathway is unique / different substrate at
   each step;
   finer control of metabolic pathways   (2 max)

5 a substrate for respiration / energy source / for ATP
       production;
       material for growth of cell walls;
       precursor for other molecules (e.g. amino acids)   (1 max)
   b glucose must be transported from the extracellular
       fluid / culture medium to the cytoplasm / transported
       to the cell;
       the transporter molecules must be located on the
       cell (surface) membrane   (2)
   c in the presence of light but no glucose, both modified and
       unmodified algae grow in the same way;
       in the presence of light and glucose, the unmodified algae
       show no change but the modified algae grow faster and
       for a longer period of time;
       in the absence of light but with glucose, the unmodified
       algae do not grow at all but the modified algae grow
       as well as when there is light and glucose   (2 max)
   d algal cells are pigmented green / have chlorophyll;
       pigments absorb light for photosynthesis;
       the more the algae grow, the more light is absorbed (so
       shading algae below them);
       unmodified algae floating deeper in the water receive less
       light / are shaded and starve;
       modified algae (given glucose) can carry on metabolising
       even if they are shaded / do not need light   (3 max)
                                                         (total 8 marks)
                                              © IB Organisation 2009

6 a 06:00 / 19:30 to 19:45   (1)
       (accept 6 am / 7:30 pm to 7:45 pm)
   b $2.3 \, mg \, CO_2 \, h^{-1}$ (±0.1) (units required)   (1)
   c more uptake at 15 °C than 30 °C during the hours of
       daylight;
       both are high during the hours of daylight / reverse argument;
       greater uptake at 30 °C than 15 °C during the hours of
       darkness;
       at only 15 °C uptake becomes negative   (3 max)
   d respiration rate greater than photosynthesis (during
       the hours of darkness)   (1)
                                                         (total 6 marks)
                                              © IB Organisation 2009

Chapter 4

1 C   (1)

2 A   (1)

3 B   (1)

4 C   (1)

5 D   (1)

6 B   (1)

7 Ludovica has alleles I^A and I^B.
   Mikhail must have alleles I^A and i because he is group A but
   his mother is group O with the genotype ii.
   Punnett grid:

		gametes from Mikhail	
		I^A	i
gametes from Ludovica	I^A	$I^A I^A$ group A	$I^A i$ group A
	I^B	$I^A I^B$ group AB	$I^B i$ group B

                                                                       (4)

8 *Responses must have at least one argument for and one argument against
   to receive full marks.*
   Arguments against cloning:
   more embryos than are needed have to be produced;
   unused embryos are destroyed;
   all embryos have the potential to develop into a human;
   human eggs need to be obtained / donated
   Arguments for cloning:
   embryonic stem cells could be used to repair damaged tissue
   or even save lives;
   the embryo is at a very early stage before any
   differentiation has taken place   (4 max)

9 *Award 7 max if no named example given. Award 5 max if both
   possible benefits and possible harmful effects are not addressed.*
   named example of desired outcome e.g. herbicide resistance;
   Possible benefits:
   specific characteristic(s) can be selected / less random than
   selective breeding;
   faster than selective breeding;
   desired characteristic(s) may not be present in gene pool /
   selective breeding cannot produce desired phenotype;
   increased crop yield / less land required for production;
   reduced use of chemicals (e.g. pesticides);
   crops that can grow in extreme conditions e.g. salt tolerance;
   drug production e.g. pharmaceuticals in milk / human
   insulin;   (4 max)
   Possible harmful effects:
   transferred gene may be harmful / cause suffering to animal;
   unknown effects of gene interaction;
   organism could escape into environment and compete with
   the naturally occurring species;

once in the environment could not be recovered / controlled;

engineered gene could cross species barriers; (4 max)

(total 8 marks)

10 *DNA profiling*:

sample of DNA / blood / saliva / semen is obtained;

PCR used to amplify / produce more copies of the DNA;

DNA broken into fragments by restriction enzymes;

DNA fragments separated by gel electrophoresis;

DNA separated into a series of bands;

bands compared between different DNA samples;

if banding pattern is the same then DNA is (almost certainly) from same source;

if some bands are similar then individuals are (almost certainly) related; (4 max)

Specific example:

testing of paternity / forensics / classification / archaeology / pedigree / another specific example; (1 max)

(total 5 marks)

11 *Application of karyotyping*:

testing for chromosome structure abnormality;

testing for chromosome number abnormality;

extra 21 indicates Down syndrome / other chromosome number abnormality (e.g. Klinefelter's syndrome); (2 max)

Obtaining chromosomes:

fetal cells obtained from amniotic fluid;

by amniocentesis / CVS;

white blood cells separated out;

allowed to divide;

mitosis / division blocked in metaphase;

slide prepared / stained (and chromosomes examined); (3 max)

(total 5 marks)

12 any two of the following: improved understanding of genetic / inherited diseases / conditions;

improved detection of (carriers of) genetic diseases;

improved drug design / pharmacogenomics / custom drugs;

gene therapy / repair or replacement of faulty gene;

study of similarities / differences between human races / populations;

study of human origins / migration / relationships with other species (2 max)

13 **a** a gene / trait / allele carried on a sex chromosome / X and Y / X / Y (1)

b recessive;

evidence from the pedigree;

e.g. individuals 2 and 3 in the 2nd generation

do not have the condition but have children who do (2 max)

c **i** X^aY where **a** = condition (1)

ii X^AX^a or X^AX^A where **A** = normal,

a = condition (*must have both*) (1)

(*If upper case letter and lower case letter are reversed then the ECF rule applies.*)

(total 5 marks)

© IB Organisation 2009

14 **a** line 3 / line III (1)

b **i** transgenic have more (%) starch than control;

transgenic have less sugar than control;

transgenic contain greater total amounts (% fresh weight) of carbohydrates than control;

greater difference between (%) starch and (%) sugar in transgenic than control (2 max)

ii transgenic contain (gene which produces) enzyme which is active and (produces more starch); (1)

stored sugar is used to produce starch so lower in transgenic (1)

c all transgenic have acceptable fry colour;

control potatoes have acceptable fry colour only after 10 days storage;

transgenic have acceptable fry colour after any length of storage / all values below 2 (2 max)

(total 7 marks)

© IB Organisation 2009

Chapter 5

1 B (1)

2 A (1)

3 D (1)

4 B (1)

5 pyramid shows three levels, widest at the bottom and narrowest at the top (*not necessarily to scale*);

lowest level labelled 'producers', middle level 'primary consumers' and top level 'secondary consumers';

calculations of energy at each level: $400\,kJ\,m^{-2}\,y^{-1}$ for bottom level (producers), $40\,kJ\,m^{-2}\,y^{-1}$ for middle level (primary consumers) and $4\,kJ\,m^{-2}\,y^{-1}$ for top level (secondary consumers) (*units required*) (3)

6 members of a population show variation;

variation has its origins in sexual reproduction / meiosis / mutation;

some variations allow an individual to be better adapted;

(better adapted varieties) more likely to survive to reproductive age;

frequency of advantageous alleles increases (over time) (3 max)

7 Any three of the following:

lack of food;

lack of breeding sites;

increase in predator numbers;

increase in disease. (3 max)

8 **a** **i** 1990 (1)

ii 1970 (1)

b **i** the higher the temperature in March and April, the earlier the date of leaf opening (1)

ii there is evidence of warming;

at the end of the twentieth century most years are warmer than the mean;

all but one of the last (12) years are warmer than the mean;

there were six colder-than-mean years in the first 15 years

and only two in the second 15 years (2 max)

c **i** date of egg laying is (always) earlier than the date of maximum caterpillar biomass / date of maximum caterpillar biomass is (always) later than the date of egg laying (1)

ii many caterpillars available to feed the young when they have hatched (1)

d date of maximum caterpillar biomass has got earlier / reduced / decreased (1)

e birds that lay eggs earlier find more caterpillars / their young are better fed;

offspring of early egg layers have a better chance of survival;

these birds inherit the early egg-laying characteristic / others are eliminated (2 max)

(total 10 marks)

© IB Organisation 2009

9 a **i** potassium / K (1)

ii sub-arctic forest (1)

b K and Ca have greater mean residence time (MRT) in chaparral (than temperate forest);

K has the shortest MRT of all nutrients in both biomes;

C, N, P and Mg have greater MRT in temperate forest than in chaparral;

MRT values for K and C show little variation between these areas (chaparral and temperate);

P shows the greatest range / difference in MRT;

temperate forest has higher MRT for all nutrients except K and Ca;

average MRT for all nutrients in the temperate forest is 3.8 and for the chaparral is 3.5;

temperate forest and chaparral have similar values for all nutrients compared to the other biomes (2 max)

c generally plant productivity increases while MRT decreases / negative correlation;

tropical rainforest biome with shortest MRT (for nutrients) has highest plant productivity / sub-arctic has low plant productivity and long MRT;

(but) chaparral has lower plant productivity than sub-arctic forest and shorter MRT for nutrients / there are exceptions to the relationship;

there is no relationship that holds true for all four biomes;

Do not accept 'no correlation'. (2 max)

d higher temperatures in tropical rainforest / lower temperatures in sub-arctic forest;

greater rate of decomposition in tropical rainforest / more saprophytes;

water availability (1 max)

(total 7 marks)

© IB Organisation 2009

10 a **i** with time, the atmospheric concentration of CO_2 has increased (1)

ii the increased use of fossil fuels / more automobiles; increased deforestation (1 max)

Do not accept 'greenhouse effect'.

b **i** any trough, clearly labelled at the bottom (1)

ii CO_2 is a raw material for photosynthesis;

there is an increase in the rate of photosynthesis in the summer;

therefore less CO_2 in the air during the summer as it is being used for photosynthesis;

increase in CO_2 in winter because there is less photosynthesis due to trees losing leaves in autumn and winter / lower temperatures / shorter days with less light (2 max)

c FCs or HFCs / CH_4 or methane / N_2O or nitrous oxide or oxides of nitrogen (1)

Do not accept 'SO_2'.

(total 6 marks)

© IB Organisation 2009

Chapter 6

1 A (1)

2 C (1)

3 C (1)

4 D (1)

5 B (1)

6 B (1)

7 *Must have at least one for each region to gain full marks.*

Stomach	Small intestine	Large intestine
provides acidic environment; provides right environment for digestive enzymes; destroys many pathogens	*provides weakly alkaline environment;* all food groups digested here; main region for absorption of end products of digestion	main region for absorption of water / water and mineral ions; contains many bacteria, which synthesise vitamin K

(4)

8 *Arteries (1 mark for each, 3 max):*

thick wall / elastic fibres to help withstand the high(er) pressure;

outer fibrous coat prevents artery from rupturing under the high pressure;

lumen small compared to wall thickness to maintain high pressure;

layers of (smooth) muscle to allow arteries to contract / elastic recoil;

smooth muscle allows the pressure to be altered (vasoconstriction and vasodilation) (3 max)

Veins (1 mark for each, 3 max):

lumen always large in relation to diameter;

thin wall / more collagen and fewer elastic fibres (than arteries) since pressure is low(er);

very little muscle since not needed for constriction;

valves to prevent back flow between pulses (3 max)

Capillaries (1 mark for each, 3 max):
no muscle / elastic tissue since pressure is very low;
endothelial layer one cell thick to allow permeability /
diffusion of chemicals / tissue fluid;
small diameter leads to exchange;
no valves since pressure very low (3 max)

(total 9 marks)

9 antigen causes an immune response to produce antibodies
specific for that antigen;
antibodies produced in lymphocytes;
lymphocytes produced in bone marrow;
lymphocytes carried in blood;
helper T-cells are needed for antibody production (3 max)

10 the skin / mucous membranes act as a physical barrier;
skin has several layers of tough / keratinised cells;
the skin is dry discouraging the growth and reproduction
of pathogens;
skin / mucous membranes host natural flora and fauna that
compete with pathogens;
the enzyme lysozyme is present on the skin's surface to
break down pathogens;
the pH of skin / mucous membranes is unfavourable to
many pathogens;
skin is a continuous layer;
mucus traps pathogens / sticky (3 max)
*Award only 2 max if either skin or mucous membranes are not
mentioned.*

11 pancreatic cells monitor blood glucose;
insulin / glucagon is a hormone;
low glucose level induces production of glucagon;
α cells of pancreatic islets produce glucagon;
glucagon stimulates the liver to break down glycogen into
glucose;
glucagon leads to increase in blood glucose level;
absorption of glucose from digestive tract causes glucose levels
to rise (after meals);
high level of blood glucose induces production of insulin;
β cells of pancreatic islets produce insulin;
insulin stimulates uptake of glucose into cells (muscles);
insulin stimulates uptake of glucose into liver / storage of
glucose as glycogen in liver;
insulin leads to decrease in blood glucose level;
homeostatic monitoring of blood glucose levels is constantly
happening;
blood glucose regulation is an example of negative feedback
(8 max)

12 *Arguments against IVF:*
fertilised egg has potential to become a person / some view a
fertilised egg as having special status;
IVF requires the production of multiple embryos;
fate of extra embryos is an ethical concern;
ethics of long-term storage;
ownership / responsibility for stored embryos is an issue;
stem-cell research is blurring the issue as other cells now have
the possibility of becoming a person;

procedure may result in multi-embryo pregnancy, which places
stress on the family resources / unwanted children;
issues of equity of access / expensive;
high rates of failure;
religious opposition / 'playing God';
Arguments favouring IVF:
only way some couples can have children / helps infertile
couples;
allows for genetic screening;
allows for surrogate mothers (8 max)
*For full marks, at least two of the points should include the
counter-argument, otherwise award 6 max.*

13 **a** obese (1)
 b 35 kg (±2) (1)
 c as height increases, body mass index decreases *or*
 as height decreases, body mass index increases (1 max)

(total 3 marks)

14 **a** blind mole rats have a lower oxygen consumption than
 white rats / numerical comparison e.g. white rats
 consume about twice as much oxygen as blind mole
 rats / *vice versa* (1)
 (*A comparison word / term is needed – just quoting numbers
 from graph is not enough.*)
 b both graphs show greater speed correlated to greater
 consumption / positive correlation / directly proportional;
 (overall) rate of increase is lower in white rats than in blind
 mole rats;
 blind mole rats consume less oxygen at lower speeds than
 white rats;
 but white rats consume less oxygen at higher speeds;
 white rat oxygen uptake slows down / stops increasing /
 reaches plateau as treadmill speed increases but blind
 mole rat oxygen uptake keeps increasing;
 blind mole rats reach a higher maximum oxygen
 consumption (3 max)
 c lowers the oxygen consumption in both types of rats;
 smaller effect on blind mole rats than on white rats;
 plateau reached in white rats at lower speed;
 blind mole rats have better ventilation systems / are better
 adapted than white rats (2 max)
 d *Command term is 'explain' so the adaptation mentioned must be
 associated with its effect / purpose.*
 greater lung volume increases amount of air / oxygen
 that can be breathed in / contained;
 greater alveolar area increases surface area for gaseous
 exchange / allows more absorption / diffusion of oxygen;
 greater capillary area means more contact / more exchange /
 larger rate of diffusion between capillaries and alveoli;
 so more oxygen can be carried away from lungs;
 greater capillary area allows more oxygen absorption /
 gaseous exchange between lungs (alveoli) and blood (3 max)

(total 9 marks)

15 a concentration rises throughout pregnancy

the rise is exponential / levels rise significantly later in pregnancy (2)

Award 0 for a description that only implies a rise.

b the CRH concentration is lower in late deliveries / higher in full-term deliveries;

differences greater / become more pronounced later in the pregnancy;

both rise gradually (2 max)

c 57 pmol dm^{-3} of plasma ($\pm$3) (1)

Value and unit needed for 1 mark.

d high concentration would indicate women at high risk of premature delivery;

low concentration would indicate women at risk of going past term / delivering late;

concentration could be used to indicate when delivery is imminent;

concentration might indicate special precautions or medical technique needed (e.g. reduce physical activity of mother or provide special incubator for likely premature birth or induce labour for past-term mothers) (2 max)

e *Low water.*

toads can mate earlier as conditions dry;

toads can move to larger ponds;

tadpole / organism cannot survive in absence of water

High water.

larger toads more resistant to predation;

larger toads more attractive to mates (3 max)

f concentrations of thyroxine and corticosterone are higher in low-water group / *vice versa*;

greater difference in thyroxine concentration / less difference in corticosterone concentration between the two groups;

in both groups thyroxine concentrations are higher than corticosterone concentrations (2 max)

Comparisons need to be made between the two hormones in the high-water environment/low-water environment.

g CRH levels would be higher in the low-water group / *vice versa*; (1)

(total 13 marks)

© IB Organisation 2009

Chapter 7

1 D (1)

2 B (1)

3 A (1)

4 A (1)

5 C (1)

6 D (1)

7 B (1)

8 three stages: initiation, elongation and termination;

mRNA translated in a 5' → 3' direction;

mRNA binds to ribosome / small subunit;

first (charged) tRNA binds to start codon / to mRNA;

tRNA anticodon binds to mRNA codon;

by complementary base pairing;

AUG is the start codon;

second (charged) tRNA binds to ribosome / to mRNA;

large subunit binds (to small subunit);

amino acid on first tRNA is joined / bonded to amino acid on second tRNA;

by condensation (reaction);

peptide bond formed;

ribosome moves (in 5' → 3' direction) by one triplet / codon;

first tRNA in exit site;

tRNA in exit site leaves and new / third (charged) tRNA binds;

repeats until reach a stop codon;

polypeptide released;

tRNA-activating enzymes join correct amino acid to its specific tRNA (9 max)

9 product of metabolic pathway can act as inhibitor of enzyme earlier in pathway;

non-competitive inhibition;

enzyme is allosteric enzyme;

allosteric enzyme has allosteric binding site / binding site other than active site;

(shape of an) allosteric enzyme alternates between active and inactive (form);

inhibitor / product binds to allosteric enzyme / site and alters shape of active site;

the more product there is, the more the pathway is inhibited;

as product gets used up inhibition decreases;

this is negative feedback (6 max)

10 a 47–49% *(units are not needed)* (1)

b *D. melanogaster / Drosophila* has few genes with one exon;

highest percentage has 2 exons;

most genes have 5 or fewer exons;

a few genes have 10 or more exons / more than 8;

maximum number of exons does not exceed 60 (2 max)

c i *S. cerevisiae* / yeast has most genes with only 1 exon while for mammals 5 exons is most frequent;

no yeast genes have more than 5 exons while some mammal genes have greater than 60 exons;

mammal genes contain more exons on average;

with a wider distribution than in yeast (2 max)

ii *S. cerevisiae* / yeast is a unicellular organism / mammals are multicellular / complex;

mammals have more transcriptional regulation;

S. cerevisiae smaller in size / more compact genome (1 max)

d gene size − mRNA size = intron size;

25.0 − 2.1 = 22.9 kb;

average size of intron = $\dfrac{22.9}{14 \text{ introns}}$ = 1.6 ($\pm$ 0.1) kb;

(unit required) (2)

e smaller genes usually have fewer introns / larger genes have more introns / relationship not clear;
dystrophin and collagen have the same number of introns but the dystrophin gene is larger;
albumin has more introns but is smaller than the gene for phenylalanine hydroxylase (2 max)

f 2.4 kb = 2400 base pairs;
1 amino acid is coded for by 3 bases;
so maximum number of amino acids = 2400 ÷ 3 = 800 amino acids
or 799 amino acids (1)

g epsilon and zeta (globin) (1)

h gamma genes (mostly) expressed before birth and beta genes expressed after birth;
beta-globin levels rise at 28(±2) weeks of gestation while gamma levels decrease / as one rises, the other falls;
gamma-globin expression starts at 0–2 weeks whereas beta-globin starts at 26(±2) weeks / gamma expression starts earlier;
one month after birth hemoglobin has equal mixture of beta-globin and gamma-globin;
gamma levels go to zero while beta becomes a regular part of hemoglobin (3 max)

i *10 weeks after gestation*:
two alpha-globins with two gamma-globins / 49 (50)% alpha and 48 (49)% gamma (1)
2 months after birth:
variety of molecules all containing alpha and two chains from the other three types / 6% delta, 14% gamma, 35% beta, 50% alpha (1)
(total 17 marks)
© IB Organisation 2009

11 a i 72.5(±1.0)% (1)
ii 40% (decrease) (1)

b both are inversely proportional / as CAA concentration increases both activity and growth decrease;
growth is more irregular at low concentrations;
ACTase activity decreases more at higher concentration / after 30 mmol dm^{-3} than growth;
both show linear decreases between 10 and 30 mmol dm^{-3} (2 max)

Any other valid comparisons.

c end product is slowing enzyme activity;
allostery / non-competitive inhibition (2)

d use CAA to control / inhibit bacterial growth / antibiotic functions *or*
use CAA to treat *H. pylori* infection (1)
(total 7 marks)
© IB Organisation 2009

Chapter 8

1 B (1)
2 A (1)
3 A (1)
4 D (1)
5 C (1)
6 D (1)
7 B (1)

8 a greater surface area for the pigments / chlorophyll
more light (energy) can be absorbed (2)

b tree leaves reduce amount of light reaching ground level
light has already passed through leaves so most of the useful wavelengths / red and blue light has been removed
or converse only green / yellow / orange light remains (2)

c catalyses first reaction in the Calvin cycle;
used for carbon fixation;
carbon fixation is essential to the plant / carbon dioxide needed for synthesis of sugars (2 max)
(total 6 marks)

9 pyruvate enters the mitochondrion;
pyruvate is converted to acetyl CoA;
by oxidation (and decarboxylation) / NADH + H$^+$ and CO$_2$ formed;
acetyl CoA enters the Krebs cycle / coenzyme A release for recycling;
during one Krebs cycle (2) further (decarboxylation) reactions remove CO$_2$;
during Krebs cycle hydrogen is removed by NAD$^+$ and FAD to form NADH + H$^+$ and FADH$_2$;
occurs in mitochondrial matrix;
electrons released from NADH + H$^+$ and FADH$_2$ onto electron transport chain (ETC);
ETC proteins on inner mitochondrial membrane / cristae;
energy released from electrons flowing along chain pump protons into inter-membrane space;
protons flow (passively) from inter-membrane space back to matrix through ATP synthase;
oxygen is final electron acceptor and is water produced (using protons) (8 max)

10 light-independent reaction fixes CO$_2$;
to make glycerate 3-phosphate;
glycerate 3-phosphate / GP becomes reduced;
to triose phosphate;
using NADPH + H$^+$;
using ATP;
from the light-dependent reactions;
ATP needed to regenerate RuBP (5 max)

11 a i increasing fructose 6-phosphate concentration (initially) causes an increase in activity;
activity levels out / remains constant as (substrate) concentration continues to rise (2)
ii more collisions with active site as concentration rises;
at high substrate levels all active sites are occupied so no further increase in rate / enzyme working at maximum rate (2)

b **i** decreases activity;

at all fructose 6-phosphate concentrations;

most effect at intermediate fructose 6-phosphate concentrations / little difference at high fructose 6-phosphate concentrations;

ATP acts as an inhibitor (2 max)

ii end-product inhibition, respiration rate decreased if ATP already available (1)

(total 7 marks)

© IB Organisation 2009

12 a rate of photosynthesis increases (rapidly) / directly proportional;

rate of photosynthesis levels off / increases slightly after 10 000 lumen m^{-2} (2)

b maximum photosynthetic rate is highest with highest CO_2 concentration;

at low light levels, higher CO_2 slightly increases the photosynthetic rate;

at low CO_2 / 280 ppm, the photosynthetic rate reaches its maximum at low light levels / constant over most light intensity / at 280 ppm CO_2 concentration limits photosynthesis;

at 500 and 1300 ppm CO_2 the curve is the same shape but with different maximum rates / each higher light intensity requires a higher CO_2 concentration to reach maximum rate;

maximum rate of photosynthesis from 280 to 500 ppm / increases 5 to 6 times while 500 to 1300 ppm increases 1.5 times (3 max)

c the rate of photosynthesis will increase (over the rate at 370 ppm);

the photosynthetic rate will at least double (but less than 5–6 times);

not linear;

bigger plants / more growth / more grain / greater yield (2 max)

d $\dfrac{4.3 - 3.8}{3.8} \times 100 = 13.16\%$ (*accept 13.2%*) (1)

e shade leaves receive less light than sun leaves;

to capture sunlight, shade leaves produce more chlorophyll;

to capture sunlight, shade leaves have greater leaf area (2 max)

(total 10 marks)

© IB Organisation 2009

Chapter 9

1 A (1)

2 B (1)

3 A (1)

4 D (1)

5 shoot is illuminated from one side;

auxin produced in shoot tip;

auxin accumulates on shaded side / transported to shaded side;

auxin stimulates increased growth on shaded side;

by stimulating cell elongation (*reject 'stimulating cell division/mitosis'*) (3 max)

6 *Transport*:

xylem vessels transport the water;

water molecules held together by cohesion/hydrogen bonding;

creates continuous column of water between leaf and root / in xylem;

water evaporates from leaves;

creates transpiration pull;

transpiration stream is flow of water through xylem / within plant;

capillarity / adhesion (to xylem walls) raises water (a short distance)

osmosis / osmotic pressure raises water (a short distance) (3 max)

Abiotic factors (accept opposites):

temperature – higher temperature increases evaporation therefore increasing transpiration flow

wind – increasing wind/air speed increases evaporation therefore increasing transpiration flow

light – increasing light intensity opens stomata/expands guard cells increasing evaporation therefore increasing transpiration flow

humidity – higher humidity decreases evaporation therefore decreasing transpiration flow (3 max)

(total 6 marks)

7 flowering plants are either short-day / require short days to flower;

or long-day / require long days to flower;

key factor is length of dark period;

key factor is wavelength of light / far red light / 730 nm;

plants are grown in buildings where day length can be controlled;

short-day plants have artificially shortened day;

long-day plants have artificially lengthened day;

dark period need only be interrupted briefly / for a few minutes by light for long-day plants;

regulated by phytochrome / P_{fr} (6 max)

8 water absorbed through the micropyle;

gibberellin formed in cotyledon;

gibberellin stimulates formation of enzymes / amylase (in aleurone layer);

amylase breaks down / digests starch in cotyledon to maltose / enzymes break down / digest food stores in cotyledon;

nutrients / soluble food molecules moved to embryo for growth / transport (4 max)

9 phloem is composed of sieve tube cells and companion cells;

companion cells synthesise ATP;

transport occurs both up and down phloem / bi-directional;

transports sugars / (soluble) organic molecules;

tissues can act as either source or sink;

molecules move from source to sink;

named example of source and sink;

ATP used to pump sugar / organic molecules into / out of sieve cell;

water follows by osmosis;

creates pressure gradient / mass flow / pressure flow in sieve cell   (6 max)

10 a i height 0.54 m: 40–59 cm / 0.40–0.59 m (from the plant)

    ii height 10.8 m: 0–2.9 m (from the plant) (*units needed for both parts of the answer*)   (1)

b the greater the height from which the seed fell, the further it travelled from the parent plant   (1)

c *At the greater height:*

seed can catch the wind to travel further / updrafts / more wind at greater height;

farther to the ground and does not travel straight down / more time to be blown before hitting the ground;

At lower height:

seed can fall straight down;

seed can hit downdraft and fall faster;   (2 max)

Any point must explain the difference in distance travelled from the two heights.

d *Agrostis stolonifera*   (1)

e *Poa trivialis*   (1)

f *Poa* produces seed earliest in the summer / June;

Holcus produces most seed in July;

Agrostis and *Festuca* produce seed in (late July to) August;

Holcus and *Poa* have a peak time of seed fall / short period of seed fall;

Agrostis and *Festuca* may continue to increase in seed production to September   (3 max)

Accept any of these points made conversely as an alternative.

g *Award 1 mark each for any two of the following.*

to avoid predation / disperse at times when other species are dispersing their seeds;

to avoid competition;

late in the year to allow seeds to germinate over winter / better germination conditions;

better dispersal conditions / more wind / animals for dispersal;

photoperiod – required day length for flowering;

more energy stored at the end of the summer for seed production;

more light / warmth / better conditions for seedling photosynthesis / growth   (2 max)

h *Award 1 mark each for any two of the following.*

tropical fruits have higher lipid content than temperate fruits;

temperate fruits (80%) have greater carbohydrate content than tropical fruits (55%);

protein levels are similar in both groups of fruits / slightly higher in temperate fruits than tropical fruits

(*must make it clear that the difference is slight*)   (2 max)

i mistletoe

high proportion of lipid and carbohydrate (lipid has approximately twice the energy content of protein and carbohydrate)   (2)

j *Animal dispersal advantage:*

travel further / digestion cracks seed coat for better

germination / deposited in faeces with organic matter / better in areas with little wind   (1 max)

Animal dispersal disadvantage:

predation / seeds eaten / deposited in poor environment / buried too deep / buried too shallow (if deposited with faeces) / animal might become extinct / scarce   (1 max)

(total 17 marks)

© IB Organisation 2009

Chapter 10

1 A   (1)

2 D   (1)

3 C   (1)

4 D   (1)

5 crossing over / chiasmata;

exchanges / mixes alleles;

random orientation of chromosomes;

at metaphase I;

at metaphase II   (2 max)

6 linked genes occur on the same chromosome / chromatid;

genes / alleles inherited together / not separated / do not segregate / do not assort independently;

diagram to show crossing over;

non-Mendelian ratio / example(s) of ratio(s);

specific example of linked genes;

Award 1 mark for each of the following examples of a cross between two linked genes:

key for alleles involved in the example of a cross;

parental genotypes and phenotypes shown;

F$_1$ genotypes and phenotypes shown;

recombinants identified;

recombinants result from crossing over;

clear diagram of cross / Punnett grid   (9 max)

7 a DdTt

all have dark body and straight bristles   (2)

b gametes are **DT**, **Dt**, **dT**, **dt** and **dt**

F$_2$ genotypes are **DdTt**, **Ddtt**, **ddTt** and **ddtt**

1 dark body, straight bristles : 1 dark body, dichaete bristles : 1 ebony body, straight bristles : 1 ebony body, dichaete bristles   (3)

c (autosomal) linkage (*reject 'sex linkage'*) / genes are on the same chromosome / genes do not assort independently;

dark body, straight bristles and ebony body, dichaete bristles are parental combinations / dark body, dichaete bristles and ebony body, straight bristles are the recombinants;

recombinants are produced by crossing over   (2 max)

(total 7 marks)

Chapter 11

1 B   (1)

2 A   (1)

3 D (1)

4 D (1)

5 antigen causes production of antibodies specific for that antigen;

antigen taken up by macrophage;

antigen presented on surface of macrophage to helper T-cell / T_H cell;

helper T-cell divides into clone(s) of (memory cells and) active cells;

active helper T-cell activates B-cell;

with antibody specific for the antigen;

B-cell activated and divides into clones of active / plasma cells and memory cells;

active B-cells / plasma cells secrete large quantities of antibody (5 max)

6 efferent arteriole has smaller diameter than afferent arteriole;

to increase (hydrostatic) blood pressure in glomerulus / glomerular capillaries;

glomerular capillaries fenestrated / have pores;

Bowman's capsule cells have processes / podocytes;

gaps between processes / feet allow filtrate to pass through easily;

basement membrane between capillaries and podocytes / Bowman's capsule cells acts as (ultra)filter;

basement membrane only allows substances below a certain size to pass through;

process of ultrafiltration is passive (4 max)

7 large surface area;

produced by microvilli and basal infoldings;

large numbers of mitochondria;

to provide energy for active transport (3 max)

8 arrival of impulse depolarises the muscle membrane;

(voltage-gated) channels are opened in the sarcoplasmic reticulum;

allowing release of calcium ions;

cross bridges form between myosin heads and (binding sites on) actin;

myosin head bends, pulling actin;

cross bridge is broken;

ATP is required;

myosin head returns to start position;

contraction stops when calcium ions are pumped back into sarcoplasmic reticulum (5 max)

9 progesterone level falls;

oxytocin (from pituitary gland) secreted;

oxytocin causes uterus muscle to contract;

estrogen makes uterus muscles more sensitive to oxytocin;

increased pressure on cervix causes further oxytocin secretion;

through nerve impulses to pituitary gland;

which further increases muscle contraction;

positive feedback (5 max)

10 a *Both answers are required for 1 mark.*

    i cooled: sour

    ii warmed: sweet (1)

b warming causes a greater sensation of sweetness than cooling;

on warming the sensation of sweetness increases (but) on cooling the sensation decreases;

on cooling sweetness becomes undetectable (but) on warming it becomes more detectable;

sensation of sweetness on warming is always 'weak' but on cooling it is always 'just detectable';

neither cooling nor warming causes moderate taste intensity (2 max)

Accept other suitable paired answers based on the data in the graph.

c *Two correct answers are required for 1 mark.*

age / gender / ethnic origin / health / sensitivity to taste / smoker (or non-smoker) / genetic (taster / non-taster) / drugs (use) / pregnancy (*not 'size / weight'*) (1)

d cooling;

because two tastes (sour and salty) are detectable (weakly) compared with only one (sweet) when warmed;

responses to cooling show the greatest changes (2 max)

e *Similarities*:

both (A and B) result in sweetness being detected;

both (A and B) result in sourness being detected;

both give a greater sensation of sweetness than sourness (2 max)

Differences:

A (chemoreceptors) give a greater sensation of sweetness than B;

B (chemoreceptors) give a greater sensation of sourness than A;

the difference between sweet and sour taste intensity for A is greater than the difference between sweet and sour for B (2 max)

(total 10 marks)

© IB Organisation 2009

11 a mean permeability for G1 (halotane) changes little / from 1.25 to 1.3 (±0.1)% but the mean permeability for G2 (isoflurane) increases / from 0.75 to 1.10 (±0.1)%;

deviation for permeability of G1 changes little / 0.7 to 0.8% but the deviation for the permeability of G2 increases / 0.4 to 0.7% (2)

b conflicting data;

G2 has difference but not G1, so cannot say inhaled anaesthetics cause change;

G3 has more difference than G1 (although not significant), so inhaled is less harmful than intravenous;

not enough data / all start at different mean / patients not all the same (3 max)

(total 5 marks)

© IB Organisation 2009

Option A

1 provide or release energy / required for cell respiration;

excess carbohydrate (glucose) can be converted into fat / glycogen (in muscles and liver) for storage;

synthesis of glycoproteins and glycolipids / combine with proteins and with lipids to form glycoproteins and glycolipids;
components of nucleic acids e.g. ribose in RNA / deoxyribose in DNA;
synthesis of some amino acids;
component of connective tissue (3 max)

2 healthy diets have less saturated lipids / less healthy diet has more saturated lipid;
saturated lipids have no double bonds / unsaturated lipids have one or more double bond(s);
saturated lipids raise LDL / cholesterol level;
saturated lipids increase risk of obesity;
obesity may lead to type II diabetes;
saturated lipids increase risk of CHD / coronary heart disease;
saturated lipids increase risk of arteriosclerosis / atherosclerosis;
arteriosclerosis / atherosclerosis leads to high blood pressure / increased risk of coronary thrombosis / stroke;
many unsaturated lipids cannot be synthesised by the body / saturated lipids can be synthesised by the body;
unsaturated lipids essential to the body / saturated lipids are not essential to the body;
omega-3 fatty acids are unsaturated and may help nerve growth / function (4 max)

3 protein and carbohydrate have similar energy content per gram;
carbohydrate has about 1760 kJ per 100 g;
protein has about 1720 kJ per 100 g;
both have approximately 1700 kJ per 100 g;
fat has about 4000 kJ per 100 g / 100 g of fat has more than twice the energy content of 100 g of carbohydrate or 100 g of protein (3 max)
Accept values if converted to 'per gram'.

4 *Causes*:
genetic component / high-risk ethnic group (Aboriginal, Asian, Pacific Islander, Maoris, Native Americans, Hispanic, Pima);
obesity (BMI greater than 27 kg/m^2) / diets high in fat / sugar (2 max)
Symptoms:
high blood glucose;
frequent urination / thirst / tiredness;
glucose present in urine (2 max)
(total 4 marks)

5 a 1977 / 1978 / 1979 (1)
b as condensed milk importation decreases (and stops in 1987), fresh product importation increases / inversely proportional (1)
c fresh milk (1)
d better refrigeration;
better forms of transportation;
changes in consumer preference;
insufficient national production;
greater consumption / demand / population growth (2 max)

e *Any two of the following for 1 mark.*
proteins / amino acids;
carbohydrates / sugars;
calcium;
lipids;
vitamin D / vitamins (1 max)
(total 6 marks)
© IB Organisation 2009

6 a coarse normal-gluten flour (1)
b the point showing the highest increase is the same / similar in both types of bread;
the point showing the greatest lowering came from the normal;
the mean shows fine high-gluten flour lowers lipids more than fine normal-gluten flour;
fine normal-gluten flour has a greater spread of values (2 max)
c cardiovascular disease can be caused by a high blood lipid level;
bread made with high-gluten flour lowered the lipid level most;
difference in lipid level is small for change in particle size / coarse and fine particles;
the hypothesis is supported by the data;
the wide spread of data may mean there is no significance and the hypothesis is not supported (3 max)
d helps peristalsis / prevents cancer / prevents obesity / prevents constipation (1)
Do not accept 'removes waste'.
(total 7 marks)
© IB Organisation 2009

7 a increased fibre intake reduces colon cancer mortality / negative correlation (1)
b i 17.3 (±0.1) deaths per 100 000 population (*units required*) (1)
ii increase of 91.0 (±5.0) g starch per day;
increase from 133 to 222 (±5.0) g starch per day;
other correct numerical example (1 max)
c fibre affects the mortality rate more than starch affects the incidence rate;
both reduce the incidence of colon cancer;
(cannot compare) as one displays incidence and the other mortality / mortality and incidence are not the same thing (2 max)
d increase in fibre intake does lower mortality;
effect may not just be caused by starch / high fibre intake;
high fibre intake usually associated with high cereal / vegetable / fruit diet;
data does not show geographical distribution / ethnic influence / gender / age;
genetic factors not taken into account (2 max)
(total 7 marks)
© IB Organisation 2009

Option B

1 cells joined with no dividing membranes;
plasma membrane called sarcolemma;
multinucleate cytoplasm;
large numbers of mitochondria;
sarcoplasmic reticulum;
bundles of protein filaments / myofibrils;
myofibrils made of actin and myosin produce banding
pattern / have light and dark bands   (5 max)

2 sarcolemma / plasma membrane depolarised (by nerve
impulse);
sarcoplasmic reticulum releases calcium ions;
calcium ions bind to thin / actin filament;
(myosin) binding sites exposed;
myosin head binds / cross-bridge forms;
head bends and pulls thin / actin filament;
sarcomere shortens / distance between Z lines shortens;
ATP binds to myosin head;
this breaks cross-bridge;
head swings back to start position   (6 max)

3 greater muscle activity / increase in respiration requires
more oxygen and glucose;
greater muscle activity / increase in respiration produces
more carbon dioxide;
tidal volume is air breathed in / out with each breath;
ventilation rate is number of breaths per minute;
increase in both is required to maintain high / steep
concentration gradients between blood and air in alveoli
for both oxygen and carbon dioxide;
high / steep concentration gradient maintains high
concentration of oxygen and low concentration of
carbon dioxide in blood   (4 max)

4 fall in blood pH (due to carbon dioxide from muscle
respiration);
detected by chemoreceptors in carotid arteries / aorta /
carotid bodies / aortic bodies / brain;
impulses sent to sinoatrial node / pacemaker;
increase in cardiac output;   (3 max for any 3)
muscle contractions squeeze veins;
increase in venous return to heart;   (1 max for final 2)
                    (total 4 marks)

5 *Must have arguments for and against for full marks.*
EPO is produced naturally by the body to stimulate
formation of red blood cells;
using EPO will increase red cell count;
more oxygen supplied to muscles could improve
performance;
especially useful for endurance events;
blood is thickened which can cause blood clot / strain
on heart;
increased risk of heart attack / stroke;
increased risk of dehydration in endurance events   (4 max)

6 ATP produced from aerobic respiration *and* anaerobic respiration
and from creatine phosphate;
creatine phosphate used for brief period / few seconds
of intense activity – e.g. 100 m sprint / similar;
anaerobic respiration used for short period / seconds to 2
minutes of intense activity – e.g. 200 m sprint / similar;
aerobic respiration used for extended period / several
minutes to hours of low level activity – e.g. long run /
cross country run / marathon / aerobic exercises   (2 max)

7 anaerobic respiration in muscle produces lactate;
lactate transferred to liver via blood;
liver converts lactate back to pyruvate;
pyruvate oxidised to carbon dioxide and water / enters
Krebs cycle;
oxygen is required;
deep breathing continues (for short time) after exercise
has ended to supply oxygen to repay debt   (4 max)

8

Fast	Slow
usually anaerobic	always aerobic
fast contraction rate	slow contraction rate
low blood supply	good blood supply
little myoglobin / white	lots of myoglobin / red
few mitochondria	many mitochondria
small glycogen store	large glycogen store
low stamina / tire quickly	high stamina / slow to tire
high strength / produce high force	low strength / produce low force

                    (5 max)

9 *Answer must include all three types of injury to gain full marks.*

Sprain	Tear	Dislocation
• damage to ligament(s) due to unusual movement of joint / movement of joint beyond normal range • small / mild tear of ligament • swelling / pain / tenderness • soft tissue damage	• damage to ligament(s) or muscle(s) due to unusual movement of joint / movement of joint beyond normal range • damage where tendon joins bone • damage greater than sprain / tear more severe • swelling / pain / tenderness • joint unstable • may take long time to heal	• bones at joint become displaced due to unusual movement of joint / movement of joint beyond normal range • damages ligaments and tendons • swelling / pain / tenderness

                    (5 max)

10 a $335 (\pm 5)$ W (*units required*) $\hspace{1cm}$ (1)

b as velocity increases power increases / positive correlation $\hspace{0.5cm}$ (1)

c both have same / similar maximum power;
both show increased power at greater velocities;
power tends to be higher at each velocity for V_{70};
there is a greater range of powers at V_{70} between 2.0
to 2.5 m s^{-1} $\hspace{1cm}$ (2 max)

d risk of heart attack / heart failure from strenuous
exercise $\hspace{1cm}$ (1)

$\hspace{4cm}$ (total 5 marks)

$\hspace{3cm}$ © IB Organisation 2009

11 a directly proportional / positive correlation / more
exercise leads to higher cardiac output $\hspace{1cm}$ (1)

b i 82.5 (± 3)% $\hspace{1cm}$ (1)

$\hspace{0.5cm}$ **ii** 5.25 / 5.3 (*units not needed*) $\hspace{1cm}$ (1)

c cardiac output to muscles / overall cardiac output increases
more in top athletes / with training;
training / top athlete decreases cardiac output to rest
of body;
training increases oxygen consumption in muscle /
overall oxygen consumption during heavy exercise;
training does not change oxygen consumption by rest
of body during heavy exercise;
training causes changes by increasing stroke volume /
lung capacity $\hspace{1cm}$ (3 max)

$\hspace{4cm}$ (total 6 marks)

$\hspace{3cm}$ © IB Organisation 2009

Option C

1 two or more polypeptides held together to form a single
protein;
same bonding as for tertiary structure;
two types of bond named – disulfide bridges / ionic /
hydrogen;
addition of a non-polypeptide structure / prosthetic group;
to form conjugated protein;
named example of quaternary structure e.g. hemoglobin
(has four polypeptides) $\hspace{1cm}$ (3 max)

2 more chlorophyll / photosynthetic pigments / photosystems; $\hspace{0.2cm}$ (1)
more light absorbed $\hspace{1cm}$ (1)

3 RuBP carboxylase catalyses addition of carbon dioxide
to RuBP;
carbon fixation;
start of / first step of the Calvin cycle;
Calvin cycle produces TP / glucose $\hspace{1cm}$ (2 max)

4 competitive inhibitors are similar to substrate molecules, and
non-competitive inhibitors are not;
competitive inhibitor attaches to the active site, non-competitive
inhibitor does not bind to the active site;
non-competitive inhibitor changes enzyme shape, competitive
inhibitor does not;
effect of competitive inhibitor is reversible $\hspace{1cm}$ (2 max)

5 fibrous proteins have a long and narrow shape, globular
proteins have rounded shape;
fibrous proteins are mostly insoluble in water, globular
proteins are soluble in water;
fibrous is mainly secondary structure, globular at least
tertiary structure;
Examples include:
collagen / actin / silk / keratin / other fibrous protein;
hemoglobin / myoglobin / any named enzyme /
other globular protein $\hspace{1cm}$ (3 max)

6 polar amino acids are hydrophilic / 'water loving';
polar amino acids form hydrophilic channels in channel proteins;
allow hydrophilic / polar / charged particle substances to pass
through the membrane;
control location of protein / hold the protein in the membrane;
polar amino acids on the surface of proteins make them
water soluble $\hspace{1cm}$ (2 max)
*Accept any of the above points if clearly explained using a
suitable diagram.*

7 electrons flow through proteins / electron transfer chain in
thylakoid membrane;
electron flow causes protons to be pumped into the
thylakoid space;
ATP synthase / synthetase located in the thylakoid
membrane / next to electron transfer chain;
protons move from the thylakoid to the stroma through
ATP synthase / synthetase;
down the concentration gradient;
ATP synthesised from ADP + P_i $\hspace{1cm}$ (4 max)

8 rate of photosynthesis rises as CO_2 concentration rises;
up to a maximum when rate levels off / labelled graph
showing outline of relationship;
when line levels off other factors become limiting;
CO_2 concentration in atmosphere is low;
CO_2 uptake reduced when stomata close to prevent
water loss $\hspace{1cm}$ (3 max)

9 a directly proportional / greater concentration, greater
rate of reaction;
at high concentrations the increase is smaller / plateaus /
levels off (at approximately 70 mmol dm^{-3}) $\hspace{0.5cm}$ (2)

b i 1 mmol dm^{-3}: 0.70 (± 0.02);
3 mmol dm^{-3}: 0.55 (± 0.02); $\hspace{1cm}$ (1)
Both needed for 1 mark. For 1 mmol dm^{-3} accept 0.7.

$\hspace{0.5cm}$ **ii** lower reaction rate at inhibitor concentration of
3 mmol dm^{-3} / the greater the inhibitor
concentration the slower the rate of reaction;
trend / overall shape are the same / increases but
then levels off;
but lower at greater concentration of inhibitor $\hspace{0.3cm}$ (1 max)

c substrate and inhibitor (structurally) similar;
inhibitor binds to active site;
prevents substrate from binding;
activity of enzyme prevented;

named example (e.g. disulfiram inhibits aldehyde dehydrogenase as it is similar to acetaldehyde, or malonate inhibits succinate dehydrogenase as it is similar to succinate)

(3 max)

(total 7 marks)

© IB Organisation 2009

10 a i 27 (±1) (1)

ii 90 (±1) (1)

b as the concentration of magnesium chloride increases the rate increases;

most rapid increase occurs between 1 and 2 mmol dm^{-3};

peaks at 4 mmol dm^{-3};

until it plateaus (at 5 mmol dm^{-3}) / no more increase / drops slightly (2 max)

c 1:4 (1)

d i membrane bound is 10 times more efficient (12 000 to 1200);

difference is (12 618 − 1215) 11 403 arbitrary units greater in membrane bound;

about 1000% greater / 938.5% greater (1 max)

ii purification could have affected structure of protein;

binding to membrane allows interactions / other molecules in membrane may help it / be acting as coenzymes (1 max)

(total 7 marks)

© IB Organisation 2009

11 a light–dark (1)

b $\left(\dfrac{1.0}{0.5} \times 100\right) = 200\%$ (1)

c dark has least of both pigments;

light has most β-carotene;

light–dark has most chlorophyll;

most total pigment in light;

light–dark is the only condition where more chlorophyll is made than β-carotene (2 max)

d pigments absorb light for photosynthesis / absorption spectrum;

more light absorbed more photosynthesis / action spectrum;

different pigments absorb different wavelengths of light;

can photosynthesise in different environmental conditions (3 max)

(total 7 marks)

© IB Organisation 2009

Option D

1 there is no mutation;

there is no natural selection;

the population is large;

all members of the population breed;

mating is random;

each mating produces the same number of offspring;

there is no immigration or emigration (3 max)

2 a $q^2 = \dfrac{1}{3600} = 0.000\,28$

frequency of the recessive allele $= q = 0.017$ (1)

b frequency of the normal allele $p = 1 - q = 0.983$ (1)

c $q^2 = \dfrac{1}{275\,000} = 0.000\,003\,6$

$q = 0.0019$

In the Jewish population the allele frequency is $\dfrac{0.017}{0.0019} = 8.9$

times more frequent than in the European population. (1)

(total 3 marks)

3 a total population is 1000, so $q^2 = \dfrac{360}{1000} = 0.36$

$q = 0.6$

frequency of the dominant allele $p = 0.4$ (1)

b the heterozygous mice are $2pq = 2 \times 0.4 \times 0.6 = 0.48$

In the population of 640 white mice 480 are heterozygous. (1)

(total 2 marks)

4 a $q^2 = \dfrac{1}{25\,000} = 0.0004$

frequency of the cystic fibrosis allele $= q = 0.02$ (1)

b Carriers are heterozygous.

frequency $= 2pq = 2 \times 0.98 \times 0.02 = 0.0392$

In a population of 10 000 there will be 392 carriers. (1)

(total 2 marks)

5 analogous structures are brought about by convergent evolution;

a cladogram is based on evolutionary / genetic relationships (2)

6 particular molecules carry out same function;

related organisms will have similar structures for particular molecules;

mutations / changes in the molecular structure occur at a particular rate;

the number of differences can be used to indicate the evolutionary distance;

amino acid sequence of cytochrome c / hemoglobin / other named protein;

base sequence of DNA / mitochondrial DNA / mtDNA;

DNA molecules can be compared using (DNA) hybridisation;

DNA is a better indicator than protein as it accumulates more mutations;

mutations occur in introns / some mutations do not cause an amino acid change;

changes / mutations do not always occur at same rate;

several different molecules can be analysed and the number of changes compared (6 max)

7 a *Award 1 mark for the comparison of both groups.*

The *Polypodium* (species) are (completely) isolated in different parts of the continent *and* the *Pleopeltis* (species) are much closer together / physically overlapping / share same habitats;

Polypodium grows in more northerly / temperate locations. (1 max)

b **i** *Polypodium* as it has lower similarity / genetic identity values / *Pleopeltis* has higher similarity / genetic identity values *(reason required to achieve 1 mark)* (1)

  ii *Pl. polylepis* and *Pl. conzattii* (1)

c geographic / ecological isolation / isolated by distance / by glacial periods / climatic changes;
reproductive or genetic separation of gene pools (led to speciation) / adaptive radiation (1 max)

d *Award 1 mark for 'Polypodium' and 1 mark for a reason.*
Polypodium (1)
more genetic difference between all three species of *Polypodium* than between the species of *Pleopeltis*;
takes time to accumulate mutations / genetic changes;
distance may have facilitated the process of reproduction isolation (1 max)
(total 6 marks)
© IB Organisation 2009

8 a lemurs / lorises (1)

b Old World monkeys closer to great apes / New World monkeys closer to lemurs / lorises;
overlap / coincide at some point (1 for these 2 points)
wider range in New World monkey cerebrotypes than in Old World monkeys (1)

c coincides with DNA tree / different to morphology;
because of exact match;
shows that *Pan* / chimp and *Homo* / human are close;
gorilla less close;
orangutan / *Pongo* further away (2 max)

d carbon dating / ^{14}C dating / ^{40}K dating;
measure the amount of isotope relative to original amount / less of the original isotope present the older the fossil / age can be calculated by knowing the half life of the isotope (2)
(total 7 marks)
© IB Organisation 2009

9 a cytochrome c (1)

b hemoglobin β-chain : fibrinopeptides = 2.8 ($\pm$0.2)% : 12.3 ($\pm$0.2)% / fibrinopeptides have (about) four times more substitutions / (about) 10% more in fibrinopeptides (1)

c sheep because fewer differences in base substitutions (1)

d mutations occur randomly;
amino acid sequences change;
differences accumulate gradually over a long time;
the differences accumulate at a (roughly) constant rate;
can be used as an evolutionary clock (2 max)
(total 5 marks)
© IB Organisation 2009

10 a some families have become extinct (1)

b Lipotidae (1)

c (mitochondrial) DNA;
amino acid sequences / proteins (1 max)

d river dolphins did not evolve from the same ancestor;
river dolphins evolved in similar environments;
river dolphins were exposed to the same selection pressures;
river dolphins adapted in the same ways;
river dolphins show convergent evolution (3 max)

e radioisotopes in the rocks where the fossils are found / in fossils;
(absolute) dates are obtained by radioisotopic dating of rocks where fossil toothed whales are found;
comparisons of molecular sequences / DNA / proteins;
(absolute) dates can be estimated from differences due to mutations in living toothed whales / molecular sequences;
position of fossils in the rocks;
(relative) dates may be obtained by comparing the positions of the fossil toothed whales relative to one another (2 max)
(total 8 marks)
© IB Organisation 2009

11 a *Carettochelys* (1)

b both have a common ancestor / common ancestor in the cretaceous / ancestral line evolved in the Jurassic;
Chelonia has three divergence points from ancestor whereas *Graptemys* has five;
Graptemys has more recently diverged than *Chelonia* / *Graptemys* evolved later than *Chelonia* (2 max)

c *Graptemys* and *Trachemys*;
(as) these separated most recently;
Graptemys and *Trachemy* are closely related to *Emys* / *Mauremys* and *Heosemys* are also closely related but diverged further back in time;
lack of fossil evidence to show that other pairs could be more closely related;
reliability of molecular dates could be questioned / reliability of fossil dates could be questioned (3 max)
(total 6 marks)
© IB Organisation 2009

12 The differences are in red.

guinea pig	gdvekgkkif vqkcaqchtv ekggkhktgp nlhglfgrkt gqaagfsytd anknkgitwg edtlmeylen pkkyipgtkm ifagikkkge radliaylkk atne
grey whale	gdvekgkkif vqkcaqchtv ekggkhktgp nlhglfgrkt gqavgfsytd anknkgitwg eetlmeylen pkkyipgtkm ifagikkkge radliaylkk atne
duck	gdvekgkkif vqkcsqchtv ekggkhktgp nlhglfgrkt gqaegfsytd anknkgitwg edtlmeylen pkkyipgtkm ifagikkkse radliaylkd atae
alligator	gdvekgkkif vqkcaqchtv ekggkhktgp nlhgligrkt gqapgfsytd anknkgitwg eetlmeylen pkkyipgtkm ifagikkkpe radliaylke atse
bullfrog	gdvekgkkif vqkcaqchtc ekggkhkvgp nlygligrkt gqaagfsytd anknkgitwg edtlmeylen pkkyipgtkm ifagikkkge rqdliaylks acse

	Guinea pig	Grey whale	Duck	Alligator
Guinea pig				
Grey whale	2			
Duck	5	6		
Alligator	6	5	7	
Bullfrog	7	9	10	8

Table is rearranged so that number of differences decreases from left to right.

	Bullfrog	Duck	Alligator	Grey whale
Bullfrog				
Duck	10			
Alligator	8	7		
Grey whale	9	6	5	
Guinea pig	7	5	6	2

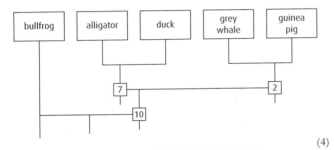

(4)

	Number of differences
bullfrog – duck	10
bullfrog – alligator	8
bullfrog – grey whale	9
bullfrog – guinea pig	7
duck – alligator	7
duck – grey whale	6
duck – guinea pig	5
alligator – grey whale	5
alligator – guinea pig	6
guinea pig – grey whale	2

(4)

(total 8 marks)

Option E

1 pain receptor detects stimulus;
sensory neuron relays impulse to CNS / spinal cord;
relay neuron connects impulse to motor neuron;
motor neuron relays impulse to effector / muscle;
effector / muscle responds by contracting to move away
from pain (3 max)
Credit annotated diagrams.

2 information from the left and right visual fields crosses over
in the brain at the optic chiasma;
the right brain / visual cortex processes information from
the left visual field / or converse (2)

3 cilia on hair cells vary in length;
each resonates to a different frequency of sound;
complex sounds are resolved into their components;
inner hair cells send messages to the brain / outer hair cells
receive signals from the brain (3 max)

4 *Innate behaviour:*
develops independently of the environmental context;
cannot be altered (1 max)
Learned behaviour:
develops as a result of experience;
can be modified (1 max)
Must have at least one from each for full marks.
(total 2 marks)

5 taxis is a directional response towards or away from a stimulus;
kinesis involves random non–directional movement / change
in rate of movement in response to a stimulus (2)

6 learning allows an animal to remember location of food
sources;
recognise predators / toxic food;
find a mate / breed successfully;
gain a competitive advantage;
learning also allows social organisation, improving individuals'
chances of survival;
leads to more efficient energy use (3 max)

7 Pavlov fed dogs and at same time rang bell / made sound;
unconditioned stimulus is food / sight or smell of food
caused salivation;
unconditioned response is salivation;
sound / ringing of bell given on own caused salivation;
conditioned stimulus caused conditioned response;
repeated association of two stimuli (food and sound) lead to a
type of learning (conditioning) (3 max)

8 pre-synaptic neuron releases neurotransmitter;
neurotransmitter binds to the post-synaptic membrane;
causes hyperpolarisation (of post-synaptic membrane) /
negatively charged chloride (Cl^-) ions move in /
potassium (K^+) ions move out;
making it more difficult to cause depolarisation (of
post-synaptic neuron) / nerve impulse transmission /
action potential (2 max)

9 increase sense of intensity of perceived sensory data / sense
of emotional well-being / concentration reduced / impaired
judgment of time and space (2)

10 addiction is dependence on a substance (such as alcohol
or other drugs) or an activity;
stopping is very difficult and causes severe physical / mental
reactions / complex behaviour;
predisposition may be determined by polygenic inheritance;
significant role of environmental factors;
dopamine released in response to reward / e.g. food;

some drugs / heroin / cocaine enhance dopamine activity;
abuse of drugs hypothesised to lead to down-regulation of
dopamine receptors;
requires increasing amounts of drug to achieve same effect
(4 max)

11 *Hypothalamus*:
maintains homeostasis;
coordinates nervous and endocrine systems;
secretes hormones for release by posterior pituitary;
secretes releasing factors into bloodstream that control
anterior pituitary (3 max)
Pituitary gland:
posterior lobe stores and releases hormones from
hypothalamus;
anterior lobe synthesises and releases hormones under
control from hypothalamus (1 max)
(total 4 marks)

12 heart rate is controlled by the autonomic nervous system (NS);
autonomic NS is composed of parasympathetic NS and
sympathetic NS;
sympathetic NS prepares body for threat / excitement
and the parasympathetic returns it to normal;
the systems are antagonistic;
acetylcholine is a neurotransmitter for parasympathetic NS;
noradrenaline / norepinephrine is a neurotransmitter for
sympathetic NS (3 max)
sympathetic system accelerates the heart rate and stimulates
glucose release (from the liver);
more blood is pumped to the muscles;
parasympathetic system slows down heart rate and stimulates
the stomach and the intestines;
body relaxes and blood flow slows down (3 max)
(total 6 marks)

13 pupil reflex is cranial reflex / ANS reflex;
shine light in eye to see if pupil constricts;
controlled by the medulla (oblongata);
absence of pupil reflex means medulla unlikely to be
functioning;
medulla controls breathing and heart activity / cannot
maintain life-sustaining activity;
person is most likely brain dead;
some drugs (barbiturates) / nerve damage may interfere with
pupil reflex (4 max)

14 bees live / interact together in a group;
arranged into castes;
each caste is specialised for a particular task that helps the
group as a whole;
castes – queen *and* males *and* sterile workers;
two examples of caste activity – building comb / locating
food / protecting hive / reproduction; (3 max)

15 a i between 110° and 120° (*units required*) (1)
      ii between 270° and 360° / upper left hand quadrant (1)
   b i 20 ms (*units required*) (1)
      ii between 2 (±1) and 56 (±1) ms (*units required*) (1)

iii e.g. different sensitivity of antennae / genetic variation
     in the species / variation in the intensity of the tap on
     the antenna / variation in the position of the tap on
     the antenna (1)
c left antenna, because approximately 110° turn only / the
   left antenna because it moves to the right (1)
d avoids danger by moving in the opposite direction to
   stimulus;
   still sees source of danger / stimulus;
   moves away at an angle of 110 / 120°;
   behaviour results in better survival rate (2 max)
(total 8 marks)
© IB Organisation 2009

16 a i 75% (±3%) (1)
      ii 25% (±3%) (1)
   b intact spiders return to housefly location while damaged
      spiders walk in different directions / no defined direction;
      only a few were very close to housefly location in damaged
      spiders / approx 25% were within 30°;
      while most intact spiders reached housefly location /
      approx 75% were 30° from housefly location (2 max)
      Accept any other comparative value.
   c innate **and** learned behaviour / both;
      Innate behaviour:
      is controlled by genes / inherited / occurs despite variation
      of environment
      spiders' ability to navigate this way is innate / could not see
      but still went back
      innate because they searched for the fly;
      innate as nearly all show responses
      Learned behaviour:
      arises from experiences during development / not inherited;
      spiders' ability to walk back is learned / without slit sense
      organs they cannot find housefly (3 max)
(total 7 marks)
© IB Organisation 2009

17 a positive correlation / directly proportional (1)
   b any value between 413 nm and 428 nm (*units must be given*) (1)
   c the percentage correct choices at 322 nm is greater than
      494 nm (1)
      *Accept any answer where the 322 nm value is higher than the
      494 nm value, even if the values given are not correct.*
   d repeat experiment after a period of time / with longer
      time between trials;
      if number of correct choices falls, information is not
      stored in long-term memory / if number of correct choices
      remains high, information is stored in long-term memory;
      if number of correct choices remains the same, repeat with
      even longer time interval (2 max)
(total 5 marks)

a 25 (±1) (1)

   b song sparrow song always longer than that of swamp sparrow;
isolation increases song sparrow song length but decreases
swamp sparrow song length (2)
Answers may be numerical.

   c innate behaviour occurs in all members of a species /
determined genetically / inherited / stereotyped behaviour /
not learned / instinctive (1)

   d innate characteristics would be the same (or nearly the
same) in normal and isolated birds;
notes per song / number of songs are very different, so
probably not innate;
number of syllables / song length similar / not so different,
so possibly innate;
hypothesis not supported for all song characteristics (3 max)
(total 7 marks)
© IB Organisation 2009

Option F

1 soya beans are soaked and boiled;
they are crushed with wheat;
a culture of *Aspergillus* sp. is added and the mixture is
incubated for several days;
at 30 °C;
salt and water are added and the mixture is fermented for
3–6 months;
finally the mixture is filtered, pasteurised and bottled (4 max)

2 Germ line therapy involves changing genes in a person's gamete
so that changes affect their offspring;
somatic therapy involves changes to targeted genes in one
person's body and only affects the person who is treated. (2)

3 **a** In the absence of OEO, the potassium concentration
outside the cell slowly decreased (by about 0.75 ppm)
over the course of the experiment;
when OEO was present, the potassium concentration
outside the cell increased (by approximately 0.9 ppm). (2)

   b In the presence of OEO both potassium and phosphate
ions are lost from the cell;
this disrupts the osmotic balance of the cell and will kill it. (2)

   c via gated channels that are blocked or disrupted by OEO (2)

   d The permeability of the cell membrane is affected so that
EB is able to enter the bacterial cell, indicating that the
cells are not healthy. (1)

   e Thymol and carvacrol are tasteless so do not affect the flavour
of food.
Cell membranes of bacteria are damaged so cells are
unlikely to survive.
Thymol and carvacrol affect both species of bacteria tested.
Any two points for full marks. (2 max)
(total 9 marks)
© IB Organisation 2009

4 **a** Biological control does not leave toxic chemicals in the
environment. / As control is achieved, the numbers of the
controlling agent fall. (1)

   b KTU-60 (1)

   c KTU-36; because it caused most deaths of larvae /
was found growing on the greatest number of larvae (2)

   d 18 (1)

   e treated in identical manner except dipped in a solution
that did not contain fungal spores (1)
(total 6 marks)
© IB Organisation 2009

Option G

1 *Maximum 3 marks for only one factor.*
1 mark for any correct named example.
Temperature:
animals can move to avoid extremes of temperature;
ectotherms limited by extremes;
endotherms more widespread as can maintain body temperature
independent of environmental temperature;
many animals hibernate to avoid cold periods;
Water:
required for survival;
obtained by drinking and with food;
some animals can survive on water from respiration / metabolic
water;
distribution of animal determined by availability of water;
some species seasonally migrate to maintain supply;
Breeding sites:
required for reproduction;
protection from predators;
source of food for young;
Food supply:
required for survival;
distribution determined by availability;
animals with varied diets can be more widespread;
animals with specialist diets restricted by distribution of specific
food;
Territory:
territory provides place to obtain food and water;
territory provides place to breed;
some animals need only a small area, others very large areas;
some animals / groups of animals defend their territory;
stronger animals / groups have larger territories (4 max)

2 quadrat positioned randomly;
using pairs of random numbers as coordinates / dividing
area into numbered grid squares and using random number
to select square;
number of a particular species within the square is counted;
5% of total area sampled;
number of that species in total area calculated by total
number counted in 5% sample × 20 / or equivalent
calculation (4 max)

3 **a** niche is unique to a species;
provides exact conditions the species is adapted to;
place where species lives *and* feeds *and* reproduces;

fundamental niche is potential niche that the species can occupy;

realised niche is the actual niche it occupies;

realised niche may be smaller than fundamental niche due to human interference / predators / disease / competition / other factor   (4 max)

4 *Competition*:

two (or more) species requiring the same resource;

the stronger one will out-compete the weaker one / weaker one has less of the resource (or vice versa);

named example   (2 max)

Parasitism:

one organism / parasite feeds in / on another organism / host;

only parasite benefits / host harmed;

parasite depends on / cannot survive without host;

named example   (2 max)

(total 4 marks)

5 *Must contain at least two examples for full marks.*

in a simple food chain organisms fit into their trophic level;

most plants are producers / a few plants are parasites / carnivorous;

e.g. dodder / yellow rattle / other parasitic plant / named carnivorous plant;

many consumers fit into two or more trophic levels depending on what they are consuming;

e.g. named herbivore may eat snails / similar when grazing, therefore is secondary consumer;

e.g. named carnivore may eat named herbivore as well as named carnivore so can be secondary or tertiary consumer;

organisms are classified on main food source   (4 max)

6 simple plants grow in new environment;

organic matter accumulates as they die;

organic matter broken down by decomposers to recycle nutrients;

larger plants can grow;

more soil trapped by plant roots;

aeration of soil improved as plant roots die and decay;

organic matter traps moisture;

erosion reduced by plant cover   (4 max)

7 *Two examples required to gain full marks.*

Economic:

many species still to be discovered;

species can be sources of useful genes / medicines / new foods / timber;

valuable for eco-tourism

Ecological:

significant effects on climate;

transpiration results in rainfall;

absorbs CO_2, which reduces greenhouse effect;

stores carbon as wood / cellulose / lignin;

reduces soil erosion / reduces flooding / reduces silting of rivers;

reduces albedo effect / reduces reflected heat

Ethical:

home to indigenous peoples;

indigenous people have vast knowledge of the medicinal uses of plants;

do humans have the right to destroy organisms which are then lost for future generations?

Aesthetic:

the rich variety of organisms is a source of wonder and beauty;

source of inspiration for art, music and writing;

once destroyed, cannot be replaced   (4 max)

8 biomagnification is process by which chemicals accumulate in food chains;

chemical is persistent / does not break down in environment / non-biodegradable;

chemicals are often pesticides;

e.g. organochlorines / DDT / DDD / dieldrin / other named example;

at concentration used, chemical is toxic to target organism / non-toxic to higher consumers;

becomes more concentrated at each trophic level;

stored in fat tissue;

becomes toxic to higher organisms due to magnification of concentration;

e.g. top carnivores such as birds of prey, herons are affected;

egg shells become thin and easily broken / chemical released during winter when fat stores used   (5 max)

9 some species can be very sensitive to their environment;

these are called indicator species;

different species have different pollution-tolerance values;

can be used to measure level of pollution / other named abiotic factor;

organisms classified according to their tolerance of pollutant / abiotic factor;

measuring change in number of indicator species indicates level of pollution;

lichens / water invertebrates / other named example   (5 max)

10 protection of species in their natural habitat;

species does not have to adapt to human-made / new habitat;

helps to maintain / does not disrupt natural ecosystem;

larger numbers in natural habitat help conserve genetic diversity

(3 max)

11 K-strategy is pattern adopted by animals and plants that produce few offspring, take longer to reach maturity, and reproduce several times during adult life;

K-strategy is favoured if environment is stable / less likelihood of sudden death;

allows organisms to spend longer time to accumulate resources / reach maturity;

fewer offspring per breeding cycle but can have several breeding cycles;

some organisms can switch to r-strategy if environmental conditions change   (3 max)

12 maximum sustainable yield is the largest proportion of fish that can be caught without endangering the population;
if fish numbers are high, could mean high MSY / or converse;
but remaining fish may be too young to breed;
continued harvesting may cause population to crash;
need to maintain breeding population;
uncertainties over calculating MSY / size of breeding population (3 max)

13 a *Must include statements of both mass and height for full marks.*
in mass there is an inverse relationship with density;
in height there is an inverse relationship with density;
at low *Populus* density, the mass is high / maximum / about 155 g
mass decreases from 160 g to 40 g;
at low *Populus* density, the height is maximum / high / 19 cm;
height decreases from 19 cm to 10 cm (3 max)
  b *Tamarix* density has very small / no effect on *Populus* height at any density / high or low density (1)
  c better underground / root growth;
to compete for water;
competition for minerals / nutrients;
greater resistance to drought / protection against dehydration / lower water needs;
resistance to higher salinity / changes in pH (2 max)
(total 6 marks)
© IB Organisation 2009

14 a primary consumer (trophic level 2) (1)
  b June to August 1994 (±1 month)
May to June 1993 (±1 month) (1 max)
  c there is a rise in the population starting every (Antarctic) summer;
every year numbers remain low from March until November / from fall / autumn until the beginning of summer;
no data available for spring 1994;
increase in numbers coincides with increase in sea temperature
decrease in numbers during fall / autumn (2 max)
  d i lowest sea water temperature is associated with highest numbers of larvae;
larvae numbers increase when temperature drops below −1.5 °C;
no larvae at temperatures above −1.5 °C;
bigger increase in numbers during July / September 1993 than in July / September 1994 although temperatures the same (2 max)
    ii global warming causes rise in sea water temperature;
lower numbers of larvae;
because larvae only present at sea water temperature below −1 °C (2 max)
(total 8 marks)
© IB Organisation 2009

15 a three (1)
  b grazing (1)
  c pollution affects more wilderness zones than climate change;
climate change affects more biomes (5) than pollution;
tropical humid forests affected by climate change but not pollution;
both affect temperate forests / wetlands / deserts / tundra;
pollution effect on deserts / wetlands greater than that of climate change;
climate change effect on tundra greater than that of pollution (3 max)
  d biodiversity is reduced due to destruction of habitats / food / breeding grounds / killing species (1)
(total 6 marks)
© IB Organisation 2009

16 a 2300 m to 3000 m (*units required*) (1)
  b any value between 2700 m and 2800 m / or 1200 m (*units required*) (1)
  c *Bolitoglossa* greater distribution, *Oedipina* less distributed;
both *Bolitoglossa* and *Oedipina* found between 1050 m and 1200 m;
between 1200 m and 1250 m only *Oedipina* is found;
Bolitoglossa is found at low and high altitudes (except between 1400 m and 1800 m), *Oedipina* is not (2 max)
  d altitude may be a determining factor in the distribution of different genera of salamanders / each genus appears to have different, preferred altitudes;
at the species level, each species (of a same genus) has a different altitude range in which it lives / not all salamanders (of same species) live at same altitude;
no two species can occupy the same niche / competitive exclusion principle;
B. striatula and *B. colonnea* share the same altitudes;
species may have different breeding sites / feeding habits / interactions with organisms (although at same altitude) (3 max)
(total 7 marks)
© IB Organisation 2009

Option H

1 osmoreceptors in hypothalamus detect increase in blood / plasma concentration / solute concentration of blood / plasma;
due to low fluid intake / fluid loss e.g. by sweating;
ADH secreted by neurosecretory cells of hypothalamus;
stored in posterior pituitary lobe;
released into blood (from posterior pituitary) when osmoreceptors stimulated;
ADH travels in blood to kidney (tubules) / nephrons;
causes collecting ducts to be made more permeable to water;
water absorbed into blood from filtrate / urine (by osmosis);
blood concentration decreases and osmoreceptors not stimulated;
ADH release stops;

ADH removed from blood by liver;

control mechanism is negative feedback / return to normal after deviation / equivalent explanation of negative feedback (5 max)

2

Protein hormones	Steroid hormones
do not enter cells / do not pass through plasma membrane	pass through plasma membrane
bind to receptors on the outside of the plasma membrane	form complex with receptors in cytoplasm
cause release of a secondary messenger inside the cell	regulate transcription of one or more genes

(2 max)

3 pepsin digests proteins;

pepsin could digest cells that secrete it;

pepsinogen is the inactive form of pepsin;

pepsinogen is activated by hydrochloric acid / HCl /

pepsinogen is converted into pepsin (active form) by HCl;

different cells in the stomach wall secrete pepsinogen and HCl (3 max)

4 inside of the alimentary canal is an aqueous environment;

lipids are hydrophobic / not soluble in water;

bile is secreted by the liver;

bile emulsifies / breaks up lipid droplets;

this increases surface area of lipid droplets for lipase to act on;

lipase (from pancreas) digests / hydrolyses lipids;

pancreatic juices are alkaline / pH 8 (approximately);

lipase works at pH 8 / optimum pH (3 max)

5 a plasma membrane of ileum (epithelial) cell pumps / uses active transport to move sodium ions from cytoplasm to (gut) lumen;

creates (sodium ion) concentration gradient between lumen and cell cytoplasm;

sodium ions diffuse back into cell along with nutrients;

facilitated diffusion / co-transport;

example of nutrient: glucose, amino acids (3 max)

b *Answer must link structure to function.*

surface area of lumen plasma membrane increased by microvilli;

facilitated diffusion (protein) channels to absorb digested molecules;

pinocytotic vesicles at base of microvilli take in fluid / solution from lumen

many mitochondria provide ATP / energy for active transport;

large amount of rER and Golgi apparatus for enzyme synthesis / secretion;

tight junctions join cells together to form barrier;

prevent intestinal juices leaking into tissue fluid (5 max)

(total 8 marks)

6 hepatic artery from aorta brings blood to liver;

hepatic portal vein from gut brings blood to the liver;

these vessels merge and branch into capillaries;

liver capillaries are called sinusoids;

sinusoids join to form hepatic vein;

hepatic vein leaves liver and joins vena cava (4 max)

7 a erythrocytes break up at end of life span / after about 120 days;

taken in to liver / Kupffer cells / hepatocytes by phagocytosis;

hepatocytes / Kupffer cells form walls of liver capillaries / sinusoids;

hemoglobin broken into globin and heme;

iron removed from heme;

remainder of heme converted to bile pigment / bilirubin;

bilirubin released into gall bladder / alimentary canal;

globin broken down / digested / hydrolysed to release amino acids (5 max)

b excess glucose stored as glycogen in liver;

iron from breakdown of red blood cells / hemoglobin;

vitamins A and D (2 max)

(total 7 marks)

8 SAN / sinoatrial node / pacemaker sends out / releases / fires electrical impulse;

when ventricle 70% / almost full;

electrical wave spreads across atria;

atrial systole;

Blood pumped / pushed into ventricles;

atrial diastole;

AVN / atrioventricular node receives electrical impulse;

AVN sends out / releases / fires electrical impulse (after brief delay);

electrical impulse passes between ventricles / down bundle of His;

electrical impulse (rapidly) spreads over ventricles in Purkinje fibres;

ventricular systole;

rise in pressure closes AV valves;

further rise in pressure opens semilunar valves;

blood pumped into arteries / aorta and pulmonary artery;

ventricular diastole;

back pressure in arteries closes semilunar valves;

pressure (difference) / lower pressure causes atrioventricular / AV valve to open;

blood drains into ventricles from atria;

heart sounds due to valves closing;

first sound is AV valves closing, second sound is semilunar valves closing (6 max)

9 a the pressure exerted by a single gas in a mixture of gases (1)

b increase in ventilation rate;

increase in number of red blood cells / erythrocytes in blood;

increase in myoglobin content of muscles;

increase in capillary networks in muscles;

increase in lung volume / vital capacity (3 max)

(total 4 marks)

10 a insulin levels at start of test were very high / $60\,\mathrm{mU\,dm^{-3}}$;
insulin levels decreased after exercise began;
insulin levels reached a minimum level at the end of the
exercise period / $5\,\mathrm{mU\,dm^{-3}}$;
insulin levels decreased most during the beginning of
the pre-load period;
insulin levels dropped and then increased at a lower rate
during pre-load period (2 max)

b overall insulin levels decreased and glucagon increased
(for both meals);
preload insulin levels decreased (for both meals) while
glucagon levels remained constant / decreased slightly
(for high fat) / decreased (for high carbohydrate);
insulin levels decreased during the incremental test while
glucagon increased;
final levels of insulin and glucagon at end of incremental
test for both meals almost equal (2 max)

c after meal glucose / fat levels increase, causing insulin
secretion;
exercise decreases blood glucose levels, causing glucagon
levels to increase;
in negative feedback, blood glucose levels that are higher /
lower than the set point cause the pancreas to secrete
insulin / glucagon (2 max)
Accept inverse statements.

(total 6 marks)

11 a $5.3\,(\pm0.3)\,\mathrm{pmol\,dm^{-3}}$ *(units needed)* (1)

b a positive correlation;
no data below $280\,\mathrm{mOsmol\,kg^{-1}}$ (1 max)

c after drinking water, blood plasma / solute concentration
decreases;
plasma ADH concentration decreases;
osmoreceptors in the hypothalamus monitor blood
solute / blood plasma / plasma concentration;
impulses passed to ADH neurosecretory cells to reduce /
limit release of ADH;
drop in ADH decreases the effect of this hormone on the
kidneys;
blood solute concentration returns to normal (2 max)

d *Award 1 mark each for any two of the following:*
vomiting / diarrhoea / blood loss;
increased salt intake;
drinking alcohol / coffee;
certain drugs / morphine / nicotine / barbiturates;
excess sweating / lack of water intake;
diabetes, as it increases glucose in blood (2 max)

(total 6 marks)

12 a as coffee consumption increases, C-peptide concentration
drops;
at all levels of coffee consumption, obese women have
higher C-peptide levels than overweight / normal
weight women;
for normal weight women, highest value of C-peptide
is at less than 1 cup of coffee per day / for obese and
overweight women the highest value is 1 cup / greatest
effect is seen when 4 or more cups are consumed (2 max)

b for all women drinking 4 or more cups of caffeinated
coffee a day, C-peptide level is lower than in those
who drink no caffeinated coffee;
the difference is greatest in obese women / smallest in
normal weight women (2)

c women should be recommended to drink 4 or more
cups of caffeinated coffee per day;
women should try to reduce their weight; (2)

(total 6 marks)

Glossary

abiotic factor   aspect of the environment that is not living – for example, humidity, temperature, salinity, wind, soil particles

absorption spectrum   the range of wavelengths of light that a pigment is able to absorb

acetyl CoA   the product of the link reaction in a mitochondrion, which enters the Krebs cycle

acetylcholine   a neurotransmitter released at some synapses in vertebrates

acinus   berry-shaped termination of an exocrine gland where its secretion is produced

acrosome   a lysosome at the tip of a sperm, containing hydrolytic enzymes that enable the sperm to penetrate the plasma membrane of a secondary oocyte

actin   globular protein that polymerises to form the thin filaments in muscle myofibrils

action potential   a rapid wave of depolarisation and repolarisation at a cell surface causing an impulse in a neuron

action spectrum   the range of wavelengths of light over which photosynthesis takes place

activation energy   the energy a substrate molecule must achieve before it can change chemically

active immunity   immunity due to the production of antibodies by an organism in response to an antigen

active site   the region on the surface of an enzyme to which the substrate binds

active transport   transport of a substance across a membrane against the concentration gradient, involving a carrier protein and energy expenditure

adaptive radiation   the evolution of diversity in a reproducing population.

adenine   one of the four nitrogenous bases found in DNA and RNA

adhesion   a force that attracts water molecules to a surface by hydrogen bonding

adrenalin (epinephrine)   the 'flight or fight' hormone produced by the medulla of the adrenal gland

aerobic respiration   respiration that requires oxygen, and produces carbon dioxide and water from the oxidation of glucose

afferent   taking towards – for example, the afferent arteriole delivers blood *to* a glomerulus

AIDS   an acquired immune deficiency syndrome caused by infection with HIV

aleurone layer   layer of specialised cells between the seed coat and endosperm of monocotyledon seeds, which produces enzymes that help to digest the food reserves for the developing embryo

algal bloom   rapid increase or accumulation in the population of algae in an aquatic ecosystem often due to the run-off of agricultural fertiliser

alimentary canal   the gut – a tube that runs from the mouth to the anus of a vertebrate in which food is digested and absorbed

allele   an alternative form of a gene found at a specific locus on a chromosome

allele frequency   the commonness of occurrence of any particular allele in a population

allopatric speciation   separating a species into two geographically isolated groups by a physical barrier so eventually they can no longer interbreed.

allosteric site   the region on the surface of an enzyme to which the allosteric effector binds

allostery   regulation of the action of an enzyme by the binding of a molecule that does not have the same structure as the substrate, at a site away from the catalytic active site

altruist   an organism which performs an action which benefits other individuals rather than itself

alveolus (*plur.* alveoli)   an air sac in the lungs where gas exchange occurs

amino acid   one of the building blocks of protein; each amino acid has an amine group $-NH_2$ and an acid carboxyl group $-COOH$, and the general formula $NH_2-CHR-COOH$, where R is one of 20 side groups

amylase   an enzyme that digests starch

anabolism   an anabolic reaction is one in which large molecules are built up from small ones

anaerobic respiration   respiration that occurs in the absence of oxygen in which glucose is broken down to lactic acid or to ethanol and carbon dioxide

analogous structures   structures with similar functions but which have different evolutionary origins

anaphase   the stage in cell division in which homologous chromosomes (in meiosis I) or chromatids (meiosis II and mitosis) separate and go to opposite poles

angiosperm   one of the flowering plants

angiospermophyta   the taxonomic group of flowering plants

anorexia nervosa   severe malnutrition brought on by a psychological condition which causes an aversion to food

antagonistic pair   a pair of muscles that work in opposition to each other at a joint

anther   pollen-bearing structures on the stamens of flowers

antibiotic   organic compounds produced by microorganisms to kill or inhibit other microorganisms

antibody   one of millions of blood proteins produced by plasma cells in response to specific antigens, which are then neutralised or destroyed

anticodon   a triplet of bases in tRNA that pair with a complementary triplet (codon) in mRNA

antidiuretic hormone (ADH)   hormone secreted by the posterior pituitary gland to control the water permeability of the collecting ducts in the kidney (also called vasopressin)

antigen   a substance, usually a protein, that stimulates the production of antibody

antigen presentation   when a phagocytic cell that takes in a pathogen, or molecules from it, presents them on the surface of its plasma membrane where they may be encountered by a lymphocyte

antiparallel   running in opposite direction; the two polynucleotide strands in a DNA molecule are antiparallel

antisense strand   the strand of DNA that is transcribed during transcription

antiseptic   substance capable of preventing infection by inhibiting the growth of bacteria or fungi

apical meristem   tissue at the tip of a stem or root that is actively undergoing mitosis

archaeabacteria   unicellular organisms, genetically different from bacteria and eukaryotes, which usually inhabit extreme environmental conditions

aquaporins   proteins embedded in a plasma membrane that regulate the movement of water through the membrane

arteriole   a small artery

artery   a muscular blood vessel that carries blood away from the heart under high pressure

asexual reproduction   reproduction that does not involve gametes or fertilisation

assimilation   uptake and use of nutrients by cells and tissues

asthma   inflammation of the bronchi and bronchioles that restricts the flow of air to the alveoli

atherosclerosis   hardening and loss of elasticity in the arteries

ATP (adenosine triphosphate)   a universal energy storage nucleotide formed in photosynthesis and respiration from ADP and P_i; when it is formed, energy is stored; when it is broken down, energy is released

ATP synthase / synthetase   an enzyme that catalyses the production of ATP

atrioventricular node (AVN)   small patch of tissue in the right atrium which acts as a pacemaker in the heart

atrioventricular valve   valve between the atrium and the ventricle

atrium (*plur.* atria)   one of the two upper chambers of the heart that receive blood from veins

autonomic nervous system (ANS)   the part of the nervous system consisting only of motor neurons; it controls involuntary functions, comprised of the sympathetic and parasympathetic nervous systems.

autosome   any chromosome other than a sex chromosome

autotroph   organism able to make its own food from simple inorganic materials and an energy source

auxin   plant growth substance, also known as indoleacetic acid (IAA)

axon   a cytoplasmic process that transmits action potentials away from the cell body of a neuron

B-cell   a type of lymphocyte involved in the immune response; B-cells develop into plasma cells, which secrete antibody

bacillus   any of the rod-shaped bacteria

bactericide   a substance that kills bacteria

bacteriostatic   able to limit the growth of bacteria by interfering with their metabolic processes

base substitution mutation   when a base in DNA or RNA is replaced with a different base

basement membrane   thin layer of cells which separates epithelium from underlying tissue

bile   alkaline liquid secreted by the liver and stored in the gall bladder before being released into the small intestine, where it emulsifies lipid

binary fission   cell division producing two genetically identical daughter cells, as in prokaryote reproduction

binomial   the two-part name that gives the genus and the species of an organism in Latin – for example, *Homo sapiens*

biochemical oxygen demand (BOD)   the uptake rate of dissolved oxygen by the biological organisms in a body of water

biofuel   any fuel derived from biomass e.g. bioethanol, biodiesel

biological control   control of a pest species by means of a natural predator or parasite

biomagnification   process in which a chemical becomes more concentrated in organisms at each higher trophic level

biomass   the total dry mass of organisms in a given area

biome   a large area of the Earth defined by its plant life and climate

bioremediation   a process which uses microorganisms to remove contaminants from the natural environment

biosphere   the inhabited part of the Earth

biotechnology   commercial application of biology, particularly the industrial use of microorganisms, enzymes and genetic engineering

biotic factor   aspect of the environment that is living – for example, predators, parasites

biotic index   a measure of the biodiversity of a given ecosystem or habitat

blastocyst   early stage in embryo development – a hollow ball of cells that implants into the endometrium

blood doping   increasing the number of red blood cells in the body using either the addition of transfused cells or by taking erythropoietin to enhance athletic performance; illegal in international competition

body mass index (BMI)   a measure of body fat $\dfrac{\text{body mass in kg}}{\text{height in m}^2}$

Bohr shift   the reduction in affinity of hemoglobin for oxygen caused by an increase in the presence of CO_2

Bowman's capsule   the cup-shaped part at the beginning of a nephron, in which ultrafiltration takes place (also known as renal capsule)

bronchiole   a small branch of a bronchus

bronchus (*plur.* bronchi)   one of the major tubes which branch from the trachea

bryophyta   mosses and liverworts

bulb   an underground storage organ of plants consisting of enlarged fleshy leaf bases

Calvin cycle   cycle of light-independent reactions in the stroma of the chloroplast in which carbon dioxide reacts with RuBP, producing GP, TP and regenerating RuBP

cambium (vascular cambium) a cylinder of cells in plant stems and roots – the cells are able to divide and produce new cells so that the stem or root grows wider

capsid protein coat covering a virus

carbohydrates organic compounds usually containing only C, H and O – examples include sugars, starch, cellulose and glycogen

cardiac cycle sequence of events in the heart during one complete heart beat

carrier an individual that has one copy of a recessive allele which causes a genetic condition in individuals that are homozygous for the allele

carrier protein one of the proteins in a plasma membrane responsible for active transport across the membrane

carrying capacity the maximum population size that can be sustained within an area

caste a specialised group carrying out a specific function within a colony of social insects or other species

catalyst a substance that changes the rate of a chemical reaction, by lowering the activation energy, but remains unchanged at the end; enzymes are biological catalysts

cell cycle the sequence of events that takes place from one cell division until the next; it is made up of interphase, mitosis and cytokinesis

cell respiration controlled release of energy from organic compounds in cells to form ATP

cell theory the theory that organisms consist of cells and that all cells come from pre-existing cells

cell wall firm structure that surrounds the plasma membrane of cells of plants, fungi and bacteria; it gives cells their shape and limits their expansion

cellulose a polymer of glucose; it is the primary constituent of most plant cell walls

central nervous system (CNS) the brain and spinal cord of a vertebrate

centriole an organelle in an animal cell that forms and organises the spindle microtubules in cell division

centromere the region of a chromosome where sister chromatids are joined and where the spindle microtubules attach during cell division

cerebellum part of the hind brain concerned with posture, movement and muscle tone

cerebral cortex a highly folded layer of nerve cell bodies that forms the surface of the cerebrum

cerebral hemispheres (cerebrum) the main part of the human brain, the co-ordinating system of the nervous system consisting of two hemispheres made of neurons and nerve fibres

charged tRNA a tRNA molecule which is carrying an amino acid

chemiosmosis the passive flow of protons down a concentration gradient from the intermembrane space of mitochondria or from the thylakoid interior of chloroplasts through a protein channel

chemoautotroph an organism that uses energy from chemical reactions to generate ATP and produce organic compounds from inorganic raw materials

chemoheterotroph an organism that uses energy from chemical reactions to generate ATP and obtains organic compounds from other organisms

chemoreceptor sensory cell that responds to pH or the concentration of a chemical such as carbon dioxide

chiasma (*plur.* chiasmata) point of crossing over between homologous chromosomes in prophase I of meiosis

chloride shift process in which bicarbonate (HCO_3^-) and chloride (Cl^-) are exchanged across the membrane of red blood cells

chlorophyll the most important photosynthetic pigment of green plants, found in the grana of chloroplasts and responsible for trapping light energy (some bacteria have a chemically different form called bacteriochlorophyll)

chloroplast organelle found in some plant cells that is the site of photosynthesis

cholesterol a lipid formed in the liver and carried in the blood as lipoprotein; it is a precursor of steroid hormones, and is also found in the plasma membrane of animal cells

chromatid one of the two copies of a chromosome after it has replicated and before the centromeres separate at anaphase

chorion outermost membrane that protects mammal embryos; it forms part of the placenta

chromosome in eukaryotes, a structure consisting of a long thread of DNA and protein that carries the genetic information of the cell; in bacteria, the DNA molecule that contains the genetic information of the cell

cilium (*plur.* cilia) microscopic extensions from the surface of a cell which are able to move

cirrhosis disease caused by excessive alcohol consumption, in which liver tissue is replaced by fibrous scar tissue leading to loss of liver function

clade all the organisms both living and fossil descended from a particular common ancestor

cladistics a way of classifying organisms which uses lines of descent rather than physical (phenotypic) similarities

cladogram diagrammatic representation of cladistic relationships

class a taxonomic group of similar orders

climax community the stable stage of a succession of communities in an ecosystem

clonal selection the way in which exposure to antigen results in activation of selected T-cell or B-cell clones producing an immune response

clone genetically identical cells or organisms produced from a common ancestor by asexual reproduction

coacervates tiny spherical droplets of assorted organic molecules held together by forces from surrounding water

coccus a spherical bacterial cell

cochlea spiral shaped tube in the inner ear, which contains sensory cells involved with hearing

codominant alleles pairs of alleles that both affect the phenotype when present in a heterozygous state

codon a triplet of three nucleotides in mRNA that specify the position of an amino acid in a polypeptide

coenzyme a non-protein substance that is required for an enzyme to catalyse a reaction

collagen fibrous protein found in bone and connective tissues

commensalism a loose feeding relationship between two different species in which one species benefits and the other is unaffected

community a group of populations of organisms living and interacting within a habitat

companion cell specialised cell found adjacent to a sieve tube cell in flowering plants

competitive inhibitor substance similar to the substrate of an enzyme, which binds to the active site and inhibits a reaction

complementary base pairing pairing of bases A–T and G–C in double-stranded DNA, of A–U and C–G between DNA and RNA during transcription, between tRNA and mRNA during translation, and in the folding of tRNA

complementary DNA (cDNA) DNA produced by reverse transcription from RNA

condensation reaction a reaction in which two molecules become bonded by a covalent bond and a molecule of water is released

conditioning a type of learning in which an animal learns to respond to a stimulus that is different from the one that normally elicits a response

conjugated protein protein combined with a non-protein group

conservation management of an ecosystem by application of ecological principles

consumer an organism that feeds on another organism

contralateral processing process in which the right brain processes information from the left visual field and vice versa

convergent evolution the appearance of similar characteristics in genetically unrelated organisms

coronary thrombosis formation of a blood clot that affects the circulation of blood to the coronary arteries of the heart

corpus luteum mass of cells which develops from an ovarian follicle after the release of the oocyte

cortex the tissue in plant stems and roots between the outer layer epidermis and the central core

cotyledon a 'seed leaf' found in a plant embryo which stores food reserves and may become the first leaf when a seed germinates

covalent bond a bond between atoms in which electrons are shared

crassulacean acid metabolism (CAM) a metabolic pathway that enables some plants to store carbon dioxide at night and then photosynthesise during the day with the stomata closed

creatine phosphate (CP) molecule that acts as a rapid reserve of high-energy phosphate in skeletal muscle

cristae folds of the inner membrane of mitochondria, where oxidative phosphorylation takes place

cross-pollination the pollination of a plant by pollen from another plant

crossing over exchange of genetic material between homologous chromosomes during meiosis

cuticle waxy layer on the outer surface of a plant or insect that restricts water loss

cyanobacteria a group of photosynthetic prokaryotes (bacteria), formerly known as blue-green algae, which use bacteriochlorophyll in photosynthesis

cytokinesis division of cytoplasm after the nucleus has divided

cytoplasm contents of a cell enclosed by the plasma membrane, not including the nucleus

deamination removal of NH_2 group from an amino acid

decarboxylation reaction removal of carbon dioxide during a chemical reaction

decomposer organism that feeds on dead plant and animal matter so that it can be recycled; most decomposers are microorganisms

denaturation a change in the structure of a protein that results in a loss (usually permanent) of its function

dendrite a short cytoplasmic process of a neuron, which conducts action potentials towards the cell body

denitrification metabolic activity of some soil bacteria by which nitrogen containing ions are reduced to nitrogen gas

deoxynucleoside triphosphate (dNTP) a building block for DNA – deoxyribose, three phosphate groups and one of the four bases

depolarise to temporarily reverse the membrane potential of an axon as an impulse is transmitted

detoxification the removal of toxic substances from the body of an organism

detritivore an organism that feeds on dead organic matter

diabetes a condition in which the blood sugar level is not maintained within normal limits either because the body does not produce sufficient insulin or because cells do not respond to insulin properly

diaphragm sheet of fibrous and muscular tissue that separates the thorax from the abdomen in mammals

diastole relaxation of the heart muscle during the cardiac cycle

dichotomous key a key in which organisms are separated into pairs of smaller and smaller groups by observation of their characteristics

dicotyledons (dicots) a class of Angiospermophyta with two seed leaves in the seed

differentiation a process by which originally similar cells follow different developmental pathways because particular genes are activated and others are switched off

diffusion passive, random movement of molecules (or other particles) from an area of high concentration to an area of lower concentration

digestion enzyme-catalysed process by which larger molecules are hydrolysed to smaller, soluble molecules

dipeptide molecule composed of two amino acid residues joined by a peptide bond

diploid cells with two sets of chromosomes in their nuclei

disaccharide molecule composed of two monosaccharide molecules linked in a condensation reaction

dissociation curve a graph which shows the release of oxygen from hemoglobin

divergent evolution accumulation of differences between two groups of organisms in a species leading to the formation of new species

DNA (deoxyribonucleic acid) the fundamental heritable material; DNA consists of two strands of nucleotide subunits containing the bases adenine, thymine, guanine and cytosine

DNA ligase   enzyme that links Okazaki fragments during DNA replication; it is also used in biotechnology to join sticky ends of double-stranded DNA fragments

DNA polymerase   one of a group of enzymes that catalyse the formation of DNA strands from a DNA template

domain   the highest rank of taxonomy of organisms; there are three domains – Archaea, Eubacteria and Eukaryota

dominant allele   an allele that has the same effect on a phenotype whether it is present in the homozygous or heterozygous condition

Down's syndrome   a condition usually caused by the presence of an additional chromosome 21, resulting from non-disjunction of chromosomes during meiosis

drone   caste of male honeybees one of which fertilises the queen

ecology   the study of the relationships between living organisms and their environment, including both the physical environment and the other organisms that live in it

ecosystem   the organisms of a particular habitat together with the physical environment in which they live – for example, a tropical rain forest

ectotherm   an organism that uses mainly behaviour to regulate its body temperature; its body temperature changes with the temperature of the environment

edge enhancement   processing by the brain so that the edge contrast of an image is enhanced

effector   an organ or cell that responds to a stimulus – for example, a muscle that contracts or a gland that produces a secretion

egestion   removal of waste from the body during defecation

electron transport chain (ETC)   a series of carriers that transport electrons along a redox pathway, enabling the synthesis of ATP during respiration

electrophoresis   separating components in a mixture of chemicals – for example, lengths of DNA – by means of an electric field

embryo   the earliest stage of development of a young animal or plant that is still contained in a protective structure such as a seed, bird egg or mammalian uterus

embryonic stem cells   cells derived from an embryo that retain the potential to differentiate into any other cell of the organism

emergent property   a property of a complex system that is more than the sum of its individual component parts

emigration   deliberate departure of an organism from the environment in which it has been living

emulsion   a mixture of two or more immiscible liquids

end–product inhibition   control of a metabolic pathway in which a product within or at the end of the pathway inhibits an enzyme found earlier in the pathway

endemic species   a species that is found naturally in only one geographic area

energy pyramid   see *pyramid of energy*

endocrine gland   a ductless hormone-producing gland that secretes its products directly into the bloodstream

endocytosis   the movement of bulk liquids or solids into a cell, by the indentation of the plasma membrane to form vesicles containing the substance; endocytosis is an active process requiring ATP

endometrium   lining of the uterus of a mammal

endoparasite   a parasite, such as a tapeworm, that lives inside another organism

endoplasmic reticulum   a folded system of membranes within the cytoplasm of a eukaryotic cell; may be smooth (sER), or rough (rER) if ribosomes are attached

endorphins   naturally occurring substances produced by the pituitary gland and hypothalamus, resembling opiates and acting as 'natural pain killers', producing feelings of well being

endosperm   the food reserves found in a seed of a monocotyledonous flowering plant

endosymbiosis   an organism that lives inside the cell or body of another organism; also, a theory which proposes that mitochondria and chloroplasts evolved from endosymbiotic bacteria

endotherm   a organism that generates heat inside the body to maintain a constant body temperature, no matter what the temperature of the environment (also known as homeotherm)

endotoxin   a molecule produced by bacteria that is recognised by the immune system

enzyme   a protein that functions as a biological catalyst

epidermis   outer layer of cells

epididymis   coiled tubules in the testes that store sperm cells and carry them from the seminiferous tubules to the vas deferens

epinephrine   alternative name for adrenaline

epithelium   a layer of cells that covers the internal or external surfaces of multicellular organisms

erythrocyte   a red blood cell

erythropoietin (EPO)   hormone produced by the kidney that promotes the formation of red blood cells in bone marrow

essential amino acid   one of a number of amino acids that cannot be synthesised in the human body and must be obtained from the diet

Eubacteria   kingdom including the great majority of bacteria (contrast with *archaebacteria*)

eukaryotic   cells which contain a membrane-bound nucleus

eutrophication   an increase in the concentration of nutrients such as nitrate in an aquatic environment so that primary production increases, which can lead to depletion of oxygen

evolution   the cumulative change in the heritable characteristics of a population

***ex situ* conservation**   conservation of species away from their natural habitat, e.g. in a zoo breeding programme

excretion   the removal of waste products of metabolism (such as urea or carbon dioxide) from the body

exocrine gland   a gland whose secretion is released via a duct

exocytosis   the movement of bulk liquids or solids out of a cell by the fusion of vesicles containing the substance with the plasma membrane; exocytosis is an active process requiring ATP

exon   a portion of the primary RNA transcript that codes for part of a polypeptide in eukaryotes (compare with *intron*)

exoparasite (ectoparasite)   organism which lives as a parasite on the outside of the body of another organism, e.g. fleas, lice

exoskeleton   inextensible outer casing of arthropods, providing support for locomotion, as well as protection

exothermic a chemical reaction in which free energy is released

exotoxin a toxin secreted by a bacterium or other microorganism which causes damage to its hosts' cells

exponential (log) phase the stage in the growth of a population in which their numbers double at regular intervals; this occurs while resources, e.g. nutrients, oxygen and space, are not limiting factors

extensor muscle muscle whose contraction results in the extension of a limb at a joint

extinction the end of a line of organisms, as the last individuals die

extracellular infection an infection caused by a pathogen which lives in the body but outside cells, produces toxins, harms or kills cells and can be detected by the immune system

extracellular matrix structure outside the cell that may function in support, adhesion and movement – for example, the plant cell wall, or glycoprotein secreted by animal cells

F_1 generation the immediate offspring of a mating; the first filial generation

F_2 generation the immediate offspring of a mating between members of the F_1 generation

facilitated diffusion diffusion across a membrane through specific protein channels in the membrane, with no energy cost

fast-twitch fibres muscle fibres which contract quickly, but tire rapidly

fat a solid lipid

fatty acid a molecule which has a long hydrocarbon tail and a carboxyl group

faeces waste that leaves the digestive system by egestion

fenestration space between the cells of a capillary which enable dissolved substances to pass through

fertilisation the fusion of male and female gametes to form a zygote

fetus a human embryo from seven weeks after fertilisation

fibrin a plasma protein that polymerises to form long threads, which provide the structure of a blood clot

fibrinogen the soluble plasma protein, produced by the liver, which is converted to fibrin during the blood-clotting process

fibrous protein protein with an elongated shape, containing a high proportion of alpha helix – for example, keratin and collagen

fitness (athletic) the ability to carry out a specific aspects of a sport or exercise

flagellum a long thin structure used to propel unicellular organisms; the structure of a flagellum in a prokaryote is different from that in a eukaryote

flexor muscle muscle whose contraction results in the flexion (bending) of a limb at a joint

fluid mosaic model the generally accepted model of the structure of a membrane that includes a phospholipid bilayer in which proteins are embedded or attached to the surface

follicle stimulating hormone (FSH) hormone produced by the anterior pituitary gland that stimulates the growth of follicles at the start of the menstrual cycle

food chain a sequence of organisms in a habitat, beginning with a producer, in which each obtains nutrients by eating the organism preceding it

food miles the distance items of food have travelled before reaching the destination where they are consumed

food web a series of interconnected food chains

fossil fuel carbon-containing fuel derived from organic material – for example, coal, gas or oil

fovea the point on the retina, directly behind the pupil, where vision is most distinct; contains only cones

G_1 and G_2 phases phases during interphase of the cell cycle

gamete haploid sex cell – for example, sperm, ovum

gas exchange the exchange of oxygen and carbon dioxide between an organism or its cells and the environment

gated channel a membrane protein channel that opens and closes in response to the binding of particular molecules or in response to a change in membrane potential

gene a heritable factor that controls a specific characteristic

gene mutation a change in the base sequence of a gene that may or may not result in a change in the characteristics of an organism or cell

gene pool all the genes and their alleles present in a breeding population

gene therapy ways in which corrected copies of genes are introduced into patients with genetic conditions or diseases

genetic modification (GM) introduction or alteration of genes, often using genes from a different species, in order to modify an organism's characteristics

genome the complete genetic information of an organism or an individual cell

genotype the exact genetic constitution of an individual feature of an organism; the alleles of an organism

genus a group of similar and closely related species

germination the growth of an embryo plant using stored food in a seed

gibberellins plant growth substances important in elongation of stems and in seed germination

global warming the hypothesis that the average temperature of the Earth is increasing due to an increase in carbon dioxide and other greenhouse gases in the atmosphere

globular protein proteins consisting of one or more chains of amino acids folded into complex shapes – for example, enzymes

glomerulus network of capillaries within the Bowman's (renal) capsule

glucagon hormone released by alpha cells of the pancreas, which stimulates the breakdown of glycogen in the liver and brings about an increase in blood glucose

gluconeogenesis the production of glucose from non-carbohydrate substances such as amino acids or lipids

glycogen polymer of glucose used as a storage carbohydrate in liver and muscle tissue

glycolysis the first (anaerobic) stage of respiration during which glucose is converted to pyruvate

goitre deficiency disease leading to enlargement of the thyroid gland and mental impairment; caused by a lack of iodine

Golgi apparatus a series of flattened membranes in the cytoplasm important in the modification of proteins produced by the rER

gradualism a form of evolutionary change whereby species slowly become new species

granum (*plur.* grana) layers of discs of membranes (thylakoids) in the chloroplast that contain photosynthetic pigments; the site of the light-dependent reactions of photosynthesis

gross primary production (GPP) the total energy captured by green plants growing in a particular area

guard cell one of a pair of modified leaf epidermis cells that control the opening of a stoma

habitat the locality or surroundings in which an organism usually lives

half-life the time taken for half of a sample of radioactive isotope to decay to its stable, nonradioactive form

haploid cells containing one set of chromosomes

Hardy–Weinberg equation allele and genotype frequencies in a population remain in equilibrium unless specific disturbing influences occur; the equation is used to calculate and model allele frequencies:
$$p^2 + 2pq + q^2 = 1$$

heart rate the number of contractions (beats) of the heart per minute

helicase an enzyme that unwinds and separates the two strands of a DNA molecule at the replication fork during replication

helper T-cells cells that activate B-cells and other T-cells in the immune response; target of the HIV virus

hemoglobin protein found in red blood cells that combines with and carries oxygen from areas of high partial pressure to areas of lower partial pressure

heterotroph an organism that feeds on organic molecules

heterozygous having two different copies of an allele of a gene

high-density lipoprotein (HDL) one of the groups of lipoproteins which enable cholesterol and triglycerides to be carried in the bloodstream

highly repetitive sequences (satellite DNA) sequences in the genome that do not code for protein but which are present in large numbers

hinge joint a joint such as the knee, which permits movement in one plane

histone one of a group of basic proteins that form nucleosomes and act as scaffolding for DNA

homeostasis maintenance of a constant internal environment

homeotherm an animal capable of maintaining a constant internal temperature (also known as endotherm)

hominids the family of great apes which includes chimpanzees, gorillas, orang-utans and humans

homologous chromosomes chromosomes in a diploid cell that contain the same sequences of genes but which are derived from different parents

homologous structures structures that are similar due to common ancestry, but which may not have the same function

homozygous having two identical copies of an allele

hormone a chemical substance produced by an endocrine gland, which is transported in the blood and which affects the physiology or biochemistry of specific target cells

host an organism that harbours a parasite and provides it with nourishment

human chorionic gonadotropin (HCG) hormone released by an implanted blastocyst, which maintains the corpus luteum so that progesterone is produced during early pregnancy; used in pregnancy-testing kits

hybrid the offspring of a cross between genetically dissimilar parents

hybridoma a cell formed by the fusion of a plasma cell and a cancer cell; it can both secrete antibodies and divide by mitosis to form other cells like itself

hydrogen bond weak bond found in biological macromolecules in large numbers, formed by the attraction of a small positive charge on a hydrogen atom and a small negative charge on an oxygen or nitrogen atom

hydrolysis reaction reaction in which hydrogen and hydroxyl ions (water) are added to a large molecule to cause it to split into smaller molecules e.g. during digestion

hydrophilic water-loving

hydrophobic water-hating

hyperglycaemia an excess of glucose in the blood

hyperpolarisation a change in the resting potential of a membrane so that the inside of the cell becomes more negative with respect to the outside

hypothalamus control centre of the autonomic nervous system and site of release of releasing factors for the pituitary hormones; it controls water balance, temperature regulation and metabolism

hypothesis a testable explanation of an observed event or phenomenon

imbibition the process by which a seed takes in water to bind to dry starch and protein

immunity resistance to the onset of a disease after infection by the agent causing the disease

in situ conservation conservation of a species in its natural habitat

in vitro a biological process occurring in cells that have been removed from the body (literally 'in glass' – as in _in vitro_ fertilisation, IVF)

indicator species species that, by their presence, abundance or lack of abundance, demonstrate some aspect of a habitat

induced fit the change in shape of the active site of an enzyme when it binds with its substrate

ingestion taking in food, eating

inhalation taking in air, breathing in

inhibitor a molecule that slows or blocks enzyme action, either by competition for the active site (competitive inhibitor) or by binding to another part of the enzyme (non-competitive inhibitor)

inhibitory synapse synapse at which the arrival of an impulse slows forward transmission of the impulse

initiation complex a combination of the small ribosomal subunit with an mRNA molecule and a charged tRNA carrying the first amino acid; formed at the start of translation

innate behaviour behaviour which is genetically determined and common to all members of a species

inorganic compounds of mineral, not biological, origin

insulin hormone produced by the beta cells in the pancreas, which lowers blood glucose levels

integral proteins proteins found embedded either fully or partially in the plasma membrane

intercostal muscles muscles between the ribs capable of raising and lowering the rib cage during breathing

interphase the period between successive nuclear divisions when the chromosomes are extended; the period when the cell is actively transcribing and translating genetic material and carrying out other biochemical processes

intracellular infection an infection caused by a pathogen which lives inside cells, does not produce toxins and is not detected by the immune system

intron a non-coding sequence of nucleotides in primary RNA in eukaryotes (compare with **exon**)

ionic bond a bond formed by the attraction between oppositely charged ions (for example, NH_3^+ and COO^-), important in tertiary and quaternary protein structure

islets of Langerhans groups of cells in the pancreas that secrete insulin and glucagon; contain alpha and beta cells

isotope different isotopes of an element contain the same number of protons in the nucleus of each atom but different numbers of neutrons – they therefore have a different atomic mass

joule the SI unit of energy; as a joule is a small unit, quantities of energy are usually expressed as kilojoules, kJ

karyogram a photographic image showing the number, shape and types of chromosomes in a cell

kinesis orientation behaviour in which an organism moves at an increasing or decreasing rate, which is not directional, in response to a stimulus

Krebs cycle a cycle of biochemical changes that occurs in the mitochondrial matrix during aerobic respiration

lagging strand the daughter strand that is synthesised discontinuously in DNA replication

landrace domesticated animals or plants adapted to the natural and cultural environment in which they live

leading strand the daughter strand that is synthesised continuously in DNA replication

leucocyte white blood cell

ligament strong fibrous tissue that connects moveable bones to one another

light-dependent reactions series of stages in photosynthesis that occur on the grana of the chloroplasts, light is used to split water, and ATP and NADPH + H^+ are produced in the Calvin cycle

light-independent reactions series of stages in photosynthesis that take place in the stroma and use the products of the light-dependent reactions to produce carbohydrate

lignin chemical found in the cellulose walls of certain plant cells, such as xylem, which gives strength and support

limiting factor a resource that influences the rate of processes (such as photosynthesis) if it is in short supply

linkage group in genetics, the genes carried on one chromosome that do not show random or independent assortment

lipid a fat, oil, wax or steroid; organic compound that is insoluble in water but soluble in organic solvents such as ethanol

lipoprotein a complex of lipid and protein which can be classified by density, e.g. LDL, low density lipoprotein and HDL, high density lipoprotein

lobule a block of liver cells, the functional unit within the liver

locus the specific location on a chromosome of a gene

long-day plants plants that require fewer than a certain number of hours of darkness in each 24-hour period to induce flowering

loop of Henle the section of a nephron between the proximal and distal convoluted tubules that dips down into the medulla and then back up into the cortex of the kidney

low-density lipoprotein (LDL) one of the groups of lipoproteins which enable cholesterol and triglycerides to be carried in the bloodstream

luteinising hormone (LH) a hormone produced by the anterior pituitary gland that stimulates the production of sex hormones by ovaries and testes

lymphocyte a type of white blood cell that is involved in the immune response; unlike phagocytes, they become active only in the presence of a particular antigen that 'matches' their specific receptors or antibodies

lysis breakdown of cells *or* splitting of hexose bisphosphate in glycolysis

lysosome a vesicle found in the cytoplasm, containing enzymes that can digest the contents of phagocytic vesicles

macromolecule a large organic molecule such as protein, nucleic acid or polysaccharide

malnutrition condition(s) caused by a diet which is not balanced and may be lacking in, or have an excess of, one or more nutrients

mature mRNA mRNA with introns removed

mean (arithmetic) the sum of a list of numbers divided by the total number of items in the list; an average

mechanoreceptor a sensory receptor that responds to mechanical pressure or distortion

medulla oblongata the part of the brain stem that connects to the spinal cord and controls breathing and other reflex actions

meiosis a nuclear division that produces genetically non-identical cells containing half the number of chromosomes of the parent cell

menstrual cycle the process of shedding the lining of the uterus at approximately monthly intervals (in humans) if fertilisation does not occur

meristem area of plant tissue that divides by mitosis to produce new cells and tissues

messenger RNA (mRNA) a single-stranded transcript of the antisense strand of DNA, which carries a sequence of codons for the production of protein

metabolic pathway a series of chemical reactions that are catalysed by enzymes

metaphase stage in nuclear division at which chromosomes become arranged on the equator of the spindle fibres

micropyle   opening in a plant ovule through which a pollen tube enters; and which is retained in the testa for imbibition

microspheres   collections of small polypeptides or phospholipids collected together to form small spheres

microvilli   folded projections of epithelial cells, such as those lining the small intestine, that increase cell surface area

mitochondrion (*plur.* **mitochondria**)   organelle in the cytoplasm of eukaryotic cells; the site of respiration reactions, the Krebs cycle and the electron transport chain

mitosis   cell division that produces two genetically identical daughter cells which are also identical to the original parent cell

monoclonal antibody   antibody produced in the laboratory by a single clone of B-cells, which gives rise to many identical antibody molecules

monocotyledons (monocots)   a class of Angiospermophyta that have an embryo with a single cotyledon – for example, grasses, maize (corn/sweetcorn)

monohybrid cross   a breeding experiment that involves one pair of genes

monosaccharide   a simple carbohydrate

morphology   the form or shape of an organism

motor neuron   nerve cell that carries impulses away from the brain

muscle fibre   a single muscle cell that is multinucleate in striated muscle

mutation   a permanent change in the base sequence of DNA

mutualism/mutualistic relationship   a type of symbiotic relationship between two organisms in which both organisms benefit

myelin sheath   a fatty covering around the axons of nerve fibres that provides insulation

myofibril   a contractile unit within a muscle fibre consisting of a bundle of myosin (thick) and actin (thin) filaments

myogenic   a contraction of heart muscle that originates in heart muscle cells

myoglobin   an oxygen-binding pigment found in muscle cells

myosin   one of the two proteins found in muscle; it makes up thick filaments

NAD (nicotinamide adenine dinucleotide)   a compound found in all living cells in two interconvertible forms: NAD^+, an oxidising agent; and NADH, a reducing agent

natural selection   the mechanism of evolution proposed by Charles Darwin in which various genetic types make different contributions to the next generation

negative feedback   a regulating mechanism in which a change in a sensed variable results in a correction that opposes the change

nephron   the functional unit of the kidney

net primary production (NPP)   total photosynthesis minus respiration by plants

neurohormones   any hormone produced and released by neurons e.g. adrenalin

neuron   a nerve cell that can carry action potentials and which makes connections to other neurons, muscles or glands by means of synapses

neurosecretory cells   cells that release neurohormones into the blood

neurotransmitter   a substance produced and released by a neuron, which passes across a synapse and affects a post-synaptic membrane

niche   the habitat an organism occupies, its feeding activities and its interactions with other species

nitrification   oxidation of ammonia to nitrites and nitrates by nitrifying bacteria

nitrogen fixation   conversion of nitrogen gas into nitrogen compounds by nitrogen fixing bacteria

nodes of Ranvier   gaps in the myelin sheath of an axon where the membrane can initiate action potentials

non-competitive inhibitor   an inhibitor of an enzyme that binds at a site away from the active site

non-disjunction   failure of sister chromatids to separate in mitosis or meiosis II, or of homologous chromosomes to separate in meiosis I

noradrenalin   a neurotransmitter used in the sympathetic nervous system

nuclear envelope   a double membrane that surrounds the nucleus in a eukaryotic cell

nucleoid   the region of a prokaryotic cell in which the genetic material is found

nucleolus   a small body found in the nucleus of eukaryotic cells where ribosomal RNA is synthesised

nucleoside   organic base (A, C, G, U or T) combined with a pentose sugar (either ribose or deoxyribose)

nucleoside triphosphate (NTP)   a building unit for RNA – a ribose nucleotide with two additional phosphates, which are chopped off during the synthesis process

nucleosome   a part of a eukaryotic chromosome made up of DNA wrapped around 8 histone proteins and held in place by another histone protein

nucleotide   the basic chemical unit of a nucleic acid – an organic base combined with pentose sugar (either ribose or deoxyribose) and phosphate

nucleus   organelle found in eukaryotic cells that controls and directs cell activities; it is bounded by a double membrane (envelope) and contains chromosomes

nutrient   a substance taken in by an organism that is required for its metabolism

obesity   having a BMI of more than 30 and being seriously overweight

Okazaki fragments   newly formed DNA fragments that form part of the lagging strand during replication and which are linked by DNA ligase to produce a continuous strand

oocyte   female sex cell that is part-way through meiosis

oogenesis   female gamete production

optic chiasma   region of the brain near the thalamus and hypothalamus at which portions of each optic nerve cross

organelle   a cell structure that carries out a specific function – for example, ribosome, nucleus, chloroplast

organic   compounds of carbon, excluding carbon dioxide and carbonates

osmoregulation   control of the water balance of the blood, tissues or cytoplasm of a living organism

osmosis   the diffusion of water molecules from an area where they are in high concentration (low solute concentration) to a area where they are in a lower concentration (high solute concentration) across a partially permeable membrane

ovary   organ in the female body in which female gametes are formed

ovulation   the release of secondary oocytes from the ovary

ovum (*plur.* ova)   a female gamete in both plants and animals

oxidation   gain of oxygen or loss of electrons or loss of hydrogen in a chemical reaction, usually associated with release of energy

oxidative phosphorylation   ATP formation in the mitochondria as electrons flow along the electron transport chain

oxygen debt   additional oxygen that must be taken into the body after exercise to remove the lactate accumulated

oxygen dissociation curve   graph showing the percentage saturation of hemoglobin or myoglobin at different partial pressures of oxygen

oxytocin   hormone produced by the posterior pituitary gland which stimulates the contraction of the uterus during the birth of a baby

ozone layer   a layer of gas in the upper atmosphere which protects living things from the harmful ultraviolet rays of the sun

pacemaker   sinoatrial node (SAN) in the wall of the right atrium, which sets the pace for the heart rate

palisade layer   a layer of photosynthetic cells found below the upper epidemis of a leaf

pancreas   a gland composed of exocrine cells that produce digestive enzymes, and the islets of Langerhans, endocrine cells which produce insulin and glucagon

pandemic   an epidemic or outbreak of an infectious disease over wide areas of the world

parasite   an organism that lives on or in a host for most of its lifecycle and derives its nutrients from it

parasympathetic nervous system   part of the autonomic (involuntary) nervous system which produces effects such as decreased blood pressure and heart rate

passive immunity   immunity due to the acquisition of antibodies from another organism in which active immunity has been stimulated

passive transport   the diffusion of substances across a plasma membrane without the expenditure of energy

pasteurisation   process of heating food (especially milk) to a specific high temperature for a definite length of time in order to kill bacteria, and then cooling it immediately

pathogen   an organism or virus that causes disease

partial pressure   the pressure exerted by each component gas in a mixture of gases

pentadactyl limbs   limbs that end in five digits

pentose   a five-carbon monosaccharide

peptide bond   a covalent linkage between two amino acid residues in which the amine group of one links to the carboxyl group of the other through a condensation reaction

peripheral nerves   parts of the nervous system not including the brain and spinal cord, which transmit information to and from the CNS

peripheral proteins   proteins that are attached to the surface of the plasma membrane

peristalsis   wave-like muscular contractions that propel food along the alimentary canal

petal   modified leaf, often brightly coloured, found in angiosperm flowers primarily to attract pollinators

phenotype   the characteristic or appearance of an organism which may be physical or biochemical

phenylketonuria (PKU)   an autosomal recessive metabolic genetic disorder characterized by a lack of enzyme needed to utilise the amino acid phenylalanine

phloem   tissue that carries sugars and other organic molecules in the stem of a plant; transports both up and down the stem

phospholipid   important constituent molecule of membranes, formed from a triglyceride in which one fatty acid is replaced by a phosphate group

photoautotroph   an organism that uses light energy to produce ATP and produces organic compounds from inorganic molecules

photolysis   the splitting of water molecules in the light-dependent stage of photosynthesis

photoheterotroph   an organism that uses light energy to generate ATP and obtains organic compounds from other organisms

photoperiodism   the control of flowering in plants in response to day length

photophosphorylation   the formation of ATP using light energy in the grana of chloroplasts

photoreceptor   a receptor which is sensitive to light

phototropism   the tropic response of plants to light

phylogenetics   a classification system based on evolutionary relationships

phylogeny   evolutionary relatedness of different groups of organisms

phytochrome   a pigment found in plants that regulates several processes including the flowering pattern in response to day length

pilus (*plur.* pili)   an extension of the surface of some bacteria, used to attach to another bacterial cell during conjugation

pinocytosis   'cell drinking', a form of endocytosis, taking extra cellular fluids into a cell by means of vesicles

pituitary gland   so-called 'master gland' whose hormones control the activities of other glands

pith   unspecialised cells found in the core of the stem

placenta   a structure of maternal and fetal tissues on the lining of the uterus; the site of exchange of materials between maternal and fetal blood systems

plaque   the build up of fatty deposits in the wall of an artery

plasma   the liquid part of blood

plasma cells   antibody-secreting cells that develop from B-cells

plasma membrane   bilayer composed mainly of phospholipids and proteins that surrounds and encloses a cell

plasmid   a small circle of DNA found in bacteria; very useful in biotechnology

platelets cell fragments found in the blood that are concerned with blood clotting

plumule part of an embryo plant that will become the shoot

pluripotent a cell that is able to differentiate into many different types of cell in the correct conditions

polar body a non-functioning nucleus produced during meiosis; three or four are produced during human oogenesis

pollen microspores containing the male gamete, formed in the anthers of flowering plants

pollination transfer of pollen from the anther to the stigma of the ovary in plants

polygene multiple loci whose alleles affect a continuously variable phenotypic characteristic, such as height in humans

polygenic inheritance inheritance of phenotypic characteristics that are determined by the collective effects of several different genes

polymerase chain reaction (PCR) process by which small quantities of DNA are multiplied for forensic or other examination

polymorphism two or more clearly different forms of a phenotype in the same population of a species

polypeptide a chain of amino acid residues linked by peptide bonds

polyploidy having more than two sets of chromosomes

polysaccharide large carbohydrates formed by condensation reactions between large numbers of monosaccharides – for example, cellulose, glycogen and starch

polysome an arrangement of many ribosomes along a molecule of mRNA

population a group of organisms of the same species that live in the same area at the same time

portal vein a vein that connects two capillary networks

positive feedback a control mechanism in which a deviation from the normal level stimulates an increase in the deviation

post-transcriptional modification a process in eukaryotic cells during which primary mRNA is converted in the nucleus to mature RNA by the removal of introns

precautionary principle principle that those responsible for change must prove that it will not do harm before they proceed

predator an organism which kills and eats other organisms to obtain nutrients

primary consumer an organism that feeds on a producer

primary succession succession which occurs on previously barren areas such as lava flows

primate the order that contains lemurs, lorises, monkeys and apes

prion a protein-based infectious particle that causes disease affecting the brain and nervous tissue

producer an autotrophic organism

progesterone a female sex hormone that maintains pregnancy

prokaryote an organism whose genetic material is not contained in a nucleus; bacteria

prolactin a hormone released by the anterior pituitary gland that stimulates lactation

prophase first stage in nuclear division by meiosis or mitosis

prostate gland male gland that produces a white alkaline secretion making up to 30% of semen volume

prosthetic group a non-protein part of a tertiary or quaternary level protein; often forms part of the active site of an enzyme

protobiont proposed, primitive coacervates containing RNA and amino acids

punctuated equilibrium a form of evolutionary change whereby species remain stable for long periods of time followed by brief periods of rapid change in response to significant environmental change; leading to the formation of new species

pure breeding an organism that is homozygous for a specified gene or genes

purine the nitrogenous bases adenine and guanine found in nucleic acids

pyramid of energy diagram which shows the total energy content at different trophic levels in an ecosystem

pyrimidine the nitrogenous bases cytosine, thymine and uracil found in nucleic acids

pyruvate a three-carbon acid produced by glycolysis that enters the Krebs cycle

quadrat a frame which encloses a sampling area.

quaternary structure the arrangement of two or more polypeptide subunits in a protein

R group any of 20 side chains that form part of an amino acid; attached to the CH section of the molecule

radicle part of an embryo plant that will become the root

radioactive dating using the proportion of different isotopes in a material to estimate the age of the material

radioisotope an atom with an unstable nucleus which decays at a constant rate and can be used to estimate the age of rocks or fossils

realised niche the actual niche occupied by an organism, differing from the fundamental niche because of competition with other species or predation

rebound malnutrition the excessive excretion of vitamin C (or other nutrient) from the body, following a period of excessive consumption, leading to an overall shortage

receptor a specialised cell or neuron ending which receives a stimulus

recessive allele an allele that has an effect on the phenotype only when present in the homozygous state

recombinant offspring in which the genetic information has been rearranged by crossing over so as to produce phenotypes which are different from the parents

recombinant DNA DNA that has been artificially changed, often involving the joining of genes from different species

recombinant DNA technology the use of biochemical techniques involving restriction enzymes and plasmids to produce specific proteins, using organisms such as bacteria

redox reaction a reaction in which reduction and oxidation occur simultaneously

reduction loss of oxygen or gain of electrons or gain of hydrogen in a chemical reaction, usually associated with released energy; the opposite of oxidation

reduction division   anaphase I of meiosis, when the chromosome number of a diploid cell is halved

reflex action   a rapid automatic response

reflex arc   a response which automatically follows a stimulus and usually involves a small number of neurons

relay neurons   neurons through which connections between sensory and motor neurons can be made

replication fork   the point at which DNA is being unzipped by helicase

residual volume   volume of air in the lungs after a maximum exhalation

respiratory pigment   substance such as hemoglobin or myoglobin that combines with oxygen

resting potential   the potential difference across the membrane of a neuron when it is not passing an impulse

restriction enzyme (endonuclease)   one of several enzymes that cut nucleic acids at specific sequences of bases

retina   the light-sensitive layer at the back of the eye

retrovirus   an RNA virus that contains reverse transcriptase

reverse transcriptase   an enzyme that catalyses the production of DNA from an mRNA template

ribosome   a small organelle that is the site of protein synthesis

rickets   deficiency disease caused by a lack of vitamin D

RNA (ribonucleic acid)   a nucleic acid that contains the pentose sugar ribose and bases adenine, guanine, cytosine and uracil

RNA polymerase   an enzyme that catalyses the formation of RNA from a DNA template

roughage (fibre)   indigestible matter found in food, e.g. cellulose and chitin

rubisco (ribulose bisphosphate carboxylase)   the enzyme in the light independent reaction that catalyses the addition of carbon dioxide to ribulose bisphosphate to form glycerate-3-phosphate (GP)

RuBP (ribulose bisphosphate)   the five-carbon acceptor molecule for carbon dioxide found in the light-independent reactions of photosynthesis

S phase   in the cell cycle, the period during interphase when DNA is replicated

saprotroph   an organism that feeds on dead organic matter

sarcolemma   plasma membrane covering of a muscle fibre

sarcomere   contractile unit of skeletal muscle between two Z-lines

sarcoplasmic reticulum   network of membranes surrounding myofibrils of a muscle fibre; stores Ca^{2+}

saturated fatty acid   a fatty acid with no double bonds

scurvy   a deficiency disease caused by a lack of vitamin C

secondary consumer   an animal that feeds on a primary consumer, a carnivore

secondary growth   in plants, growth of the vascular and cork cambium, which leads to an increase in diameter

secondary oocyte   the oocyte released from a mature follicle at ovulation

secondary structure   type of protein structure such as the α helix and the β pleated sheet

secondary succession   a succession on an area of land which had previously been colonised but suddenly cleared, e.g. by flooding

sedentary   an organism that lives attached to the substratum such as a rock; alternatively, a person who has an inactive lifestyle and takes little exercise

seed   structure formed from a fertilised ovule and containing an embryo plant together with a food store within a seed coat

segregation   separation of a pair of alleles from one another during meiosis so that each haploid cell produced contains one or other of the pair

selection pressure   varying survival or reproductive ability of different organisms in a breeding population due to the influence of the environment

self-pollination   transfer of pollen from the anther to the stigma of the same plant (often the same flower)

semen   thick, whitish liquid produced by male mammals, which contains sperm cells

semi-conservative replication   each of two partner strands of DNA in a double helix acts as a template for a new strand; after replication, each double helix consists of one old and one new strand

semilunar valves   half-moon shaped valves in the arteries leaving the heart, also found in veins

seminiferous tubules   tubules in the testes in which sperm production takes place

sense strand   the coding strand of DNA, which is not transcribed but which has the same base sequence as mRNA produced during transcription (though mRNA has uracil instead of thymine)

sensory neuron   nerve cell that carries impulses to the central nervous system

sepals   the outermost parts of a flower that protect the bud

Sertoli cells   cells in the seminiferous tubules that protect and nurture developing sperm cells

sex chromosomes   chromosomes that determine the sex of an individual

sex linkage   the pattern of inheritance of genes carried on only one of the sex chromosomes – usually the X chromosome; a different pattern of inheritance is seen in crosses where the male carries the gene from those where the female carries the gene

sexual dimorphism   difference in appearance between the different sexes of a species

sexual selection   selection by one sex of characteristics in individuals of the opposite sex

short-day plants   plants that only flower when the night is longer than a critical length

sieve tube cell   a component of the phloem containing cytoplasm but few organelles and having perforated ends known as sieve plates

sinoatrial node (SAN)   the pacemaker cells in the wall of the right atrium, which initiate the heart beat

sinusoid   small blood vessel found in the liver, similar to a capillary but with fenestrated endothelium cells

skeletal (striated) muscle   voluntary muscle tissue, which has multinucleated cells with arrangements of actin and myosin myofibrils

slow-twitch fibres   (red) muscle fibres which produce slow but long-lived contractions and are able to function for long periods of time

smooth (non-striated) muscle sheets of mononucleate cells that are stimulated by the autonomic nervous system (in gut, arteries and bladder)

sodium–potassium pump a protein in the plasma membrane of neurons that is responsible for active transport – it pumps sodium ions out and potassium ions into the cell against their concentration gradients

speciation the evolution of new species

species a group of individuals of common ancestry that closely resemble each other and are normally capable of interbreeding to produce fertile offspring

sperm cell motile male gamete of an animal (also known as spermatozoon)

spermatogenesis the production of sperm cells

spindle structure formed of microtubules which attach to centromeres during meiosis and mitosis

spirometer apparatus for measuring breathing rate and lung capacity

spongy mesophyll a layer of loosely packed photosynthetic cells in the leaf

stabilising selection selection against extreme phenotypes in a population

stable polymorphism when the frequencies of the different forms of a phenotype in a population remain steady

staple food a basic but nutritious food that forms the basis of a traditional diet

stem cell a cell capable of generating more undifferentiated stem cells and a large clone of differentiated progeny cells

standard deviation a measure of the spread of data about the mean value; the formula is:

$$s = \sqrt{\frac{\sum (x - \overline{x})^2}{n - 1}}$$

where x is the value of the measured variable, $\overline{x}$ is the mean value for x and n is the number in the sample

stigma part of the female reproductive organs of a plant, which receives pollen grains

stimulus a change in the environment that is detected by a receptor and leads to a response

stoma (*plur.* stomata) pore in the epidermis of a leaf, surrounded by two guard cells

striated muscle see *skeletal muscle*

stroke volume the volume of blood pumped out of the heart per minute

style female part of a flower, which links the stigma to the ovary

substrate the molecule on which an enzyme exerts its catalytic effect

succession the sequence of different communities that appears in a given habitat over a period of time

supercoiling additional coiling of the DNA helix that reduces the space needed for the molecule and allows the chromosomes to move easily during nuclear division

symbiosis a relationship between organisms which includes commensalism, mutualism and parasitism; living together

sympathetic nervous system part of the autonomic nervous system; effects include increasing blood pressure and heart rate

sympatric speciation separation of a species into two groups within the same geographic area; caused by some form of isolation, such as a behavioural, ecological or genetic barrier

synapse the connection between two neurons – a small gap that is bridged by a neurotransmitter

synovial fluid lubricating fluid secreted by the synovial membrane at a joint

systole contraction of the chambers of the heart during the cardiac cycle

t-test a method for deciding whether the difference between two sets of data is statistically significant; the formula for t is:

$$t = \frac{\overline{x}_1 - \overline{x}_2}{\sqrt{\dfrac{\text{var}_1}{n_1} + \dfrac{\text{var}_2}{n_2}}}$$

where x is the value of a measured variable and $\overline{x}$ is the mean value for x, var is the variance the data set, n is the number in the sample, and 1 and 2 indicate two different sets of data

taxis the movement of an organism in a particular direction in response to a stimulus

taxonomy the science of classification

telophase the phase of cell division when daughter nuclei form

tendon connective tissue that connects a muscle to a bone

tendril a specialised stem or leaf used by a plant for attachment or support

tertiary consumer consumer that feeds on a secondary consumer, often a top carnivore

tertiary structure the overall three-dimensional shape of a protein

test cross testing a suspected heterozygote by crossing with a known homozygous recessive

testa seed coat

testosterone the main sex hormone of male mammals

thermoreceptor receptor which responds to changes in temperature

thrombin enzyme that converts fibrinogen to fibrin in the final stage of blood clotting

thylakoid membranes membrane system of a chloroplast where the light dependent reactions take place

thyroxine hormone produced by the thyroid gland which influences the rate of metabolism

tidal volume volume of air normally exchanged in breathing

tight junction junction between epithelial cells where plasma membranes of adjacent cells are bonded together by integral proteins

total lung capacity volume of air in the lungs after a maximum inhalation

transcription copying a sequence of DNA bases to mRNA

transfer RNA (tRNA) short lengths of RNA that carry specific amino acids to ribosomes during protein synthesis

transect a line or belt through a habitat in order to sample the organisms present

transgenic containing recombinant DNA incorporated into an organism's genetic material

transient polymorphism changes over time in the frequencies of the different forms of a phenotype in a population, due to a change in allele frequencies

translation decoding of mRNA at a ribosome to produce a polypeptide

translocation transport of dissolved organic compounds, e.g. sugars, up and down the phloem of a plant

transpiration loss of water vapour from the leaves and stem of plants

triglyceride a simple lipid in which three fatty acids are combined with one molecule of glycerol

triplet see *codon*

trisomy containing three rather than two members of a chromosome pair

trophic level a group of organisms that obtain their food from the same part of a food web and which are all the same number of energy transfers from the source of energy (producer)

tropomyosin a protein that, together with actin and troponin, makes up the thin filaments in myofibrils

troponin a protein that, together with actin and tropomyosin, makes up the thin filaments in myofibrils

tuber an underground stem that is enlarged to act as a storage organ, for example, potato

tumour a disorganised mass of cells that occurs in plants and animals; a malignant tumour grows out of control

turgid having a high internal pressure; the turgidity of plant cells allows them to remain firm

type II diabetes diabetes which results from the body developing an insensitivity to insulin over a long time period

ultrafiltration process that occurs through tiny pores in the capillaries of the glomerulus; filtration at the molecular level

umbilical cord tissues derived from the embryo that contain and carry blood vessels between the embryo and the placenta

urea NH_2CONH_2 – a molecule formed of amino groups deaminated from excess amino acids in the liver; the main form in which nitrogen is excreted by mammals

vaccination injection of an antigen to induce antibody production before a potential infection

vacuole a liquid-filled cavity in a cell enclosed by a single membrane; usually small in animals

vascular bundle a length of vascular tissue in plants consisting of xylem, phloem and vascular cambium

vasoconstriction narrowing of arterioles supplying blood to the capillaries in the skin to reduce heat loss

vasodilation widening of arterioles supplying blood to capillaries in the skin to increase heat loss

vector a plasmid or virus that carries a piece of DNA into a bacterium during recombinant DNA technology; or an organism, such as an insect, that transmits a disease-causing organism to another species

vein a vessel that returns blood to the heart at low pressure

venous return volume of blood returning to the heart via the veins in one minute

ventilation rate the number of inhalations or exhalations in one minute

ventricle muscular lower chamber of the heart that pumps blood into the arteries

vesicle a membrane-bound sac

vital capacity the total possible change in lung volume; the maximum volume of air that can be exhaled after a maximum inhalation

vitamin an organic compound that an organism requires for its metabolism; plants make all their own vitamins but animals require most of them in their diet

VO₂ an indicator of the body's ability to use oxygen

VO₂ max a person's maximum rate of oxygen consumption

xerophyte a plant that is adapted to withstand drought conditions

xylem water-carrying vessels of plants that transport up the stem only

zygote the diploid cell produced by the fusion of two gametes

Index

Acknowledgements

The author and publishers are grateful for the permissions granted to reproduce materials in either the original or adapted form. While every effort has been made, it has not always been possible to identify the sources of all the materials used, or to trace all copyright holders. If any omissions are brought to our notice, we will be happy to include the appropriate acknowledgements on reprinting.

IB questions and mark schemes from the IB Questionbank: Biology 2nd Edition (2009) and assessment statements from IB Biology guide (2007) © International Baccalaureate Organization – thanks to the International Baccalaureate Organization for permission to reproduce its intellectual property.

Artwork illustrations throughout © Cambridge University Press or © Geoff Jones.

p.467 excerpt adapted from "Stanley B. Prusiner – Autobiography" Nobelprize.org © The Nobel Foundation, 1997

Cover image: Eye of Science/SPL; p. 13*l* Gerd Guenther/SPL; p. 13*r* Susumu Nishinaga/SPL; pp. 18, 148, 275 Astrid & Hans-Freider Michler/SPL; p. 21 BSIP, SERCOMI/SPL; p. 23*l* Phototake Inc/Alamy; p. 23*r* Herve Conge/ISM/Phototake; p. 24 Medimage/SPL; p. 25 Anton Page, Biomedical Imaging Unit, University of Southampton; p. 35 *all* Michael Abbey/SPL; pp. 39,197, 254, 344 CNRI/SPL; p. 61 Giphotostock/SPL; p. 63 Nigel Cattlin/Alamy; pp. 67, 226*b* Power and Syred/SPL; pp. 69, 221 Eye of Science/SPL; p. 75*tr* Pixtal Images/Photolibrary; pp. 75*bl*, 75*br* Soverign, ISM/SPL; pp. 86, 136, 139*b* SPL; p. 89 J.C. Revy/ISM/SPL; p. 114*t* Image Source/Alamy; p. 114*b* Natural Visions/Alamy; p. 115 J.S & S. Bottomley/ardea.com; pp. 118*l*, 118*r* John Mason/ardea.com; p. 119 John Durham/SPL; p. 120 Sheila Terry/SPL; p. 121 Greg Vaughn/Alamy; p. 122*l* Bob gibbons/Alamy; p. 122*r* Matthew Oldfield/SPL; p. 123*t* Peter Scoones/SPL; p. 123*c* David Fleetham, Visuals Unlimited/SPL; p. 123*b* Animals Animals/Earth Sciences/Photolibrary; pp. 134*l*, 520, 525*l* Steve Gschmeissner/SPL; p. 134*r*, 525*r* Dennis Kunkel/Phototake Sciences/Photolibrary; p. 139*t* Ed Reschke, Peter Arnold Images/SPL; p. 141 Pasieka/SPL; p. 142 Science Source/SPL; pp. 202, 220, 349 Dr Jeremy Burgess/SPL; pp. 206, 353 Lawrence Berkeley Nat'l Lab; p. 216*l* Modesigns58/iStock; p. 216*r* Brian Bowes/SPL; p. 217*t* Gustoimages/SPL; p. 217*b* Scott Camazine/SPL; p. 225 Dirk Wiersma/SPL; p. 226*t* Ian West/Photolibrary; p. 226*c* Sidney Moulds/SPL; p. 245 Herman Eisenbeiss/SPL; pp. 262, 313 Manfred Kage/SPL; pp. 266, 316 University of Edinburgh/Wellcome Images; p. 278 Garry Delong/SPL; p. 289 Andy Crump, TDR, WHO/SPL; p. 294 Biophoto Associates/SPL; p. 295 John Paul Kay, Peter Arnold Inc./SPL; p. 298*t* Tom Myers/AGSTOCKUSA/SPL; p. 298*ct* TH Foto-Werbung/SPL; p. 298*cb* Chris Knapton/SPL; pp. 298*b*, 301 Gustoimages/SPL; p. 306 Martin Bond/SPL; p. 317 David Williams/Alamy; p. 326*t* Cephas Picture Library/Alamy; p. 326*b* Alistair Scott/Alamy; p. 330 DU Cane Medicalimaging Ltd/SPL; p. 335 Kenneth Edward/Biografx/SPL; p. 363 Dynamic Light USA/Alamy; p. 368*l* Tom & Pat Leeson/ardea.com; p. 368*r* Dennis Avon/ardea.com; p. 369 Custom Life Science Images/Alamy; p. 380 *all* © Bone Clones www.boneclones.com; pp. 404*t*, 404*b*, 428 Oxford Scientific/Photolibrary; p. 415*t* Steve Bloom Images/Alamy; p. 415*b* Ria Novosti/SPL; p. 417 Robert Shantz/Alamy; p. 424 US National Library of Medicine/SPL; p. 425 Philippe Psaila/SPL; p. 429 Neil Bromhall/SPL; p. 431 Helen Williams/SPL; p. 444 Nigel Cattlin/SPL; p. 451 Peter Arnold Inc./Photolibrary; p. 454 Cordelia Molloy/SPL; p. 458 CDC/SPL; p. 462 Russell Knightly/SPL; p. 465 Dr Gopal Murti/SPL; p. 466 Sean Sprague/Still Pictures; p. 472 Mauro Fermariello/SPL; p. 473 Marvin Dembinsky Photo Associates/Alamy; p. 474 imagebroker/Alamy; p. 475 Chris Howes Wild Places Photography/Alamy; p. 476 Martyn F. Chillmaid/SPL; p. 479 Clouds Hill Imaging/SPL; p. 484 John Beatty/SPL; p. 485 Arctic Images/Alamy; p. 486*l* Arco Images GmbH/Alamy; p. 486*r* David Whitaker/Alamy; p. 488*t* Sue Clark/Alamy; p. 488*b* CuboImages srl/Alamy; p. 489 Bob Gibbons/Alamy; p. 493 Peter Yates/SPL; p. 495 deadlyphoto.com/Alamy; p. 499 Photo Researchers/SPL; p. 502 David Chapman/Alamy; p. 503 Brian Hartshorn/Alamy; p. 505*t* nagelestock.com/Alamy; p. 505*b* Ron Austin/SPL; p. 525 Phototake Science/Photolibrary; p. 529 Simon Fraser/Freeman Hospital, Newcastle-Upon-Tyne/ SPL

Key

SPL – Science Photo Library
l = left, *r* = right, *t* = top, *b* = bottom, *c* = centre